FISHES OF HAWAII

THE BRIDGE BUILDER

An old man, going a lone highway,
Came at the evening, cold and gray,
To a chasm, vast and deep and wide,
Through which was flowing a sullen tide.
The old man crossed in the twilight dim —
That sullen stream had no fears for him;
But he turned, when he reached the other side,
And built a bridge to span the tide.

"Old man," said a fellow pilgrim near,
"You are wasting strength in building here.
Your journey will end with the ending day;
You never again must pass this way.
You have crossed the chasm, deep and wide,
Why build you the bridge at the eventide?"

The builder lifted his old grey head.
"Good friend, in the path I have come," he said,
"There followeth after me today
A youth whose feet must pass this way.
This chasm that has been naught to me
To that fair-haired youth may a pitfall be.
He, too, must cross in the twilight dim;
Good friend, I am building the bridge for *him*."

                                        WILL ALLEN DROMGOOLE.

The Pacific Big-mouth Shark. The above photo is of the only specimen of this rare, deep-water shark that has ever been seen. It measured over eleven feet in length, weighed about 1,600 pounds, and was captured about 25 miles northeast of Honolulu. For additional information see the Appendix page 522.

FISHES OF HAWAII

A Handbook of the Marine Fishes

of

Hawaii and the Central Pacific Ocean

By
Spencer Wilkie Tinker
Director
Waikiki Aquarium
1940 - 1972

With Color Photographs By
Frank W. Adams, Scott Johnson, and James H. O'Neill

Published By

HAWAIIAN SERVICE, INC,
P. O. Box 2835, Honolulu, Hawaii 96803

First Printing: August, 1978
Second Printing: June, 1982

Published and Distributed
by

HAWAIIAN SERVICE, INC.
Publishers of Hawaiiana
P. O. Box 2835
Honolulu, Hawaii 96803

The black and white photographs were taken by John Bowles, Robert A. Morris, John E. Randall, and the author.

The drawings were made by Charles J. DeLuca, Y. Oda, Gordon Sing Chan Chun, Herbert Rosenbush, and the author.

Additional color photographs were taken by Dougles Faulkner, Karl Frogner, John E. Randall, and the author.

The graphic preparation was made by Glenda E. Farley.

The index was prepared by Mrs. Grace Hollander Littlejohn.

ISBN 0-930492-02-1
ISBN 0-930492-14-5 pbk.

Library of Congress Catalog Card No. 77-93337

Printed in Honolulu, Hawaii, U.S.A.

TABLE OF CONTENTS

PART II

THE BONY FISHES

Class Osteichthyes (Pisces) - The Bony Fishes

Subclass Sarcopterygii The Flesh-finned or Primitive Bony Fishes

Order Coelacanthiformes - The Coelacanth Fishes

Order Ceratodiformes - The Australian Lungfish

Order Lepidosireniformes - The South American and
African Lungfishes

Subclass Brachiopterygii - The Short-finned or Bichir Fishes

Order Polypteriformes - The Bichir Fishes

Subclass Actinopterygii - The Ray-finned Fishes

Superorder Chondrostei - The Sturgeons and Paddle Fishes

Order Acipenseriformes - The Sturgeons and Paddle Fishes

Superorder Teleostei - The Modern Ray-finned Fishes

Order Lepidosteiformes - The Gar Fishes

Order Amiiformes - The Bowfin Fishes

Order Clupeiformes - The Herrings and Related Families

Order Ophiocephaliformes - The Snake-head Fishes and
Related Families

Order Synbranchiformes - The Rice-field Eels and Related Families

Order Perciformes - The Perch-like Fishes and Related Families

PREFACE

This book on Pacific Ocean fishes is intended to serve as a handbook of the marine fishes of the Hawaiian Islands and the warm waters of the surrounding tropical, central Pacific Ocean. It is written for the use of fishermen, amateur naturalists, schools, and others who are interested in identifying their specimens and learning a little about them.

I hope each person who uses this book will read *The Bridge Builder*, the short poem at the beginning of the book. It explains my feeling about the purpose of this book. I want this book to be a bridge across the chasm that separates the beginning or amateur naturalist from the seemingly involved and difficult world of fish names and fish classification. I want it to be simple enough for beginners to read in order that, through it, they may be able to move on to more complex materials.

The Table of Contents has been enlarged to include a fairly complete presentation of the classification of fishes in the larger catagories. This arrangement includes the major groups above the *family*, except for the *sub-orders* which have been omitted for reasons of simplicity. This outline should be very useful to students because it presents the Hawaiian species in the total classification scheme. It will be noted that the only *family* groups listed are those which have representatives in the Hawaiian area.

I would like to call the attention of students to the scientific name of each species and to have them note that the scientific name includes the name of a man and a date. The name is that of the person who first made a written description of this species, assigned a name to it, and then published this name and the description in some book or journal; the date is the year of this publication. These names and dates complete the scientific name of a species and also are a convenience to those persons who may wish to refer to the orginal description of a species. Knowing these facts, a student may then go to a very large library and there seek out the *Zoological Record* for that year and, in the section on fishes, look under the name of the author to find the reference to the book or journal in which this orginal description was first published.

Students who are interested in a detailed historical review of the early ichthyological investigations in the central Pacific area will find a very good account and a bibliography in the introductory pages in the following reference: David Starr Jordan and Barton Warren Evermann. The Aquatic Resources of the Hawaiian Islands, Part I — The Shore Fishes, *Bull. U.S. Fish Commission* Vol. 23 for 1903, (Issued July 29, 1905), pp. 3-30.

A great multitude of individuals, both living and dead, have laid the ground work for this modest effort and each, in turn, is due special recognition and thanks for his contribution, assistance, or encouragement with this project. Among the many scholars who have studied and written about Hawaiian species, the following are among the most important: Mr. Vernon E. Brock, Dr. Thomas A. Clark, Mr. John N. Cobb, Mr. Frank Cramer, Dr. Barton Warren Evermann, Dr. Henry Weed Fowler, Mr. Andrew Garrett, Dr. Charles Henry Gilbert, Dr. William A. Gosline, Dr. Albert Gunther, Dr. Earl S. Herald, Mr. Edward Y. Hosaka, Dr. Oliver P. Jenkins,

Dr. David Starr Jordan, Mr. John T. Nichols, Dr. Victor Pietschmann, Dr. John E. Randall, Dr. Leonard Peter Schultz, Mr. Alvin Seale, Dr. John Otterbein Snyder, Dr. Franz Steindachner, and Dr. Paul J. Struhsaker.

Several employees of the Waikiki Aquarium were very helpful in keeping an alert lookout for uncommon species and in bringing them to the attention of the author. These persons include Mr. Matsuo Maruya, Mr. Kenneth A. Wong, and Mr. Horace Hokama. In addition, Mr. John Bowles, Ph.D., and Mr. Robert A. Morris, D.V.M., brought their scientific backgrounds to aid in this effort.

Various recreational and commercial fishermen have offered rare and unusual specimens to be studied or photographed. These have included Mr. Lloyd Blaine, Mr. Raymond Chun, Mr. Tatsuo Hayashi, Mr. Horace Ichimasa, Mr. John Kala, Mr. Samuel Kaololo, Mr. George Kansaki, Mr. Takichi Kawasuna, Mr. Paul Kimura, Mr. Edward Kokubun, Mr. Hoichi Matsubara, Mr. Haruyoshi Matsunaga, Mr. Eugene Mioi, Mr. Tagao Miyoii, Mr. Naosuke Nakamoto, Mr. Joseph Soffra, Mr. Phillip Tanaka, Mr. Matsu Tanna, Mr. Kazu Tsubota, Mr. Harry Yagi, Mr. John Yanagawa, Mr. Walter P. Young, Mr. Yoshimoto of the *Sandra Ann*, and Mr. Lester Zukeran. Special mention must be made here of the long and unselfish contribution of Mr. Fernando Leonida in supplying the Waikiki Aquarium with specimens. His resourcefulness in obtaining specimens, his alertness in recognizing rare and uncommon species, and his steady, continuous supply of specimens have brought to light many new records for Hawaii and a few new species.

The drawings and photographs of the various species are from many sources; these sources are usually indicated.

A bibliography has not been included because of the time and cost involved and because most of the references which it would contain are only available in very large libraries.

No book of this sort is ever complete, accurate, or up to date. The number of species is continually increasing, while the known species are being restudied, rearranged, and renamed by many scholars. So I have decided to issue this volume regardless of its errors and completeness and to allow the next generation to make the additions and corrections in their books and publications.

I have chosen to dedicate this book to four friends of my early residence in Honolulu, all of whom were scholars and administrators associated with the formative years of the University of Hawaii.

Spencer Wilkie Tinker

1121 Hunakai Street
Honolulu, Hawaii 96816
United States of America

INTRODUCTION

This introduction is written to give the students of fishes an opportunity to learn something of the history of ichthyology and to know the names of a few of the many great men who have studied the fishes of the world and helped to classify them. Mention has been made of a few ancient writers and several of the European ichthyological scholars, but far more names have been omitted than have been included. Brief glimpses of ichthyology in America have been included together with a short biography of David Starr Jordan. Mention is also made of a few students who pioneered the study of fishes in the great, tropical Indo-Pacific area of which Hawaii is a part.

The task of catching, studying, and naming the fishes of the world is a very large project which has taken the time and effort of many scholars for many years and which is still not completed. There are many reasons for this delay.

The fishes are the largest group of the vertebrates and may number as many as 25,000 species; they are more numerous than the amphibians (2,500 ±), the reptiles (6,000 ±), the birds (8,600 ±), or the mammals (4,000 ±). Their great diversity has required ichthyological scholars to prepare the largest and most complex classification scheme of the vertebrates and their capture has not been as easy as the other vertebrate groups because some of the fishes live in places almost inaccessible to man.

The study of fishes has occupied the mind of man from very ancient times. Originally, man was concerned with fishes as a source of food, but, as language developed and scholars were able to record their thoughts in writing, we find mankind beginning to record the names, habits, and uses of fishes and more recently to study their anatomy, their physiology, their relationships to each other, and finally their relation to the place in which they live.

EARLY STUDENTS OF ICHTHYOLOGY

The first man to write a creditable treatise on fishes was the great Greek philosopher Aristotle (384-322 B.C.). He studied the anatomy of fishes, as well as the anatomy of other animals, and made observations on their habits. These studies seem to have been based upon about 115 species which were native to the Aegean Sea. His observations were accurate, and his writings on ichthyology, which were preserved in his *Historium Animalium*, were the authoritative references on fishes as well as other branches of zoology for nearly eighteen centuries.

Following Aristotle, Greek science entered a long period of decline beginning about 200 A.D., during which time very little original work was accomplished in ichthyology. However, before passing on to more modern students of fishes, mention should be made of three other ancient scholars who had an interest in fishes in addition to other areas of their culture.

(1) Gaius Plinius Secundus (c. 23-70 A.D.), better known as Pliny The Elder, was a versatile Roman scholar who produced a large work on natural

history titled *Naturalis historia.*

(2) Athenaeus was a Greek scholar who lived in the Greek city of Naucratis in northern Egypt at the end of the 2nd century A. D. Athenaeus wrote voluminously on many subjects including fishes.

(3) Aelian or Claudius Aelianus, a Roman author and teacher of rhetoric of the 3rd century A. D., issued a collection of stories of animals under the title *On The Nature of Animals.*

SIXTEENTH CENTURY ICHTHYOLOGY

The next naturalist to study and write extensively about fishes was a Frenchman by the name of Pierre Belon (1517-1564). He was trained a physician, but found travel and natural history more alluring. Between 1547 and 1550, he traveled through Greece, Asia Minor, Palestine, Arabia, and Egypt observing and collecting living things; he then returned to France to write and later publish an account of his journeys and his scientific observations. His observations on fishes, which were illustrated with drawings, were included in *L'histoire naturelle des estranges poissons*, published in 1551, and also in *De aquatilibus libri duo*, published in 1553 in Paris.

Another physician by the name of Ippolito Salviani (1514-1572) prepared and issued the first popular book on fishes. It included an account of 92 species from the waters of Italy and contained an excellent illustration of each species. Salviani's book, *Aquatilium animalium historia*, was issued in Rome beginning in 1554.

In addition to being the physician to three popes, Salviani was a very able scholar and his book was an important contribution to the study of fishes; but, because his interest lay in the economic and natural history aspects of each species, Salviani did not add anything to the classification of this group.

A third European physician, Guillaume Rondelet (1507-1557) of France, published two books on fishes; they were *Libri de Piscibus Marinis*, published in 1554 and 1555, and *Universae aquatilium historiae pars altera*, published in 1555; both were issued at Lyons in southeastern France. Rondelet's treatise included 187 marine and 47 fresh water species of which most were either of European origin or from the Mediterranean Sea. It was a well illustrated work and contained descriptions of the species, but it added very little to the classification of fishes.

THE BEGINNING OF MODERN ICHTHYOLOGY

An English clergyman by the name of John Ray, or John Wray, (1628 - 1705) made the next significant contribution to the description and classification of fishes. Ray was a very remarkable man; he was born the son of a blacksmith and, showing great promise as a scholar, was sent to Trinity College at Cambridge, England. Here he studied the usual subjects of Greek, mathematics, theology, etc., but he soon gave up the church for a life devoted to the study of natural history.

During his sojourn as a teacher at Trinity College, Ray made the acquaintance and friendship of a student named Francis Willughby (1635-1672). These two men agreed to jointly undertake a project of improving the classification of the plant and animal kingdoms. Together, they travelled extensively over Great Britain and Europe collecting specimens and information and thereafter returned to England to study and write. In the beginning, Ray worked with plants and Willughby studied the animals. Willughby, however, died at the age of 37 years and Ray completed, edited, and published his *Historia piscium* at Oxford in 1686; this book contained descriptions and drawings of 420 species of fishes.

In their studies and writings on animals, Ray and Willughby introduced some important improvements in the science of animal classification. They decided that all classification had to be based on structure; they developed a concept of a "species" and defined it; and they were very careful to reject all myths, hearsay, etc., and to include only that information which has a basis in facts.

Of these two men, Willughby seems to have been the leader and Ray the follower. Willughby had come from a titled English family and apparently provided the financial support for their undertakings. It is interesting to note that Willughby left Ray the sum of L60 per year and requested that Ray attend to the education of his two sons. The Ray Society of England was founded in his honor in 1844 for the publication of material on natural history.

THE FOUNDATION OF CLASSIFICATION

The credit for devising the basic classification scheme for fishes belongs to a Swedish naturalist and ichthyologist named Peter Artedi (1705-1735). He began his professional career by studying theology at Upsala University, but he soon turned to medicine and natural history. While engaged in his studies at Upsala, he met and developed a friendship with Carl von Linne (Linnaeus). Together they made an agreement that, should either die, the books, papers, and writings of the deceased partner would go to the survivor. Shortly thereafter Artedi was accidentally drowned in 1735 at Amsterdam, where he had gone to classify the specimens in a private museum. Thereupon, Linnaeus inherited Artedi's writings which he edited and thereafter published. These works included the following:

Bibliotheca ichthyologica . . . .a list of all preceeding authors who had written upon fishes with comments on their work;

Philosophia ichthyologica . . . .an anatomical work on fishes including terminology and a discussion of his principles of classification;

Genera piscium . . . . .a description of 45 genera;

Species piscium . . . . .a description of 72 species, and

Synonymia piscium . . . . .a list of species with the names of all previous authors who had written about them.

Linnaeus adopted Artedi's classification scheme for fishes and, with a minimum of changes including the addition of binomial names, incorporated it into his *Systema Natura.*

The greatest advance in the preparation and publication of a systematic approach to the classification of plants and animals was made by a Swede named Carl von Linne (1707-1778), also known as Linnaeus. Although he was primarily a botanist, Linnaeus established a method of organizing the various species of both plants and animals which was to gain immediate acceptance and which was to start a stampede of biologists to gather, study, and publish descriptions of the many species of plants and animals from all over the world. This classification scheme was set forth in a work called the *Systema Natura,* which first appeared in 1735 and in many subsequent editions (1740, 1748, 1758, and 1766). The 10th edition, published in 1758, was the first edition to consistently use the binomial system of nomenclature; for this reason, this 1758 edition has been accepted as the starting point for the scientific naming of plants and animals.

A German physician, Mark Eliezer Bloch (1723-1799), of Jewish lineage and living in Berlin, took a fancy to ichthyology late in life and, beginning at the age of 56 wrote and published a series of works on fishes. These included a work on the fishes of Germany which was published in Berlin between 1782 and 1784 and another work on foreign fishes published between 1785 and 1795; both of these works were scholarly and beautifully illustrated. Unfortunately, Bloch's work on foreign fishes is not entirely dependable because Bloch obtained much of his material from travellers and others who did not supply him with accurate information.

Bloch next prepared a large work of 1,519 species in which he presented his system of classification. It was titled *M. E. Blochii Systema ichthyologia iconibus* . . . and was edited and published after Bloch's death by Johann Gottlob Scheider (1750-1822), a classical scholar and naturalist.

An extremely talented French nobleman by the name of Compte De Bernard Germain Etienne De La Villa Lacepede (1756-1825) had an eventful career in each of the three areas of music, science, and politics and, within each of these very different fields, he was exceedingly active and productive. His scientific studies included physics, whales, reptiles, and fishes. His *Histoire naturelle des poissons* consisted of five volumes which were published in Paris between 1798 and 1803. The interruptions of the French Revolution hindered his studies, effected their accuracy, and reduced their use following publication. He was, none the less, a man of remarkable talents.

With the beginning of the nineteenth century the science of ichthyology took a slightly different direction. Where it had been primarily concerned with the description and classification of species, it now turned toward the study of the anatomy of fishes and other vertebrates with the appearance on the scene of another talented French nobleman by the name of Baron Georges Leopold Chretien Frederic Dagobert Cuvier (1769-1832). Cuvier, somewhat like Lacepede, began his professional career in educational and scientific circles and shifted to the political arena in his later years. Cuvier's greatest works were *Regne Animal . . .,* which appeared in four octavo volumes in 1817 and in a second edition of five volumes in 1829 and 1830, and the *Histoire naturelle des poissons,* the first volume of which made its appearance in 1828.

Cuvier began the study of fishes about 1801 and later renewed his interest in them in association with one of his pupils, Achille Valenciennes (1794-1865). The first volume of the *Histoire naturelle des poissons* appeared in 1828 and continued intermittently through 1848 at which time the twenty second volume was left unfinished. With the death of Cuvier in 1832, the entire project became the work of Valenciennes, who pursued it with diminishing vigor until 1848. This treatise on fishes contained 5,000 species and, although unfinished, is one of the great classics of biological science. Although Valenciennes was overshadowed by Cuvier, great credit is due him for his part in the production of this study.

OTHER EUROPEAN ICHTHYOLOGISTS

The science of the classification of fishes which began with Artedi and Linnaeus, has produced a continuing array of European scholars in this field. Of this group, special attention should be given to the work of Albert Carl Ludwig Gotthilf Gunther (1830-1914) of the British Museum (Natural History). Gunther's most famous work was a *Catalogue of the Fishes of the British Museum*, 1857-1870. Gunther had set out to develop a classification system but ended with a classification system and a treatise on the fishes of the world. Because of its great scope, it became the basic authority on systematic ichthyology for many years. The volumes were issued periodically over many years, but the work was never completed.

Gunther studied the dredged and trawled fishes which were collected by the *Challenger* Expedition and issued them in a report titled *The Deep-Sea Fishes of the Challenger Expedition*, 1887. This was an early and important treatise of deep-sea fishes. In addition, Gunther prepared the expedition reports* on the pelagic fishes and the shore fishes.

The list of noteworthy European ichthyologists who made significant contributions to the classification of fishes is long, but the following deserve to be mentioned: A. Alcock, S. Berg, G. A. Boulenger, R. Collett, L. Doderlein, A. Fraser-Brunner, P. H. Greenwood, E. Lonnberg, C. Lutken, N. B. Marshall, John R. Norman, C. Tate Regan, Antoine Risso, Franz Steindachner, R. H. Traquair, Ethelwynn Trewavas, L. Vaillant, and others.

AGASSIZ, THE EURO-AMERICAN

Mention should be made of the studies and teaching of Louis Jean Rudolphe Agassiz (1807-1873), a native of Switzerland, who was trained in medicine but soon transferred his scientific affections to geology and zoology. He began his ichthyological inquiries by studying a collection of fresh water fishes from Brazil; this study, which was completed and published in 1829, bore the title of *Selecta Genera et Species Piscium*. In 1830, Agassiz issued a prospectus of a *History of the Fresh Water Fishes of Central Europe*, which was later enlarged and published in 1839 and 1842. Meanwhile, a five volume work on fossil fishes, including 1700 species and titled *Recherches sur les poissons fossiles*, was issued in sections between 1833 and 1843. With the publication of these works and others of equally

*See *Challenger Reports* Section V, Vol. 1, Part 6 (shore fishes); Section V, Vol. 22 (deep sea fishes); Section V, Vol. 31, Part 2 (pelagic fishes).

high quality in both zoology and geology, Agassiz became very well known in Europe and America.

In 1846, Louis Agassiz came to the United States to deliver a series of lectures and here accepted a position as Professor of Zoology and Geology at Harvard University, where he remained for the rest of his life. At Harvard, he founded the Museum of Comparative Zoology (The Agassiz Museum) and established a biological station on Pekinese Island in Buzzard's Bay off the eastern coast of Massachusetts, although he did not live long enough to make much use of this station.

Agassiz, through Harvard and his teaching, had a profound effect on biology and geology in the United States, because nearly all the great biologists and geologists of the last half of the nineteenth century were his students at this institution.

EARLY ICHTHYOLOGY IN AMERICA

The development of ichthyology in America received its greatest impetus from the inspiration and teaching of Louis Agassiz. There was, however, another European naturalist who preceded Agassiz and whose studies and writings should be mentioned.

The earliest scholar to classify American fresh water fishes was an erudite, eccentric European by the name of Constantine Samuel Rafinesque (1784-1840). Rafinesque was born in Constantinople, lived as a boy and youth in southern France, and then came to Philadelphia at the beginning of the French Revolution; he then returned to Sicily in 1805 and remained in business there for about ten years. On his return to America, he was ship-wrecked off New London and on landing lost all of his money and possessions.

Rafinesque traveled widely in eastern America collecting specimens, observing wildlife, and writing. He lived for a time at New Harmony, an early science center on the Wabash River in Indiana. This was followed by an appointment for a time as Professor of Natural History and Modern Languages at Transylvania University at Lexington, Kentucky. In his later years, he centered his activities around Philadelphia where he died.

Rafinesque described many plants and animals including many fresh water fishes. His best work is doubtless his account of the fishes of the Ohio River and its tributaries, but his enthusiasm for new species caused him to describe many species more than once and thereby clutter the literature with duplicate names or synonyms. Although he was a strange, lonely, solitary figure in American science, he described a large number of America's fresh water fishes.

One of the very earliest students of fishes in the United States was David Humphrey Storer, a physician of Boston. His most important publication was titled a *Synopsis of the Fishes of North America* and was published in the *Memoirs of the Academy of Arts and Science of Boston* in 1846. This book listed 739 species in 221 genera and included principally those species of the eastern United States, since very little was known about the other areas of North America.

Another early naturalist in the United States was James Ellsworth

DeKay, a zoologist. DeKay issued a large treatise on the state of New York which he titled *Natural History of New York* (1842); included in this set was a volume on the reptiles and fishes of that state.

Of the many students of Louis Agassiz, at least four were involved in the development of ichthyology in Western America and in the Pacific Ocean; these were Alexander Agassiz, Charles Dana, Samuel Garman, and David Starr Jordan.

Alexander Emanuel Agassiz (1835-1910), the son of Louis Agassiz, studied chemistry and engineering and later became very wealthy from his interest in copper mines near Lake Superior; from this fortune, he gave approximately $500,000 to Harvard University for the Museum of Comparative Zoology.

Agassiz was interested in the fauna of the deep sea and wrote the two volume *Review of the Echini* (echinoderms) covering the materials collected by the British *Challenger* Expedition (1872-1876). He also took part in three deep sea dredging expeditions of the U. S. Coast Guard steamer *Blake* between 1877 and 1880.

In 1887, Agassiz took charge of the biological work of the Coast Survey. This work was carried on aboard the steamer *Albatross* in the Atlantic Ocean until 1888, in which year the *Albatross* was moved to the Pacific Ocean. In the same year (1888), Agassiz issued his report on the ichthyological work of the Coast Survey and the Fish Commission. It was titled *Contributions To American Thalassography* (oceanography).

Agassiz accompanied the steamer *Albatross* of the U. S. Fish Commission on many of its dredging cruises in the Pacific Ocean. Most of these writings of Agassiz, which are not contained in government reports, appear in publications of the Museum of Comparative Zoology.

A significant contribution of Alexander Agassiz to ichthyology has gone almost unnoticed and unheralded. Agassiz had a talent for improving oceanographic gear and greatly advanced the collecting of fishes and other specimens by designing better nets and trawls. He was a pioneer in deep-sea dredging and was the first to use steel cables for dredging at great depths.

James Dwight Dana (1813-1895) was an American geologist, mineralogist, and zoologist. He had studied at Yale, spent two years teaching mathematics as a midshipman in the Navy, and then returned to Yale for an additional two years in the chemistry laboratory. He was next appointed as the mineralogist, geologist, and naturalist of the U. S. Exploring Expedition (1838-1843) under the command of Captain Charles Wilkes. He spent most of the next thirteen years preparing the reports of the expedition; his reports included the *Zoophytes* (1846), *Geology of the Pacific Area* (1849), and two volumes on *Crustacea* (1852-1854). In 1850, he was appointed Professor of Natural History and Geology at Yale University, where he remained until 1892. Dana revisited Hawaii in 1887 to again study volcanoes; this study resulted in a quarto volume titled *Characteristics of Volcanoes* which was published in 1890.

Samuel Garman was a vertebrate naturalist who was born in 1846 in west-central Pennsylvania, attended college in Illinois, and thereafter taught natural sciences for a time in that state. In 1872, Garman became a special student of Louis Agassiz and attended the famous 1873 summer school of Agassiz at Pekinese Island; he thereafter became a specialist in fishes, amphibians, and reptiles under the supervision of Agassiz at Harvard's Museum of Comparative Zoology. Garman wrote many papers on the above animal groups, most of which were included in the publications of the Museum of Comparative Zoology. Garman is probably best remembered in the Pacific area for his *Deep Sea Fishes*, 1899, which included the dredgings of 1891 which the steamer *Albatross* made off the western coast of Central America.

The United States has produced a large array of ichthyologists. In addition to those previously named, the following should be remembered: Spencer Fullerton Baird, Tarleton H. Bean, William Beebe, Henry B. Bigelow, Edwin D. Cope, Bashford Dean, Barton Warren Evermann, Theodore Gill, George Brown Goode, William C. Schroeder, Leonard Peter Schultz, and John Tee-Van.

DAVID STARR JORDAN, AMERICA'S GREATEST BIOLOGIST

Without a doubt, the greatest of the American ichthyologists was David Starr Jordan* (1851-1931), a New Englander, who was born on a farm near Gainesville in western New York on January 19, 1851. Jordan had an exceedingly interesting life, so we will trace it briefly in order that the reader may see the various scenes and places through which Jordan passed.

Following completion of his secondary schooling, we find Jordan teaching school for a time; this was of short duration. In 1869, at the age of 18, Jordan entered Cornell University and was graduated three years later in 1872. During these three years, his academic interest was in the natural sciences, particularly botany.

Beginning with his graduation, Jordan began a series of moves in his employment career which was to take him through one high school and five colleges. In the fall of 1873, Jordan accepted a position teaching natural sciences at Lombard College in Galesburg, Illinois; he remained there but one year. During the following summer of 1873, Jordan attended the now famous summer school of Agassiz at Pekinese Island off Massachusetts where he studied marine algae. It was here that Agassiz suggested that Jordan should review the fishes of the area and, from this project, Jordan became familiar with fishes and the literature about them.

In the autumn of 1873, Jordan accepted a job for a year teaching at the Appleton Collegiate Institute in Appleton, Wisconsin. The following summer he returned again to Pekinese Island and there had the good fortune to meet various members of the new U.S. Fish Commission, who were later to be his employers.

In the fall of 1874, Jordan accepted a job teaching in a high school at Indianapolis, Indiana. He stayed at this school for only one term, but it was here that he met Charles Henry Gilbert, then a student, who was to be associated with Jordan for the most of his life. During the summer of 1875

*Much of this material on David Starr Jordan has been taken from an article by George Sprague Myers titled "David Starr Jordan, Ichthyologist, 1851-1932". *Stanford Ichthyological Bulletin* 4:1, 1951, pp. 2-6.

which followed, Jordan went to the Harvard Summer School of Geology which met in Tennessee.

His third collegiate appointment came in the fall of 1875 when he accepted a post as a professor at Butler College in Indianapolis. He remained at this school for three years. It was here that he issued his first sizable monograph which was titled the *Manual of the Vertebrates of the Northern United States*, 1876-1929. This book went through thirteen editions in Jordan's lifetime.

During the summer of 1876, Jordan and Gilbert went to Georgia to study the fishes of that area. This trip was followed in 1879, 1881, and 1883 by excursions with students to Europe, where they travelled from England to Italy and made the acquaintance of Europe's leading ichthyologists.

The fourth collegiate appointment came in the fall of 1879 when Jordan accepted a position as Professor of Natural Sciences at the University of Indiana in Bloomington. His teaching here was immediately interrupted in December of 1879 for a time while Jordan and Gilbert went to the Pacific coast to survey the fisheries of that area for the U.S. Fish Commission. This survey took nine months and extended from Seattle to San Diego.

Jordan was next chosen President of the University of Indiana and assumed that office in January, 1885, and Gilbert was subsequently appointed Professor of Zoology. Travel, small expeditions, and writing occupied Jordan's time during the period from 1879 to 1891, while he was still at Indiana. One progressive innovation in the college curriculum should be noted here. President Jordan established the principle of elective courses in the curriculum, thereby developing a wider perspective in his students.

When the California railroad baron and U.S. Senator, Leland Stanford, decided to establish a university in memory of his son, he chose Jordan to be its first president. In the move from Indiana to California, Jordan took with him to the new school two men who were to be closely associated with Jordan for many years to come; they were Dr. Charles Henry Gilbert to be head of the Department of Zoology and Oliver Peebles Jenkins, a physiologist. They were also followed by various students, the most colorful of whom was probably Alvin Seale, who is reported to have ridden most of the way from Indiana to California on a new bicycle. John Otterbein Snyder, a student at Indiana, also transferred to Stanford.

Stanford suddenly became the center of ichthyological study in the United States, particularly those studies relating to the classification of fishes, and many of the students trained there later became leaders in the field of biology. These students included Henry Weed Fowler, Albert W.C.T. Herre, Carl Leavitt Hubbs, Alvin Seale, Edwin Chapin Stark, John Otterbein Snyder, William Francis Thompson, and others.

While at Stanford, Jordan and Evermann issued their largest and most important work, *The Fishes of North and Middle America*, 1896-1900, (U.S. Natl. Mus. Bull. 47). This work consisted of four volumes of fine print with over 4,000 pages and contained 3,263 species and 133 subspecies, a total of 3,396 fishes. Jordan had begun this work with Gilbert; the latter, however, became involved with the dredgings of the steamer *Albatross* and Evermann, then ichthyologist for the U. S. Fish Commission, did the final editorial work.

Jordan and various members of his staff continued to travel; they visited Puget Sound, Alaska, Mexico (1894-5), Japan (1901, 1911, 1922), Korea, Formosa, Hawaii (1901, 1902), Samoa (1902), Australia (1907, 1914), and New Zealand (1907), and from each of these excursions a publication on fishes of the area usually resulted.

With the beginning of the twentieth century, Jordan became increasingly interested in world affairs and by 1910 was well known for his interest in world peace. He retired as President of Stanford in 1913, assuming the title of Chancellor until his retirement in 1916, in order to spend time touring Europe and lecturing against war, aggression, and imperialism.

With the outbreak of World War I, Jordan returned to Stanford, resumed the study of fishes, and issued *The Genera of Fishes*, 1917-1920, which appeared in four parts. This was followed by *A Classification of Fishes* in 1923. These two publications were great forward steps in bringing order and stability to the classification of fishes.

Jordan spent the remaining years of his life near Stanford University and died there on September 16, 1931.

Jordan had a talent for leadership found in few men. He was able to gather able students around him, inspire them to achieve success, to arrange for their employment, and to raise money for the study of science. He was able to identify the "voids" and "areas of need" in natural science and to organize studies within these areas that resulted in useful contributions to human knowledge. As a lecturer, he was a "spell-binder" and attracted large audiences. He was a man of large stature, about six feet tall, and only moderately robust. His features were regular, a bit lean, and his nose and ears were larger than usual. He was poised, direct, and unassuming.

Jordan's accomplishments may be summarized in about three areas: (1) he added a vast quantity of material to our knowledge of the natural world, including 50 books; (2) he trained many biologists, including many of the leaders in biology in the United States during the first half of the twentieth century; and (3) he gave the study of natural science in the United States enough momentum to carry it forward for half a century.

EUROPEANS IN THE INDO-PACIFIC

As the interest in ichthyology increased in Europe, the European biologists began to turn their attention to more remote regions. Of these, the largest, most conspicuous, and most remote region was the vast Indo-Pacific area from the Red Sea and the coast of Africa eastward across the Indian and Pacific Oceans to the western coast of the Americas; this is the famous Indian Ocean-Tropical Western Pacific Faunal Area. To collect in these distant places, these biologists had to depend upon the captains, crews, or passengers aboard sailing ships or personally accompany these vessels upon their long and tedious journeys. Both methods were productive, but soon it became the pattern for European nations to send out ships on expeditions of discovery and to recruit naturalists of various interests to accompany these voyages.

In the beginning, the interest in Indo-Pacific fishes was confined to the scholars of European nations, possibly because these European nations were engaged in colonial expansion in this area. However, the enthusiasm of Europeans for Indo-Pacific fishes declined by 1900 and this area became the center of increasing activity for American and Japanese scholars. Many nineteenth century Europeans should be mentioned here for their interest in this area, but only five or six produced a large, scholarly, or monumental work on the fishes of this area.

One of the very earliest scientific adventurers to produce a creditable account of Indo-Pacific fishes was a Dane named Petrus Forskal. He obtained specimens from the area of the Red Sea and incorporated them into a book titled *Descriptiones Animalium quae in Itinere Orientali Observit*, 1775. Forskal's work was edited and published after his death by Carsten Niebuhr.

An early contributor to our knowledge of western Pacific fishes was a nineteenth century naturalist named Philipp Franz von Siebold (1796-1866). He was a physician employed by the Netherlands East Indian Army and from there was detached for service with a small garrison in Japan. During six years of residence in Japan, von Siebold collected many specimens and a large amount of information. Following his expulsion from Japan, he returned to Europe where he published the results of his collecting and study in a large work titled the *Fauna Japonica*, 1832. This treatise contained a section on fishes which was prepared by K. J. Temminck of Amsterdam and Professor Hermann Schlegel, both European naturalists and ornithologists.

Dr. Pieter Bleeker (1819-1878) was a Dutch citizen of humble origin who trained himself to be an apothecary and later a physician. He developed an interest in museums, but found employment as a physician with The Netherlands East Indian Army. He then moved to Batavia where he lived almost continuously from 1842 to 1860; it is here that he developed his great curiosity about the fishes of the area and set to work studying them. In his lifetime, Bleeker wrote over 500 articles of which 432 are on East Indian fishes. His greatest work was a treatise titled *Atlas ichthyologique des Indes orientales*, which was issued in Amsterdam between 1862 and 1877. This work consists of nine volumes, but it was never finished; it also lacks an index to the synonyms used in the book. Weber and De Beaufort prepared an index to the many papers written by Bleeker and issued this index as Volume 1 of their *Fishes of the Indo-Australian Archipeligo*, 1911.

An Englishman by the name of Francis Day produced a large work titled *The Fishes of India* (including Ceylon and Burma), which was published in London in 1878-1888. This work contained over 800 pages and an atlas of 198 plates.

Following Bleeker, another treatise on the fishes of the East Indies was prepared by Max Wilhelm Carl Weber (1852-1937) and Dr. Lieven Ferdinand De Beaufort, both Professors at the University of Amsterdam. This large work was titled *The Fishes of the Indo-Australian Archipelago*. It consists of 11 volumes and was issued periodically between 1911 and 1962.

ANDREW GARRETT, A PIONEER IN POLYNESIA

The most amazing person to collect and to study the fishes of the central Pacific Ocean was an American named Andrew Garrett. Because so little is known or has been written about this Pacific pioneer, special mention is made of his Pacific career.

This naturalist was an American sailor from New England, who single handed, without any formal education, and at a time when transportation was difficult, set an early record of exploration and scientific study in Polynesia which has not been equalled.

Andrew Garrett was born in 1823 at Middlebury, Vermont, and was apprenticed at the age of eleven to an iron moulder in order that he might eventually establish himself as a tradesman. The foundry had no lure for Garrett compared to the world of nature, so we find Garrett at the age of sixteen going to sea as a blacksmith to begin a new life to be spent in the study of plants and animals, in drawing and painting, and in wandering and shipwrecks that was to take him over the entire world. These travels, which extended over many years, took him through the West Indies, the Azores and the Cape Verde Islands in the Atlantic, along both coasts of North and South America, through the Pacific to Hawaii, the Mariannas, and the Bonin Islands, through the East Indies, along Australia, and finally into central Polynesia. He settled for a time in Hawaii, but later moved on to the island of Huahine near Tahiti in the Society Islands; here he died of cancer on November 1, 1887.

Garrett lived for a time in Hilo, where he came in contact with Dr Charles Hinckley Wetmore, a physician and pharmacist of that city. Dr Wetmore was interested in natural history and purchased many of Garrett's paintings. These paintings eventually came to rest in the Library of the Hawaiian Mission Children's Society in Honolulu.

During his stay in Polynesia, Andrew Garrett received at times a small retainer fee from various museums together with a supply of alcohol to aid in preserving his specimens. There are stories which relate that Andrew Garrett was helped in his collecting by various lady friends with whom he left containers of alcohol and that periodically he would make the rounds, collect the specimens, and renew their supply of alcohol.

While in Polynesia and the central Pacific area, Garrett visited and explored Tahiti, Moorea, Raiatea, Borabora, Fiji, the Cook Islands, the Tuamotus, Samoa, and countless other islands in search of his heart's desire — beautiful fishes and shells.

Here with the aid of his meager education he taught himself the ways of science. He learned to observe at first hand the phenomena of nature and to keep a record of these observations. He corresponded with the leading biologists of his time in both America and Europe. He described in a simple scientific manner nearly all of the fishes and shells of Polynesia, but, unfortunately very little of this material was ever printed. And then, as if to climax his life of labor and study, Andrew Garrett taught himself to draw and to paint. The wielding of a brush was a difficult task to calloused, horny hands trained in a foundry and his early drawings show the intense application and labor which were required to produce a drawing. But perseverence so characterized the life of this naturalist that it was not long before he was drawing and painting reproductions of fishes and shells in natural color which were both beautiful and lifelike. These paintings, which he must have turned out literally by the hundreds, were sent to various scientists in America and Europe. Unfortunately, out of Andrew Garrett's vast collection of specimens and drawings, only one major treatise resulted.

Eventually Garrett established contact with Dr. Albert Gunther, who was then at the Museum Godeffroy in Hamburg and who was later to become the curator of fishes in the British Museum. The Museum Godeffroy was the private project of a large trading company, known as Caesar Godeffroy and Sohn, which had shipping activities in the Pacific Ocean centered at Apia. Gunther assembled and edited Garrett's material and thereafter printed a beautiful three volume treatise in German which he titled Andrew Garrett's *Die Fische der Sudsee* and issued it as the *Journal des Museum Godeffroy* between 1873 and 1881; two volumes were issued before Garrett's death. This treatise listed 439 species from Polynesia; of this number 78 were Hawaiian. Meanwhile, the Godeffroy firm suffered financial reverses and *Die Fische der Sudsee* was discontinued in the family *Labridae*. This book by Garrett and Gunther, in spite of its shortcomings, was the first significant publications on the fishes of the tropical, central Pacific Ocean.

Today, Andrew Garrett is nearly forgotten; he is remembered by a sea shell collection in the Bernice Pauahi Bishop Museum in Honolulu, by hundreds of preserved fishes in the bottles of various museums, by a few paintings laid away in a few libraries, and by a plaque in the public square on Huahine. Students of Pacific fishes owe a debt to Andrew Garrett for his biological pioneering; the least we can do is remember his name.

THE BEGINNING OF SCIENTIFIC EXPEDITIONS

Exploring expeditions for the discovery of new lands, new resources, and new peoples began in ancient times, but explorations for scientific collecting and observation probably had their formal beginning with the first voyage (1768-1771) of Captain James Cook (1728-1779) aboard the *Endeavor;* on this journey, he was accompanied by Sir Joseph Banks as naturalist and by Daniel Solander, a young Swedish botanist and friend of Banks. In the century following Cook, other expeditions were organized for scientific explorations or for similar reasons; of these, the following ships are the most important and should be mentioned with their dates and naturalists: the *Beagle* (1831-1836) with Charles Darwin as naturalist; the *Porpoise* (1838-1842) of the U. S. Exploring Expedition with James Dwight Dana as naturalist; the *Erebus* and *Terror* (1839-1843) with Joseph Hooker as naturalist; the *Rattlesnake* (1846-1850) with Thomas Henry Huxley as naturalist; the *Bulldog* (1860) with G. C. Wallich as naturalist; the *Lightning* (1868) with Wyville Thompson as naturalist; the *Porcupine* (1869-1870) with Wyville Thompson as naturalist; and the *Challenger* (1872-1876) with Wyville Thompson as naturalist.

The United States Exploring Expedition (1838-1842) was authorized by Congress in 1836 for the purpose of exploring and surveying the southern seas. The expedition included six vessels: the *Vincennes* and the *Peacock*, both sloops of war, the *Porpoise*, a brig, the *Relief*, a store ship, and two tenders. This expedition left Hampton Roads, Virginia, on August 18, 1838, under the command of Lieutenant Charles Wilkes (1798-1877), and proceeded to Madeira, Rio de Janeiro, Tierra del Fuego, Chile, Peru, the Tuamoto Islands, Samoa, Sydney, the Antarctic Ocean (December, 1839), Fiji, Hawaii (1840), the northwest coast of the United States, the San Francisco Bay area (1841), the Philippines, the Sulu Archipelago, Borneo, Singapore, the Cape of Good Hope, and finaly arrived at New York City on June 10, 1842. The expedition had a staff of scientists aboard, under the supervision of naturalist James Dwight Dana, who gathered information and prepared the reports. These reports were planned to include 28 volumes, but only 19 volumes were published. Wilkes wrote the *Narrative* (six volumes in the 1845 edition and five in the 1850 edition).

The *Challenger* Deep-sea Exploring Expedition (1872-1876), the first major oceanographic expedition for oceanic exploration of the Atlantic and Pacific Oceans, was a joint effort of the British government and the Royal Society. The British government supplied the *Challenger*, a wooden-hulled, steam-powered corvette of 2,306 tons, and a navy crew under the command of Captain George Nares. The scientific staff and its work were supervised by Charles Wyville Thompson (1830-1882) and after 1882 by John Murray (1841-1914). After leaving Portsmouth (December, 1872), the expedition spent a year in the Atlantic Ocean during which time they visited the Canary Islands, Bermuda, the Azores, Madeira, the Cape Verde Islands, and Tristan da Cunha; thereafter they continued to Capetown (October, 1873), then eastward to Kerguelen Island (January, 1874), then to Melbourne, New Zealand, Fiji, Torres Strait, the Banda Sea, the China Sea, Hong Kong, Yokohama, Honolulu*, Tahiti, Valparaiso, Montevideo, Ascension Island, the Azores, and finally Sheerness (May, 1876) in the mouth of the River Thames. The report of the expedition, known as the *Challenger Report** covered many subjects and consisted of 50 quarto volumes which were issued in London between 1880 and 1895. That part of the report known as *The Deep-sea Fishes of the Challenger Expedition* was prepared by Albert C. L. G. Gunther and was issued in London in 1887. Gunther also prepared the smaller reports on the pelagic fishes and the shore fishes.

Prince Albert I of Monaco (1842-1922) was one of the modern pioneer oceanographers. He studied the Mediterranean Sea and the Atlantic Ocean aboard a succession of small vessels including the *Hirondelle* and the *Princess Alice*. To store and to exhibit his oceanographic collections, Prince Albert I built the Institut Oceanographique at Monaco. It was opened in 1910 and contains exhibit halls, a marine laboratory, lecture halls, a public aquarium, and other facilities.

With the beginning of the twentieth century, oceanic expeditions became commonplace with many nations and scientific institutions entering

* The *Challenger* arrived in Honolulu on July 27, 1875, and left on August 11th for Hilo; they arrived in Hilo on August 14th and departed on August 19th.

* The full title is *Report on the Scientific Results of the Voyage of H. M. S. Challenger*, 1880-1895.

he field; today many of these institutions support oceanographic ships and personnel on a continuing basis. These will not be discussed in this introduction.

Mention should be made of a new approach to oceanographic exploration which is marked by a departure from the traditional collecting, storing, studying, publishing routine. This new field might be termed *popular oceanography* or *educational oceanography*. The most successful person to develop public interest in oceanography by means of motion pictures and television was a Frenchman by the name of Jacques-Yves Cousteau of the Institut Oceanographique at Monaco. Using the *Calypso* and other ships, Cousteau prepared and presented a series of movies and television shows depicting his oceanic adventures of the 1950s, 1960s, and 1970s. A few popular books also resulted from the voyages.

UNITED STATES INVESTIGATIONS IN THE PACIFIC AREA

At the end of the 19th century the United States* acquired an interest in several Pacific Islands (in addition to Puerto Rico in the Atlantic area). These included the Hawaiian Islands, the eastern part of Samoa, and the Philippine Islands. The United States Fish Commission sent an exploratory team of naturalists to each of these areas to study the marine fauna.

The fishes and fisheries of Samoa were investigated in the summer of 1902 by a small expedition supported by the U.S. Bureau of Fisheries and under the supervision of Dr. David Starr Jordan of Stanford University. Soon thereafter David Starr Jordan and Alvin Seale issued *The Fishes of Samoa* which appeared in the Bulletin of the *U.S. Bureau of Fisheries* Volume 25 for 1905 (1906).

After the U.S. Bureau of Fisheries completed its surveys of Hawaii (1901, 1902) and Samoa (1902), it turned its attention to the Philippine Islands. The steamer *Albatross* was brought to the Philippines and spent from 1907 to 1910 sampling various deep-water areas of these islands. They collected a large quantity of specimens, most of which were sent to Washington, D.C. Alvin Seale was employed by the Philippine Bureau of Science and, during the period from 1906 to 1916, made extensive fish collections for that office.

The publications resulting from the Philippine collections of the *Albatross* have emerged rather slowly. Several have appeared as a series of volumes of *U.S. National Museum Bulletin 100;* these have been prepared by various authors. Several check lists of Philippine fishes have been published. David Starr Jordan and R. E. Richardson prepared the first useful check list of 830 species which they issued in 1910. Albert Herre prepared a check list if 1,900 species; this list was mysteriously destroyed in 1927. Hilario A. Roxas prepared a list of 1,918 species which was issued in 1937. Albert Herre prepared a second list titled *Check List of Philippine Fishes*, 1953,

* All persons who are interested in the earlier history of ichthyology in the central Pacific Ocean, are urged to read the "Historical Review" written in 1903 by Jordan and Evermann.

See Jordan, David Starr and Barton Warren Evermann. "The Aquatic Resources of The Hawaiian Islands, Part I — The Shore Fishes". *Bulletin of the U.S. Fish Commission* vol. 23 for 1903 (1905), pp. 3-30.

(Fish and Wildlife Service Report 20); this list contains 2,145 species and consists of 977 pages; it is an excellent work.

Fisheries investigations in the Philippine Islands came to an abrupt halt during World War II. The Japanese army completely destroyed the Bureau of Science in Manila including the library. This library, which had its beginning in the previous century during the period of Spanish influence, was one of the best in the world.

The investigation of the Hawaiian area was conducted during the summers of 1901 and 1902. The work of the first summer was based on shore, principally in Honolulu, and was conducted under the supervision of Dr. David Starr Jordan, President of Stanford University, and Dr. Barton Warren Evermann, an ichthyologist with the U.S. Fish Commission. This group spent the summer collecting and studying specimens and thereafter returned to the mainland United States to complete their report. This report was titled "The Aquatic Resources of the Hawaiian Islands, Part I — The Shore Fishes". *Bulletin of the U. S. Fish Commission* vol. 23 for 1903 (1905), and was issued as the first volume of the three volume treatise on Hawaii. This report treated 447 species and contained 234 text figures, 65 black and white plate, and 73 colored plates.

Included with this staff was John N. Cobb of the U. S. Fish Commission, a specialist in commercial fisheries. Cobb's report, titled *Sect. III— The Commercial Fisheries of the Hawaiian Islands*, was bound together with *Sect. II — The Deep-sea Fishes*, to form the second volume of the three which comprise *The Aquatic Resources of the Hawaiian Islands*, 1903 (1905). Cobb's report was a summary of the status of fishing in Hawaii at the beginning of this century. He included a description of the fishing vessels in use, fishing methods, nets and other gear, fish products and fish marketing, a list of the existing fish ponds in Hawaii, and some details of the commercial catch for the year 1900. It is interesting to note that Cobb recorded 178 fish ponds in 1901. The ponds which he listed were distributed as follows: Kauai, 7 ponds; Oahu, 78 ponds; Molokai, 53 ponds; Maui, 4 ponds; and Hawaii, 16 ponds; Niihau, Lanai, and Kahoolawe were not listed.

In 1902, the investigations of the Hawaiian area were directed toward deeper water. The U.S. Fish Commission steamer *Albatross* was sent to the Hawaiian Islands for the spring and summer from March through August, 1902. During this period, they made 344 deep water samplings extending from the Island of Hawaii to Laysan Island. They explored the depth, nature, and configuration of the bottom, and recorded the fauna which they captured. From these samples, they recovered 111 species of fishes which inhabit the sea below 100 fathoms. These fishes were studied by Dr. Charles Henry Gilbert, Professor of Zoology at Leland Stanford Junior University and the naturalist in charge of the expedition; this study was then issued as *Section III* of *Part II—The Deep-sea Fishes.*

In addition to the studies of the Hawaiian fishes which the U.S. Fish Commission undertook, ten other miscellaneous groups of animals were studied and a report made upon them. These reports were assembled as *Part III — Miscellaneous Papers* and issued in 1906 to form the third volume of *The Aquatic Resources of the Hawaiian Islands.* These subjects included birds, a dolphin, isopods, crabs and lobsters, etc., hydroids, schizopods, nemertean worms, starfishes, medusae, and polychaet worms.

SOME PACIFIC - AMERICAN ICHTHYOLOGISTS

The study of Indo-Pacific fishes has attracted the attention and interest of some of the best taxonomic talent in America. This is understandable because this area has the world's largest marine fauna, it is the least known, and it is without doubt the most varied and colorful in the tropical world. During the middle years of the twentieth century, there have been at least four American taxonomists who deserve mention for their studies on Indo-Pacific fishes; they are Fowler, Schultz, Gosline, and Randall.

Dr. Henry Weed Fowler, (1878-19   ) an ichthyologist at the Academy of Natural Sciences of Philadelphia, had maintained a life-long interest in Indo-Pacific fishes beginning just before 1900. He studied this fauna in various museums and in several Indo-Pacific areas and published many smaller reports on these fishes. Dr. Fowler climaxed his Indo-Pacific studies in 1928 with the publication by the Bishop Museum of a large work, *The Fishes of Oceania*. This treatise contained 540 pages, 82 text figures, and 49 black and white plates. It was followed by three additions: Supplement I of 71 pages in 1931, Supplement II of 84 pages in 1934, and Supplement III of 152 pages in 1949.

Dr. Leonard Peter Schultz, (1901-19   ), longtime Curator of Fishes at the U. S. National Museum, was a very able taxonomist and added immeasurably to the knowledge of the Indo-Pacific fishes through numerous publications on this area. His *Fishes Of The Phoenix and Samoan Islands . . .*, a book of 316 pages, appeared in 1943 as *U. S. N. M. Bulletin 180*. This was followed by *The Fishes of The Marshall and Marianas Islands*, a larger work which appeared in three volumes as follows: *U.S.N.M. Bull. 202*, volume 1 of 685 pages in 1953; *U.S.N.M. Bull. 202*, volume 2 of 438 pages in 1960; and *U.S.N.M. Bull. 202*, volume 3 of 176 pages in 1966. This last work greatly improved the classification of central Pacific fishes and remains a very useful taxonomic guide.

Toward the close of World War II, two professional ichthyologists arrived to make their home in Hawaii. They were Vernon E. Brock (1912-1971), a tuna specialist, who became Director of the Division of Fish and Game, Department of Agriculture, State of Hawaii, and Dr. William Alonzo Gosline III (1915-19   ), a taxonomist, who became Professor of Zoology at the University of Hawaii. Gosline and Brock prepared a very useful guide, titled *Handbook of Hawaiian Fishes*, which was issued by the University in 1960. It included 372 pages with 279 figures and treated 584 species of which 136 were regarded as deep water forms and 448 as inshore or surface species.

Dr. John E. Randall (1924-19   ) came from California as a young man to study the fishes of the central Pacific area. Except for a period of about ten years at various locations in the Caribbean area, he has concentrated on the study of the Indo-Pacific fauna. He has issued various publications on Caribbean fishes including *Caribbean Reef Fishes*, a handbook of 318 pages which discusses and illustrates about 300 species of the reef and shore line areas. In the tropical Pacific, Dr. Randall has collected, studied, revised, and published materials on various family groups including the *Acanthuridae*, the *Labridae*, the *Scorpaenidae*, various groups of eels, and others.

THE APPROACHING END OF THE ERA OF CLASSIFICATION

For over three centuries, scientists have been busily engaged in discovering and describing the fishes of the world and in arranging them within a classification scheme. During this time, they have explored most of the remote areas of the earth with the exception of a very few isolated interior regions and much of the bottom of the sea. As a result of this activity, the number of new and undescribed species has diminished each year until the discovery of a new species has now become an uncommon event. This means that those persons who are interested in the classification of fishes are shifting their attention and energies from the search for new species to the redescription and rearrangement of the known species. This trend, in due time, will lead toward a more stable, less changeable classification scheme for fishes and the end of this exciting phase in the era of classification.

PART I
THE CARTILAGINOUS FISHES
(Class Chondrichthyes)
including
The Sharks, Rays, and Chimeras

INTRODUCTION TO
THE SHARKS, RAYS, AND CHIMERAS

Of all the fishes in the sea, the sharks and rays hold a very special place in the attention of man because of the fear and horror which they engender. Their attacks upon swimmers and others together with their savage teeth and fearsome appearance make them the most feared of all aquatic animals. In addition to their man-eating tendencies, sharks are of interest to us because of their evolutionary background, their unusual structure and size, their habits and mode of life, their economic value, and because of the many stories associated with them.

In addition to the sharks and rays that are living today, many ancient species are known from fossils. Fossil teeth and other remains of these prehistoric species are evidence that these fishes existed in very ancient times. Some of these fossil records go back to the Paleozoic Era and are here found in the Devonian Period, known as the Age of Fishes, and also in the earlier Silurian Period of this ancient era. This means that primitive, well formed, recognizable, ancestral sharks and rays existed well over 350,000,000 years ago, and their ancestors, in turn, must have existed many millions of years before them. Even in these early times, there were many kinds of sharks and rays ranging in length from small forms of less than two or three feet to gigantic species exceeding 50 feet in length.

In the world today there are probably about 600 kinds of sharks and rays; of these there are approximately 250 species of sharks and about 350 kinds of rays. These 600 species contain a wide variety of forms and sizes. They range in length from less than 12 inches long when fully grown to the great whale shark which measures about 45 to 50 feet in length. There is also to be found among them a great diversity of form. Some, like the frilled shark with its six gill slits, still resemble their ancient ancestors in many ways, while others, like the basking shark and the whale shark, have developed specialized structures within their mouths for straining food from the sea. These specialized structures are much more recent developments that were not found in their prehistoric ancestors.

Sharks and rays are grouped together by a most unusual anatomical characteristic; this is a skeleton made of cartilage. Their bodies are without

1

bone as we know it and are, therefore, without hard parts except for their teeth, the dermal denticles embedded in their skin, and their spines. This skeleton of cartilage, which is found in all sharks and rays, separates the sharks and rays from the other fishes which have skeletons of bone and which are therefore known as the "bony fishes".

Present-day sharks and rays live everywhere. Most modern sharks and rays live in the sea, but a few species do occur in river mouths and estuaries, and one species, which lives in Lake Nicaragua, has become a permanent resident in fresh water. Within the ocean, sharks and rays live in both cold and warm water, but they are more numerous in the temperate and warmer seas. They are found living at the surface, both along the shorelines and far out at sea, and also upon the ocean bottom, from shallow water down to the dark and cold abyssal depths of the ocean.

The food of these fishes varies with their habitat, for they must eat whatever is plentiful in their area. Bottom living forms such as the rays and some sharks must eat the mollusks, crustaceans, and other bottom dwelling groups while oceanic sharks and rays must feed upon the surface fishes and other animals of the open sea.

In their reproductive habits, sharks and rays exhibit two general patterns. Their young may be developed within the body of the mother and thereafter be born as miniature adults, or, in other sharks and rays, the eggs are placed within an egg case which is thereafter dropped upon the ocean floor or attached to rocks or seaweeds. Here they undergo their development and escape from their egg case when they have achieved their adult form.

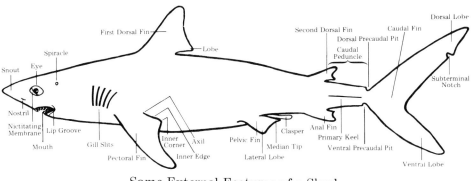

Some External Features of a Shark

Sharks and rays have always been of importance to man as food and as a source of raw materials. The flesh of sharks is eaten by people in various countries of the world where it is sun-dried, salted, made into fish cake, or into some other food product. Although it can be made palatable, many people find its odor objectionable or do not wish to take the time to properly prepare the flesh; shark flesh is therefore not eagerly sought after as human food. However, shark flesh does find a ready use and market as fish meal, fertilizer, and as a protein component in various animal foods. Shark liver is rich in an oil which is high in vitamin A and was once eagerly sought after as a source of this vitamin, particularly when cod liver oil was in short supply. In recent years most vitamin A has been produced synthetically and the market for shark liver oil has declined.

Sharks have a tough skin which is very durable and lasting because of the many small denticles embedded in it. Known in medieval times as shagreen, this shark leather was used to bind large books, to make scabbards and sword handles, and for other uses where a tough, durable leather was required.

The hard teeth of sharks and the pointed spines of sting rays have been used by many primitive peoples. The teeth, because of their sharp points and edges, were made into cutting tools, fastened to weapons, or hung as ornaments upon their bodies; the spines of sting rays were usually attached to the forward end of spears.

In recent years large numbers of sharks have been used in biology and zoology classes of colleges and universities as specimens to demonstrate the structures of simple vertebrate animals. Sharks, both living and dead, are sought for study and display purposes by museums, marine laboratories, and public aquaria.

THE FAMILIES OF
THE SHARKS, RAYS, AND CHIMERAS

THE SIX-GILL AND SEVEN-GILL SHARK FAMILY
1 *Family Hexanchidae (Heptranchidae)*

This family of primitive sharks includes fishes which possess either six or seven pairs of gill slits in contrast to more modern sharks which have only five pairs. The members of this group are mostly of moderate size with long, flat heads and protruding snouts. There is only one spineless dorsal fin on the back and the anal fin is present directly below it on the ventral side. The caudal fin extends backward with but little elevation and is marked by a notch near its end. In this family there are no precaudal pits on the caudal peduncle at the base of the tail. The eyes lack the nictitating membrane and a small spiracle is present. The teeth in the upper and lower jaws are different; the upper teeth are sharp, with slender, curved primary cusps; the lower teeth are more blade-like, quadrate or triangular in shape, and possess several smaller cusps on their margins. These sharks are known from fossils in the Cretaceous and Tertiary Periods. Today this family is represented by a few species which are found chiefly in warmer temperate and tropical seas.

THE SIX-GILL SHARK
Also known as the Bull Shark, Bulldog Shark, Cow Shark,
Gray Shark, and Mud Shark
1—1 *Hexanchus griseus* (Bonnaterre), 1780

Drawn from Kato, Springer, and Wagner

The six-gill shark is a fairly large species with a cylindrical body which becomes a bit flattened toward the rear where it tapers to a very long tail. This tail extends almost straight backward and is not angled upward to any appreciable degree. The head is thick, heavy, broad, flattened above, and bears a snout which is broadly rounded in front. The vertical fins of the body are small; there are no pits on the caudal peduncle as in some sharks; and the spiracle, located near the corner of the mouth, is very small. In

4

color, this shark is very dark gray or gray-brown above and shades gradually to a paler gray or whitish on the belly. This shark is reported to mature at about six or seven feet and will reach 14 or 15 feet in length. Reports of longer specimens, some reaching as much as 25 feet, are viewed with suspicion.

Apparently a slow-moving bottom dweller, this fish is rarely seen. It seems to live at depths of over 600 feet and has been captured as deep as 5,000 feet. Here it feeds upon other bottom living creatures including crustacea, rays, and other fishes. It is ovo-viviparous in its reproductive habits and gives birth to litters of 40 or more living young which may measure from 16 to 26 inches in length.

This shark is of very little value to man at present.

The six-gill shark apparently occurs in all warm seas and in most warmer areas of the temperate regions.

THE FRILLED SHARK FAMILY
2 Family Chlamydoselachidae

To this family belongs a single living species known as the frilled shark. In this species there are six pairs of gill slits, of which the first pair extends downward and connects across the throat below the head; this feature, together with its ruffled edge, gives this shark the appearance of having a fringe or frill around its head. The body of this shark is slender and elongated and the head is wide and depressed. The eye lacks the nictitating membrane and the spiracle nearby is quite small. The tail and the caudal fin are long and are but little raised above the longitudinal axis of the body; the caudal fin is not notched and there are no pits at its base. The pectoral and pelvic fins in this species are broad and rounded and the anal fin is located directly below the dorsal fin.

This is a primitive family of sharks of which only a single species survives. Fossils of its ancestors have been found in the strata of the Miocene and Pliocene Epochs.

THE FRILLED SHARK
Also known as the Frilled-gilled Shark
2—1 *Chlamydoselachus anguineus* Garman, 1884

Drawn from Kato, Springer, and Wagner

The frilled shark is a fish of moderate size with a long, slender body and a long tail which is raised but little above the longitudinal axis of the body. It has but a single, spineless, dorsal fin which is located at the back end of the body directly above the anal fin. The mouth is large and contains sharp teeth, each of which has three curved points. This fish is a famous biological curiosity because of its six gill slits and because the first gill slit nearly encircles the head to give the fish the appearance of wearing a frilled collar around its neck. In color this fish is light brown or dusky. This shark reaches a length of six or seven feet.

In its reproductive habits, this species is ovo-viviparous and gives birth to perhaps a dozen young, each of which developed from an egg within the body of the mother before being born. The frilled shark inhabits deeper water where it is reported to feed upon squid and various fishes.

This shark has no value to man.

The distribution of this shark is probably world-wide in tropical seas and in warmer temperate regions.

THE SAND TIGER SHARK FAMILY
3 *Family Odontaspidae (Carchariidae)*

Sand sharks have rather elongated, compressed bodies which lack significant surface markings including any longitudinal dermal ridges often found on the sides of some species in the area anterior to the anal fins. The body tapers backward quite uniformly to form a long, compressed tail, the axis of which is inclined only slightly upward from the axis of the body. The caudal peduncle is not greatly flattened, is without lateral folds, and bears a caudal pit above but not on its lower surface.

The head is depressed and tapering and leads gradually into a snout which is short and tapering and which terminates in a sharply pointed tip. The mouth is large, wide, and greatly arched and possesses a labial fold on the lower jaw. These jaws are not greatly extendible as in some species. The teeth are large, long, slender, and awl-shaped and have their bases composed of two roots; these teeth may or may not bear a small, sharp denticle on each side at their base. The nostrils in this family are transverse in position, are without barbels on their anterior margins, and are entirely separate from the mouth. All five gill openings are wide and the fifth gill slit lies anterior to the origin of the pectoral fin; the gill arches within are without gill rakers.

The body bears two dorsal fins; the first of these is placed at the middle of the trunk or just behind the middle and has the posterior end of its base terminating anterior to or slightly behind the origin of the pelvic fins. The caudal fin is not lunate in shape as in the *Isuridae;* it is elongated but measures less than one-third of the total length, is notched at the tip, and has the lower anterior corner of the fin drawn out into a lobe. The pectoral fins are quite short and the inner margins of the pelvic fins are more or less united posterior to the cloaca; this is more apparent in the male than in the female. These sharks are moderate to large in size; some will exceed ten feet in length.

The members of this family are bottom living forms and seem to have the habit of swimming continuously. They are voracious, predatory species, regardless of their size, and should never be trusted.

In their reproductive habits these sharks are ovo-viviparous and bring forth their young fully formed. Apparently the young develop two at a time, with each side of the uterus occupied by a single individual. After each of these embryonic sharks has absorbed the egg to which it is attached and has grown to nearly the size at which it is born, it then develops an astonishing, predacious, cannibalistic habit for a time of eating the eggs which thereafter come sliding down the uterus.

In modern times this family seems to have been reduced to but one genus of about a half dozen species which are distributed in most tropical and temperate seas.

Many fossil forms are known from teeth which are scattered from the Cretaceous Period of the Mesozoic Era down through the Tertiary Period of the Cenezoic Era.

Of this family, at least one species is known from this area.

The sand sharks have long been known under the name of *Carchariidae* and will therefore be found in most books under this name. The name *Odontaspidae* is now regarded as a more correct name for these sharks, so that books of the last few years and of the future will probably have the members of this family listed under the name of *Odontaspidae*.

The following species are not described or illustrated:

Odontaspis kamoharai (Matsubara), 1936. Kamohara's shark was first reported from the Sea of Japan; this specimen measured about 30 inches in length. It has been reported from the Hawaiian area.

THE RAGGED-TOOTH SHARK OR FIERCE SHARK
3—1 *Odontaspis ferox* (Risso), 1810

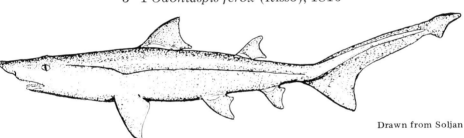

Drawn from Soljan

Like the other members of this family, the body of this species is quite elongated, somewhat compressed, and tapers uniformly toward the tail which is angled upward slightly from the longitudinal axis of the body. This tail possesses a pit at its base on the upper surface where it joins the caudal peduncle, but there is no pit on the lower surface. The upper lobe of the tail fin is notched on its posterior margin and the lower forward corner of this fin is drawn out into a sizeable angular lobe.

The teeth of this species are useful in its identification. In the upper jaw the first tooth on each side is noteably smaller than the second and third teeth; the third tooth in turn is followed by three or four teeth which are very much smaller than the second and third teeth. These teeth are typically five-pointed and possess a large, straight, central cusp and two, small, straight cusps on each side at the base of the large central cusp; this means that each tooth is usually five-pointed.

The color of the body is a reddish-greyish hue above and is marked by a few large, darker, possibly blackish areas which extend downward onto the body. The lower surface is a grayish, metallic-red color. Large specimens will reach a length of about 12 feet.

The distribution of this species includes the Mediterranean Sea and the warm waters of the eastern Atlantic Ocean: it has been reported from California and the Hawaiian area. Its distribution is doubtless much wider than indicated above.

In all except the most recent publications, this species will appear under the name of *Carcharias ferox* Risso, 1810. *Odontaspis* has been decreed a more correct name for this genus.

THE MACKEREL SHARK FAMILY
4 Family Isuridae (Lamnidae)

This is a family of large sharks and includes many of the vicious and voracious species which are dangerous to man. Their bodies are generally stout, heavy, robust, fusiform or spindle-shaped, and do not have any longitudinal dermal ridges on the body except at the tail. The caudal peduncle at the base of the tail is flattened dorso-ventrally, has a pit both above and below, and has a wide prominent keel on each side which extends backward onto the tail and forward a short distance onto the body. The axis of the tail is greatly elevated to support the upper lobe of the tail, which is notched on its lower border a short distance from the tip; the lower lobe of the tail in this family is nearly as large as the upper lobe. There are two dorsal fins and an anal fin in all members of the family. The head of these sharks is conical in shape and contains a large mouth equipped with sharp teeth. The eyes are without nictitating membranes, the spiracle may be either present or absent, and the nostrils are separate from the mouth.

They are reported to be ovo-viviparous and to give birth to living young.

This is a family with many fossil forms, many of which have been found in the strata of the Cretaceous and later periods.

The sharks of this family inhabit all temperate and tropical oceans of the world from shore line areas to deeper water.

THE GREAT WHITE SHARK
Also known as the Man-eater Shark, White Pointer and Ma-no Ni-u-hi
4—1 Carcharodon carcharias (Linnaeus), 1758

The great white shark is a large species with a spindle-shaped body which is somewhat heavier toward the head. The snout is pointed and bears beneath it a large mouth containing large, triangular, coarsely-serrated teeth which are similar in both jaws. The caudal peduncle is flattened vertically and bears a prominent keel on each side which extends forward some distance onto the body; the caudal peduncle also bears a transverse furrow above and below which is located just in front of the base of the caudal fin. The spiracle, found in most sharks, is either very small or absent.

In color, this species is a dull leaden-gray, slate-gray, slaty-brown or bluish above and shades gradually to a dirty white color on the lower sides and belly. There is a dark area in the axil of the pectoral fins and the dorsal and caudal fins are darker along their posterior margins. The tip of the pectoral fin is darker in color and often has dark spots nearby.

This species is most easily identified by its large size, the nearly equal lobes of the tail with its lunate margins, and the large, serrated, triangular teeth. This shark will reach a length of at least 21 feet and has been reported to grow much longer. Reports of larger specimens should be questioned.

Of all known sharks, the great white shark is probably the most feared by man. It is a fierce, fearless, voracious, active, strong fish which has been described as the world's most ferocious animal. It inhabits the open sea and occasionally skirts the shore line areas in its search for food. It will eat almost anything from fish, seals, dolphins, birds, and turtles, to man, domestic animals, and garbage. It is a tough fish, fights when captured, and may even attack boats when hooked or injured.

The young of this shark are developed from eggs within the body of the mother and are born at a length of about 50 inches.

The white shark is important to man because of its fierce habits, its effect on fishing, and the value of its animal products.

It is a pelagic species and is distributed world-wide in tropical and sub-tropical seas.

THE SHORT - FINNED MAKO SHARK
Also known as the Bonito Shark, the Blue Pointer,
and the Sharp-nosed Mackerel Shark
4—2 *Isurus oxyrinchus* Rafinesque, 1810

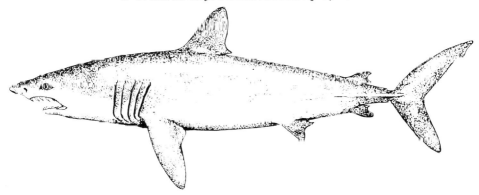

The mako shark is a fairly large species with a moderately slender, spindle-shaped body and a head and snout which are very pointed and conical in shape. The caudal peduncle is flattened dorso-ventrally to form broad, sharp-edged keels on the sides and the precaudal pits form deep crosswise furrows on the upper and lower sides at the base of the tail.

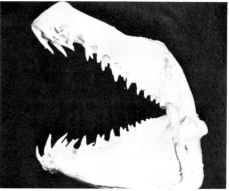

The teeth of this species are distinctive and will serve to identify it. They have a single, slender, inward-curving blade without secondary cusps and without serrations along their edges. It should be noted that in this species the two central teeth in the front of each jaw are more slender than the other teeth in the jaws. The color of this shark when living is a deep cobalt or ultramarine blue or blue-gray above and white beneath. This shark will reach a length of 13 or 14 feet.

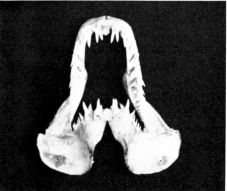

The mako shark is an offshore species which is only occasionally seen in shallow water. It is an active, strong, fierce, and dangerous species, which struggles and fights when hooked and jumps from the water in its attempts to dislodge the hook. It appears to enjoy the surface and is often seen swimming with the tips of its dorsal fin and the tail above the surface.

The mako shark is an edible species and is often sold in fish markets. It is also an interesting game fish for sportsmen because of its habit of leaping when hooked.

The distribution of the mako shark is world-wide in tropical and warmer temperate seas.

This fish seems to bear two names. In the Atlantic Ocean it is called *Isurus oxyrinchus* Rafinesque, while in the Pacific Ocean it is often known as *Isurus glaucus* (Muller and Henle). It should not be confused with *Prionace glauca* (Linnaeus), the Great Blue Shark.

THE LONG-FINNED MAKO SHARK
4—3 *Isurus paucus* Guitart-Manday, 1966

The long-finned mako shark has a slender trunk, a long head, and long pectoral fins which are approximately equal in length to the head. The mouth is large, the gill openings are very large, and the eyes are also large and circular in outline. The caudal peduncle of the tail is flattened vertically, bears precaudal pits both above and below, and possesses a sharp-edged keel on each side. The teeth are narrow, triangular, and fearsome, and are alike in both jaws. The color of this species, like that of *I. oxyrinchus*, is blue or grayish blue above and white beneath. The body of this shark will reach a length of at least nine feet.

Drawn from Guitart-Manday

This species very closely resembles *Isurus oxyrinchus* but may be separated from *I. oxyrinchus* by its long pectoral fins; also, those specimens of *I. paucus* which are over five feet in length have dark blotches on the underside of the head and body, while *I. oxyrinchus* is white beneath.

This is an uncommon oceanic species which occurs in the western and central Pacific Ocean including the Hawaiian Islands.

This species is found in some books under the name of *Isurus alatus* J. A. F. Garrick, 1967, and *Lamna punctata* DeKay, 1872.

THE BASKING SHARK FAMILY
5 Family Cetorhinidae (Halsydridae)

This family contains but a single species, the basking shark which, next to the whale shark, is the second largest fish of modern times. It has an elongated, massive body and a large head which bears an unusual, elongated snout. The head is marked off from the body by great long gill slits which extend from the upper regions of the head to nearly the midline of the throat. The eyes are small and without a nictitating membrane and the spiracles are likewise small. The teeth are very small and the back of the mouth contains numerous gill rakers which are long, slender, and horny. The anal fin is present and the caudal peduncle has well developed keels along its sides.

The basking shark and its relatives have left fossil teeth and other remains in strata of the Cretaceous and later periods.

THE BASKING SHARK
Also known as the Bone Shark
5—1 Cetorhinus maximus (Gunnerus), 1765

The basking shark, the world's second largest fish, has a short head and a robust, massive, spindle-shaped body. It is easily identified by its great size, by a very wide mouth which occupies most of the lower surface of the head, by the long gill slits which extend from high on the back to well under the throat, and by its small, numerous teeth. In addition, the head bears a

11

well-developed snout and a longitudinal keel extends along each side of the body in front of the tail.

This shark is developed for feeding on plankton. The teeth have become reduced in size, are alike in both jaws, and are without cusps or serrations. The mouth and gill slits are large to permit the passage of great quantities of water, and the gills through which the water passes have elaborate, long, slender, horny, sieve-like gill rakers for straining out the food on which it feeds.

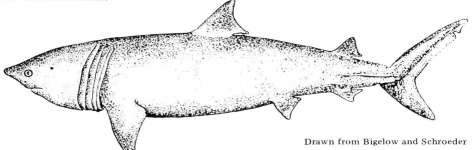

Drawn from Bigelow and Schroeder

The color of this shark appears to vary. It has been reported as grayish brown to slaty gray above and may sometimes be a very dark color approaching black. The sides and belly may be the same color as the back or they may gradually shade to lighter hues on the sides and even to white below.

This shark is usually less than 30 feet long, although there are reports of specimens approaching 45 feet in length.

The basking shark is a sluggish, harmless, plankton feeder usually seen lying at the surface with possibly the snout, dorsal fin, and tip of the tail protruding. It occasionally gathers into schools of 100 or more individuals and is thought by some to migrate to cooler waters in the summer seasons. It is ovo-viviparous and gives birth to living young which measure about five or six feet in length.

This shark has been hunted and captured for the oil contained in its liver.

This is a pelagic species which is world-wide in temperate and cooler waters; it occasionally wanders into sub-tropical areas.

THE THRESHER SHARK FAMILY
6 *Family Alopiidae*

The thresher sharks may be recognized immediately from all other fishes by their astonishing tail which is about equal in length to the body and is greatly elevated and arched. Their bodies are moderately long and are somewhat fusiform, spindle, or torpedo-shaped. The head and mouth of these sharks are small compared to other sharks. The gill arches within the mouth are without gill rakers, and the teeth, which are alike in both jaws, are small, simple, flat, and triangular with smooth edges. There are two dorsal fins; the first one is large and the second one is very small. The anal fin is present but there are no keels at the base of the caudal fin. The spiracle is present near the eye.

Their development is ovo-viviparous and the young, therefore, are not born until they are fully formed.

These are oceanic fishes which inhabit tropical and sub-tropical seas and are not often seen near shore.

The family contains one genus and possibly five or six species which are presently distinguished by the position of the fins, the cusps of the teeth, and the size of the eyes.

Young Thresher Shark (*Alopias* sp.)

THE COMMON THRESHER SHARK
Also known as the Fox Shark, Whip-tailed Shark, Thrasher Shark,
Ma-no Hi-'u-ka, and Ma-no La-u Ka Hi-u
6—1 *Alopias vulpinus* (Bonnaterre), 1788

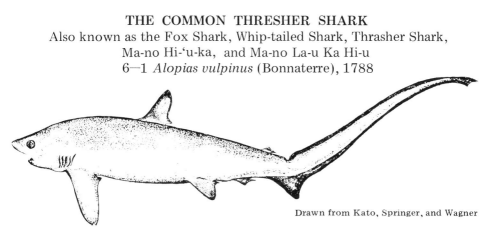

Drawn from Kato, Springer, and Wagner

The common thresher shark has a rather stout, solid body which is slightly flattened on the sides and which tapers rather uniformly from its center to the base of the tail. The mouth is not particularly large and the teeth within it are simple, smooth, and sharp-edged. The body color on the back varies from almost black through various shades of slate, blue, leaden blues, and grays to brown and then shades gradually to white on the belly. In addition, there are various irregular spots, areas, and mottlings scattered over the body. In length, this shark may reach as much as 20 feet, but most individuals are less than 18 feet in length.

Thresher sharks are harmless, pelagic fishes and are rarely seen near shore. They roam the oceans feeding upon squids and smaller schooling fishes which they are reported to somehow encircle and to herd into more compact schools by the thrashing action of their long tails. The thresher is reported to feed on the outer edge of the school as it swims around it. It is reported to continue to feed in this manner until the school scatters or is consumed or until the appetite of the shark is satisfied.

These sharks are ovo-viviparous; the eggs are retained within the body of the mother where the young complete their development prior to birth. Litters of thresher sharks are reported to contain fewer young than the litters of other large sharks. The young at birth vary in length from 30 inches to five feet.

These sharks are occasionally taken on hook and line by fishermen and sometimes are entangled in fishing nets. They are a good sport fish and usually fight when hooked.

The common thresher shark is world-wide in warmer temperate and sub-tropical seas.

THE WHALE SHARK FAMILY
7 *Family Rhincodontidae*
This family contains but one living species, the famous whale shark, the world's largest fish of modern times. The body of this fish is large and massive and tapers gradually toward the tail. The head is large, flattened, and wide and bears five gill slits of unusual length. The mouth is wide and situated at the very front of the head. There are small eyes located close to the corners of the mouth and a small spiracle is nearby, but there are no regular oro-nasal grooves connecting the nostrils and the mouth. The two dorsal fins are without spines, the anal fin is present, and the tail is large but lacks a notch on its rear border. The caudal peduncle bears horizontal keels on the sides and contains a pit on the upper surface at the base of the tail.

This family contains but one genus and a single known living species.

THE WHALE SHARK
7—1 *Rhincodon typus* Smith, 1829

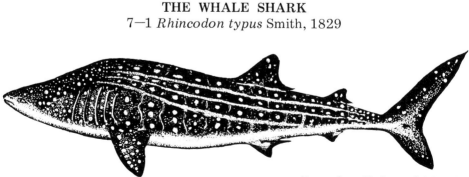

Drawn from Bigelow and Schroeder

The whale shark is the world's largest fish although larger species undoubtedly lived in prehistoric times. It has a gigantic body which is thickest in the area of the gills and tapers gradually toward the tail. This body bears long, longitudinal ridges of skin which arise in the area above the gill openings and extend to the base of the tail. The head is very wide and flattened and bears a very wide mouth situated across the very front of the head. Within this mouth are a myriad of small teeth arranged in rows and an elaborate branchial sieve that strains the food particles from the water as it passes on out through the gill slits.

The color of the body has been variously described as purplish blue, dark gray, reddish brown, and greenish brown above and yellowish or white beneath. The back and sides are marked by both longitudinal and vertical lines of light yellow or white to form a somewhat reticulated pattern on the body. Light spots, usually white or yellowish, are scattered over the entire upper surface and sides of the body.

This shark is usually less than 35 feet in length although reports exist of sharks of 40, 50, and 60 feet in length.

Whale sharks are sluggish, slow moving fishes which often lie motionless at the surface. They feed upon small fishes, crustaceans, squids, and other animals and are occasionally seen feeding in a vertical position.

Whale sharks do not bear their young alive, but encase the egg in an egg capsule and release this capsule to develop and hatch in the ocean outside of the body of the mother.

Except for their great size, whale sharks are absolutely harmless to swimmers and boats. They are occasionally rammed by steamers as they lie floating at the surface and are thereafter carried impaled upon the bow for a time. In some areas, including the western coast of India, where these fishes have been numerous, they have been hunted for food.

The whale shark occurs in all of the tropical seas of the world.

THE CAT SHARK FAMILY
Also known as the Lazy Sharks
8 *Family Scyliorhinidae*

The cat sharks are a large family of rather small species. Their bodies are usually slender, elongated, and spindle-shaped and taper toward the tail which is not angled upward to an appreciable degree. Most species have two dorsal fins without spines, although one or two species have but a single dorsal fin. The caudal peduncle has no keels upon its sides and also lacks the precaudal pits on its upper and lower surfaces. The anal fin is present in this family. The head of most species lacks the oro-nasal grooves connecting the nostrils and the mouth, a spiracle is present behind the eye, and there is no nictitating membrane over the eye. The teeth are small and usually possess three cusps.

These fishes are variously colored with brown, black, white, and other colors. Some are uniformly colored and others have various types of patterns. The deeper water species are usually darker.

This family contains small sharks most of which are bottom dwellers. They are found from the shallow waters of the shore line to depths well below 500 feet where they live a sluggish life feeding upon bottom-dwelling creatures including crustaceans, worms, molluscs and almost any other substance which might serve as food. Some forms are nocturnal and feed at night and may sometimes be seen swimming in shallow water during the hours of darkness.

Cat sharks rear their young in a curious way. They lay their eggs in a rather large, quadrate-shaped, leathery egg case with prehensile tendrils at the corners. These tendrils then attach to seaweeds, stones, and other objects to keep the egg case from drifting away. A few cat sharks are reported to bring forth their young alive.

There are reported to be over 50 species in this family, most of which live in tropical and temperate seas of the world; many are found in the tropical Indo-Pacific region.

THE SPONGE-HEADED CAT SHARK
8—1 *Aprinsturus spongiceps* (Gilbert), 1905

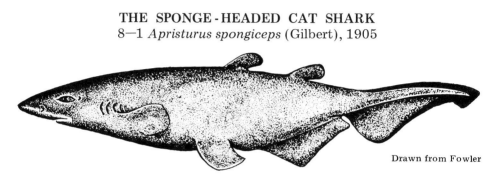

Drawn from Fowler

This cat shark is a small species with a deep, compressed body which leads gradually into the tail, the axis of which points almost directly backward. The head is flattened, the snout is reported to be soft and flabby, and a small spiracle is present near the eye. The teeth bear cusps, of which there are usually five, although some teeth with three and four cusps are present. The color of this little shark is reported to be a dull gray-brown. The body of this shark is small and measures about 20 inches in length. It is a rare fish and very little is known about it. This little shark is a deep water species from the Hawaiian Islands and doubtless elsewhere in the Pacific Ocean.

THE FALSE CAT SHARK FAMILY
9 *Family Pseudotriakidae*
The false cat sharks are a small family of large sharks with two dorsal fins of which the first is very long and low. The anal fin is present and the caudal peduncle is not flattened dorso-ventrally. On the head, the nostrils are not connected to the mouth by a groove, a spiracle is present, the teeth are small and numerous, and the gill arches are without gill rakers. These are deep water sharks and are reported to be ovo-viviparous. This family contains but one genus and apparently two species, one living in the north Atlantic Ocean and the other in the north Pacific Ocean.

THE PACIFIC FALSE CAT SHARK
Also known as the Dumb Shark or Oshizame (Japanese)
9—1 *Pseudotriakis acrages* Jordan and Snyder, 1904

Drawn from Jordan and Snyder

In this shark the body is elongated, the head is wide and flattened, and the snout is short, rounded, and flattened. The mouth is wide and large and contains many small teeth. The eyes are large and the spiracle is present nearby. The body bears a small dermal ridge along the midline of the back just in front of the dorsal fin. The tail extends almost directly backward from the body and is elevated only slightly. The caudal peduncle bears no precaudal pits, the paired pelvic fins are small, and the margin of the tail fin is notched near its posterior end. The teeth each bear a cusp at their center and one or two smaller lateral cusps on each side. These teeth are very small and are arranged in a mosaic pattern in the mouth.

The color of the body is dark gray or dark brown, both above and below; the body is also marked on the sides with vertical streaks of grayish brown. The posterior margins of the second dorsal fin, the anal fin, and the caudal fin are edged with a darker color. This shark measures eight or nine feet in length.

At present this species is known only from Hawaii, Japan, and the cooler waters of the western Pacific Ocean.

THE SMOOTH DOGFISH SHARK FAMILY
Also known as the Smoothhounds
10 *Family Triakidae*

The smooth dogfish sharks are a family of smaller, somewhat slender sharks with two dorsal fins and an anal fin. As a rule the species of this

The White-tipped Reef Shark showing its slender body and short snout.

17

family lack the upper and lower precaudal pits in front of the tail, but a few species do have a precaudal pit on the upper side only. There are no keels on the caudal peduncle at the base of the tail. In most species the nictitating membrane of the eye is usually lacking, but it is present in a few forms. The spiracle may be either present or absent, the gill arches are without gill rakers, and the teeth are either small and rounded or with two or three distinct cusps.

The members of this family are reported to be ovo-viviparous and to bring forth their young alive.

This family is widely distributed in the tropical and warmer temperate seas of the world from the shallow coastal waters down to moderate depths. The family includes about seven genera and nearly 30 species.

THE WHITE - TIPPED REEF SHARK
10—1 *Triaenodon obesus* (Ruppell), 1835

The white-tipped reef shark is a fish of medium size with a smooth skin and a rather slender body which tapers quite uniformly from the head to the tail. The head is short, flat, and wide, the eyes are small with a nictitating membrane, and there is no spiracle. The caudal peduncle has a precaudal pit above, but there is no precaudal pit below, and there are no keels on its sides. The teeth of this shark have a large central cusp and a smaller cusp on each side; they are small in size and alike in both jaws.

In color the body is uniformly grayish or brownish above and whitish below. White tips on both dorsal fins and the caudal fin help to distinguish this shark.

This shark reaches a length of about seven feet, although most specimens are smaller.

This is a shore line species which frequents shallow water areas but is not common throughout all of the areas of its range.

The liver of this species has been reported as toxic to humans in the Gilbert Islands.

Occasionally this fish is included in the *Carcharhinidae.* This species should not be confused with *Pterolamiops longimanus* (Poey), the oceanic white-tipped shark.

The white-tipped reef shark occurs in tropical and sub-tropical waters from the Red Sea eastward across the Indian Ocean, through the East Indies, and across the entire Pacific Ocean.

THE GRAY SHARK FAMILY
Also known as the Requiem Sharks, the Whaler Sharks, and the
Typical Sharks
11 *Family Carcharhinidae (Galeorhinidae)*

The gray sharks make up the largest family of sharks and include the majority of modern species. They are of moderate or large size and have rather elongated, compressed bodies and tails. Their snout is usually short, sharp, and tapering and the spiracle behind the eye is usually present, although in a few species it is very small or entirely absent. The nostrils are not connected to the mouth and there are no gill rakers present. In this family all of the species except one, *G. japonicus*, bear the nictitating membrane. There are two dorsal fins without spines and all members of this family possess the anal fin. The caudal fin is elongated and compressed, bears a notch just below its tip, and is never lunate in shape. The caudal peduncle is without keels on its sides and the caudal pits at the base of the tail are present on both the upper and lower sides. The teeth are blade-like with only one cusp.

These sharks are usually large or of moderate size and include both harmless species and others that are very dangerous to man. Although a few of the smaller species may be harmless, the larger species live a roving, predatory life.

Some species are of commercial importance for their livers, their skins, or their flesh. The livers of these and other sharks have often been the source of vitamin-rich oil. Their skins have also been a valuable article of commerce, known as shagreen, and have been used for binding books, making sword handles and scabbards, for polishing wood, and other uses.

The members of this family are reported to be ovo-viviparous and to bring forth their young alive.

Most species live in tropical or sub-tropical seas both along the shore line and in the open sea. A few inhabit fresh water.

There are about 16 genera within this family and possibly about 60 species.

THE TIGER SHARK
Also known as the Leopard Shark and Ma-no Pa-'e-le
11—1 *Galeocerdo cuvieri* (Peron and Lesueur), 1822

The tiger shark is a large fish with a robust, elongated body and a short, blunt snout which is broadly rounded. It is probably most easily identified by its teeth which are curved to the side, notched on their outer margins, and coarsely serrated. These teeth, which are alike in both jaws, are largest in front and decrease in size toward the corners of the mouth. A spiracle is present on the side of the head near the eye. The caudal peduncle has low, hard keels along its sides and the upper fork of the tail ends in a point with a notch just below the tip. This shark is gray or grayish brown above and lighter below. It is often marked, particularly in younger specimens, with short, vertical bars which slowly disappear with age. This shark usually measures 12 or 13 feet in length and is known to reach at least 18 feet; in addition, there are reports which indicate this shark may reach more than 20 feet.

Tiger sharks are strong, active fishes which roam the oceans in search of food. They will eat almost anything including fishes, other sharks, rays, turtles, seals, sea lions, dolphins, birds, crabs, garbage, and carrion. They are savage beasts and are reported to even take bites out of each other when tangled in a net. They will attack bathers, wreck nets and fishing gear, and destroy food fishes and other animals. They are apparently more active during the night.

These sharks are ovo-viviparous and retain the developing young within

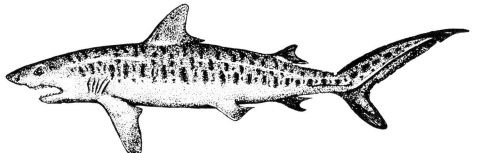

the body of the mother. They are born when 18 or 20 inches in length in litters ranging from 30 to 50 or more, although some litters may be much smaller.

These are important fishes because of their size, their dangerous habits, and because of the products which they contain. They are fished for fun and also for their high grade oil and skins.

The tiger shark is both an oceanic and a shore line species which occurs world-wide in tropical and sub-tropical seas. These are warm water sharks and seem to move northward and southward with the seasons.

THE SOUP FIN SHARK
Also known as the Oil Shark
11—2 *Galeorhinus zyopterus* Jordan and Gilbert, 1883

This is a shark of medium size with a snout which is long, depressed, and rounded at the tip. The eyes are large and the spiracle, which is small, is located beside the eye. The pectoral fins are of moderate size with concave posterior margins and somewhat pointed tips. The first dorsal fin is located midway between the pectoral and ventral fins. The second dorsal fin is about one-fourth the size of the first dorsal fin, is slightly larger than the anal fin, and is located slightly nearer the tail.

The teeth, which are similar in both jaws, number about 32 above and 30 below. The lateral teeth have their points directed toward the sides of the mouth. These teeth contain a deep notch on the middle of the anterior margin, below which are a series of two to five small, sharp cusps or serrations; the main cusps are not serrated. The four or five teeth nearest the center of the mouth are smaller than the lateral teeth, while the median tooth of each jaw is smallest of all and lacks the basal cusps.

The color of the body is dusky grayish. Both dorsal fins are black anteriorly, the pectoral fins are dark over most of their surface, and the caudal fin is dark-tipped. This shark reaches six or seven feet in length.

The soup fin shark is ovo-viviparous and retains the developing eggs within the body to be born later as fully formed miniature sharks. These litters have been reported to contain from six to as many as 52 young sharks.

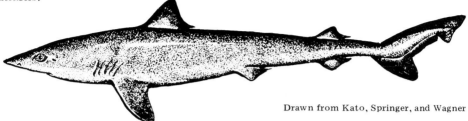

Drawn from Kato, Springer, and Wagner

This shark was once valued for the oil contained in its liver. The fins of this species are used for shark fin soup which is eaten by the Chinese and others.

The distribution of this species includes the temperate and tropical seas of the central and eastern Pacific Ocean.

THE GREAT BLUE SHARK
Also known as the Blue Whaler
11—3 *Prionace glauca* (Linnaeus), 1758

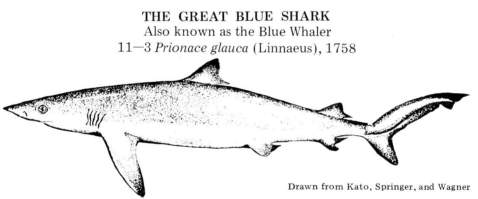

Drawn from Kato, Springer, and Wagner

Blue sharks are large in size and have long heads and long, slender bodies. Their pectoral fins are large, long, and falcate or sickle-shaped, while the remaining fins of the body are only of moderate size. The tail has the usual notch just below the end of the upper lobe and there is a nictitating membrane over the eye. The teeth are large and unlike in the two jaws. The upper teeth are sub-triangular in outline and have serrated edges; the lower teeth are narrower, more erect, and also possess serrated edges.

In life, the color of this species is a brilliant, dark, indigo blue on the upper parts of the body and thereafter shades to a light blue on the sides, and then to pure white on the belly. The tips of the fins are also usually lighter in color. Some individuals of this species have been reported as slaty gray or gray-black in color above and whitish or dirty white below; these may possible have been dead. This shark is known for certain to reach 12 or 13 feet in length and has been reported to reach 20 feet.

This shark is an oceanic species, pelagic in its habits, and is rarely seen near shore. It is a moderately active fish except when feeding; at this time it becomes very active and voracious and will attack fishing nets and other gear. It feeds upon a wide variety of food including various fishes, small sharks, squids, birds, and garbage. When actively hunting food, it is reported to have the habit of moving the nictitating membrane up and down over the eye.

This is an ovo-viviparous species and retains the young within the mother until fully formed. They are then released in litters numbering from about 25 to 50 at about 20 inches in length.

Although fairly numerous, this shark does not have much commercial value. It interferes with commercial fishermen and does some damage to their fishing gear. A few are caught for sport and for their flesh.

The distribution of this species is world-wide in tropical and warmer temperate seas.

THE OCEANIC WHITE-TIPPED SHARK
11—4 *Pterolamiops longimanus* (Poey), 1861

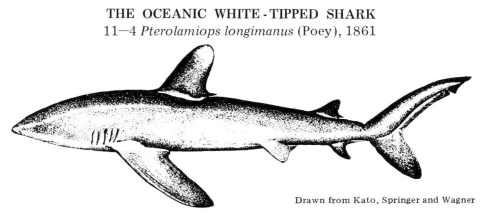

Drawn from Kato, Springer and Wagner

The oceanic white-tipped shark is a medium-sized species with a trunk which is moderately stout, a snout which is broadly rounded in front, and with the horizontal keels absent on the sides of the caudal peduncle. The first dorsal fin and the paired pectoral fins are very large and long and are broadly rounded at their tips. A low ridge of skin is present on the midline of the back between the dorsal fins. The spiracle found in most sharks is absent in this species. The upper teeth are broadly triangular and serrated on the edges, while the teeth of the lower jaw are more slender, particularly toward the front of the jaw.

In color, this shark is bluish, grayish, or a copper brown above and yellowish or dirty white below. The tips of the dorsal fins are marked with white and sometimes there are white markings on the tips or margins of the tail, pectoral and pelvic fins. The anal fin is black-tipped. The lower surface of the pectoral fins and both the upper and lower surfaces of the pelvic fins are sometimes spotted with gray. Young specimens may have dusky fin tips. There is some variation in the color patterns. Sometimes the white tip of the first dorsal fin is mottled with tiny darker spots and sometimes the dorsal and pectoral fins are not white-tipped at all.

This shark matures at five or six feet. Although most specimens are less than ten feet, there are reports of specimens two or three feet longer.

The oceanic white-tipped shark is an active, dangerous, voracious species which feeds upon all manner of marine animals including fishes, squids, and even garbage. This shark is a nuisance to commercial fishermen because it eats their bait and other fishes which have been caught upon their lines.

In its reproductive habits it is ovo-viviparous and retains the developing young within the body of the mother until they are fully formed. The young are born in small litters which number from six to eight and measure about 27 inches at birth.

The oceanic white-tipped shark occurs in tropical and sub-tropical seas of the world. It is a truly pelagic species which is rarely seen in shore line areas.

There are many references to the oceanic white-tipped shark under the older name of *Carcharhinus longimanus* (Poey). This species should not be confused with *Triaenodon obesus* (Ruppell), the white-tipped reef shark.

THE WHITE-MARGINED SHARK
Also known as Ruppell's White-tip Shark and Silver-tip Shark
11—5 *Carcharhinus albimarginatus* (Ruppell), 1835

The body of the white-margined shark is of medium size and moderately slender and tapers quite uniformly from the mid-section toward both the head and tail. The head is likewise of moderate length and bears a short, bluntly rounded snout. The teeth are blade-like and have single cusps which are oblique; those of the upper jaw are narrow and serrated. The first dorsal fin, which is of average size, begins directly above the axil of the pectoral fin. The caudal peduncle bears caudal pits on both its upper and lower sides. There are no lateral keels or ridges on the caudal peduncle. Large specimens of this species will reach a length of about nine feet.

The white-margined shark is most easily recognized by the color pattern of its body. It is in general a dark gray color above with brownish hues and a pure white color beneath. The fins are marked by white tips and by narrower, white, posterior margins; these margins, which may be of various widths, contrast rather sharply with the darker areas of the fins. These white markings are the largest on the tip of the first dorsal fin, the tips of the pectoral fins, and on the upper and lower tips of the caudal fin. Both the pectoral and pelvic fins are darker below and become darker toward their posterior borders. The anal fin is lighter in color and the white edge along its posterior border is faint and indistinct. It is helpful to know that this color pattern of white tips and white margins is the same in both young and adult individuals and in both sexes.

The habitat of the white-margined shark is in the offshore waters. Although both adults and young have been observed in shore line areas, it appears to shun this area and to make its home over deeper water. In this offshore habitat, it ranges from the surface down to depths of at least 1200 or 1300 feet in search for food and is known to eat fishes from the surface waters, from mid-water areas, and from the ocean bottom.

The reproductive pattern of this shark is ovo-viviparous; it mates, retains the eggs within the body of the female, and gives birth to the young approximately one year later. These young are usually born in litters of five or six; they may occasionally be fewer in number, but probably do not exceed a dozen in any one litter. They are approximately two feet long when born and mature by the time they reach five or six feet in length.

The distribution of this species extends across the entire tropical and warmer temperate Pacific and Indian Oceans. It extends from the Red Sea southward along the eastern coast of Africa, across the Indian Ocean,

WHITE MARKINGS ON THREE PACIFIC WHITE-TIPPED SHARKS

	Carcharhinus albimarginatus	Carcharhinus longimanus	Triaenodon obesus
First Dorsal Fin	White-tipped with a white posterior margin	A high, rounded fin which is white-tipped and often covered with darker mottlings	White-tipped
Caudal Fin	White-tipped above and below	White-tipped above and below and often covered with darker mottlings	White-tipped above
Anal Fin	Pale with indistinct white tip and trailing edge	Black-tipped	Dark or dusky in color
Pectoral Fin	White-tipped with very narrow white posterior margin	Usually white-tipped but sometimes mottled or clouded	Never white-tipped

through the East Indies including the Philippine Islands, through Micronesia, and on eastward across the tropical and warmer temperate Pacific Ocean to the Revillagigedo and Galapagos Islands in the eastern Pacific Ocean. It is believed to occur in the Hawaiian area although this occurrance has not been well documented.

THE BIG-NOSED SHARK
Also known as Knopp's Shark
11—6 *Carcharhinus altimus* (S. Springer), 1950

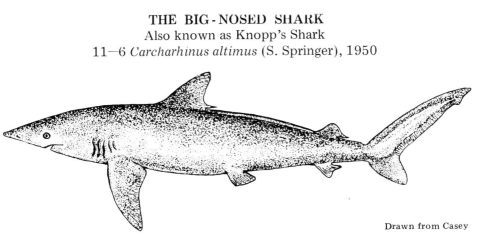

Drawn from Casey

The big-nosed shark is a large species with a long head and a long snout with a broadly rounded tip which is but little flattened. The eyes are of moderate size, the spiracle is missing, and there are no lateral ridges on the sides of the caudal peduncle. The ridge of skin found on the midline of the back between the dorsal fins is present but may not extend the full distance between these fins. The first and fourth gill slits are of about equal length, but the fifth gill slit is only about two-thirds the length of the first four gill slits. The teeth of the upper and lower jaws are different. Those of the upper jaw have wider cusps which are somewhat flattened and have serrated edges. The teeth of the lower jaw are narrow and slender with serrated or finely serrated margins and are set upon broad bases. The teeth of the upper jaw usually number 15 on each side and have either one or two small, median teeth; those of the lower jaw number 14 on each side and have but a single, small, median tooth. In life, the color of this shark is light gray on the upper parts of the body and a whitish color below. The tips of the pectoral fins are darker on the lower sides. This species reaches nine feet in length.

This shark seems to prefer water which is 100 or more feet deep and is rarely seen or taken in shallow water. It seems to prefer to live beyond the outer edge of the insular or continental shelf and has been captured as deep as 1100 feet.

The young are born when two feet or larger and in litters which number seven, eight, or more.

The big-nosed shark occurs in the tropical Atlantic Ocean, the southwestern Indian Ocean, and in the tropical eastern and central Pacific Ocean including the Hawaiian area.

THE GRAY REEF SHARK
Also known as The Long-nosed Black-tail Shark
11—7 *Carcharhinus amblyrhynchos* (Bleeker), 1856

The gray reef shark is a medium-sized species with a fairly robust smooth-skinned body, a depressed head, and no spiracle. In this species the teeth of the two jaws are different. The upper teeth are triangular in shape, with large cusps, and are not directed outward; the teeth of the lower jaw are smaller, slender with a broad base, erect, and serrated. The body is gray or grayish colored above and shades to white on the belly. The second dorsal and anal fins are usually dark, the pectoral fins are usually dark below, and the pelvic and caudal fins are margined with black. This shark may reach seven or possibly eight feet in length, but most specimens are shorter. This shark lives in the deeper waters on the outer edge of the reef. It is a shore line species of warmer latitudes. Like its relatives, it is a predatory species and has been known to attack swimmers.

It is ovo-viviparous in its reproductive habits and retains the developing young within the body of the mother until they are fully formed.

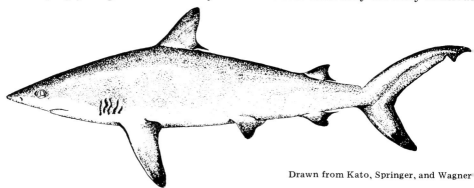

Drawn from Kato, Springer, and Wagner

The distribution of the gray reef shark includes the warm tropical waters from the Red Sea eastward across the Indian Ocean, through the East Indies, and across the tropical Pacific Ocean as far as the Hawaiian area.

This species is found in some books under the name of *Carcharhinus menisorrah* (Muller and Henle), 1841.

THE SILKY SHARK
Also known as the Sickle Shark
11—8 *Carcharhinus falciformis* (Muller and Henle), 1841

The silky shark is a species of medium size with a slender, spindle-shaped trunk and a broad, rounded, flattened snout. There is a low dermal ridge between the first and second dorsal fins and both the second dorsal fin and the anal fin have long free tips. The eye is small and nearly circular in outline and the caudal peduncle contains a pit both above and below. The teeth differ in the two jaws. The upper teeth, which number from 14 to 17 on each side, are larger, nearly triangular, and serrated; the lower teeth are more slender, with a broad base, and with either smooth or very weakly serrated edges. There is also one or more minute, slender teeth in the front center of the lower jaw. The color of the body varies from shining black to a dark gray above; below, the color is a dirty white or grayish white.

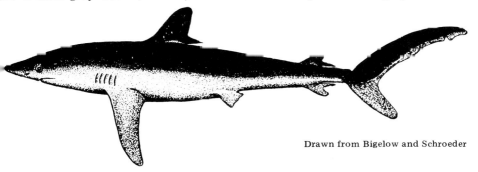

Drawn from Bigelow and Schroeder

This shark reaches a maximum size of about ten feet; however, most specimens are much smaller.

This shark seems to be an offshore species which is more abundant at depths below 100 feet. This species, like most sharks, is used for food and its skin is suitable for processing into leather. It is one of the species that appears in most fisheries. It gets its common name from the fact that the skin is smooth and feels silky to the touch.

The silky shark occurs in all tropical seas of the world.

The name of *Carcharhinus floridanus* Bigelow, Schroeder, and Springer, 1943, was used to describe one of the growth stages of this species and so should be replaced by *C. falciformis.*

THE GALAPAGOS SHARK
11—9 *Carcharhinus galapagensis* (Snodgrass and Heller), 1905

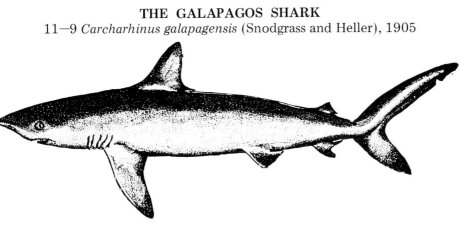

The Galapagos shark is one of the larger oceanic species. Its body is quite robust, particularly toward the anterior end, and the snout is quite short and broadly rounded. The back is marked by a dermal ridge between the fins, but the body lacks the keels on the sides at the base of the caudal peduncle. The upper teeth are serrated, broadly triangular in outline, and usually number 14 on each side with one or occasionally two, small, median teeth; the teeth of the lower jaw are usually the same as the upper jaw in number, but are much more slender. The body of this shark is gray in color It resembles *Carcharhinus obscurus* (Lesueur) but has smaller gill slits and a "more erect, pointed apex of the first dorsal fin".

The young are usually born in litters of nine or ten and measure between 24 and 30 inches at birth. This shark reaches a length of about ten or 12 feet.

There are records of this species attacking swimmers and bathers. It is an active, voracious, predatory species.

The Galapagos shark occurs in the tropical Atlantic Ocean, the tropical and sub-tropical western Indian Ocean, the tropical and sub-tropical eastern Pacific Ocean, Hawaii, and doubtless elsewhere in warmer latitudes.

THE SMALL BLACK-TIPPED SHARK
Also known as the Volador
11—10 *Carcharhinus limbatus* (Muller and Henle), 1841

Drawn from Kato, Springer, and Wagner

The small black-tipped shark is a fish of medium size with a moderately slender body and without a dermal ridge on the midline of the back between the fins. The caudal peduncle bears a pit on its lower side, but lacks the horizontal keels on the sides. The teeth of both the upper and lower jaws are narrow, triangular, and serrated in adult specimens. The body is gray, bluish, grayish, or a bronze-gray color above and changes to white or yellowish white below. Two darker, longitudinal, wedge-shaped bands, separated by a lighter band, mark the sides of the body. The fins are dark colored at the tips, particularly the lower side of the pectoral tip; the anal fin usually lacks these dark markings; in young sharks these tips are nearly black and become lighter in older individuals. This fish matures at four or five feet in length, usually measures between five and seven feet as an adult, and may reach a length of eight feet.

This shark is a surface dweller, both at sea and along coast lines. It is an active, rapid swimmer and has been reported to sometimes gather into schools where it may be seen jumping and rolling in the air. It feeds on a wide variety of food including smaller fishes, sting rays, squids, and doubtless other animals. This species is ovo-viviparous in its reproductive habits and gives birth to fully developed young. These young are born in small litters and measure about two feet in length.

The small black-tipped shark inhabits the tropical and sub-tropical seas of the world.

This species should not be confused with two other black-tipped sharks; these are the large Atlantic Black-tipped Shark, *Carcharhinus maculipinnis* (Poey), and the Black-tipped Reef Shark, *Carcharhinus melanopterus* (Quoy and Gaimard).

THE BLACK-TIPPED REEF SHARK

11—11 *Carcharhinus melanopterus* (Quoy and Gaimard), 1824

The black-tipped reef shark is a medium-sized species with an elongated body, a depressed head, and a short snout. The back is somewhat higher than most sharks, and there is no ridge of skin between the dorsal fins; nor is there a ridge on the sides of the caudal peduncle at the base of the tail.

Photo by John Randall, Ph.D.

The teeth in the upper jaw are broadly triangular and serrated. The most noticeable features of this shark are the dark tips and margins of the fins. The body is uniformly gray, grayish brown, or lemon-brown above and shades to white below. The sides of the body are marked by longitudinal white streaks with a darker band between them. This shark is usually less than six feet in length, although it has been reported to reach ten feet.

This reef shark is a small, harmless species which is commonly seen by swimmers and divers in the tropical Pacific Ocean. It is curious about swimmers and divers and always lingers nearby to watch their activities.

The black-tipped reef shark occurs in warm tropical waters from the Red Sea eastward across the western Pacific Ocean to Hawaii. It is not known from the eastern Pacific Ocean.

There are other black-tipped sharks which should not be confused with this species. These include the small Atlantic and Pacific Black-tipped Shark, *Carcharhinus limbatus* (Muller and Henle) and the large Atlantic Black-tipped Shark, *Carcharhinus maculipinnis* (Poey).

MILBERT'S SANDBAR SHARK
Also known as the Brown Shark
11—12 *Carcharhinus milberti* (Muller and Henle), 1841

The sandbar shark is a medium-sized species with a comparatively stout body and a very broad snout. It can be recognized by the large, erect dorsal

fin which is placed far forward on the body, by the ridge of skin on the midline of the back between the dorsal fins, and by the free trailing corner of the second dorsal fin. The teeth of the two jaws differ. The upper teeth are larger, nearly triangular in shape, and possess very finely serrated margins; the lower teeth are slender with broad bases and very finely serrated margins. The color of the body is a slate gray or brownish gray above and shades gradually to white on the belly. This shark usually measures about five feet in length; a few specimens may reach six feet in length.

This shark is a common shore line species in most areas where it occurs. It will enter harbors and bays in search of food and is therefore easily captured. It feeds upon free swimming fishes and also upon bottom dwelling fishes, crustacea, and mollusca including octopods.

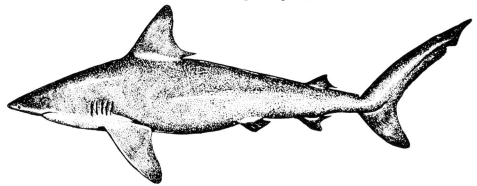

The adults mate in the summer and give birth nine or ten months later to living young which measure about 22 inches; these are released in the summer-time in small litters of a dozen or less.

The sandbar shark occurs in the tropical and warmer temperate waters of the Atlantic, Pacific, and Indian Oceans.

THE ISLAND SHARK
11—13 *Carcharhinus nesiotes* (Snyder), 1904
The island shark is a medium-sized species with all of the features of the gray shark family but without many special features to identify it. The first

dorsal fin is pointed at the apex and the second dorsal fin and anal fin are equal in size. The caudal fin has a notch on its margin below the tip and the caudal peduncle is marked above by a crosswise furrow at the base of the tail. The pectoral fins are pointed at the tips, there is no median longitudinal ridge on the top of the back, and the spiracle is absent. The teeth of the upper jaw are symmetrical in the front of the mouth but become more curved and notched toward the sides of the jaw. The lower teeth are narrow,

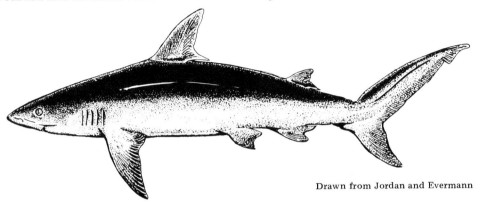

Drawn from Jordan and Evermann

with a wide base, and with either smooth edges or fine serrations. The color of the body is bluish gray above and lighter below. The fins get slowly darker toward their tips. This shark reaches a length of five or six feet. Very little is known of its habits.

This species occurs in Hawaii and elsewhere in the tropical Pacific Ocean.

THE DUSKY SHARK
Also known as the Shovel Nose or Bay Shark
11—14 *Carcharhinus obscurus* Lesueur, 1818

Drawn from Kato, Springer, and Wagner

The dusky shark is of medium size with a moderately slender body and a broad, rounded snout. It possesses a dermal ridge on the midline of the back between the two dorsal fins and the caudal peduncle bears a precaudal pit both above and below. The teeth are unlike in the upper and lower jaws. The upper teeth are nearly triangular in shape and are serrated; the lower teeth are more slender, have a broad base, and are more finely serrated than

31

the upper teeth. The color of the body is variously described as blue-gray or leaden gray above and white or grayish white below. This shark usually measures ten or eleven feet in length, although some have been reported to reach 14 feet.

The dusky shark lives both far at sea and along shore lines. It therefore feeds upon fishes which are both pelagic forms and bottom living species.

The young are born fully formed in litters of six to 14 and measure about three feet in length at birth.

This species is caught with other sharks in the shark fishery and is sold for its flesh, oil, and skin.

The dusky shark occurs in the tropical and warmer temperate waters of the Atlantic Ocean, the western Indian Ocean, and the eastern Pacific Ocean including Hawaii.

The dusky shark is very difficult to distinguish from *C. milberti* (Muller and Henle) and *C. falciformis* (Muller and Henle).

THE HAMMER-HEAD SHARK FAMILY
12 *Family Sphyrnidae*

The hammer-head and bonnet-head sharks are most amazing fishes for they have a head which is flattened dorso-ventrally and greatly expanded to the sides giving them the outline of a hammer when viewed from above. In other ways they look like carcharhinid sharks. They are of quite large size and have bodies which are compressed laterally. They possess large pectoral fins, two dorsal fins of which the first is large and the second is very small, and a small anal fin. The caudal fin is quite long and bears a notch just below its tip, while the caudal peduncle usually contains a pit both above and below the base of the caudal fin. The eyes, which are placed at the outer edge of the head, have a nictitating membrane, but the spiracle usually found near the eye is absent in this group. In addition, the groove that connects the nostrils and the mouth in some sharks is entirely absent in this family.

These sharks are active swimmers, voracious in their feeding habits, and dangerous to man. In the northern summer they enter warm shallow bays to give birth to their young. They are ovo-viviparous and may release from 20 to 40 young measuring about 18 or 20 inches in length.

Although a few members of this family are found in cooler waters, they prefer warmer water. They occur in nearly all warm oceans of the world. Some seem to be oceanic in their habits while others seem to be inhabitants of the shore line.

Fossils of these fishes are known from early Tertiary times; today the family includes about nine species.

THE SCALLOPED HAMMER-HEAD SHARK
Also known as Ma-no Ki-hi-ki-hi
12—1 *Sphyrna lewini* (Griffith and Smith), 1834

The scalloped hammer-head shark is a large species with a robust body

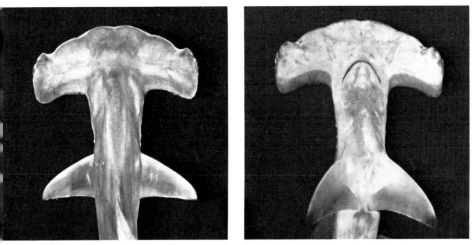

The Scalloped Hammer-head Shark, showing front margin of head.

which is laterally compressed behind the head. This species is distinguished from other hammer-heads by the front margin of the head which, when viewed from above, is distinctly undulated and divided into four low lobes by very shallow depressions. The color of the body is a deep olive or brownish gray above and shades gradually to white on the belly. The pectoral fins are tipped with black below. This shark reaches a length of 12 or 13 feet and some have been reported to reach 15 feet in length.

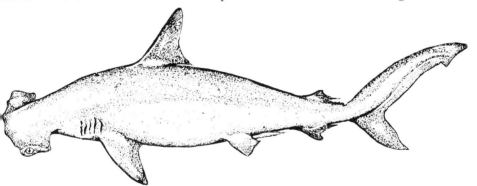

This species occurs both along shore lines and far at sea. It prefers warmer waters but is reported to wander into cooler latitudes. It is an active shark and feeds upon all manner of surface fish and bottom fish alike. The young are held in the body of the mother until fully formed at which time they will measure 17 or 18 inches in length. The adult sharks are often seen in shallow bays and inlets during the spring and summer, and the young, which they release at this time, are often taken in the nets of fishermen.

The scalloped hammer-head shark occurs world-wide in tropical and warmer temperate seas.

This shark was named for Mr. John William Lewin (1770-1819), a natural history painter and coroner of New South Wales, Australia.

THE COMMON HAMMER - HEAD SHARK
Also known as the Smooth Hammer-head or Mano Kihi-kihi
12—2 *Sphyrna zygaena* (Linnaeus), 1758

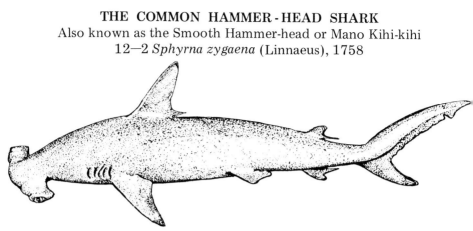

The common hammer-head shark is a large species with a body which is strongly compressed behind the head. The front margin of the head is undulating and is divided into three lobes of which the central lobe is almost straight and only very slightly rounded. This anterior margin is not indented at the center as in *S. lewini* and is therefore useful in separating these species. The back of this shark lacks a ridge of skin between the dorsal fins and there is no well-defined precaudal pit on the lower side of the caudal peduncle. The teeth are quite similar in the upper and lower jaws; they are notched and, with the exception of one or two central teeth, are directed toward the side. The color of the body is olive gray or brownish gray above and shades downward to grayish white or white on the belly. The median fins are darker edged and the pectoral fins may sometimes be dusky or dark tipped on their lower surfaces. This shark usually measures from nine to eleven feet, but specimens have been captured as long as 14 feet.

The common hammer-head occurs along shore lines and also far at sea. It will enter bays and harbors where it is often seen swimming with its first dorsal and caudal fins out of the water. This shark is an aggressive and ferocious fish and a voracious feeder upon a wide variety of both free-swimming and bottom-living fishes and other animals.

The young are retained within the mother until fully formed and are then born in shallow bays in litters of 30 to 35 "pups" when they are about 20 inches in length.

The common hammer-head shark occurs in the sub-tropical and warmer temperate seas of the world.

THE DOGFISH SHARK FAMILY
Also known as the Dogfishes or Skittledogs
13 *Family Squalidae*

The dogfish sharks are a family of small sharks with no anal fin and with two dorsal fins which usually contain a spine along their anterior margins. They have depressed heads, eyes without a nictitating membrane, and possess a spiracle adjacent to the eye. Their teeth vary from one to several cusps. It should also be noted that their five gill slits are all located anterior to the pectoral fin. All are regarded as harmless and are of value as food. These sharks live in the cooler waters of the world and are found from shallow water down to considerable depths. A few have been captured at depths between 1500 and 3000 feet. There are ancient records of these sharks in late Tertiary times in the form of fossil teeth and fossil spines.

BLAINVILLE'S DOGFISH SHARK
13—1 *Squalus blainvillei* Risso, 1826

Blainville's dogfish shark is a small species with a slender body, with no anal fin, and without a notch on the caudal fin below the tip of the tail. The teeth possess but a single cusp and are similar in both jaws. This species is very difficult to distinguish from *Squalus fernandinus* Molina, but they may be separated by the spine on the second dorsal fin. In *S. blainvillei* the second dorsal spine reaches to the tip of the second dorsal fins; in *S. fernandinus* the second dorsal spine reaches only two-thirds of the way to the tip of the second dorsal fin. The color of the body is plain gray or brownish gray. There are white edges on the posterior margins of the pectoral fins, the first dorsal fin, and the caudal fin. This shark reaches about four feet in length.

Blainville's dogfish shark occurs in the tropical and sub-tropical waters of the eastern Pacific Ocean, in the Hawaiian Islands, and doubtless elsewhere in the tropical Pacific Ocean.

THE DOGFISH SHARK
13—2 *Squalus fernandinus* Molina, 1782

This spiny dogfish shark is a small species with a slender body, a cylindrical trunk which is somewhat flattened below, with no anal fin, and with a small spiracle near the eye. The teeth contain a single cusp each and are alike in both jaws. This species is very difficult to distinguish from *Squalus blainvillei* Risso, but they may be separated by the spine on the second dorsal fin. In *S. blainvillei* the second dorsal spine reaches the tip of the second dorsal fin, in *S. fernandinus* the second dorsal spine reaches only two-thirds of the distance to the tip of the second dorsal fin.

The color of the body is grayish or brownish gray above and lighter below. The dorsal fins are darker toward their tips and lighter toward their bases. The caudal fin is reported to be darker medially and to be a pale yellowish gray on the lobes of the fin. This shark reaches a length of three or three and one-half feet.

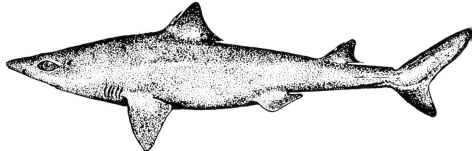

This is an edible species which is both tasty and nourishing when properly prepared.

This dogfish shark is apparently distributed throughout the temperate and sub-tropical waters of the world.

THE GRANULAR SHARK
13—3 *Centroscyllium granulosum* Gunther, 1880

Drawn from Kato, Springer, and Wagner

This squalid shark is a very small species with large eyes and a large spiracle nearby. The teeth within the mouth bear between three and five cusps each and are similar in both jaws. There are two dorsal fins with a spine on the anterior border of each fin. These spines are sharp along their forward edge and are flat along their back side. The second dorsal spine has been reported to extend considerably beyond the tip of the second dorsal fin. The color of the body is black except for white areas along the tips or margins of the fins. This shark is a small species and measures between 12 and 18 inches in length.

The distribution of this little shark is apparently world-wide in tropical and sub-tropical waters.

This species is found in books under several names including *Centroscyllium nigrum* Garman, 1899, from near Cocos Island and *Centroscyllium ruscosum* Gilbert, 1905, from near Kauai, Hawaii.

THE BLACK SHARK
13—4 *Centroscyllium nigrum* Garman, 1899

The black shark is a very small, slender species with large eyes and a large spiracle. The head is large, broad, and depressed, and the mouth is wide. The two dorsal fins each bear a long, slender spine along their anterior border. These spines are sharp on their front edge, flat on their back side, and have grooves along each side. The tip of the caudal fin is truncated and there is a definite subterminal notch. The teeth bear from three to five cusps each and are quite similar in both jaws. The color of this little shark in life is reported as a dark brown to black and to be darker on the lower surface. The body is covered with very small dusky to blackish brown dots; these are more numerous on the lower surface and less numerous over the back of the body. The fins are dark in color and are bordered with whitish margins and areas. This shark measures a foot or less in length.

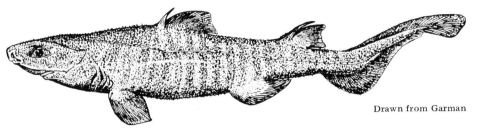

Drawn from Garman

This is a deep water species; specimens have been taken at depths of about 3000 feet.

This little shark is known to occur in the tropical and sub-tropical waters of the eastern Pacific Ocean, the Hawaiian Islands, and doubtless elsewhere in the Pacific basin.

THE TESSELLATED DEEP-WATER SHARK
13—5 *Centrophorus tessellatus* Garman, 1906

This small, deep-water shark has a slender body which tapers uniformly toward the tail. The two dorsal fins each possess a spine on their forward margin; the posterior spine is slightly longer than the first spine and both have longitudinal grooves along their lateral surfaces. The caudal peduncle is without both precaudal pits and lateral ridges. A large spiracle is located above and behind the eye at a distance of about one and one-half times the diameter of the spiracle. The nostrils are without barbels. The dermal denticles in the skin are block-like, closely set but not overlapping, and are marked posteriorly with low, radiating ridges somewhat like a pecten shell; this tessellated arrangement of the denticles is doubtless the source of the scientific name.

The upper and lower teeth are unlike and number about 42 above and 31 below. These teeth are compressed or flattened, contain but one cusp or point, and have either smooth edges or very finely serrated edges, particularly along the lower portions of their cutting edges. There is a median tooth in both the upper and lower jaws. The upper teeth have slender, sharp-pointed cusps and are more numerous and more erect than the lower teeth; they are quite erect in the front of the jaw and become slightly and increasingly tilted backward toward the corners of the mouth. The lower teeth present a long, serrated cutting edge leading laterally to a single cusp which is directed laterally and in turn followed by a deep notch.

The color of the body is light brownish on the back and sides and white below; there are white bands at the margins of the fins and gill clefts. This shark may reach a length of about three feet.

Drawn from Bigelow and Schroeder

Records of this rare fish indicate that it inhabits deep water from possibly 300 or 400 feet down to depths of over 2,000 feet.

The distribution of this species thus far includes the western Pacific Ocean from Japan to Hawaii and doubtless adjoining areas.

This species closely resembles *C. granulosus* Bloch and Schneider, 1801. Persons wishing to study these sharks should consult Garman's original description in *Harvard University, Bulletin of the Museum of Comparative Zoology* 46:11, 1906, p. 205, and also studies of the squalid sharks by Bigelow and Schroeder in the same bulletin Volume 117:1, 1957, pp. 1—150.

THE LUCIFER SHARK
13—6 *Etmopterus lucifer* Jordan and Snyder, 1902

Drawn from Kato, Springer, and Wagner

This squalid shark is a small species with a slender, tapering trunk and with both large eyes and large spiracles. The caudal peduncle is without lateral keels or ridges and there are no precaudal pits. There are two dorsal fins with spines; of these, both the second dorsal fin and its spine are larger than the first dorsal fin and its spine. The teeth of the upper and lower jaws differ; those of the upper jaw have several cusps, while those of the lower jaw have but a single cusp. The color of the body is very dark brown or black and often exhibits a variegated pattern of light and dark areas, especially in the pelvic region. The fins are paler in color and the caudal fin is dark at the end. This shark measures less than two feet in length.

This little shark is a deep water form and appears to live at depths between 1,000 and 2,000 feet.

The distribution of this species extends from the Red Sea, across the Indian Ocean, through the East Indies, and across the tropical western Pacific Ocean to Hawaii.

THE HAWAIIAN SHARK
13—7 *Etmopterus villosus* Gilbert, 1905

Drawn from Gilbert

This squalid shark is a small species with a slender trunk, large eyes, and a large spiracle. The caudal peduncle is without lateral ridges or keels and there are no precaudal pits. The body bears two dorsal fins with a spine each; of these two, the second dorsal fin and its spine are the longer. The teeth of the upper and lower jaws are unlike; the upper teeth have several cusps each, while the lower teeth have but a single cusp. The color of the body is a dark brown above; the belly is reported to be darker than the back. The dorsal fins are a dull blackish color at their bases and are broadly whitish at their extremities; the other fins are darker basally and paler terminally. The gill openings are blackish. This shark is a small species which measures less than one foot in length.

This species has long been known from a single specimen taken in Hawaii off the south coast of Molokai between 222 and 498 fathoms in 1902. It doubtless occurs in other areas in the Pacific Ocean.

THE SLIME SHARK
13—8 *Euprotomicrus bispinatus* (Quoy and Gaimard), 1824

Drawn from Kato, Springer, and Wagner

The slime shark is a very small and uncommon shark with a slender, fusiform body. The head is blunt and bears a short snout. The spiracles are large and the eyes, which lack the nictitating membrane, have a yellow iris. There are two dorsal fins, both without spines, located far to the back of the body. Of these, the first fin has a short base and the second fin has a very long base. The body extends backwards to terminate in a tapering central axis which extends through the caudal fin. There are no precaudal pits and the anal fin is absent. The teeth are different in the two jaws. The upper teeth are thin, pointed, and spike-like. The lower teeth, which number about 22, are wider, asymmetrical, with the cusps directed outward, not serrate, and with their outer margins notched. The color of the body is a uniform brown, brownish gray, or blackish. The edges of the fins do not have dermal denticles and are therefore transparent. This is a luminous fish and is reported to radiate an even pale greenish light from the lower surface, particularly along the midline of the body. This shark measures about ten inches or less in length. It is one of the very smallest species of sharks

This species is ovo-viviparous and brings forth its young fully formed.

The distribution of this shark extends through the tropical and temperate Pacific and Indian Oceans.

THE SLEEPER OR SPINELESS DOGFISH SHARK FAMILY
14 *Family Dalatiidae*

The members of this family resemble the dogfish sharks and are sometimes included with them in the family *Squalidae*. They are mostly small sharks without an anal fin and with two small dorsal fins; some species are equipped with a spine on the first dorsal fin. The eyes are without a nictitating membrane and a small spiracle is present nearby. The teeth have one cusp each, but they are very unlike in the upper and lower jaws. The upper teeth are narrow and long, while the lower teeth are expanded laterally to form a cutting edge. There are no pits on the caudal peduncle at the base of the tail.

This family contains about six genera and possibly a dozen species.

BONNATERRE'S DEEP-WATER SHARK
14—1 *Dalatias licha* (Bonnaterre), 1788

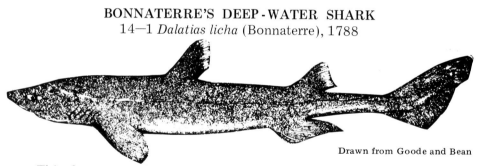

Drawn from Goode and Bean

This deep-water shark has a body which is quite long and slender and which tapers very gradually toward the tail. The head, which is strongly flattened above, bears a thick, fleshy snout which is rounded in front and very short in front of the mouth; in fact, this distance from the mouth to the tip of the snout is about equal to the width of the mouth. The lips are thick and fleshy and do not have any supporting cartilage in them near the corners of the mouth. The upper lip is joined to the gums along the central third of the jaw, but the lower lip is entirely free of this attachment. The gill openings are small; the eyes are oval and are placed with their midpoints just anterior to the mouth; and the spiracles, which are about one-half as long as the eyes, are placed upon the dorsal side of the head a little above the level of the eyes.

The teeth are very different in the upper and lower jaws. The upper teeth are long, slender, and thorn-like and rest upon a two-pronged base. The first tooth is slightly smaller than the others and all teeth curve

40

backward; this backward tilt increases toward the sides of the mouth. The lower teeth are blade-like with a squarish base and a single, broad, triangular cusp or point which has uniformly serrated edges; each tooth in turn overlaps the tooth behind it. These teeth are larger and more erect in the front of the mouth and become somewhat smaller and more slanting toward the rear of the mouth.

The fins are quite small and are without the spines often found in related species. The first dorsal fin is small, brush-like, rounded on top, and possesses a straight, vertical margin. The second dorsal fin resembles the first although it is somewhat larger. The caudal peduncle, which is without precaudal pits or lateral ridges, leads upward into a caudal fin in which the apex is rounded and the posterior margin is quite straight, diagonal, and deeply notched; the lower corner of this fin has an angle of about 90°. The pectoral fins are rather small, paddle-shaped, and rounded at their tips. The pelvic fins are larger than either dorsal fin, possess nearly straight sides, have a rounded lower angle, and a pointed tip at the rear.

The color of the body is uniformly dark brownish above and below; the body fins have lighter margins and the caudal fin is black tipped. There are reports of "poorly defined blackish spots in life" in some specimens. Large specimens will reach a length of at least six feet.

The habits of this species are not well known. It lives in deep water where it has usually been captured at depths between 1,000 and 2,000 feet. However, a few have been captured in water as shallow as 300 feet and others at a depth of more than 3,000 feet. It is apparently a bottom living species and must therefore feed upon a variety of bottom fishes and other animals which occur at those depths.

In their reproductive habits, these sharks are ovo-viviparous and retain the eggs within the body of the mother until the young are fully formed miniature adults. The broods of these young sharks are reported to contain from ten to at least 16 young.

The distribution of this species seems to be nearly world-wide. It is known from the Mediterranean Sea, both sides of the Atlantic Ocean, and in the Pacific Ocean from Hawaii and Japan to New Zealand and Australia.

THE BRAZILIAN SHARK
Also known as the Cigar Shark
14—2. *Isistius brasiliensis* (Quoy and Gaimard), 1824

The Brazilian shark is a small species with a slender, tapering body and two spineless dorsal fins located far back on the trunk. The anal fin is not present. The body extends backward to form a central axis which extends through the caudal fin. The eyes are large with bright green, nearly round pupils and do not possess the nictitating membrane. The spiracles in this species are large and are located on the top of the head. The teeth are unlike in the two jaws. The teeth of the upper jaw are slender, thorn-like, bent outward, and very widely spaced; the lower teeth are wider, large, flattened, straight, symmetrical, triangularly pointed, overlapping, and number between 25 and 31.

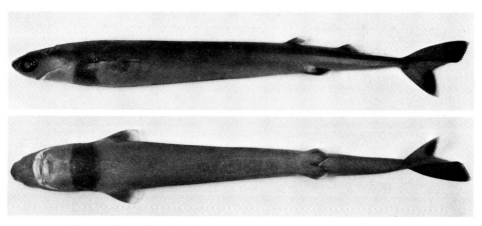

The small Brazilian Shark showing its distinctive dark throat band.

The color of the body is a dark gray-brown above and a lighter brown below. The pectoral, pelvic, and dorsal fins are darker in front and transparent toward their free margin. The caudal fin is marked by dark areas on both the upper and lower lobes. The body is marked by a very unusual, wide, ribbon-like band of a darker color which encircles the body just in front of the pectoral fins. The body of this shark measures about 18 or 20 inches in length, although most specimens are smaller.

The habits of this shark are not well known. It is an uncommon pelagic species which is believed to be associated with various larger fishes including tunas from which it is believed to take bites of flesh. Its principal food seems to be squids. This shark is a luminous species and is reported to radiate light for as much as three hours after its death. It is ovo-viviparous in its habits and brings forth its young fully formed.

The Brazilian shark occurs in the tropical and sub-tropical seas of the world.

THE NORTH PACIFIC SLEEPER SHARK
14—3 *Somniosus pacificus* Bigelow and Schroeder, 1944

The North Pacific Sleeper Shark is a large species with a robust, elongated body and a rather small, short head. The dorsal fins are small, brush-like, about equal in size, and are without spines; the first dorsal fin is placed near the middle of the body at a location which is farther back than in most sharks. The pectoral fins are likewise small, short, and rounded. The ventral fins are nearly opposite the second dorsal fin and the anal fin is absent. The caudal peduncle is without precaudal pits and leads almost

42

horizontally into a tail with an upper and lower lobe. The upper lobe of the tail is somewhat longer than the lower lobe and both are truncated behind. The head bears a comparatively short snout, a transverse mouth with grooves extending forward and backward from its corners, and a pair of spiracles above and behind the eyes; there is no nictitating membrane on the eyes. The skin of the entire body is uniformly covered with fine tubercles. The teeth of the upper jaw are small, narrow, and lancet-shaped, while those of the lower jaw are quadrangular in shape and have their tips directed laterally so that the side of each cusp faces upward and presents a horizontal cutting edge; each of these lower teeth overlaps the adjoining tooth. There are five or six rows of teeth in the upper jaw, each of which bears about 26 teeth on each side; the lower jaw has two rows of teeth and about 30 teeth in a single row on each side.

The color of the body is reported as gray with bluish hues. A few dark blotches occur around the bases of the fins. The length of this species is still uncertain, but it is known to reach a length of at least eight feet.

Sleeper sharks are very sluggish species which seem to prefer the deeper water of colder seas, although they do surface to feed upon any edible materials. They are very easy to catch and do not struggle when hooked, speared, or otherwise molested. The flesh contains a type of toxin which, when eaten, produces the symptoms of drunkedness; this poison is weakened by cooking, by storage, and by drying. The flesh of other species is often used as food for dogs and is occasionally eaten by humans in some areas.

The biology of sleeper sharks is not well known. They are apparently oviparous in their reproduction. Female sharks develop large numbers of soft, globular eggs which measure about two inches and are without any horny, protective covering; these are deposited upon the ocean floor.

The distribution of this shark includes the Bering Sea and the North Pacific Ocean as far south as Japan and California.

In addition to the above species, at least three other sleeper sharks are known. They are *Somniosus microcephalus* (Bloch and Schneider), 1801, the famous Greenland or Gurry Shark of the North Atlantic and Arctic Oceans; *S. rostratus* Risso, 1826, a species known from the Mediterranean Sea, Portugal, and adjoining areas; and *S. antarcticus* Whitley, 1939, a species known from but a single specimen which was beached in 1912 on Macquarie Island to the southwest of New Zealand.

THE BRAMBLE SHARK FAMILY
15 *Family Echinorhinidae*

This family contains a single genus with but a few living species in the modern world. These sharks are of moderate size, have two dorsal fins without spines, and no anal fin. The teeth are alike in both jaws. Each tooth bears three to seven cusps of which the large central cusp points toward the side of the mouth. These sharks resemble the members of both the *Squalidae* and the *Dalatiidae* and are included with these families in some books. Except for fossils from Tertiary times, only two species are known from the modern world.

THE COMMON BRAMBLE SHARK
Also known as the Spiny Shark, the Prickle Shark, and the Alligator Dogfish Shark
15—1 *Echinorhinus brucus* (Bonnaterre), 1788

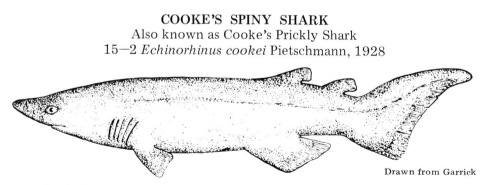

Drawn from Bigelow and Schroeder

The common bramble shark is a medium sized, elongated species with a solid, heavy, robust body which is marked by two, small, brush-like, spineless dorsal fins which are placed far to the rear. The head is depressed, a minute spiracle is present, the eyes lack the nictitating membrane, and the gill openings are large. The longitudinal axis of the tail is only slightly elevated and the caudal peduncle bears neither lateral keels nor precaudal pits. The surface of the body is covered by curious, scattered, shield-like, white, dermal denticles of various sizes. The teeth contain several cusps, usually from three to seven, of which the large central cusp is directed toward the side of the mouth to form a continuous cutting edge.

The color of the body is a dark gray, dull olive, or brown above with reflections of various colors; it may also sometimes include reddish or blackish blotches of color. Below, the body is lighter in color and may be a paler brown, grayish, or even whitish. This shark usually measures from six to eight feet in length, but it occasionally may reach a length of ten feet.

The bramble shark is a bottom dweller and lives from shallow water down to a depth of at least one mile. It is a bottom feeder and subsists on small fishes, other smaller sharks, crustacea, and other animals.

The distribution of the bramble shark is world-wide in tropical and temperate seas.

COOKE'S SPINY SHARK
Also known as Cooke's Prickly Shark
15—2 *Echinorhinus cookei* Pietschmann, 1928

Drawn from Garrick

Cooke's spiny shark is a medium to large sized species with a stout trunk in the adult, although the younger individuals are more slender in form. The head is depressed, flat above and below, and the snout is pointed. The eyes are small and the spiracle, located just behind the eye, is minute in size. The posterior part of the trunk and the caudal peduncle are compressed and the caudal peduncle lacks both the lateral keels and the precaudal pits. The dorsal fins are small, of nearly equal size, brush-shaped, and are located far to the back of the body. The pectoral fins are somewhat square at their ends, while the pelvic fins are large and triangular in shape with a long base of attachment to the body. The anal fin is missing. The caudal fin is curved and tapering, convex above, concave below, with a bluntly pointed tip, and without a subterminal notch. The body is covered rather uniformly with bucklers, measuring between two and four millimeters in diameter; they are conical in shape, radially ridged, and bear scalloped margins; these denticles are never joined together as in *E. brucus*. The teeth are small, with broad bases, similar in both jaws, and bear one large cusp which points toward the side of the mouth. The lateral line (in both this species and *E. brucus*) is open for most of its length and is supported by incomplete bony rings which end in pointed spines.

The color of the body is grayish brown in life; the snout is white on the lower side and a white area borders the mouth; the fins are black on their distal margins. Specimens have been captured that measured 13 feet, but most have been much smaller. This shark is a rare species from deeper water.

Cooke's Spiny Shark has long been confused with the common bramble shark, *E. brucus*. *E. cookei* differs from *E. brucus* by having only a few small denticles under the snout and around the mouth and also by having the bucklers of uniform size and never joined together.

Cooke's shark was first described from an Hawaiian specimen by Dr. Victor Pietschmann in 1928 and named by him for Mr. Charles Montague Cooke, Jr., Ph.D., of the Bernice Pauahi Bishop Museum in Honolulu.

Cooke's spiny shark is distributed in the tropical and temperate areas of the Pacific Ocean.

THE ELECTRIC RAY FAMILY
16 *Family Torpedinidae*

Among the sharks and rays, two groups of fishes are able to produce electricity in reasonably large amounts. They are the torpedo or electric rays and certain skates of the Family *Rajidae*. In the rays, the electricity is developed in kidney-shaped banks of cells located in the "wings" near the head, while in the skates the electricity is developed in the tail regions. When this electricity is discharged, the upper side of the "wing" has the positive charge while the lower side is negative. This charge, which rarely exceeds 100 volts and is usually much less, gets weaker with repeated discharges; it is then slowly recharged and restored by a rest of several days.

Electric rays, like other ray fishes, have depressed, flattened bodies, but unlike them have outlines which are nearly circular. The body and tail are usually without scales and there are no spines on the tail. The eyes are not well developed; some have small eyes, in some the eyes are vestigial, and in some the eyes are non-functional so that the ray is blind.

Electric rays vary in the number of dorsal fins which they possess on top of the tail. Some have two dorsal fins, some only one, and some have none. Sometimes scholars place all of these rays in the Family *Torpedinidae;* however, some ichthyologists limit this family to those rays with two dorsal fins and place those rays with one dorsal fin in the Family *Narkidae* and finally those with no dorsal fins in the Family *Temeridae.*

The habitat of these fishes is on the ocean bottom from shallow water to depths in excess of 3,000 feet. Here they move slowly over the muddy or sandy bottoms searching for small fishes and crustaceans which they cover with their "wings", shock with their electricity, and subsequently devour.

In rearing their young, these rays are ovo-viviparous in their habits. This means that they retain the fertilized eggs within the female until they complete their development, at which time they are released to live and swim independently like their parents.

About 40 species of electric rays are known; these range in length from about 18 inches to over five feet and in weight from a few pounds to perhaps 175 pounds.

Their distribution is world-wide in the tropical and temperate seas of the world.

The Hawaiian area has no species in this family which live in the shallow, shore line areas; however, one species has been discovered in the deeper waters surrounding the islands. Four specimens have been captured with trawls off Maui at almost 1500 feet and at about 800 feet in the Kalohi Channel which lies to the southwest between Molokai and Lanai.

THE FIN-TAILED STING RAY FAMILY
17 *Family Urolophidae*

These sting rays are closely related to those of the Family *Dasyatidae.* However, these rays have a long, narrow caudal fin on their tail which has radial, cartilaginous supports. This fin, which is on both the upper and lower side of the tail is not found in the *Dasyatidae.* This tail is usually about as long as the body and, like the *Dasyatidae*, bears a large, saw-edged spine midway on its upper side.

The distribution of this family is being extended by deep water fishing. Species are known from the Florida-Caribbean area, East Africa, Hawaii, from Japan to Tasmania, from California to Chile, and doubtless elsewhere.

The family contains about 25 species of which at least one is known from this area.

DAVIES' STING RAY
17—1 *Urotrygon daviesi* Wallace, 1967

The body disc of this ray is quite shallow or flat and is usually about as wide as long, although some specimens are slightly longer than wide. The forward tip of the disc is pointed and makes an angle of about 110° with the two sides forming it. The margins of the disc tends to be quite straight along their anterior edges and thereafter become rather uniformly rounded along

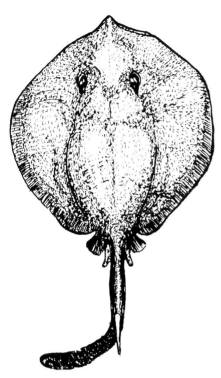

their lateral and posterior margins. The tail is wide and flat from its base to the dorsal spine and is laterally compressed from the area of the spine to its tip. The tail is about 12 times as long as its width at the base. The spine is serrated along its margins and lies nearly midway along the top of the tail. The small dorsal fin, usually found on the body anterior to the tail spine, is absent in this species, but there is a long caudal fin reinforced with radial cartilagenous rays extending along both the upper and lower margins of the tail; these upper and lower fins meet and encircle the tip of the tail. The small upper tail fin begins behind the spine, while the small lower tail fin begins just slightly anterior to the middle of the spine. Small closely set prickles cover the upper and lower surfaces of the disc, the tail, and the caudal fins; they are sparse on the pelvic fins and are absent along the lower margin of the disc, on the nasal flaps, and on the claspers. This species does not have large tubercles along the midline of the back, around the eyes, or on the tail. Adult specimens appear to range in width from three to five feet.

The color of the body is grayish black above and white beneath. The lower surface of the tail is gray and the pelvic fins are margined posteriorly with gray. The lower side of the disc is margined with a blackish color.

The habitat of this ray is in the deeper water beyond the reef. It has been captured in dredges and trawls at depths between 150 and nearly 1,500 feet below the surface.

The distribution of this ray includes the shore lines of East Africa, the Hawaiian Islands, and doubtless many areas between them.

The name of this ray honors Dr. David H. Davies, Director (1967) of The Oceanographic Research Institute in Durban, South Africa.

THE STING RAY FAMILY

18 *Family Dasyatidae*

This is a very large family of rays and includes both large and small species. Their body is typically a large, flat, round, or slightly angular disc composed principally of the pectoral fins which extend along the sides of the body and unite in front of the head. These pectoral fins are rounded at the sides and are therefore unlike those of the eagle rays which are quite pointed. The upper surface of this disc may be either smooth or roughened with tubercles and spines. The tail is slender, tapering, sometimes long and whip-like, and is usually longer than the body. The rays possess one or more venomous spines on the upper part of the tail; these are placed farther to the rear than are those of the eagle rays. A longitudinal fold of skin is present on the tail of some species, but not in other species. This fold, which runs lengthwise on the midline of the tail, may occur only on the upper surface, only on the lower surface, or in some species on both surfaces. The dorsal fin and caudal fin are lacking. The head of these rays bears a pair of eyes on its upper surface and a large spiracle for the intake of water is located close behind each eye. In these fishes the water enters the spiracles on top of the head and, after passing through the gills, is discharged through the gill slits on the lower surface. The mouth contains many very small teeth which are very closely set and which occur in numerous series in the mouth. In addition, the floor of the mouth is covered by numerous fleshy papillae which are set in transverse rows. The largest member of the family is reported to reach 15 feet in length.

In their reproductive habits, the members of this family are ovoviviparous and retain the developing young within the body of the parent until it is fully formed.

Most sting rays inhabit the coast lines of the world, particularly those with warmer climates; here they live in the shallow offshore waters or enter bays, estuaries, lagoons, and even the mouths of rivers to feed. They are bottom dwellers and forage upon the various animals which inhabit these areas. They are particularly fond of mollusca although they do eat worms, crustacea, and occasionally smaller fisher. This food, which is often dug from the mud or sand, is ground in the mouth, the hard parts discarded, and is thereafter swallowed. They are particularly numerous over clam and oyster beds where they are quite often destructive. When they are not feeding, sting rays spend considerable time lying concealed upon the bottom; they lie covered over with a light layer of sand or mud with only their eyes, spiracles, tail, and sting exposed. It is at these times that they are occasionally and accidentally stepped on by bathers. In these instances the sting ray usually tries to drive the spine of its tail into the foot of the bather. When this happens, it results in a very serious and painful wound.

The spines of sting rays were highly prized by most primitive peoples and were used by them as tips on spears and other weapons. Aristotle is reported to have said that "nothing is more terrible than the spine that arms the tail of Trygon." Odysseus (Ulysses), the famous mythological king of ancient Ithaca, was reported to have been killed by his son, Telegonus, with a spear tipped with a spine of a ray.

This family contains between 90 and 100 species.

THE HAWAIIAN STING RAY
Also known as Lu-pe or Hi-hi-ma-nu
18—1 *Dasyatis hawaiiensis* Jenkins, 1903

The Hawaiian sting ray has a broad, flat, disc-shaped body which is composed principally of the expanded pectoral fins. Because these fins are a bit angular at their edge and also where they unite in front of the head, they give the body a somewhat square appearance when viewed from above;

but, it should be noted that the margins of these four sides are slightly convex in outline. The upper surface bears a pair of eyes and just behind them a pair of spiracles. These spiracles, which are much larger than the eyes, are the openings through which the water enters the gills. The tail is long and slender and in most specimens will ususally be longer than the body. This tail bears the usual poisonous spine upon its upper surface. The tail lacks the caudal fin but may possess very small remnants of the dorsal and anal fins still persisting near the spine. In addition, this species has a single, long, longitudinal fold of skin in the midline of both the top and bottom sides of the tail and extending nearly the full length of the tail; this feature is very useful in helping to identify this species and to separate it from *Dasyatis latus*, which has a keel only on the lower side. The teeth are small in size and are grouped together in a broad band in both the upper and lower jaws. The skin of this species is quite smooth; it is a uniform brown color above, paler at the outer edge of the disc, and is whitish below. In size, this ray is known to exceed four feet in width.

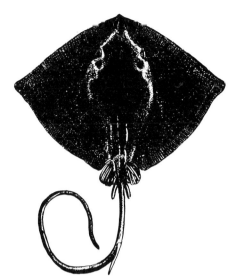

This ray is a bottom living species which spends its time searching for mollusks on which it prefers to feed.

These rays are ovo-viviparous in the rearing of their young and retain the developing young within the body of the mother until they are fully formed.

This species is known from California, Peru, Hawaii, and doubtless elsewhere in the tropical Pacific area.

THE BROWN STING RAY
Also known as Lu-pe or Hi-hi-ma-nu
18—2 *Dasyatis latus* (Garman), 1880

Like the previous species and the other members of this family, this ray has a large, flat, disc-like body which is composed of the enlarged pectoral fins. These pectoral fins are somewhat angular at their outer edges and also where they join in front of the head and therefore give the large flat body a somewhat square appearance. The eyes and the spiracles through which the water enters the gills are located on the top of the head. The tail is slender and is usually longer than the body. It lacks the caudal fins, and the dorsal fin, when present, is very short and small. This species bears a poisonous spine in the usual place on the upper side of the tail and a fleshy longitudinal ridge or keel on the lower side only. This fleshy keel or ridge of skin is very

49

Dorsal View

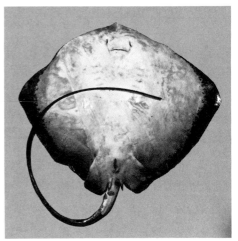

Ventral View

useful in identifying this species. The teeth are very small and lie in a broad band in both the upper and lower jaws. The skin, which is smooth over most of the body, is colored a uniform brownish above and whitish below with pale brownish markings on the outer margins of the pectoral fins. It is believed to reach a width of at least three feet.

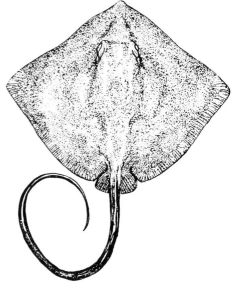

This species is a bottom dwelling form; here it may be observed swimming about, lying half concealed in mud or sand, or digging with its "nose" in the sand for the shellfish on which it feeds.

In its reproductive habits this ray is ovo-viparous and retains the developing young within the body of the parent until it is fully formed.

The distribution of this species extends from Hawaii southward through the tropical Pacific Ocean to Australia and doubtless elsewhere in the tropical Indo-Pacific area.

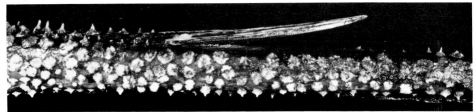

The dried tail of a ray showing the spine on its dorsal surface.

THE MANTA RAY FAMILY
19 *Family Mobulidae*

The manta rays are a small family of surface living fishes, most of which are of large size. Their head is flat, broad, and low and bears a mouth located either at the very front of the head or just below it. The eyes are located on the sides of the head and the spiracles, which in these fishes are very small, are located just posterior to the eyes. A pair of strange, fleshy appendages, called cephalic fins, project forward from each side of the head and serve to assist the ray in getting prospective food into its mouth. They are moveable and are usually shown curved toward the center, although they may be extended directly forward or held horizontally for swimming. The teeth of this group are small and pavement-like and, depending upon the species, may be found either in both jaws or only in the lower jaw.

Within this family the members of the Genus *Mobula* may be distinguished from the members of the Genus *Manta* by the location of the mouth and by the teeth. In the species of *Mobula* the mouth lies across the lower surface of the head, while in the species of *Manta* the mouth lies across the front of the head. The teeth in the species of *Mobula* occur in both the upper and lower jaw, while in the species of *Manta* they are found only in the lower jaw.

In ancient times these rays were doubtless bottom living forms. But they seem to have moved to the surface and to have slowly changed some of their body structures to suit their surface existence. The spiracles, through which water entered the gills for breathing, have become small and this water now enters through the mouth. They have developed a rather elaborate meshwork in their gills to strain out the small organisms which occur in their surface waters and on which they now feed. They have also developed the cephalic fins to assist in the capture of this small food.

Manta rays feed mostly upon small planktonic animal forms including small fishes, crustacea, and various other drifting animals of the sea. These rays are sometimes seen in very shallow water near the shore line; at these times they appear to be driving schools of small fishes into shallower water where they may be more easily captured.

In their reproductive habits, these large rays are ovo-viviparous and retain the young within the parent until they have been fully formed.

This family ranges from species four or five feet across to some which measure over 20 feet and weigh in excess of 3,000 pounds.

ALFRED'S MANTA RAY
Also known as Ha-ha-lu-a
19—1 *Manta alfredi* (Kiefft), 1808

Prince Alfred's manta ray is a large species and quite closely resembles the other large manta rays. Like them, it possesses the greatly widened pectoral fins and the two horn-like cephalic fins projecting forward from the head on each side of the mouth. The mouth is very wide and extends across the entire width of the head; it is situated at the very front of the head, rather than below it as in the species of *Mobula*. The teeth occupy a wide, ribbon-like band across the entire width of the lower jaw; the upper jaw is without teeth. The tail is tapering and whip-like and is usually about as long as the body. It posses a small triangular fin at its base on the upper side, but there is no spine at the base of the tail.

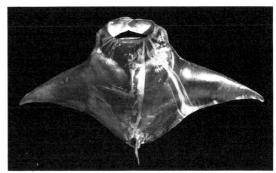

Dorsal View: Note the large cephalic lobes or fins and the wide mouth.

The color of the upper surface is a slate gray, dark bluish, or black and usually contains a pair of very faint lighter patches on the shoulders. The lower surface is white in color with a few scattered dark steel blue or black blotches and a dark margin at the edge of the disc. There are three irregular dark spots on the midline of the lower surface between the

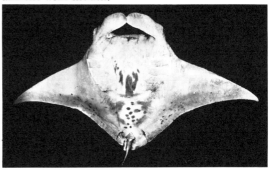

Ventral View: This species is most easily identified by the scattered dark spots on the lower surface.

gill slits; there are also many small irregular black spots on the lower side of the last third of the body. This ray will reach a width of at least twelve feet.

This large fish is distributed from the Hawaiian Islands southward to Australia and westward through the tropical western Pacific Ocean. It doubtless occurs elsewhere in warm waters.

This species is named for Prince Alfred Ernest Albert (1844 - 1900), the fourth child of Queen Victoria of Great Britain.

THE GIANT DEVIL RAY OR MANTA
Also known as Ha-ha-lu-a
19—2 *Manta birostris* (Donndorff), 1798

In the manta rays, the body is very wide and the enlarged pectoral fins do not encircle the head to join at its front as in the smaller rays. These broad fins are slightly convex on their anterior margins, concave on their posterior margins, and rather pointed at the sides. The head of this ray is very wide and bears a pair of fleshy, muscular, horn-like appendages called cephalic fins which are located on each side of the mouth. In this species, the mouth is wide and extends across the front of the head (rather than below the head as in the species of *Mobula*) and contains within it a large number of small teeth which are arranged in a broad pavement-like band across the lower jaw; the upper jaw is without teeth. The tail is short, whip-like, and tapering, and bears a small triangular fin on the upper surface of its base. This species lacks a spine at the base of the tail.

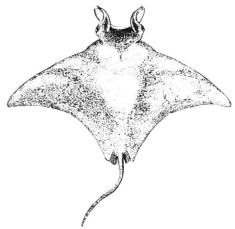

The skin is dark olive or black above, white below and is roughened with small tubercles. The back is sometimes marked with faint lighter areas. Some specimens exhibit two faint V-shaped bands which are pointed toward the back of the body. Dark bluish spots are scattered over the posterior part of the lower surface; but there are no dark spots on the midline of the ventral surface between the gills as in *Manta alfredi* (Krefft). This great ray will reach a width of over 20 feet and some have been estimated at 30 feet; these large individuals will weigh 4,000 pounds or more.

This manta ray is an oceanic form which lives in surface waters where it feeds upon surface fishes and other animals. It is rarely seen near shore. It is reported to swim at times with the tips of the pectoral fins or wings showing above the surface.

This large ray is found in all of the tropical seas of the world.

THE JAPANESE DEVIL RAY
Also known as Ha-ha-lu-a
19—3 *Mobula japanica* (Muller and Henle), 1841

The Japanese devil ray is one of the larger members of the family of manta rays and, like the other members of this family, bears a pair of fleshy appendages called cephalic fins which are located at the front of the head on each side of the mouth. The body of this ray is large, broad, somewhat square, and consists of the enlarged and widened pectoral fins. These wide pectoral fins are convex on the forward margin and concave on the posterior margin. The skin of this ray is dark, dusky brown in color above, creamy white below, and is somewhat roughened with

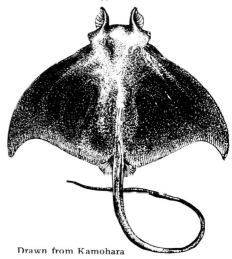

Drawn from Kamohara

spines. The teeth of this species are minute in size and occur in a band in both the upper and lower jaws. The tail is about twice the length of the body, unless accidentally shortened, and bears both a spine and a small triangular dorsal fin at its base on the upper side. This ray will reach at least eight feet in width.

This ray is a surface dwelling or pelagic species which feeds upon small fishes and crustacea in the surface waters.

The Japanese devil ray is native to the tropical Pacific Ocean.

THE EAGLE RAY FAMILY
20 *Family Myliobatidae*

The rays of this family have pectoral fins or "wings" which form a very wide disc of which the lateral edges or "wing tips" are pointed. In this family the pectoral fins do not extend forward and envelop the head as in the sting rays *(Dasyatidae)*, but end at the side of the head, so these rays appear to have a head which is distinct from the remainder of their body. The surface of this disc is usually smooth except for a few tubercles around the eyes and along the midline of the back in the males. The tail is long, slender, and tapering; it may or may not contain a spine on its dorsal surface. A very small dorsal fin is present on the tail whenever a spine is present; but there is no caudal fin. The spine, in those species in which it occurs, is venomous and is placed closer to the body than in the typical sting ray family *(Dasyatidae)*. The head bears a pair of eyes and a pair of spiracles which are located upon the sides of the head. The teeth in this family are flat, pavement-like, and are set in one or more series to form a roll of flat, grinding teeth in each jaw.

In their reproductive habits, these fishes are ovo-viviparous and bring forth their young after they are fully formed.

These rays are shore line forms that live in the shallow coastal waters of tropical seas; they feed upon mollusks and other sand dwelling forms.

THE SPOTTED EAGLE RAY
Also known as the Spotted Duck-billed Ray or Hi-hi-ma-nu
20—1 *Aetobatus narinari* (Euphrasen), 1790

The spotted eagle ray is very easily identified by the many white or bluish white spots which are scattered over the upper surface of the body. Much of the body of this ray consists, as in most rays, of the expanded pectoral fins; but in this species these fins are pointed at the tips and also do not encircle the head to meet in front. The head of

Ventral View

54

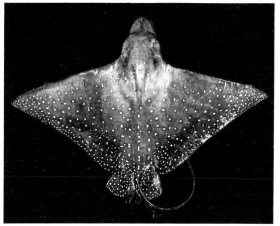

Dorsal View

this ray is large and prominent and bears a fleshy, muscular snout at its front. In addition, the eyes and spiracles, which in most rays lie on the top of the head, are in this species placed upon the sides of the head. The color of the body above is a slate gray or slate brown color while the entire under surface is white in color. The skin is smooth. The teeth of this species are united together to form a single, coarse, large, grinding plate in each jaw. The tail is very long and slender and sometimes may be as much as four times the length of the body; however, it is nearly always much shorter. This tail bears a small poisonous spine at its base on its upper surface and a small dorsal fin is present just in front of the spine. Although most specimens usually measure between two and four feet in diameter, some have been known to exceed seven feet across.

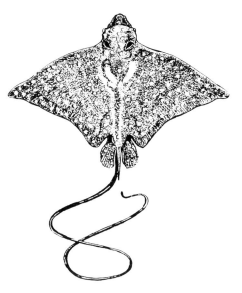

In its reproductive habits, this species is ovo-viviparous and brings forth the young after they have been fully formed. Litters are reported to number from six to ten young.

The spotted eagle ray is a shore line species that frequents sandy bottoms. Here it searches for the bivalves and other mollusca on which it feeds by digging in the sand with its fleshy lower jaw.

The spotted eagle ray inhabits all warm seas of the Atlantic, Pacific, and Indian Oceans.

THE CHIMAERA FAMILY
21 Family Chimaeridae

The chimaeras, like the sharks, are a very ancient group of fishes and like them have a skeleton within their bodies which is made up of cartilage rather than bone. The gill openings in these fishes are covered by a common fold of skin and open through a single opening which is placed low on the side of the body near the base of the pectoral fin. The teeth of chimaeras are represented by two plates in the upper jaw and by a single plate in the lower jaw.

Chimaeras are mostly small, sluggish, bottom dwelling species which feed upon a variety of small fishes and invertebrate animals. They are oviparous in their reproductive habits and deposit large eggs which are enclosed in a large, brown, horny capsule. These capsules are then dropped upon the floor of the sea where they develop independently of the parents.

Chimaeras inhabit many areas of the world's oceans, but seem to prefer cooler and deeper water. They are a small family and contain only about 25 species.

THE PURPLE CHIMAERA
21—1 *Hydrolagus purpurescens* (Gilbert), 1905

Drawn from Gilbert

This chimaera has a large head with a distinct snout and large eyes. The body is quite large, is somewhat flattened laterally and tapers gradually toward the tail. A long, slender, nearly straight spine is present along the entire anterior margin of the first dorsal fin. It will reach a length of three feet. The color of the body was described as "uniform purplish or plum colored."

This species was described from a specimen which was dredged in 1902 by the steamer *Albatross* off the island of Kauai between 957 and 1,067 fathoms.

This species is found in some books under the name of *Chimaera gilberti* Garman, 1911.

10—1 *Triaenodon obesus*   Photo by Scott Johnson

37—2 *Saurida gracilis*   Photo by Scott Johnson

Photo by Scott Johnson
37—2 *Saurida gracilis*

Photo by Scott Johnson
50 2 *Uropterygius tigrinus*

Plate 1

50—8 *Echidna zebra*

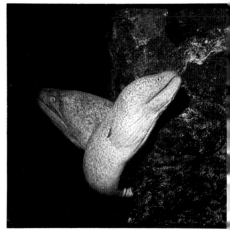

50—11 *Gymnothorax flavimarginatus*

50—14 *Gymnothorax meleagris*

50—16 *Gymnothorax steindachneri*

50—10 *Gymnothorax eurostus*

Plate 2

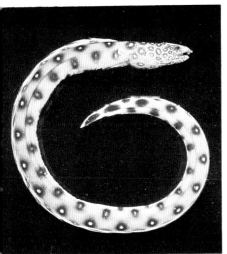

Photo by John Randall
55—6 *Ophichthus polyophthalmus*

Photo by Karl Frogner
68—1 *Hippocampus kuda*

79—9 *Adioryx xantherythrus*

Photo by Frank W. Adams

Plate 3

79—10 *Ostichthys pillwaxi*

79—11 *Holotrachys lima*

79—13 *Myripristis murdjan*

Plate 4

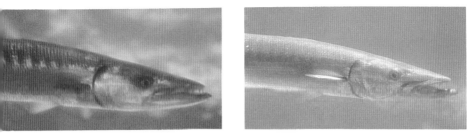

84—1 *Sphyraena barracuda*

92—9 *Apogon snyderi*   Photo by James H. O'Neill

88—11 *Cephalopholis argus*   Photo by James H. O'Neill

Plate 5

98—8 *Parupeneus multifasciatus*

Photo by James H. O'Neill

98—8 *Parupeneus multifasciatus*

Photo by Scott Johnson

Photo by Frank W. Adams
98—2 *Mulloidichthys auriflamma*

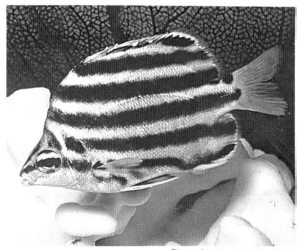

Photo by Douglas Faulkner
103—1 *Microcanthus strigatus*

Plate 6

104—2 *Holacanthus arcuatus*

Photo by Frank W. Adams

104—5 *Centropyge loriculus*

Photo by Scott Johnson

104—7 *Centropyge potteri*

Photo by Frank W. Adams

Plate 7

104—8 *Forcipiger flavissimus*
Photo by Frank W. Adams

Photo by James H. O'Neill
104—9 *F. longirostris* (young dark phase)

Photo by James H. O'Neill
104—9 *Forcipiger longirostris* (dark)

Photo by James H. O'Neill
Upper: 104—8 *F. flavissimus* (adult)
Lower: 104—9 *F. longirostris*

Photo by Frank W. Adams
104—10 *Heniochus acuminatus*

Plate 8

104—10 *Heniochus diphreutes*

Photo by Frank W. Adams

104—12 *Hemitaurichthys polylepis*

Photo by Frank W. Adams

Plate 9

Photo by Scott Johnson
104—13 *Chaetodon auriga*

Photo by Frank W. Adams
104—15 *Chaetodon kleini*

104—14 *Chaetodon citrinellus*

Photo by James H. O'Neill

Plate 10

104—17 *Chaetodon fremblii*

Photo by Frank W. Adams

Photo by Scott Johnson

104—16 *Chaetodon ephippium*

Photo by Scott Johnson

104—18 *Chaetodon lineolatus*

Plate 11

104—19 *Chaetodon lunula*

Photo by Frank W. Adams

104—20 *Chaetodon miliaris*

Photo by Frank W. Adams

Plate 12

104—22 *Chaetodon multicinctus*   Photo by Frank W. Adams

Photo by Scott Johnson
104—23 *Chaetodon ornatissimus*
Day time color

Photo by Scott Johnson
104—23 *Chaetodon ornatissimus*
Night time color

Plate 13

104—22 *Chaetodon multicinctus*, (upper)
Photo by Frank W. Adams
104—20 *Chaetodon miliaris*, (middle)
104—15 *Chaetodon kleini* (lower)

Plate 14

104—24 *Chaetodon quadrimaculatus*   Photo by James H. O'Neill

104—25 *Chaetodon reticulatus*   Photo by James H. O'Neill

Plate 15

104—26 *Chaetodon tinkeri*

Photo by James H. O'Neill

Photo by James H. O'Neill
104—27 *Chaetodon trifasciatus*

Photo by Scott Johnson
104—28 *Chaetodon unimaculatus*
Night time

Plate 16

PART II

THE BONY FISHES
(Class Osteichthyes)
including
The Ancient and Modern Finned Fishes

INTRODUCTION TO
THE BONY FISHES

The bony fishes include by far the greatest number of modern day species. Although no one really knows the total number of living species of fishes, they have been estimated to include perhaps 25,000 species. Of this large number, only about 600 species or about 2.4% are sharks and rays; this means that over 97% of all present day species belong in the group of the bony fishes.

While the present day sharks and rays are divided between 35 to 40 families, the present day bony fishes, because of their immense numbers and great diversity, are divided into about 500 family groups. These various families of fishes are arranged on the basis of their anatomical structure, so that the members of a family share similar structures and therefore resemble each other. These scientific family groups vary in size from families containing but a single species, like the broad-bill sword fish, to very large groups like the carp family which probably contains over 1,500 species.

The distribution of the bony fishes over the face of the earth is extremely wide. They inhabit all of the oceans and seas of the world from the surface waters down to the dark, abyssal depths of the ocean bottoms. They extend from the warmer tropical climates to the frigid polar regions. In addition, they have invaded the inland rivers, streams, lakes, and marshes wherever possible from the warmer regions to the harsh climates of the polar regions. Over this vast area they extend from sea level up the various rivers and streams into the higher elevations of mountainous regions and even to the lower melting edges of snow fields and glaciers. This wide distribution of fishes is scarcely equalled by any other living group.

The bony fishes are of great importance to man for they furnish him with valuable food and other products. The tuna fishes, salmon, trout, herring, sword fish, halibut, and many others are captured, sold, and eaten over nearly the entire world. In addition, these fishes produce some valuable products; these include fertilizers, oils, vitamins, animal feeds, and other products of lesser value. Fishing is also an important recreational activity of mankind and many people find rest, quiet, and peace of mind while fishing, in addition to any fish which they might catch.

INTRODUCTION TO THE PACIFIC FAUNA

The Pacific Ocean is an exceedingly enormous and vast expanse of water and occupies over 64,000,000 square miles; it covers more than 32% of the entire surface of the earth and contains almost one-half (46%) of the earth's water.

Within this great area are several different geographical regions with very different characteristics. The central Pacific area is warm with comparatively little land area; the northern and southern boundaries of the Pacific Ocean are cold and border upon Arctic and Antarctic lands and seas; while both the eastern and western boundaries of the Pacific Ocean are bordered by great continents which have underwater shelves extending outward from them in many places.

In addition, the ocean varies from the surface downward to the bottom While the surface waters of the central Pacific Ocean are warm and sunny this sunlight and warmth diminish as the depth increases. The sunlight becomes dimmer in an uneven manner; the light at the red end of the spectrum is filtered out more rapidly in the surface waters than blue light; finally, even the light from the blue end of the spectrum diminishes until total darkness i reached. Consequently, the entire lower portion of the ocean is in total darkness with only small, weak, and occasional glows of luminescence visible from the animals of this dark domain.

The warmth of the surface waters likewise diminishes as the depth increases. But in this instance, the temperature of the deeper waters does not get much colder than 4°C (39.2°F). This is due to a remarkable physical property of water in which water occupies its smallest volume or space at 4°C. Water shrinks in volume as it cools until it reaches 4°C and thereafter increases in volume as it gets colder. This tells us that, when water is subjected to great pressure, it tends or tries to occupy the smallest possible space and in so doing gives off its excess heat until its temperature is reduced to 4°C. As a result of this phenomenon, all of the great depths of the sea and the bottom water of large and deep lakes usually approach 4°C in temperature.

Within this vast ocean, the fishes inhabit those geographical areas to which they have become accustomed over long periods of time and which most nearly meet their particular needs for sufficient food, a suitable temperature, the proper depth, light, salinity, and other life-sustaining factors This need for a suitable environment for each species of fish has limited the distribution of each species. No fish or any other animal occurs throughout all of the oceans of the world, but each is restricted to a certain geographical area which provides the particular type of environment which that species requires. Some species are surface dwellers and live in the sea without any need for either a shore line or a bottom; some prefer to be near a shore line and there select a depth and the type of bottom most suitable to them, including some fishes which have moved downward along the bottom into very deep water; and some live in the mid-water between the surface and the bottom and there exist without the need for either the shore line, the surface, or the bottom.

1. THE SURFACE, PELAGIC, OR OCEANIC FISHES

The surface, pelagic, or oceanic fishes occur in the upper layers of the sea from the surface downward to a depth of about 500 feet or 150 meters.

These fishes are usually of medium or large size, active swimmers, and voracious feeders, and are usually of a gun-metal blue color above and silvery below. They are most numerous in tropical seas and diminish in kinds and numbers in both northward and southward directions as the waters become cooler in the temperate and polar regions.

This group includes some sharks, the tuna fishes, the flying fishes, the sword fish and spear fishes, the dorado or dolphin fish, many uncommon species, and finally a few forms which belong and live in the deeper water below, but which rise upward toward the surface each night during the hours of darkness and descend again during the daylight.

These surface fishes include many species which are world-wide in warm and temperate seas and other species which occur across an entire ocean or at least a large portion of an ocean. They are limited in an east-west direction by continents and other large land masses, and in a north-south direction by more cooler waters. They are also limited by ocean currents, by the availability of food, and by other factors. Although the northward and southward range of each species is different, it might be stated that very general northern and southern boundaries for these tropical surface fishes lie along the isotherm (temperature line) where the surface water is about 20°C during the coldest months of the year. This boundary line is not a straight line and usually lies between the latitudes of about 20° and 30° in both the North Pacific and South Pacific Oceans, although it is not confined between these latitudes.

2. THE MID-WATER OR BATHY-PELAGIC FISHES

The mid-water or bathy-pelagic fishes live in the middle or intermediate areas between the surface or pelagic fishes and those deep-sea, bottom-dwelling forms which are called the abyssal fishes. This mid-water area extends from approximately 500 feet or 150 meters below the surface downward to about 500 meters (1,640 feet) or more, below which the fauna slowly changes to those species which are more closely associated with the bottom.

These bathy-pelagic or mid-water fishes are mostly of small size, are usually mostly silvery in color, and contain many species with large eyes. These fishes are extremely numerous in both the number of species and in their populations, but are predominantly members of only a very few families, of which the lantern fishes (Myctophidae) are best known.

These fishes feed upon fish eggs and fish larvae, copepods and the larvae of other crustacea, miscellaneous animals of the plankton, and other bits and pieces which have come filtering down from the lighted surface areas above.

Many of these fishes also migrate vertically; it is their habit to move upward during the hours of darkness and to descend again during the daylight hours.

The distribution of this group is still imperfectly known because it is difficult to explore and to study this area of the sea. However, many species are world-wide or nearly so in temperate and tropical seas, and still others are known to inhabit wide and extensive areas of a single ocean.

3. THE ABYSSAL FISHES

The abyssal fishes live in the deeper parts of the sea. This area is best described as a vast, rolling plain with occasional mountains, ridges, basins, and trenches. It is composed principally of great basins with very gentle contours, but it is lacking in most of the abrupt and rugged topographic features which are found on the land.

In addition, much of the bottom area is covered with a deposit of some sort which is spread over the ocean bottom like a blanket. Near the shore line the bottom may contain layers of silt or mud which have been carried down from the land by its rivers. Farther from shore, the bottom is covered in some areas by the accumulated skeletons of microscopic plants and animals which once lived in the upper layers of the sea. These are mostly the silica shells of various diatoms and *Radiolaria* and the calcium carbonate shells of various species of *Foraminifera*; there are also extensive deposits of red clay. This is an area of total darkness and is only weakly lighted by the faint and occasional glow of luminescent animals.

The fishes which inhabit this bottom area are usually very specialized species which have moved into deeper water ages ago. Most of their ancestors were once bottom-dwelling forms which lived along the shore line and which gradually moved downward along the continental slopes into the deeper water. Here they developed into very unusual forms and so today are quite unlike the shallow-water, shore line fishes from which they are descended. They are mostly small or medium in size and dark in color. Their skeletons are light and fragile, although nearly all species have large heads and jaws and may have rather fearsome and formidable teeth. In some, the jaws and stomach are designed to accept very large fish and other food, suggesting that meals are often infrequent in their world. Their eyes are usually small and sometimes are without sight; in other species, the eyes may be large and exceedingly well developed to gather any light which is available.

4. THE SHORE LINE FISHES

The fishes which inhabit the shore line and coastal waters of the oceans are quite different from those which live in the open sea or in the deeper offshore waters. In general, they occupy the region from the shore line outward to the edge of the continental or island shelf and downward to a depth of about 500 or 600 feet. They represent different family groups and include many more species than are found in either the pelagic fauna or in

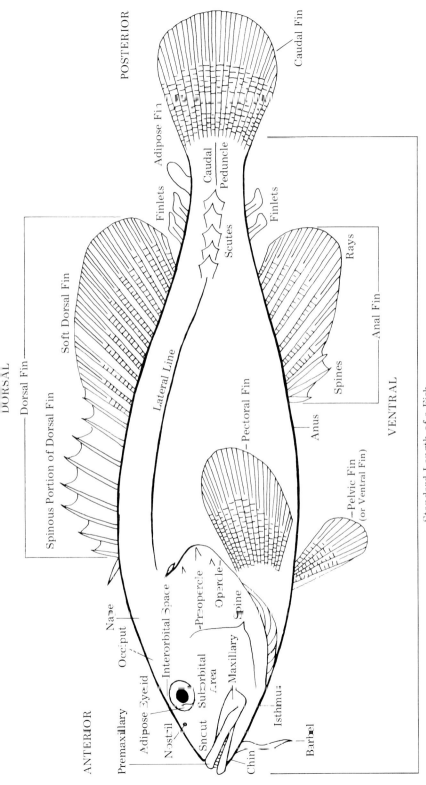

External Features of a Bony Fish

61

the deeper areas of the sea, although their gross or total numbers are less than can be found in these other groups. The areas which the shore line fishes occupy vary widely in such physical and chemical properties as temperature, salinity, turbidity, currents, available oxygen, etc., and also in their biological properties.

As a result we find that the shore line fishes of the sea, in response to their needs, have also grouped themselves into suitable regions in the sea which we call "marine shore line faunal areas." These areas are of different sizes and contain different species of fishes. Their boundaries are not exact and definite, but instead merge gradually into other adjoining areas. Within the shore line fauna, the number of species is greatest in the warmer tropical waters and diminishes gradually in both northerly and southerly directions, although some species in these cooler areas may have very large populations.

The Origin Of The Tropical Shore Line Fauna. In the Mesozoic Era the equatorial regions of the world were encircled by a great body of water called the Tethys Sea (named for Tethys, a Titan goddess of Greek mythology and the wife of the god Oceanus). This Tethys Sea extended from the eastern Pacific Ocean through Central America, across the tropical Atlantic Ocean and the Mediterranean Sea, across parts of Asia Minor and India, into the Indian Ocean, and finally joined the western Pacific Ocean. As the land arose from the sea, new shore lines were formed and the fauna which inhabited this world-wide tropical sea was subsequently divided into large marine faunal areas. Of these, the most important are the Tropical Western Atlantic Faunal Area and the Tropical Western Pacific and Indian Ocean Faunal Area, which is usually called the Indo-Pacific Area.

The fauna of the Tropical Western Atlantic Region occupies the Gulf of Mexico, the Caribbean Sea, and waters adjoining the West Indian Islands; it also extends northward along the Atlantic coast of a few southern states and southward along the coast of South America to Brazil. It has also contributed a few species to the tropical fauna of the western coast of Africa and so, in addition, has some affinities with that area.

The most interesting development in this area occurred on the western or Central American side of this Tropical Western Atlantic Faunal Area. Central America was under water in Mesozoic times so that the Atlantic and Pacific Oceans were joined in this region and these fishes were free to range over this entire area. This submergence continued into the Tertiary Period and extended through the Paleocene, Eocene, Oligocene, Miocene, and into the older or lower part of the Pliocene Epoch. Then in the lower Pliocene Epoch, the land of Central America was lifted from the sea and divided the ocean and its fishes into a tropical western Atlantic fauna on the east and a tropical eastern Pacific fauna on the western side.

Today the fishes which live in the tropical shore line area of the Pacific Ocean to the west of Central America exhibit a very close resemblance to those fishes which live in the Caribbean Sea to the east of Central America. This, of course, is due to the fact that they were once a single faunal unit in late Tertiary times.

It is now customary to divide this great, world-wide, tropical, marine, shore line fauna into four large areas consisting of the Indo-West Pacific, the Eastern Pacific, the Western Atlantic, and the Eastern Atlantic areas. These large areas are in turn subdivided into smaller areas, usually called "provinces," because they possess similar or closely related faunal elements or characteristics.

The Indo-West Pacific Faunal Area And The Hawaiian Islands. The Indo-Pacific Faunal Area extends over one-half of the distance around the earth and is by far the largest faunal area in the world. It extends from the Red Sea on the eastern coast of Africa southward along this coast to about the latitude (30°S) of Durban, South Africa, and then eastward across the entire tropical Indian Ocean to the islands of the East Indies. It extends across the entire northern coast of Australia, southward along the western coast about as far south as Shark Bay (25°S), and also southward along the eastern coast to about the latitude (34°S) of the city of Sydney. In the western Pacific, the northern boundary extends to the islands of southern Japan, but is somewhat irregular in this area because of the many islands and various cooler ocean currents. From the western Pacific, this area continues eastward through the many islands of Micronesia, Melanesia, and Polynesia as far as the Hawaiian Islands to the northeast and to the Marquesas Islands, the Tuamotu Islands, and lonely Easter Island to the extreme east.

Within this great area, the islands with the most numerous species seem to lie in the area to the east of the Malay Peninsula including Borneo, the southern Philippines, and adjacent island groups. Scientists believe that the tropical Pacific shore line fauna, which occupies the many islands of the Pacific Ocean to the eastward, came from this central East Indian area in ancient times. Various species from this area spread in which ever direction they were able. Fishes with larvae which drift in the plankton were spread in some directions by currents and by winds, while other fishes may have drifted along with floating logs or with patches of seaweed which were also carried by currents or winds.

Those islands which were nearest to this population center today have more species than those islands which were more distant, and those fishes which had habits and life cycles which best suited them to spread to nearby shore lines, are now the most widely distributed.

So during countless centuries these Indo-Pacific fishes have spread from island to island in an uneven manner until many species reached the eastern limits of Polynesia, and are today found in the Hawaiian area, the Marquesas and Tuamotu Islands, and some as distant as Easter Island.

The migration routes leading to Hawaii and the other central Pacific islands were doubtless many, but it is quite obvious that the eastward currents which cross the equatorial latitudes were primarily responsible for the eastward spread of these marine animals to the Hawaiian area.

To the eastward beyond Hawaii lies a wide expanse of ocean of over 2,000 miles which forms a barrier to the continued eastward migration of these fishes. Because there are no islands in this ocean to the east, this distance was too great for the continued migration of most of these fishes and so most species living in Hawaii are not found any farther eastward. However, about two dozen or more of these Hawaiian fishes have been found among the islands along the western borders of Mexico, Central, and South America. Of these fishes, the best known is the Moorish Idol, *Zanclus canescens* Linnaeus, 1758, which has performed the remarkable feat of extending its range eastward from the Red Sea across the Indian and Pacific Oceans to the coast of the Americas.

The following pages contain 151 families and more than 600 species of bony fishes which occur in the Hawaiian area and the surrounding central Pacific Ocean.

THE FAMILIES OF
THE BONY FISHES

THE TARPON OR TEN-POUNDER FISH FAMILY
22 *Family Elopidae*

This is a small family of silvery, herring-like fishes which have elongated, somewhat compressed bodies which are covered with large, smooth, silvery scales. The eyes are large, the tail is deeply forked, and the spineless dorsal fin is located at the center of the back. They are among the most primitive of the bony fishes.

Although these fishes are edible, they are not usually sought after as food.

This family is widely distributed in tropical and sub-tropical seas.

THE HAWAIIAN TARPON
Also known as A-wa-a-wa or A-wa-'a-u-a
22—1 *Elops hawaiensis* Regan, 1909

This tarpon-like fish has a long, slender body with a widely forked tail and a single dorsal fin located in the middle of the back. The entire body is silvery in color. It will reach about 24 inches in length. It inhabits the waters of the shore line where it may be found in brackish water including fish ponds.

Its distribution beyond this area is not completely known.

THE BONE FISH FAMILY
23 *Family Albulidae*

The bone fishes or lady fishes are brilliant, silvery fishes of moderate size which are most easily recognized by their semi-transparent snout, deeply forked tail, and single dorsal fin. This is a small family of probably only two species which occur in most tropical seas.

THE BONE FISH
Also known as 'O-i-'o
23—1 *Albula vulpes* (Linnaeus), 1758

The head of this fish is useful in its identification because it extends forward of the mouth to form a snout which is somewhat transparent. Large specimens will reach a length of about three feet.

The common bone fish is one of the best game fishes, although it is not regarded as particularly good to eat. It is commonly sought by sport fishermen who capture it by hook and line; however, most specimens which appear in markets are caught in various types of nets.

The bone fish occurs in the shore line areas of all tropical seas.

THE HERRING FISH FAMILY
24 *Family Clupeidae*
The true herring family is a large group of fishes in which the body is laterally compressed and the belly is usually sharply V-shaped. There is but a single dorsal fin on the back, the tail is deeply forked, and the scales of the body fall off very freely.

This is a family of important food fishes and includes the herrings, shads, sardines, pilchards, the alewife, the menhaden, and others.

Some scholars create a separate family for those species of herring in which the belly is rounded in contrast to the V-shaped belly of the true herrings *(Clupeidae)*. These round herrings, which include about 15 species, are then placed in a separate family called the *Dussumieriidae*. These round herring are a small group of small, silvery, cigar-shaped fishes which live in tropical and warmer temperate seas.

Of more than 150 species in this family, at least two species are native to this area and at least two additional species have been introduced into Hawaii.

THE ROUND HERRING
Also known as the Japanese Herring, Ma-ki-a-wa, Mi-ki-a-wa, and 'O-ma-ka
24—1 *Etrumeus micropus* (Schlegel), 1846

This species is a small, cigar-shaped, stream-lined fish with a rather long body. The head is quite long and pointed and bears large eyes which are covered with a thick, transparent membrane. The pectoral and pelvic fins are a bit unusual for they fold beneath a sheath of scales. It should also be noted that these pelvic or ventral fins are placed to the rear of the single dorsal fin. The color of this fish is bluish and brownish above and bright silvery on the sides and belly. The scales of the back are each marked with a brownish spot. Most specimens measure between six and ten inches in length.

The distribution of this species extends from tropical America westward across the tropical Pacific Ocean to Japan; it occurs in the tropical western Pacific and extends across the Indian Ocean to the coast of Africa.

THE SMALL ROUND HERRING
Also known as the Pi-ha and Blue-backed Sprat
24—2 *Spratelloides delicatulus* (Bennett), 1831

This little herring is a round-bellied, spindle-shaped species which measures from two and one-half to four inches in length. It is slate colored above and silvery

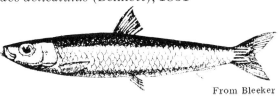

From Bleeker

white below and is probably most easily recognized by four, dark, horizontal lines at the base of the tail.

The distribution of this round herring extends from the tropical central and western Pacific southward to Australia and westward across the Indian Ocean to the region of Mauritius.

THE MARQUESAN SARDINE
24—3 *Sardinella marquesensis* Berry and Whitehead, 1968
This sardine is a small fish with a body which is strongly compressed and bordered by a sharp-edged belly, it is covered with large, thin, smooth-edged scales which are easily rubbed off. The mouth is large, there is no

lateral line, and the tail is widely forked. The body is silvery in color and bears blackish areas upon the tips of the tail.

This fish was introduced into Hawaii with the hope that it might become established and later be used as a bait fish for the tuna fishermen. The introduction of this species was made by the United States government at the request of the Division of Fish and Game, Department of Agriculture, State of Hawaii. The Pacific Oceanic Fisheries Investigation office in Honolulu made eight shipments of these sardines from the Marquesas Islands and liberated all of them around Oahu. These shipments extended over four years and totalled about 143,800 specimens. They arrived as follows: 7,500 in December of 1955; 7,900 in the fall of 1956; 24,000 in March of 1957; 32,000 in December of 1957; 56,000 in February of 1958; 9,400 in May of 1958; 3,000 in June of 1958; and 4,000 in March of 1959. It was the first imported marine fish to become established in the Hawaiian Islands.

This fish, when first introduced into Hawaii, was thought to be *Harangula vittata* (Cuvier and Valenciennes) and so the early references to it in Hawaii use this name. It was later discovered to be an undescribed species and was described and named *S. marquesensis* in 1968.

The distribution of this species includes the Marquesas Islands and doubtless other adjoining areas of the tropical Pacific to the westward.

THE THREAD-FIN SHAD OR GIZZARD SHAD
24—4 *Dorosoma petenense* (Gunther), 1868

The gizzard shads are a small group of less than a dozen species which are very closely related to many kinds of herrings, sardines, shads, and similar fishes found in the herring family (*Clupeidae*). However, they differ from these other fishes in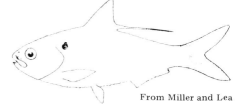

From Miller and Lea

having a very short, muscular stomach which resembles the gizzard of a chicken and from which they get their common name. For this reason the gizzard shad are placed by some scholars in a separate family called the *Dorosomidae*. As a group they have short, deep bodies which are strongly compressed or flattened and covered with loose scales. The head is short and without scales, the mouth is small and without teeth, and the jaws are about equal in length. Gizzard shads range in length from five to about 20 inches.

D. petenense is a small species about five or six inches in length and bright silvery in color with a round, black spot on the side of the body behind the head. The body is flattened, the head and mouth are small, and the eyes are covered by adipose eyelids. The dorsal fin, located midway on the body, has 14 or 15 rays of which the last ray extends as a filament nearly to the end of the anal fin. The anal fin has 20 to 23 rays, the tail is widely forked, and there is neither a lateral line nor an adipose fin on the back.

D. petenense, a North American species, was first introduced into Hawaii on April 10, 1958, by Vernon Brock, Director of the Division of Fish and Game of the State of Hawaii Department of Agriculture. Subsequent introductions were made jointly by the Honolulu Office of the National Marine Fisheries Service and the State Division of Fish and Game so that this fish is now well established in various reservoirs and in some streams.

Gizzard shads are mostly shore line fishes and live in both fresh and salt water; they inhabit lakes, reservoirs, rivers, estuaries, and the marine waters of coast lines. However, in Hawaii they do not show any inclination to inhabit the marine environments.

Gizzard shads resemble mullet in their feeding habits and like them forage over the bottom for bits of organic material and other detritus.

THE ANCHOVY FISH FAMILY
25 *Family Engraulidae*

The anchovies are a family of small, weak, carnivorous fishes of shore line areas. They have a single dorsal fin on the back, a deeply notched tail, and in many ways resemble the round herrings in appearance.

Anchovies lay oval, floating eggs which hatch within a few days. Thereafter the young anchovies feed almost continuously upon the floating larvae of crustacea and grow rapidly into their adult form.

Anchovies are gregarious fishes and gather into large schools at which time they are captured in nets for use as food or bait.

This family of approximately 75 species is widely distributed in tropical, sub-tropical, and warmer temperate seas.

It should be noted that a new species from this area was described as *Anchoviella mauii* Fowler and Bean, 1924; this is an error and should be ignored.

At least two species are known from this area.

THE HAWAIIAN ANCHOVY
Also known as the Ne-hu
25 1 *Stolephorus purpureus* Fowler, 1900

This anchovy is a small, frail, weak, little fish with a compressed body, a rounded belly, and a widely forked tail. The color of the body in life is

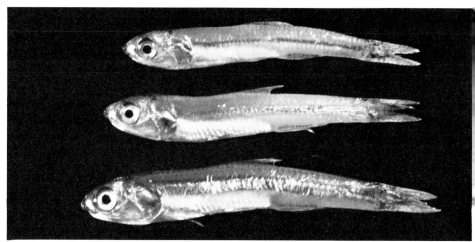

greenish or brownish and there is a wide, silvery white stripe extending along each side of the body from the head to the tail. It will reach a length of about four inches.

The nehu inhabits the quiet waters of bays and estuaries where it feeds upon the floating larvae of various crustacea. This is a very important bait fish in Hawaii and is preferred to all other fish as bait for chumming tuna.

The distribution of this species is believed to be limited to the Hawaiian area.

THE ROUND - HEADED ANCHOVY
25—2 *Stolephorus buccaneeri* Strasburg, 1960

This anchovy is a small fish which is very similar in general appearance to the preceeding species, although it differs from it in having a shorter head, a smaller mouth, a shorter maxillary bone above the mouth, and in having the pectoral and pelvic fins closer together. The scales are very loosely attached.

The color of the body in life is reported as purplish blue. The sides of the body are marked by a horizontal stripe about as wide as the eye; this stripe extends from the eye to the base of the tail. The tips of the snout and jaw are blackish in color; the scale pockets on the upper side of the body are margined with black; and the rays of the dorsal and caudal fins are spotted with black. It ranges in length from one and one-half to two and one-half inches.

This fish occurs in bays and estuaries and in adjoining offshore areas where it gathers into schools. It is carnivorous in its eating habits. White opaque eggs are released into the plankton and drift with it until hatching, after which the young feed continuously upon copepods and other small drifting forms.

This anchovy is named for the M/V Buccaneer, a Honolulu tuna boat captained in 1958 by Captain Noboru Tsue.

The distribution of this species includes the Hawaiian area, southern Africa, and probably adjoining waters.

THE SAND FISH FAMILY
26 *Family Gonorhynchidae*

This is a primitive family of slender fishes of shore line areas. Their body is long and has the fins placed well toward the back. The head is pointed and bears a single barbel at the tip of the snout.

There is probably only one widely distributed species in the Indo-Pacific region.

THE SAND FISH
Also known as the Sand Eel or Beaked Salmon
26—1 *Gonorhynchus gonorhynchus* (Linnaeus), 1766

The sand fish is a very slender species with a small, toothless mouth located under the head. The lips are thick and there is an unusual, single barbel under the snout in front of the mouth. The inside of the mouth is dark in color, the tail is marked with black, and the lower surface of the body is reddish white in color. Although larger specimens have been reported, most individuals do not exceed 15 inches.

The sand fish lives along shore line areas where there are sandy bottoms in which it can dig for its food.

This species is known to occur along the shore lines of South Africa, New Zealand, Australia, Japan, and Hawaii.

THE MILK FISH FAMILY
27 *Family Chanidae*

This family seems to contain but a single species, the famous milk fish of the tropical Pacific and Indian Oceans.

THE MILK FISH
Also known as the A-wa
27—1 *Chanos chanos* (Forskal), 1775

The milk fish or awa has a spindle-shaped body with a single, prominent, dorsal fin and a widely forked tail. The head is small and there are no teeth in the mouth. The entire body is a brilliant, metallic, silvery color; it is somewhat bluish, greenish or grayish above, silvery on the sides, and nearly white beneath. It will exceed three feet in length.

Because this fish feeds on vegetable food, it is raised in fish ponds in Hawaii, Asia, and elsewhere. It is usually caught in nets along the shore line

while young, transferred to enclosed ponds, and thereafter harvested when it reaches marketable size.

The milk fish is found throughout the tropical Pacific and Indian Oceans.

THE DEEP-SEA SMELT OR ARGENTINE FISH FAMILY
28 *Family Argentinidae*

The deep-sea smelts are closely related to the true smelts of the family *Osmeridae* and resemble them in general appearance. They comprise a small family of rather small fishes and have bodies which are flat or compressed and covered with large, firm, cycloid scales which are usually rough and spiny. In this family, the side of the body bears a lateral line. The head is wedge-shaped, is without scales, and bears a small or medium-sized mouth which is located at the front of the head. The eyes are large and are located on the sides of the head. The single dorsal fin is short and is located at approximately the middle of the body; the pectoral fins are located low on the body, while the ventral fins are located almost directly beneath the dorsal fin. A large air bladder is present.

The deep-sea smelt inhabit the mid-water depths of the ocean. They are most common in the northern hemisphere, although they occur in all seas including the Mediterranean Sea. Some species ascend rivers to lay their eggs and in this habit resemble the salmon and trout to which they are closely related.

STRUHSAKER'S DEEP-SEA SMELT
28—1 *Glossanodon struhsakeri* Cohen, 1970

Struhsaker's deep-sea smelt is a small, frail fish with a large, long, wedge-shaped head and a body which tapers gradually and uniformly toward the tail and is quite rectangular in cross section. The scales, which cover the body except for the head, are loose and easily rubbed off. The pectoral fins are placed low on the body, the pelvic fins are almost directly beneath the dorsal fin, and the tail is quite deeply forked.

The light colored body is marked by a wide, darker band which extends from the head to the tail. This band is darker above than below and is marked with darker areas distributed along its length. Most specimens measure between three and five inches in length.

The habitat of this species is in the mid-water regions of the sea. It is usually captured by the use of special deep-water trawling gear.

Drawn from Cohen

The name of this fish honors Dr. Paul Struhsaker, an ichthyologist employed by the Honolulu Laboratory of the National Marine Fisheries Service.

The distribution of this fish includes the Hawaiian area and doubtless adjoining areas.

THE BRISTLE-MOUTH OR LIGHT FISH FAMILY
29 *Family Gonostomatidae (Gonostomidae, Maurolicidae)*

The bristle-mouths resemble miniature herring. Their heads and bodies are compressed, barbels are absent on the chin, and the gill openings are very wide. The eyes range from small to large, an adipose fin may be either present or absent, and the scales are either large, thin, and deciduous or entirely absent. They are small, delicate fishes with photophores along the sides of their bodies and usually measure less than three inches in length.

These fishes live in large numbers in deeper water and are rarely seen unless captured by special equipment. They lay spherical eggs which float in the plankton and which hatch into sardine-like larvae before assuming their adult form.

When the 1950 lava flow from Mauna Loa volcano on the island of Hawaii ran into the sea, it killed a great many fishes of which some were undescribed species and others were new records for this area. These 1950 specimens were described by Marion Gray in 1961 in *Pacific Science* 15(2):462-476, figs. 1-5. They included the following species of this family:

Araiophos gracilis Gray, 1961
Argyripnus atlanticus Maul, 1952
Cyclothone species
Danaphos oculatus (Garman), 1899
Gonostoma atlanticum Norman, 1930

Of about 40 species, at least a dozen are known from this area.

THE ELONGATED BRISTLE-MOUTH FISH
29—1 *Gonostoma elongatum* Gunther, 1878

This bristle-mouth is a small to medium sized, slender, tapering species with small eyes and a small, adipose fin on the back. The body bears a very few, thin, transparent scales behind the head and numerous photophores along the ventral side of the body. In color, it is brownish black above and jet black below; the inside of the mouth is also black in color. This species will reach about 11 inches in length, but most specimens are six or seven inches or less. It inhabits deep water.

From Gilbert

This species is known from the western temperate and tropical North Atlantic Ocean and from the eastern and central tropical and temperate North Pacific Ocean and doubtless elsewhere.

THE DEEP-WATER BRISTLE-MOUTH FISH
29—2 *Cyclothone atraria* Gilbert, 1905

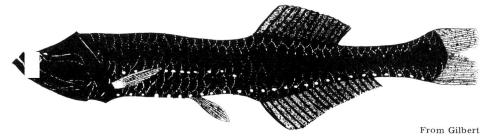

From Gilbert

This bristle-mouth is uniformly black over the entire body. It contains photophores along the lower side of the body and measures about three inches in length. It is a deep-water species which is only captured with special equipment.

It is known from the Hawaiian area and doubtless elsewhere in deep water.

GILBERT'S DEEP-WATER BRISTLE-MOUTH FISH
29—3 *Cyclothone canina* Gilbert, 1905

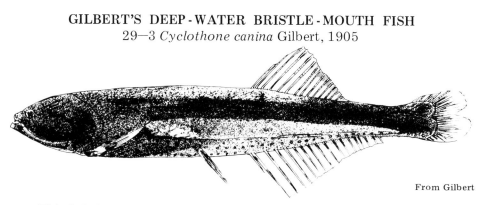

From Gilbert

This bristle-mouth is a small, slender species with a few large scales on the body, without an adipose fin, and with photophores on the lower surface. The body is dark brown above and on the sides; the sides of the head and the lower surface are black. It reaches a length of nearly three inches and inhabits deep water.

This species is known from the Hawaiian area and doubtless elsewhere in deep water.

THE WORLD WIDE BRISTLE-MOUTH FISH
29—4 *Vinciguerria nimbaria* (Jordan and Williams), 1895

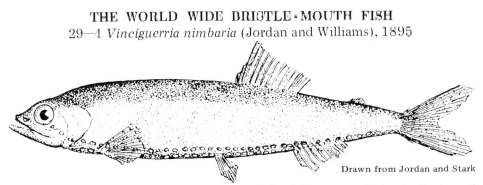

Drawn from Jordan and Stark

This is a small, slender, deep-water fish with a somewhat spindle-shaped body which tapers gradually toward the tail. The mouth is large, the teeth are slender, the eyes are very large and round, the gill openings are wide, and the adipose fin is present. The ground color of the body is brownish above and silvery on the sides. The photophores are large and conspicuous and are arranged in two rows along each side of the belly; the upper row ends in front of the anal fin, while the lower row continues to the tail. There is one pair of photophores near the symphysis of the lower jaw; these symphyseal photophores are absent in *V. poweriae*. It measures about two and one-half inches in length.

This is a deep-water form which is very widely distributed. It is known to occur in the Red Sea, the Arabian Sea, southern Africa, the Indian Ocean, from Hawaii to California, in the tropical and temperate western North Atlantic Ocean, and doubtless elsewhere.

POWER'S DEEP-WATER BRISTLE-MOUTH FISH
29—5 *Vinciguerria poweriae* (Cocco), 1838

This bristle-mouth is a small, deep-water species with a slender body, a large mouth, large eyes, and wide gill openings. The photophores are present and number between 13 and 15 on each side of the body. This fish resembles *V. nimbaria* very closely, but it may be separated from that species by the fact that it lacks the pair of symphyseal photophores near the symphysis of the lower jaw which are found in *V. nimbaria*.

It is known from the Mediterranean Sea, the tropical and sub-tropical western Atlantic, the tropical and sub-tropical eastern and central Pacific Ocean, and doubtless elsewhere.

BROCK'S BRISTLE-MOUTH FISH
29—6 *Argyripnus brocki* Struhsaker, 1973

This small species has a large head set with large eyes and a body which is deepest behind the head and thereafter tapers uniformly toward the tail. Rows of photophores adorn the lower sides of the body. Adult specimens range in length from one and one-half to three and one-half inches. Dark pigmented areas occur on the upper sides of the body behind the head and on the sides of the caudal peduncle; elsewhere the body has a translucent appearance.

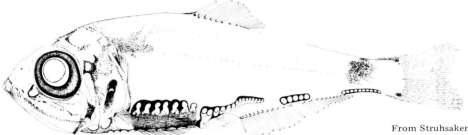

From Struhsaker

The habitat of this species is near the bottom in moderately shallow water. It has been captured during the daytime at depths between about 600 and 900 feet.

The distribution of this species thus far includes the Hawaiian area and doubtless adjacent surrounding areas.

This species was named for Vernon E. Brock (June 24, 1912—January 31, 1971), ichthyologist and oceanographer, gentleman and friend, and a resident of Honolulu from 1944 until his death.

Persons interested in studying this species should consult Dr. Paul Struhsaker's original description in *Fishery Bulletin* 71:3, 1973, pp. 827-836 (1 fig.).

GILBERT AND CRAMER'S BRISTLE-MOUTH FISH
29—7 *Argyripnus ephippiatus* Gilbert and Cramer, 1897

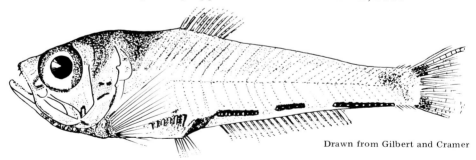

Drawn from Gilbert and Cramer

This bristle-mouth is a small, deep-water species with a strongly compressed body and large eyes. The mouth is wide and the teeth are short, slender, and in a single series. The scales are large, very thin, and flexible and an adipose fin is present on the back. It measures about three and one-half inches in length.

This species is known from the Pacific Ocean and doubtless elsewhere in the deep sea.

THE BIG-EYED BRISTLE-MOUTH FISH
29—8 *Danaphos oculatus* Garman, 1899

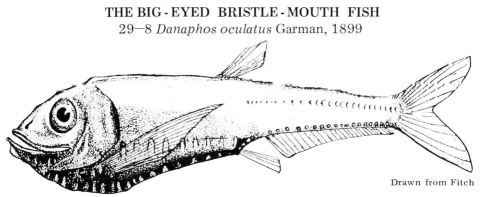

Drawn from Fitch

This little fish has a slender, tapering body with a large head and a large mouth. The eyes are large, the gill openings are very wide, and there is no barbel trailing from the lower jaw. Specimens of this fish will reach two and one-fourth inches in length, although most specimens are usually about one and one-half inches in length. This fish has been taken at depths around 1200 feet.

It is known from the North Pacific and Indian Oceans, but is undoubtedly more widely distributed.

MUELLER'S BRISTLE-MOUTH FISH
29—9 *Maurolicus muelleri* (Gmelin), 1789

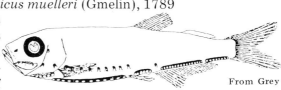

From Grey

Mueller's bristle-mouth is a small fish which measures between one and one-half and two inches in length. It inhabits the middle depths of the ocean from less than 1,000 feet down to at least 5,000 feet.

In Hawaii, specimens have been taken off the Hamakua coast of Hawaii, off Maui, and in the Kealaikahiki Channel between Lanai and Kahoolawe.

The distribution of this species includes the Atlantic and Pacific Oceans.

THE HATCHET FISH FAMILY
30 *Family Sternoptychidae*

The hatchet fishes are a small family of small fishes which inhabit the deep sea. Their bodies are short, deep, and compressed and are either scaleless or are covered with very thin scales which fall off readily. The eyes are large and in some species are telescopic and are directed upward. The teeth are very small in this family and luminescent organs occurs in groups over the body. The members of this family are separated from all other fishes by the presence of a dorsal blade in front of the dorsal fin. This blade may be a plate *(Argyropelecus)*, a pair of bony keels *(Polyipnus)*, or a single elongated spine *(Sternoptyx)*.

Hatchet fishes are world-wide in tropical and temperate seas where they inhabit the deeper waters.

Of about 25 or more species, at least six are known from this area.

The following species are not described or illustrated:

Argyropeleus affinis Garman, 1899. This species was reported among those fishes killed by the 1950 lava flow from Mauna Kea volcano, but some scholars doubt its identity.

THE DIAPHANOUS HATCHET FISH
30—1 *Sternoptyx diaphana* Hermann, 1781

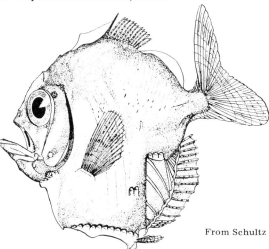

From Schultz

This hatchet fish has a body which is very short, deep, and laterally compressed. Scales are present over the body, but they are very thin and easily lost. The dorsal blade is present in front of the fin as a single, enlarged spine. The color of the body is generally silvery; it is darker above than below. The fins are translucent and doubtless served as the inspiration for the selection of the name *diaphana* (transparent) for this species. Large individuals will reach about two or more inches in length, but most are somewhat smaller. It has been captured at depths greater than one and one-half miles.

This hatchet fish is widely distributed. It occurs in the western north temperate and tropical Atlantic Ocean, in the Indian Ocean, through the East Indies, and over most of the temperate and tropical Pacific Ocean.

NUTTING'S HATCHET FISH
30—2 *Polyipnus nuttingi* Gilbert, 1905

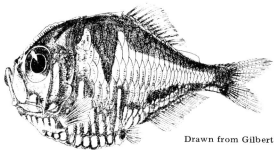

Drawn from Gilbert

The body of this hatchet fish is deep in front and thereafter narrows abruptly to a slender, tapering tail. The eyes of this fish are large, telescopic, and directed upward. The mouth is large with a cleft which opens vertically and contains minute teeth and long, slender gill rakers. A small adipose dorsal fin is present. The body is colored a dark brown above and silvery on the sides. Most specimens measure between one and one-half and three inches in length. It has been captured at depths of 1,800 feet. Stomach contents indicate that it eats *Globigerina*, *Foraminifera*, and copepods.

The scientific name honors Professor Charles C. Nutting of the University of Iowa, who participated in the collecting of the steamer *Albatross* in 1902 and later wrote the articles on the hydroids of the Hawaiian Islands.

This hatchet fish is known from the Hawaiian area, the central Pacific Ocean, and doubtless elsewhere.

THE HAWAIIAN HATCHET FISH
30—3 *Argyropelecus hawaiensis* Schultz, 1960

This species is a close relative of *A. lynchus* and will appear in some books as a subspecies designated *A. lynchus hawaiensis* Schultz, 1960. It has the dorsal blade and other characteristics typical of hatchet fishes. An adipose fin is present and photophores are

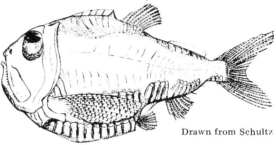

Drawn from Schultz

present in groups on the lower part of the body. Larger specimens measured about two and one-half inches.

This species is based on a few specimens from Hawaii and adjacent areas.

HEATH'S HATCHET FISH
30—4 *Argyropelecus heathi* Gilbert, 1905

Heath's hatchet fish is a small species with a deep body to which is attached a slender caudal peduncle and a forked tail. The mouth is far forward and opens almost vertically. They eyes are large and lateral in position, but are telescopic in

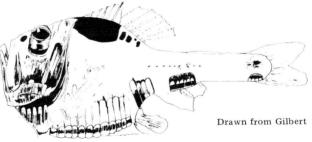

Drawn from Gilbert

appearance and are directed upward. The dorsal blade is present in this species as a thin plate located just in front of the dorsal fin. The body scales are very thin. In color, the head and trunk are mostly black; the middle of the trunk is silvery green, and the caudal peduncle is whitish. The mouth is whitish in front, but its interior and the gill cavity are black. This fish measures less than one and one-half inches in length. Its habitat seems to be at depths of about 2,000 feet.

In distribution, this seems to be a Pacific species which occurs about Hawaii and in the eastern Pacific Ocean.

THE PACIFIC HATCHET FISH
30—5 *Argyropelecus pacificus* Schultz, 1960

The Pacific hatchet fish, like other members of the family, contains the dorsal blade in front of the dorsal fin; in this species the blade takes the form of a thin plate. The body is compressed; the head is large and contains a large mouth which opens

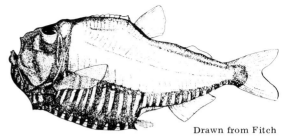

Drawn from Fitch

almost vertically; the eyes, which are telescopic, are directed upward. The parallel rows of photophores along the lower side help to identify this species. Specimens will reach a length of four inches, although most individuals are a little less than three inches long.

It is known to live at depths in excess of a mile. Examinations of the stomach content of various specimens reveal that this little fish feeds upon larval crustacea and larval fishes.

The distribution of this species extends from Hawaii to Oregon and southward along the Pacific coast to the equator.

SLADEN'S HATCHET FISH
30—6 *Argyropelecus sladeni* Regan, 1908

This hatchet fish is a small species with a deep body and a slender tail. Like other members of this family, a dorsal blade is present as a thin plate on the midline of the back in front of the dorsal fin. The eyes are telescopic in appearance and are pointed upward. It measures about two and one-half inches in length.

The distribution of this fish is probably world-wide. It has been found in the Atlantic, Antarctic, and Indian Oceans, and also in the eastern, central, and western Pacific Ocean.

Some scholars regard this fish as a subspecies of *A. lynchus* and will include it under the name of *Argyropelecus lynchus sladeni* Regan, 1908.

THE VIPER FISH FAMILY
31 *Family Chauliodontidae*

The deep sea fishes of this family have a slender, elongated, tapering body which ends in a large, widely-forked tail. The sides of the body are covered with loosely attached scales which are large, thin, and angular in shape. The sides of the body bear a lateral line and two rows of photophores which are placed low on the body and extend from the head to the tail. The dorsal fin bears a very long filament which is an extension of the first fin ray. The pectoral and ventral fins are well developed and there is both a dorsal and a ventral adipose fin. The head is very large in comparison to the body, is compressed in shape, and is composed of thin, ossified bones. The mouth is large and wide and is set with many, long, slender, sharp teeth of various lengths; the gill openings are likewise very wide. The barbel on the chin is either absent or very rudimentary. Most species are comparatively small; the largest measure about eight or ten inches in length.

It seems to be the habit of these fishes to migrate vertically; some are known to come within 1,500 feet of the surface during the night and to descend as deep as 7,500 feet during the daytime.

The distribution of the family is world-wide in deep water, although they are more numerous in the temperate and tropical seas.

This is a small family of less than ten species, of which at least one is known from this area.

SLOAN'S VIPER FISH

31—1 *Chauliodus sloani* Bloch and Schneider, 1801

From Goode and Bean

Sloan's viper fish has the slender, elongated body which is characteristic of this family. This body is covered with near-hexagonal scales, bears a lateral line, and exhibits many, small, dot-like photophores extending in longitudinal series from the chin to the anal fin. The dorsal fin, which is located rather close to the head, contains six or seven rays; the first ray extends as a long filament. An adipose fin is present on the back just forward of the tail and opposite the anal fin. The pectoral fins are quite short, but the ventral or pelvic fins are elongated. The head is short and deep and bears a mouth full of viper-like teeth; those teeth on the tips of the jaws remain outside of the mouth when the jaws are closed. The dark colored body is greenish above, silvery on the sides, and blackish below. It will reach a length of about nine or ten inches.

This viper fish is rarely seen or captured because it usually inhabits water from about 2,000 to at least 9,000 feet in depth. Although an occasional specimen is captured at the surface, most specimens are obtained by special collecting gear aboard oceanographic vessels.

The distribution of this fish seems to be almost world-wide. It occurs in the temperate and tropical Atlantic, Pacific, and Indian Oceans.

THE ASTRONESTHID FISH FAMILY

32 *Family Astronesthidae*

These fishes are small in size, have elongated, scaleless bodies, and usually possess an adipose fin. Their mouth is large, their teeth are long and sharp, and they possess a stomach of large size. A barbel is attached to the chin, although it may be missing in many specimens. Photophores are present and occur on each side of the body in two rows of various groupings. Some species will reach six inches in length, but most are much smaller.

The members of this family are world-wide in the deeper waters of tropical and temperate seas.

Of about 40 species, several are known from the Pacific Ocean and at least one is known from this area.

THE PACIFIC ASTRONESTHID FISH
32—1 *Astronesthes lucifer* Gilbert, 1905

This little fish has a slender, tapering, scaleless body, eyes of moderate size, and an adipose fin. The fins are translucent and rows of photophores are present on the lower side. The body is brownish black above, silvery

Drawn from Gilbert

on the sides, and black below. It reaches a length of about six inches.

This species was originally described from two specimens dredged off Oahu and Kauai in 1902 by the steamer *Albatross* at depths of about 1500 feet. It seems to inhabit the areas between 300 or 400 feet and about 2,000 feet.

The distribution of this species includes the Hawaiian area and Japan; it doubtless extends far beyond this area.

THE SCALY DRAGON FISH FAMILY
33 *Family Stomiatidae (Stomiidae)*

The scaly dragon fishes have long, slender, tapering bodies which are covered with scales. These scales are very loosely attached to the body and the whole body and scales are enveloped by a thin, gelatinous membrane. They have large eyes which are directed forward, no adipose fin on the back, and usually have a barbel trailing from the lower jaw. Their mouths are

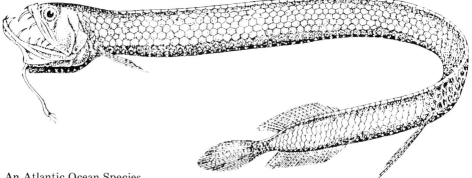

An Atlantic Ocean Species,
Stomias boa (Risso), 1810.

From Goode and Bean

large and are equipped with fang-like teeth and their bodies are either black or dark in color in keeping with their habitat. Judging from their fang-like teeth and distensible stomachs, they are doubtless aggressive, voracious fishes.

They inhabit the deep water of all oceans. Although most are believed to live between 1,000 and 1,500 feet in depth, they are known to inhabit waters exceeding one mile in depth.

Of more than one dozen species, several are known from the Pacific and Indian Oceans and also from this area.

No Pacific species are listed here.

THE SCALELESS DRAGON FISH FAMILY
Also known as the Hinged Heads, Loose-jawed Fishes
or Black Dragon Fishes
34 *Family Melanostomiatidae (Malacosteidae)*

The members of this family of dragon fishes usually have elongated, slender bodies, usually lack an adipose fin, and have no scales covering the body. The head is usually short with large jaws and depressible teeth. A barbel is present on the chin and photophores are present in various arrangements. They are dark colored, degenerate fishes of the deep sea. Although some specimens have been taken at depths in excess of two miles, most species live nearer the surface.

Of over 100 species in this family, at least two are known at present from this area and many more species will doubtless come to light as deep water exploration continues.

THE VALDIVIA BLACK DRAGON FISH
34—1 *Melanostomias valdiviae* Brauer, 1902

From Brauer

This black dragon fish is typical of its family in having a slender trunk, a short snout, large jaws, long and depressible teeth, and a barbel on its chin. It will reach a length of about eight inches, but most specimens are much smaller.

This species is probably world wide in tropical and temperate seas. It has been captured from deep water in the Hawaiian area.

The name of this species begins with Pedro de Valdivia (c. 1498-1554), an early Spanish governor of Chile. Valdivia is a city and province in southern Chile and the name of the vessel used in 1898 and 1899 by the German deep sea scientific expedition.

THE LONG-THREADED DRAGON FISH
34 2 *Leptostomias macronema* Gilbert, 1905

Drawn from Gilbert

This dragon fish has a long, slender, tapering body with fang-like teeth, transparent fins, a long barbel on its chin, and rows of photophores on the lower part of the body. It is jet black in color.

This species was described from a single little specimen which was taken in a dredge by the steamer *Albatross* at over 2,000 feet off Niihau in 1902. It is doubtless much more widely distributed.

THE BLACK DRAGON FISH FAMILY
35 *Family Idiacanthidae*

Black dragon fishes are astonishing in their appearance because they look more like snakes than like fishes. Their bodies are extremely long and slender and are without scales, although two rows of photophores extend low along each side of the body; the upper row extends from the head to the caudal fin, but the lower row is shorter. The head, which is considerably larger than the body and compressed, bears a very large mouth which in turn is filled with large, barbed, depressible teeth. The eyes are quite small and a long barbel trails downward from the chin. The dorsal and anal fins are very long, the pectoral fins are absent, and the caudal fin is deeply forked. Very unusual spiny processes from the front of the vertebrae project upward through the skin of the back. Most species are black in color. Some will reach 15 inches in length.

The members of this family go through a weird larval stage in which the eyes of the fish are carried for a time upon the ends of very long eye-stalks, which are later slowly shortened and the eyes are drawn back to the skull.

The habitat of the dragon fishes is in very deep water including depths in excess of three miles.

The distribution of this family is world-wide.

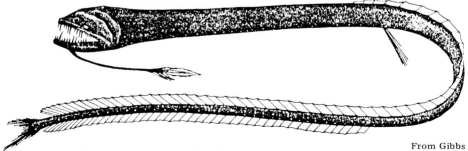

From Gibbs

Idiacanthus fasciola, adult female, an Atlantic Ocean species.

Of about a half dozen known species, at least one species is known from this area.

No Pacific Ocean species are listed here.

THE BARREL-EYE FISH FAMILY
36 Family Opisthoproctidae

Although the fishes in this group have telescopic or barrel-like eyes, they are named for the fact that their anus is placed far to the rear of the body (*opisth* = to the rear; *proct* = anus). Some species have elongated bodies, while the bodies of others are short and robust; but they all possess a pad of skin on the belly which gives them a flattened ventral surface. On the head, the suborbital bone below the eye is unusually large and covers the cheek and part of the eye. The premaxillary and maxillary bones, which compose the upper jaw, are either rudimentary or missing. The lateral line is present and extends in a straight course along the side of the body, but it does not enter the caudal fin.

This is truly a very weird group of small fishes which inhabit very deep water.

Less than a dozen species are known. At least one has been captured in this area.

THE BARREL-EYE OR SPOOK FISH
36—1 Opisthoproctus soleatus (Vaillant), 1888

From Cohen

The body of this barrel-eye fish is quite short and robust, but is deformed from the usual shape of most fishes. The last two vertebrae are angled upward so that the caudal fin has been dislocated, reduced in size, and now points almost vertically; the anal fin has shifted to the rear of the body and increased in size so that it now performs the function of propelling the body. The lower surface of the body has the unusual ventral pad of skin extending from beneath the head to the anal fin. The eyes are telescopic and the suborbital bone is large and covers parts of both the cheek and the eye. The bones of the upper jaw are absent so there are no teeth in this species.

The first known specimen from this area measured about three inches in length and came from a depth of about 2,000 feet in the Kaiwi Channel between Oahu and Molokai.

The distribution of this fish includes both the Atlantic and Pacific Oceans.

THE LIZARD FISH FAMILY
37 *Family Synodidae (Synodontidae, Sauridae)*

The lizard fishes are a family of small, slender, cylindrical species in which the entire head and body are covered with scales. The head is lizard-like in appearance and bears a pointed snout and a large mouth containing many teeth upon the jaws and tongue. A small adipose fin is present on the back and the caudal fin is widely forked.

These fishes live along the shore lines of tropical and warmer, temperate seas. They prefer shallow water with sandy bottoms; here they may be found resting propped upon their pelvic fins or buried in the sand up to their snout and eyes.

Of less than 40 species, at least seven are known from this area.

FORSTER'S LIZARD FISH
Also known as 'U-la-e and We-le-'a
37—1 *Trachinocephalus myops* (Forster), 1801

This lizard fish is most easily recognized by the short snout, by the eyes placed far forward on the head, and by the mouth which is directed upward at an angle. The body is slender and cylindrical and has a small adipose fin, a large mouth, and closely

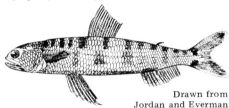

Drawn from
Jordan and Everman

set teeth. It usually measures about eight inches in length, although large specimens will reach 12 inches. The body is grayish above and is marked on the sides by three, irregular, yellow stripes; the lower surface is silvery or whitish. There is a distinctive dark spot on the side of the body just behind the head.

The habitat of this fish is in the deeper waters on the outer slopes of the reef and downward for several hundred feet.

This species seems to be nearly world-wide in warm water. It occurs in the western Atlantic Ocean from Massachusetts to Florida and Cuba, and from Hawaii, Japan, and the Philippines westward to southern Africa.

THE SLENDER LIZARD FISH
Also known as 'U-la-e
37—2 *Saurida gracilis* (Quoy and Gaimard), 1824

This lizard fish has the unusual, slender, cylindrical body which is typical of this family. It may be recognized by three or more rows of teeth showing along the outer edge of the lips and by the single row of teeth along the median ridge of the tongue. The body is brownish in color above and is marked by irregular, vertical bands of darker color. The body is silvery below and the fins are marked with brown cross bands. It will exceed 12 inches in length.

This species lives over sandy areas and is known to enter the brackish water of bays and estuaries wherever there is a sandy bottom.

The distribution of this species extends from East Africa eastward across the Indian Ocean, through the East Indies, and across the tropical Pacific Ocean to Hawaii and Tahiti.

From Schultz

THE TWO-SPOT LIZARD FISH
37—3 *Synodus binotatus* Schultz, 1953

This species is most easily identified by the double, median, dark spot on the tip of the snout. The ground color is light and the body is marked by a pattern of darker,

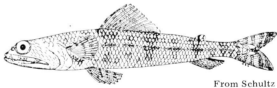

From Schultz

irregular, vertical markings which form about ten vertical bars on the back and sides; these alternate in intensity and do not extend onto the lower side.

This is a bottom dwelling form which does not exceed five inches in length.

It is known from Hawaii and the central Pacific area.

FOWLER'S LIZARD FISH
Also known as 'U-la-e
37—4 *Synodus dermatogenys* Fowler, 1911

This species resembles *S. variegatus* and is hard to identify with certainty; it has 13 or 14 dorsal fin rays, while *S. variegatus* has but 11 or 12. It has but a single row of teeth showing along the edges of the

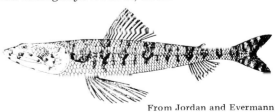

From Jordan and Evermann

lips. It is a common species and reaches as much as 16 inches in length. The name *dermatogenus* means "skin-jaw"

This species is known from the Hawaiian Islands and doubtless elsewhere in the Pacific area.

GUNTHER'S LIZARD FISH
37—5 *Synodus kaianus* (Gunther), 1880

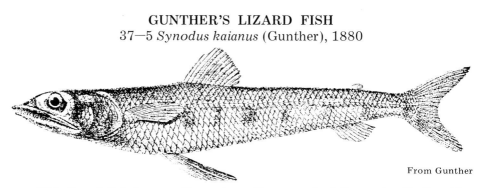

From Gunther

This lizard fish is a small species with unmarked fins and with the sides of the body marked by a series of black spots. It is also one of a few species in which the peritoneum is black or gray-black in color. Specimens range in length from four to 11 inches.

It prefers to live in deeper water and those specimens known from this area have been taken from a dredge at depths in excess of 100 fathoms.

The distribution of this species extends from Hawaii to Japan and the East Indies.

THE RED LIZARD FISH
Also known as 'U-la-e
37—6 *Synodus ulae* Schultz, 1953

From Jordan and Evermann

This species is a reddish form which resembles *S. variegatus* in many ways. It has the typical, tubular, tapering body of lizard fishes and is identified only after rather detailed study of its external anatomy. It has been recorded to reach over 13 inches in length, although most specimens are from six to eight inches long. See the original description contained in Schultz, Leonard P., *Fishes Of The Marshall and Marianas Islands*, 1953, page 38; this is *U. S. National Museum Bulletin* No. 202.

The distribution of this species extends from Hawaii to Japan and doubtless elsewhere in the tropical Pacific area.

THE VARIEGATED LIZARD FISH
Also known as 'U-la-e
37—7 *Synodus variegatus* (Lacepede), 1803

This species very closely resembles *S. dermatogenys* but may be distinguished from it because it has but 11 or 12 rays in the dorsal fin, while *S. dermatogenys* has 13 or 14 rays. The body is brownish in color above and is marked with eight or nine bands which extend across the back and onto the sides, sometimes with interruptions. The ventral and anal fins are yellow and the tail fin is clear. Most individuals grow to about 10 inches, although it may reach 14 inches.

This is one of the common species in shore line areas.

It is distributed from the Red Sea and Zanzibar eastward across the Indian Ocean, through the East Indies, and eastward into the Pacific Ocean as far as Japan, Hawaii, and Tahiti.

THE THREAD-SAIL FISH FAMILY
38 *Family Aulopidae (Chlorophthalmidae)*

The thread-sail fishes resemble the lizard fishes (*Synodidae*) in many ways and are closely related to them. Their ventral fins are placed far forward, a small adipose fin is usually present, and they lack the photophores. Most of these fishes are small in size, although there is one species in Australia which is reported to reach about two feet in length.

Most species inhabit the deeper waters of the Atlantic, Pacific, and Indian Oceans.

Of less than a dozen species, at least two are known from this area.

AGASSIZ'S THREAD-SAIL FISH
Also known as the Short-nosed Green-eye
38—1 *Chlorophthalmus agassizi* Bonaparte, 1840

Agassiz's thread-sail fish is a small species with a long, slender, tapering body and large eyes. An adipose fin is present and scales cover the body.

The body color is a dusky, grayish, silvery hue and black speckles are scattered over the body; the back of the mouth and the peritoneum are also black. This species ranges in size from about three and one-half to seven inches in length.

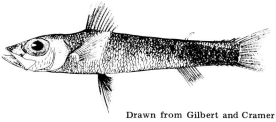

Most specimens of this fish have been taken at depths between 1,200 and 2,000 feet.

This species is obviously named for Louis John Rudolph Agassiz, 1807 - 1873, famous European and American naturalist.

Drawn from Gilbert and Cramer

In some books this species will be carried under the name of *C. proridens*, Gilbert and Cramer, 1897.

This species is known from Hawaii and doubtless elsewhere in deeper waters.

THE JAPANESE THREAD - SAIL FISH
38—2 *Hime japonicus* (Gunther), 1880

The body of this fish is slender and tapering and bears a large mouth and large eyes. The dorsal fin is large and long and the tail fin is quite deeply forked. The body is reddish brown above, silvery white beneath, and marked by four, large, dark brown, saddle-shaped areas. Reddish speckles and blotches occur on the head and body; yellow colors mark the pelvic, anal, and part of the caudal fins.

This species was first known in Hawaii from a single specimen measuring about nine inches in length which was caught in 1962 by Mr. Kuni Sakamoto off the M/V "Koun Maru" of Honolulu between Lanai and Kahoolawe at about 780 feet.

The distribution of this species includes Hawaii, Japan, and the western Pacific Ocean.

THE PEARL-EYE FISH FAMILY
39 *Family Scopelarchidae*

The pearl-eye fishes are a small family of deep-water fishes which resemble the barracudina family *(Paralepidae)*. They have large heads and their bodies, which taper rather uniformly to the tail, are covered with scales and bear an adipose fin. They are best recognized by their eyes and teeth. Their eyes, which are telescopic in varying degrees, are directed forward and upward and bear a most unusual, shining, white spot. The teeth on the tongue are large, compressed and hooked. Most species are less than six or eight inches in length.

Pearl-eyed fishes are rarely captured, possibly because of their agility, and so are seldom found in the stomachs of larger deep-sea fishes or in deep-water trawls.

The habitat of this family includes the deep waters of the world from 500 or 600 feet down to at least 7,500 feet. They do not occur along shore lines or over the submerged shelves which border continents and islands.

When they are young, their food consists of copepods and other small forms, but as they grow larger their diet shifts to small fishes.

This family contains at least 20 species, some of which will doubtless be reported from this area.

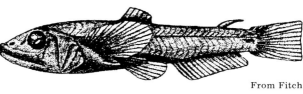

From Fitch

Longfin Pearleye, *Benthalbella linguidens*

THE PIKE SMELT OR BARRACUDINA FISH FAMILY
40 *Family Paralepididae (Sudidae)*

The members of this family resemble the barracudas in general appearance. They are elongated, slender-bodied, large-toothed fishes with an adipose fin and a rather long anal fin. Most of the members are lacking in photophores, although there are light organs in the species of *Lestidium*. They are pale or silvery in color and are usually of small size, although one species is reported to reach a length of 24 inches.

Pike smelt are oceanic fishes of voracious habits which are found down to depths of about two miles.

Of about 50 species, at least four are known from this area.

THE STRANGE PIKE SMELT
40—1 *Lestidium mirabile* (Ege), 1933

This species somewhat resembles a barracuda in body outline and shape. The body is elongated, somewhat compressed, and tapers toward the tail. The head is quite long, broad, and pointed and contains an array of sharp teeth. The origin of the dorsal fin is in front of the pelvic fins; these pelvic fins have the inner rays longer than the outer rays. The color, which is brownish, is darker on the head and body; the anal and caudal fins are also pigmented. Hawaiian specimens have measured from about five to nearly seven inches in length.

Drawn from Harry

This species has been recorded from Hawaii and the East Indies; it doubtless occurs over the vast area separating these places.

THE DEEP WATER PIKE SMELT
40—2 *Lestidium nudum* Gilbert, 1905

This pike smelt has a long, slender, compressed body which tapers toward the tail. The head and snout are long and pointed and an adipose fin is present. The body lacks scales except for a row of small scales along the

Drawn from Gilbert

lateral line which are embedded in the skin. The beginning of the dorsal fin is above the anus and the anal fin has 30 or 31 soft rays. The color of the body is translucent with faint silvery reflections. There are black markings on the top of the eye, the nape, and on the area of the caudal peduncle in front of the tail.

This uncommon species was first described from a specimen measuring about eight inches in length which was caught in a trawl at a depth of about 1,600 feet in Pailolo Channel between Molokai and Maui in 1902.

The distribution of this species is probably limited to the North Pacific Ocean.

THE FIERCE PIKE SMELT
40—3 *Sudis atrox* Harry, 1963

From Berry and Perkins

The body of this paralepid fish is long, slender, and oval in cross-section and tapers very gradually from the center of the body to the tail. The head is likewise long, slender, and tapering and bears a large and prominent snout. A lateral line extends the length of the body to end at the tail. The dorsal fin is quite high and short and is followed by a small adipose fin just anterior to the tail. The caudal fin is deeply forked. The pelvic fins are small and are located forward of the dorsal fin. The anal fin is rather long and is located posterior to the dorsal fin. The pectoral fins are large and pointed. The color of the body includes light brownish and grayish hues.

The type specimen measured about three inches in length and came from the stomach of an *Alepisaurus* which was captured midway between Hawaii and Baja California.

The distribution of this species includes the eastern Pacific area between Hawaii, California, and Baja California; it doubtless extends to adjoining areas.

THE CHRISTMAS ISLAND PIKE SMELT
40—4 *Sudis pofi* (Harry), 1953

Like other members of this family, the body of this species is elongated and compressed and tapers uniformly from the head to the caudal peduncle. The body is without scales and there is a small ridge of skin extending along the belly from the head to the pelvic fins. A small dorsal fin is placed behind the middle of the body and behind the pelvic fins. The pelvic fins are likewise small and have the inner rays longer than the outer rays. The anal fin is about as long as the head and usually contains 33 fin rays. The color of the body is light and translucent and has only a light pigmentation. There is a dark spot in front of the eye and the peritonium is black with a silvery layer beneath. The length of the body is about five inches.

This species was first known from two specimens "collected . . . by night light and dipnet at the surface in the littoral waters of Christmas Island, Line Islands, in May, 1950, by T. J. Roseberry."

From Harry

The name of *pofi* is derived from the initial letters of the Pacific Oceanic Fisheries Investigation.

The distribution of this species at present includes the central Pacific area.

THE LANCET FISH FAMILY
Also known as Hand-saw Fishes and Wolf Fishes
41 *Family Alepisauridae*

This is a small family of long, slender, tapering fishes of the open sea. Their bodies are laterally compressed, lack scales, and have a high dorsal fin which extends for two-thirds of the length of the body and is in turn followed by a small adipose fin. Their head is quite large, angular, laterally compressed and contains a large, long mouth within which are many large, sharp, angular teeth. Some specimens have been reported which reached a length of seven feet.

Lancet fishes are oceanic species which live from the surface down to at least 1,000 feet. In their habits they are active, carnivorous, and voracious; because of their sharp teeth, they may be a bit dangerous to handle.

This is a small family which appears to include only a few species, the most common of which are *A. ferox* Lowe, 1833, from Atlantic waters and *A. borealis* (Gill), 1862, from the Pacific Ocean.

THE NORTHERN LANCET FISH
41—1 *Alepisaurus borealis* (Gill), 1862

This lancet fish is a very long, slender, light weight species. The body has a large head and tapers gradually to a forked tail in which the upper lobe is longer than the lower lobe. The dorsal fin is very high, extends for about two-third the length of the body, and is followed by a small adipose fin. The head is quite angular in appearance; it bears a large eye and a long mouth which is lined with large, sharp, angular teeth. The body is without scales and the lateral line is raised on the surface of the body.

The specimen in the photograph was 30 inches long and was captured on the hook of a flag line off Hawaii at a depth of 600 feet.

This species is widely distributed in the warmer waters of the Pacific Ocean and possibly elsewhere.

THE LANTERN FISH FAMILY
42 *Family Myctophidae*

The lantern fishes are a large family of small species which inhabit the deep sea. In general, they are fishes with quite a large head and a body which tapers rather uniformly toward the tail. The body is covered with scales, the adipose fin is present on the back, and there are no barbels under the chin. The head bears large eyes, a large mouth, and many small teeth. Photophores are present on the body; these are usually placed in a single row along the ventral side of the body or are sometimes scattered in groups below the lateral line. They are small shining fishes which measure from one to six inches in length.

Lantern fishes inhabit the open oceans of the world from polar to tropical seas. They may be found from the surface down to depths of at least a mile. Many species move toward the surface during the night and return to deeper water during the daytime. They are often caught with lights suspended from boats at sea.

More than 200 species are known; of this number probably more than 60 are known from this area.

In addition to their usual anatomical features, these fishes are classified on the number and location of the photophores or light organs on the body. This information is too detailed and too tedious for inclusion here. Because the *Myctophidae* is a very large and exceeding complex family with a special terminology for describing the photophores, persons who are trying to identify lantern fishes may find it necessary to seek out the help of specialists. These specialists are few in number, but may usually be located with the help of staff members in the departments of zoology or oceanography in large universities or museums. In addition, the literature on these fishes will probably only be found in large scientific libraries.

The following species are not described or illustrated:

Benthosema suborbitale (Gilbert), 1913. This is a small species which measures less than one and one-half inches in length. It occurs in Hawaii, Japan, and doubtless in surrounding areas.

Bolinichthys distofax Johnson, 1975. This lantern fish measures from one and one-half to three inches in length. Its distribution as presently known includes the western and central North Pacific Ocean. See *Copeia* 1975 (1): 53—60.

Bolinichthys longipes (Brauer), 1906. This small fish measures about one inch in length. It has been captured at depths between one-half and one mile. It occurs in both the Atlantic and Pacific Oceans.

Bolinichthys supralateralis (Parr), 1928. This species is known from the Atlantic Ocean and was thought to also occur in the Pacific Ocean; but recent studies suggest that the Pacific specimens are another species and have been described and named *B. distofax*.

Diaphus dumerili (Bleeker), 1856. The length of this species ranges from about two inches to about three and one-half inches. It inhabits depths of about one mile in the temperate and tropical waters of the Atlantic and Pacific Oceans.

Diaphus schmidti Taaning, 1932. The type specimen from which this species was described was captured near the Tokelau Islands just north of Samoa. It reaches a length of nearly two inches.

Diaphus theta Eigenmann and Eigenmann, 1890. The distribution of this species includes the San Pedro Basin, its adjoining areas, and the Hawaiian area.

Diogenichthys atlanticus (Taaning), 1928. This small species measures about one inch in length. It inhabits the warmer waters of both the Atlantic and Pacific Oceans.

Hygophum proximum Becker, 1965. This is a small species which usually measures less than two inches. It resembles *H. macrochir* (Gunther), 1864, and *H. taaningi* Becker, 1965. It is widely distributed in the tropical and sub-tropical waters of the Pacific and Indian Oceans.

Lampadena anomela Parr, 1928. This species measures about one inch in length and inhabits areas between one-half and one mile in depth. It occurs in both the Atlantic and Pacific Oceans.

Lampadena luminosa (Garman), 1899. The distribution of this species includes the Indian Ocean and the Pacific Ocean including the Hawaiian area.

Lampadena urophaos Paxton, 1963. The type specimen, obtained off California, measured about three inches in length. The distribution of this species includes the western Atlantic, the eastern Pacific, and the central North Pacific Oceans.

Lampanyctus nobilis Taaning, 1928. This small species measures about one inch in length. It has been captured at depths of one mile. It occurs in both the Atlantic and Pacific Oceans.

Lampanyctus steinbecki Bolin, 1939. This species was first described from a single specimen 35.5 mm long which was collected in 1918 off Santa Catalina Island at a depth of 800 feet. Its name honors Mr. John Steinbeck (1902-1968), a California writer.

Lampanyctus tenuiformis (Brauer), 1906. This fish measures at least one inch in length and inhabits depths between one-half and one mile. It occurs in the temperate and tropical Atlantic, Indian, and Pacific Oceans.

Myctophum coccoi (Cocco), 1829. This species inhabits all temperate and tropical seas, including the Mediterranean Sea, from the surface to depths of at least one mile.

Myctophum nitidulum Garman, 1899. The body color of this species is dark blue above and lighter below. It reaches about two inches in length.

Myctophum obtusirostrum Taaning, 1928. This species is dark blue above and lighter below. It approaches three inches in length.

Notoscopelus caudispinosus (Johnson), 1863. This species was first described from a single specimen measuring about six inches in length from the Island of Madeira. It is known from the Atlantic and Pacific Oceans.

Notolychnus valdiviae (Brauer), 1904. This small species measures about one inch in length. It has been captured at depths of about one mile. It occurs in the temperate and tropical waters of the Atlantic and Pacific Oceans.

Protomyctophum (Hierops) beckeri Wisner, 1971. This species is named in honor of Dr. V. E. Becker (Bekker) of the Institute of Oceanology in Moscow. It is an uncommon species which very closely resembles *P. chilensis* Wisner, 1971, and *P. crockeri* (Bolin), 1939.

Taaningichthys bathyphilus (Taaning), 1928. This lantern fish will reach a length of about three inches. It is world-wide in distribution in tropical and warmer temperate seas at depths below 1500 feet.

Taaningichthys minimum (Taaning), 1928. This fish is the smallest of three within this genus and measures as much as two and one-half inches in length. It is world-wide in its distribution in tropical and warmer temperate seas. It is usually found at depths of about 1,500 feet.

Taaningichthys paurolychnus Davy, 1972. This lantern fish will reach nearly four inches in length. It is found world-wide in tropical and warmer temperate waters at depths below about 1,800 feet.

Triphoturus nigrescens (Brauer), 1904. The distribution of this species includes the Indian Ocean and the central Pacific area.

THE LARGE-SCALED LANTERN FISH
42—1 *Neoscopelus macrolepidotus* Johnson, 1863

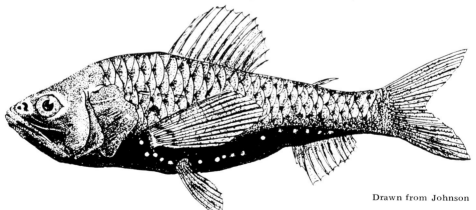

Drawn from Johnson

Among the lantern fishes, this species is regarded as one of the more primitive forms. The profile of the head is less curved than in most species and the eyes are large. In addition, the dorsal and the anal fins are more widely separated than in most lantern fishes. The dorsal fin contains 12 or 13 rays, but no spines. The photophores are present only on the lower half of the body where they appear as a nearly continuous double series; a series is also present along the mid-line of the belly. The color of the body has been described as silvery with a pink sheen; the fins are pink and there are violet colored areas about the photophores. The length of this species varies from about four inches to about ten inches.

It has been captured in dredge hauls at depths between about 1,000 and 9,000 feet.

The distribution of this lantern fish is apparently world-world in temperate and tropical seas.

GILBERT AND CRAMER'S LANTERN FISH
42—2 *Benthosema fibulata* (Gilbert and Cramer), 1897

This lantern fish has a compressed body and a blunt head which bears large eyes. The body is brown to black in color and is covered with silvery, blue, irridescent scales which are loosely attached. It measures four or more inches in length.

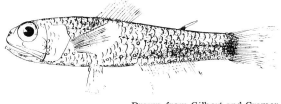

Drawn from Gilbert and Cramer

Specimens have been captured from the surface downward to depths of 1,500 feet or more. It is a common species.

The distribution of this species includes the tropical and temperate waters of the Pacific, Indian, and North Atlantic Oceans.

REINHARDT'S LANTERN FISH
42—3 *Hygophum reinhardti* Lutken, 1892

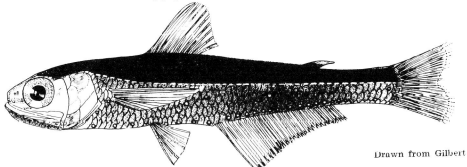

Drawn from Gilbert

Reinhardt's lantern fish is a very slender species with thin scales, very large eyes, and a short, pointed snout. The mouth is slightly oblique and the gape is slightly recurved. The body is dark in color with bluish reflections. The fins are transparent with the exception of the caudal fin which has a dark area at the base of each lobe. The body will measure two or more inches in length.

The distribution of this fish includes the tropical and temperate Atlantic, Indian, and Pacific Oceans and the Mediterranean Sea.

LUTKEN'S LANTERN FISH
42—4 *Myctophum affine* Lutken, 1892

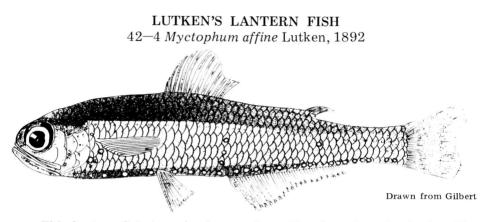

Drawn from Gilbert

This lantern fish is a slender species with a long tapering body. The body and head are compressed, the eyes are very large, and the mouth is large with the lower jaw protruding very slightly. The body is grayish brown in color and will measure from three to four inches or more.

The distribution of this species includes the tropical and temperate waters of the Atlantic, Pacific, and Indian Oceans.

Most scholars regard *M. margaritatum* Gilbert, 1905, and *Rhinoscopelus oceanicus* Jordan and Evermann, 1903, as synonyms of this species.

THE SHORT-JAWED LANTERN FISH
42—5 *Myctophum brachygnathos* Bleeker, 1856

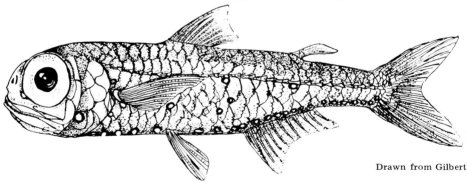

Drawn from Gilbert

The body of this lantern fish is elongated and compressed and tapers gradually to the tail. The head is heavy and compressed and is capped with a short, bluntly-rounded snout. The eyes are large and circular. The opercle is thin, with a posterior margin which is rounded, and bears only a slight, blunt point; the preopercle has a posterior margin which is nearly vertical. The scales which cover the body are large and firm and have edges which are strongly toothed. The length of the body is about two and one-half inches.

The color of the back and top of the head is black, while the snout is yellowish white. Silvery colors occur on the cheek, the opercle, the lower side of the jaw, and on the sides of the body. All scales have a metallic luster. The mouth is black within and the peritoneum is likewise very dark in color.

This is an abundant species and is caught at the surface.

The distribution of this lantern fish includes a wide area in the tropical and temperate Pacific Ocean.

Scholars regard *Dasyscopelus pristilepis* Gilbert and Cramer, 1897, as a synonym of this species.

HONOLULU LANTERN FISH
42—6 *Myctophum hollandi* Jordan and Jordan, 1922

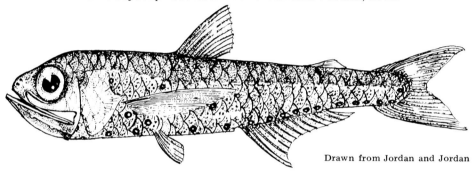

Drawn from Jordan and Jordan

The body of this lantern fish is moderatly elongated, is covered with rather large scales, and bears a well developed lateral line. The pectoral fins are large and long, the dorsal fin is high, the adipose fin is small, and the caudal fin is rather deeply forked. The head is quite large and bears a very short snout and a large, oblique mouth with jaws which are approximately equal. Like most other members of this family, the eyes are large. The color of the body is blackish above and paler below. The luminous spots are ringed with black. The type specimen measured four and one-half inches in length and was obtained by a Mr. Grinnell in the Honolulu fish market.

This species is known from Hawaii and doubtless elsewhere in the Pacific area.

WISNER'S LANTERN FISH
42—7 *Myctophum selenoides* Wisner, 1971

The body of this species is typical of this family. It is possibly a bit shorter than most, moderately deep, and somewhat compressed. The head is large and deep and bears eyes which are large, slightly ovoid in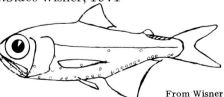

From Wisner

shape, and which contain distinctly ovoid pupils; the long axis of the eyes is tilted slightly forward of vertical. The jaws are terminal, are of about equal length, and bear small teeth which are arranged in bands. Most specimens exceed two inches in length.

The type specimen was captured on July 14, 1960, about 8 miles off Keahole Point on the western side of the island of Hawaii somewhere between the surface and 4,800 feet.

This species resembles *M. selenops* Taaning, 1928, from the Atlantic Ocean and was named for that resemblance.

The distribution of this species includes the Hawaiian area, adjoining equatorial waters, and possibly other adjoining areas.

THE SPINY LANTERN FISH
42—8 *Myctophum spinosum* (Steindachner), 1867

The body of this lantern fish is elongated, compressed, and covered with scales. The eyes and the mouth are both large and the snout is described as obtuse. The color of the

Drawn from Fraser-Brunner

body is violet on the back and exhibits bright, shining reflections on the sides and belly. The iris is silvery white and the fins are grayish in color. The photophores are small in size, yellowish in color, and are surrounded by black areas. The Hawaiian specimens, which the steamer *Albatross* captured in 1902, were all taken at the surface; the largest was about two and three-fourths inches in length.

The distribution of this species includes the eastern and south Atlantic, the Indian, and the western Pacific Oceans including Hawaii.

EVERMANN'S LANTERN FISH
42—9 *Symbolophorus evermanni* (Gilbert), 1905

Drawn from Gilbert

Evermann's lantern fish is a small species with a slender, compressed body, a tapering head, and thin scales. The color of the body is blackish in general, although the sides of the head are lighter in color. Large specimens will reach a length of three inches. These larger specimens are often captured at night between about 150 and 300 feet.

The distribution of this species includes the Pacific Ocean.

The name of this species honors Dr. Barton Warren Evermann (1853—1932), an American ichthyologist, long associated with the California Academy of Sciences and noted for his studies of Pacific fishes, many of which were made with Dr. David Starr Jordan.

LAURA'S LANTERN FISH
42—10 *Loweina laurae* Wisner, 1971

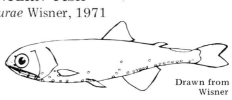

Drawn from Wisner

The body of this lantern fish is moderately robust and laterally compressed. The dorsal fin originates just behind the middle of the body and the supra-caudal gland is large. The lateral line is incomplete and bears pores only at the anterior end. This is a small species and reaches a length between one and one-half and two inches. It is an uncommon species which comes to the surface at night.

The distribution of this species includes the eastern Pacific Ocean from Hawaii eastward to the Americas and from Baja California southward to Chile.

The name of this species honors Mrs. Laura Clark Hubbs of La Jolle, California.

LUTKEN'S LANTERN FISH
42—11 *Centrobranchus andrae* (Lutken), 1892

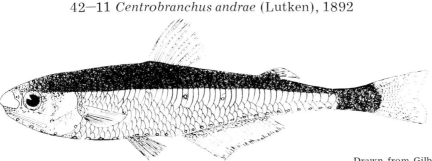

Drawn from Gilbert

Specimens of this little lantern fish from the Hawaiian Islands were first described as a new species by Charles Henry Gilbert under the name of *Centrobranchus gracilicaudus* Gilbert, 1905, from specimens collected at the surface by the steamer *Albatross* in 1902. The type specimen measured about one and one-third inches in length. More recent scholars believe this fish to be identical with *C. andrae*, a species which is widely distributed in the Atlantic Ocean.

The distribution of this species now includes the Atlantic and Pacific Oceans.

THE PIG-HEADED LANTERN FISH
42—12 *Centrobranchus choerocephalus* Fowler, 1904

This lantern fish has a slender body and small eyes. The body is dark in color above, silvery below, and measures in excess of an inch.

Some scholars think that this species is identical with *C. nigro-ocellatus* (Gunther), 1889.

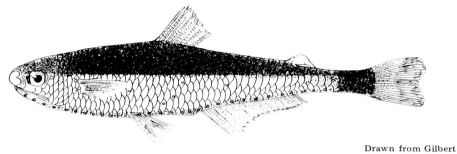

The specimens from which this species was described were captured in 1902 by the steamer *Albatross* at the surface at a location south of Oahu.

COCCO'S LANTERN FISH
42—13 *Lobianchia gemellari* (Cocco), 1838

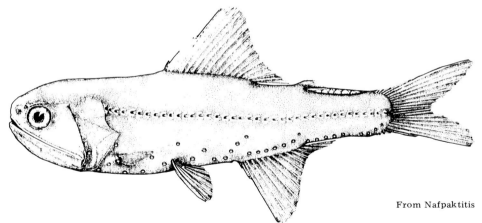

The body of this lantern fish is quite robust and tapers uniformly from the dorsal fin toward the tail. The outlines of the front of the body curve rather uniformly forward to a short, blunt snout. The mouth is large, is located terminally at the end of the head, and exhibits an oblique cleft. The eyes are of medium size. The dorsal fin contains 17 rays (occasionally 18) and originates slightly in advance of the pelvic fins below it. The pectoral fins are small. The body usually measures about two inches in length, but it may reach as much as four inches in length.

The distribution of this species includes a wide area in the warmer waters of the north Atlantic Ocean, the central Pacific Ocean, and doubtless adjoining areas.

THE SHINING-TAILED LANTERN FISH
42—14 *Lobianchia urolampa* (Gilbert and Cramer), 1897

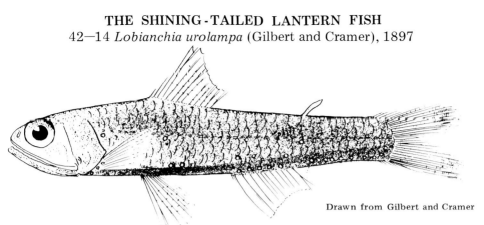

Drawn from Gilbert and Cramer

The body of this lantern fish is elongated and slender and is covered with thin, loosely attached scales. The body and head are compressed and the snout is short and blunt. The eye is quite large. The color of the body is dark with lighter, silvery areas on the head. The bases of the fins are dark but their extremities are light in color. Specimens have measured from two to more than four inches in length and were caught at depths of about 1,500 to 1,800 feet near the Hawaiian Islands.

The distribution of this species includes the Hawaiian area.

GILBERT'S LARGE LANTERN FISH
42—15 *Diaphos adenomus* Gilbert, 1905

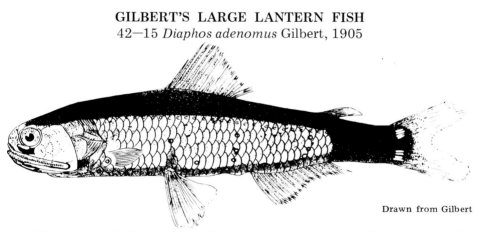

Drawn from Gilbert

The body of this lantern fish is quite elongated and tapers from its center to the tail which is quite deeply forked. The head and snout are blunt and bear eyes of moderate size and a very large mouth. The pectoral fins are smaller than in most other species and the pelvic fins are larger. The color of the body is dark with a whitish snout, silvery cheeks, and a black opercle. A dark spot is present below the eye. The interior of the mouth and the peritoneum are black. The body of full grown specimens will measure six inches or more in length. It is one of the largest lantern fishes.

Specimens were taken in dredges off the Hawaiian Islands in 1902 by the steamer *Albatross* at depths between about 1,500 and 2,000 feet.

The distribution of this species includes the Hawaiian area.

ANDERSEN'S LANTERN FISH
42—16 *Diaphus anderseni* Taaning, 1932

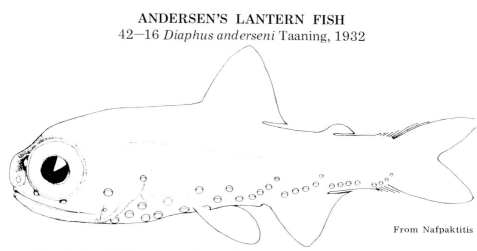

From Nafpaktitis

The body of this species is small and the head is relatively large. The upper profile of the head bears a depression above the front of the eyes. The mouth is large and the cleft is slightly oblique in position. The dorsal fin contains 12 or 13 rays each; and the pelvic or ventral fins have 8 rays each.

This species was first described from a single specimen measuring 20.5 mm which was captured just northeast of the island of Martinique in the Caribbean.

The distribution of this species includes the north Atlantic Ocean and the central Pacific area.

THE SHORT - HEADED LANTERN FISH
42—17 *Diaphus brachycephalus* Taaning, 1928

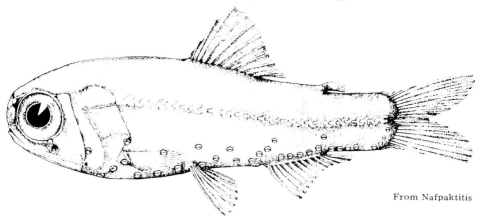

From Nafpaktitis

The body of this lantern fish is small, deep, and short and tapers to a caudal peduncle which is likewise deep and short. The dorsal and ventral outlines are uniformly rounded and about equal. The head is quite large and bears a snout which is blunt, rounded, and very short. The mouth is large and its cleft is slightly oblique. The eyes are very large. The dorsal fin usually contains 12 rays and begins almost directly above the base of the pelvic fins; the anal fin begins just behind the end of the dorsal fin. Most specimens measure between one and two inches in length.

The distribution of this species includes the warmer parts of the Atlantic Ocean and the central Pacific Ocean.

THE GOLDEN - NOSED LANTERN FISH
42—18 *Diaphus chrysorhynchus* Gilbert and Cramer, 1897

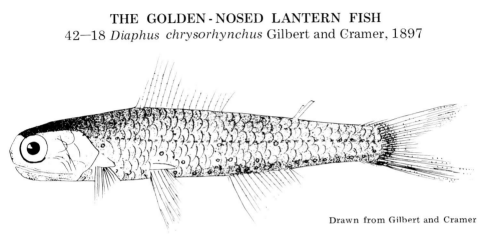

Drawn from Gilbert and Cramer

The body of this lantern fish is compressed and elongated and tapers uniformly to a tail which is widely forked. The head is compressed and bears large eyes and a large mouth; the snout is very short and blunt. The opercle bears a long, triangular, pointed lobe along its posterior edge. The body is generally dark in color and both the inside of the mouth and the peritoneum are likewise dark colored. Specimens measuring from three to three and three-fourths inches have been taken in surface tows in various areas.

This species is known from the tropical and temperate Pacific Ocean.

THE TRANSPARENT LANTERN FISH
42—19 *Diaphus elucens* (Brauer), 1904

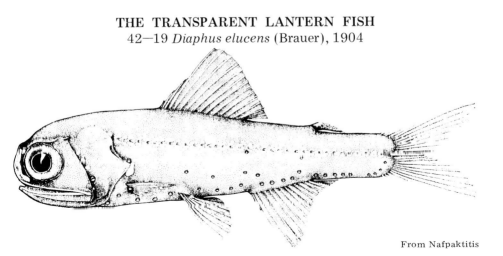

From Nafpaktitis

This lantern fish is of medium size and has a robust body which tapers gently from the dorsal fin to the tail. The head is rather deep and bears a very short snout which is bluntly rounded. The mouth is only moderately large and is only slightly oblique in position. The dorsal fin usually has 16 rays and originates well in advance of the base of the pelvic fins. The anal fin originates behind the end of the dorsal fin. Most specimens measure from two to two and one-half inches in length.

The distribution of this species includes the Pacific and Indian Oceans.

THE FRAGILE LANTERN FISH
42—20 *Diaphus fragilis* Taaning, 1928

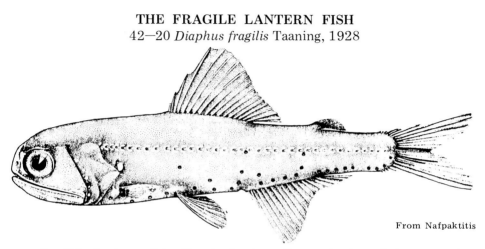

From Nafpaktitis

In this lantern fish the body is rather robust and tapers rather uniformly from the dorsal fin to the caudal peduncle. The profile of the head is uniform and evenly rounded. The head is rounded and the snout is short and blunt. The mouth and the eyes are both large. The dorsal fin contains 17 or 18 rays (occasionally 19) and begins just ahead of the pelvic fins below it. The pectoral fins are small. The anal fin contains 17 rays and begins directly below the end of the dorsal fin. Most specimens measure between two and one-half and three inches in length.

The distribution of this species includes the tropical Atlantic and the tropical Pacific Oceans.

THE SPOT-HEADED LANTERN FISH
42—21 *Diaphus metopoclampus* (Cocco), 1829

The body of this species, which is oblong in shape and compressed, tapers quite uniformly from the front to the back. The head is short and the snout is short and blunt with a profile which is almost perpendicular. The eyes are quite large and the cleft of the mouth is only slightly oblique. The dorsal fin is large and begins directly above the beginning of the pelvic fins. The scales which cover the body are quite large and smooth; they number 40 along the lateral line. Adult specimens will measure about three inches in length.

The body is dark in color and is marked by a light, luminous area on the front of the head. This luminous area occupies the front of the head between the eyes and extends backward between the eye and the jaw to a point about below the middle of the eye. This species was named for this spot; *metopo* means forehead and *clampus* means a patch.

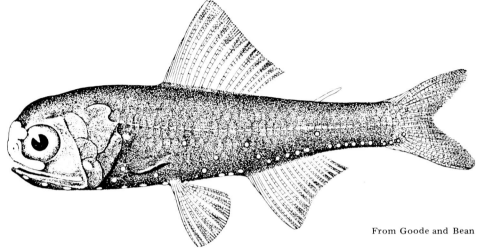

From Goode and Bean

Specimens have been captured at depths between one-half and one mile.

The distribution of this species includes the Atlantic and Pacific Oceans.

BOLIN'S LANTERN FISH
42—22 *Diaphus rolfbolini* Wisner 1971

Bolin's lantern fish is a species of moderate size with a body which is somewhat robust, moderately deep, and laterally compressed. The head is long, the orbits and eyes are large, and the snout extends well beyond the upper

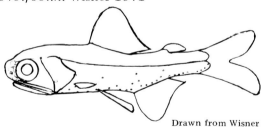

Drawn from Wisner

jaw. Large specimens will reach a length of about three inches.

This is an uncommon species which occupies waters of moderate depth and which seems to migrate vertically between about 150 and 1,500 feet.

The distribution of this fish extends over a very large area in the central, tropical Pacific Ocean.

The name of this species honors Dr. Rolf L. Bolin, an ichthyologist at Stanford University in California.

TAANING'S LANTERN FISH
42—23 *Diaphus termophilus* Taaning, 1928

The body of this species tapers rather uniformly toward the caudal peduncle which is quite rectangular in cross section. The outline of the head is uniformly curved below, but there is a pronounced depression in the dorsal profile directly above the eyes. The head is large, the snout is short, the mouth is large and terminal in location, and the eyes are rather

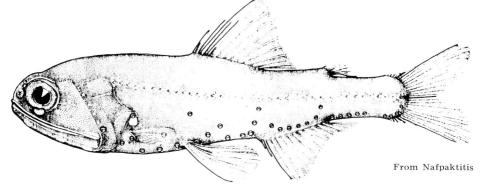

From Nafpaktitis

large. The dorsal fin contains 14 rays (occasionally 13). Most specimens are of small or medium size and range from two to three inches in length.

The distribution of this species includes the warm waters of the Atlantic Ocean and the central Pacific area.

THE BLACK LANTERN FISH
42—24 *Lampanyctus niger* (Gunther), 1887

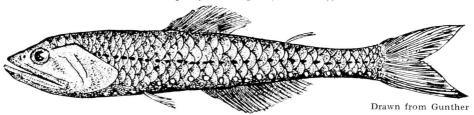

Drawn from Gunther

The black lantern fish has an elongated, slender body which tapers gradually toward a deeply forked tail. The head is less blunt than in other species and the eyes are only of moderate size. The mouth is very large and slightly oblique in position. The pectoral fins are very short in this species and do not reach to the beginning of the ventral fins. The color of the body is uniformly black including the basal parts of the fins. The type specimen measured four and one-half inches and was captured by the Challenger Expedition (1872 - 1876) south of the Philippine Islands at a depth of about 3,000 feet.

The distribution of this species appears to be nearly world-wide in tropical and temperate seas. It occurs in the Atlantic and Indian Oceans and in the Pacific Ocean from the East Indies to Japan, Hawaii, and California.

WARMING'S LANTERN FISH
42—25 *Ceratoscopelus warmingi* (Lutken), 1892
This rather small species has a body which tapers quite uniformly

toward the tail. The head measures about one-third of the total length, which is rather long for a lantern fish. The dorsal profile of the head is moderately uniform except for a depressed area above the eyes. There are no spines above the orbit. The snout is also quite long for a lantern fish and the mouth is likewise long and exhibits a cleft which becomes increasingly oblique toward the snout. The dorsal fin contains 13 or 14 rays and originates directly above the base of the pelvic fins. The anal fin contains 14 or 15 rays and originates slightly in advance of the end of the dorsal fin. The pelvic fins contain seven rays each. The pectoral fins, which contain 13 rays each, are extremely long and extend backward to nearly the middle of the anal fin. There are between 36 and 38 scales along

From Parr

the lateral line. Most specimens measure one and one-half inches in length.

Specimens have been captured at depths between one-half and one mile.

The distribution of this species includes the Atlantic, Indian, and Pacific Oceans.

THE BLACK-CHIN FISH FAMILY
43 *Family Neoscopelidae*
This small family is often used to include a few fishes which are related to the lantern fishes (*Myctophidae*), but which some scholars thinks should be placed in a separate family.

The fishes placed in this family have a compressed body which is covered with loose scales. Phosphorescent organs are present on the head and body, but they are not placed in groups. An adipose fin is present and the remaining fins are without spines. They are small in size and inhabit deep water.

The most abundant species in this area which is sometimes included in this family is *Neoscopelus macrolepidotus*; however, in this book this species is listed with the lantern fishes *(Myctophidae).*

THE SPIDER FISH FAMILY
44 *Family Bathypteridae (Benthosauridae)*
The spider fishes are a small family of elongated fishes of the deep sea. Their bodies are long and tapering and are covered with small scales. The pectoral and pelvic fins are usually elongated. The pectoral fins often have the first ray developed into a long streamer which may reach as far as the tail. The first rays of the pelvic fins are elongated and strengthened and are used by the fish to hold its body off the ocean floor.

This family is world-wide in distribution and inhabits the deeper waters of all oceans.

Of about 13 species, at least one is known from this area.

THE ATTENUATED SPIDER FISH
44—1 *Bathypterois attenuatus* Gilbert, 1905

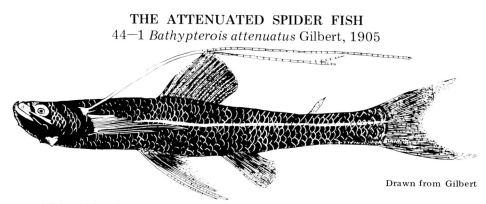

Drawn from Gilbert

This spider fish has an elongated body, an adipose fin, small eyes, and weak teeth. The first ray of the pectoral fin is developed into a long, white streamer and the pelvic fins contain firm rays which are used as props to rest upon the bottom. The body is a brownish black color; the inside of the mouth, gill cavity, and peritoneum are also black in color. This is a species of small size; Hawaiian specimens taken in 1902 measured six and one-half and eight inches in length.

The habitat of spider fishes is in deep water; this species is known to occur at depths in excess of one mile.

It is doubtless widely distributed in the deep sea.

THE ATELEOPID FISH FAMILY
45 *Family Ateleopidae (Guentheridae)*

The ateleopids are a small family of slender fishes which inhabit deep water. Their bodies are elongated, compressed, and taper rather uniformly toward the tail. The surface of these fishes is slimy and they are usually without scales. The fins are quite unusual. The dorsal fin is short and high and is placed far forward on the body. The pelvic fins are reduced to one or two rays and are also placed far forward. The anal fin is very long and is continuous with the caudal fin. The flesh of the body is not firm and there is a semi-transparent aspect to it. The skeleton is somewhat degenerate for the bones are not well developed and remain as cartilage or are not ossified in the adult. The eyes are very small and the teeth are small and weak. Some members of this family will reach a length of at least six feet.

The members of this family inhabit the deep waters of the Atlantic, Pacific, and Indian Oceans.

THE DEEP WATER ATELEOPID FISH
45—1 *Ijimaia plicatellus* (Gilbert), 1905

This deep water species has an elongated, compressed body which tapers gradually and uniformly toward the tail. The dorsal fin is short, high, and placed far forward on the body; the ventral fins are reduced to one or two rays and are located beneath the head; the anal fin is very short and is continuous with the caudal fin. The head bears a blunt snout which overhangs a wide, horizontal mouth. The surface of the body is scaleless and the skin is very delicate and easily broken. A lateral line is present but it is very poorly marked. The color of the body is a uniform, dusky gray, the fins are all jet black, and the lips are margined with white. The inside of the mouth, the gill cavity, and the peritoneum are pale in color.

Drawn from Gilbert

The first Hawaiian specimens were taken in a dredge by the steamer *Albatross* in 1902 off southern Oahu and in the Pailolo Channel between Maui and Molokai at depths in excess of 1,500 feet.

Although known at present from only a few Hawaiian specimens, this species will doubtless prove to be much more widely distributed.

In most books, particularly the older ones, this species will be listed under the name of *Ateleopus plicatellus* Gilbert, 1905.

THE GIGANTURID FISH FAMILY
46 *Family Giganturidae*

The giganturid fishes lack some of the anatomical structures found in most fishes. The pelvis, the paired pelvic fins, and the scales are missing in this group and some of the fins are not in their usual locations. The paired pectoral fins are placed very high on the body and close to the head, the single dorsal and anal fins are farther back than usual, and the tail fin has a long, extended lower lobe.

This family includes a very few species of small, voracious, deep-sea fishes which live at depths of one-half mile to beyond two miles. Very few have been captured.

The distribution of this family is world-wide in the deeper parts of the ocean.

LISA'S PACIFIC TELESCOPE FISH
46—1 *Bathyleptus lisae* Walters, 1961

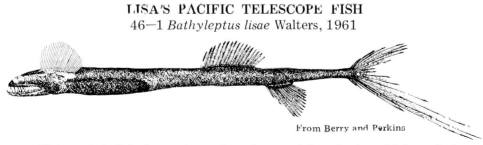

From Berry and Perkins

This weird fish has a long, tapering, scaleless body which ends in a deeply forked tail of which the lower lobe may be extended as a trailing

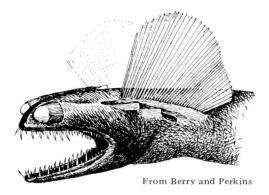

From Berry and Perkins

ribbon. The head is of moderate size and bears upon it a pair of large, tubular, telescopic eyes which are forward looking; but most of the head is occupied by a very large mouth which is filled with slender, sharp, curved, depressible teeth. The dorsal and anal fins are located quite far back on the body; there are no ventral fins. The pectoral fins are large, fan-shaped, nearly horizontal in their attachment, and are placed high upon the body, close behind the head and above the gill openings. The luminous organs found in many deep-sea fishes are absent in this species. Large specimens will measure about eight inches in length.

The habitat of this rare fish is in deep water; it has been captured at various depths between 2,000 and 12,000 feet. Hawaiian specimens have been caught in trawls off the Hamakua or north-east coast of the Island of Hawaii at depths of about 2,500 feet.

The distribution of this species extends from California and Hawaii southward to Chile and New Zealand and doubtless elsewhere in the Pacific area.

The name *lisae* is derived from the author's wife, whose name seems to have been Mrs. Lisa Walters.

THE GULPER EEL FAMILY
47 *Family Eurypharyngidae*

The gulpers are eel-like in general appearance, but are not closely related to any of the eel groups. Although their heads are of comparatively large size, their jaws and related bones are truly gigantic and out of proportion to the head to which they are attached. These jaws are capable of great expansion and are by far the most significant feature of this family. The head is large, long, flat on top, and bears an angular margin around the front. The eyes, which are small, are placed above the margin and far forward on the head. The teeth which line the jaws are very small and feeble; however, there are two larger teeth placed in the very front of the lower jaw. The surface of the body is without scales, the gill openings are small, round holes located quite far back from the angle of the mouth, the pectoral fins are very small, and the pelvic fins are absent.

This family is believed to have but one known species.

THE PELICAN GULPER FISH
47—1 *Eurypharynx pelecanoides* Vaillant, 1882

Because of its extremely bizarre appearance, the pelican gulper is one of the strangest fishes in the sea. It begins with a large head, continues as a short body, and ends in a very long, slender, tapering tail which is capped by a small, luminous nubbin. Suspended beneath the head is a pair of gigantic jaws which are light and frail, yet capable of great expansion; it is this great mouth and jaws which give this fish some resemblance to the bill and mouth of a pelican. Adult specimens are deep black in color and will reach 30 inches in length.

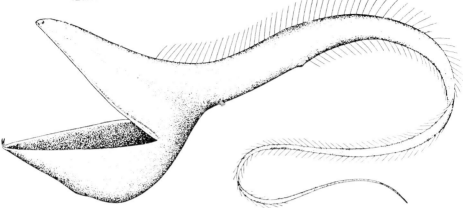

From Goode and Bean

This fish is voracious in its habits and is reported to feed upon both large and small forms which it is able to capture in its cavernous mouth and hold in its expansible stomach.

The habitat of this fish is in the deep, dark depths of the sea from about 500 feet to depths of at least two miles.

The distribution of this gulper fish includes the deeper parts of all temperate and tropical seas.

THE NECK EEL FAMILY
48 Family Derichthyidae

Members of this small family are most easily distinguished by a constriction or neck between the head and the pectoral fins. They are eel-like in shape, although some ichthyologists believe that they are not closely related to other eel families. Their bodies are slender, eel-shaped, without scales, and are marked by a lateral line which begins high behind the head and becomes lower on the posterior part of the body. The head is small and snake-like and bears rather large eyes on the front half of the head, and well developed jaws which are of equal length and which extend backward well beyond the eyes. The nostrils in this family are not tubular as in many families of eels.

This is a very small family of just a few species which are world-wide in the depths of the sea.

THE DEEP-WATER NECK EEL
48—1 *Derichthys serpentinus* Gill, 1887

The name of this eel comes from its fancied resemblance to a serpent, although it is a true fish. In this species the dorsal fin begins back on the body about halfway between the snout and the anus and continues backward to join the caudal fin; the anal fin likewise is joined to the caudal fin so that all of the median fins form one continuous, confluent fin. The pectoral fins are placed quite high on the sides of the body above and behind the gill openings. There are also rows of pores upon the head. The color in life is reported as a ruddy brown. Large specimens have measured less than 12 inches in length.

From Goode and Bean

Adults are reported to lay about 4,000 eggs which measure about 0.75 mm in diameter; these are released to drift in the sea and develop into a leptocephalus-type larvae, and thereafter transform to their adult form when they have reached a length of about two inches. The food of this eel consists of small fishes and crustacea. This is a rare fish and has been captured at depths from about 1,500 feet to well beyond one mile.

The distribution of this species is world-wide in warm water.

THE XENOCONGRID EEL FAMILY
49 *Family Xenocongridae*

The xenocongrid eels are a small family of small species which live in tropical seas. Their bodies have no scales, the pectoral fins are absent in most species, and the gill opening is a small hole similar to that of the moray eels. The lower lip in this family has a folded flap of skin along its outer margin and the vomerine teeth within the mouth are in two distinct rows. There are two nostrils; of these, the posterior one is unusual because it opens into the mouth from inside the upper lip.

Some species in this group are sometimes listed within the *Echelidae*, the worm eels.

At least two species occur in this area.

THE DOUBLE-TOOTHED XENOCONGRID EEL
49—1 *Kaupichthys diodontus* Schultz, 1943

This is a small and insignificant species which has no scales on the body and which presents a small pectoral fin located just above a round gill opening. The tail is twice the length of the body (the anus-to-tail length is twice the snout-to-anus length). The head presents a snout which is flattened, smooth, and rounded dorsally. The jaws contain pores located at various places and the eyes are quite large. The anterior nostrils are located near the corners of the snout and the posterior nostrils are located in the lip below the eye and are covered by a flap of skin. The color of the body is brown; the fins are likewise brown at their bases but paler toward their margins. This is an uncommon species and reaches a length of about 8 inches.

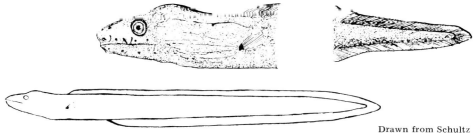

Drawn from Schultz

The distribution of this eel extends from Hawaii southward to central Polynesia and westward through Micronesia.

Dr. Leonard Schultz named this species *diodontus* because of the double row of teeth on the vomer.

THE FLAT-NOSED XENOCONGRID EEL
49—2 *Chilorhinus platyrhynchus* (Norman), 1922

This insignificant species has no pectoral fins and the tail is equal in length to the body. The head bears a very short, flat snout which is rounded anteriorly; the mouth, which is very wide, has a horizontal cleft which extends to the rear border of the eye. The color of the body is brownish above and paler below. There is a very narrow, pale margin bordering the caudal fin. This is a small eel and will reach a length of seven inches.

It is known from Hawaii and the tropical, south Pacific Ocean.

THE MORAY EEL FAMILY
50* *Family Muraenidae (Echidnidae)*

Moray eels are true bony fishes in which the body has become modified to suit their mode of life; as a result their bodies have become elongated, robust, and muscular. The paired pectoral and pelvic fins have disappeared leaving only the median dorsal, anal, and caudal fins and in some species even these fins are greatly reduced or absent. The skin has become thickened and toughened and covers the fins; even the scales have been entirely lost in some species or remain as minute remnants buried in the skin. The head is rather elongated and bears a large mouth with a wide cleft. The mouth usually contains a large number of sharp teeth, although some species have teeth which are adapted for grinding. The nostrils consist of an anterior pair and a posterior pair; of these, the anterior pair and often the posterior pair are fitted with fleshy tubes. Moray eels present many colors from dark to light and from uniform patterns to unusual arrangements of spots, blotches, bars, and net-like markings.

* See Appendix.

Moray eels are usually eaters of fish which they seek out during the hours of darkness. They are strong, fierce, and aggressive animals and have few enemies in the coral reef where they live. The larvae of eels are called *Leptocephalus* (small head) larvae; they are long and ribbon-like and have very small heads. After a period of drifting in the plankton, they assume their adult form and begin a life on the ocean bottom. They should be treated with respect for their sharp teeth can inflict very severe wounds upon the hands or feet of careless swimmers or fishermen.

At least eighty species are known which range in length from a few inches to possibly ten feet.

Moray eels are common in tropical regions and a few occur in temperate seas.

The following species of moray eels are mostly small forms and are not discussed or illustrated:

Anarchias allardicei Jordan and Stark, 1906. This eel is light brown in color, measures about six or seven inches and is uncommon.

Anarchias cantonensis (Schultz), 1943. This eel is light in ground color and is covered by a reticulated network of darker markings. It measures about eight inches in length.

Anarchias leucurus (Snyder), 1904. This is a small brown eel which is finely spotted with white. It measures about ten inches.

Gymnothorax buroensis (Bleeker), 1857. This eel is a small species which is widely distributed in the western tropical Pacific and Indian Oceans. It exhibits a great variety of color patterns and intensities in brown and black and is therefore difficult to recognize. It will reach 12 or 14 inches.

Gymnothorax gracilicaudus Jenkins, 1903. This is a small, slender, light colored species which measures less than a foot in length.

Gymnothorax hilonis Jordan and Evermann, 1905. This is a species of uncertain identity. It is dark in color and measures one foot or less.

Gymnothorax melatremus Schultz, 1953. This is a small eel possibly reaching one foot in length. It is bright yellow or orange in color with variable markings and a black gill opening.

Gymnothorax moluccensis (Bleeker), 1864. This eel is uniformly brown in color and lacks a light border on the fins. There is single, enlarged tooth in the middle of the upper jaw; the other teeth are serrated. It may reach 18 inches.

Gymnothorax mucifer Snyder, 1904. This is a species of uncertain identity. It is known from one specimen described in 1904 which measured about 30 inches in length.

Gymnothorax pictus (Ahl), 1789. This eel is light colored and is covered over the back and sides with small, very dark spots. It will grow to about two feet.

Rabula fuscomaculata Schultz, 1953. This is a brown spotted eel which measures about seven inches in length. *Gymnothorax* is now the correct genus.

Uropterygius fuscoguttatus Schultz, 1953. This brown spotted species measures about 12 inches in length.

Uropterygius inornatus Gosline, 1958. This is a plain brown eel which measures about eight inches in length.

Uropterygius knighti (Jordan and Stark), 1906. This species is dark colored with lighter markings. It reaches 12 or 14 inches in length.

Uropterygius polyspilus (Regan), 1909. This is a pale, reddish species marked with dark spots arranged in two or three irregular rows. It has been recorded to reach 17 inches, although most specimens are less than one foot in length.

Uropterygius supraforatus (Regan), 1909. This eel is brown anteriorly and dark brown spotted posteriorly. It reaches 18 inches.

SEALE'S MORAY EEL
50—1 *Uropterygius sealei* Whitley, 1932

This moray eel is probably most easily recognized by its size, its color, and the location of the anus. The body is elongated and tapers very little until the last fifth of the body.

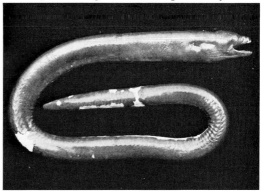

The dorsal and anal fins are not apparent and the anus is located two-thirds of the body length from the head. The body color is a plain, dark, yellow-brown or brown and is without markings; the markings on the accompanying illustration are believed to be abnormal. It will reach a length of at least three feet.

The distribution of this eel includes Hawaii, central Polynesia, and doubtless adjoining areas.

The name of this eel honors Mr. Alvin Seale, zoologist, ichthyologist, explorer, and scientist of San Francisco, Hawaii, and the South Seas. This species was originally described as *Scuticaria unicolor* Seale, 1917.

THE TIGER MORAY EEL
50—2 *Uropterygius tigrinus* (Lesson), 1829

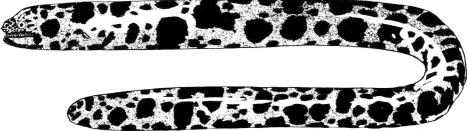

Drawn from Jordan and Evermann

The body of this eel is round or cylindrical in shape and is not compressed except at the tail. The head, snout and the end of the tail are blunt and rounded. The nostrils are

represented by pairs of anterior and posterior tubes; of these the anterior pair is the longer. The eyes are very small. The location of the anus is farther toward the back of the body than in most morays. This eel is of striking coloration; the ground color is light and the entire body is covered with irregular, round, dark markings of various sizes.

This species will reach at least four feet in length.

The distribution of this eel extends from Hawaii southward into Polynesia and westward across the entire tropical Pacific and Indian Oceans to the coast of Africa.

THE LEOPARD MORAY EEL
Also known as Pu-hi a-o, Pu-hi 'o-'a, and Pu-hi we-la
50—3 *Muraena pardalis* Schlegel, 1846

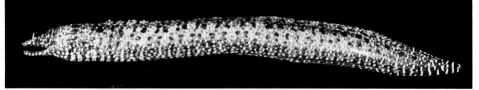

This moray eel is typical of the family and easily identified. The body is long and slender, the head is small, and the dorsal, anal, and caudal fins are  well developed. The mouth contains a large number of sharp teeth and the lower jaw cannot be completely closed because it is curved. The nose tubes are erect and give this eel an unusual appearance. The color of the body is the most vivid, complex, and unusual of all moray eels. It consists principally of white spots and spots of other colors spread upon a light background. Specimens will reach at least three feet in length.

The distribution of this species extends from Hawaii and southern Japan southward to central Polynesia.

Other names for this eel appearing in books include *Muraena kailuae* Jordan and Evermann, 1903, *Muraena lampra* Jenkins, 1903, and *Muraena kauila* Jenkins, 1903.

THE CANINE-TOOTHED MORAY EEL
Also known as Pu-hi ka-u-i-la
50—4 *Enchelynassa canina* (Quoy and Gaimard), 1824

This moray eel can be mistaken for no other eel because of its color and jaws. The body is quite robust and possesses dorsal, anal, and caudal fins. The head is of normal size and exhibits two long arching jaws which touch at their tips but do not close at their middle. The mouth is full of a large number of long, sharp teeth which are readily visible. The color of

Drawn from Jordan and Everman

118

the body is a uniform, dark, rich, red-brown hue. Individuals will reach five feet or more in length.

The distribution of this species extends from Hawaii southward to central Polynesia and westward through the East Indies.

THE WHITE-BANDED MORAY EEL
50—5 *Echidna leucotaenia* Schultz, 1943

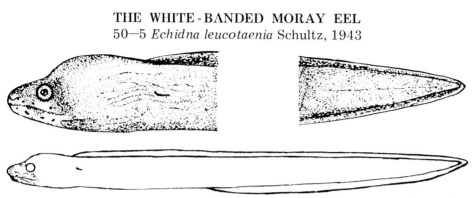

Drawn from Schultz

The body of this moray eel is very long and slender and tapers but little until just ahead of the tail. The anus is located at about the middle of the body so that the tail is equal in length to the head and trunk combined. The dorsal fin is very long and has its origin a short distance in front of the gill opening. The color of the body is plain brown throughout except for a narrow white margin on the outer edge of the dorsal, caudal, and anal fins. There are white areas upon the chin which may extend onto the upper jaw. It is reported to reach a length of at least 21 inches.

The distribution of this eel extends from Johnston Island and possibly Hawaii southward to central Polynesia and westward through the Marshall and Marianas Islands.

THE NEBULOUS MORAY EEL
Also known as Pu-hi ka-pa
50—6 *Echidna nebulosa* (Ahl), 1789

Of all moray eels, this species is one of the most beautiful and easy to identify. The entire body is a very light brown-orange color and is marked with irregular, black blotches each having a white center. The ground color of the lower side is white. This is an uncommon species and will probably reach a maximum length of about three feet. Jordan and Evermann

state that this eel has a reputation of making havoc among all kinds of fishes. The Hawaiians compared Kamehameha with this eel and named him "puhi kapa" because he was victorious over all.

The distribution of this eel extends from Hawaii southward to Australia, westward through the islands of the tropical Pacific to the East Indies, and across the Indian Ocean to the coast of Africa.

THE MANY BANDED MORAY EEL
Also known as Pu-hi le-i ha-la
50—7 *Echidna polyzona* (Richardson), 1844

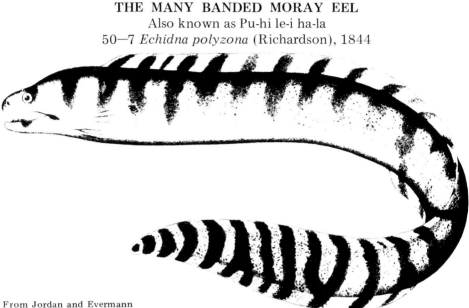

From Jordan and Evermann

The teeth of this eel are rounded for grinding and are not long and sharp as in most moray eels; these teeth may be seen grouped on the roof of the mouth. This is a dark eel which, when young, is marked by alternating light and dark vertical bands. As the eel grows older this banding disappears and the eel assumes a uniformly dark color. Adults will reach a length of at least two feet. This is a shore line species which inhabits the reef and in-shore water.

The distribution of this species extends from Hawaii southward to central Polynesia, westward across the tropical western Pacific Ocean, through the East Indies, and across the Indian Ocean to the coast of Africa and the Red Sea.

THE ZEBRA MORAY EEL
50—8 *Echidna zebra* (Shaw), 1797

The body of this eel is long, slender, and only slightly compressed. The dorsal and anal fins are reduced in length and are found as small remnants near the tail. The anus is located quite far posteriorly on the body. The head is short and bears a blunt snout with a medium-sized mouth. Identification of this species is simple because of its color pattern. The body is a dark

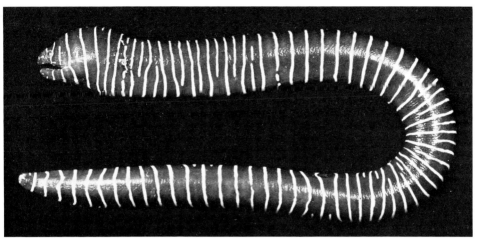

reddish brown or black and is encircled by a large number of yellowish lines. Each of the yellow lines is bordered by a vague, indistinct, darker band on each side. The *Echidna* eels differ from other morays by having grinding teeth in the mouth with which they are reported to crush the shells of the animals on which they feed.

The distribution of this eel extends from the Hawaiian Islands southward to Polynesia, westward across the tropical Pacific Ocean to the Philippines and the East Indies, and across the Indian Ocean to the coast of Africa. It also occurs off Panama, the Galapagos Islands, and Mexico.

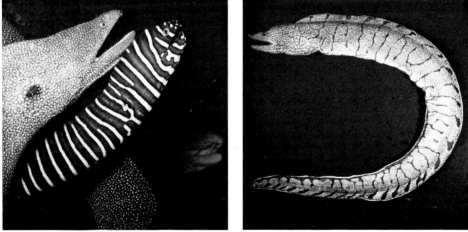

Echidna zebra   *Gymnothorax berndti*

BERNDT'S MORAY EEL
50—9 *Gymnothorax berndti* Snyder, 1904

Berndt's moray eel is a large, somewhat slender species which may best be recognized by its color pattern. The light gray body is covered by a fine, reticulated pattern of lines and is also marked off into larger rectangular areas by a series of narrow, vertical, irregular, dark brown lines. The caudal fin is narrowly outlined in white. It will reach a length of at least three feet.

The distribution extends from Hawaii and Japan southward through the East Indies and across the Indian Ocean to Mauritius and Reunion Island.

The scientific name of this eel honors the memory of Mr. E. Louis Berndt, an inspector in the Honolulu fish market at the beginning of the 20th century.

ABBOTT'S MORAY EEL
50—10* *Gymnothorax eurostus* (Abbott), 1860

This moray eel is a difficult species to identify without an inspection of its teeth. Dr. William A. Gosline states "It is only necessary to open the mouth far to see whether there are two or more long rows of teeth on each side of the upper jaw in the area below the eye. Any mottled fish with such rows belongs to this species. There are other morays that have an inner row of as many as five teeth on the maxillary, but *Gymnothorax eurostus* always (along with *G. buroensis* and often *G. meleagris)* has nine or more. The mottling on the head, throat, and body, in addition to the white spots when these are present, will serve to distinguish *G. eurostus* from both *G. meleagris* and *G. buroensis.*" The color of the body alone cannot be used for positive identification for it is a mottled pattern varying from light gray through brown to black and, in addition, possesses light spotting in young individuals. It will reach a length of about two feet.

This is a common shore line species in the Hawaiian Islands.

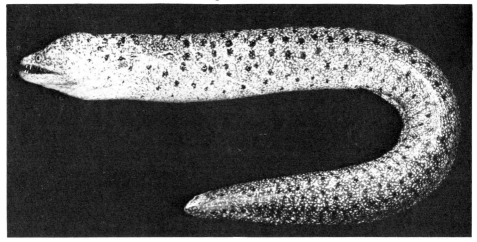

THE YELLOW-MARGINED MORAY EEL
Also known as Pu-hi ka-pa
50—11 *Gymnothorax flavimarginatus* (Ruppell), 1828

The body of this eel is large, heavy, and robust with a short head and snout. The color of the body is brown with darker brown marblings covering it. The gill opening is black and a distinctive, bright, narrow, green-yellow line borders the outer edge of the fins. This is a large and strong eel which

* See Appendix.

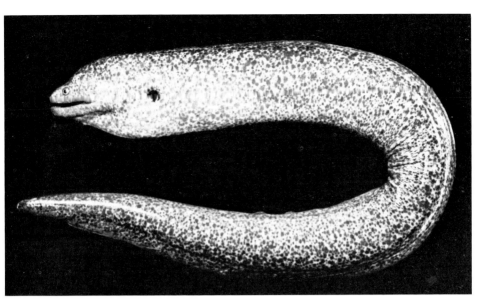

will reach a length of at least four feet.

The distribution of this eel extends from Hawaii southward into Polynesia, westward across the tropical Pacific Ocean, through the East Indies, and across the Indian Ocean to the coast of Africa.

GOLDSBOROUGH'S MORAY EEL

50—12* *Gymnothorax goldsboroughi* Jordan and Evermann, 1903

Goldsborough's moray eel is an uncommon species of uncertain classification. It is of medium size with a somewhat slender, compressed body and a dorsal fin which begins far forward on the body. The head is short, the mouth is large, and the eyes are small. The color of the body is brownish; white spots are scattered along the full length of the body. It will reach a length of at least 21 inches.

At present it is known only from the Hawaiian Islands.

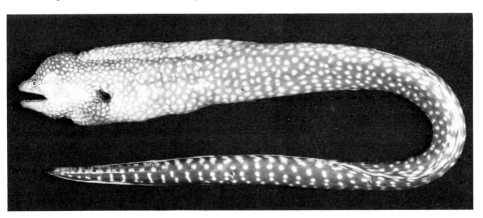

* See Appendix.

THE LIVER-COLORED MORAY EEL
50—13 *Gymnothorax hepaticus* Ruppell, 1828

The body of this species is long and slender; it is of uniform diameter from the head to the anus and then tapers gradually to the tail. The anus is located in the posterior half of the body so that the head and trunk are longer than the tail. The color of the body is a uniform, light brown and there is a narrow white line bordering the median fins except at the beginning of the dorsal fin. The iris of the eye is a golden color. There is a row of four or five white spots along the edge of the lower jaw and a similar row of four spots on the upper jaw. Large specimens will measure between 36 and 40 inches.

This is an uncommon species known from the Red Sea, Hawaii, and doubtless many areas in between.

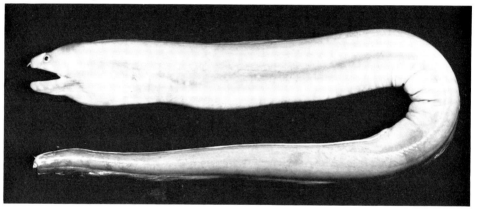

THE GUINEA MORAY EEL
50—14 *Gymnothorax meleagris* (Shaw and Nodder), 1795

The guinea moray eel has a fairly robust body which becomes increasingly compressed toward the tail. The anus is forward of the center of the body so that the tail is longer than the head and trunk combined. The entire body is covered by white or light colored, rounded spots set upon a dark or black background. The gill opening is black. This species will reach about three feet in length.

The distribution of this eel extends from Hawaii southward into central Polynesia, westward across the tropical western Pacific Ocean,

hrough the East Indies, and across the Indian Ocean to the coast of Africa.

The species known as *Gymnothorax nuttingi* Snyder, 1904, is regarded s a synonym of *G. meleagris*.

THE YELLOW - HEADED MORAY EEL
50 15" *Gymnothorax pelelli* (Bleeker), 1856

The yellow-headed moray is an eel of moderate size with a body typical f the family. The snout and front of the head are marked with yellowish ues and the body is marked by wide, encircling, black bands which are ften incomplete on the belly. These bands become less distinct in older)ecimens. It will reach three feet in length.

The distribution of this eel extends from Hawaii southward into olynesia, westward across the tropical western Pacific Ocean, through the ast Indies, and across the Indian Ocean to the coast of Africa and the Red ea.

STEINDACHNER'S MORAY EEL
50—16 *Gymnothorax steindachneri* Jordan and Evermann, 1903

Steindachner's moray eel is a medium sized, slender species in whic the body is quite strongly compressed. The head is small and is quite lon and slender; the mouth is likewise long. The color of this eel is light browr it is marked by irregular, dark, brown spots which cover the entire body The gill opening is marked by an area of black and a horizontal series of dar lines is present along the lower side of the head between the mouth and th gill openings. It will reach a length in excess of two feet.

This eel is known from Hawaii and doubtless elsewhere in the tropica western Pacific Ocean.

The authors named this species in honor of Dr. Franz Steindachner, German ichthyologist, who studied Hawaiian and Samoan fishes during th last half of the 19th century.

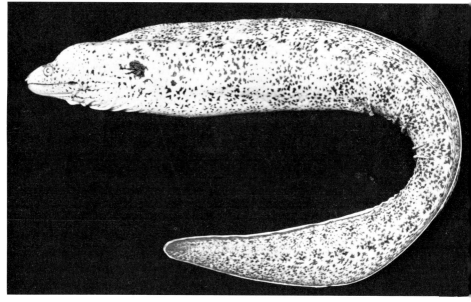

THE COMMON MORAY EEL
Also known as Pu-hi la-u mi-lo
50—17 *Gymnothorax undulatus* (Lacepede), 1803

The common moray eel is dark in color and is marked over the entire body by a network of irregular, white lines. This pattern seems to disappear on the sides of the head and on the belly. It will reach a length of about three feet. Of the larger eels, this species is probably the most

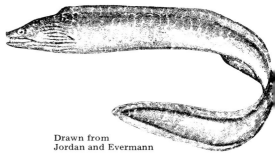

Drawn from
Jordan and Evermann

ommon in the Hawaiian Islands.

The distribution of this species extends from Hawaii southward into 'olynesia, westward across the tropical Pacific Ocean, through the East ndies, and across the Indian Ocean to the coast of Africa.

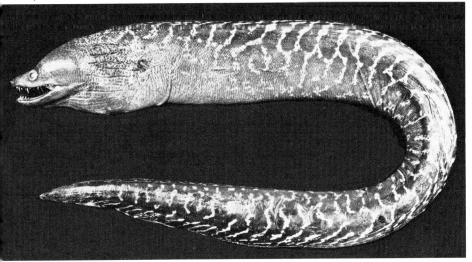

THE YELLOW-MOUTHED MORAY EEL
50—18* *Gymnothorax xanthostomus* Snyder, 1904

The body of this eel resembles that of *G. meleagris* for it is heavy and 'obust and possesses a short head and snout. The background color pattern of the body is yellowish olive anteriorly and changes to brown posteriorly. This background is covered with white spots which are very small on the lead and increase in size toward the tail where they change somewhat from

* See Appendix.

white to a cream color. There are no spots on the belly and the opercle is
ringed with brown or black. The interior of the mouth is an orange-yellow
color and helps to identify this species. It will reach about three feet in
length.

It is known from Hawaii and probably elsewhere in the tropical western
Pacific Ocean.

In some books this eel will be listed under the name of *G. nudivome*
(Gunther), 1866.

THE THREAD EEL FAMILY
Also known as the Whip Eels
51* *Family Moringuidae (Ratabouridae, Stilbiscidae)*

The thread eels have elongated, slender, cylindrical, worm-like bodies
which are scaleless and in which the anus is located in the posterior one-third
of the body. The dorsal and anal fins are present but are usually very small,
the pectoral fins may be present as small appendages or they may be absent,
the caudal fin is separated from the dorsal and anal fins by a space. In this
family, the chin of the lower jaw protrudes beyond the upper jaw, although
the upper lip usually overhangs the lower lip. The eyes are small, the mouth
is small, and the teeth are small and in one row. The gill openings are small,
narrow, and located low on the body. The males and females differ in
appearance.

This is a family of degenerate eels which live in the sand.

More than 20 species are known from the tropical seas of the world.
Several occur in this area.

THE THREAD EEL OR WHIP EEL
51—1 *Moringua macrochir* Bleeker, 1853

This thread eel, like the
other members of its family,
has a long, slender, scaleless
body which ends in a pointed
tail. The pectoral fins,
although present, are rudimentary. The cleft of the mouth
is long and the lower jaw

Drawn from
Jordan and Evermann

projects beyond the upper jaw. The eyes are small and probably degenerate.
The color of the body changes with age. When the fish is young, it is
yellowish in color, but as it matures it becomes black above and silvery
beneath. Full grown eels will reach a length of about 18 inches. The young
forms are sand dwelling.

The distribution of this species extends from Hawaii southward and
westward across the tropical Pacific Ocean to the East Indies.

* See Appendix.

THE DUCK-BILLED EEL FAMILY
52 *Family Nettastomidae*

Duck-billed eels are a small group of fishes with fragile, elongated, scale-less bodies. The dorsal fin begins far forward on the back and extends to the tail which ends in a slender filament. The pectoral fins are absent. The snout is long and projects beyond the lower jaw. The mouth is large and the left is long. Together the snout and mouth resemble the bill of a duck; from this resemblance the family has received its common name.

This is a deep water family which is found principally in tropical and temperate seas. A few species have been recorded from deep water in this area.

THE DUCK-BILLED EEL
52—1 *Metopomycter denticulatus* Gilbert, 1905

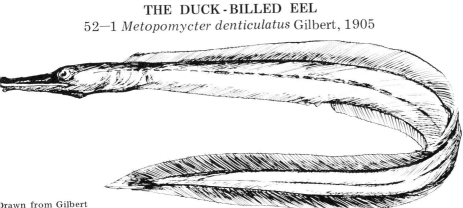

Drawn from Gilbert

This duck-billed eel has a slender head and body and a tail which tapers posteriorly to end at the caudal fin. The snout is depressed and flattened above and the mouth contains very small teeth in wide bands. The color of the body is olive brown and becomes darker posteriorly and also on the head. There are also blue-black markings on the snout, jaws, opercle, and vent.

This species is known from only one specimen 30.5 inches long which was obtained by the steamer *Albatross* in 1902 off the island of Kauai at a depth of about one-half mile.

Although presently known only from the Hawaiian Islands, it is doubtless much more widely distributed.

THE CONGER EEL FAMILY
53* *Family Congridae*
(*Leptocephalidae, Heterocongridae, Macrocephenchelyidae*)

The bodies of conger eels are long and cylindrical anteriorly and compressed posteriorly. Pectoral fins are present and quite well developed; the dorsal and anal fins are also quite large and join with the caudal fin to make a continuous fin from behind the head, down the back, around the tail, and forward to the anus. The snout is long, the mouth is large, and the lips have

* See Appendix.

free edges of skin that fold against the outer edge of each jaw. The gill openings are quite large and are located low on the body. There are no scales in this family. The color of conger eels is usually grayish over the back and sides and light gray or white beneath. In size, they range from a few inches to over six feet.

Conger eels inhabit the shore lines of tropical and sub-tropical seas.

The following species are not described or illustrated:

Ariosoma bowersi (Jenkins), 1903. This conger eel is a sand dwelling form measuring from 12 to 16 inches in length. Its eye, which is larger than the eye of most eels, is covered by transparent protective tissue.

Conger oligoporus Kanazawa, 1958. This is a large species which reaches about five feet. This species has been listed in some books under the name of *Conger wilsoni* (Schneider), 1801.

Congrellus aequoreus (Gilbert and Cramer), 1897. This species reaches a length of about 24 inches. It appears to live in depths below 500 feet.

Promyllantor alcocki Gilbert and Cramer, 1897. This conger eel is an uncommon species, measures about ten inches in length, and inhabits waters between about 1,000 and 2,000 feet in depth.

Veternio verrens Snyder, 1904. This conger eel lacks teeth, measures about 20 inches in length, and is known from a very few specimens.

THE ASH - COLORED CONGER EEL
Also known as Pu-hi u-ha
53—01* *Conger cinereus* Ruppell, 1828

This conger eel has a cylindrical body and a tapering, compressed tail. The head and snout are long, pointed, and depressed and the mouth is large. The gill openings are quite large and are located low on the body. The scales are absent and the skin is smooth. The lips are fleshy and possess a fold of skin which is folded back along their outer margins. The color of this species is grayish to brownish and is lighter on the lower side. There are two significant dark marking on this species. The first is a black border along the upper lip below the eye; the second is a dark area on the pectoral

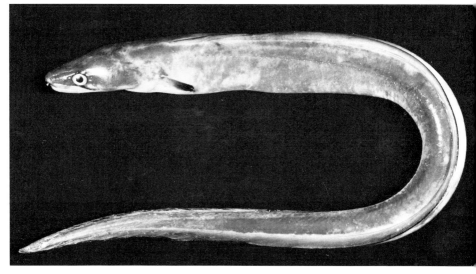

in. The young individuals of this species often show very faint, wide, vertical bars along their bodies. The size of adult specimens will exceed three feet and may reach as much as five feet.

The distribution of this species extends from Hawaii southward into Polynesia and westward across the tropical Pacific and Indian Oceans to the coast of Africa and the Red Sea.

Some books will include this species under the name of *C. marginatus* Valenciennes, 1841.

THE WORM EEL FAMILY
54 *Family Echelidae (Myridae)*

The worm eels are a heterogeneous, complex assemblage of various types of eels. Many of the species formerly found in this family have been studied and reclassified and are now placed in other families of fishes including the *Xenocongridae* and the *Ophichthidae*.

None are discussed or illustrated here. However, the following species may be of interest to individuals who wish to study this group:

Chilorhinus brocki Gosline, 1951. This little eel, measuring less then four inches, is described in *COPEIA* 1951(3), pp. 195-202. Its name honors Mr. Vernon E. Brock (1912-1971) ichthyologist, oceanographer, and resident of California and Hawaii.

THE SNAKE EEL FAMILY
55* *Family Ophichthidae (Ophichthyidae)*

Snake eels are slender fishes with long cylindrical bodies, without scales or pelvic fins, and usually without pectoral fins. Most snake eels have no fin rays at the end of the tail and the tail itself ends in a firm, fleshy, muscular point which is used in digging backward into the sand. The dorsal fin starts just behind the head and extends the full length of the body, while the anal fin is much shorter. Most species are less than 36 inches in length and many are brightly colored.

Snake eels live over sandy bottoms along the shore lines of tropical and sub-tropical seas.

Of more than 200 species, at least 18 are known from this area.

The following species are not discussed or illustrated:

Brachysomophis sauropsis Schultz, 1943. This is a small, uncommon species which measures about 14 to 18 inches in length. Its eyes are located far forward on the snout.

Caecula flavicauda (Snyder), 1904. This is a very slender species which reaches a length of about one and one-half feet. It occurs from the surface to depths of at least 700 feet. At present it is known only from the Hawaiian area. A more recent and more correct name for this species is *Verma flavicauda* (Snyder), 1904.

Caecula platyrhynchus Gosline, 1951. This is a common, sand-dwelling species which is pink in color and measures between six and 15 inches in length.

Cirrhimuraena macgregori (Jenkins), 1903. This is a small, plain-colored eel which measures less than one foot in length. Pectoral fins are present and the dorsal fin begins far forward of the gill openings.

* See Appendix.

Leptenchelys labialis (Seale), 1917. This is a small species and measures betwee[n] 5 and 7 inches in length. Now called *Schismorhynchus labialis* (Seale), 1917[.]

Muraenichthys cookei Fowler, 1928. This is a yellow species which measure[s] between five and ten inches in length.

Muraenichthys gymnotus Bleeker, 1864. This is another small species of a fe[w] inches in which the dorsal fin is short and begins behind the anus.

Muraenichthys macropterus Bleeker, 1857. This small eel will measure at lea[st] 15 inches in length. It was first described from the East Indies but, in add[i]tion, is distributed from the Philippine Islands to Hawaii and southward t[o] New Caledonia and Australia.

Muraenichthys schultzei Bleeker, 1857. This eel measures about five inches i[n] length. It is a robust species known from the East Indies, Micronesia, an[d] Johnston Island; it doubtless occurs in adjoining areas.

Myrichthys bleekeri Gosline, 1951. This is a small, uncommon species whic[h] measures about 12 to 14 inches and is marked by darker saddle-shaped areas[.]

Phyllophichthus xenodontus Gosline, 1951. This is a small, uncommon specie[s] from Hawaii and the Marshall Islands. It measures about ten inches in lengt[h] and has an unusual leaf-like flap at the anterior nostril.

Schultzidia johnstonensis (Schultz and Woods), 1949. This is a small eel whic[h] measures about 12 inches in length. It is dark colored above and lighte[r] below.

HENSHAW'S SNAKE EEL
55—1 *Brachysomophis henshawi* Jordan and Snyder, 1904

Henshaw's snake eel is a large species with a large head and large jaw[s]. The body is brown in color above and is marked with scattered brown dot[s] and by a single longitudinal row of dark brown spots along the side of th[e] body. The lower side of the body is a light, yellowish color. This specie[s] will reach at least 44 inches in length.

The distribution of this eel includes the Hawaiian Islands and doubtles[s] adjoining areas in the tropical, western Pacific Ocean.

The scientific name of this eel honors Mr. Henry W. Henshaw, a famou[s] naturalist who lived in Hilo at the beginning of the 20th century.

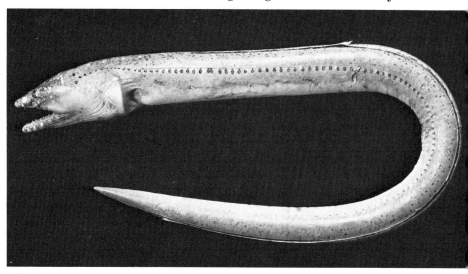

THE YELLOW-SPOTTED SNAKE EEL
55—2 *Callechelys luteus* Snyder, 1904

This snake eels has an unusually long and slender body, no paired fins, and a dorsal fin which begins ahead of the gill openings. The color of the body is white to bluish-white and is marked with small, oval, black spots and scattered yellow spots which are smaller and more numerous on the gill covers.

The specimen in the illustration is exceptionally large and measured 41 inches in length.

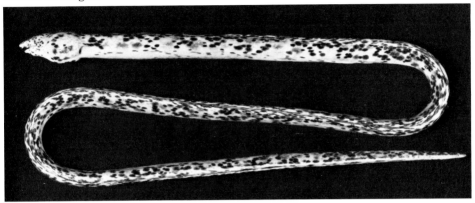

THE HALF-BANDED SNAKE EEL
55—3 *Leiuranus semicinctus* (Lay and Bennett), 1839

This snake eel has a very long, slender, cylindrical body and a small head. The color of the body is white below and becomes somewhat yellowish toward the back. It is conspicuously marked by about 24 or 25, black, saddle-shaped areas. It will reach a length of at least 20 inches.

The distribution of this eel extends from Hawaii southward into Polynesia and across the tropical Pacific Ocean to include the East Indies.

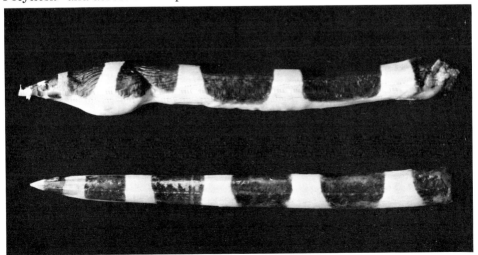

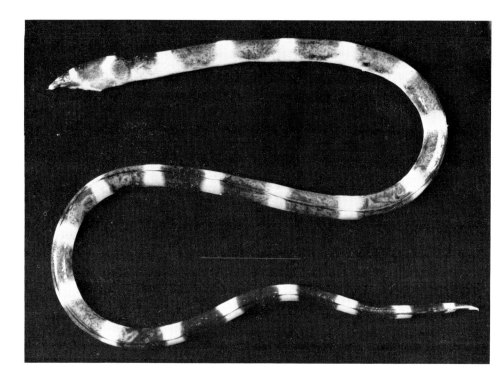

FOWLER'S SNAKE EEL

55—4 *Microdonophis fowleri* Jordan and Evermann, 1903

Fowler's eel is a large and beautiful species with an elongated, cylindrical body, a head of moderate size, and the usual pointed tail. The color of the body is light with many, round, brown spots and about 16 faint, darker, vertical cross-bars. This uncommon species will reach a length of at least 40 inches.

It occurs in Hawaii and doubtless in the adjoining areas of the tropical western Pacific Ocean.

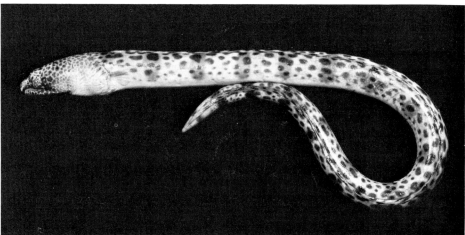

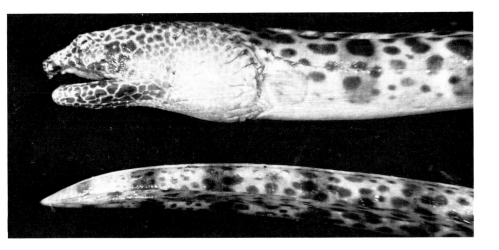

THE SPOTTED SNAKE EEL
55—5 *Myrichthys maculosus* (Cuvier), 1817

The spotted snake eel has a very long, cylindrical body and a small head. The dorsal fin originates on the head and the tail ends in a stiff point as in other ophichthids. The color of the body is a light yellowish white; it is marked by large, oval spots of various sizes which are arranged in an alternating pattern; these spots vary from green to brown to black in color. Large specimens will reach about three feet in length. It is nocturnal in its habits.

The distribution of this eel extends from Hawaii southward into Polynesia, westward through Melanesia and Micronesia, through the East Indies, and across the Indian Ocean to the coast of Africa and the Red Sea.

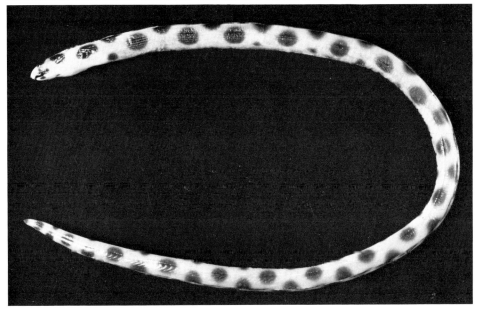

THE MANY-EYED SNAKE EEL
55—6 *Ophichthus polyophthalmus* Bleeker, 1864

This snake eels is an elongated species with a cylindrical body and a small head. The tail ends in the usual, hard, firm point. The body is light in color and is marked by round, dark, brownish spots which may or may not be arranged in a regular pattern. These spots are usually in four rows on the side, extend onto the dorsal fin, and are smaller on the belly. This eel will reach a length of at least 40 inches.

The distribution of this species extends from Hawaiii southward into central Polynesia and westward across the tropical western Pacific Ocean to the East Indies.

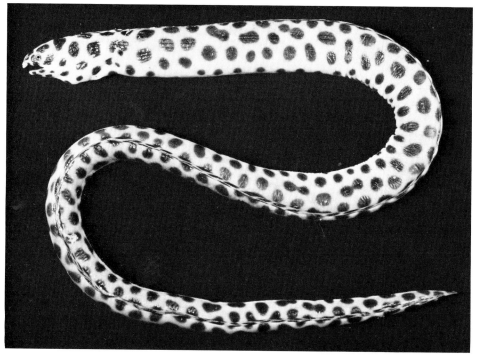

THE SYNAPHOBRANCHID EEL FAMILY
56 *Family Synaphobranchidae*

The synaphobranchid eels are a small family of marine species. They possess pectoral fins, have scales on the body, and have their gill openings placed low on the head so that they may converge below the head. Most synaphobranchid eels inhabit deep water in the Atlantic, Pacific, and Indian Oceans.

Of about a dozen known species, at least one occurs in this area.

GILBERT'S SYNAPHOBRANCHID EEL
56—1 *Synaphobranchus brachysomus* Gilbert, 1905

This synaphobranchid eel has a short body and a relatively long tail.

The head is slender and flattened and has a fleshy snout at its tip. Scales cover most of the body with the exception of the fins, the snout, and the lower side of the head. A lateral line with many small pores is plainly visible.

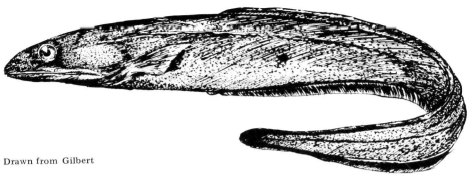

Drawn from Gilbert

The color of the body was described as a warm brown but was darker on the head and on the fins. The edges of the fins are marked by a narrow, white margin.

Several specimens were caught around Hawaii by the steamer *Albatross* in 1902; most of these specimens were found at depths between one-quarter and one-half mile. The largest specimen measured about 29 inches in length.

THE SERRIVOMERID EEL FAMILY

57 *Family Serrivomeridae (Gavialicipitidae)*

The serrivomerid eels are a small family of deep-water forms which are rarely seen or captured. They have slender, elongated bodies which are without scales or a lateral line and which taper to a point or slender tip at the tail. The dorsal fin is shorter than the anal fin and begins some distance behind the head. The dorsal, caudal, and anal fins are continuous and the pectoral fins are small and are located high on the sides of the body. The head bears an elongated pair of jaws which taper to a point.

The family includes about a dozen species of which at least two are known from this area.

BEAN'S SERRIVOMERID EEL

57 1 *Serrivomer beani* Gill and Ryder, 1883

Bean's serrivomerid eel is an elongated, slender species with a body which tapers gradually to the tail. Although slender, the head and trunk of the body are rather short compared to the tail. The dorsal fin begins some distance behind the anus and both it and the anal fin continue without interruption to the tail. The head is long and bears a pair of long, slender jaws of which the lower jaw is somewhat the longer. This species will reach a length of at least two feet.

In 1902, the steamer *Albatross* obtained three specimens, one off Kauai, one off Bird Island, and one off Oahu; they were captured at depths between 1,800 and 6,000 feet.

The distribution of this species includes the deep waters of both the Atlantic and Pacific Oceans.

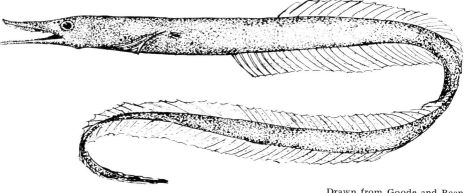

Drawn from Goode and Bean

THE BLACK SERRIVOMERID EEL
57—2 *Stemonidium hypomelas* Gilbert, 1905

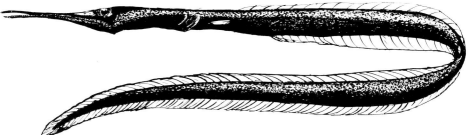

Drawn from Gilbert

The body of this deep-water eel is long, narrow, and band-shaped. The pectoral fins are present, although small, and are located rather high on the sides of the body. The dorsal, anal, and caudal fins are joined and continuous. The head bears a pair of very small eyes and a pair of jaws which are long, slender, and tapering with delicate tips. The color of the body is light grayish on the upper half and is covered with fine, black, pigment specks. The head and the lower half of the body are jet black. The fins are all transparent.

This species was described from one specimen, measuring about seven inches in length, which was taken in a dredge by the steamer *Albatross* in 1902 at a depth of about 3,000 feet off Niihau. It is doubtless more widely distributed.

THE SNIPE EEL FAMILY
58 *Family Nemichthyidae (Avocettinidae)*

The snipe eels are a small family of fishes with long bodies which taper posteriorly toward a long, pointed tail which may end in a filament and also anteriorly toward a neck-like constriction and a small head. Their bodies are somewhat translucent, without scales, and possess a pair of small pectoral fins in addition to the median fins. The jaws of these fishes are very unusual for they are recurved in such a manner that they do not close along much of their length.

Snipe eels are an oceanic group which lives in the deep water of tropical and warm temperate seas.

They include less than a dozen species of which at least one is known from this area.

THE POLYGON-SPOTTED SNIPE EEL
58—1 *Nematoprora polygonifera* Gilbert, 1905

Drawn from Gilbert

The body of this eel is very long and slender and tapers from its middle toward both the head and tail. The head is small and is separated from the body by a distinct neck-like constriction. The jaws of this species, like the other members of this family, are long, slender, and recurved at their ends. The color of the body is whitish on the upper half, while the lower side of the body is covered by blackish, polygonal-shaped spots. In addition, there is a single row of these dark spots extending along the upper side of the lateral line.

This species is known from a single specimen, measuring about 12 inches in length, which was caught in a dredge between 1,800 and 4,800 feet off Bird Island by the steamer *Albatross* in 1902.

THE HALOSAURID FISH FAMILY
59 *Family Halosauridae*

The halosaurid fishes are a small group of eel-like fishes, although they are unrelated to the eels. Their bodies are long and tapering and bear upon their sides a double series of scutes which extend from the head to the tail; it is by this unusual feature that they are most easily identified. The dorsal fin is short and composed of nine to 12 rays and the anal fin is unusually long. The pectoral fins are placed high upon the body and the pelvic fins may be placed far forward on the abdomen. The gill openings are wide.

Halosaurid fishes live in the colder, deeper waters of all oceans.

At least three species are known from this area.

THE KAUAI HALOSAURID FISH
59—1 *Aldrovandia kauaiensis* (Gilbert), 1905

The Kauai halosaurid is a fairly large, slender fish with scutes extending along the sides of the body from the head to the tail and with large, arrow-shaped teeth. Elliptical photophores are present. The color of the body is dark brown on the back and sides and blue-black on the sides of the head and below. The type specimen measured more than 26 inches in length.

Because this species resembles *H. verticalis*, it is helpful to know that *A. kauaiensis* has a shorter snout than *H. verticalis*.

Hawaiian specimens have been captured between about 2,300 and 4,800 feet in depth.

This species is known from the Hawaiian areas and doubtless elsewhere in the Pacific area.

In older books this species will be listed under the name of *Halosauropsis kauaiensis* Gilbert, 1905.

GILBERT'S HALOSAURID FISH
59—2 *Halosauropsis proboscidea* Gilbert, 1905

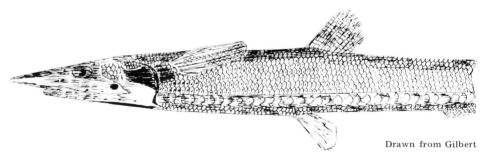

The body of this halosaurid resembles those of the preceeding species; it is long, slender, and tapering and is marked on the sides by longitudinal series of scutes which extend from the head to the tail. The head is more elongated and the snout more pointed than in the preceeding species. The color of the body was described as light grayish brown with faint bluish tinges. Other parts of the body, including the head, a narrow streak on the belly, the lower side of the tail, and the interiors of the mouth and gill cavity are blue-black. The type specimen measured almost 17 inches in length.

The steamer *Albatross* caught several specimens in several locations around Hawaii, all of which were taken at depths below 2,400 feet.

The distribution of this species includes the Hawaiian Islands and doubtless a much larger area in the Pacific basin.

THE HAWAIIAN HALOSAURID FISH
59—3 *Halosauropsis verticalis* Gilbert, 1905

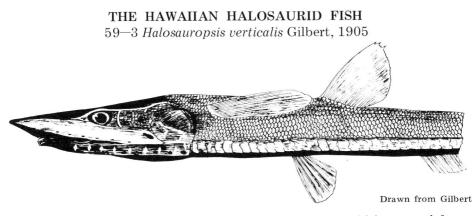

Drawn from Gilbert

The body of this fish resembles the Kauai halosaurid in general form, but the proportions are somewhat different and the snout is longer. Photophores are also present in this species. The color of the body is brownish black on the back and sides and there is a dark streak on the midline of the back behind the dorsal fin. The head, the lower sides of the body and the belly, and the interiors of the mouth and gill covers are all blue-black in color. The type specimen measured slightly more than 11 inches in length. Hawaiian specimens have been captured at depths between 1,800 and 4,800 feet.

This species occurs in the Hawaiian area and doubtless elsewhere in the Pacific basin.

THE NEEDLE FISH FAMILY
Also known as the Hound Fishes, Gar Fishes, Salt Water Gars, Bill Fishes,
and Long Tom Fishes
60 *Family Belonidae*

The needle fishes are a large family of fishes with slender, elongated bodies and long, slender jaws. The shape of their bodies somewhat resembles that of the barracudas, although they are not closely related. The dorsal and anal fins are opposite each other and are located at the rear of the trunk; the caudal fin is symmetrical and forked and the pelvic fins are located midway along the belly. The lateral line begins at the gill opening, extends low along the side of the body, and terminates at the caudal peduncle. The head contains a pair of large eyes and a set of remarkably long jaws armed with sharp teeth; the lower jaw is slightly the longer. The larger species will exceed four feet in length and possibly reach a length of six feet.

The needle fishes are a voracious and carnivorous group of surface

141

fishes with appearance and habits much like the barracudas, pikes, and gar fishes. They appear to be easily excited, to jump out of the water at the slightest provocation, and to occasionally crash into the sides of ships. Because they attain a fair speed, needle fishes are a source of danger to swimmers and fishermen and some have been known to pierce the bodies of people in the course of their wild leaps. Most of the needle fishes are good eating. Their flesh is snow-white, firm and of good taste. These fishes have sometimes been avoided because the bones and occasionally the flesh of some of the larger species are greenish in color.

Of more than two dozen species, at least four are known from this area.

THE GAPING NEEDLE FISH
Also known as 'A-ha
60—1 *Ablennes hians* (Cuvier and Valenciennes), 1846

This needle fish is one of the larger species; it has an elongated body and sides which are flattened and compressed. The head is flat on top and strongly compressed. The eyes are large and the scales are small. The lateral line extends along the ventral surface of the body and caudal peduncle. The caudal peduncle is compressed, lacks a lateral keel, and leads into a tail fin in which the upper lobe is smaller than the lower lobe. The color of the body is greenish on the back and silvery on the sides and belly. The sides of the body are often marked by a single row of large, dark, quadrate spots; these may be apparent along much of the side of the body or be visible only in the area in front of the tail. Large specimens will reach a length of at least 40 inches.

The distribution of this species is circumtropical.

THE FLAT-TAILED NEEDLE FISH
Also known as 'A-ha and 'A-ha 'a-ha (young)
60—2 *Belone platyura* Bennett, 1830

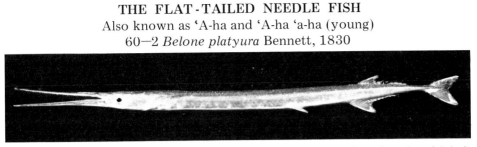

This species is most easily identified by the caudal peduncle which is very broad and flattened and bears a sharp keel along its lateral margin. The body is long and slender and bears a lateral line extending low along the side of the body. The eyes are quite large and slightly oval. The jaws are long, straight, and toothed. The color of the body is greenish or brownish above and on the sides and silvery white below; it bears a silvery, bluish, lateral streak. The fins are brownish and the iris is white. Young individuals exhibit a black, lateral band. It will reach a length of at least 18 inches.

The distribution of this species extends from Guam to Hawaii, southward into central Polynesia, and westward through much of the tropical Indo-Pacific area.

THE KEEL-JAWED NEEDLE FISH
60—3 *Strongylura appendiculata* (Klunzinger), 1871

This needle fish may be immediately separated from all others by the presence of a small, flat, bony keel at the front end of the lower jaw just below the tip. The body, head, and jaws are elongated and typical of this family. The caudal peduncle bears lateral keels and the lower lobe of the caudal fin is larger than the upper lobe. The eye is marked by a distinguishing, black spot at its upper edge. The color of the body is greenish above and silvery beneath. It will reach a length of about four feet.

The distribution of this species extends from Hawaii southward and westward across the entire tropical central and western Pacific Ocean and westward across the Indian Ocean to the Red Sea.

THE GIANT NEEDLE FISH
Also known as 'A-ha
60—4 *Strongylura gigantea* (Temminck and Schlegel), 1846

This needle fish is a large species with a tubular body which is not greatly compressed. The head is long with compressed sides and a somewhat flattened top; it is marked by bony striae. The jaws are long, toothed, and stronger than in other species. The lateral line runs along the lower side of the body and rises up near the caudal peduncle to help form a lateral keel. The tail is forked with the lower lobe being slightly longer than the upper lobe. The color of the body is greenish above and silvery and silvery white below. It will reach a length of at least 40 inches.

The distribution of this species extends from Hawaii and the sub-tropical, central Pacific southward to central Polynesia and westward to the East Indies.

THE SAURY FISH FAMILY
61 *Family Scomberesocidae*

The sauries are oceanic fishes which are closely related to the needle-fishes and half-beaks; the sauries, however, do not have elongated jaws. Their bodies are very long, slender, and stream-lined to reduce the friction of the surrounding water. The pectoral fins are small and are placed quite high on the sides of the body; the pelvic fins are likewise quite small and are placed just behind the center of the body. The dorsal and anal fins are about equal in size and opposite in position and are followed by finlets of which five are dorsal and seven are ventral in position.

Sauries inhabit the surface waters of the large oceans including the Mediterranean Sea.

This is a small family of about a half-dozen species of which at least two occur in the North Pacific Ocean.

The following species is not described or illustrated:

Cololabis adocetus Bohlke, 1951. This species was first described from a specimen caught off the coast of Peru. A few Hawaiian specimens have measured about two inches in length. It seems to be uncommon in Hawaii.

THE PACIFIC SAURY
61—1 *Cololabis saira* (Brevoort), 1850

From Tanaka

The body of this saury is very long and quite straight in outline. The upper and lower contours are nearly parallel in the middle of the body and then taper very gently toward the head and tail. The dorsal and anal fins are placed about opposite and are followed by small finlets of which five are dorsal and seven are ventral in position. The pectoral and pelvic fins are both small. The position of the pelvic fins near the mid-point of the body is useful in recognizing these fishes. This species will reach a length of at least 14 inches.

The name of *saira* is one of several common names for this fish in Japan.

The distribution of this saury includes both sides of the North Pacific Ocean.

THE HALF-BEAK FISH FAMILY
Also known as the Balaos or Herbivorous Balaos
62 *Family Hemiramphidae*

The half-beaks are a family of elongated, slender fishes with compressed, silvery bodies. These fishes take their common name from their unusual jaws which are quite unlike and most unequal in length. The lower jaw is usually long and pointed as in the needle fishes, while the upper jaw is short and rounded in front. Like the needle fishes and the flying fishes, the lateral line runs low along the side of the body. Likewise, the lower lobe of the tail is longer than the upper lobe and is used in their attempts to skitter along the surface of the water.

Most members of this family are marine and live in small schools at the surface of the water, usually along the shore line. A few species are truly pelagic and inhabit the open sea. They are herbivorous in their feeding habits and subsist upon marine algae. The young are hatched from eggs which are attached to marine plants in quiet waters along the shore line. When small, they possess equal jaws, but soon develop the elongated lower jaw. Like both flying fishes and needle fishes, they will jump and attempt to skim along the surface of the water.

The family contains more than 60 species; of this number at least three species are known from this area.

The following species is not described or illustrated:

Hyporhamphus acutus (Gunther), 1871. This half-beak was first described from a specimen obtained at Rarotonga in the Cook Islands. It now appears that there are really two forms of this species. Gunther's species, now known as *H. acutus acutus* (Gunther), 1871, usually has slightly fewer vertebrae and fewer fins rays than the other subspecies and is distributed from Wake Island southeastward to Easter Island. The other subspecies, known as *H. acutus pacificus* (Steindachner), 1900, has slightly more vertebrae and fin rays; it is known from the Hawaiian area.

THE GREEN HALF-BEAK FISH
Also known as I-he i-he and Me-'e me-'e
62—1 *Euleptorhamphus viridis* (van Hasselt), 1824

Drawn from Jordan and Evermann

The green half-beak has a body which is very long, greatly compressed, and flattened on the sides. The head is likewise compressed, flat on top, and very narrow below. It may be most easily identified by its large and long pectoral fins, by its small ventral fins, and by the dorsal and anal fins which are long and opposite. The caudal fin of this fish is deeply forked and the lower lobe is much the larger. The color of the body is a pale bluish silvery hue above and silvery on the lower sides and belly. The sides are marked by a broad, longitudinal, silvery, mid-lateral band. It will reach a length of at least 20 inches.

This fish is an offshore species and is pelagic in the open sea.

The distribution of this fish is believed to span the entire tropical western Pacific and Indian Oceans.

THE TROPICAL HALF-BEAK FISH
Also known as I-he i-he and Me-'e me-'e
62—2 *Hemiramphus depauperatus* Lay and Bennett, 1839

The body of this half-beak is moderately elongated, is somewhat thick and deep-bodies, and has the sides of the body compressed and flattened. The head is likewise compressed, somewhat flattened on top, and narrow beneath. The dorsal fin is longer than the anal fin and begins anterior to it. It is helpful in identifying this species to know that the base of the anal fin is shorter than the greatest depth of the body. The pelvic fins are small and their tips just reach the base of the dorsal fin. The color of the body is bluish above and silvery on the lower sides and belly. It will reach at least 15 inches in length.

The distribution of this species includes the tropical and sub-tropical waters of the Pacific Ocean and possibly adjoining areas.

THE PACIFIC HALF-BEAK FISH
Also known as I-he i-he and Me-'e me-'e
62—3 *Hyporhamphus pacificus* (Steindachner), 1900

Drawn from Jordan and Everman

The Pacific half-beak has an elongated, cigar-shaped body which is laterally compressed. The head is flattened above, compressed on the sides, and has a narrow, lower surface. This species is best identified by the dorsal and anal fins which are about opposite and nearly equal. The anal fin has more rays than the dorsal fin and its base is longer than the height of the body. The ventral fins are small, the caudal peduncle is compressed, and the lower lobe of the caudal fin is larger than the upper lobe. The pelvic fins are small and do not reach the origin of the dorsal fin. The color of the body is greenish blue above and the sides are marked by a horizontal, dark line and by a silvery band which extends from the pectoral region to the tail. It will reach a length of at least ten inches.

The distribution of this species extends from the Hawaiian Islands southward to equatorial waters and possibly elsewhere in the tropical Pacific area.

Some scholars have concluded from recent studies that this species should be considered a subspecies of *H. acutus* and therefore known as *Hyporhamphus acutus pacificus* (Steindachner), 1900. The other subspecies is known as *H. acutus acutus* (Gunther), 1871, and occupies an area extending from Wake Island southeastward as far as Easter Island.

THE FLYING FISH FAMILY
63 *Family Exocoetidae (Oxyporhamphidae)*
Flying fishes have cylindrical, oblong bodies with a flattened lower surface. The pectoral fins of most species are unusually large, are placed high upon the body, and in a few species reach to the tail. The pelvic or ventral fins are located on the abdomen and are also enlarged in some species. The dorsal fin and the anal fin are usually about opposite in

position and usually of about equal size. The caudal fin is deeply forked and the lower lobe is much larger than the upper lobe. None of the fins have spines and there are no dorsal finlets behind the dorsal fin. The lateral line extends low along the side of the body as in the half-beaks and needle fishes. The jaws of flying fishes are quite normal and are not extended as in the half-beaks and the needle fishes. Most flying fishes are less than a foot in length; a few of the larger species will measure 18 or 20 inches in length when mature.

The home of most flying fishes is the open ocean in all tropical seas, although a few do seem associated with shore lines. Here they inhabit the surface water feeding upon both animal and plant foods. They have many enemies including dolphins, porpoises, the dolphin fish, and various tuna fishes. The eggs are attached to floating seaweeds. The young individuals of this family are often quite different from the adults; they have large, flap-like whiskers attached to the lower jaw which disappear as the fish matures.

Of about 45 or 50 species, at least ten are known from this area.

The following species is not discussed or illustrated:

Fodiator rostratus (Gunther), 1866. This species is known from a single specimen from Hawaii measuring about six and one-half inches. It is in the British Museum. It was named for its unusually long snout.

JENKIN'S FLYING FISH
63—1 *Cypselurus atrisignis* Jenkins, 1903

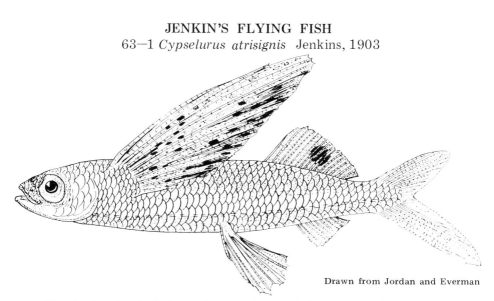

Drawn from Jordan and Everman

The body of this flying fish is slender and elongated; it is broad dorsally and narrow ventrally. The pectoral fins are long and reach to the tip of the last ray of the dorsal fin. They are also marked by two groups of scattered dark spots in the pectoral membrane. The pelvic fins are quite large and reach to about the middle of the anal fin. A significant, black spot on the dorsal fin together with the scattered small spots on the pectoral fin will help to identify this species. Specimens will reach a length of at least 14 inches.

The distribution of this fish includes the Hawaiian area, Micronesia, and doubtless adjoining areas in the tropical Pacific Ocean.

THE SHORT-NOSED FLYING FISH
63—2 *Cypselurus simus* (Cuvier and Valenciennes), 1846

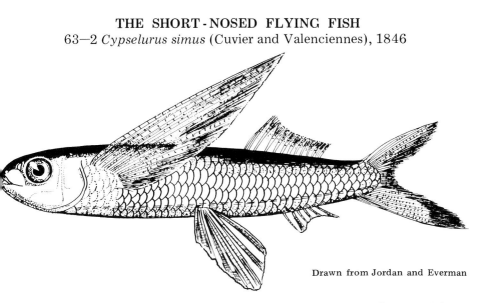

Drawn from Jordan and Everman

The body of this species is elongated, compressed, and flattened from side to side. The snout is short, rounded, and blunt. The eyes are large. The pectoral fins are very long, reach nearly to the base of the caudal fin, and are covered with many, small, black spots. The pelvic fins are quite large and reach nearly to the posterior base of the anal fin. The caudal peduncle is deep vertically and much compressed laterally. The color of the body is reddish purple above and white below. Specimens will reach about 14 inches in length. This is a common species in Hawaii.

The distribution of this fish includes the Hawaiian area and the warm, tropical waters to the south and west.

CUVIER'S FLYING FISH
63—3 *Cypselurus speculiger* (Cuvier and Valenciennes), 1846
The body of this flying fish is similar to others in this family. The

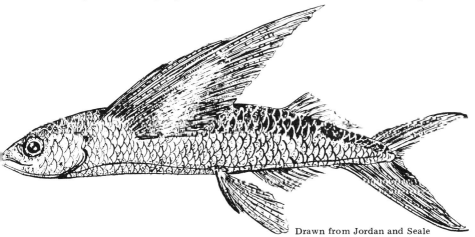

Drawn from Jordan and Seale

149

pectoral fins are long and reach beyond the middle of the base of the dorsal fin; they contain between 17 and 19 rays of which the second and subsequent rays are branched. The pelvic fins are long and reach beyond the origin of the anal fin. This species exhibits a wedge-shaped, light colored area on the pectoral fins. Specimens are known to reach at least 15 inches in length.

It is an uncommon species and is known to occur off Hawaii and in the Tasman Sea off Australia.

BLEEKER'S FLYING FISH
63—4 *Cypselurus spilonotopterus* (Bleeker), 1866

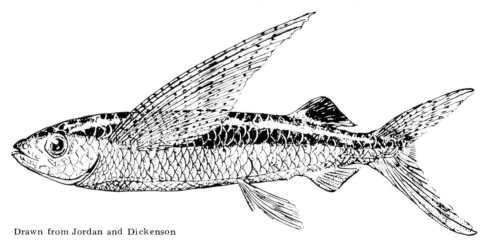

Drawn from Jordan and Dickenson

The body of this species is elongated, laterally compressed, and flattened and bears a head which is rather long for this group. The pectoral fins are very long and reach beyond the middle of the base of the dorsal fin. The pelvic fins are likewise long and reach beyond the origin of the anal fin. In color, the pectoral fins have been described as reddish brown in life and as uniformly dark. There is a significant dark blotch on the dorsal fin. Specimens will reach more than 18 inches in length. It appears to be a rather common species.

The distribution of this fish extends from Hawaii southward to central Polynesia, westward to the East Indies, and doubtless to adjoining areas.

THE SPOTTED - WING FLYING FISH
63—5 *Cypselurus spilopterus* (Cuvier and Valenciennes), 1846

This flying fish has long pectoral and pelvic fins and in most particulars resembles *C. atrisignis.* Both have small dark spots on the pectoral fins, but *C. spilopterus* lacks the round dark spot found on the dorsal fin of *C. atrisignis.* It is apparently uncommon in Hawaii and only a few specimens are known.

The distribution of this fish extends from the Hawaiian area southward to central Polynesia, westward into Micronesia, and possibly surrounding areas.

LINNE'S FLYING FISH
63—6 *Exocoetus volitans* Linnaeus, 1758

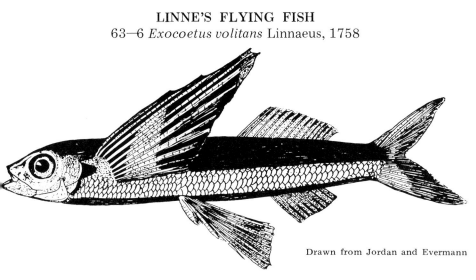

Drawn from Jordan and Evermann

The body of this flying fish is elongated and has compressed and flattened sides. The pectoral fins are very long and extend to the base of the caudal fin; the second and third pectoral rays are the longest and the second ray is divided. The anal fin is very small and is located quite far forward on the belly. The color of the upper surface is dark bluish; the lower surface is silvery. It will reach a length of at least ten inches.

The distribution of this fish includes the tropical and sub-tropical waters of the world.

The drawing by Jordan and Evermann was made from a specimen which measured six inches in length.

THE SMALL-WINGED FLYING FISH
Also known as the Ma-lo-lo
63—7 *Oxyporhamphus micropterus* (Cuvier and Valenciennes), 1846

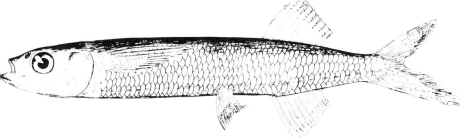

Drawn from Jordan and Evermann

This flying fish is typical of the family and has an elongated, compressed body and a rather elongated, pointed head. It is most easily recognized by its short pectoral fins and by its small size which is usually eight inches or less.

This species occurs in the tropical and sub-tropical Atlantic and Pacific Oceans.

THE SHORT-WINGED FLYING FISH
Also known as Ma-lo-lo, Pu-ki ki-'i, Pu-hi ki-'i (young),
'O-lo-la, and Le-le po
63—8 *Parexocoetus brachypterus* (Richardson), 1846

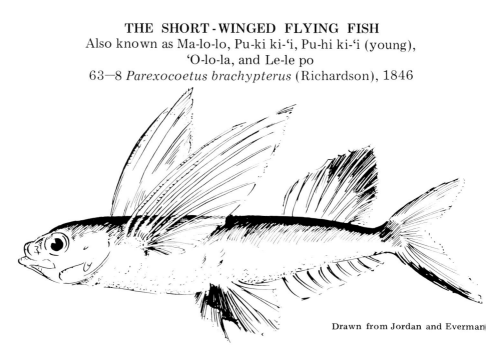

Drawn from Jordan and Everman

The body of this flying fish is elongated, spindle-shaped, and laterally compressed; the head is also elongated, compressed, and pointed. The pectoral fins are relatively short and the dorsal fin is long in its posterior half and marked by a black area at its tip. The color of the body is blue above and silvery white beneath. It reaches a length of six, seven, or eight inches. This is one of the more abundant species in this area.

The distribution of this fish includes most warm seas.

GILBERT'S FLYING FISH
63—9 *Prognichthys gilberti* (Snyder), 1904
The body of this flying fish is elongated as in the members of this family, but is rather square in cross section. The pectoral fins are distinct in having 17 or 18 rays; the second of these rays is unbranched and shorter than the succeeding rays. The color of the body is steel blue above and silvery below. It will reach a length of 12 inches.

The distribution of this species includes the Hawaiian Islands and probably adjacent areas.

This species is known from a very few specimens. It is named for Dr. Charles Henry Gilbert, Professor of Zoology at Leland Stanford Junior University, ichthyologist, and student of Hawaiian fishes.

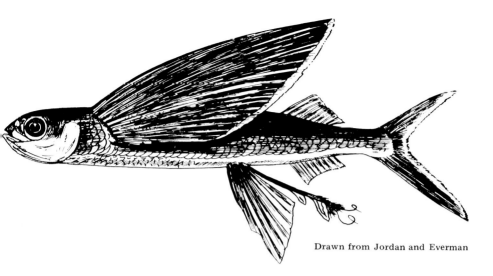

Drawn from Jordan and Everman

THE TRUMPET FISH FAMILY

64 *Family Aulostomidae*

Trumpet fishes are a very small family of long, band-shaped fishes. They have a long head with a tubular snout which extends forward to end in a small mouth with a barbel attached to the tip of the lower jaw. They have a spinous dorsal fin along the middle of the back. The soft dorsal and anal fins are about equal and opposite and are placed far to the back of the trunk. The caudal fin is rhomboid in shape and lacks the long filament found in the cornet fishes. The pectoral fins are rounded and the pelvic fins are located about midway on the trunk.

Members of this family inhabit the tropical shore line waters of the Indo-Pacific area and both sides of the Atlantic Ocean.

This family includes about four species, of which at least one is known from the Hawaiian area.

THE CHINESE TRUMPET FISH
Also known as Nu-nu or Nu-hu
64—1 *Aulostoma chinensis* (Linnaeus), 1766

Trumpet fishes are easily identified because of their unusual appearance. This species varies in color and may be either brownish, greenish, or orange. Some are longitudinally striped, some show evidence of wide vertical bands, and some will exhibit two rows of vertical spots at the end of the trunk. The tail usually contains two dark spots. It will reach a length of at least two feet.

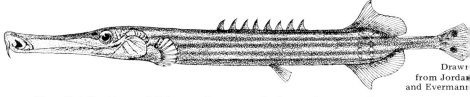

Drawn
from Jordan
and Evermann

The distribution of this species extends from the Hawaii area southward and westward across the entire, tropical, western Pacific and Indian Oceans to the coast of Africa.

THE CORNET FISH FAMILY
Also known as the Flute Mouth Fishes
65 *Family Fistulariidae*

The cornet fishes have very long, slender, flat bodies and a long, tube like snout ending in a pair of small jaws. The pectoral and pelvic fins are small, the spinous dorsal fin is absent, and the soft dorsal fin and the anal fin are about equal in size and opposite in position. The tail bears a slender filament from its center by which members of this family may be identified. The color of their bodies is either red, pink, brown, or green. One species approaches six feet in length.

Cornet fishes are carnivorous species which inhabit the coastal waters of warm, tropical seas.

This family contains about five species of which two are known from this area.

The following species is not discussed or illustrated:

Fistularia villosa Klunzinger, 1871. This is the red cornet fish, a large species which approaches six feet in length. It inhabits waters to depths of at least 500 feet

LACEPEDE'S CORNET FISH
Also known as Nu-nu Pe-ke
65—1 *Fistularia petimba* Lacepede, 1803

This cornet fish is easily recognized by its long body, long snout, and the long filament extending from the tail. The body is greenish above and lighter below. It reaches about four feet in length. It is a surface dwelling species.

The distribution of this cornet fish extends from Hawaii southward into central Polynesia and westward across the entire tropical Pacific and Indian Oceans to the coast of Africa.

THE SNIPE FISH FAMILY

66 *Family Macrorhamphosidae*

The snipe fishes have short, deep, compressed bodies which are partly covered along the sides of the back with two series of bony plates. The snout is long and contains a pair of toothless jaws at the end. The dorsal fin possesses a long, serrated spine in this family. The lateral line is absent. Most snipe fishes are small in size and even the largest species are about ten inches or less.

They are a marine family which inhabits tropical and temperate seas from moderate depths into deep water.

Of about a dozen known species, at least one is known from this area.

THE SLENDER SNIPE FISH
66—1 *Macrorhamphosus gracilis* Lowe, 1839

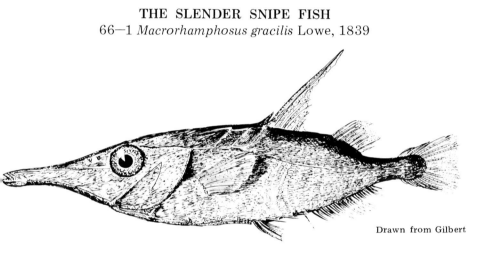

Drawn from Gilbert

The slender snipe fish is a small species in which the color of the body is a dark slate on the back and top of the head and silvery over the remainder of the body. It will reach a length of about six inches although Hawaiian specimens have measured a bit less.

The steamer *Albatross* captured the first two Hawaiian specimens in 1902 off Laysan Island at depths beyond 350 feet.

The distribution of this species extends from California and Hawaii southward and westward across the tropical Pacific and Indian Oceans to the coast of Africa.

In some books this species may appear under the name of *M. hawaiiensis* Gilbert, 1905.

THE SHRIMP FISH FAMILY

67 *Family Centriscidae*

Shrimp fishes are among the most unusual of fishes. Their body is compressed and knife-like in shape and is covered with thin horny or bony plates which render it immobile. The snout is long and tubular and contains a small pair of toothless jaws at the end. The position of the fins is very unusual in this family; the spine of the first dorsal fin is at the posterior end of the body and the remainder of the dorsal fin and the caudal fin are along the ventral side.

The members of this family occur from Hawaii southward and westward across the tropical, western Pacific and Indian Oceans to the coast of Africa; they do not occur in the Atlantic Ocean.

Of four known species, at least one is known from this area.

THE STRIPED SHRIMP FISH
67—1 *Centriscus strigatus* (Gunther), 1861

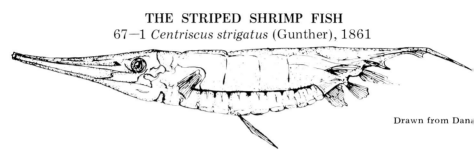

Drawn from Dana

A black stripe, which extends along the side of the body from the head to the tail, and a yellowish brown body will distinguish this species from other shrimp fishes. Specimens will reach a length of at least five or six inches.

These fishes live in shore line water, often in small schools, and are associated at times with sea urchins.

The distribution of this species extends from Hawaii southward and westward through Micronesia and Melanesia, through the East Indies, and across the Indian Ocean to the Persian Gulf.

THE PIPE FISH AND SEA HORSE FAMILY
68 *Family Syngnathidae (Hippocampidae, Siphostomidae)*

The pipe fishes and sea horses have slender, elongated bodies and long tails either with or without a caudal fin. A single dorsal fin is present, the pectoral fins are either small or absent, and the anal fin is very small. Pipe fishes range in length from one to over 20 inches; sea horses measure between one and one-half and eight inches in length.

The male fishes in this family carry the incubating eggs either in a brood pouch on the belly or variously attached to the surface of the belly or tail. All sea horses are marine and live in shallower waters of the shore line. Most pipe fishes are marine, but some are found in fresh water and some live in intermediate brackish areas. Both sea horses and pipe fishes are often found in beds of seaweed or in floating patches of *Sargassum* and other species.

Of about 24 kinds of sea horses, at least two are known from this area.
The following species are not described or illustrated:
Hippocampus histrix Kaup, 1856. This widely distributed Indo-Pacific sea horse is recorded from Hawaii on the basis of one poorly preserved specimen from Maui in the Agassiz Museum.

Dunckerocampus baldwini Herald and Randall, 1972. This Hawaiian species of pipe fish was described from twenty specimens ranging in length from two and one-half to five inches. The body is reddish with a long, red stripe along the body; the tail is also reddish and has white edges. It occurs at depths between 20 and 160 feet. Persons wishing to study this and related species should consult the article by Herald and Randall in *California Academy of Science Proceedings*, Fourth Series, 39 (11), 1972, pp. 121-140.

Micrognathus brachyrhinus Herald, 1953. This species of pipe fish is based upon two specimens. The first Hawaiian specimen was captured by the steamer *Albatross* in 1902 in a plankton net off Oahu at a depth in excess of 400 feet. It was immature and measured about one and one-fourth inches in length. The Philippine specimen was captured by the Steamer *Albatross* in 1908 at Ticao Island. It was also a juvenile and measured less than one inch in length.

BLEEKER'S SEA HORSE
68—1 *Hippocampus kuda* Bleeker, 1852

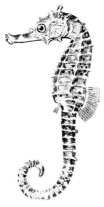

This species, often called the spotted sea horse, has spine above its eye and tubercles or blunt knobs on the body at the intersections of the ridges between the various plates which cover the body. The color in life seems to vary from dark to light and includes blackish, brown, orange, golden, and reddish colors. Black spots are scattered over the head and body. This sea horse is reported to reach 12 inches in length, although most Hawaiian specimens have been less than one-third that length.

It inhabits the shore line in marine and brackish areas.

Drawn from Jordan and Evermann

The distribution of this fish extends from Hawaii southward and westward across the tropical western Pacific and Indian Oceans to the coast of Africa.

THE BLACK-SIDED PIPE FISH
68—2 *Doryrhamphus melanopleura* (Bleeker), 1958

From Jordan and Evermann

The body of this species is much longer than the tail, but the feature most readily observed and most useful in its identification will be a large, fan-shaped, caudal fin. The body is gray or brown in color and is marked with a long, dark, lateral band along the side which extends from the snout to the tail. It is a small species and will measure at least two and one-half inches in length.

The distribution of this fish extends from the coast of Mexico and Columbia across the entire tropical Pacific and Indian Oceans.

THE RED PIPE FISH
68—3 *Ichthyocampus erythraeus* Gilbert, 1905

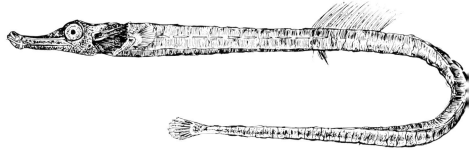

Drawn from Gilbert

Dr. Charles Henry Gilbert described this species from a single specimen taken by the steamer *Albatross* in 1902 off the coast of Molokai. It had a short snout, was brick red in color, and measured about two and one-fourth inches in length. It has since been found in Japanese waters.

EDMONDSON'S PIPE FISH
68—4 *Micrognathus edmondsoni* (Pietschmann), 1938

Drawn from Pietschmann

Edmondson's pipe fish is an elongated species which will reach a length of at least seven inches. It inhabits the shallow waters of the shore line and has been captured in tide pools. At present it is known only from the Hawaiian area.

It is named for Dr. Charles Howard Edmondson (October 14, 1876 — August 29, 1970), long time Zoologist at the Bernice Pauahi Bishop Museum, Professor of Zoology at the University of Hawaii, and Director of the Cooke Marine Laboratory in Honolulu.

BALL'S PIPE FISH
68—5 *Syngnathus balli* (Fowler), 1925

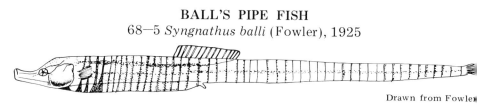

Drawn from Fowler

Ball's pipe fish is a small shore line species which reaches about four inches in length. At present it is known only from Hawaii. It is named in honor of Stanley C. Ball.

THE MOON FISH OR OPAH FISH FAMILY
69 *Family Lampridae*

This family contains a single species called the opah or moon fish. It
s a fish of large size with a compressed, ovate body, a forked caudal fin,
minute scales and no teeth

THE MOON FISH OR OPAH
Also known as the Mariposa, Jerusalem Haddock, and Kingfish
69—1 *Lampris regius* (Bonnaterre), 1788

The body of this fish is large, short, and deep and the sides are strongly
compressed. The skeleton is strong and there are no teeth in the mouth.
The color of the body is silvery blue-gray above, rose red below, vermillion
on the jaws and fins, and golden around the eyes. The entire body is covered
with round, silvery spots. It will reach a length of about six feet and a
weight of about 600 pounds.

The habits of this fish are not well known. It is an oceanic species
which lives at or near the surface where it swims slowly feeding upon squids,
various crustacea, and other animals of the surface waters.

This is an edible fish. The flesh is firm, rich, of a reddish shade somewhat like the tunnies, and unsurpassed as food; it has been described as rich,
firm, delicate, and oily.

The distribution of the moon fish includes all temperate and tropical
seas. It is nowhere common.

THE FAN FISH FAMILY
70 *Family Veliferidae*

The veil-fin fishes are a very small family of one genus and about a half dozen species. They are flat, deep bodied fishes with long, high dorsal and anal fins and with pectoral fins containing less than 13 rays. The anus and the ventral fins are placed quite far forward on the ventral surface.

They appear to live in moderately deep water which borders land. They occur in both the Pacific and Indian Oceans.

THE MANY-SPINED VEIL-FIN FISH
70—1 *Velifer multispinosus* J. L. B. Smith, 1951

The body of this veil-fin fish is deep and flat and measures about eight inches in length. The dorsal and anal fins are very long and contain about 22 and 18 spines respectively. The body is silvery gray in color and exhibits a light, barred pattern on the tail.

The distribution of this species extends from Hawaii and Japan to Madagascar.

THE OAR FISH FAMILY
71 *Family Regalecidae*
This family contains a single species known as the oar fish. It is one of the most unusual curiosities of the marine world and evokes great interest wherever it occurs. It is separated from related families of fishes by the presence of the pelvic fins and by their development into single, long filaments with a small, paddle-like enlargement at their ends.

THE GIANT OAR FISH
71—1 *Regalecus glesne* (Ascanius), 1788

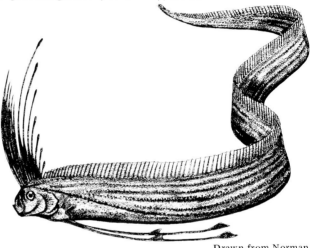

The giant oar fish has a very long, slender, ribbon-like body. The dorsal fin begins on the head with some longer elements, which can be erected to form a crest, and thereafter continues unbroken to the tail. The ventral fins are placed far forward on the body and consist of two long, slender filaments with paddle-like enlargements at their tips. The caudal fin is absent and the

Drawn from Norman

lateral line is low on the side of the body. The head is short and the snout is short and truncated. The cleft of the mouth is vertical and the upper jaw is protractile. The stomach is reported to resemble a long sack and to extend to the tail. The color of living specimens appears to be a silvery gray with a vermillion colored crest and fins. It is reported to reach lengths in excess of 25 feet.

The distribution of the oar fish is world-wide in temperate and tropical seas.

THE RIBBON FISH FAMILY
72 *Family Trachypteridae (Radiicephalidae)*
The ribbon fishes are a group of bizarre species in which the body is greatly elongated, compressed, and generally ribbon-shaped. The head, which is short, is followed by a dorsal fin which extends the entire length of the body. The lower profile is nearly straight, while the upper profile descends uniformly to the tail which is turned rather abruptly upward and bears a small caudal fin which lies above the horizontal axis of the body. The pelvic or ventral fins are either small or absent, in some species they grow for a time and thereafter atrophy. There is no anal fin. In general, these fishes are very fragile and weak-bodied.

The habitat of ribbon fishes seems to be in the deeper waters where their fragile bodies do not have to withstand the forces of waves and currents. They are occasionally seen swimming slowly in shallow water or found dead upon the beach. They are sometimes caught in nets and plankton tows or regurgitated by larger fishes.

The distribution of this family appears to be world-wide in deep water.

This is a small family of less than a dozen species. Several members have been reported from this area.

The following species are not described or illustrated:

> *Trachypterus woodi* Smith, 1953. Persons wishing to read about this species should consult *Pacific Science* 10(1), 1956, pp. 22-23 and a short account in J. L. B. Smith - *The Sea Fishes of Southern Africa*, 1953, Appendix, p. 504. Both references have small illustrations.

> *Desmodema polystictum* (Ogilby). A good account of this ribbon fish may be found in the *Deep-water Teleostean Fishes of California* by John E. Fitch and Robert J. Lavenberg which was issued in 1968 by the University of California Press at Berkeley.

THE IRIS RIBBON FISH
72—1 *Trachypterus iris* (Walbaum), 1792

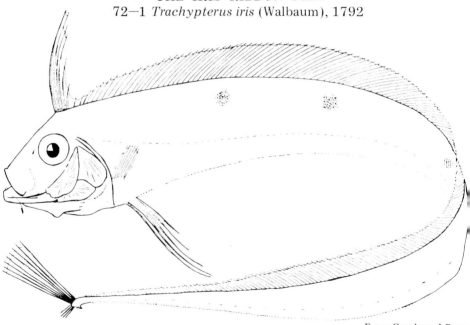

From Goode and Bean

The body of this ribbon fish is long, slender, compressed, and ribbon-like. The lower margin of the body is nearly straight, while the upper margin is likewise straight but descends slowly toward the tail. The first rays of the dorsal fin are longer than those following and form a crest. The head has a steep profile and bears a protractile mouth. The caudal fin is very small in size, lies above the horizontal axis of the body, and is divided into two unequal parts; the upper part is the larger and projects upward, while the lower part is much smaller in size and is directed downward. The color of the body is a silvery white; it is marked with a few, large, round, black spots.

t will reach a length of at least five feet.

The habitat of this ribbon fish is in deep water to depths of at least hree miles.

The distribution of this species is believed to be world-wide.

THE CREST FISH OR BAND FISH FAMILY
73 *Family Lophotidae*

The crest fishes and band fishes are a very small group of elongated, :ompressed, ribbon-like fishes which inhabit the deeper waters of the sea. They have a head which is elevated in front to form a high, triangular crest which bears a long, strong spine. The dorsal fin is very long and extends from the crest of the head backward to the tail. The ventral fins are absent, he caudal fin is small, and the anal fin is small and located at the end of the ower surface. The snout is short, the eyes are large, and the body is without scales.

The members of this family are world-wide in tropical and temperate seas. A few species are known from this area.

The following species are not described or illustrated:

Lophotus cristatus Johnson, 1963. This crest fish is silvery colored with crimson fins. It is an uncommon species which will exceed three or four feet in length. It is world-wide in distribution.

Eumecichthys fiski (Gunther, 1890) Regan. The body of this crest fish is compressed and of nearly uniform depth from head to tail. The body is silvery in color and is marked with about 30 irregular bars. It will exceed 4 feet in length. Specimens are known from both the Atlantic and Pacific Oceans. Interested persons should consult *Pacific Science* 10(1), 1956, pp. 20-22.

SCHLEGEL'S LOPHOTID FISH
73—1 *Lophotes capellei* Schlegel, 1845

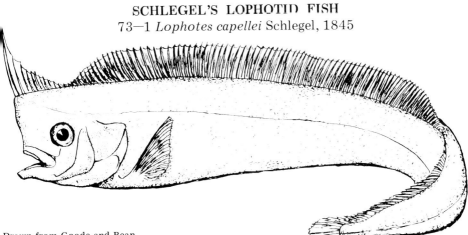

Drawn from Goode and Bean

The body of this fish is ribbon-like and bears a head with a crest on the top of which stands a long, strong spine. The dorsal fin extends the full length of the body, the ventral fins are absent, and the caudal and anal fins are small. The color of the body is blackish blue upon the head, pale blue upon the upper surfaces, and shades to white below. The fins are blood red in color and the eye is silvery white with bluish hues.

This is an edible species and the flesh is good.

The distribution is believed to be world-wide in the surface waters o tropical and temperate seas.

THE MELAMPHAID OR BIG-SCALE FISH FAMILY
74 *Family Melamphaidae*

The melamphaid fishes are a small family of deep water species. They have large, rough, thick, bony heads with small teeth. There is but a single dorsal fin and the caudal fin has a spine at the base of its upper and lower margins.

This family includes about three dozen species of which a few are known from this area.

THE ONE-HORNED MELAMPHAID FISH
74—1 *Melamphaes unicornis* Gilbert, 1905

Drawn from Gilbert

The body of this fish is small and bears a very large, rough, bony head on which is placed a slender, horn-like spine. The color of the head is black and the body is possibly a bit lighter in color. It is a very small fish and reaches a length of at least one and one-fourth inches.

The species was first known from two specimens captured by the steamer *Albatross* in 1902 in a dredge off Kauai at depths between one-half mile and one mile.

THE YAWNING OR LISTLESS MELAMPHAID FISH
74—2 *Poromitra oscitans* Eberling, 1975

This fish is a small species with a large head and a stout body which leads into a long, slender caudal peduncle. The body is covered with large scales. The head is rough and ridged and bears a single, small, median spine forward of the eyes. The mouth is large and the eyes are small. It will reach a length of three inches.

The habitat of this fish is in the bathypelagic zone below about 5,000 feet, although young specimens seem to prefer shallower water.

The distribution of this species extends across the warmer temperate and tropical areas of the Pacific and Indian Oceans from the east coast of

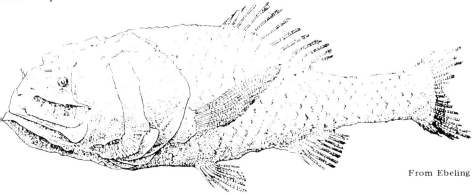

From Ebeling

Africa eastward to the western coasts of California, Mexico, Central America, and South America.

Members of this genus may be identified by reference to *Copeia* 1975 (2), pp. 306-315.

THE BARBUDO OR BEARD FISH FAMILY
75 *Family Polymixiidae*

The barbudos are a small family of moderate sized fishes which may be recognized by the single dorsal fin, the two barbels hanging from the chin, the small scales, and the black spot at the forward tip of the dorsal fin. They occur in all tropical seas at depths from possibly 500 to 1,000 feet.

At least one species is known from this area.

BERNDT'S BARBUDO FISH
75-1 *Polymixia berndti* Gilbert, 1905

Berndt's barbudo has a rather robust body which is covered with small scales. The dorsal fin is single and contains a dark spot at the forward tip; the caudal fin is deeply forked. The head bears a pair of large eyes and a pair of rather long barbels beneath the chin. The color of the body is blue-green above with a shining, metallic iridescence; this color becomes lighter on the belly. The snout is somewhat blue-green in color. The specimen in the photograph measured nine inches in length; it will reach at least twice that length.

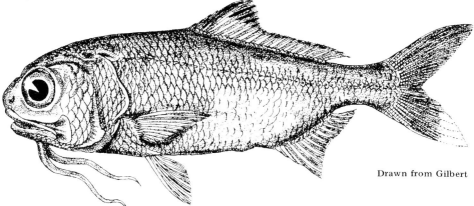

Drawn from Gilbert

The distribution of this species includes the Hawaiian area, Japan, and the tropical Indo-Pacific area as far west as the coast of Africa.

In some books this species has been treated as a synonym of *P. japonicus* Gunther, 1877.

The name of this fish honors the memory of Mr. E. Louis Berndt, who was the inspector of the Honolulu fish market at the time of the investigations by the U. S. Fish Commission in 1901-1902.

THE ALFONSINOS FISH FAMILY
76 *Family Berycidae*
The alfonsinos resemble the squirrel fishes in form and color. They have a short, compressed body with an elongated caudal peduncle and a forked caudal fin. In this family the dorsal fin contains four spines and there is no notch between the spinous part of the fin and the soft posterior part. The dorsal fin is always shorter than the anal fin and the ventral fins have between six or seven and 13 soft rays. The color of these fishes is usually red or black.

Members of this family live in the deeper waters of all seas.

One species is known from this area.

CUVIER'S BERYCID FISH
76—1 *Beryx decadactylus* Cuvier and Valenciennes, 1829
The body of this fish is deep and strongly compressed. The caudal peduncle is quite long and the tail is large and deeply forked. The color of

Photograph of a mounted specimen.

the body is a uniform, bright, rose red. Individuals will reach a length of at least 24 inches.

The distribution of this species includes Hawaii, Japan, and doubtless the adjoining areas.

THE SLIME-HEAD FISH FAMILY
77 Family Trachichthyidae

In this small family, the body is deep and strongly compressed and bears a large, compressed head which is deeper than long. The suborbital bones below the eyes are very wide and cover the cheeks. All of the surface bones of the head are thin and are crossed by bony ridges which border, separate, and define the mucous cavities on the head. The preopercle bone of the head has flat spines, while the opercle has radiating ridges, but no spines. The mouth is wide and obliquely placed, the gill openings are wide, and there are no barbels upon the chin. The body is covered with ctenoid scales of small or moderate size and the lateral line is present. The abdomen bears dermal scutes ventrally which form a ridge or a serrated ventral margin. The dorsal fin bears from four to eight spines and from 12 to 15 soft rays. The anal fin bears three spines and from eight to eleven rays; the pelvic or ventral fins bear one spine and six or seven soft rays; the anal fin has three spines and from 8 to 11 rays. The caudal fin is forked and bears spines on its upper and lower margins. Most of the fishes within this family are of a reddish color.

The distribution of this small family includes the deep waters of the Atlantic, Pacific, and Indian Oceans.

At least two species of this family are known from this area. An unidentified specimen of *Paratrachichthys* has been seen in deep water in the Hawaiian area.

167

THE MEDITERRANEAN SLIME-HEAD FISH
77-1 *Hoplostethus mediterraneus* Cuvier and Valenciennes, 1829

From Goode and Bean

The body of this slime-head fish is quite deep and compressed. The head is large, compressed, deeper than long, and bears large eyes and a large mouth which is oblique in position. There are 15 slender gill rakers. The dorsal fin bears six spines and between 12 and 15 soft rays; the anal fin has three spines and from 9 to 11 rays; the ventral fins have but a single spine and six soft rays. The enlarged scutes along the belly vary from 11 to 13. Specimens will measure at least a foot in length. The color of the body is a silvery rose hue in life. It is of a darker reddish hue on the upper half of the body and lighter below and on the anal fin; the other fins are somewhat scarlet in color. The inside of the mouth and the peritoneum are black in color.

The habitat of this species is in deep water from about 500 feet down to at least 3,000 feet.

The distribution of this fish is world-wide in all oceans.

THE FANG-TOOTH FISH FAMILY
78 *Family Anoplogasteridae (Caulolepidae)*

The fang-tooth fishes are a family of deep water fishes with deep bodies and large bony heads which are covered with bony ridges. Like the berycid fishes, there is but a single dorsal fin on the body. The front of the mouth contains long, slender, fang-like teeth. The body is black in color to match their deep-water habitat.

The family occurs in the deep waters of the Atlantic and Pacific Oceans.

At least one species is known from the Hawaiian area.

THE HORNED FANG-TOOTH FISH
78—1 *Anoplogaster cornuta* (Cuvier and Valenciennes), 1839

This fang-tooth fish is a small species with a very deep body and a large

168

head which is marked by bony ridges. The teeth in the front of the mouth are long and slender. It is uniformly black in color and, when fully grown, will reach a length of about six inches. Young individuals have a few long spines on the head and it is from these spines that the fish was given the name of *cornuta* which means "horn".

The habitat of this fish is in deep water to depths of over a mile. The steamer *Albatross* captured a single specimen in 1902 off Hawaii at a depth in excess of 7,000 feet.

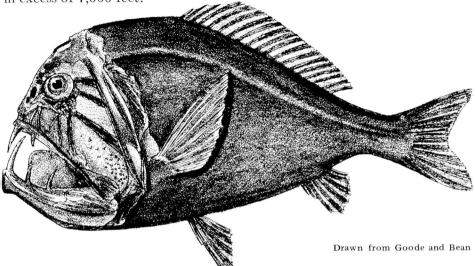

Drawn from Goode and Bean

The distribution of this species includes the Atlantic Ocean, the eastern Pacific Ocean, the Hawaiian area, and doubtless adjoining areas.

In many books this species will be listed under the name of *Caulolepis longidens* Gill, 1884.

THE SQUIRREL FISH FAMILY

Also known as Soldier Fishes, Welshmen, Soldados, and Matajuelos

79 *Family Holocentridae*

The squirrel fishes are a family of small to moderate sized fishes which have large eyes and are covered over the head and body with spines and rough, prickly scales. The dorsal fins have 11 or 12 spines; the pelvic fins have one spine and seven soft rays and are located quite far forward on the body; the anal fin has four spines of which the third spine is usually the largest and strongest. A lateral line is present and there are no barbels on the chin. Most species are brightly colored, usually red and yellow, and are often marked with lighter, longitudinal lines and stripes.

Squirrel fishes are distributed throughout the tropical seas of the world where they live near rocks and ledges. They are nocturnal in their habits and some live in schools. The young, which are found drifting in the plankton, have sharp, pointed snouts and do not resemble the adults. They are a good food fish and are usually caught on hook and line.

The Hawaiian people had two names for these fishes. The pure red

169

forms *(Myripristis)* were called 'U-'u and the striped species *(Adioryx)* were known as 'A-la-'i-hi.

About 70 species are known in this family; of these, about 20 species are known from this area.

The following species are not described or illustrated:

Adioryx caudimaculatus (Ruppell), 1835. This species is identified by a white spot or area on top of the caudal peduncle. It is found from Hawaii and Tahiti westward to the Red Sea. It is listed in most books under the name of *Holocentrus caudimaculatus* Ruppell, 1835.

Adioryx tieroides (Bleeker), 1853. This species, found in most books under the name of *Holocentrus tieroides* Bleeker, 1853, has 11 dorsal spines, ten distinct, light, horizontal lines, and pale fins without patterns. It measures about eight inches in length. It occurs in Hawaii, the Marshall Islands, the Philippine Islands, Tahiti, and central Polynesia.

Myripristis sealei Jenkins, 1903. This species, described from Hawaiian materials, is believed to represent an error. It should be disregarded.

THE BLOOD-SPOT SQUIRREL FISH
79—1 *Flammeo sammara* (Forskal), 1775

This species is most easily identified by the large, dark spot on the dorsal fin. The body is a silvery white or reddish color and the head and opercle are a darker reddish brown. There are black spots beneath the eye and about nine of ten lengthwise rows of black spots along the side of the body. Most specimens are about six inches or less, but some authors report this species to reach a length of 12 inches.

The distribution of this species extends from Hawaii southward into Polynesia and westward across the entire tropical Pacific and Indian Oceans to the coast of Africa.

Some books may list this species under the name of *Holocentrus sammara* (Forskal), 1775.

JORDAN'S SQUIRREL FISH
Also known as 'A-la-'i-hi and 'A-'a-la-'i-hi (young)
79—2 *Flammeo scythrops* Jordan and Evermann, 1903

This squirrel fish is a medium-sized species which may be recognized by the long anal spine which is longer than any of the succeeding anal rays. The lower jaw is quite prominent and extends well in front of the upper jaw. The body is longitudinally striped with orange and yellow. It is a beautiful species which will reach a length of about ten inches. It was first described from Honolulu.

Some books may list this species under the name of *Holocentrus scythrops* (Jordan and Evermann), 1903.

THE CROWNED SQUIRREL FISH
79—3 *Adioryx diadema* (Lacepede), 1802

The body of this fish may range in color from a deep red to a light orange-red and is marked on the sides with about nine, narrow, longitudinal, white stripes. There is a diagonal white stripe under the eye from the snout to the base of a large preopercular spine. The throat is white and the breast becomes darker posteriorly. The dorsal fin is a very dark red or black in color and is marked with distinctive, white bands on the membranes between the spines. The front band begins low and extends diagonally upward across about five membranes, followed by a completely black membrance between the sixth and seventh spine; the posterior band is narrower and extends along the outer margin of the membranes. Another distinctive mark is a dark red membrane on the anal fin between the large third spine and the fourth spine. Specimens are usually about six inches long, although they have been reported to reach about nine inches.

The habitat of this fish is the coral reef on the outside of the breakers; it is one of the more numerous squirrel fishes.

The distribution of this species extends from Hawaii southward into Polynesia and westward across the entire tropical Pacific and Indian Oceans to the coast of Africa and the Red Sea.

This species appears in older books under the name of *Holocentrus diadema* Lacepede, 1802.

HAWAIIAN SQUIRREL FISH
79—4 *Adioryx ensifer* (Jordan and Evermann), 1903

The body of this holocentrid is reddish in color and is marked by longitudinal, yellow bands. The most distinctive feature of this fish is a single, large spine on the opercle at the level of the eye and just behind it. It is a

beautiful species and will reach a length of about nine inches. In Hawaii it is less common than the smaller species.

Older publications will list this species under the name of *Holocentrus ensifer* Jordan and Evermann, 1903.

THE WHITE-SPOTTED SQUIRREL FISH
Also known as 'A-la-'i-hi and 'A-'a-la-'i-hi (Young)
79—5 *Adioryx lacteoguttatus* (Cuvier and Valenciennes), 1829

The body of this species is rosy red in color above with a brownish tinge on the back and silvery white beneath. It is also speckled over the body with brown or black pigment. The dorsal fin is useful in identifying this fish. The outer border of the fin is a brick red color, the base of the fin is reddish, and the central area of the fin is marked by a series of white spots. The iris of the eye is bright yellow in life. There are two spines on the edge of the opercle just posterior to the eye. It reaches about five inches in length.

This species inhabits the shore line waters and is often captured in the shallow water on the inside of the reef.

The distribution of this species extends from Hawaii southward into Polynesia and westward across the entire tropical Pacific and Indian Oceans to the coast of Africa and the Red Sea.

Older publications will list this species under the name of *Holocentrus lacteoguttatus* Cuvier, 1829.

THE SMALL MOUTH SQUIRREL FISH
79—6 *Adioryx microstomus* (Gunther), 1859

In life this fish has a brick red head and body. It has a white belly and is marked on the sides by six or seven white or pale yellow, longitudinal lines. The head is marked by a white, vertical bar behind the eye along the margin of the preopercle. The dorsal fin is distinctive in having membranes with white edges and a series of dark spots extending the length of the spinous dorsal fin, but diminishing in size posteriorly. The first three anal spines are white in color; the fourth anal spine and the first and second soft anal rays are red in color; the remainder of the anal fin is either yellowish or pale. Specimens reach a length of five or six inches.

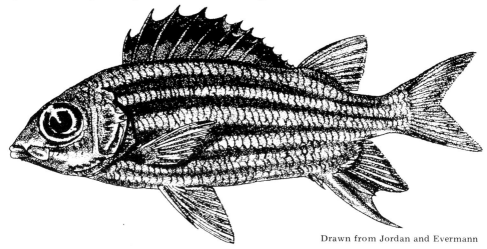

Drawn from Jordan and Evermann

The distribution of this species includes Hawaii and the tropical areas of the Pacific Ocean to the south and west.

In older books this species will be listed under the name of *Holocentrus microstomus* Gunther, 1859.

THE SPINE-BEARING SQUIRREL FISH
Also known as 'U-'u ka-ne po-u
79—7 *Adioryx spinifer* (Forskal), 1775
The body of this fish is deep and compressed and terminates quite

abruptly in a rather slender caudal peduncle. The color of the body varies from deep red to light red with silvery colors. There are one or more spots behind the eye. The spinous dorsal fin is a bright vermillion color, while the remaining fins are yellowish with red shadings. Most specimens approach a foot in length, but they will occasionally reach as much as two feet.

The distribution of this fish extends from Hawaii southward into Polynesia and westward across the tropical Pacific and Indian Oceans to the coast of Africa and the Red Sea.

Older publications will list this species under the name of *Holocentrus spinifer* Forskal, 1775.

THE TAHITIAN SQUIRREL FISH
79—8 *Adioryx tiere* Cuvier and Valenciennes, 1829

The large spine at the base of the preopercle, the two unequal spines behind the eye at the edge of the opercle, and the six and one-half rows of scales between the lateral line and the midline of the belly should help to identify this species. In addition, there is a row of distinctive light spots on the membrane of the spinous dorsal fin. The color of the body varies from a deep blood red to light red with silvery hues. Usually, it is deep red in life and lighter when dead. In life, the body is marked upon its sides by eight or nine, longitudinal, iridescent, blue lines. Of these, the two lines on the belly seem the most conspicuous. Specimens will reach a length of nine or ten inches.

The distribution of this species includes the tropical central and western Pacific Ocean.

Older publications will list this species under the name of *Holocentrus tiere* Cuvier and Valenciennes, 1829.

THE YELLOW-RED SQUIRREL FISH
79—9 *Adioryx xantherythrus* (Jordan and Evermann), 1903

The body of this holocentrid is bright red on the sides and is marked with about ten, longitudinal, white lines. The belly is silvery white. On the head, a diagonal white line extends below the eye from the snout to the base of the preopercular spine. The spinous dorsal fin is uniformly, deep red in color and contains two distinctive marks which are useful in identifying this species. First, there is a small spot on the membrane just behind the base of the first spine; second, the membranes behind the third or fourth spine have a small, white area just behind the tip of the spine. Specimens are usually between five and six inches in length, but are reported to reach as much as seven inches.

This is probably the most abundant holocentrid in Hawaii.

At present, its known distribution does not extend beyond the Hawaiian area.

In older books this species may be listed under the name of *Holocentrus xantherythrus* Jordan and Evermann, 1903.

THE LARGE-SCALED SQUIRREL FISH
79—10 *Ostichthys oligolepis* (Whitley), 1941

The body of this species is more oblong than other squirrel fishes and narrows rather abruptly posteriorly where it continues as a slender caudal peduncle. The head and the mouth are both large and there is an unusual groove on the skull down the front of the head between the eyes. It is light red in color and is unmistakably marked along the sides of the body by about ten, longitudinal rows of white spots. It will reach a length of five or six inches.

This is a very beautiful species which lives in the deeper waters on the outer side of the reef.

Hawaiian specimens have long been listed under the name of *O. japonicus* (Cuvier), 1829. However, *O. japonicus* is a species from the western Pacific which will reach a length of at least 12 inches; the Hawaiian fish is a smaller species.

THE ROUGH-SCALED SQUIRREL FISH

79—11 *Holotrachys lima* (Cuvier and Valenciennes), 1831

The body of this species is oblong in shape and narrows abruptly at the rear to continue as a slender caudal peduncle. The mouth is large and the

eyes, which are a bit smaller than most squirrel fishes, are set high upon the head and are directed upward. The body is a solid, reddish color which becomes lighter below. Specimens are reported to reach a length of about seven inches; most are smaller.

The distribution of this species extends from Hawaii southward into central Polynesia and westward across the entire tropical western Pacific and Indian Oceans to the island of Mauritius.

Recent books may list this species under the name of *Plectrypops lima* (Cuvier and Valenciennes), 1831.

CASTELNAU'S SQUIRREL FISH
Also known as 'U-'u
79—12* *Myripristis amaenus* (Castelnau), 1873

This 'u-'u resembles *M. murdjan* and is difficult to distinguish from it. The body is bright pink or red and has faint, silvery hues on the sides, belly, and cheeks. The eyes are white with a copper-colored iris and a purple bar extending upward from the pupil. The membranes of the spinous dorsal fin are red on their outer borders and pink at their bases. In life, the caudal fin is a deep, blood-red color on the outer rays. This fish is reported to reach a length of 14 inches, but most specimens are about one-half this length.

It is a common species on the outside of the reef.

This species is known from the western and central Pacific area.

BERNDT'S SQUIRREL FISH
Also known as 'U-'u
79—13* *Myripristis berndti* Jordan and Evermann, 1903

Berndt's squirrel fish is uniformly red in color like the other species of *Myripristis*, but it is possible to identify some specimens by the white

* See Appendix.

borders on the fins. In this species there is a narrow white edge on the anterior border of the soft dorsal fin and on the anterior ray of the anal fin; the caudal fin is narrowly bordered by white on its upper and lower margin. This fish is reported to reach a length of 14 inches; most specimens are much smaller.

The distribution of this species extends from East Africa eastward across the entire tropical Indian and Pacific Oceans to the Galapagos Islands.

THE GOLDEN - FINNED SQUIRREL FISH
Also known as 'U-'u
79—14 *Myripristis chryseres* Jordan and Evermann, 1903
The squirrel fishes of the Genus *Myripristis* are hard to identify. This

species, however, is a bit more slender than most and may be distinguished by its color. The body and the pectoral fins are red, but the remaining fins are golden in color and are variously edged or bordered with red. In addition, there is a black bar on the body just behind the edge of the opercle; this bar continues downward into the axil of the pectoral fin where it becomes a red spot. Specimens are reported to reach a length of ten inches; most are smaller. This species was described from Hawaii.

CUVIER'S SQUIRREL FISH
79—15* *Myripristis kuntee* Cuvier and Valenciennes, 1831

The body of this species is uniformly red in color and lighter below. It may sometimes be identified by the markings of the fins. The first ray of the dorsal fin is white; the spines of the anal fin are white; and the spine and its membrane in the pelvic fin are likewise white. This is a small species which may reach seven inches.

The distribution of this fish extends from Hawaii westward and southward through the warm waters of the western Pacific and Indian Oceans.

Some books may list this species under the name of *Myripristis borbonicus* Cuvier and Valenciennes, 1831.

THE JOHN DORY FISH FAMILY
80 Family Zeidae

The bodies of these fishes are short, deep, and compressed and bear a series of unusual, bony plates along the belly. The mouth is large and extensible, the pectoral fins are usually small, short, and rounded and the scales of the body may be either small or absent.

These are oceanic fishes which seem to live at moderate depths.

* See Appendix.

Of less than twenty species, at least two occur in this area.

GILBERT'S ZEID FISH
80—1 *Stethopristes eos* Gilbert, 1905

The body of this zeid fish is small, deep, and compressed, and bears a large head with large eyes. The pectoral fins are small in contrast to the much larger pelvic fins. It measures at least five inches in length and is a silvery color with lighter rose hues.

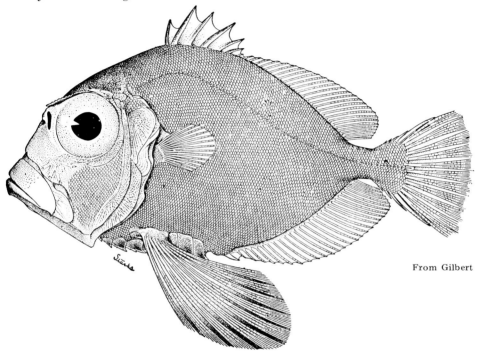

From Gilbert

This species was first known from a few specimens caught in a dredge by the steamer *Albatross* in 1902 between Maui and Molokai at depths between about 1,300 and 2,000 feet.

The distribution of this species includes the Hawaiian Island area and doubtless surrounding areas.

THE NEBULOUS ZEID FISH
80—2 *Zenopsis nebulosus* (Schlegel), 1847

This zeid fish is a very unusual species. The body is rather high, short, and compressed, and bears a large head with an extensible mouth. One of its most unusual features is a series of bony plates extending along the dorsal and anal fins. Each of these plates is armed with a projecting hook. The dorsal fin has nine spines and 27 rays, while the anal fin has three spines and 26 rays. Most specimens measure between 24 and 30 inches in length. The color of the body is silvery gray.

The distribution of this fish includes Hawaii, Japan, and undoubtedly a large area in the western Pacific Ocean.

THE GRAMMICOLEPID FISH FAMILY
81 *Family Grammicolepidae*
The members of this family have a high, compressed body with a small head and a small mouth. The most unusual features of this small family is the type of scales which cover the body; they are vertically elongated, vertically striated, and paper-like in quality.

The family at present contains only two species, one of which occurs in this area.

POEY'S GRAMMICOLEPID FISH
81—1 *Grammicolepis brachiusculus* Poey, 1873
The body of this species is oval in shape, high, and compressed. The head and mouth are both small. The scales which cover the body are paper-like in quality and are vertically elongated and vertically striated.

The first specimen known from Hawaii measured over 13 inches in length, was a uniform, slaty gray in color, and was obtained off the island of Hawaii at the time of the 1919 eruption of Mauna Loa.

This species was first discovered near Cuba and may therefore be widely distributed in deeper water. At present, it is known from only these two areas.

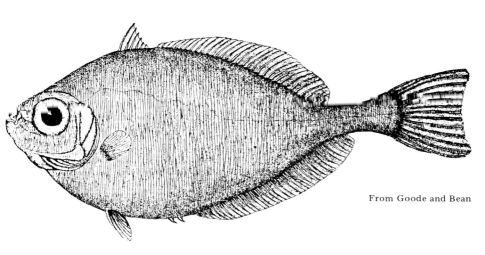

From Goode and Bean

THE CAPROID FISH FAMILY

82 *Family Caproidae*

Members of this small family are sometimes included with the family *Zeidae*. They lack the abdominal plates of the zeid fishes and for this and other reasons may appear in some books as a distinct family.

In some recent books the members of the Family *Antigoniidae*, the boar fishes, are included within the *Caproidae*. Here they are listed separately in the next family under *Antigoniidae*.

At least one species of the *Caproidae* is known from this area.

GILBERT'S CAPROID FISH

82—1 *Cyttomimus stelgis* Gilbert, 1905

This small fish has a deep, compressed, diamond-shaped body with a

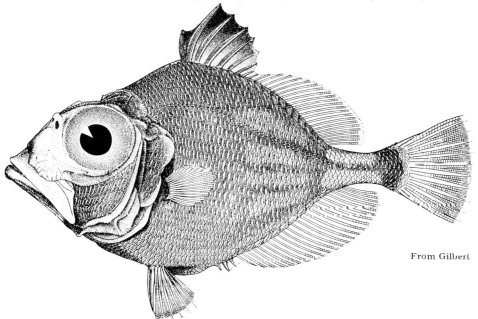

From Gilbert

large head and large eyes. The pectoral fins are small and the scales which cover the body are likewise small. The color is a grayish silvery hue. It will reach at least three and one-half inches in length.

This species is known from a single specimen which was obtained in a dredge by the steamer *Albatross* in 1902 off Barbers Point, Oahu, at a depth between about 1,100 and 2,100 feet. At this time it is known only from Oahu.

THE BOAR FISH FAMILY
83 *Family Antigoniidae*

The bodies of these fishes are very deep and diamond-shaped, extremely flattened, and possess three distinct spines just forward of the soft rays of the anal fin. The color of their bodies is bright red.

The name of boar fish is also applied to the *Histiopteridae (Pentacerotidae)*.

In some recent books the members of this family will be found within the family *Caproidae*.

At least two members of this family occur in this area.

GILBERT'S ANTIGONIID FISH
83—1 *Antigonia eos* Gilbert, 1905

Like the following species, this fish has a diamond - shaped body which is very flat. The dorsal fin has nine spines and, although deeply notched, is continuous between its anterior and posterior parts. The anal spines and the anal rays are likewise joined by a narrow membrane. The color of the body is light reddish above and silvery below; the iris and the membranes of the pelvic fins are yellow. It will reach a length of at least three and one-half inches.

In some areas it is quite abundant at depths between 300 and 700 feet.

The distribution of this species includes the Hawaiian Islands and doubtless adjoining areas.

STEINDACHNER'S ANTIGONIID FISH
83—2 *Antigonia steindachneri* Jordan and Evermann, 1903

The body of this species is diamond-shaped and very flat. There are eight dorsal spines in the dorsal fin and these are separated from the soft dorsal rays which follow. There are three spines in front of the anal fin which are likewise separated from the anal rays. The color of the body is pink or reddish, the iris is light red or orange in color, and the membranes of the pelvic fin are black. Specimens will measure at least seven inches in length.

The distribution of this species includes the Hawaiian Islands and probably surrounding areas in the tropical, western Pacific Ocean.

Jordan and Evermann named this

Drawn from
Jordan and Evermann

species for Dr. Franz Steindachner, a native of Germany, who studied the fishes of the tropical, western Pacific area during the latter part of the 19th century.

THE BARRACUDA FISH FAMILY
84 *Family Sphyraenidae*

The barracuda fishes have long, spindle-shaped bodies, a long head with long jaws, and large, sharp teeth. The dorsal fin is helpful in identifying these fishes. The spinous dorsal fin has five spines and is widely separated from the soft dorsal fin which has but one spine and about nine rays. The large teeth, however, make this an unmistakable family.

Barracudas are carnivorous and voracious in their habits and live upon all manner of fishes; they eat sardines, anchovies, silversides, mackerel, and their own young. They are brave and formidable and seem to fear nothing in the ocean. When they are young they travel in schools, but as they grow larger, they become more solitary in their habits.

They are edible fishes and are eaten wherever they occur.

Most species live in the shore line areas of the tropics, some live far from shore, and some occur in warmer, temperate areas.

About 21 species are known; of these at least two are known from this area.

The following species is not described or illustrated:

Sphyraena forsteri Cuvier and Valenciennes, 1829. This species is widely distributed from Hawaii and the Marshall Island southward to central Polynesia and westward through the East Indies to India.

THE GREAT BARRACUDA
Also known as Ka-ku or Ku-pa-la
84—1 *Sphyraena barracuda* (Walbaum), 1792

All barracudas look much alike for they all possess long, spindle-shaped bodies with long heads and jaws which are equipped with large, sharp teeth. The color of the body is an olive-brown hue above and changes gradually to silvery on the sides and belly. It may be marked upon the sides with darker vertical bars or large spots. This species may be separated from *S. helleri* by its relatively thicker head, its smaller eye, its larger scales, its pectoral fin tips reaching beyond the base of the pelvic fins, and about 85 scales in the lateral line as opposed to about 135 in *S. helleri*. Large specimens will reach a length of six feet and there are reports of this species reaching as much as eight feet in length.

The young fish frequent the shore lines, but larger individuals move seaward as they mature.

The distribution of this species is probably world-wide in warm water except for the eastern Pacific Ocean. It occurs from Hawaii westward to the Red Sea and in the western, tropical Atlantic Ocean.

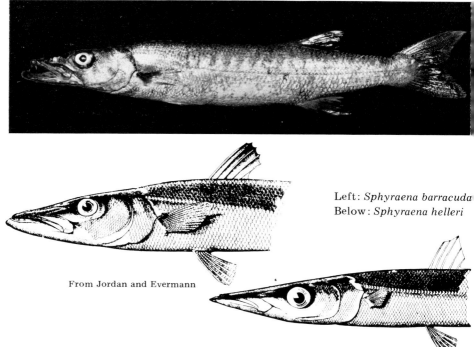

Left: *Sphyraena barracuda*
Below: *Sphyraena helleri*

From Jordan and Evermann

HELLER'S BARRACUDA
Also known as Ka-we-le-'a
84—2 *Sphyraena helleri* Jenkins, 1901

Heller's barracuda has a more slender head and a relatively larger eye than *S. barracuda*. It is a silvery olive color above and gradually becomes silvery on the sides and belly. In life, the sides are marked by two, longitudinal yellowish or golden stripes. It will reach a length of about 24 inches or less.

The distribution of this fish extends from Hawaii westward to the Marshall Islands and doubtless other adjoining areas.

This species was named for Mr. Edmund Heller, a student of the fishes of the Galapagos Islands.

THE MULLET FISH FAMILY
85 *Family Mugilidae*

Mullet fishes are spindled-shaped and have a head which is bluntly rounded in front. Their teeth are either minute or absent and when present are set in the lips rather than in the jaws. They lack a lateral line and the body is covered with large scales. In many ways they resemble the silversides (*Atherinidae*), but lack the broad stripe found on the sides of these fishes. Most members of this group are silvery, silvery gray, or bluish silvery in color and measure between about 12 and 24 inches in length.

Mullet live in tropical and temperate seas where they inhabit the shore line waters; a few species invade brackish and fresh waters, and a few species live entirely in fresh water.

Of more than 100 known species, at least five are known from this area. The following species are not described or illustrated:

Chelon engeli (Bleeker), 1858-59. Engel's mullet is a small species which measures about six inches in length. It was introduced into Hawaii in the decade following World War II. It now occurs from Hawaii and the Marshall Islands southward to central Polynesia and westward through the East Indies.

Chelon vaigiensis (Quoy and Gaimard), 1825. This mullet may be recognized by its black pectoral fins. It is very widely distributed. It occurs from Hawaii and the Marshall Islands southward to Australia and westward to China, through the East Indies, and across the Indian Ocean to the coast of Africa and the Red Sea.

Crenimugil crenilabis (Forskal), 1775. This mullet may be recognized according to Dr. Leonard Schultz by "the papillae on the outer surface of the upper lip and the folded edge of the lower lip, features that make it unlike any other species of *Mugilidae* yet found." It occurs from Hawaii and the Marshall Islands southward to central Polynesia, westward to Japan, through the East Indies, and across the Indian Ocean to the Red Sea.

THE STRIPED MULLET
Also known as the 'A-ma-'a-ma
85—1 *Mugil cephalus* Linnaeus, 1758

The common, striped mullet has a spindle-shaped body and a head

which is rounded in front. The eyes are covered in front and behind by transparent, adipose eyelids. The body is a shining, silvery color, either greenish or brownish above, and changing to white on the belly. It normally measures 18 or 20 inches in length when full grown, but it has been reported to reach as much as three feet in length.

This species seems to prefer shore line areas which are slightly brackish. For this reason it is common in bays, river mouths, and estuaries. It is also the species most commonly reared in fish ponds. Mullet are bottom feeders and cruise along over the bottom feeding upon all manner of organic detritus. The young of these fishes are found drifting in the plankton during the spring months.

Mullet was one of the most important food fishes in old Hawaii and, as a consequence, had many names. Mrs. Pukui lists the following names and the growth stage for each name: Pu-a 'a-ma, Pu-a 'a-ma 'a-ma, Pu-a po-'o-la and 'O-'o-la were of finger length; Ka-ha-la was of hand length; 'A-ma 'a-ma measured about eight inches; and 'A-na-e were mullet larger than 12 inches.

The distribution of this species is world-wide in warm, tropical seas.

CHAPTALL'S MULLET
Also known as the U-o-u-o-a
85—2 *Neomyxus chaptalli* (Eydoux and Souleyet), 1841
This mullet resembles other members of this family in most particulars.

Drawn from Jordan and Evermann

188

It can be distinguished from *M. cephalus* because it lacks the transparent, adipose eyelid on the front and back sides of the eye and by the presence of a bright, yellow spot located on the dorsal edge of the base of the pectoral fin. The color of the body is a plain, gray color dorsally, silvery on the sides, and white ventrally. It will reach a length of about 18 or 20 inches.

This is an abundant fish and is common along sandy shores and in tide pools.

The distribution of this species extends from Hawaii westward through the Marshall and Marianas Islands and doubtless elsewhere in the tropical western Pacific area.

Recent studies indicate that this species should be called *Neomyxus leuciscus* (Gunther), 1871.

THE SILVER-SIDE FISH FAMILY
86 *Family Atherinidae (Melanotaenidae)*

Silver-sides are small, elongated, translucent, green-hued fishes with no lateral line and with two, widely-separated, dorsal fins. They get their name from a wide, prominent, longitudinal, silvery band along the side of the body. They are sometimes called white-bait and are occasionally erroneously called smelt, but they should never be confused with the true osmerid smelts from which they differ by having two dorsal fins, while the osmerid smelt have a single dorsal fin and a small adipose fin far to the rear.

These fishes live in schools, often in great numbers, along the shore lines of tropical and warmer, temperate seas. Some are strictly marine, some live in brackish waters, and a few live in rivers and lakes. Their eggs possess a sticky filament by which they are attached to plants until they hatch.

About 150 species are included in this family; of these at least two are known from this area.

THE ISLAND SILVER-SIDE FISH
Also known as 'I-a-o
86—1 *Pranesus insularum* (Jordan and Evermann), 1903

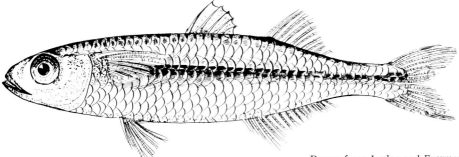

Drawn from Jordan and Everman

This is a small fish with an oblong, compressed body. The two dorsal fins are widely separated and the pectoral fins are placed high on the sides of the body. The color of the body is rather olive-green above and the edges of

189

the scales are darker. The stripe along the side of the body is steel blue above and fades away to silvery on the belly. In length, the 'iao measures between one and one-half and three and one-half or four inches. This is a schooling fish which frequents the shore line areas.

THE SMALL SILVER-SIDE FISH
86—2 *Iso hawaiiensis* Gosline, 1952

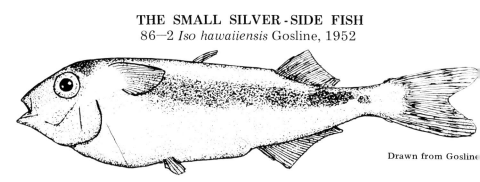

Drawn from Gosline

This little silver-side may be recognized by the position of the pectoral fins, which, together with the lateral band, are placed very high upon the side of the body. In addition, there are no teeth and the ventral margin of the belly is angular and sharp. The body is a brilliant silvery color in life. The lateral band ends midway on the caudal peduncle and is followed by a small spot of the same color.

The distribution of this fish includes the Hawaiian area.

THE THREAD-FIN FISH FAMILY
87 *Family Polynemidae*
The thread-fin fishes are a small group with fairly robust, compressed bodies, with two widely separated dorsal fins, and with a lateral line and a forked tail. The snout is somewhat translucent and overhangs the mouth, while the eyes possess adipose eyelids similar to some of the mullets. They are most easily recognized by their pectoral fins; the lower rays of these fins are separated from the rest of the fin and are developed into long, slender filaments. These filaments are usually held against the belly but are often extended forward in a curved, fan-like position to trail over the bottom.

Thread-fins are marine, shore line fishes which occur in the tropical Atlantic Ocean and in the tropical Indo-Pacific area.

Less than 40 species are known; of these, at least one occurs in this area.

THE PACIFIC THREAD-FIN FISH
Also known as Mo-i and Mo-i li-'i
87—1 *Polydactylus sexfilis* (Cuvier and Valenciennes), 1831
The body of this thread-fin in quite deep and compressed like other members of this family. Because the pectoral fins in this species have six

filaments, the Latin name of *sexfilis* is derived from this anatomical feature. The color of the body is a dull silvery above and shades gradually to white on the belly. The pectoral fins are black and the anal fin has a dark, dusky margin. It will reach a length of nearly three feet.

In old Hawaii the small moi of two or three inches in length were known as mo-i li-'i. Intermediate sizes of about five inches were known as pa-la mo-i on Kauai and as ma-na mo-i on Hawaii.

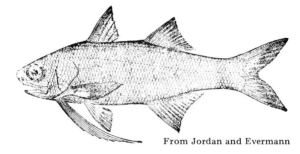

From Jordan and Evermann

The distribution of this species extends from Hawaii southward and westward across the Indian Ocean to Mauritius.

THE GROUPER FISH FAMILY
88* *Family Serranidae*

The groupers are a large family of fishes, usually with robust bodies, a large mouth, small teeth, and a projecting lower jaw. The dorsal fin is usually single, although it may be deeply notched; the pelvic fins possess one spine and five soft rays; the anal fin contains three spines. They range in color from dull to bright and some possess the ability to change colors to a limited degree. Their size likewise varies greatly; there are species which measure a couple of inches in length and some which weigh more than 1,000 pounds.

They are a family of carnivorous, marine fishes of both active and sedentary habits. Most of them are edible and may be captured with hook and line.

The family is widely distributed throughout the tropical and warmer temperate seas of the world and a few do ascend the rivers of these regions. There are no species, however, in polar seas.

The groupers include about 400 species of which at least 25 occur in this area.

* See Appendix.

The following species are not described or illustrated:

Gracila albomarginata (Fowler and Bean), 1930. A description of this fish may be found in *Pacific Science* 18(3), 1964, p. 282. It is of moderate size and extends from Central Polynesia to East Africa. It is found in most books under the name of *Cephalopholis albomarginatus* Fowler and Bean, 1930.

THE LAYSAN ISLAND GROUPER
88—1 *Grammatonotus laysanus* Gilbert, 1905

This species is light purplish red above and silvery below. It is known from a single specimen about an inch and one-half long which was obtained from a dredge between about 600 and 1,200 feet off Laysan Island by the steamer *Albatross* in 1902.

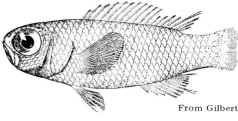

From Gilbert

SCHLEGEL'S GROUPER
88—2 *Caprodon schlegeli* Gunther, 1859

Schlegel's grouper is a medium sized fish with a fleshy, robust body. The pectoral fins are long, the tail is large, and the dorsal and anal fins are low and heavily scaled. The color of the body is crimson and yellow. There are two yellow stripes in front of the eyes and another yellow stripe running from the eyes to the pectoral fins. It will reach about 17 or 18 inches in length. It is caught at depths of about 500 feet.

The distribution of this fish includes Hawaii, Japan, and doubtless many intervening areas.

THE STRIPED GROUPER
88—3 *Epinephelus fasciatus* (Forskal), 1775

This South Sea grouper may be recognized by a black ring around its eye, by a black margin on the dorsal fin, and by the absence of spots or marks of any type upon the soft dorsal fin, the caudal fin, and the pectoral fins.

From Katayama

An introduction of this fish into the Hawaiian Islands was made by the State of Hawaii in 1958. In that year, 51 fishes from the Marquesas Islands were liberated on June 27th off Brown's Camp, Oahu; this site is just south of Kahe Point on the southwestern shore of Oahu.

The distribution of this species extends from central Polynesia westward through Micronesia to Japan and China, through the East Indies, and across the Indian Ocean to the coast of Africa.

THE BROWN-SPOTTED GROUPER
88—4 *Epinephelus fuscoguttatus* (Forskal), 1775

The body of this grouper is marked over the back at the base of the dorsal fin by about five, darker, saddle-shaped areas. There is also a black

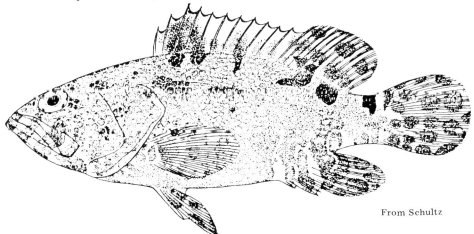

From Schultz

saddle on the caudal peduncle. The body and fins are covered with closely set, round spots. The fins are darker toward their outer edges.

This is a large species which was brought from Palmyra Island to Hawai in the 1950's. See *Pacific Science* 18 (3), 1964, p. 289.

The distribution of this species extends from central Polynesia west ward through the East Indies to the coast of Africa.

THE SPOTTED GROUPER
88—5 *Epinephelus hexagonatus* (Bloch and Schneider), 1801

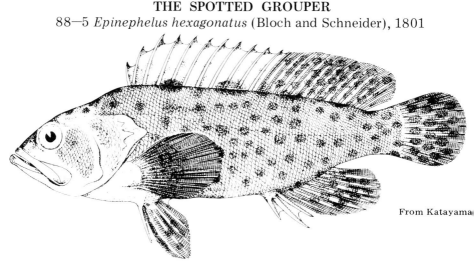

From Katayama

This species resembles *E. spilotoceps;* however, the notes given under that species should be helpful in separating them. In addition, this species is often confused with *E. merra* and is often listed as a synonym of it. The background color of the body is a creamy white. The upper part of the body is marked by three or four dark blotches along the base of the dorsal fin and by a black saddle over the caudal peduncle. The pattern of the body is composed of grayish or brownish hexagonal spots which have smaller, white, triangular spots at their corners.

The State of Hawaii introduced 113 of these fishes into Hawaii on October 11, 1956; they were brought from Moorea in the Society Islands and liberated off La Perouse Bay on Maui. In December 1961, another school of 865 fishes from Moorea was released in Maunalua Bay on Oahu.

BLOCH'S GROUPER
88—6 *Epinephelus merra* Bloch, 1793

The ground color of this species is white and its body is not as heavily pigmented as most other species. The body is covered with spots of various shapes; however, there are no large blotches along the base of the dorsal fin and there is no black saddle on the caudal peduncle. Small, round, black dots cover the soft dorsal, caudal, anal, and pectoral fins.

The State of Hawaii introduced this fish into the Hawaiian area in 1956. Specimens, which were procured from Moorea in the Society Islands,

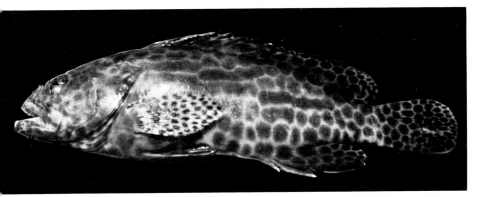

were liberated as follows: on October 10, 1956, a school of 469 was released off Moku O Loe in Kaneohe Bay, Oahu; on October 17, 1956, a school of 132 was released off Wainini on Kauai; and in December, 1961, a school of 1033 fishes were released in Maunalua Bay on Oahu.

SEALE'S GROUPER
Also known as Ha-pu-'u and Ha-pu-'u-pu-'u (young)
88—7 *Epinephelus quernus* Seale, 1901

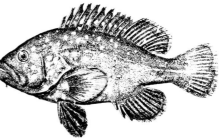

This grouper is typical of the family and has a robust, deep body which is somewhat compressed. The body is dark, purplish brown in color and is covered over the sides with small, light, pearly white spots. This fish is an edible species which will reach about three feet in length. It is usually caught by hook and line at depths below 300 feet.

Drawn from Jordan and Evermann

The distribution of this grouper seems to be limited to the Hawaiian area.

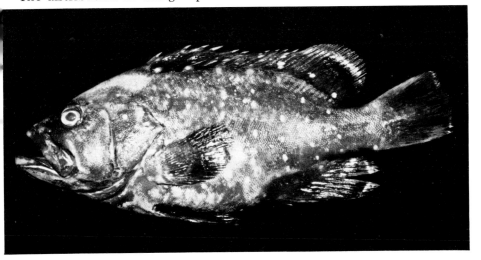

THE SPOTTED-HEAD GROUPER
88—8 *Epinephelus spilotoceps* Schultz, 1953
This grouper resembles *E. hexagonatus* but may be distinguished from
it according to Dr. Leonard Schultz by "the small black spots dorsally on the

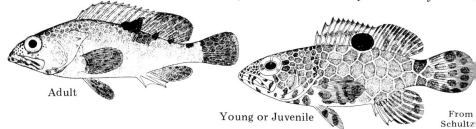

Adult

Young or Juvenile

From Schultz

front part of the head" and by "the presence of the two to four intensely
black dorsal blotches". The background color of the body is creamy white;
upon this background are placed brown to gray hexagonal spots which are
bordered or defined by white lines. These hexagonal spots extend onto the
fins and belly, but in these areas they tend to become more rounded in
outline.

The specimens from which this species was originally described came
from the Marshall Islands. The figure with the very dark oval spot is a young
specimen.

GUNTHER'S GROUPER
88—9 *Epinephelus spiniger* (Gunther), 1859
The coloration of this grouper helps to identify it. The spinous dorsal
fin has a black edge and the soft dorsal fin, the anal fin, and the caudal fin
are all marked with a narrow, white edge.

The State of Hawaii introduced a few specimens of this fish into the
Hawaiian area. A school of 22 fishes, which was captured in the Marquesas
Islands, was released on June 27, 1958, off Brown's Camp, a small locality
just south of Kahe Point on the southwest shore of Oahu.

196

THE GIANT GROUPER
88—10 *Epinephelus tauvina* (Forskal), 1775

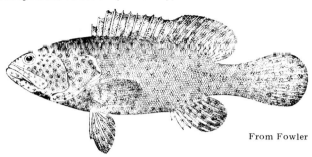

From Fowler

This is a very large grouper which is difficult to distinguish. The body is olive-green to brownish in color and, in addition, bears about six, blackish, saddle-shaped blotches extending along the back as far as the caudal peduncle. The entire body is covered with orange-red or brown spots and the fins are without lighter borders. The bands and the spots diminish with age and tend to disappear in large specimens. It may reach seven feet in length.

The distribution of this fish extends from Hawaii southward and westward across the tropical Pacific and Indian Oceans to the coast of Africa and the Red Sea.

THE ARGUS GROUPER
88—11 *Cephalopholis argus* Bloch and Schneider, 1801

The body of this grouper is described as a "dark brownish or purplish black" and covered over the entire surface with small, bright, blue spots. In some specimens and at some times the body is marked with five, six, or seven wide, vertical bands, particularly toward the posterior end of the body. The body is darker anteriorly and lighter posteriorly. In life, the caudal fin has a yellow margin which becomes white after death; in addition, the soft dorsal, anal, and pectoral fins are likewise edged with yellow in life.

The State of Hawaii introduced this fish from Moorea in the Society Islands into the Hawaiian area. They released 171 fishes at Brown's Camp near Kahe Point on Oahu on October 10, 1956, and about 400 fishes at Keahole Point on the island of Hawaii on October 11, 1956. In December,

1961, a total of 1,814 fishes from Moorea were released in Maunalua Bay on Oahu.

This species was named for the ancient god Argus, who had a hundred shining eyes of which only two slept at any one time.

In the Society Islands this fish is known as "roi".

THE STRIPED-TAIL GROUPER
88—12 *Cephalopholis urodelis* (Bloch and Schneider), 1801

The background color of this fish is light to dark brown and is darker posteriorly. There is a distinct, black blotch on the upper part of the operculum just behind the eye. The head, body, and fins are often speckled with orange spots which turn white after death. The most significant and reliable marking of this species is a pair of diagonal stripes across the tail.

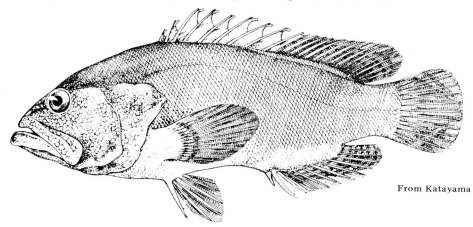

From Katayama

The State of Hawaii on June 27, 1958, liberated eight fishes from the Marquesas Islands off Brown's Camp south of Kahe Point on Oahu. Later, in December, 1961, the State released 1,803 fishes from Moorea in the Society Islands into Maunalua Bay on Oahu.

The distribution of this species extends from central Polynesia westward through the East Indies and across the Indian Ocean to the coast of Africa.

In the Society Islands this fish is known by the name of "tahiatatai".

THE RED GROUPER
Also known as 'U-'u
88—13 *Pikea aurora* Jordan and Evermann, 1903

The body of this fish, including the head, is more slender than that of most other groupers. It is most easily identified by its astonishing colors. The color of the body is rosy red above and paler beneath. There is a yellow stripe through the eye, a horizontal, yellow stripe through the dorsal and anal fins, and a single, horizontal, yellow stripe at both the top and bottom of the tail. It will reach a length of about eight inches.

The distribution of this species includes the Hawaiian area and doubtless other nearby areas in the tropical western Pacific Ocean.

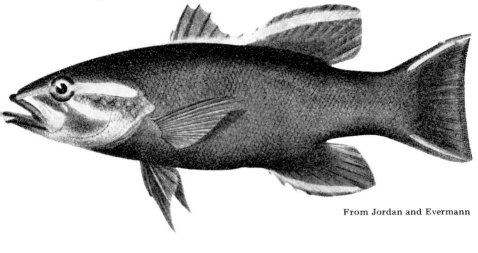

From Jordan and Evermann

THE SPOTTED GROUPER
88—14 *Pikea maculata* Doderlein and Steindachner, 1883

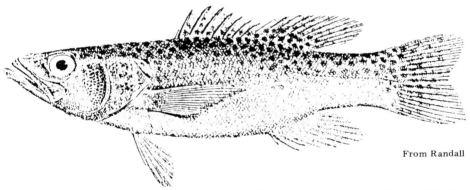

From Randall

This small, rare grouper has a body which is pink on the sides and belly and has the upper part of the body covered with many spots of reddish and yellowish hues. It measures less than a foot in length.

The distribution as presently known includes Japan, the Hawaiian area, and doubtless many adjacent areas.

THOMPSON'S GROUPER
88—15 *Caesioperca thompsoni* Fowler, 1923

Thompson's grouper is a small, somewhat slender species with a long filament trailing from the end of the dorsal fin and from the top and bottom of the tail fin. The body is a uniform, rosy-pinkish color and the fins are marked with red. It will reach a length of about seven or eight inches.

At present the known distribution of this species is limited to the

Hawaiian area.

This species was named in honor of Mr. John W. Thompson, a long time museum technician and artist at the Bishop Museum in Hono-

lulu. Mr. Thompson was best known for his beautiful fish casts and his limber elbow.

Some scholars believe the name of this fish should be *Pseudanthias thompsoni* (Fowler), 1923.

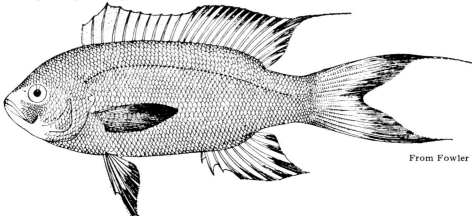

From Fowler

KELLOGG'S GROUPER
88—16 *Pseudanthias kelloggi* (Jordan and Evermann), 1903

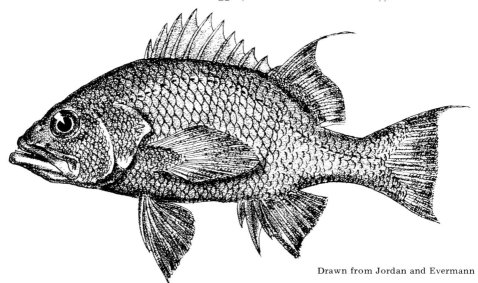

Drawn from Jordan and Evermann

The body of this grouper has the typical shape of the members of this family. It is probably most easily recognized by the color pattern of the body. The upper side of the body is marked by wide, vertical bands of white and red which are narrower and less well defined toward the tail and which end on the middle of the side. The entire lower half of the fish is white. It will reach about eight or nine inches in length. It is a small and uncommon species from deeper water.

The known distribution of this species is limited to the Hawaiian area.

This species is named in honor of Dr. Vernon Lyman Kellogg, professor of entomology at Stanford University.

Some scholars believe a more correct name for this species is *Zalanthias kelloggi* (Jordan and Evermann), 1903.

Pseudanthias kelloggi   Odontanthias elizabethae

ELIZABETH'S GROUPER
88—17 *Odontanthias elizabethae* Fowler, 1923

The body of this grouper is oval in shape and laterally compressed; it contains a short head with a short snout and large eyes. This fish is most

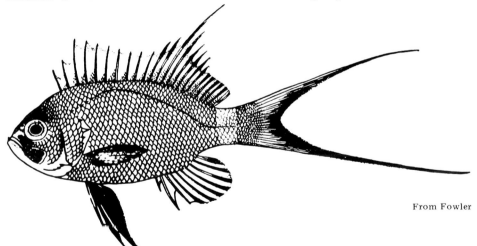

From Fowler

easily identified by the white band which encircles the caudal peduncle. It reaches six or seven inches in length.

The known distribution of this species seems to include only the Hawaiian area.

This species is named in honor of Mrs. Elizabeth K. Fowler, wife of Henry W. Fowler. Dr. Fowler was for many years the ichthyologist of the

Academy of Natural Sciences of Philadelphia and a long time student of Indo-Pacific fishes.

THE DARK - FINNED GROUPER
88—18 *Odontanthias fuscipinnis* Jenkins, 1901

The body of this grouper is deep and laterally compressed compared to other members of the family. Unlike most groupers, the tail is deeply

forked. The third dorsal spine is much longer than the rest and helps to identify this species with certainty. The color of the body is orange to yellow with pink shadings. The fins are variously marked with crimson, golden, yellow, or olive-green hues. Specimens range in length from seven to more than nine inches. It inhabits the deeper waters on the outer edge of the reef.

The known distribution of this species is limited to the Hawaiian area.

THE SMALL LONG - FINNED GROUPER
88—19 *Pteranthias longimanus* Weber, 1913

This little grouper is quite typical of the family body contours and features. It may be most easily recognized by the very long pectoral fins for which it is named, by the fifth and longest spine of the dorsal fin, and by its markings. A single white spot is located on the side of the body above the center and below the third ray of the soft dorsal fin. There are two dark spots each followed by a white spot at the top and bottom of the base of the tail. There is also a single dark spot followed by a white spot behind both the dorsal and anal fins. This is a small species which reaches a length of at least two inches.

It seems to live over sandy or coral bottoms at depths between 25 and 150 feet.

The known distribution of this species includes the East Indies and the Hawaiian Islands.

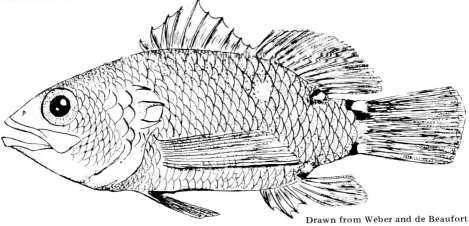

Drawn from Weber and de Beaufort

THE GRAMMISTID OR SOAP FISH FAMILY
89 *Family Grammistidae*

The fishes in this family resemble the groupers *(Serranidae)* in many ways and have often been included within that large family. Two common features possessed by them and by which they may be separated from the *Serranidae* include an incomplete or interrupted lateral line and a single, enlarged spine on the head at the upper end of the border of the operculum.

Some authors have included various species of this group within the family *Pseudochromidae*. For a discussion of this problem see *Pacific Science* 14(1), 1960, pp. 28—38.

The common name of this family comes from a soap-like mucous which these fishes exude when they are disturbed.

The soap fishes include about 30 species; of this number at least three are known from this area.

The following species are not described or illustrated:

Pseudogramma polyacanthus (Bleeker), 1856. This fish is a small species which measures about three inches. It occurs in Hawaii, the Marshall Islands, Samoa, and doubtless in adjoining areas.

Suttonia lineata Gosline, 1960. This fish was described from a few specimens collected off Oahu. They measured less than four inches in length.

THE TWO LINED GRAMMISTID FISH
89—1 *Aporops bilinearis* Schultz, 1943

The name assigned to this species by Dr. Leonard P. Schultz calls attention to the two, lateral lines which this species and its relatives exhibit. The first or upper part of the lateral line arches along the upper side of the body and ends under the middle of the soft dorsal fin. The posterior and lower part of the lateral line begins some distance below the end of the first part of this line and continues straight down the mid-axis of the body and caudal peduncle to the tail. This species measures less than four inches in length.

The distribution of this species includes Hawaii, the Marshall Islands, Samoa, and doubtless many adjoining areas.

THE FLAG-TAIL FISH FAMILY
Also known as the Aholehole, Saboti, and Mountain Bass
90 *Family Kuhliidae (Duleidae)*

The kuhliid fishes are perch-like in appearance with fairly deep bodies, large eyes, and an oblique mouth. They have a single dorsal fin which is continuous, although a deep notch between the spinous portion of the fin and the soft portion makes it appear as two separate fins. The various species range in size from small to some which may reach as much as 18 inches.

They live in a variety of habitats from pure sea water through estuaries, lagoons, and river mouths into fresh water. The marine species are silvery in color, while those species which inhabit fresh water exhibit various color patterns.

These are good food fishes and enter into the diet of people wherever they occur.

This family, which is limited to the central and western Pacific and Indian Oceans, contains about a dozen species of which at least three are native to this area and a fourth species has been introduced.

The following species are not described or illustrated:

Kuhlia marginata (Cuvier and Valenciennes), 1829. This species reaches eight or nine inches in length and is bluish or brownish above; the upper half of the body is marked by dark brown spots in the posterior quadrant. It is widely distributed in the Indo-Pacific area from the Phoenix Islands and Polynesia westward.

Kuhlia ruprestris (Lacepede), 1802. This species was introduced from Guam into Hawaii by the State of Hawaii, Department of Agriculture, Division of Fish and Game. In 1957 they imported 43 fishes which they held in their tanks for study. In 1958 they imported 170 fishes of which 104 were subsequently released in a small stream near Bellows Field, Oahu. It is a dusky silver color, grows to about 16 or 18 inches, and is widely distributed from Polynesia and Micronesia westward to the coast of Africa.

THE HAWAIIAN FLAG-TAIL FISH
Also known as A-ho-le and A-ho-le-ho-le (young)
90—1 *Kuhlia sandvicensis* (Steindachner), 1876

The aholehole is a small fish with an oblong, compressed body, a short, blunt snout, an oblique mouth, and very large eyes. The body is a bright silvery color throughout life and is marked with bluish shades on the back. It usually reaches a length of eight or nine inches.

The young inhabit shallow water along the shore line and may be found in tide pools, streams, and estuaries. When they reach their adult size, they move to the outer edge of the reef where they may be observed in schools.

This is an edible fish and is captured for food.

The distribution of this species may possibly be limited to the Hawaiian area. It or a similar species has been reported from central Polynesia and Fiji and from some of the islands between this area and Hawaii, but some uncertainty is attached to these reports.

THE BANDED FLAG-TAIL FISH
90—2 *Kuhlia taeniura* (Cuvier and Valenciennes), 1829

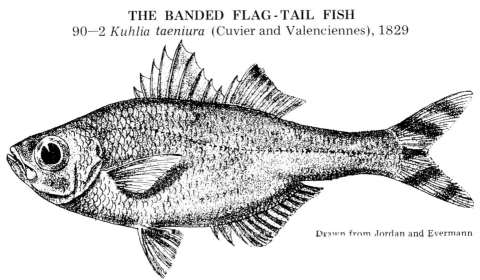

Drawn from Jordan and Evermann

This shore line fish is silvery in color and is easily recognized by the five, horizontal, black stripes on the tail. It will reach a length of eight or nine inches. The young are found in tide pools and shallow water areas.

The distribution of this species extends from the Revillagigedo Islands of Mexico across the tropical Pacific Ocean, including Johnston Island and central Polynesia, through the East Indies, and across the Indian Ocean to the coast of Africa.

THE BIG-EYE FISH FAMILY
Also known as the Catalufas, Scads, and Bullseyes
91 *Family Priacanthidae*
The body of the priacanthids is oval, ovoid, or oblong in shape and strongly compressed. The eyes are very large, the mouth is large and oblique in position, and the lower jaw is very prominent and protruding. The scales which cover the body are very small, thin, and rough and the lateral line is complete. There is a single dorsal fin consisting of ten spines anteriorly and between 11 and 15 rays posteriorly; this fin arises in a groove into which it may be depressed. The caudal fin is truncated or nearly so at its extremity. The anal fin possesses three spines at its anterior end. The pectoral fins are small, but the pelvic fins are large and have their inner border joined to the abdomen by a broad membrane. The members of this family are nearly all reddish in color and are fishes of small to moderate size; the largest species will reach a length of about two feet.

In habits these fishes are carnivorous, nocturnal, marine bottom dwellers and, although not particularly common, are eaten for their white flesh. They inhabit the shore lines of most tropical and sub-tropical seas.

The family contains less than two dozen species of which at least four have been reported from this area.

SCHNEIDER'S BIG-EYE FISH
Also known as 'A-we-o-we-o, 'A-la-u-wa, and 'A-la-la-u-wa (young)
91—1 *Priacanthus boops* (Schneider), 1801
This priacanthid fish has a body which is somewhat oval, compressed, and covered with small scales. The head is large and bears large eyes and a large mouth which opens nearly vertically. Its distinctive features are very large pelvic fins and a long soft-dorsal fin. The color of the body is quite uniformly reddish. It will reach a length of about 20 inches.

The distribution of this species appears to extend from Hawaii through the tropical western Pacific, across the Indian Ocean, and into the tropical Atlantic Ocean.

This species will appear in some books under the name of *Cookeolus boops* (Schneider), 1801.

THE BLOOD-COLORED BIG-EYE FISH
Also known as 'A-we-o-we-o, 'A-la-u-wa, and 'A-la-la-u-wa (young)
91—2 *Priacanthus cruentatus* (Lacepede), 1801

The body of this big-eye is oval in outline like the other members of this family. It differs from some in having but 13 soft rays on the dorsal fin and in its color. The body is normally a mottled silvery and red color, but may apparently vary in color from pink to red. It will reach a length of about 12 inches.

This species will enter shallow water and appears to be by far the commonest of the species in this area.

The distribution of this fish seems to be world-wide; it inhabits all warm seas.

FORSKAL'S BIG-EYE FISH
Also known as 'A-we-o-we-o, 'A-la-u-wa, and 'A-la-la-u-wa (young)
91—3 *Priacanthus hamrur* (Forskal), 1775

This fish has long been known under the name of *Priacanthus ululuuu* Jordan and Evermann, 1903. Although it may be a distinct species, many authorities regard it as identical to *P. hamrur* which was described over a century earlier from the Red Sea.

The body of this fish is oval in shape, compressed, and covered with very small scales. The body is variously colored with silvery, olive, and reddish hues. The dorsal fin is an olive-yellow color; the pelvic fins are nearly black and have lighter colored rays; the fins bears no spots as in some other species. It will reach a length of about 16 inches. It is a species from deeper water.

The distribution of this species extends from Hawaii southward and westward across the tropical western Pacific and Indian Oceans to the coast of Africa and the Red Sea.

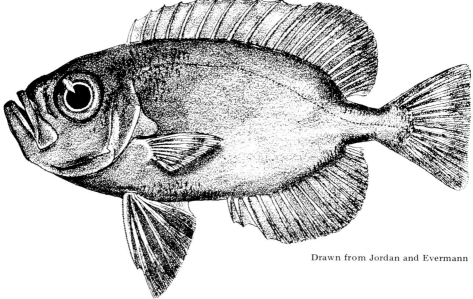

Drawn from Jordan and Evermann

MEEK'S BIG-EYE FISH

Also known as 'A-we-o-we-o, 'A-la-u-wa, and 'A-la-la-u-wa (young)

91—4 *Priacanthus meeki* Jenkins, 1903

Meek's big-eye has an oval or oblong body which is compressed and covered with small scales. The head is large and bears a pair of large eyes

and a large mouth which is oblique in position. The entire body is deep red in color and is without spots, blotches, or bands, except for about 15 faint spots scattered along the lateral line. The inside of the mouth is an orange-red color. This species is darker in color than the preceeding species mentioned here. The dorsal and anal fins are darker than other species and there is a black margin on the tail. It will reach a length of about 12 inches.

The distribution of *P. meeki* seems limited at present to the Hawaiian area.

Dr. Jenkins named this fish in honor of Dr. Seth Eugene Meek, at that time Assistant Curator of Zoology in the Field Columbian Museum.

Some authors regard *P. meeki* as identical to *P. macracanthus* Cuvier, 1829, a species which extends from Hawaii to southern Japan, Australia, and the East Indies.

THE CARDINAL FISH FAMILY
92 *Family Apogonidae*
(Amiidae, Cheilodipteridae, Apogonichthyidae)

Cardinal fishes are small to moderate in size. They have oblong bodies which are sometimes compressed and which are covered with large scales. The mouth is large and oblique in position and the eyes are likewise large. There are two completely separate dorsal fins of which the second or soft dorsal has ten or fewer soft rays. The anal fin is short and contains but two anal spines. The bodies of the various species are usually marked with shades of red or brown. They are active, carnivorous fishes and include many species in which the males and/or females are mouth brooders.

Cardinal fishes are found in all warm tropical seas where they occupy a variety of habitats. Some are marine and live along the shore line, some live in brackish water including mangrove swamps, and some species live in fresh water including some of the higher, tropical Pacific Islands. It should be noted that a few marine species inhabit waters at depths in excess of 1,000 feet.

The family contains more than 150 species of which at least ten are known from this area.

THE SMELT-LIKE CARDINAL FISH
92—1 *Epigonus atherinoides* (Gilbert), 1905

The body of this fish is very elongated and bears straight and parallel sides which cause it to superficially resemble the members of the smelt family. The eyes are large and the mouth is comparatively small and does not reach as far as the pupils of the eyes. The caudal fin is forked. The color of the body is dark gray or dusky. It is lighter below than above and is without significant markings, although there are dusky markings upon the snout. It will reach about seven inches in length.

This is an uncommon species. The type specimen was captured in a dredge in Pailolo Channel between Molokai and Maui by the streamer *Albatross* in 1902 at a depth in excess of 1,700 feet. Other specimens have been obtained from the Honolulu market where they were presumed to have been disgorged by larger carnivorous fishes.

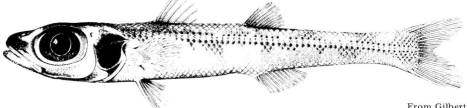

From Gilbert

The distribution of this species extends from Hawaii southwestward through the tropical Pacific and Indian Oceans to the coast of Africa.

Some books will list this species under the name of *Hynnodus atherinoides* (Gilbert), 1905.

THE SLENDER-TAILED CARDINAL FISH
92—2 *Pseudamiops gracilicauda* (Lachner), 1953

This species will probably pass unnoticed by most swimmers because it is very transparent and therefor very difficult to see in the water. It has an elongated body with a long caudal peduncle and a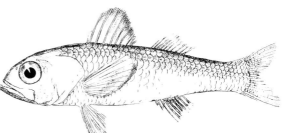

Drawn from Schultz

long caudal fin which is rounded at the end. It has no scales and the canine teeth are enlarged. It measures less than two inches in length.

The distribution of this species includes Hawaii, Johnston Island, the Marshall Islands, and doubtless surrounding areas.

THE SILVERY-COLORED CARDINAL FISH
92—3 *Synagrops argyrea* (Gilbert and Cramer), 1896

The body of this cardinal fish is elongated and compressed and bears a caudal fin which is deeply forked. The eyes are quite large and the canine teeth are likewise enlarged. The color of the body is a silvery hue, darker above than below, and contains darker areas on top

Drawn from Gilbert and Cramer

of the head and snout. The dorsal fin is also darker along its outer border. It will reach a length of about six inches.

This is an uncommon species and is known from only a few specimens, most of which were captured in a dredge at depths in excess of 1,000 feet.

The distribution of this species includes Hawaii, Guam, and undoubtedly many adjoining areas.

THE SHORT-LINED CARDINAL FISH
92—4 *Apogon brachygrammus* (Jenkins), 1903

The body of this cardinal fish is shorter, deeper, and more compressed than others illustrated here. It may be rather positively identified by the facts that the lateral line appears to end below the soft dorsal fin. Specimens will reach a length of about three inches. This appears to be an abundant species around dead coral in some areas.

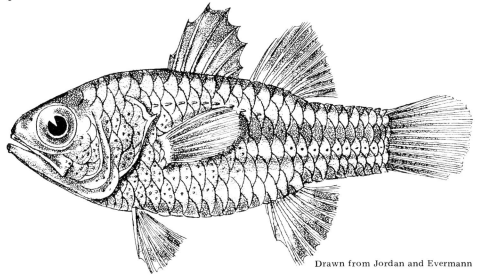

Drawn from Jordan and Evermann

The distribution of this fish includes Hawaii, central Polynesia, Melanesia, and other Indo-Pacific areas.

THE REDDISH CARDINAL FISH
92—5 *Apogon erythrinus* Snyder, 1904

The reddish cardinal fish is a plump little species with a long caudal peduncle and a forked tail. It may be distinguished from other species by its dorsal spines (of which the second is the largest), by the absence of spots or bars on the body or fins, and by its light, reddish pink or orange-red color.

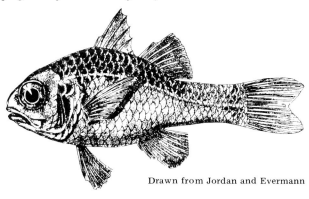

Drawn from Jordan and Evermann

It will reach a length of about three and one-half inches.

This species is widely distributed although nowhere abundant. It occurs from Hawaii and Guam southward to central Polynesia and westward across the tropical western Pacific and Indian Oceans to the coast of Africa.

EVERMANN'S CARDINAL FISH
92—6 *Apogon evermanni* Jordan and Snyder, 1904

Evermann's cardinal fish is based upon a single specimen obtained in 1902 from the Honolulu Market by Mr. E. Louis Berndt, the market inspector.

The body is quite slender, the caudal peduncle is long, and the tail is forked. The head, mouth, and eyes are large and all of the fins have rounded extremities. The species may be identified by the scales along the lateral line which are larger than the scales above and below the line. The color of the body and fins is red. A dark, horizontal band extends backward from the eye to the free edge of the operculum. A dark spot is present at the posterior base of the soft dorsal fin; a smaller yellow spot is placed just behind it. The body of the type specimen measured 5.6 inches in length and was marked by five, indistinct, vertical bands.

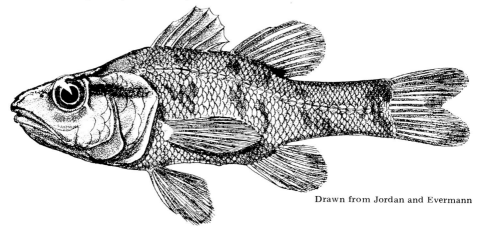

Drawn from Jordan and Evermann

It is a deep water species which so far is known only from the Hawaiian Island area.

This species is named in honor of Dr. Barton Warren Evermann (1853-1932), California ichthyologist, long time staff member of the California Academy of Sciences and the Steinhart Aquarium, and scientific associate of Dr. David Starr Jordan.

THE SPOTTED CARDINAL FISH
Also known as 'U-pa-pa-lu, 'U-pa-lu-pa-lu, and 'U-pa-pa-lu ma-ka nu-i
92—7 *Apogon maculifera* Garrett, 1863

The body of this cardinal fish is short and deep and moderately compressed. The head is pointed and the eyes are large. The species is most easily recognized by the rows of dark spots on the sides of the body. The color of the body is mostly reddish; it has been described by some as a very pale purplish gray, the head as dusky reddish orange, and the belly as pale orange. It will reach a length of about six inches.

The known distribution of this species at present seems to be limited to the Hawaiian area.

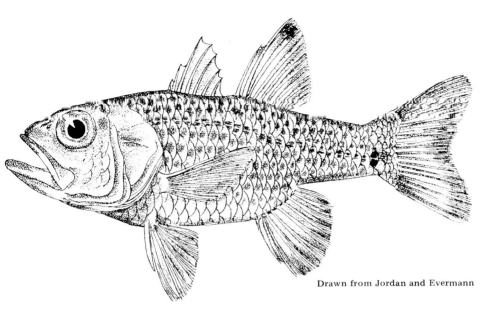

Drawn from Jordan and Evermann

JENKIN'S CARDINAL FISH
Also known as 'U-pa-pa-lu, 'U-pa-lu-pa-lu, and 'U-pa-pa-lu ma-ka nu-i
92—8 *Apogon menesemus* Jenkins, 1903

The body shape and general resemblance of this species to *A. snyderi* should be noted. The two dorsal fins and the anal fin each have a black band; the caudal fin bears a dark longitudinal bar on its upper and lower edge and a dark vertical bar along its anterior border. The body will reach a length of about nine inches. This is a common species in the Hawaiian area.

The distribution of this species at the present time includes the Hawaiian area, Johnston Island, and Palmyra.

Drawn from
Jordan and Evermann

SNYDER'S CARDINAL FISH
Also known as 'U-pa-pa-lu, 'U-pa-lu-pa-lu, and 'U-pa-pa-lu ma-ka nu-i
92—9 *Apogon snyderi* Jordan and Evermann, 1903

Snyder's cardinal fish is a short, stout species which closely resembles *A. menesemus*. The body is a pale reddish or brownish color and is marked by a narrow, dark border at the upper and lower edges of the caudal fin; this border may be entirely absent, but when present is much narrower than in

213

From
Jordan and Evermann

A. menesemus. There is a black band, likewise resembling *A. menesemus*, on the dorsal and anal fins in the young only; these bands disappear in the adult. A dark spot may be present on the side of the caudal peduncle just forward of the tail. The body will reach a length of about nine inches. This is a common shore line species in this area.

The distribution of this species extends from the Hawaiian area and central Polynesia westward through Micronesia to the East Indies, and across the Indian Ocean to the Red Sea.

This species was named in honor of Dr. John O. Snyder, Assistant Professor of Physiology at Stanford University.

Recent studies suggest that this species should be known as *Apogon kallopterus* (Bleeker), 1878.

THE WAIKIKI CARDINAL FISH
92—10 *Apogon waikiki* (Jordan and Evermann), 1903

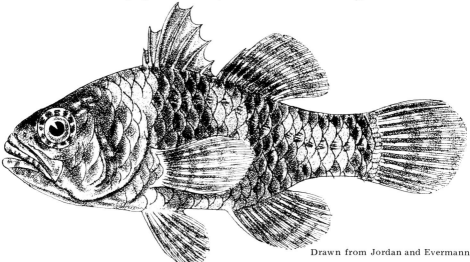

Drawn from Jordan and Evermann

The cardinal fish which bears the name of Hawaii's famous tourist resort is a small species with a short, deep, stout, compressed body. It may be identified by the smooth border of the preopercle and by the fins which have rounded outlines and are colored dark brown with narrow, gray borders. It reaches a length of about four inches. It is not a common species.

The known distribution of this species appears for the present time to be limited to the Hawaiian Islands and Johnston Island to the south.

THE BLANQUILLOS FISH FAMILY
Also known as Sand-fish and Tile-fish
93 *Family Malacanthidae*

The blanquillos are slender, elongated fishes of small or medium size which have their bodies covered by small scales. The dorsal fin is unusually long and is continuous from just behind the head to the beginning of the tail; the anal fin is likewise very long. The pectoral fins are pointed and the pelvic fins are placed far forward (thoracic) on the body. The lips are fleshy and there is a prominent spine on the preopercle. Most of these fishes are beautifully colored.

They inhabit the temperate and tropical seas of the Atlantic and Indo-Pacific areas.

The family includes about 15 species of which at least two occur in this area.

THE BANDED BLANQUILLO
Also known as Ma-ka-'a and 'U-la-e ma-hi-ma-hi
93—1 *Malacanthus hoedtii* Bleeker, 1859

This slender, elongated fish is easily recognized by its color markings. The body is light olive-green above and silvery white below with about 20 short, darker bars extending downward along the upper side of the body. The tail is white at the center and is marked with two, black, horizontal stripes placed one above and the other below the white center stripe. The dorsal fin is pinkish and has a narrow yellow border; the other fins are somewhat yellowish in color. It will reach a length of at least 12 inches.

The maka'a is a shore line, shallow water, bottom-living species which is very active and beautiful. It is edible and will take a hook, but it will use its teeth and spines on the hands of anyone attempting to hold it while alive.

The distribution of this fish extends from the Hawaiian area southward and westward through central Polynesia, Micronesia, Melanesia, the East Indies, and across the Indian Ocean to Mauritius.

THE STRIPED BLANQUILLO
93—2 *Malacanthus latovittatus* (Lacepede), 1802

The body of this blanquillo is long, slender, and covered with small scales; the snout is long and conical and the lips are fleshy. It is most easily recognized by its unusual color pattern. The head and back are black; the side of the head, the upper side of the body, and the pectoral fins are a brilliant sky blue, while the lower side of the body and the pelvic and anal fins are white. The side of the body is marked by a longitudinal black band. It will reach a length of at least 16 inches. This is a shore line species which is reported to enter the mouths of rivers.

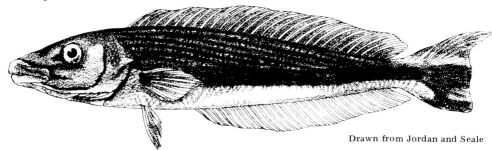

Drawn from Jordan and Seale

The distribution of this species extends from the Hawaiian area southward and westward through central Polynesia, Micronesia, Melanesia, and the East Indies, and across the Indian Ocean to the coast of Africa. The occurrence of this species in Hawaii needs verification.

THE BOGA FISH FAMILY

94 *Family Emmelichthyidae (Erythrichthyidae, Dipterygonotidae)*

The fishes within this family are small or medium in size and have bodies which are elongated and quite rounded although noticeably compressed. Their tail is deeply forked and the two dorsal fins appear to be separate, but they are usually (but not always) connected by a small, low membrane along the back. In some species the dorsal fin is in three parts; in these fishes the middle section consists of two, three, or four, short, disconnected spines. The soft dorsal fin and the anal fin fit into a scale-covered groove or sheath at their base. These fishes resemble the snappers *(Lutjanidae)* in many ways and, like them, are eaten wherever they occur.

The members of this family are uncommon inhabitants of deeper water in the West Indies and Indo-Pacific areas.

This is a very small family of which at least one species occurs in this area.

SCHLEGEL'S BOGA FISH

94—1 *Erythrocles schlegelii* (Gunther), 1859

The body of this fish is slender and spindle-shaped with only a minimum amount of lateral compression. The body is reddish yellow in color; the upper areas are more orange and the lower surfaces are more pink. The head, dorsal fins, and the tail are orange in color. The upper side of the body is marked by alternating pink and orange zigzag lines. It will reach a length of 15 inches. It is an uncommon food fish from deeper waters.

The distribution of this species includes the Hawaiian area and Japan; in time, it will doubtless be reported from adjoining areas.

Recent studies indicate that the correct name of this Hawaiian species is *Erythrocles scintillans* (Jordan and Thompson), 1912.

The species is named for H. Schlegel, who was the author of the section on fishes in Philipp Franz von Siebold's *Fauna Japonica*, 1845.

THE SNAPPER FISH FAMILY
Also known as the Pig Fishes
95 *Family Lutjanidae*
(Aphareidae, Aprionidae, Denticidae, Hoplopagridae, Haemulidae, Lethrinidae, Lutianidae, Nemipteridae, Plectorhynchidae, Pristipomidae, Verilidae, Xenichthyidae)

The snappers comprise an assortment of fishes which have often been placed in other families. In general, they are medium to large in size and possess oblong bodies. They have large heads, nearly equal jaws, and a flat area on top of the snout. The dorsal fin is usually single and continuous, although it may be deeply notched or even divided in some species into two separate fins; this dorsal fin arises from a groove into which it may be depressed. The anal fin posses three strong spines and the tail fin is usually forked, although it is sometimes truncated or emarginated on its posterior border. Snappers are usually brightly colored with red or yellow hues. Most species are reasonably uniform in their color, although a few do have definite color patterns. The members range in size from a few inches to some forms which measures two or three feet in length.

Snappers are active, carnivorous, voracious fishes which inhabit the shallow, shore line waters of most tropical and a few temperate seas.

This family includes about 250 species, of which possibly 20 are known from this area.

The following species are not described or illustrated:

Lutjanus bohar (Forskal), 1775. This snapper is marked by two, large, pearly white spots on the upper side of the body and by many smaller, pale, silvery white spots on the back. The body is brownish with reddish hues; the head has yellowish hues. It lives on the outer side of the reef in deeper water.

Lethrinus miniatus (Bloch and Schneider), 1801. This species has an elongated, pointed snout and conical teeth in the jaws. The insides of the mouth and gill cavity are orange or scarlet in color. The scales of the upper part of the body have blue centers and there are two or three bluish lines running from the eye forward and downward across the snout. Some specimens may reach

32 inches in length.

A group of three fishes from Moorea in the Society Islands was importe
and released on October 10, 1956, off Moku O Loe, Kaneohe Bay, Oah
Another school of 17 fishes from Moorea was released in December, 1961, i
Maunalua Bay off southeastern Oahu.

The distribution of this fish extends from Polynesia westward to the Re
Sea.

Symphysanodon maunaloae Anderson, 1970. This little fish has a slender, taperin
body with a large head and large eyes. The largest specimen known was le
than four inches long. The species is based on specimens which we
captured in trawls below 500 feet or were picked up dead following a lav
flow which entered the sea off the island of Hawaii. It is named for th
volcano of Mauna Loa.

Persons interested in this and related species should read Wm. I
Anderson's article in *Fishery Bulletin* 68(2), 1970, pp. 325-346.

BLEEKER'S SNAPPER FISH
95—1 *Symphysanodon typus* Bleeker, 1878

This snapper has an elongated body which is strongly compressed,
short snout, and very large eyes. The caudal peduncle is also strongl
flattened. The species may be most easily recognized by two sharp knob
placed on the front of the lower jaw; it should be noted that these are absen
in small specimens. In addition, the scales completely cover the top of th
head as far forward as the nostrils; the anal fin has but seven soft rays; an
the lower profile of the lower jaw has a pronounced upward jog about two
third of its length from the front. The color of this fish is quite uniforml
greenish. It will reach a length of at least 12 inches.

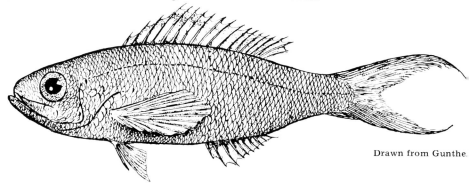

Drawn from Gunthe

This species appears to live in deeper water; most specimens from thi
area have been killed by lava flows in the sea.

The distribution at present includes the Hawaiian area and the Eas
Indies.

BRIGHAM'S SNAPPER FISH
Also known as Ka-le-ka-le and 'U-ki-ki-ki
95—2 *Rooseveltia brighami* (Seale), 1901

The identity of this snapper is easily established by its deep body anc
brilliant color pattern. The color of the body in life is light red to which are

218

added about four, wide, yellow, saddle-shaped bands which extends downward from the back to below the midline of the body. It will reach a length of at least 20 inches.

This food fish lives in deeper water and is caught on hook and line along with the other members of this family.

This species is named in honor of William Tufts Brigham (1841 - 1926), attorney, botanist, geologist, geographer, ethnologist, and the first Director (1890 - 1918) of the Bernice Pauahi Bishop Museum in Honolulu.

Drawn from Jordan and Evermann

This fish may be found in some books under the name of *Tropidinus zonatus* (Cuvier and Valenciennes), 1830, or *Pristipomoides zonatus* (Cuvier and Valenciennes), 1830.

THE FORK - TAILED SNAPPER FISH
95—3 *Aphareus furcatus* (Lacepede), 1802

The body of this species is quite long and slender, quite compressed, and entirely covered by small scales. The upper and lower profiles of the body are long, gentle curves which end in a rather long caudal peduncle and a tail which is deeply forked. The mouth is large and contains small teeth only in the jaws; none of these teeth are enlarged. There are no teeth on the vomer, the palatines, or the tongue. The dorsal fin is continuous along the back and contains ten spines of which the third is the longest. The anal fin has three spines of which the third is the longest. The color of the body is rather uniformly steel blue, dirty violet, or purplish and there is a yellow border on the anal fin. The body will reach about two feet in length, although most specimens measure about 12 inches.

The habitat of this species is in the deeper water on the outer edge o
the reef.

The distribution of this fish includes the Hawaiian Islands, central Poly
nesia, and undoubtedly surrounding areas.

In some books this species will appear under the name of *Aphareu:*
flavivultus Jenkins, 1901.

THE REDDISH SNAPPER FISH
95—4 *Aphareus rutilans* Cuvier and Valenciennes, 1830

The body of this snapper is quite elongated and presents uniformly
curved upper and lower profiles which terminate posteriorly in a long
slender caudal peduncle and a long, deeply-forked tail. The eyes are o
medium size and are placed high on the head. The teeth are all small and o
nearly equal size. The color of the body is uniformly, dull pink above and
silvery below. The fins are mostly reddish in color; the dorsal fin has a yellowish border and yellow spots on its margins, and the tail has yellowish
hues. Large specimens will reach a length of at least three feet.

This species resembles *A. furcatus* somewhat, but is more slender,
larger, and more reddish in color.

The distribution of this species extends from Hawaii southward into
Polynesia and westward across the entire tropical Pacific and Indian Oceans
to the Red Sea.

THE BLUE-GREEN SNAPPER FISH
Also known as U-ku
95—5 *Aprion virescens* Cuvier and Valenciennes, 1830

The uku is a rather large, elongated, slender fish with a body which is only slightly compressed. The upper and lower outlines of the body curve uniformly to a tail which is deeply forked. The pectoral fins are short and rounded. The front of each jaw contains a pair of enlarged canine teeth which are accompanied by a few smaller teeth farther along in the jaw. This species may be quite readily recognized by the eyes which are somewhat smaller than other snappers and are placed higher upon the head.

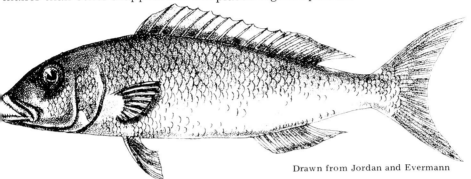

Drawn from Jordan and Evermann

The color of the body is a light gray, bluish, or greenish tint with bluish reflections above; it becomes much lighter on the lower surface. The membrane of the spinous dorsal fin is marked at its base with violet colored blotches. The body of large specimens will reach a length of about 40 inches.

This is an active fish which inhabits the shore line; it is a fine food fish and is captured on hook and line.

The distribution of this species extends from the Hawaiian area southward and westward through the tropical western Pacific Ocean, through the East Indies, and across the Indian Ocean to the coast of Africa.

THE SMALL-SCALED SNAPPER FISH
Also known as the 'O-pa-ka-pa-ka
95—6 *Pristipomoides microlepis* (Bleeker), 1869

The body of this snapper is large, rotund, quite slender and elongated, and has dorsal and ventral profiles which curve gently from the head to a tail

which is widely forked. This species very closely resembles the kale-kale *(F siboldii)* but is larger, slightly thicker bodied, has a larger and less obliqu mouth, a relatively smaller eye, and is without any teeth on the roof of th mouth. The color of the body is an uncertain, reddish olive hue with add tional violet hues coming from the center of each scale along the back of th body. The dorsal, pectoral, and caudal fins are generally flesh colored an often present faint hues of other colors along their borders. Large specimen will reach a length of at least three feet.

The habitat of this fish is in the deeper offshore water beyond the reef It is an important food fish and is captured by hook and line.

The distribution of this species extends from Hawaii southward t central Polynesia and westward across the tropical western Pacific Ocean t the East Indies.

The ancient Hawaiians had four names for the growth stages of th 'opakapaka; they were 'ukikiki, pakale, opakapaka, and kalekale.

VON SIEBOLD'S SNAPPER FISH
Also known as Ka-le-ka-le
95—7 *Pristipomoides sieboldii* (Bleeker), 1857

The kale-kale is a slender, medium-sized fish with large eyes and a deeply forked tail. The body color is silvery red with faint, longitudinal blue lines. The dorsal and pectoral fins have a yellowish cast, the ventral and anal fins are clear, and the tail fin is reddish. Large individuals will reach a length of 24 inches. The photo is of a specimen ten inches in length.

Although the known distribution of this species includes Hawaii and Japan, it is doubtless more widely distributed in the western tropical Pacific Ocean.

The name of this species honors the memory of Philipp Franz voi Siebold, 1796-1866, German physician and naturalist, who, while employec by The Netherland's East Indian Army, made extensive visits to Japan and in 1832 published the *Fauna Japonica.*

This species is found in some books under the name of *Bowersia ulaulc* Jordan and Everman, 1903.

THE RUBY-COLORED SNAPPER FISH
Also known as 'U-la-'u-la
95—8 *Etelis carbunculus* Cuvier, 1828

The 'ula-'ula has a rather slender body which terminates in a long caudal peduncle and a long, deeply-forked tail with tapering lobes. The eyes are large and each jaw bears a pair of enlarged teeth in front; the remainders of the jaws are lined along their edges with many, small, sharp teeth. The color of the body is reddish above and the interior of the mouth is pinkish within. It lacks the yellowish lateral line found in *E. marshi*. Large specimens will reach 30 or possibly 36 inches in length.

This important food fish inhabits the deeper waters beyond the reef.

The distribution of this species extends from Hawaii to Japan, through the East Indies, and across the Indian Ocean to Africa; it also occurs in the tropical Atlantic Ocean.

Some books list this species under the name of *Etelis evurus* Jordan and Evermann, 1903.

MARSH'S SNAPPER FISH
Also known as 'U-la-'u-la
95—9 *Etelis marshi* (Jenkins), 1903

The 'ula-'ula has a body which tapers rather uniformly toward the tail and which is only slightly compressed. The head is quite large and bears rather large eyes. The teeth are helpful in identifying this species; there are usually about five, sharp, slender teeth on each side of the mouth in both upper and lower jaws; they are rather widely spaced and are slightly larger toward the front of the mouth. The body is reddish in color above and is marked along the side with a narrow, yellow line running lengthwise through the red area. The lower parts of the sides and belly are lighter and somewhat silvery. The pelvic fins are bright yellow with black margins. The interior of the mouth lacks the red color found in *E. carbunculus*. Adult specimens will reach at least 24 inches in length.

This food fish inhabits the deeper waters beyond the reef.

The distribution of this species includes the Hawaiian Islands and doubtless surrounding areas in the western tropical Pacific Ocean.

The name of this species perpetuates the memory of Mr. Millard Caleb Marsh, an ichthyologist employed by the United States Fish Commission and co-author of *The Fishes of Porto Rico* published in 1900.

THE RED AND GREEN SNAPPER FISH
Also known as To-a-u (Tahiti)
95—10 *Lutjanus fulvus* (Bloch and Schneider), 1801

The body of this snapper is quite deep and moderately compressed. The dorsal fin is continuous and the caudal fin is wide and slightly concave on its posterior margin. The upper profile of the head is long and straight and the snout is somewhat elongated. The body is rosy or greenish in color and is marked with six or more golden, longitudinal lines on the side of the body. The dorsal fin has a dark red border; the pectoral, ventral, and anal fins are yellow; and the soft dorsal and anal fins bear a narrow, white margin. Large specimens may reach 24 inches in length.

The distribution of this fish includes Polynesia and Melanesia.

Several introductions of this fish have been made into the Hawaiian area. On October 10, 1956, a school of 239 fishes from Moorea in the Society Islands was released off Moku O Lo'e in Kaneohe Bay, Oahu; on June 24, 1958, a small school of 23 fishes was released in the same area. During August, 1961, a school of 148 fishes from Canton Island was released n Ko'ohi Lagoon, Oahu. During December, 1961, a school of 1,782 fishes from Moorea was released in Maunalua Bay off southeastern Oahu.

This fish has often been listed under the name of *Lutjanus vaigiensis* (Quoy and Gaimard), 1824.

THE HUMPED SNAPPER FISH
Also known as the Paddle-tailed Snapper Fish
95—11 *Lutjanus gibbus* (Forskal), 1775

This snapper fish is deep bodied and has a large, deeply-forked tail. The dorsal profile of the head becomes indented with age in the area in front of the eyes so that this fish appears to have a protruding snout. The "upper parts of the head and body are brownish" and the pectoral fins are light in color. It will reach about 24 inches in length.

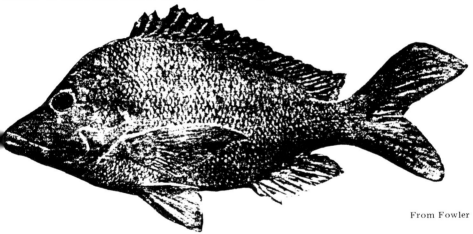

From Fowler

It inhabits the deeper water on the outside of the reef.

This species has been introduced into the Hawaiian area. On June 24, 1958, a school of 40 fishes from the Marquesas Islands was released off Moku O Lo'e, Oahu. Another introduction was made on December, 1961, when 137 fishes from Moorea in the Society Islands were released in Maunalua Bay, Oahu.

The distribution of this species includes Polynesia, Micronesia, Melanesia, the East Indies, and the areas westward to the Red Sea.

THE SPOTTED ROSE SNAPPER FISH
Also known as Pargo Flamenco, Pargo Chibato, Flamenco,
and Mutton Snapper
95—12 *Lutjanus guttatus* (Steindachner), 1869

This American snapper may be best identified by an anchor-shaped patch of teeth on the roof of the mouth and by its color. The body is a rose pink color on the back and sides and shades gradually to golden yellow or the belly. The body is marked by a large, dark spot (often vague) on the upper side of the body just below the beginning of the soft dorsal fin. Some specimens will reach a length of 30 inches, although most are much smaller.

This is a valuable food fish wherever it occurs.

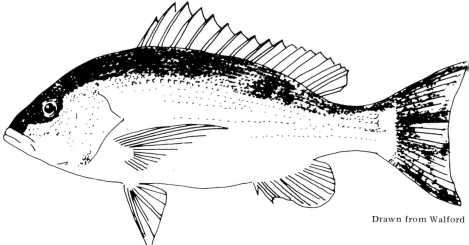

Drawn from Walford

This American fish has been introduced into the Hawaiian area. In May, 1960, a shipment of these fishes was brought from Manzanillo, Mexico, and released. A school of 3,000 fishes was released off Ilio Point, Molokai, and another smaller school of 439 fishes was released at Kewalo Basin, Oahu.

The distribution of this snapper extends along the coast from Baja California to Equador.

THE BLUE-LINED SNAPPER FISH
95—13 *Lutjanus kasmira* (Forskal), 1775
The color pattern of this fish makes it easily identified. The body and

he fins are yellowish in color and there are four, lengthwise, light blue tripes with narrow, brown borders extending lengthwise of the body. It will reach a length of about 15 inches.

This fish has been imported into the Hawaiian Islands and released. On June 23, 1958, about 1,400 of these fishes from the Marquesas Islands were released off Moku O Lo'e Island in Kaneohe Bay, Oahu. The following day, June 24, 1958, a second school of 1,035 fishes from the Marquesas Islands was released off Moku O Lo'e. A few years later in December, 1961, a school of 728 fishes from Moorea in the Society Islands was released in Maunalua Bay, Oahu.

The distribution of this species includes Polynesia, Micronesia, Melanesia, the East Indies, and the areas westward to the Red Sea.

THE TRIPLE-TAIL FISH FAMILY
96 *Family Lobotidae*

The triple-tails are deep-bodied fishes in which the posterior ends of the soft dorsal fin and anal fin are rounded and enlarged so that they are almost as large as the caudal fin. This makes the fish appear at first glance to have three tails and has given rise to its common name of triple-tail. In this family, the dorsal fin arises from a sheath and is continuous from the spinous dorsal through the soft dorsal fin. The teeth are small and are in bands in the jaws.

The life history of this family includes a stage in which the young fishes of two or three inches are camouflaged to appear like a leaf drifting in the water. These fishes are carnivorous, will fight when captured, and are good eating.

They occur in tropical and temperate seas in both brackish and fresh waters.

The triple-tails comprise a very small family of less than a half-dozen species of which at least one is known from this area.

THE SURINAM TRIPLE-TAIL FISH
96—1 *Lobotes surinamensis* (Bloch), 1790

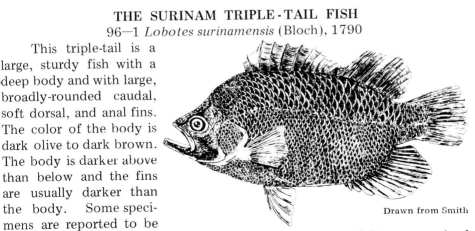

This triple-tail is a large, sturdy fish with a deep body and with large, broadly-rounded caudal, soft dorsal, and anal fins. The color of the body is dark olive to dark brown. The body is darker above than below and the fins are usually darker than the body. Some specimens are reported to be mottled on the body. The second dorsal fin and the anal fin are margined

Drawn from Smith

with whitish markings in young specimens. The pectoral fins are reported to have yellowish hues. Large specimens are reported to reach 40 inches in length.

The distribution of this species is almost world-wide in warmer waters. It has been reported from the West Indies in the Atlantic, Hawaii and Tahiti in Polynesia, Japan, the East Indies, and the eastern coast of Africa.

THE PORGY FISH FAMILY
Including the Sea Breams and Mussel Crackers
97 *Family Sparidae (Denticidae, Girellidae)*

The porgies are a family of fishes with deep, compressed bodies, and a continuous dorsal fin. They possess quite strong canine or incisor teeth and rather unusual molar or grinding teeth. They resemble the snappers *(Lutjanidae)* in most features except for their grinding teeth. Since it has been discovered that these grinding teeth are secondary developments from conical teeth, it is possible that some or all of this family should be combined with the snappers.

Porgies are bottom dwelling fishes of tropical and sub-tropical areas. Most species live in warmer marine waters, but a few occur in cooler marine areas and a few live in fresh water. They are good food fishes, although a few have been known to cause tropical fish poisoning.

The family contains approximately 100 species of which at least one is known from this area.

THE GRAND-EYED PORGY FISH
Also known as the Mu
97—1 *Monotaxis grandoculis* (Forskal), 1775

The mu is a medium sized fish with a high, compressed body, a continuous dorsal fin, and a large, deeply-forked tail. The eyes and mouth are quite large and the mouth contains the grinding teeth for which this species is most famous. The color of the body is an indefinite olive-gray or greenish above and shades to silvery below. The sides of the body are marked by about four, light, vertical bands; of these the first and the last tend to be

ndistinct and are often not visible. The interior of the mouth is red in color. The color pattern becomes fainter in older specimens. Large specimens are reported to reach a length of 24 to 30 inches.

This is a good food fish but has been known to cause tropical fish poisoning.

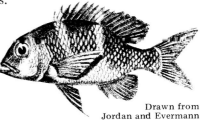

Drawn from
Jordan and Evermann

The distribution of this species extends from Hawaii southward to Australia and westward through Melanesia, Micronesia, and the East Indies, and onward across the Indian Ocean to the coast of Africa.

In some publications this species is listed with the *Pentapodidae* or the *Nemipteridae*.

THE GOAT FISH FAMILY
Including the Surmullets and the Red Mullets
98 *Family Mullidae*

The goat fishes have elongated, tapering bodies which terminate in a deeply forked tail. The two dorsal fins are well separated and the ventral fins are placed far forward on the body. The head bears a pair of small eyes and a small, protractile mouth which contains many, fine, weak teeth. This family is most easily recognized by a pair of barbels or whiskers which are attached to the tip of the lower jaw; when not in use, these barbels are carried against the lower jaw. They are usually extended forward and used as feelers in the search for food. Most goat fishes are brightly colored with red or reddish hues and, in addition, exhibit various markings of black, yellow, or white.

Goat fishes are bottom dwelling and occur in these areas either singly or in small schools. They are a tasty food fish and are eaten wherever they occur. In some areas, the head of these fishes is not eaten because it is regarded as poisonous.

The family inhabits the tropical and warmer seas of the world.

This group contains more than 50 species of which at least ten species are known to occur in this area.

THE BAND - TAILED GOAT FISH
Also known as We-ke pu-e-o, We-ke pa-hu-lu, and We-ke a-hu-lu
98—1 *Upeneus arge* Jordan and Evermann, 1903

This goat fish is very easily identified by its color marking. It is greenish above and whitish below, and bears horizontal black and white stripes upon the tail. It will reach a length of about 12 inches.

The distribution of this species extends from Hawaii southward into central Polynesia and westward into Micronesia and Melanesia.

THE GOLDEN - BANDED GOAT FISH
Also known as We-ke and We-ke 'u-la
98—2 *Mulloidichthys auriflamma* (Forskal), 1775

This goat fish has a rather slender, tapering body. In life, the body color is light with yellow and silvery hues; it becomes reddish in color when

dead. It is prominently marked by a long, horizontal, reddish, golden yellow band which extends along the side of the body from the eye to the base of the tail. The inner lining of the abdomen in this species is black. It will reach a length of about 16 inches.

The distribution of this fish extends from Hawaii southward into Polynesia, westward through Micronesia, Melanesia and the East Indies, and onward across the Indian Ocean to the coast of Africa and the Red Sea.

The old name of *M. auriflamma* has been suppressed by the International Commission for Zoological Nomenclature Opinion 846 and the name of *M. vanicolensis* (Cuvier and Valenciennes), 1830, should now be used for this species.

PFLUGER'S GOAT FISH
Also known as We-ke 'u-la
98—3 *Mulloidichthys pflugeri* (Steindachner), 1900

Pfluger's goat fish is a large, robust species in which the body is quite uniformly red in color. In contrast to the preceeding species, the lining of the abdomen is white. This is a common species from deeper water and is a very good food fish. Large specimens will reach about 24 inches in length.

At present this species is known from the Hawaiian Islands and central Polynesia; it is doubtless much more widely distributed.

THE SAMOAN GOAT FISH
Also known as We-ke, We-ke-'a, and We-ke-'a-'a
98—4 *Mulloidichthys samoensis* (Gunther), 1874

The Samoan goat fish is a very slender species which is marked by a

black spot on the side of the body below the first dorsal fin and by another dark spot on the inside of the gill cover. The body color is reddish, yellowish, and whitish; there is also a yellow line from the head to the tail. The tail becomes yellow after death. Large specimens will reach 18 inches in length.

This is a common shore line species and is most often seen in the spring when the silvery colored young appear in shallow water.

The distribution of this species extends from Hawaii southward to central Polynesia, westward through Micronesia, Melanesia, and the East Indies, and onward across the Indian Ocean to the coast of Africa and the Red Sea.

Recent studies reveal that an earlier and therefor more correct name for this species is *M. flavolineatus* (Lacepede), 1801.

THE TWO-STRIPED GOAT FISH
Also known as Mu-nu and Mo-a-no
98—5 *Parupeneus bifasciatus* (Lacepede), 1802

The munu is a medium sized goat fish of typical color and body proportions. It is probably most easily recognized by the dark area bordering the eye, by a black triangular saddle under each dorsal fin, and by a smaller, fainter saddle on the caudal peduncle. The barbels on the chin are

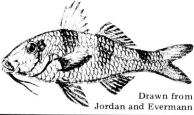

Drawn from
Jordan and Evermann

somewhat shorter and darker than in other species. These fishes are more easily recognized after they approach their adult form and the color pattern has become established. Adult specimens will reach a length of at least 11 inches.

The distribution of this species extends from Hawaii southward into central Polynesia, westward through Micronesia, Melanesia and the East Indies, and onward across the Indian Ocean.

THE YELLOW-TAILED GOAT FISH
Also known as the Mo-a-no
98—6 *Parupeneus chryserydros* (Lacepede), 1802

The body of this fish is moderately slender, bears a longer snout than most goat fishes, and exhibits a pair of unusually long barbels beneath its chin. The color of the body is a purplish hue and contains red shadings. The caudal peduncle is yellow and provides an easy method of identification. Large specimens are reported to reach 24 inches in length; most specimens are much smaller.

The distribution of this species extends from Hawaii southward into central Polynesia, westward through Micronesia (including Guam), Melanesia and the East Indies, and onward across the Indian Ocean to Mauritius.

THE YELLOW-THREADED GOAT FISH
98—7 *Parupeneus chrysonemus* (Jordan and Evermann), 1903

The body of this species is somewhat more slender than others in this family and exhibits very gently curving profiles. Identification of this species can be facilitated by a scale count; there should be about 30 scales along the lateral line and two and one-half scales from the lateral line to the midline of the back between the dorsal fins. The color of the body is reddish brown above and lighter beneath with various yellow markings. There is a pale streak from the eye backward along the upper side of the body parallel to the outline of the back. The caudal fin is reddish at the

base and yellowish at the tip. The barbels are completely yellow and account for the name of *chrysonemus.* It will reach at least nine inches in length.

The distribution of this species includes the Hawaiian area and doubtless other adjoining warm water areas.

THE RED AND BLACK BANDED GOAT FISH
Also known as Mo-a-no
98—8 *Parupeneus multifasciatus* (Quoy and Gaimard), 1824

This is a fish of moderate size and only moderately robust proportions. The body is colored with various shades of black and red with yellow and white hues and markings. There are small, black markings behind the eyes and at the bases of the pectoral fins; there are larger, black, saddle-shaped areas in front of the dorsal fin, between the dorsal fins, and below the soft dorsal fin; there is also a fainter, black, saddle-shaped marking toward the end of the caudal peduncle. The barbels are long and light yellow in color. Large specimens might reach as much as 12 inches in length.

The distribution of this fish extends from Hawaii southward through-out central Polynesia, westward through Micronesia, Melanesia and the East Indies, and onward across the Indian Ocean at least as far as India.

THE SPOTTED GOAT FISH
98—9 *Parupeneus pleurostigma* (Bennett), 1831

The most significant marking of this species is a black spot on the side of the body above the center and at the end of the first dorsal fin. This fish is easily confused with *M. samoensis* but may be separated by the following features: the body is deeper, the spot on the side is larger, the base of the soft dorsal fin is dark, and there are two, dark, triangular saddle-shaped marks behind the soft dorsal fin. The body color is reddish above with yellowish markings and hues and nearly white on the lower side. It will reach a length of about 16 inches, although most specimens are much smaller.

The distribution of this species extends from Hawaii southward into central Polynesia, westward through Micronesia, Melanesia and the East Indies, and onward across the Indian Ocean to the coast of Africa.

THE PURPLISH GOAT FISH
Also known as Ku-mu
98—10 *Parupeneus porphyreus* (Jenkins), 1903

The body of this goat fish is variously colored from greenish to reddish above and is nearly white beneath. It offers a few color markings by which it can be identified. There is a dark, diagonal line running through the eye from the direction of the snout toward the dorsal fin; there is a small, white saddle immediately behind the soft dorsal fin; this light saddle spot is

followed by a dark saddle, then by a large light area at the end of the caudal peduncle, and finally by a dark area at the very base of the tail. The maximum size of this species is reported to be about 16 inches, but most are far smaller.

The young of this species are common in shallow water during the summer months.

The distribution of this species extends from Hawaii southward to central Polynesia and doubtless includes other adjoining areas.

THE RUDDER FISH FAMILY
Also known as the Chubs, the Sea Chubs, the Chopas, and the Pilot Fishes
99 *Family Kyphosidae*

The rudder fishes have bodies which are deep and compressed and which bear a large tail at one end and a small head with a small mouth and fine teeth at the other. The bases of both the dorsal and anal fins are enclosed by a sheath of scales.

These fishes feed on plant food, a fact which accounts for their small mouth and long digestive tract. They live on the bottom in shallow water where they feed upon various marine plants. Because of their diet, their flesh is somewhat less palatable than that of carnivorous fishes.

The family inhabits all tropical and warmer temperate seas. They include about a dozen species of which at least two are known from this area.

THE ASH-COLORED RUDDER FISH
Also known as Ne-nu-e, Na-nu-e, E-ne-nu-e, and Ma-na-lo-a
99—1 *Kyphosus cinerescens* (Forskal), 1775

The nenue has a body which is high and compressed, a small head and mouth, and a large tail. The color of the body is an ash-colored, silvery gray; the fins are darker in color. Occasionally a nenue will be seen which is golden yellow above and white beneath; it is known as nenue pala (yellow) and represents a color phase of this species. Adults when fully grown may reach a length of 24 inches.

The distribution of this species extends from Hawaii southward into Polynesia and westward from Easter Island across the entire tropical Pacific and Indian Oceans to the coast of Africa and the Red Sea.

This species will appear in some books under the name of *Kyphosus fuscus* Lacepede, 1803, and *K. bigibbus* Lacepede, 1802.

THE AZURE RUDDER FISH
99—2 *Sectator azureus* Jordan and Evermann, 1903

The body outlines of this fish are uniformly curved from the small mouth to the tail. The body is a metallic yellow-green color above and is marked along the sides by longitudinal lines of blue and gold; the lower surface is white. This is an unusually rare fish and only a few specimens have been seen. It will reach a length of at least 15 inches.

At present it is known from Hawaii and a few widely scattered areas.

THE GREGORY'S FISH FAMILY
100 *Family Gregoryinidae*

This family consists of only one species of which only one specimen is known. In some ways it resembles the *Kyphosidae* and may someday be grouped with them.

The family was named for Dr. Herbert Gregory, geologist and former Director of the Bernice Pauahi Bishop Museum in Honolulu.

GREGORY'S FISH
100—1 *Gregoryina gygis* Fowler and Ball, 1924

This little fish is known from but a single specimen about two inches in length from Laysan Island which was "brought to the nest of a white tern" on May 12, 1923. This is an example of the extreme depravity to which scientists will descend to obtain a new species, namely, taking food from a

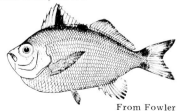

From Fowler

little bird.

The name *gygis* is taken from the name of the white tern, *Gygis alba.*

THE BOAR FISH FAMILY
101 *Family Pentacerotidae (Histiopteridae)*

The boar fishes are a curious group of high-bodied, compressed fishes which live in the deeper waters beyond the shore line. This family is found principally in the warmer waters of the Pacific and Indian Oceans where a few of them are captured for food.

It is a small group of which at least one species occurs in this area.

THE BOAR FISH
101—1 *Histiopterus typus* Temminck and Schlegel, 1844

This boar fish has a body which is deep and compressed. The profile of the head is steep and leads upward to the dorsal fin which contains four spines and about 28 rays. The snout is conical and there is a lump in front of the eyes. A curious group of short whiskers or barbels are attached beneath the chin. The body is gray-black in color and is marked by four, nearly white, wide, vertical stripes across the body and one stripe across the

caudal peduncle. Large specimens will reach at least 18 inches in length.

This is an edible species which appears to live in the deeper waters beyond the shore line.

The distribution of this fish extends from Hawaii and Japan to Australia.

Some authors prefer to use the name of *Histiopterus acutirostris* Temminck and Schlegel, 1844, for this species.

THE OPLEGNATHID FISH FAMILY
102 *Family Oplegnathidae (Hoplegnathidae)*

The members of this obscure family are sometimes called parrot fishes or false parrot fishes, although they are quite unrelated to the true parrot fishes *(Scaridae)* of the tropics. These fishes have a parrot-like beak which is formed from separate incisiform teeth which begin as separate teeth and later fuse into a beak as the fish matures.

They are marine forms which are distributed through most of the tropical and temperate waters of the Pacific and Indian Oceans.

THE STRIPED OPLEGNATHID FISH
102—1 *Oplegnathus fasciatus* (Schlegel), 1844

The body of this fish is deep, compressed, and somewhat elliptical in outline. The color of the body is a somber, dull, brownish color with greenish hues on the back; it turns to a whitish shade on the belly. In young individuals the body is marked by about seven, darker, vertical bands; these disappear with age and become practically invisible in the adults. It will reach a length of about 24 inches.

The distribution of this North Pacific species includes Japan and Hawaii.

The only specimen known from Hawaii measured about 18 inches in length and was reported by Dr.

Drawn from von Siebold

Franz Steindachner in a paper published in Vienna in 1893. No one has seen a specimen since; perhaps he got his labels mixed.

THE BUTTER FISH AND STONE BREAM FAMILY
103 *Family Scorpidae (Scorpididae)*

The butter fishes have deep bodies which are strongly compressed and which are covered by a tough skin and small scales. These are marine fishes of the surf and shore line which occur in the tropical Pacific and Indian Oceans.

Of this small family, only one species is known from this area.

THE STRIPED SCORPID FISH
103—1 *Microcanthus strigatus* (Cuvier and Valenciennes), 1831

The body of this fish is deep, shorter than usual, and compressed. The head and mouth are small and the eyes are large. There is also a scaly sheath at the base of the dorsal fin. The color pattern consists of a series of five or six, wide, horizontal, blackish bands upon a silvery white or creamy white background. Adults will reach six inches in length.

The young of this species are found in the shallow waters of the shore line in April and May and move into the deeper water on the outer side of the reef as they mature.

The distribution of this species extends from Hawaii and Japan to Australia and doubtless includes most of the island groups in this vast area.

This species has been previously included within several families by various authors including the Family *Chaetodontidae* and the Family *Kyphosidae.*

THE BUTTERFLY FISH FAMILY
Including the Angel Fishes and Coral Fishes
104 *Family Chaetodontidae (Pomacanthidae)*

The family of the butterfly fishes is a large and well known group of tropical species. They are mostly of small size with oval-shaped bodies which are deep and greatly compressed. The dorsal fin is continuous along the back and is not divided between the anterior spinous part and the spineless posterior portion. The tail may be rounded, truncated, or emarginated on its posterior border, but it is never forked. The head bears a small mouth which contains flexible, brush-like or comb-like teeth.

Within this family, some members bear a sharp spine on the lower posterior corner of the preopercle. These are the true angel fishes and, by means of this spine, may be distinguished and separated from the true butterfly fishes which lack this spine. These angel fishes are often separated from the butterfly fishes and placed in a separate family, the *Pomacanthidae.*

Butterfly fishes and angel fishes are variously colored with bright and vivid hues of yellow, blue, red, orange, black and white. A few are of somber colors and many possess a dark stripe through the eye.

Most of these fishes live a solitary life or wander through the reef in small groups of two or three. They are nibblers and feed upon small animal and plant life which they pluck from the reef. These fish are edible and are captured for food in many areas.

This family occurs in all tropical seas, but by far the largest number occurs in the tropical western Pacific and Indian Oceans. Of about 190 species, nearly 30 are known from this area.

THE IMPERIAL ANGEL FISH
104—1 *Pomacanthus imperator* (Bloch), 1787

The imperial angel fish is quite rectangular in outline and is easily recognized by its fantastic and complex color patterns. The body is generally a dark blue or purplish color. A curved, triangular, black band with a narrow, blue border passes vertically through the eye; this is separated by a green area from a second oval-shaped, blue-edged black area behind and above the pectoral fins. The entire side of the trunk is covered by many, somewhat horizontal and somewhat 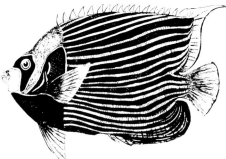 parallel, narrow, yellow lines. Large specimens will reach about 15 inches in length.

The distribution of this species extends from Hawaii and central Polynesia westward through Micronesia, Melanesia and the East Indies, and onward across the Indian Ocean to the coast of Africa and the Red Sea.

The first specimen known from Hawaii was captured by Mr. Fernando Leonida on January 10, 1948, in about 90 feet of water off Ewa, Oahu.

THE BLACK-BANDED ANGEL FISH
104—2 *Holacanthus arcuatus* Gray, 1831

The body of this fish is oval in shape and compressed and bears a small head. It is white in color below, light brown above, and marked along the sides of the body by a wide, horizontal, black stripe which extends from forward of the eye to the end of the dorsal fin. The white areas are variable in color. The caudal and anal fins are black with white trimmings. Large specimens will reach a length of about seven inches.

The distribution of this species is limited at present to the Hawaiian area.

THE MASKED ANGEL FISH
104—3 *Genicanthus personatus* Randall, 1975

This species of angel fish was first discovered by divers in Hawaii in 1972 in the deeper waters on the outer edge of the reef.

Photo by John E. Randall

The body of this fish is deep and very strongly compressed. The head bears a small mouth, small eyes, and the curved spine on the lower edge of the preopercle which is characteristic of the angel fishes. The lateral line extends the full length of the body, although it may be obscure toward the rear of the body. The dorsal fin has 14 spines and 17 or occasionally 18 rays. The anal fin has four spines and 16 soft rays, although some specimens may have three spines and 17 rays. The pectoral fin has 17 rays. The caudal fin is very slightly emarginated or indented on its posterior margin.

The sexes are of different colors. The females are described by Dr. John Randall as having a light gray body on which each scale had a white, crescent-shaped spot. The head and the base of the tail are black. The dorsal fin, anal fin, and the edge of the caudal fin have a bluish hue. The pelvic fins are whitish at their base and the remainder is of a yellowish color.

The male fish has a more elongated body, a more lunate margin on the caudal fin and a different color pattern. In the males, the front of the head is yellow and an orange-yellow color adorns the dorsal, anal, pectoral, and pelvic fins. The body is known to reach a length of at least five inches.

The habitat of this fish is in the deeper water on the outer edge of the reef at depths from about 75 to over 250 feet.

The distribution of this species at present includes only the Hawaiian area.

FISHER'S ANGEL FISH
104—4 *Centropyge fisheri* (Snyder), 1904

This fish is oval in shape and may be recognized by its size, color, and spines. The preopercle bears a long, slightly curved spine at its lower corner and about two smaller spines anterior to it. There are also about three small spines below the eye. The color of the body is a bright reddish orange, the tail is a lemon yellow color toward the center, the pectoral fins are orange in color, and the ventral fins are orange with a blue anterior edge. Most specimens are three inches or less in length.

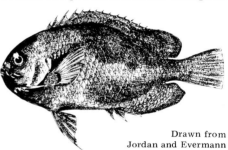

The habitat of this fish seems to be in the deeper waters on the outer edge of the reef.

The distribution of this fish at the present seems limited to the Hawaiian area.

Drawn from
Jordan and Evermann

The scientific name of this species honors Mr. Walter K. Fisher, zoologist of Leland Stanford Junior University, who studied Hawaiian starfishes and birds in the years around 1902.

THE RED ANGEL FISH
104—5 *Centropyge loriculus* Gunther, 1874

This angel fish is easily recognized by its oval, brightly colored body. The sides of the body are uniformly red in color; the tail is a lighter reddish yellow color. The sides of the body are marked with about six, irregular, vertical, black stripes; the mouth is also black and the soft dorsal and anal fins are black posteriorly; the

dorsal fin also exhibits some scattered black spots. Large specimens are reported to reach a length of five inches, but most are much smaller.

The habitat of this little fish is around the coral heads in the deeper water on the outer edge of the reef.

The distribution of this species extends from Guam eastward to Hawaii,

Tahiti, and the Marquesas Islands.

Some books use the name of *Centropyge flammeus* Woods and Schultz, 1953, for this species.

THE BLACK-SPOTTED ANGEL FISH
104—6 *Centropyge nigriocellus* Schultz, 1953

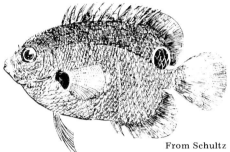

This little fish has an oval-shaped body. It exhibits the typical spine at the base of the preopercle with smaller spines below it and other smaller spines below the eye. The body is variously colored and is marked by two, large, intense, round, black spots, one at the base of the pectoral fin and the other at the base of the soft dorsal fin.

From Schultz

This uncommon fish was described from a single specimen almost two inches in length from Johnston Island.

POTTER'S ANGEL FISH
104—7 *Centropyge potteri* (Jordan and Metz), 1912

Potter's angel fish has an oval body which is brilliantly colored with orange over the front and upper sides. It is marked by many, vertical lines of dark blue or black which sometimes are so dense as to make the lower and posterior parts of the body appear as a solid, deep blue color. Most specimens measure three or four inches in length.

The distribution of this species at present is limited to the Hawaiian area.

The scientific name of this species honor the memory of Mr. Frederick A. Potter (1874-1961), who served from 1903 to 1940 as the first Director of the Waikiki Aquarium. Mr. Potter was born in Michigan on November 5, 1874, and learned the printing trade in his youth. He first came to Honolulu in 1896, at the age of 21, bringing with him the first linotype machine in Hawaii. He worked at the printing trade and later as a clerk for the Honolulu Rapid Transit Company. When the Rapid Transit Company built the "Honolulu Aquarium" in 1903, Mr. Potter transferred from their office to the new Aquarium. He retired from the Aquarium at the end of May, 1940, and immediately moved to Berkeley, California, where he died on March 31, 1961, at the age of 86.

THE COMMON LONG-NOSED BUTTERFLY FISH
Also known as La-u wi-li-wi-li nu-ku-nu-ku 'o-i 'o-i and La-u ha-u
104—8 *Forcipiger flavissimus* Jordan and McGregor, 1898

This butterfly fish has the distinction of having the longest Hawaiian fish name known to the author. The translation means the leaf (lau) of the wili-wili tree with a long or sharp ('oi-'oi) nose (nuku-nuku). The body is quite deep and strongly compressed and the head leads into a long, tubular snout with a small mouth at the end. The color of the body is a bright yellow; the head is brown or black above and white below; there are also small, black areas at the posterior edges of the soft dorsal fin, the caudal fin, and the anal fin. It is reported to reach a length of nine inches, although most specimens are about four or five inches in length. It inhabits the calmer waters on the outer side of the reef.

The distribution of this species extends from Hawaii and the Revilla-gigedo Islands southward into eastern and central Polynesia and then west-ward across the tropical Pacific Ocean, through the East Indies, and across the Indian Ocean to the coast of Africa and the Red Sea.

The use of the name *Forcipiger longirostris* Broussonet, 1782, which has been used for this common long-nosed species, is now incorrect.

THE RARE LONG-NOSED BUTTERFLY FISH
104—9 *Forcipiger longirostris* (Broussonet), 1782

The name of *F. longirostris* has long been used for a fish which is different than the one originally described by Broussonet in 1782. The true *F. longirostris* of Broussonet is an uncommon species which is dark colored when young. This fish and the more common species, *F. flavissimus*, may be

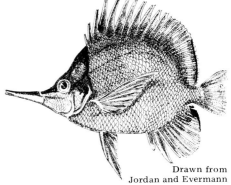

separated by counting the spines and rays of the dorsal fin. *F. longirostris* usually has 11 spines and from 25 to 28 soft rays, while *F. flavissimus* usually has 12 spines and from 22 to 24 soft rays. Both have a yellow body, a head which is black above, and a black margin at the rear edge of the soft dorsal and anal fins. Dr. John Randall notes that there are some minor color differences on the head of these two species. "There is a mid-

Drawn from
Jordan and Evermann

dorsal band on the snout of *longirostris*, extending forward from the inter-orbital space; this band is absent on *flavissimus.*" Large specimens will reach a length of about six inches.

The habitat of this species is in the deeper waters on the outer side of the reef.

The distribution of this species extends from Hawaii southeastward to the Tuamotu Islands and westward through Micronesia, Melanesia, and the East Indies.

It should be noted that the name of *F. inornatus* Randall, 1961, is the juvenile, dark color phase of *F. longirostris* and is therefor a synonym. *F. cyrano* Randall, 1961, is also a synonym of *F. longirostris.*

THE BLACK AND WHITE BUTTERFLY FISH
104—10 *Heniochus acuminatus* (Linne), 1758

This beautiful butter-fly fish has a body which is very high and very com-pressed and which bears a long, arched filament trailing from the fourth dorsal spine. The head is small with a very steep profile and the mouth is unusually small. The color of the body is bas-ically white; it is marked with two, wide, vertical, black stripes and by small, black areas above the eyes and snout. The soft dorsal fin and the caudal fin are yellow. Large specimens will reach about seven inches in length and there are reports of some specimens reaching as much as ten inches.

This fish inhabits the shore line waters on the outer side of the reef. It is edible and is usually caught in wire traps. The distribution of this species extends from Hawaii and Japan southward to central Polynesia and northern Australia and westward across the entire tropical Pacific Ocean, through the East Indies, and across the Indian Ocean to the coast of Africa and the Red Sea. Recent studies indicate that *Heniochus acuminatus* does not occur in Hawaii and that the Hawaiian species is *Heniochus diphreutes* Jordan, Tanaka, and Snyder, 1913.

THOMPSON'S BUTTERFLY FISH
104—11 *Hemitaurichthys thompsoni* Fowler, 1923

Thompson's butterfly fish has an oval body which is very deep and greatly compressed, and a head and mouth which are very small. This is a very drab species and has been described as "deep uniform neutral dusky". It is a deep gray color with some areas, including the ventral fins, approaching black. This is a shore line fish which lives beyond the reef.

The distribution of this fish extends from Guam to the Hawaiian area.

Mr. Henry Weed Fowler first obtained specimens of this fish from Mr. John W. Thompson, preparator and technician at the Bishop Museum, and subsequently named it in his honor.

THE BANDED BUTTERFLY FISH
104—12* *Hemitaurichthys polylepis* (Bleeker), 1857

The body of this butterfly fish is deep, extremely flattened, and bears the unusually small head and very small mouth of this family. It is easily recognized by its color pattern. The side of the body is a beautiful white color while the head, the area above the head, the soft dorsal fin, and the anal fin are all of a golden yellow or orange color. There are some

tinges of black on the tail. Adults are usually from five to seven inches long. This butterfly fish inhabits the deeper water on the outside of the reef.

The distribution of this species extends from Hawaii to the East Indies including New Guinea. It doubtless occurs in adjoining areas.

In some books this species is listed under the name of *Hemitaurichthys zoster* (Bennett), 1831.

Polylepis is a Greek word meaning "many scales" and *zoster* is the Greek word for "band or girdle".

THE YELLOW BUTTERFLY FISH
Also known as La-u ha-u and Ki-ka ka-pu
104—13 *Chaetodon auriga* Forskal, 1775

The yellow butterfly fish is one of the larger species of the family. It is most easily identified by the filament of the soft dorsal fin and by the black spot below it. The body is a grayish white color in front, white below,

* See Appendix.

and yellow in the upper posterior areas. There is a vertical, black stripe through the eye and a pattern on the body consisting of two sets of parallel dusky stripes which are almost at right angles to each other. This is a large species and will reach six and perhaps as much as nine inches in length.

The distribution of this fish extends from Hawaii southward to central Polynesia and Australia and westward through Micronesia, Melanesia, the East Indies, and across the Indian Ocean to the coast of Africa and the Red Sea.

In some books this fish is described under the name of *Chaetodon setifer* Bloch, 1788.

THE LEMON-COLORED BUTTERFLY FISH
104—14 *Chaetodon citrinellus* Cuvier and Valenciennes, 1831

This is a small, frail species with a strongly compressed body. It is yellow colored on the upper part of the body and lighter below. The sides of the body are covered with many, small, dark spots, each of which is located in the center of a scale. It will reach a length of about four inches.

The distribution of this species extends from Hawaii southward to central Polynesia and northern Australia and westward through Micronesia, Melanesia, and the East Indies.

KLEIN'S BUTTERFLY FISH
104—15 *Chaetodon kleini* Bloch, 1790

This butterfly fish is a small, frail, thin species without distinctive markings. The head is marked by a dark, vertical band through the eye, while the remainder of the body is a dusky, greenish brown hue with scattered darker spots. It reaches about four inches in length.

It inhabits deeper water on the outer side of the reef.

The distribution of this species extends from Hawaii westward to the coast of Africa.

Some authors have previously listed this species as *Chaetodon corallicola* Snyder, 1904.

Chaetodon kleini   Chaetodon ephippium

THE SADDLE-MARKED BUTTERFLY FISH
104—16 *Chaetodon ephippium* Cuvier and Valenciennes, 1831

This butterfly differs from others in having a longer snout and also a slender filament extending backward from the soft dorsal fin. The body is conspicuously marked by a large, black, saddle-like spot at the upper, rear corner of the body; this spot is separated from the remainder of the body by a white border. The body is generally grayish in front with six or more, faint, horizontal stripes along the abdomen. The lower side of the head is orange, there is a faint vertical stripe through the eye, and the fins are yellow. It will reach a length of about six inches.

The distribution of this species extends from Hawaii southward into central Polynesia, westward through Micronesia and Melanesia, and through the East Indies.

THE BLUE-LINED BUTTERFLY FISH
Also known as La-u ha-u, Ki-ka ka-pu, and Ka-pu hi-li
104—17 *Chaetodon fremblii* Bennett, 1829

The body of this species is yellow in color and is marked by eight or nine, horizontal, blue stripes. In addition, the body is marked by two black spots, one of which is located above the eye and the other at the base of the tail. It will reach about six inches in length.

At present this fish is known only from the Hawaiian area.

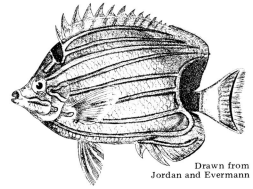

Drawn from
Jordan and Evermann

THE LINED BUTTERFLY FISH
Also known as La-u ha-u, Ki-ka ka-pu, and Ka-pu hi-li
104—18 *Chaetodon lineolatus* Cuvier and Valenciennes, 1831

This butterfly fish is a large species. It has a grayish white body which is marked on the sides by about 16 or more, narrow, vertical, black lines. There is a vertical, black band through the eye and a wider, black border on the body just below the dorsal fin. The fins are yellow in color. Large specimens will reach 12 inches in length.

The distribution of this species extends from Hawaii and central Polynesia westward through Micronesia, Melanesia, the East Indies, and across the Indian Ocean to the coast of Africa and the Red Sea.

Chaetodon lineolatus   *Chaetodon lunula*

THE LUNULE OR CRESCENT - MASKED BUTTERFLY FISH
Also known as La-u ha-u, Ki-ka ka-pu, and Ka-pu hi-li
104—19 *Chaetodon lunula* (Lacepede), 1802

The body of this butterfly fish is slightly more robust than that of other species. It is colored with various shades of yellow and is marked by three, significant, black bands. There is a vertical black band through the eye, a second black moon-shaped band which curves from the upper side of the body toward the eye, and a third black area at the base of the tail. Large specimens will reach six or seven inches in length and some have been reported to reach eight inches. Young specimens have a circular, white-edged, black spot on the soft dorsal fin and are therefor often mistaken for other species.

The distribution of this species extends from Hawaii and central Polynesia westward through Micronesia, Melanesia, the East Indies, and across the Indian Ocean to the coast of Africa and the Red Sea.

THE SPOTTED OR MILLET SEED BUTTERFLY FISH
104—20 *Chaetodon miliaris* Quoy and Gaimard, 1825

The spotted butterfly fish is a rather small, flat species with a bright yellow body which is marked by many, small, round, dark spots which are arranged in vertical rows. In addition, there is a black, vertical band through the eye and a black band on the caudal peduncle. Large specimens will reach about five inches in length.

The distribution of this species extends from Hawaii southward to central Polynesia, westward through Micronesia, Melanesia and the East Indies, and on across the Indian Ocean to the coast of Africa.

The authors seem to have assigned the name *miliaris* to this species because the small, black spots resembled the seed of millet.

THE BANDED BUTTERFLY FISH
104—21 *Chaetodon modestus* Temminck and Schlegel, 1842

The body of this rare fish is oval in shape, deep, and compressed. The spines on the dorsal fin are quite long compared to most fishes of this group. The body is conspicuously marked by wide, alternating, vertical bands of white and a golden brownish color. A round, black spot with a narrow,

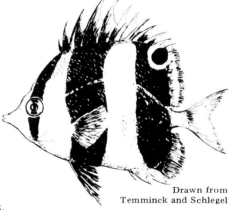

white border is located at the upper, posterior edge of the body and upon the dorsal fin. Most specimens measure about two inches in length.

The habitat of this small fish seems to be in the deeper, shore line waters beyond the reef at depths ranging from about 300 feet to at least 600 feet. It is therefore seldom seen.

The distribution of this butterfly fish extends from Japan southward through the Philippine Islands to Singapore. It occurs in Hawaii and doubtless in many other adjoining areas.

Drawn from
Temminck and Schlegel

The first specimen known from Hawaii was found floating dead in the ocean off the Kau district on the island of Hawaii at the time of the eruption of Mauna Loa in 1919. It was described as a new species and so will also be found in books under the name of *Loa excelsa* Jordan, 1922, and also as *Heniochus excelsa* (Jordan), 1922.

THE MANY-BANDED BUTTERFLY FISH
104—22 *Chaetodon multicinctus* Garrett, 1863

This butterfly fish is small, strongly compressed, and lightly colored; it has the body marked by a series of five or six, dark but faint, parallel, vertical bands and by a great multitude of small spots, some of which are in vertical and horizontal rows. Adult specimens will measure as much as four inches in length.

At present this species is known only from the Hawaiian area; it is doubtless more widely distributed.

Chaetodon multicinctus is often confused with a very similar species, *C. punctato-fasciatus* Cuvier and Valenciennes, 1831. Persons who wish to clearly distinguish these species should read Schultz, Leonard P. 1953. Fishes of the Marshall and Marianas Islands. *U.S. Nat'l Mus. Bull.* 202(1):596.

Chaetodon multicinctus   Chaetodon ornatissimus

THE ORNATE BUTTERFLY FISH
Also known as Ki-ka ka-pu
104—23 *Chaetodon ornatissimus* Cuvier and Valenciennes, 1831

Without a doubt this fish is one of the most beautiful species in the sea. The body is a silvery white color and is marked by six, diagonal, parallel, orange stripes. The fins are yellow in color and the head, which is likewise yellow, is marked by five, vertical, black lines. Large specimens will reach a length of about seven inches.

The distribution of this fish extends from Hawaii southward to central Polynesia and westward through Micronesia, Melanesia, and the East Indies.

THE FOUR-SPOTTED BUTTERFLY FISH
104—24 *Chaetodon quadrimaculatus* Gray, 1831

The four-spotted butterfly fish is unmistakable and cannot be confused with any other species. The body is black above and marked with oval, white spots; the lower part of the body and the fins are yellow or yellowish in color. A vertical band passes through the eye and there are darker lines upon the fins. It is a medium-sized species and will

reach about six inches in length.

The distribution of this fish extends from Hawaii southward into central Polynesia.

THE RETICULATED BUTTERFLY FISH
104—25 *Chaetodon reticulatus* Cuvier and Valenciennes, 1831

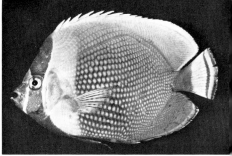

The reticulated butterfly fish is named for the net-like pattern of light spots which mark the black, posterior part of the body. The head is marked by a vertical, black band through the eye. The remainder of the body is variously colored with gray, yellow, and red markings. It will reach a length of about six inches.

The distribution of this species extends from Hawaii and Japan southward to central Polynesia and westward through Micronesia, Melanesia, the East Indies, and across the Bay of Bengal to India.

TINKER'S BUTTERFLY FISH
104—26 *Chaetodon tinkeri* Schultz, 1951

The body of this fish is oval in shape, deep, strongly compressed, and possesses the small head and small mouth which are typical of the butterfly fishes. The color of the anterior and lower portion of the body is white, while the upper and posterior portion is black. There is a vertical, yellow band through the eye and the caudal fin is yellow. It will reach about six inches in length.

The habitat of this species is in the calmer waters on the outside of the reef at depths below 100 feet and particularly in those areas which abound in the black coral (*Antipathes*).

The distribution of this species is limited to the Hawaiian area.

This species is named for Spencer Wilkie Tinker, (1909 -   ) biologist, author of this book, and Director of the Waikiki Aquarium in Honolulu from 1940 to 1972.

THE THREE-BANDED BUTTERFLY FISH
Also known as Ka-pu hi-li
104—27 *Chaetodon trifasciatus* Mungo Park, 1797

This species is slightly darker in color than most butterfly fishes. The body is a yellowish color but is darkened by 18 or more, long, interrupted, black stripes. There are three, black, vertical stripes on the head; the center stripe, which is the widest, passes through the eye. There is also a black band with a yellow border on the soft dorsal fin, the caudal fin, and the anal fin. Large specimens will reach about six inches in length.

The distribution of this species extends from Hawaii southward to central Polynesia and Australia and then westward through Micronesia, Melanesia and the East Indies, and onward across the Indian Ocean to the coast of Africa and the Red Sea.

Chaetodon trifasciatus   *Chaetodon unimaculatus*

THE ONE-SPOT BUTTERFLY FISH
Also known as La-u ha-u and Ki-ka ka-pu
104—28 *Chaetodon unimaculatus* Bloch, 1787

The body of this fish is colored with various shades of yellow and is marked with a large, round, black spot on the upper center of the body. There are also two, vertical, black stripes, one of which passes through the eye and the other through the ends of the dorsal fin, the caudal peduncle, and the anal fin. The maximum length of this fish is reported to be seven inches; most are much shorter.

The distribution of this species extends from Hawaii southward to central Polynesia and westward through Micronesia, Melanesia, and the East Indies, and then on across the Indian Ocean to the coast of Africa.

THE JACK FISH FAMILY
Including the Pompanos, Cavallas, and Runners
105 *Family Carangidae (Seriolidae)*

The jacks and their relatives vary in the shape of their bodies from species which are slender and spindle-shaped to others which are short, deep bodied, and very compressed. They possess both a spinous dorsal and a soft dorsal fin. The spinous dorsal fin is situated in a groove in the back and is not as strong and well developed as in many other families of fishes; in older individuals of some species these spines often become embedded in the flesh and are scarcely visible. The members of this family possess two spines located just in front of the anal fin; these spines likewise originate in a groove and so may not always be visible. In this group, the caudal peduncle is small and leads to a tail which is either forked or occasionally has a lunate margin. Nearly all of these fishes bear hard, bony plates called scutes along the sides of the caudal peduncle; these scutes follow the lateral line forward onto the body where they gradually diminish in size and end at various locations depending upon the species. The pectoral fins are usually narrow and often falcate in shape. In coloration, these fishes are usually bluish or silvery above and lighter below. The group includes small, medium, and large species, some of which will exceed six feet in length.

In their habits they are active, fast swimming, carnivorous predators which feed upon a wide variety of fish and crustacea. Most prefer to live in schools and will either form schools of their own or join the schools of other species. The largest number of species of this family live about the reef and shore line areas of tropical and sub-tropical seas. The young live closer to the reef and shore line for protection and move toward deeper water as they mature. Many will enter bays and estuaries and a few live in fresh water.

The family includes more than 200 species of which more than 25 species are known from this area.

THE LEATHER - BACK FISH
Also known as La-i, Runner, Queenfish, and Saint Peter's Leather-skin
105—1 *Scombroides sancti-petri* (Cuvier), 1831

The lai is a very slender, compressed fish with a spindle-shaped profile and a widely forked tail. The dorsal and anal fins are equal and opposite and each ends in a series of about six or seven finlets. This fish does not have the hard scutes along the caudal peduncle and the lateral line as do many other members of this family. The color of the upper part of the body is a shining slaty blue with silvery reflections; this changes gradually to silvery white on the belly. The fins may be tinged with yellow. Adult specimens will reach a length of at least 25 inches.

The habitat of the lai is in the surface waters bordering the coast line where they forage upon smaller fishes. It is considered a game fish and is caught for food, although it is not particularly tasty. Their tough skin is used to make fishing lures.

The distribution of this species extends from Hawaii southward to central Polynesia, westward through Micronesia, Melanesia and the East

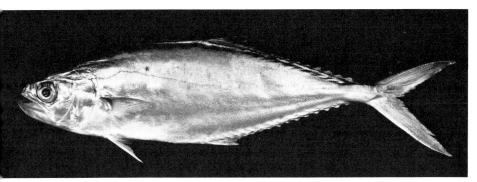

Indies, and on across the Indian Ocean to the coast of Africa and the Red Sea.

This species may appear in some books under the name of *Chorinemus tolooparah* (Ruppell), 1828.

THE RAINBOW RUNNER FISH
Also known as Ka-ma-nu, Yellow-tail, Shoe-maker, Sea Salmon, and Hawaiian Salmon
105—2 *Elagatis bipinnulatus* (Quoy and Gaimard), 1824

The rainbow runner has a body which is long, slender, and spindle or cigar-shaped. The dorsal and anal fins are both long and are each followed by a single, separate finlet. The heavy scales or scutes found along the sides of the body at the base of the tail are absent in this species. The color is a beautiful, deep blue above; below this blue area is a long, horizontal, yellow stripe; below this stripe is a thin blue stripe; and below it is the lighter colored abdomen. Large specimens will reach a length of four feet.

The runner is an edible species which is occasionally captured by trolling.

This is a pelagic species which seems to be circumtropical in distribution.

THE PILOT FISH
Also known as the Annexation Fish (Hawaii)
105—3 *Naucrates ductor* (Linne), 1758

The pilot fish is most easily recognized by the wide, vertical bands which mark the body. It lacks the bony scutes found on the sides of the

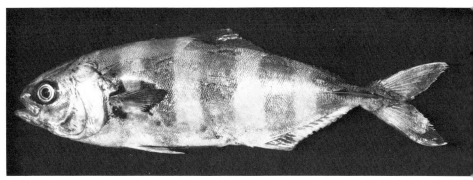

caudal peduncle in most members of this family, but in their place the body bears a hard, lateral keel on the caudal peduncle. Large specimens will reach 24 inches in length.

The pilot fish lives in the open sea. The young seek refuge beneath floating seaweed, jelly-fishes, logs, and any other object which affords protection. As they grow older they join larger fishes, particularly sharks, and follow them about, enjoying their protection and feeding upon their food scraps and faeces.

In Hawaii, this species is known as the Annexation Fish because it appeared in some numbers at the time of the annexation of Hawaii to the United States.

The pilot fish occurs in all warm and temperate seas of the world, but it does not enter colder water. It is an uncommon species.

THE AMBER-JACK OR YELLOW-TAIL FISH
Also known as Ka-ha-la, A-mu-ka, Mo-ku-le-'i-a, Ka-ha-la ma-o-li,
Ka-ha-la 'o-pi-o (young), Atlantic Amber-jack, and Greater Amber-jack
105—4 *Seriola dumerili* (Risso), 1810

The body of the kahala is long, somewhat spindle-shaped in outline and laterally compressed. The dorsal and anal fins do not have any separate finlets behind them and there are no hard, bony scutes on the side of the body at the base of the tail. The color of the body is light brown with some metallic and purplish tinges. A horizontal, yellow band extends along the

side of the body from the head to the base of the tail; there is also a dark, diagonal streak through the eye. Large specimens will reach a length of about six feet.

The kahala is usually caught on hook and line at depths of 400 or 500 feet. It seems to be a bottom-living fish and apparently feeds off other bottom-living forms at those depths.

The distribution of this species is probably world-wide in warm water.

This species very closely resembles *Seriola rivoliana* Cuvier and Valenciennes, 1833, the common Almaco Jack of the Atlantic Ocean. Some scholars believe that they are identical and that *S. rivoliana* is the correct name for this world-wide species.

THE GOLDEN-STRIPED AMBER-JACK FISH
Also known as Ka-ha-la ʻo-pi-o (young)
105—5 *Seriola aureovittata* Schlegel, 1842

Drawn from Jordan and Evermann

The body of this amber-jack is long, spindle-shaped, and not especially compressed. It resembles *Seriola dumerili* but differs from it in some details including the presence of a dense patch of scales on the upper part of the opercle near the eye. The only known Hawaiian specimen measured ten and one-half inches in length.

The distribution of this fish includes Hawaii and Japan.

THE TORPEDO CAVALLA FISH
105—6 *Megalaspis cordyla* (Linne), 1758
The body of this fish is torpedo-shaped like the bodies of the tuna fishes. It has a thin caudal peduncle and between six and nine detached finlets behind the dorsal fin and the anal fin. The color is bluish green above and silvery below; the fins are yellowish, usually fringed with black; and there is a prominent black spot on the upper corner of the operculum. The eyes have an adipose eyelid which gives the eye of this species a somewhat cat-like appearance. Adult specimens measure between 12 and 20 inches in length and live in large schools near the surface.

The distribution of this species extends from Hawaii southward to central Polynesia, westward across the tropical Pacific Ocean, through the

East Indies, and across the Indian Ocean to the coast of Africa and the Red Sea.

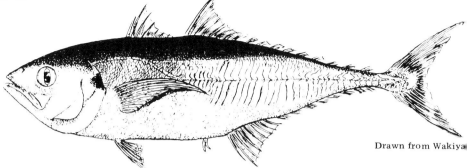

Drawn from Wakiya

THE MACKEREL SCAD FISH
Also known as the 'O-pe-lu
105—7 *Decapterus pinnulatus* (Eydoux & Souleyet), 1841

This scad has a truly spindle-shaped body, for it is evenly and uniformly tapered from the center toward both ends. There is a single, detached finlet behind both the dorsal fin and the anal fin. There are scutes along the posterior part of the lateral line; this feature is useful in separating *D. pinnulatus* from *D. maruadsi* since *D. pinnulatus* has between 20 and 27 scutes, while *D. maruadsi* has between 32 and 37 scutes on the lateral line. The body is bluish on the upper one-third and silvery white below; some specimens are greenish yellow above and white beneath. A dark spot on the upper edge of the gill cover is also useful in identifying this species.

The distribution of this species seems to be nearly world-wide in warm water. It will reach 20 inches in length, although most specimens are less than ten inches.

THE SMALLER MACKEREL SCAD FISH
Also known as the 'O-pe-lu
105—8 *Decapterus maruadsi* (Schlegel), 1844

This scad has a spindle-shaped body and a single, detached finlet behind both the soft dorsal fin and the anal fin. It very closely resembles the other scads, but may be distinguished from them by its yellow fins and by the

258

white border on the soft dorsal fin. Large specimens will reach a length of about 12 inches. This is an uncommon species which is found within the schools of the common 'opelu.

The distribution of this species extends from Hawaii to Japan.

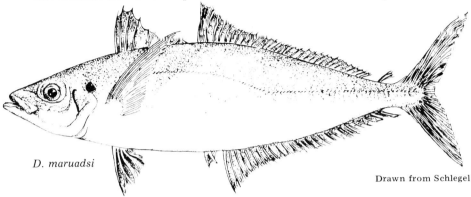

D. maruadsi

Drawn from Schlegel

THE BIG-EYED SCAD FISH
Also known as A-ku-le and Ha-la-lu
105—9 *Trachiurops crumenophthalmus* (Bloch), 1793

The body of the akule is quite spindle-shaped and resembles in general the shape of the mackerel fishes. It has exceedingly large eyes and is usually identified by this feature. For more positive identification, it may be helpful to inspect the shoulder girdle just beneath the gill cover. Bend the gill cover forward and glance along the posterior margin of the gill opening; if this margin has a notch toward its lower border, it is doubtless this species. The color of the body is a silvery blue above and a silvery white beneath. The caudal fin is yellow in color. It will reach 14 or 15 inches in length.

The akule is a food fish which is caught by hand lines at night and by beach seines and other types of nets.

The distribution of this fish is world-wide in warm water.

In old Hawaii the names of the growth stages of this species were as follows: pa-'a-'a (young of 2 or 3 inches), ha-la-lu or ha-ha-la-lu (intermediate size), and a-ku-le (adult).

THE YELLOW JACK FISH
Also known as U-lu-a pa-'o pa-'o, U-lu-a ka-ni-'o (striped), and Yellow Ulua
105—10 *Gnathanodon speciosus* (Forskal), 1775

This jack may be easily identified by its color. The body is a creamy, yellowish color with silvery and bluish hues and is marked by a series of darker, greenish, vertical stripes. These stripes vary in number from about eight to twelve, become fainter with age, and slowly fade away. The scutes on the lateral line are small and weak in this species and there are no teeth in the jaws of the adults. Large specimens will reach a length of 36 to 40 inches.

The distribution of this species extends from Hawaii southward to central Polynesia, westward through Micronesia and Melanesia, through the East Indies, and across the Indian Ocean to the coast of Africa.

THE THREAD-FIN JACK FISH
Also known as U-lu-a ki-hi ki-hi, Thread-fin Ulua, Thread Fish,
and Cobbler Fish
105—11 *Alectis ciliaris* (Bloch), 1787

This is without a doubt one of the world's most beautiful fishes. The body is diamond-shaped, extremely compressed, and possesses long, trailing filaments from its dorsal and anal fins. These filaments are longest in the younger fish and become progressively shorter with age. The color of the body is silvery blue above and brilliant silvery below. It will reach a length of at least 12 and possibly 15 inches.

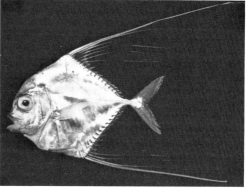

The distribution of this species extends from Hawaii southward into central Polynesia, westward through Micronesia and Melanesia, through the East Indies, and across the Indian Ocean to the coast of

Africa.

In some books this fish may be listed under the name of *Selar ciliaris* (Bloch), 1787. The following comparison is from Gosline and Brock.

From Gosline
and Brock

Alectis ciliaris
The depth of the preorbital is not greater than the diameter of the eye; the gill rakers are long and slender.

Alectis indica
The depth of the preorbital is nearly twice the diameter of the eye; the gill rakers are short and stout.

THE LARGE THREAD-FIN JACK FISH
Also known as U-lu-a ki-hi ki-hi
105—12 *Alectis indica* (Ruppell), 1828

This fish is a larger species of the thread-fin jack and not as startling and beautiful as the preceeding species. It also has a diamond-shaped body, but is more elongated than *A. ciliaris.* The body is compressed like the preceeding species, but the streamers are not as long or as numerous. The color of the body is a combination of bluish, greenish, and yellowish hues above and a dull, silvery color below. It will reach over two feet in length and has been reported to measure as much as five feet.

The habitat of this fish is in the deeper, calmer waters off the outer edge of the reef. It is an uncommon species, although it used to appear occasionally in island markets.

The distribution of this species extends from Hawaii southward into Polynesia, westward through Micronesia and Melanesia, through the East Indies, and across the Indian Ocean to the coast of Africa and the Red Sea.

THE WHITE JACK FISH
Also known as the White U-lu-a, U-lu-a ke-a, and U-lu-a a-u-ke-a
105—13 *Carangoides* species

The white ulua is a stocky species with a compressed body and a steep profile on the front of the head. It is silvery in color with fainter, darker hues above and lighter below. It is a large species and will reach from 36 to 42 inches in length when fully grown.

This is a common species which frequents the shore line and which is caught by casting from shore, by nets, and in wire traps.

The distribution of this species seems limited to the Hawaiian area.

The name of *Carangoides ajax* Snyder, 1904, has been used for this species. Uncertainty surrounds its identity.

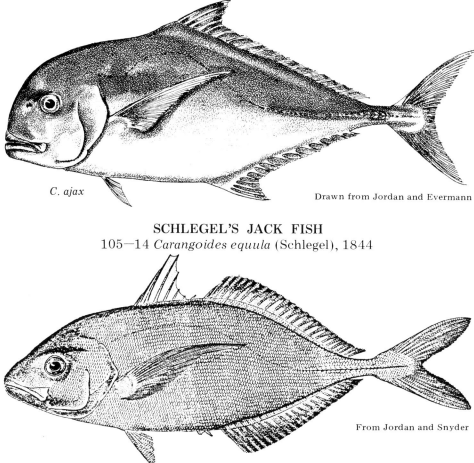

C. ajax

Drawn from Jordan and Evermann

SCHLEGEL'S JACK FISH
105—14 *Carangoides equula* (Schlegel), 1844

From Jordan and Snyder

The body of this species is typical of most jacks. The dorsal profile is a low sweeping curve with low dorsal and anal fins. The breast is scaled and there are between 21 and 27 scutes along the posterior, straight portion of the lateral lines. There are about 23 dorsal rays and about 21 anal rays. The color is a silvery greenish above and silvery below. The dorsal and anal fins are dusky with their anterior portions approaching black. Some authors report five or six, wide, darker, vertical bands on the sides of the body, possibly in younger specimens. Specimens have been reported from ten to 21 inches in length.

The distribution of this fish extends from Hawaii and Japan southward to the East Indies and westward to the coast of Africa.

FORSKAL'S JACK FISH
Also known as 'O-mi-lu
105—15 *Carangoides ferdau* (Forskal), 1775
The body of this species is robust and the profile is quite uniformly

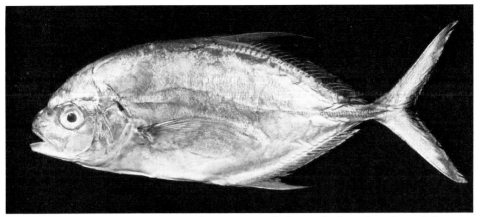

curved above and below. The front rays of the soft dorsal and anal fins are longer than usual and the breast is without scales. The color of the body is silvery bluish above and lighter below with bluish and golden hues on the fins. The sides of the body are marked with a few, round, lemon-colored spots with darker centers. These spots vary in number and location and tend to disappear in older individuals. It will reach a length of about 24 inches.

This is an edible shore line species which is solitary in its habits.

The distribution of this species extends from Hawaii southward to central Polynesia, westward through Micronesia and Melanesia, through the East Indies, and across the Indian Ocean to the coast of Africa and the Red Sea.

Some scholars believe that this species with the yellow spots is in reality *Carangoides orthogrammus* (Jordan and Gilbert) and that the name of *C. ferdau* belongs to a species with a barred color pattern.

BLEEKER'S JACK FISH
105—16 *Carangoides gymnostethoides* Bleeker, 1852

The body of this jack is slender, elliptical in shape, and compressed. The head is quite long and the dorsal and ventral profiles are gently sweeping curves. The breast is without scales (naked), the pectoral fins are long, and the caudal peduncle is quite slender. The arched part of the lateral line is slightly

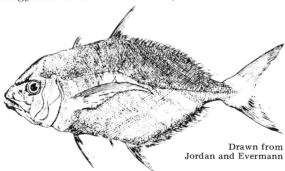

Drawn from
Jordan and Evermann

longer than the straight part. The color of the body is greenish above and silvery below. The second dorsal fin and the anal fin are greenish with black marks. There is no well-defined spot on the operculum as in some species, but the area above and behind the eye is darkened. Large specimens are reported to reach about 30 inches in length.

263

The distribution of this uncommon species extends from Hawaii southward into central Polynesia, westward through the East Indies, and across the Indian Ocean to the coast of Africa.

THE REVERSED-SPINE JACK FISH
105—17 *Uraspis reversa* Jordan, Evermann and Wakiya, 1927

This species was described in 1927 from a few small specimens. It was described as having a moderately deep body in which the straight, posterior part of the lateral line bore 26 scutes; these scutes were very unusual because the blunt spines were directed forward rather than backward as in other members of this family. The color of the body was described as "more or less dusky, with dark cross-bars." One museum specimen measured six inches

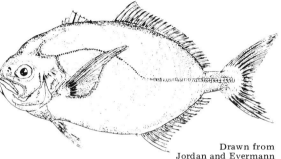

Drawn from
Jordan and Evermann

in length. It is supposed to resemble *Caranx helvolus*. Very little is known about it.

THE THICK-LIPPED JACK FISH
Also known as Thick-lipped Pig Ulua, Buta-guchi (pig mouth), and Buta Ulua
105—18 *Caranx cheilio* (Snyder), 1904

The thick-lipped ulua is most easily identified by its pointed, conical snout and its thick, fleshy lips. In addition, the dorsal profile is concave in the area in front of the eyes. The color of the body is silvery and, as in most fishes, is darker above and lighter beneath. There is a dark spot about one-half the size of the eye at the upper edge of the opercle. Young specimens

are marked with a horizontal, yellow streak which passes through the eye and continues along the body to the tail. Large specimens will reach 36 inches in length.

The distribution of this species extends from the leeward islands of Hawaii southward to central Polynesia, eastward to Easter Island, and doubtless elsewhere in the tropical Indo-Pacific area.

THE DARK OR DUSKY JACK FISH
Also known as U-lu-a la-u-li (dark)
105—19 *Caranx helvolus* (Forster), 1775

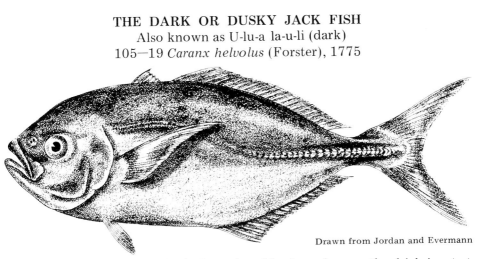

Drawn from Jordan and Evermann

This species has a dark, dusky-colored body and a mouth which is set at a steep angle. The identifying feature of this fish is the color of the inside of the mouth and tongue. The tongue and the roof of the mouth are white, while the back of the mouth, the pharynx, and the inner surfaces of the gill openings are blue-black. Adults will reach a length of at least 30 inches.

The distribution of this species includes the Hawaiian area and doubtless adjoining areas.

THE WHITE ULUA OR FORSKAL'S INDO-PACIFIC JACK FISH
105—20 *Caranx ignobilis* (Forskal), 1775

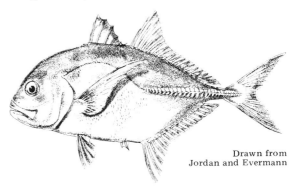

Drawn from
Jordan and Evermann

The body of this species is short, robust, deep, and compressed. The head has a steep dorsal profile and the mouth is large and nearly horizontal. The breast is without scales except for a small patch in front of the pelvic fins. The straight part of the lateral line begins directly above the origin of the anal fin and continues with 30 to 33 well-developed scutes along the entire straight portion to the tail. The color of the body is a silvery, dusky, gray-green above with a greenish head and becomes increasingly silvery white toward the belly. There is no spot on the opercle and the base or axil of the pectoral fins is dark or blackish. The caudal fin is blackish on the upper lobe and yellow on the lower lobe; the remaining fins are yellowish. Adults will measure 36 and possibly as much as 44 inches in length. This is a common species.

The distribution of this fish extends from Hawaii southward to central Polynesia, westward through Micronesia and Melanesia, through the East Indies, and across the Indian Ocean to the coast of Africa.

THE GOLDEN SCAD FISH
105—21 *Caranx kalla* Cuvier, 1832

The body of this fish is slender and has the general shape of the akule and the 'omaka. The lateral line has about ten scales followed by about 40 to 46 scutes. The color of the body is greenish silvery to bluish green above with yellow reflections. There are about seven, faint, darker cross-bars above the lateral line. The lower half of the body is silvery in color with pearly reflections. The caudal fin is yellow in color. There is a significant, black spot at the upper corner of the operculum. Most specimens measure about ten inches in length, although some will reach as much as 15 inches.

The distribution of this species extends from Hawaii southward to Australia and westward across the Indian Ocean to the Red Sea.

THE BLACK JACK FISH
Also known as the Black Ulua
105—22 *Caranx lugubris* Poey, 1861

From Schultz

In this fish the scutes on the lateral line number from 27 to 34, are black in color, and begin immediately at the straight portion of the lateral line. The breast is covered with scales and there is but a single row of teeth in the upper jaw (*C. sexfasciatus* has two rows). The body is dark in color and the head is almost black. Large specimens will reach between 36 and 48 inches in length.

The distribution of this species is circumtropical.

THE YELLOW-TAILED SCAD FISH
Also known as 'O-ma-ka
105—23 *Caranx mate* Cuvier and Valenciennes, 1833

The 'omaka is a rather slender, fusiform fish with gently curving profiles which are almost identical on the upper and lower margins of the body. The straight posterior portion of the lateral line bears from 6 to 14 scales which are followed in turn by 25 to 36 scutes which continue backward to the tail. There is a small finlet at the end of both the soft dorsal and anal fins which is only partly detached or separated from the fins. The body is multi-colored; the upper part of the body is silvery with darker, greenish yellow markings; these are arranged in nine or ten, darker, vertical bars which are distributed along the body from the head to the tail. The lower surface is silvery. A significant black spot, located directly behind the eye, marks the posterior corner of the operculum.

The habitat of this fish is the quiet, shallow bays and estuaries of the shore line; it is never found in the open sea. Young individuals are occasionally found under jelly-fishes.

The distribution of the 'omaka extends from Hawaii southward to central Polynesia, westward through Micronesia and Melanesia, through the East Indies, and across the Indian Ocean to the coast of Africa and the Red Sea.

THE BLUE JACK FISH
Also known as 'O-mi-lu, 'O-mi-lu-mi-lu, Blue Ulua, and Hoshi (star) Ulua
105—24 *Caranx melampygus* Cuvier and Valenciennes, 1833

The blue ulua has a body which is comparatively slender when compared with that of the white ulua; the profile of the head is also more gently sloping. In the blue ulua, the breast is covered with scales and the first four or five scales of the lateral line are not modified into scutes. This species changes color with age. When it is young, the body is bright, silvery, blue-green above and silvery beneath, and the pectoral fins are yellowish. As the fish grows larger, blue-black spots appear scattered over the body; these increase in number until they practically cover the body.

This species will reach a length of about 36 inches.

The distribution of this fish extends from Hawaii southward into central Polynesia, eastward to western Central America, and westward through Micronesia and Melanesia, through the East Indies, and across the Indian Ocean to the coast of Africa.

Previously the name of *C. melampygus* was given only to small, young, blue ulua and the name of *Caranx stellatus* Eydoux and Souleyet, 1841, was given to the older, larger, darker individuals. You will therefore find this fish listed in some books under both names.

THE SIX-BANDED JACK FISH
Also known as U-lu-a
105—25 *Caranx sexfasciatus* Quoy and Gaimard, 1825

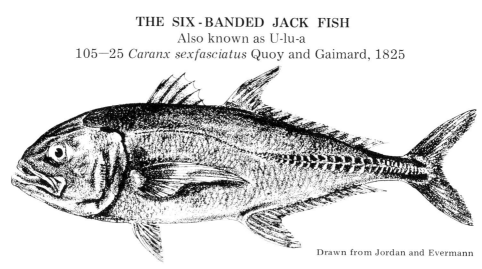

Drawn from Jordan and Evermann

This ulua is a large and relatively slender species. The breast is scaly, the pectoral fins are long and falcate, and the lateral line has from 27 to 35 scutes which begin at the very beginning of the straight portion and extends backward in a straight row to the tail. The eye is relatively large and the posterior adipose eyelid, which is far larger than the anterior one, extends rather far forward, but does not cover the pupil of the eye. The upper jaw contains two rows of teeth; the teeth of the outer row are canine-like and are widely separated, while those of the inner row are in a narrow band. The color of the body is blue-green with golden hues above and yellowish green to silvery hues beneath. Young specimens are marked with dark, vertical bands from four to seven in number; it is from these bands that the scientific name is taken. A round, dark spot is present at the upper corner of the operculum. The caudal fin is yellowish below, become darker dorsally, and is black at the upper tip. The color of this fin and the round spot on the opercle are useful in identifying this species. This is a common species which will possibly reach 60 inches in length.

The distribution of this fish extends from Hawaii southward into central Polynesia, westward through Micronesia and Melanesia, through the East Indies, and across the Indian Ocean to the coast of Africa.

THE POMFRET FISH FAMILY
106 *Family Bramidae (Steinegeriidae)*
The pomfrets are deep-bodied, compressed fishes with an ovate outline, with steep dorsal and ventral profiles, and with an oblique mouth. The dorsal fin and usually the anal fin are both elevated in front and often falcate; the caudal fin is deeply forked with long lobes and the pectoral fins are long and falcate. The appearance of these fishes changes as they mature. The young have spines on the scales and upon the head which disappear as they grow older. The lateral line is not apparent in this family. Most species are small, dark colored, and without dramatic appearance. They inhabit the high seas and some occur in deeper water.

The family is widely distributed in the Atlantic, Pacific, and Indian Oceans. It is a small group of which at least five species are known from this area.

The following species is not described or illustrated:
Taractes rubescens (Jordan and Evermann), 1887. An account of this fish in this area may be found in *Fishery Bulletin* 71:3, 1973, pp. 900-902. It is an uncommon, off-shore, deep-water species.

STEINDACHNER'S POMFRET FISH
106—1 *Taractes steindachneri* (Doderlein), 1884
The body of this pomfret is somewhat ovate in shape and has rather uniformly curving dorsal and ventral profiles. The body is compressed and the eyes are large. There is a specimen in the Bernice P. Bishop Museum in Honolulu obtained July 7, 1906, which measures about 24 inches in length, is uniformly deep brown,

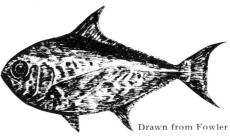

Drawn from Fowler

and has fins which are paler toward the margins. Other specimens have been reported as "grey, with coppery iridescence." The maximum length is about three feet.

The distribution of this fish includes the Atlantic, Indian, and Pacific

Oceans.

This species was long listed in books under the name of *Taractes longipinnis* (Lowe), 1843.

THE SILVER POMFRET FISH
106—2 *Collybus drachme* Snyder, 1903

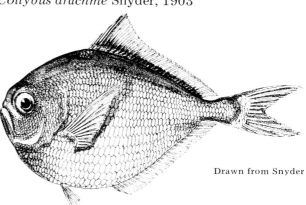

Drawn from Snyder

The body of this pomfret is shaped somewhat like a tear drop for it has an outline which is uniformly curved. The body is compressed, the lateral line is absent, and the mouth opens at a nearly vertical angle. The color of the body is bright silvery with blackish shades over the head and back. The fins are mostly dusky and the caudal fin has a central, whitish yellow area. An unusual, round, silvery spot about the size of the pupil is situated on the back at the beginning of the dorsal fin. Adult specimens seem to range in length from about three to eight inches. It is an uncommon species from the open sea.

It is known from the Hawaiian area, the south Pacific Ocean and doubtless other areas.

The scientific name of this fish comes from the Greek word *drachma*, an ancient Greek silver coin.

THE LUSTROUS POMFRET FISH
106—3 *Eumegistus illustris* Jordan and Jordan, 1922

This species is known from a very few specimens. It is a deep-bodied fish, ovoid in outline, and has uniformly curving profiles. The eyes are quite large and the cleft of the mouth is nearly vertical. The color of the body was described as "lustrous brownish black". The dorsal and anal fins were paler and had a black border along their free edge. The caudal, pectoral, and pelvic fins had white margins.

The specimen on which this species is based was found by Dr. David

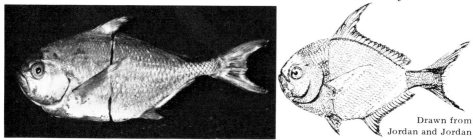

Drawn from
Jordan and Jordan

Starr Jordan in the Honolulu market in the process of being cut up for sale and his drawing of it shows that someone had cut a large filet from the side of the specimen. Jordan's fish measured 24 inches in length and weighed nine pounds.

The specimen shown in the photo was captured by Mr. Peter E. Russell of Honolulu in October, 1972, off the island of Oahu near the bottom at a depth of 900 feet. It measured 28 inches in length and weighed ten pounds; it was of a "clean steel" gray color and was mottled with black. The photo of this fish was taken after it had been scaled and cut into halves.

The distribution of this species includes Hawaii, Japan, and undoubtedly most of the area between these islands.

Some scholars regard this species as identical to *Brama raii* (Bloch), 1791, and have listed it accordingly.

THE FAN FISH FAMILY
107 *Family Pteraclidae*

The fan fishes are a small family of oceanic species which have very high dorsal and anal fins. The pelvic fins and the anus are placed far forward on the body and the lateral line is rudimentary or absent.

The family is world-wide in distribution.

Of this small group, only one species is known from this area.

THE SAIL - FIN FISH OR FAN FISH
107—1 *Pteracles velifer* (Pallas), 1769

The body of this fish is elongated, tapering, and compressed. The cleft of the mouth is wide and oblique, the eyes are large, and the lateral line is absent. The dorsal and anal fins are phenomenally large. The dorsal fin extends nearly the entire length of the body and is very high and sail-like. The anal fin likewise extends nearly the entire length of the body. This is an amazing fish from the deep sea which is known to reach a length of at least 24 inches.

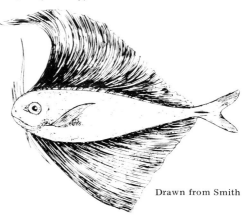

Drawn from Smith

The distribution includes the Atlantic, Indian, and Pacific Oceans.

In Hawaii, it is known at this time from a single specimen which measured only four inches in length and which was taken from the stomach of a tuna fish.

THE DORADO OR DOLPHIN FISH FAMILY
108 *Family Coryphaenidae*

The dolphin fishes are slender, possess compressed heads and bodies, and bear a long dorsal fin which extends for nearly the full length of the body. The head bears a bony crest, the lateral line is present, and the body is covered with small scales. The pectoral fins are rather small and falcate in shape; the ventral fins are placed far forward on the body and fold into a groove on the belly.

These fishes are found in all tropical and temperate seas. It is a small group and probably contains only two species.

The dolphin fishes should not be confused with the true dolphins which are miniature whales.

THE COMMON DOLPHIN FISH OR DORADO
Also known as Ma-hi ma-hi, Ma-hi-hi,
Ma-hi ma-hi la-pa (male), and Ma-hi ma-hi o-ma
108—1 *Coryphaena hippurus* Linne, 1758

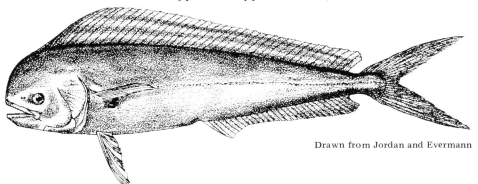

Drawn from Jordan and Evermann

The mahi-mahi has a long, slender body with long dorsal and anal fins and a widely forked tail. The head and body are greatly compressed and give the fish a somewhat ribbon-like aspect. The head bears a median bony crest which becomes high in the male and gives this sex a nearly vertical profile. The color of the body is a brilliant blue or green above and apple green or white beneath. The entire body is covered by emerald green or light blue spots. The dorsal fin is somewhat purplish in color, while the other fins are yellowish. During life and when the fish is dying, these colors are so brilliant that it is a sight not soon forgotten. Large specimens will reach a length of about six feet and a weight of about 70 pounds.

These fishes inhabit the surface waters where they feed upon most all forms of small surface fishes and other animals of the plankton. They are in turn pursued and eaten by larger fishes and small whales. It has been reported that a mahi-mahi was seen "impaled on the spear of a marlin off Kona, Hawaii". The mahi-mahi is an active fish, is attracted to fishing lures, fights when hooked, and is an excellent food fish.

The distribution of this species is world-wide in tropical and warm temperate seas.

This fish should always be called "the dolphin **fish**" to separate it from the true dolphins which are small whales. To refer to it as a "dolphin" is incorrect.

THE SMALL DOLPHIN FISH
Also known as Mu hi ma-hi
108—2 *Coryphaena equisetis* Linne, 1758

This species resembles the common mahi-mahi in general appearance and in most details. It is therefore not often observed and may even be over-looked because of its resemblance to the larger, common mahi-mahi. This species has a broad, square-cut tongue, while the common mahi-mahi has a tongue which is narrower and rounder in front. Full grown specimens are thought to reach a maximum length of about 30 inches.

The distribution of this fish is believed to be world-wide in warm water.

THE DAMSEL FISH FAMILY
Including the Coral Fishes and the Anemone Fishes
109 *Family Pomacentridae (Amphiprionidae, Premnidae, Chromidae)*

The damsel fishes are a large group of small fishes with bodies which are deep, ovoid in outline, and compressed. The lateral line usually ends below the soft dorsal fin or is interrupted in some species. The soft dorsal, anal, and caudal fins are scaly at the base, the mouth is small, and a single nostril is located on each side of the snout. It should be noted that the single nostril is a useful feature in identifying members of this family, since it is found only in this group and in the *Cichlidae*. Most members of this group are brightly colored with orange, blue, and red. Most are small in size, although a few species do exceed six or more inches in length.

Damsel fishes are active inhabitants of the shore line and, like the butterfly fishes, spend their life leisurely nibbling on the flora and fauna of the reef.

This is a large tropical family which includes about 225 species; at least 16 or more are known from this area.

The following species are not described or illustrated:

Chromis acares Randall and Swerdloff, 1973. This species resembles *C. vanderbilti* and *C. lineatus*, although it is more slender than *C. vanderbilti*. It is blue in life with lighter colors below. It ranges widely from Hawaii southward to Australia. See *Pacific Science* 27(4), 1973, pp. 331—335 for original description and photograph.

Chromis agilis Smith, 1960. This small fish will reach three inches in length. It is orange brown in color with bluish hues and is marked by a large, black spot at the base of the pectoral fin. It is distributed from Hawaii southward and westward to the Indian Ocean. See *Pacific Science* 27(4), 1973, pp. 336—338 for details and photograph.

Chromis hanui Randall and Swerdloff, 1973. This small species is described as "... dark yellowish brown, abruptly white on caudal peduncle ..." At present it is known only from the Hawaiian area. See *Pacific Science* 27(4), 1973, pp. 338—341 for original description and photograph.

Chromis struhsakeri Randall and Swerdloff, 1973. The eye of this species is large, the tail is light in color, and there is a distinct, light spot on the upper edge of the caudal peduncle at the rear base of the soft dorsal fin. This is a small fish which will exceed three inches in length. It lives below 300 feet. At present it is known only from the Hawaiian area. See *Pacific Science* 27(4) 1973, pp. 344—348 for original description and photographs.

The name of this fish honors Dr. Paul Struhsaker of the National Marine Fisheries Service in Honolulu.

THE WHITE-SPOTTED DAMSEL FISH
Also known as A-lo-'i-lo-'i, A-lo-'i-lo-'i pa-'a-pa-'a, Lo-'i-lo-'i, 'a (young), and 'A-'a (young)
109—1 *Dascyllus albisella* Gill, 1862

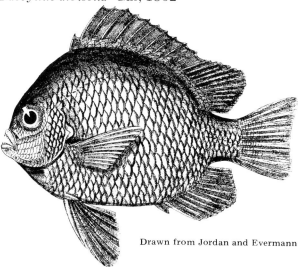

The body of this damsel fish is oval in outline and compressed. The head and mouth are small and the dorsal profile is steep. The color is usually black, although it may be altered at will by the fish and made a lighter grayish color. A nearly round, white spot is present on the upper side of the body and a single, white spot is located on the midline in front of the dorsal fin. These spots are most apparent in young specimens and become less intense with age. Large specimens will reach five and possibly six inches in length.

Drawn from Jordan and Evermann

The newly hatched young of this species form colonies around coral heads of *Pocillopora* in areas of quiet water and seem to feed upon small crustacea. This species is easily confused with *Dascyllus trimaculatus* (Ruppell), 1828. In *D. trimaculatus* the spot on the side of the body is about the same size as the eye; while in *D. albisella* this spot is considerably larger than the eye.

THE GREEN DAMSEL FISH
Also known as Ma-mo, Ma-ma-mo, Ma-mo-'o, Ma-o-ma-o, and Ma-mo po-ho-le
109—2 *Abudefduf abdominalis* (Quoy and Gaimard), 1824

The mao-mao has an oval-shaped, deep, compressed body which bears a small head and mouth. The color of the body is a pale brassy green which becomes much lighter on the belly. The sides of the body are marked with about five, darker, bluish black, vertical bands which become narrower ventrally and tend to disappear. Large specimens will reach a length of about nine inches.

This is an active shore line fish which is found in tide pools and in areas of quiet water along the shore.

The distribution of this species extends from Hawaii southward to central Polynesia.

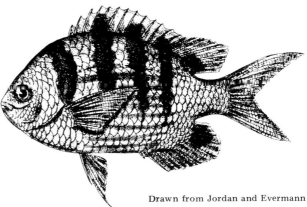

Drawn from Jordan and Evermann

THE SMALL DAMSEL FISH
109—3* *Abudefduf imparipennis* (Vaillant and Sauvage), 1875

This damsel fish is a small species with a body which is elliptical in outline. The color of the body is generally yellowish and is without any special markings. There are black areas on the eye above and below the pupil which will help to identify it. It does not appear to exceed three inches in length.

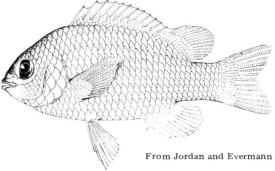

From Jordan and Evermann

The habitat of this fish is in the surge areas of the shore line where waves and rocks meet.

The distribution of this fish extends from Hawaii to central Polynesia.

THE PHOENIX ISLANDS DAMSEL FISH
109—4* *Abudefduf phoenixensis* Schultz, 1943

The damsel fish noted here is a small species from the central Pacific area. The body is quite typical of the members of this genus but differs in its coloration. The body is dark blackish or brownish and is marked with two, three or four, light vertical stripes; there is also a prominent black spot at the upper posterior corner of the soft dorsal fin. The caudal peduncle is dark in color and the tail is light colored. Adult specimens will reach about four inches in length.

The distribution of this fish includes Johnston Island, Wake Island, the Phoenix Islands, and doubtless other adjoining areas. An illustration follows.

* See Appendix.

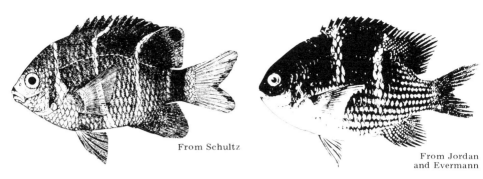

From Schultz

From Jordan
and Evermann

Abudefduf phoenixensis   *Abudefduf sindonis*

SINDO'S DAMSEL FISH
109—5* *Abudefduf sindonis* (Jordan and Evermann), 1903

This small, uncommon species passes through several color changes as it matures. Dr. William A. Gosline reports that, when under two inches in length, it exhibits a black spot with a white border on its soft dorsal fin. Between two and three inches the fish has lost the black spot and exhibits two, vertical, white bands on the side of the body. When it reaches a length of about four inches the fish is plain black in color. Large specimens will reach a length of about five inches.

The habitat of this fish is in the surge areas where the waves and rocks meet.

The name of this species honors the memory of Mr. Michitaro Sindo who first discovered this fish at Kailua, Oahu, in 1901.

THE GRAY DAMSEL FISH
Also known as Ku-pi-pi, 'O-'o nu-i, and 'A-o 'a-o nu-i (young)
109—6 *Abudefduf sordidus* (Forskal), 1775

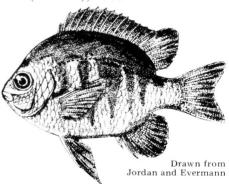

Drawn from
Jordan and Evermann

The body of this damsel fish is somewhat oval in outline, short, deep, and compressed. The color of the body is brownish gray with lighter, silvery, yellowish colors below. The sides of the body are marked with five or six, lighter, vertical bands. There is a distinct dark spot on the upper side of the caudal peduncle and a dark spot at the base of the pectoral fin. Large specimens may reach a length of about nine inches.

This is an active, alert, pugnancious, little fish of the tide pools and shallow waters of the shore line and reef.

The distribution of this species extends from Hawaii southward to central Polynesia, westward through Micronesia and Melanesia, through the East Indies, and across the Indian Ocean to the coast of Africa and the Red Sea.

* See Appendix.

THE JOHNSTON ISLAND DAMSEL FISH
109—7 *Plectroglyphidodon johnstonianus* Fowler and Ball, 1924

The Johnston Island damsel fish is a small species with a body which is deep, oval-shaped, and greatly compressed. The head and the mouth are small and the soft dorsal fin, anal fin, and caudal fin are covered with fine scales. It is reported to reach a length of about four inches.

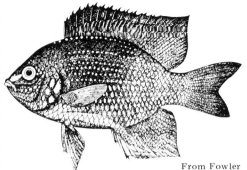

From Fowler

Dr. William Gosline reports that it inhabits water between 15 and 50 feet in depth.

The distribution of this fish seems limited to the Hawaiian area at this time.

This species is named for Johnston Island southwest of the Hawaiian Islands.

JENKINS' DAMSEL FISH
109—8* *Pomacentrus jenkinsi* Jordan and Evermann, 1903

Jenkins' damsel fish is a small, plain, dark brown species with a yellowish eye in life. Large specimens may reach five inches in length. It is an active, solitary, reef dweller in quiet water.

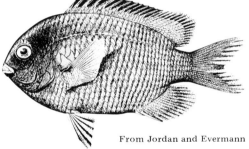

From Jordan and Evermann

It is known from Hawaii, the Marshall Islands, and undoubtedly elsewhere in the central Pacific area.

This species is named in honor of Dr. Oliver P. Jenkins, Professor of Physiology at Stanford University, who collected a series of these fishes in Hawaii in 1899.

THE DARK DAMSEL FISH
109—9* *Chromis leucurus* Gilbert, 1905

The body of this damsel fish is elliptical in outline and compressed. The head and the mouth are small and the tail is deeply forked. The color of the body is a brownish black anteriorly and white on the posterior half of the caudal peduncle and caudal fin. Adults will reach a length of at least two inches.

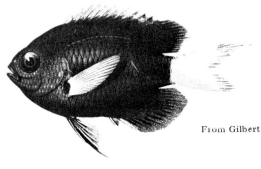

From Gilbert

* See Appendix.

277

Only a few specimens are known.

The habitat of this fish is in the waters beyond the reef from 15 feet to at least 200 feet in depth.

It is known from Hawaii and eastern Polynesia.

See *Pacific Science* 27(4), 1973, pp. 335-336, for description and photograph.

THE OVAL DAMSEL FISH
109—10 *Chromis ovalis* (Steindachner), 1900

The body of this damsel fish is elliptical in outline and quite strongly compressed. The tail is deeply forked and the upper lobe is slightly longer than the lower. The color of the body is described as steel blue to silvery. There is a black area at the base of each pectoral fin and the dorsal fin has dark or black membranes. The upper side of the body is marked by about eight, darker, narrow, longitudinal lines. Large specimens will reach a length of about six inches.

The habitat of this species seems to be in the shore line waters between 20 and 150 feet in depth.

The distribution of this species includes the Hawaiian area and doubtless other adjoining areas.

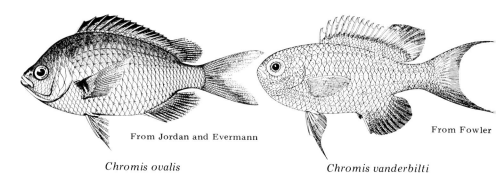

From Jordan and Evermann

From Fowler

Chromis ovalis

Chromis vanderbilti

VANDERBILT'S DAMSEL FISH
109—11 *Chromis vanderbilti* (Fowler), 1941

This damsel fish is a small species with an elongated, elliptical body. The head and mouth are small, the eye is fairly large, and the upper and lower edges of the caudal fin are elongated. It lacks significant features, but may be identified by the dark, lower edge of the caudal fin and by the anal fin rays which are nearly black except for the last few which are abruptly lighter in color. The body is yellowish in color and is marked by blue spots along the rows of scales. Large specimens will reach a length of about two and one-half inches.

The distribution of this species includes the area from Hawaii to Guam and from eastern Polynesia to Melanesia.

This species was named for Mr. George Vanderbilt.

THE BLACK DAMSEL FISH
109—12 *Chromis verator* Jordan and Metz, 1912

The body of this damsel fish is oval in outline and strongly compressed.
The head and mouth are small and the
upper lobe of the caudal fin is slightly
longer than the lower. The color of
the body is plain dark grey to black in
life and there are three white spots on
each side near the tail. They are
located at the posterior base of the
soft dorsal fin, at the posterior base of
the anal fin, and on the middle of the
side of the caudal peduncle where it

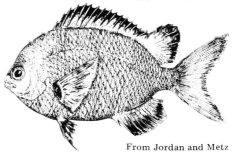

From Jordan and Metz

joins the caudal fin. The body fades rapidly on dying and the spots disappear. Adults may reach as much as nine inches in length.

The habitat of this species seems to be on the outer side of the reef in depths beyond 30 or 40 feet.

The distribution of this species includes the Hawaiian area and probably nearby adjoining areas.

THE WRASSE FISH FAMILY
Also known as the Rainbow Fishes
110 *Family Labridae (Coridae, Neolabridae, Bodianidae)*

The wrasse fishes have a greater variety of species included within their family than do most other groups. Their bodies vary in shape from species which are elongated and somewhat spindle-shaped to species whose bodies are deep and compressed. The dorsal fin is usually continuous and the caudal fin, although variously shaped, is never forked at its extremity. The pelvic fins always have one spine and five rays, are placed far forward on the body, and are separated from each other. The mouth of most species is small, contains separate teeth in the front, and usually includes projecting canine teeth in the front corners of the mouth.

The species are nearly all brightly colored, often with vivid hues of blue, green, yellow, and red. The colors found in adult fishes are usually quite different from those of immature individuals; for this reason young wrasse fishes are often difficult to recognize.

In length, wrasse fishes vary from small forms of about three inches in length to some which reach at least seven feet and possibly as much as ten feet in *Cheilinus undulatus* Ruppell, 1835, the largest of the group.

Wrasse fishes are primarily carnivorous but do ingest some plant food. They inhabit the coral reefs, seaweeds, and rocks of all warm seas, although most are confined to the tropics. They live a leisurely, solitary life and do not form into schools as many species do. With a few exceptions, most species spend the night "asleep" in the sand or, where sand is absent, simply lying outstretched upon the bottom.

The wrasse fishes are a large family and include about 600 species. Of this number, about fifty species are known from this area.

The following species are not described or illustrated:

Pseudojuloides cerasinus (Snyder), 1904. The body of this fish is three or fou inches in length and cherry red in small specimens. See color Plate 17.

Novaculichthys bifer (Lay and Bennett), 1839. This species is now known to be the young, immature stage of *Novaculichthys taeniourus* (Lacepede), 1802.

Thalassoma melanochir (Bleeker), 1857. This species has a blunt head, reaches a length of at least six inches, and occurs in the tropical central and western Pacific Ocean.

Thalassoma quinquevittata (Lay and Bennett), 1839. The body of this fish is green ish above and yellowish below, has dark red stripes around the eyes, a red line along the side of the body, and a purple spot at the front of the dorsa fin. It is common in the Marshall Islands and occurs at Johnston Island. I reaches five inches in length.

Wetmorella albofasciata Schultz and Marshall, 1954. This is a small, uncommon species which resembles *W. ocellatatus* Schultz and Marshall, 1954. It is named for the white bar which passes vertically across the body between the black ocellate spot in the soft dorsal fin and a similar black spot in the ana fin; this bar is useful in identifying this species. Specimens measure about 1.5 to 2 inches. See *Proc. U.S. National Museum* Vol. 103:3327, 1954 pp. 439-447.

THE SPINDLE-SHAPED WRASSE
Also known as Ku-po-u, Ku-po-u-po-u, Ku-po-u-po-u le-le (yellow)
and the Unarmed Wrasse
110—1 *Cheilio inermis* (Forskal), 1775

The ku-pou-pou has a slender, elongated, cylindrical body and a pointed head and snout. Young individuals are greenish above and whitish below. The adults are somewhat greenish above and somewhat bluish below with yellow hues. There is often a poorly-defined, yellow area on the upper side of the body at about the middle which contains a few black spots. The color is variable. Adults will reach a length of about 20 inches.

The distribution of this species extends from Hawaii and southern Japan to Easter Island and northern Australia, through the East Indies, and westward across the Indian Ocean to the coast of Africa and the Red Sea.

THE BLACK-SPOT WRASSE FISH
Also known as 'A-'a-wa and Po-'o-u
110—2 *Bodianus bilunulatus* (Lacepede), 1802

The 'a'awa has an elongated, compressed body which bears a tapering head and snout. The dorsal fin has 12 spines and, like the anal fin, is covered

at its base by a heavy sheath of several rows of scales; the caudal fin is nearly straight on its posterior margin.

The color of this fish varies with age. Young individuals have a large, black spot at the back of the body. As they grow older, this spot disappears and a black spot appears on the upper side of the body at the base of the soft dorsal fin. In addition, younger fishes will have a small, dark spot between the first and third dorsal spines and two, short, horizontal, black lines on the side of the head, one level with the eye and the other extending backward from the corner of the mouth. At this intermediate age and size, the body of the fish is predominately white and the markings are yellow and reddish. Older fishes loose their brilliance and become a bluish-black color. Large individuals will reach a length of about 24 inches.

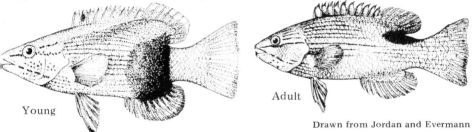

Young

Adult

Drawn from Jordan and Evermann

The distribution of this species extends from Hawaii southward to central Polynesia and westward though the East Indies and across the Indian Ocean to Mauritius.

THE SHARP-HEADED WRASSE FISH
110—3 *Bodianus oxycephalus* (Bleeker), 1862

This unusual wrasse fish has an elongated compressed body, an elongated head, and a pig-like snout. The body color is reddish or pinkish brown and is marked with longitudinal rows of spots. The dorsal fin bears a prominent black spot at its base between

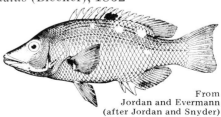

From
Jordan and Evermann
(after Jordan and Snyder)

the sixth and the tenth spines. Large specimens will reach a length of abou'
24 inches.

The specimen in the adjoining photo measured 16 inches and was cap
tured at a depth of 900 feet.

The distribution of this species extends from Hawaii and southern
Japan to Queensland and the East Indies.

RUSSELL'S WRASSE FISH
110—4* *Bodianus russelli* Gomon and Randall, 1975

This rare wrasse fish is pink in color and is marked on the sides of the
body by three, longitudinal, yellow stripes. A large spot, orange-red in color
is located at the base of the tail just above the midline of the body.

This species is known from a very few specimens, one of which was
captured by Mr. Peter E. Russell of Honolulu on March 26, 1974, off
Mokapu, Oahu, at a depth of about 800 feet. It measured 15 inches in
length.

This species is known from Hawaii and the western Pacific area.

Photo by Honolulu Star Bulletir

RARE WRASSE FISH
110—5 *Verriculus sanguineus* Jordan and Evermann, 1903
This rare wrasse fish is a small species with an elongated, compressed

* See Appendix.

body and a head and snout which is quite long and tapering. The colors of this species are brilliant reds and yellows. The upper and lower sides of the body and the anal fin are a deep red color. A horizontal, golden yellow stripe extends along the upper side of the body from the eye to the tail. The pelvic fins and the caudal fin are yellow. There is a dark spot on the side of the caudal peduncle near the tail.

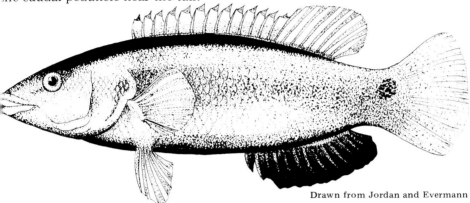

Drawn from Jordan and Evermann

This species was first known from a single specimen caught in deep water off Hilo in 1901.

At present it is known only from the Hawaiian area.

Some books may list this fish as *Bodianus sanguineus* (Jordan and Evermann), 1903.

THE LOUSE-EATING WRASSE OR CLEANER WRASSE FISH
110—6 *Labroides phthirophagus* Randall, 1958

This little wrasse fish has an elongated, compressed body. The head is tapering and bears a pointed snout with a small mouth and thick lips. In life, this fish is brilliantly colored. The front half of the body is yellow above and below; a black band, extending from the mouth to the tail, passes through the eye and extends along the side of the body to the midpoint where it widens to include most of the body except for a purplish margin above and below. Large specimens will reach a length of five inches.

This unusual fish feeds upon parasitic copepods and isopods which it picks from the skin, fins, gills, and mouth of other fishes. The pattern of swimming of this fish is of a dancing, flitting nature and is quite unlike that of other wrasse fishes. While most wrasse fishes burrow into the sand at night, this species forms a balloon-like, mucous cocoon, similar to those formed by parrot fishes, and spends the night resting within it.

The distribution of this species is currently limited to the Hawaiian area.

WRASSE FISH OR TELESCOPE FISH
110—7 *Epibulus insidiator* (Pallas), 1770

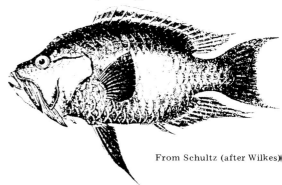

From Schultz (after Wilkes)

This wrasse fish has a heavy, deep, compressed body which is covered by large scales. The jaws of this fish are amazing. The lower jaw is extremely long and may, with the upper jaw, be extended to form a tube for the capture of its food. The color of the body is uniform but variable and ranges from light yellow to chocolate brown. The dorsal fin in some individuals may bear a dark spot at its anterior end and a horizontal brown band. Large specimens may reach as much as 24 inches in length. It is a shore line species.

The distribution of this fish extends from Hawaii southward to Queensland and westward through Micronesia and Melanesia, through the East Indies, and across the Indian Ocean to the coast of Africa.

JORDAN'S WRASSE FISH
110—8 *Cirrhilabrus jordani* Snyder, 1904

This little fish has a slender body and a tapering head and snout. The dorsal and anal fins are high and the caudal fin is rounded at its margin. The

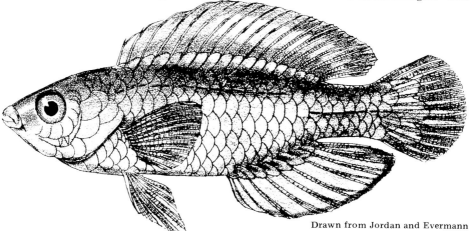

Drawn from Jordan and Evermann

dorsal spines are 11 in number and do not extend the full height of the fin. The body color is reddish and the anal fin is edged in black. There are a few light spots along the upper part of the body below the dorsal fin and a few, faint, light, longitudinal lines along the abdomen. It will reach about four inches in length.

It is an uncommon fish of surge pools and deeper shore line waters.

The distribution of this species is at present limited to the Hawaiian rea.

This species was named for Dr. David Starr Jordan (1851-1931), amous American ichthyologist and the first President of Leland Stanford 'unior University.

THE TWO - SPOT WRASSE FISH
Also known as Po-'o-u, Pi-li-ko-'a, and Pi-li-ko-'a li-'i li-'i
110—9 *Cheilinus bimaculatus* Cuvier and Valenciennes, 1839

This little wrasse fish is reddish in color above, brownish below, and is overed with short, orange-red lines at the edges of the scales. In adult fishes he caudal fin is pointed in the center and the upper ray is extended to form . short streamer. There is a dark spot behind the eye and an intense, black pot in the middle of the side in adult individuals. It will reach a length of .bout six inches.

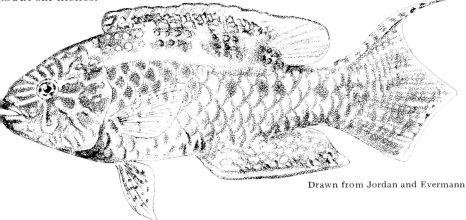

Drawn from Jordan and Evermann

The distribution of this species extends from Hawaii southward and vestward to the East Indies.

THE ROSE - COLORED WRASSE FISH
Also known as Po-'o-u
110—10 *Cheilinus rhodochrous* Gunther, 1866

The po'ou has a body which is quite heavy and compressed. The caudal 3eduncle is quite deep and the posterior margin of the tail is nearly straight. The lower jaw is quite heavy and projects beyond the upper jaw. The color of this fish changes with age; the older individuals are usually plain in color ind have black areas at the bases of the soft dorsal and anal fins and extend-ng onto the fin membranes; the pelvic fins are black. In most specimens, :here is a white, vertical stripe at the front of the caudal peduncle and a 3luish spot in the center of the caudal peduncle. There is usually a stripe from the eye to the base of the pectoral fin.

The distribution of this fish extends from Hawaii southward to central Polynesia, westward through Micronesia and Melanesia, through the East

Indies, and across the Indian Ocean to the coast of Africa.

SMALL WRASSE FISH
110—11 *Pseudocheilinus evanidus* Jordan and Evermann, 1903

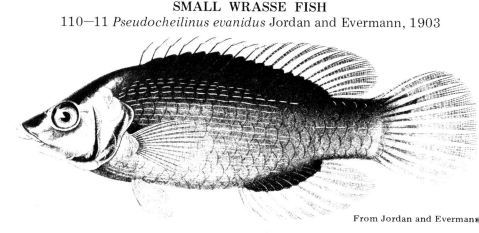

This little fish has a body which is quite deep and compressed and which bears a tapering head and snout. The body is colored a dull brick red above and purplish below and has the sides marked by about 17 yellow horizontal, thread-like lines which extend from the head toward the tail. I will reach a length of about four inches.

This species occurs from Hawaii westward to East Africa.

THE EIGHT-LINED WRASSE FISH
110—12 *Pseudocheilinus octotaenia* Jenkins, 1900

This little wrasse fish is brownish red over the front of the body and more gray in color posteriorly. The sides of the body are marked by eight narrow, horizontal bands. Adult specimens will reach six inches in length.

The distribution of this species extends from Hawaii and the Marshal Islands westward to the Red Sea.

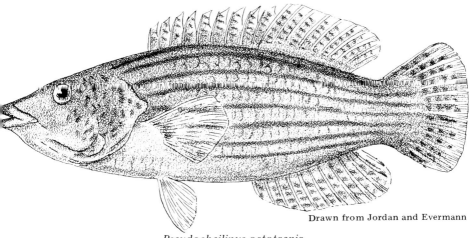

Pseudocheilinus octotaenia

Drawn from Jordan and Evermann

THE FOUR - LINED WRASSE FISH
110—13 *Pseudocheilinus tetrataenia* Schultz, 1959

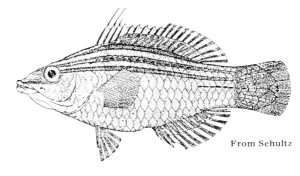

From Schultz

The body of this little wrasse fish is bright blue in color and is marked along its upper sides by four, narrow, longitudinal bands. It measures at least two inches in length.

The distribution of this fish includes Hawaii, the Marshall Islands, and adjoining areas.

BALDWIN'S WRASSE FISH
Also known as La-e ni-hi
110—14 *Hemipteronotus baldwini* Jordan and Evermann, 1903

Baldwin's wrasse fish is a deep-bodied species with a large head and a nearly vertical profile. The body is yellowish white with other additional hues. A prominent dark spot is located in the upper middle of the side and there is a black spot at the end of the anal fin in the males. The dorsal and anal fins have many diagonal blue lines. It will reach a length of about nine inches.

The distribution of this species includes the Hawaiian area.

"This species is named for Mr. Albertus H. Baldwin in recognition of his paintings of American and Hawaiian fishes."

287

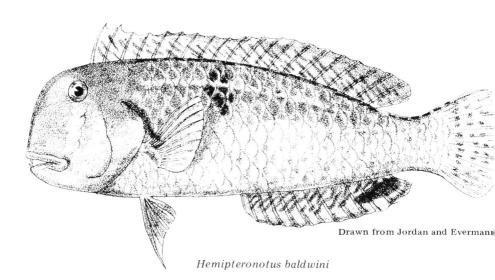

Drawn from Jordan and Everman[...]

Hemipteronotus baldwini

THE SHARP-HEADED WRASSE FISH
Also known as La-e ni-hi
110—15 *Hemipteronotus leclusei* (Quoy and Gaimard), 1824

This is a slender wrasse fish with a compressed body and a head with a sharp, steep profile. It is uniformly green in color above and white below. It has a very significant, small, black spot on the side of the caudal peduncle at its upper, posterior corner. It will reach at least six and occasionally seven inches in length.

The distribution of this species extends from Hawaii southward to central Polynesia, westward through Micronesia, Melanesia and the East Indies, and across the Indian Ocean to the coast of Africa.

The Hawaiian name of lae-nihi means "sharp forehead".

This species has long been known under the name of *Cymolutes leclusei* (Quoy and Gaimard), 1824.

THE BLACK RAZOR WRASSE FISH
Also known as La-e ni-hi 'e-le-'e-le
110—16 *Hemipteronotus niger* (Steindachner), 1900

The black lae-nihi has a deep, compressed body, a large head with a

steep profile, and eyes which are small and high on the head. The color of
the body is black or dark brown on the body and fins except for the
posterior border of the caudal fin which is a transparent, rosy white color.
The belly may show some purplish hues on some specimens. An occasional
fish will exhibit an unusual scale on the upper side of the body just below
the fourth dorsal spine; this scale which is black with a blue border, suggests
a relationship with *H. pavoninus* which has a dark scale in about the same
location. It will reach a length of at least eight inches.

The distribution of this species includes the Hawaiian area.

In older books this species may be listed as *Iniistius niger* (Steindachner), 1900.

THE WHITE-SIDE RAZOR WRASSE FISH
Also known as La-e ni-hi
110—17 *Hemipteronotus niveilatus* (Jordan and Evermann), 1903

The body of this razor fish
is short, deep, and compressed;
the head is large with a steep
profile; and the eyes are small
and are set high upon the head.
The ground color of the body
seems to be grayish with four,
wide, faint, vertical bands of a
darker hue with lighter areas
between them. The body is

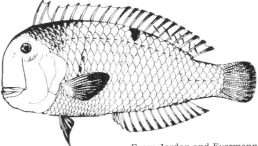

From Jordan and Evermann

289

marked and trimmed with yellow and orange, red and violet, and blue and white in a variety of ways. One distinctive mark will identify this species this mark is a small, black area on the upper side of the body just below the beginning of the soft dorsal fin. Large individuals will measure at least ten inches in length.

The distribution of this species includes the Hawaiian area.

The name *niveilatus* is Latin and means "snowy side"; it doubtless refers to the large, white area on the side of the body.

In older books this species may be listed as *Xyrichthys niveilatus* Jordan and Evermann, 1903.

THE PEACOCK WRASSE FISH
Also known as La-e ni-hi
110—18 *Hemipteronotus pavoninus* (Cuvier and Valenciennes), 1839

Like the other lae-nihi or razor wrasse fishes, this species has a deep, compressed body with a large head and steep profile. On the dorsal fin, the first two spines are elongated and separated from the remainder of the fin. There is but a single row of scales on the cheek below the eye. The body is blue-green in color and

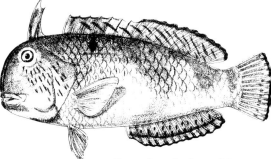

Drawn from Jordan and Evermann

s marked with about three, faint, vertical crossbands with lighter areas between them; of these lighter areas, the one just behind the pectoral fin is the lightest. There is an unusual black spot the size of a single scale located just below the membrane which connects the fourth and fifth dorsal spines. The anal fin has a longitudinal, yellow, sub-marginal stripe. It will reach a length of about 15 inches.

The distribution of this species extends from Hawaii southward to central Polynesia, westward through Micronesia and Melanesia, through the East Indies, and across the Indian Ocean to the coast of Africa and the Red Sea.

In older books this species may be listed as *Iniistius pavoninus* (Cuvier and Valenciennes), 1839.

THE STRIPED WRASSE OR CLOWN WRASSE FISH
110—19 *Hemipteronotus taeniourus* (Lacepede), 1802
The body of this fish is somewhat elongated and compressed and bears

Young, above; Adult, below.

a small head with a pointed snout. Recognition of the adults of this specie is possible from the color alone. Each scale on the sides bears an oval, white spots so that the entire fish, with the exception of the head and tail, i spotted with white upon a brown background. There are about four, brown gray-edged bands radiating out from the eyes and a large, nearly black area in the axil of the pectoral fin. The tail is marked with a vertical whitish area.

The young of this species were long unrecognized and hence were described under a separate name, *Novaculichthys bifer* Lay and Bennett 1839. The color change from the young *(N. bifer)* to the adult is gradua and is usually about complete by the time the fish reaches four inches in length. Adult specimens will reach a length of about 12 inches.

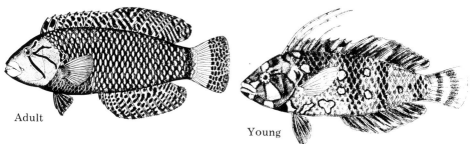

Adult

Young

Drawn from Jordan and Evermann

The distribution of this species extends from Hawaii southward to central Polynesia, westward through Micronesia and Melanesia, through the East Indies, and across the Indian Ocean to the coast of Africa.

In older books this species may be listed as *Novaculichthys taeniourus* (Lacepede), 1802.

THE RAZOR WRASSE FISH
Also known as La-e ni-hi
110—20 *Hemipteronotus umbrilatus* Jenkins, 1900

This lae-nihi has a body which is deep and greatly compressed and a head which is quite large and which has a nearly vertical profile. The first two rays of the dorsal fin are more or less separated from the remainder of the fin. A large, dark area covers the upper side of the middle of the body. The scales in the area of this dark blotch and below it have white edges. Adults will reach a length of ten or twelve inches.

These fishes inhabit the quiet sandy bottoms beyond the reef. They are caught with hook and line.

The distribution of this fish includes the Hawaiian area.

Drawn from
Jordan and Evermann

WOOD'S WRASSE FISH
110—21 *Hemipteronotus woodi* (Jenkins), 1900
This wrasse fish is a small, elongated species which is greatly compressed. The color of the body is generally a pale violet with various rosy areas. The spinous dorsal fin is a violet-blue color and contains about nine, blue-black spots on the membranes of the spinous dorsal fin. The pelvic fins are light in color. Large specimens will measure about five inches in length.

 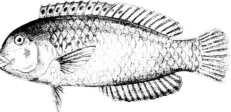

Drawn from Jordan and Evermann

The distribution of this species includes Hawaii and Easter Island.

The name of this species honors Dr. Thomas Denison Wood, professor of hygiene at Stanford University, who collected specimens of this fish in 1898.

BALLIEU'S WRASSE FISH
Also known as Hi-na-le-a lu-a-hi-ne
110—22 *Thalassoma ballieui* (Vaillant and Sauvage), 1875
The body of this wrasse fish is rather long, slender, and compressed and bears a fairly long head and snout. The body is brownish or grayish in color and is marked by many, short, vertical, brownish marks. Large specimens are reported to reach a length of about 24 inches, although most are less than 12 inches.

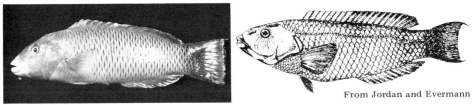

From Jordan and Evermann

The distribution of this species extends from Hawaii and Guam southward through Micronesia, Melanesia, and Polynesia.

This fish was named for M. Ballieu, a French consul to the Hawaiian Islands sometime prior to 1875.

DUPERREY'S WRASSE OR THE SADDLE WRASSE FISH
Also known as Hi-na-le-a la-u wi-li and Hi-na-le-a la-u i-li
110—23 *Thalassoma duperrey* Quoy and Gaimard, 1824
This hinalea has a slender, compressed body and a small head and mouth. The coloration of the adult fish is unmistakable. The body is

green and is marked with many, short, vertical, purple-red bars and by a wide, reddish orange, saddle-like band around the body just behind the head. Adult specimens will reach a length of about 12 inches.

The distribution of this species includes the Hawaiian area.

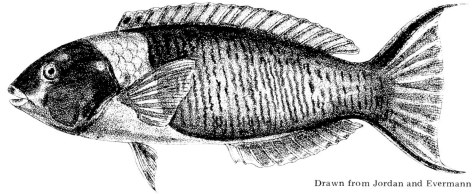

The name of this fish honors M. Louis Isidore Duperrey, a midshipman aboard the royal French corvette *Uranie.* This ship made a voyage around the world beginning September 17, 1817, at Toulon, France. During this voyage they visited Hawaii, Maui, and Oahu in August, 1819, and while in Hawaii collected 22 species of fishes of which 21 species were later described as new species.

THE BROWN WRASSE FISH
Also known as 'A-we-la
110—24 *Thalassoma fuscum* (Lacepede), 1802

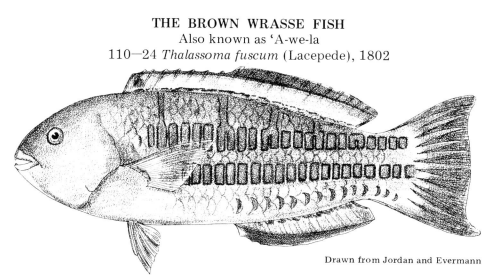

The body of the 'awela is uniformly curved on both dorsal and ventral profiles, the caudal fin is nearly straight at its outer edge, and the eyes are small. This species is most easily identified by its color pattern, although the color changes when the fish dies. There are two, horizontal, parallel rows of distinctive, blue-edged, green, quadrate spots extending along each side of the body from the pectoral fins to the tail. The remainder of the body is variously marked with green, orange, red, yellow, and blue. It will

reach a length of about 12 inches.

The distribution of this species extends from Hawaii southward to central Polynesia, westward through Micronesia and Melanesia, through the East Indies, and across the Indian Ocean to the coast of Africa.

The name *fuscum* is Latin for "brown" and was probably chosen because this fish changes to a brown color after death.

Recent studies by Dr. John E. Randall and others indicate that "*T. fuscum* is the terminal male of a labrid fish almost indistinguishable from *umbrostygma*". So in this species the males and females are of different color patterns.

THE MOON WRASSE FISH
110—25 *Thalassoma lunare* (Linne), 1758

The body of this wrasse is elongated, compressed, and somewhat rectangular in outline. The caudal peduncle is almost as deep as the body and the tail, which is lunate or moon-shaped on its posterior margin, has the upper and lower rays extended to form filaments. The color of the adult fish is a blue-green hue with red markings in various areas. Each scale is marked with a short, vertical, red line; the dorsal and anal fins have longitudinal red bands; the head is marked with red bands; and the pectoral fins bear a red, club-shaped mark along their anterior margin. Young specimens have a dark spot of varying intensity at the base of the upper caudal rays.

After death, this fish fades to a blue color. Adult specimens will reach a length of at least 12 inches.

The distribution of this species extends from Hawaii southward to Queensland, westward through Micronesia and Melanesia, through the East Indies, and across the Indian Ocean to the coast of Africa and the Red Sea.

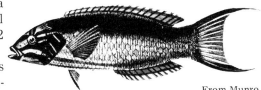

From Munro

THE YELLOWISH BROWN WRASSE FISH
110—26 *Thalassoma lutescens* Lay and Bennett, 1839

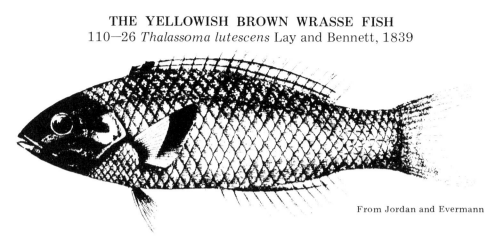

From Jordan and Evermann

The body of this fish very closely resembles *T. duperreyi* in anatomical details but differs from it in color; it is therefore suspected by some that they may be of the same species. The color of the body is yellowish brown when small (50 mm), reddish orange when larger (100 mm), and green when they reach their adult coloration (125 mm). The scales of the body are marked with narrow, vertical, often faint, dusky lines. The head is marked by four or five stripes; there is an area of purplish black on the outer, upper edge of the pectoral fins; and there is a black spot on the dorsal fin between the second and third spines. Adult individuals will reach a length of about seven inches.

The distribution of this species extends from Hawaii and Japan southward through Micronesia, Melanesia, and Polynesia to Australia.

THE PURPLE WRASSE FISH
Also known as Ho-u
110—27 *Thalassoma purpureum* (Forskal), 1775

In this species the male and female fishes are of different color patterns. The fish pictured here shows the "terminal male" color pattern for the

species which we also know as *T. umbrostygma.* So the name of *T. purpureum* includes but one species with different color patterns depending upon their age and sex. Since *T. purpureum* was described in 1775, it is the oldest name in use and should now include and replace the name of *T. umbrostygma.*

The body of the hou is bright green in color and is marked along the sides by two rows of rectangular, green spots and by two, long, horizontal, red bands. The entire lower surface is bluish in color. The head is green in color, but this changes to red upon the snout. The lips are green and there is a green stripe across the snout just behind the upper lip. There is an orange band from the eye backward and downward across the operculum. The dorsal and anal fins are green with longitudinal stripes of red or pink and blue or blue-green. The colors of this fish are not identical in all specimens and fade and change with death. Large specimens will reach a length of about 18 inches.

This species is distributed from Hawaii southward to Polynesia and westward through Micronesia and Melanesia, through the East Indies, and across the Indian Ocean to the coast of Africa and the Red Sea.

RUPPELL'S WRASSE FISH
110—28 *Thalassoma umbrostygma* (Ruppell), 1838

Recent studies by Dr. John E. Randall and others indicate that the males and females in this species are of different colors and that *T. purpureum* is the terminal male of this species. Since these two fishes *(T. purpureum* and *T. umbrostigma)* are the same species and since *T. purpureum,* the male, was described over 60 years earlier, the correct name for both of these fishes should probably be *Thalassoma purpureum* (Forskal), 1775.

This wrasse fish is a more elongated and slender species than the 'awela. The basic color of the body is green and it is variously trimmed in many different shades and hues of red. The head is spotted and longitudinal, green bands run through the dorsal and anal fins. It will measure about 11 inches when fully grown.

The distribution of this species extends from Hawaii southward to central Polynesia, westward through Micronesia and Melanesia, through the

East Indies, and across the Indian Ocean to the coast of Africa and the Red Sea.

The name *umbrostygma* is a Latin word meaning "shady spots" and undoubtedly refers to the markings of this fish.

THE BIRD WRASSE FISH
Also known as Hi-na-le-a nu-ku 'i-'i-wi
110—29 *Gomphosus varius* Lacepede, 1801

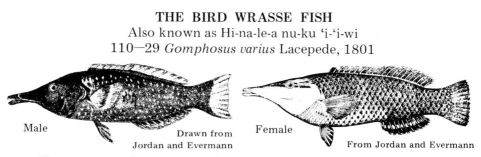

Male
Drawn from
Jordan and Evermann

Female
From Jordan and Evermann

There are two forms of this long-nosed fish; one is dark bluish green in color, the other is lighter colored on the head and lower parts of the body. These two forms were for years regarded as two separate species; it now appears that the dark colored form *(G. tricolor)* is the male and the lighter colored form *(G. varius)* is the female. The males are dark green or greenish blue and the females are a creamy white color in front and nearly black posteriorly. Large specimens of this fish will reach a length of about 11 inches.

The distribution of this species extends from Hawaii southward to central Polynesia and westward to Micronesia, Melanesia and southern

Above: Male   Below: Female

Japan, through the East Indies, and across the Indian Ocean to the coast of Africa and the Red Sea.

THE LIGHT COLORED WRASSE FISH
Also known as Ma-la-ma-la-ma
110—30 *Coris ballieui* Vaillant and Sauvage, 1875

This species varies in color and was therefore originally regarded as two separate species. The name of *C. ballieui* was given to the bluish form, while the form colored with white, yellow, pink, and occasionally blue was listed as *C. rosea* Vaillant and Sauvage, 1875. Both should hence forth be known as *C. ballieui*. Specimens will reach a length of about 14 inches.

Above: Bluish Male (*C. ballieui*)   Below: Yellow-white Female (formerly *C. rosea*)

The distribution of this species includes the Hawaiian area.

This fish is named for M. Ballieu who was a French consul in Hawaii sometime prior to 1875.

THE BLACK - STRIPED WRASSE FISH
Also known as Hi-na-le-a hi-lu and Hi-lu
110—31 *Coris flavovittata* (Bennett), 1829

The body of the hilu is elongated and compressed and bears a small head and small eyes. The mouth bears two, strong, prominent teeth in the

front of the mouth in each jaw. The body is principally white in color and is marked above by longitudinal, black stripes. The belly is white in life and turns to a salmon reddish color on death. Young fishes, which are smaller than about five inches in length, have longitudinal stripes both above and below. Large specimens will reach a length of about 18 inches.

Recent studies by John Randall indicate that this is the female color form of *Coris flavovittata;* the male was formerly known as *Coris lepomis.*

GAIMARD'S WRASSE FISH
Also known as Hi-na-le-a ʻa-ki-lo-lo
110—32 *Coris gaimardi* (Quoy and Gaimard), 1824

This is a typical wrasse fish with a slender, compressed body and a small head. The colors of the young and the adult are amazing. The young are brick red with about five, light areas along the back; of these, two are

located on the head, two on the trunk, and one on the caudal peduncle. These young were previously known as *C. greenovii.* The adults are reddish in front, darker posteriorly where they are covered with many brilliant blue spots, and a brilliant yellow on the tail. Large specimens will reach a length of about 15 inches.

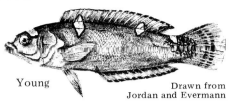

Young   Drawn from
Jordan and Evermann

The distribution of this fish extends from Hawaii and Guam southward to central Polynesia, westward through Micronesia and Melanesia, through the East Indies, and across the Indian Ocean to the coast of Africa and the Red Sea.

The name of this fish honors M. Joseph Paul Gaimard, who was the second surgeon aboard the royal French corvette *Uranie* during its voyage around the world. The fishes which he and others collected in Hawaii in August, 1819, were later studied and their descriptions published in 1824.

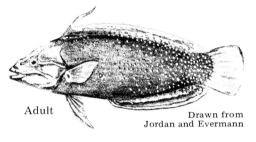

Adult   Drawn from
Jordan and Evermann

THE BLUE AND GREEN WRASSE FISH
Also known as Hi-lu la-u wi-li
110—33 *Coris lepomis* (Jenkins), 1900

This wrasse fish is a large species with a robust, compressed body, and a small head; the eyes are likewise small and are placed high upon the head. The color of the body is greenish with blue hues and shadings. There is a significant blue-black spot on the end of the operculum. There are also six or eight, irregular, vertical, black blotches on the side of the body near its center. Large specimens might possibly reach 24 inches in length. Recent studies by John Randall indicate this is the male of *C. flavovittata.*

THE ELEGANT WRASSE FISH
110—34 *Coris venusta* Vaillant and Sauvage, 1875

The body of this wrasse fish is elongated and compressed and bears a long head with small eyes located high upon it. The color of the body is variable, but consists mostly of brownish shades. The sides of the body below the midline are marked by a parallel series of diagonal cross-bars. Large specimens are reported to reach six inches in length.

The distribution of this species includes the Hawaiian area.

THE SMALL GREEN WRASSE FISH
Also known as 'O-hu-a and 'O-ma-ka
110—35 *Stethojulis balteata* (Quoy and Gaimard), 1824

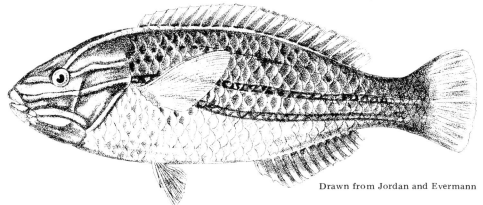

Drawn from Jordan and Evermann

This fish has previously been a very confusing species because it has two color phases. The problem has now been resolved through the work of Dr. John Randall and others and the correct name of *S. balteata* assigned to it.

The name of *S. axillaris* (Quoy and Gaimard), 1824, has long been applied to the "primary phase" in which the color of the body was a light green when young and greenish brown as the fish became larger in size. These individuals are marked by a black area at the base of the pectoral fin and by a bright cream or yellow colored spot just above the base of the

pectoral fin. In addition, there are usually two (occasionally one or three), small, black spots on the side of the caudal peduncle. In this color phase, the fish will reach a length of about five inches. This fish was known as the 'omaka.

The name of *S. albovittata* (Bonnaterre), 1788, has been used for the "terminal phase" in which the body is greenish or brownish above and a yellowish white beneath. In this color stage, there is a wide reddish or orange stripe, which is bordered above and below by a blue line, extending from the pectoral fin backward to the lower edge of the tail. In addition, the head is marked with about four, horizontal, blue lines, one of which extends along the base of the dorsal fin, and another extends along the middle of the body to the tail. These fishes will reach a length of about seven inches. This fish was known as the 'ohua.

The habitat of this wrasse fish extends from the shallow waters of the shore line to the outer edge of the reef.

The distribution of this species includes the Hawaiian area and Johnston Island.

GEOFFROY'S WRASSE FISH
Also known as Hi-na-le-a 'a-ki-lo-lo
110—36 *Macropharyngodon geoffroyi* (Quoy and Gaimard), 1824

The body of this small fish is deep and compressed and bears a short head with small eyes. There are four, strong teeth in each jaw and the second tooth of the upper jaw on each side points backward. The background color of the body is brown or brownish. Each scale on the

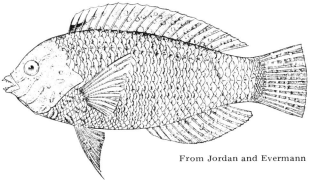

From Jordan and Evermann

side of the body is marked with a blue and a black stripe which align themselves to form longitudinal bands upon the body. The head is covered with many, curved, blue stripes; these turn brown after death. Adults will reach a length of about five or six inches.

The distribution of this species extends from Hawaii southward to central Polynesia, westward through Micronesia and Melanesia, and through the East Indies.

THE SPECKLED WRASSE FISH
110—37 *Macropharyngodon meleagris* (Cuvier and Valenciennes), 1839

The speckled wrasse is a small species which may be recognized by its color pattern. Its dark colored background is marked by longitudinal rows of pale blue spots with brown edges. The head is marked by orange brown stripes. Adults will reach a length of five or six inches.

The males and females in this species are of different colors. The accompanying photo is of the male *(M. meleagris)*, while the species known as *M. pardalis* (Kner), 1867, represents the other color phase.

The distribution of this species extends from Hawaii southward to central Polynesia and westward through Micronesia, Melanesia and doubtless into adjoining areas.

THE GOLDEN-HEADED WRASSE FISH
110—38 *Anampses chrysocephalus* Randall, 1958

The golden-headed wrasse is typical of the group and possesses a compressed body with a small head, mouth, and eyes. The jaws each have a single pair of large, protruding teeth and the tail is truncated or nearly so.

In this amazing species, the male and female fishes are of different colors. The color of the male fish is a dark orange-brown and each scale upon the side of the body is marked with a grayish green posterior border. The head is a brilliant, light, orange color and is rather distinctly marked off from the orange-brown of the body. The head is marked by several, irides-cent, black-bordered, bluish spots and bands.

Top Photo: Female. Bottom Photo: Male.

The female fish, which was originally described as *Anampses rubrocaudata* Randall, 1958, may be identified by its chocolate brown color and by the many white spots which cover the body. These spots are smaller on the head and back and larger on the sides where they form into longitudinal rows on the lower side of the body. The caudal fin is marked with a wide, white, vertical band at its base and by a significant, bright red band at the end. Specimens will reach at least seven inches in length.

The distribution of this species includes the Hawaiian area.

The first female specimen of this fish was obtained by the author from a fisherman on Oahu and subsequently described by Dr. John E. Randall, ichthyologist and long time student of Indo-Pacific marine fishes.

CUVIER'S WRASSE OR SPOTTED WRASSE FISH
Also known as 'O-pu-le, 'O-pu-le-pu-le la-u-li, and 'O-pu-le-pu-le u-li
110—39 *Anampses cuvier* Quoy and Gaimard, 1824
This beautiful and dainty fish has a rather elongated, compressed body which bears a conical head and snout.

In this astonishing species the male and female fishes are of different color patterns. The color pattern in the female fish is one of many round, light colored spots upon a dark, somewhat brownish background. In some

Top Photo: Female. Bottom Photo: Male.

areas of the body these spots tend to run together and form into lines like a string of beads. The lower surface is reddish in color and the dorsal fin is orange-red. Young specimens of less than two or three inches are light green and plain, although they do have two, oval, black spots located at the posterior ends of the dorsal and anal fins.

In the male fish, previously known as *A. godeffroyi* Gunther, 1881, the color of the body is a reddish, greenish, gray combination with blue stripes on the head and with the sides of the body covered by narrow, vertical, blue lines on each scale. There are tinges of red and yellow on the pectoral and caudal fins. Large specimens will reach 15 inches in length, however, most specimens are nine or ten inches long.

The distribution of this species includes the Hawaiian area.

Mr. Albert Gunther named the male fish in honor of the Godeffroy brothers who were Hamburg business men engaged in shipping. They also operated a museum called the Museum Godeffroy in which Mr. Gunther was employed and from which institution Mr. Gunther published the material sent him from the South Seas by Andrew Garrett, an early naturalist in this area.

The female fish was named in honor of Baron Georges Cuvier (1769-1832), a famous French biologist.

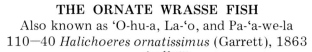

THE ORNATE WRASSE FISH
Also known as 'O-hu-a, La-'o, and Pa-'a-we-la
110—40 *Halichoeres ornatissimus* (Garrett), 1863

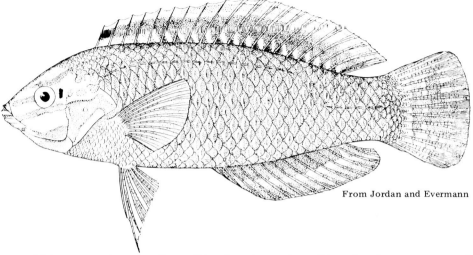

From Jordan and Evermann

This wrasse is a small, multi-colored species with a slender, compressed body and with dorsal and ventral profiles which are about equal and opposite. The head, mouth, and eyes are small and there are two, strong, canine teeth in the front of each jaw. The colors of the body are many. The head is red and is marked with horizontal, green bands; the throat and belly are blue; and each scale is marked by a vertical, crescent-shaped stripe followed by blue. The dorsal fin is dark red and has a row of dark, green, oblong spots on the lower part of the membranes; the outer part of the fin is marked with a green band and the very edge has a narrow, blue line. A significant, dark spot is present on the membrane between the first and second dorsal spines. By far the most significant and useful spot in the identification of this species is a small, vertical, black mark just behind the eye. Adult specimens will reach a length of about seven inches.

The distribution of this species includes the Hawaiian area, Johnston Island, and central Polynesia.

THE PARROT FISH FAMILY

111 *Family Scaridae (Callyodontidae, Sparisomidae, Scarichthyidae)*

The parrot fishes are related to the wrasse fishes and, like them, have bodies which are somewhat oblong and moderately compressed. Their bodies are covered with large scales and the dorsal fin is continuous as in most wrasse fishes. Parrot fishes get their name from the fact that the teeth of both jaws are fused to form a parrot-like beak; in addition, these fishes have grinding plates known as pharyngeal teeth which are located farther back in the mouth and which are used to grind the material taken into the mouth.

Of all of the many families of fishes, the parrot fishes have been one of the most difficult to classify. Fortunately, Dr. Leonard P. Schultz, long time Curator of Fishes in the United States National Museum, has reorganized this group. These fishes are difficult to classify because the males and females may be of different colors and because these fishes may pass through one, two, or three color phases before reaching the final adult pattern. In general, the males tend to be the more colorful and are usually green or blue-green in color, while the females and some males are usually brown or red in color.

The adult fish of this family vary in length from species well under one foot in length to species which measure six feet or more in length.

In their habits, parrot fishes are principally herbivorous and feed upon marine algae; they also eat coral polyps and other living forms. They spend the night resting upon the bottom, often within a transparent, veil-like, balloon-like, mucous bubble.

The family contains about 80 species which inhabit all shallow tropical seas; of this number, about a dozen species are known from this area.

THE RED AND VIOLET PARROT FISH
111—1 *Scarops rubroviolaceus* (Bleeker), 1849

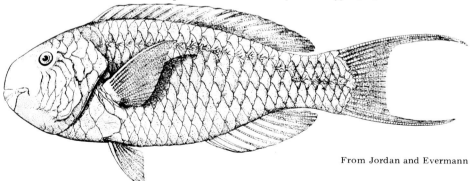

From Jordan and Evermann

In this species the males and females are of different colors; however, the following features are the same in both sexes. There are from five to seven scales on the back in front of the dorsal fin; the cheek has three horizontal rows of scales with the lower row containing but two scales. The teeth are white in the young and in the females and blue or green in the adult males; the pharyngeal teeth in the throat have but a single row of enlarged teeth above.

The adult males are orange to purplish on the upper part of the body and green to blue below. The dorsal fin is orange with a blue or green, narrow, outer border; the anal fin is orange or pink with a blue or green border; the pectoral fin is purplish to brown above and bears a green dorsal edge; the pelvic fins are green-edged. The head is orange below, usually with a blue or green blotch. The upper lip is red to orange; from it a narrow stripe extends backward to below the eye; the lower lip is blue to green.

The adult females are purplish red or dark brownish red in color. The dorsal fin has a dark blue stripe along its outer border; the pectoral fin is bluish with a red dorsal streak; the remaining fins are red in color. The juvenile stages are all reddish brown in color. This species will reach at least 28 inches in length.

The distribution of this species extends from the tropical eastern Pacific (including Cocos Island, Socorra Island, and Roqueto Island) westward through Hawaii and the tropical central and western Pacific, through the East Indies, and into the Indian Ocean.

The males of this species have appeared in books under the name of *Pseudoscarus jordani* Jenkins, 1900.

THE BROWN PARROT FISH
111—2 *Scarus dubius* Bennett, 1828

From Schultz

The identification of this species may be made after a study of the following features. There are four, median, predorsal scales on the back and there are three rows of scales on the cheek, of which the lower row has but a single scale and it is often missing. The teeth are white and the lips do not quite cover them. The color of the body is brownish in both sexes and it is marked by about three, horizontal, light streaks upon the abdomen. The pectoral fin bears a significant, black spot or area at the dorsal edge of its base. The dorsal and caudal fins and the caudal peduncle are usually yellowish in color. The dorsal and anal fins bear a narrow, blue edge. Adult specimens will reach a length of at least 12 inches.

The distribution of this species extends from Hawaii southward to central Polynesia and westward across the tropical Pacific Ocean to the East Indies, and possibly to adjoining areas.

THE FORMOSAN PARROT FISH
111—3 *Scarus formosus* Cuvier and Valenciennes, 1839

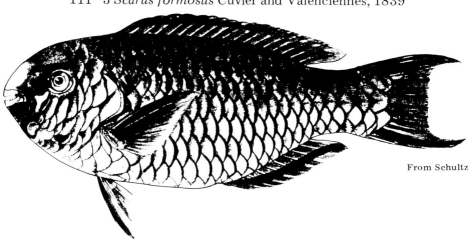

From Schultz

A tentative identification of this species may be made by reviewing the following features. There are four, median rows of predorsal scales and three rows of scales on the cheek with the lower row containing only one or two scales. The teeth are white and the lips do not quite cover them. Large adults are known to develop an enlarged forehead. The color of the body is green, the scales are trimmed with a rose-colored border, and there are three significant spots on the midline of the belly anterior to the base of the pelvic fins. The dorsal and anal fins are marked with three, longitudinal bands; they are a green band at the base, an orange center band, and a blue band at the outside border. Adults will reach a length of at least 12 inches.

The distribution of this species extends from Hawaii southward to central Polynesia, westward through Micronesia and Melanesia, through the East Indies, and across the Indian Ocean.

FORSTER'S PARROT FISH
111—4 *Scarus forsteri* Cuvier and Valenciennes, 1839

An examination of this species should reveal four predorsal scales, two rows of scales on the cheek, and white teeth which are nearly covered by the lips. The body has a greenish color from the scales which are green with brown borders. The cheeks and the chest are salmon colored, and the dorsal and anal fins are salmon colored at the base, bluish along their margins, and marked with a dark line just inside of the blue marginal stripe. There is a black spot at the upper base of the pectoral fin. Both lips are green edged; the green edge of the upper lip continues as a line to the area below the eye. This species exceeds one foot in length.

The distribution of this species extends from Hawaii southward to central Polynesia, westward through Micronesia and Melanesia, through the East Indies, and into the Indian Ocean.

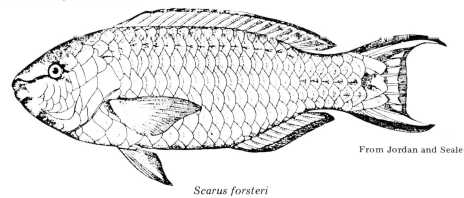

From Jordan and Seale

Scarus forsteri

THE HAWAIIAN PARROT FISH
Also known as La-u-i-a
111—5 *Scarus lauia* Jordan and Evermann, 1903

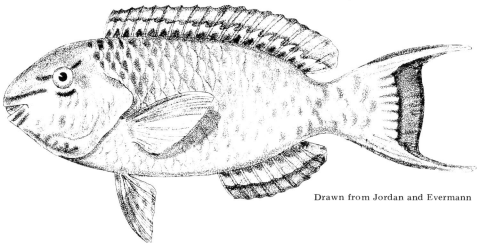

Drawn from Jordan and Evermann

The lauia has but four, median, predorsal scales and three rows of scales on the cheek with only two scales in the lower row. The teeth are white and are nearly covered by the lips. The body is light yellow in color and is marked with bluish and greenish hues. The margins of the lips are blue and there is a blue streak from the tip of the snout to below the eye. The dorsal and anal fins are longitudinally marked with a green border, a central orange band, and a row of green spots at the base. The caudal fin is edged with blue-green. Adult specimens will reach a length of at least 14 inches.

The distribution of this species includes the Hawaiian area.

THE LARGE BLUE PARROT FISH
Also known as U-hu u-li-u-li
111—6 *Scarus perspicillatus* Steindachner, 1879

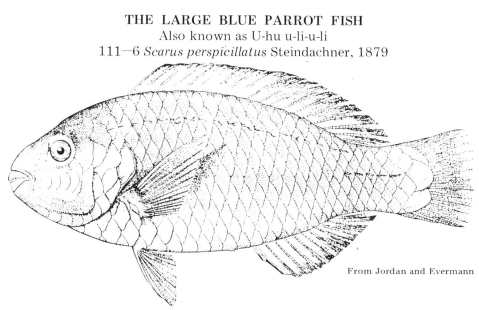

From Jordan and Evermann

This uhu or parrot fish is an amazingly beautiful species. There are four, median, predorsal scales and two rows of scales on the cheek with the lower row containing one, two, three or occasionally no scales. The teeth are white and are not covered by the lips.

Adult males are colored with brilliant green and blue hues. The body is green above with more blue on the belly and tail. In the adult males, the snout is enlarged and is crossed by a wide band in front of the eyes.

The females are rather uniformly reddish brown with a pale caudal peduncle. The females of this species appear in many publications under the name of *Scarus ahula* Jenkins, 1899, and were called uhu-'ula (red) and pa-nuhu-nuhu (second growth stage) in Hawaii.

The young resemble the females but lack the pale caudal peduncle; they have appeared in print under the name of *Scarus barborus* Jordan and

vermann, 1902, and were called pa-nuhu by the Hawaiians, a name for the second growth stage of the uhu or parrot fish. Large adults will reach a length of at least two feet.

The distribution of this species is limited by present knowledge to the Hawaiian area including Johnston Island to the south.

THE SORDID PARROT FISH
111—7 *Scarus sordidus* Forskal, 1775

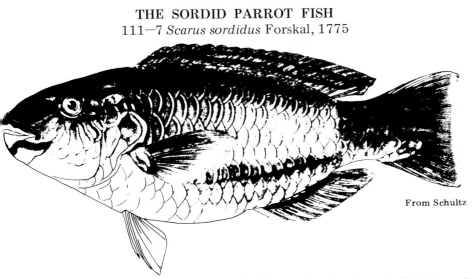

From Schultz

One of the significant features of this species is a long, bullet-shaped head with equal dorsal and ventral profiles. There are four, median, predorsal scales and two rows of scales on the cheek. The teeth are white in the young forms, greenish in the green adult males, and are not covered by the lips.

During growth this species passes through three color phases. The young are striped, the intermediate sizes are brown, and the old and large individuals are greenish. The juveniles may be brown to reddish brown with a pink caudal area which contains a round, dark blotch at the base on the caudal fin. The lips are yellowish to pink when alive. The old males are green and possess an ill-defined darker area behind the eye. Adult specimens will reach at least 18 inches in length.

This is a common species which inhabits the shallow water areas from the shore line down to at least 50 feet.

The distribution of this species extends from Hawaii southward to central Polynesia, westward through Micronesia and Melanesia, through the East Indies, and across the Indian Ocean to the Red Sea.

THE BAND-TAILED PARROT FISH
111—8 *Scarus taeniurus* Cuvier and Valenciennes, 1839

This parrot fish bears four, median, predorsal scales and has two rows of scales upon the cheeks. The teeth are white and are covered by the lips. There is a significant black spot at the upper base of the pectoral fin. Adult males have a body which is brownish green anteriorly and light green posteriorly. The edges of the lips are green and the cheek has a bright yellow area at the center.

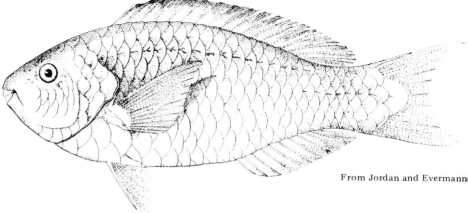

Readers with fishes appearing to be this species should consult the writings of Dr. Leonard Schultz including *U.S. National Museum Bulletin* 214, 1958, and *Smithsonian Contributions to Zoology* No. 17, 1969.

The distribution of this species extends from Hawaii southward to central Polynesia, westward through Micronesia and Melanesia, through the East Indies, and across the Indian Ocean to the coast of Africa and the Red Sea.

JENKIN'S PARROT FISH
111—9 *Calotomus zonarcha* (Jenkins), 1903

This genus contains but a single species which has four, median, predorsal scales, one row of scales on the cheek, teeth which are incompletely fused in four plates, and dorsal spines which are stiff and sharp.

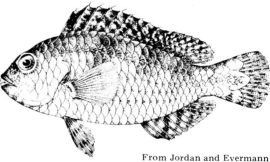

The distribution of this species as presently known seems limited to the Hawaiian area.

THE JAPANESE PARROT FISH
111—10 *Calotomus japonicus* (Cuvier and Valenciennes), 1839

The Japanese parrot fish has four, median, predorsal scales and the cheek has but one row of four scales. The margin of the caudal fin is rounded. The background color of the body is reddish brown; the adult females retain reddish hues, while the adult males show some bluish shades. The scales bear tiny, white spots and there are numerous, white spots on the head. The side of the body is marked with larger, white spots on the upper side and by two rows of white spots on the lower side. Adults will reach a length of at least 14 inches.

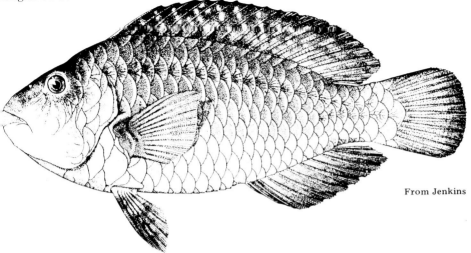

From Jenkins

The distribution of this species extends from Hawaii southward to central Polynesia, westward through Micronesia and Melanesia, through the East Indies, and into the Indian Ocean.

QUOY AND GAIMARD'S PARROT FISH
111—11 *Calotomus spinidens* (Quoy and Gaimard), 1824

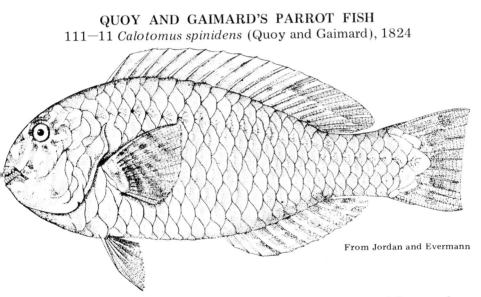

From Jordan and Evermann

This parrot fish has four, predorsal scales and one row of three or four scales on the cheek. The background color of the body is a mottled, reddish brown; the lower surfaces are purplish; and there are red bands radiating from the eye including two to the rear edge of the mouth. There may also be red blotches on the lower jaw. Juvenile forms have a dark pectoral base and a black blotch between the anterior dorsal spines. Adults will reach 20 inches in length.

This species is distributed from the Revillagigedos Islands and Hawaii southward to central Polynesia, westward through Micronesia and Melanesia, through the East Indies, and across the Indian Ocean to the coast of Africa and the Red Sea.

THE HAWK FISH FAMILY
112 *Family Cirrhitidae*

The hawk fishes are small or moderate in size and possess bodies which are not particularly elongated and which are usually compressed. Their pectoral fins are a bit unusual; the upper rays are thin, while the lower rays are thickened and elongated beyond the margins of the fins. The dorsal fin is single and continuous and the caudal fin is never forked. The mouth is of medium size and contains fine, pointed teeth.

As a group, hawk fishes are brightly colored, carnivorous, sedentary fishes which live in shallow areas about the reef. They spend most of their time perched upon a rock or coral head and from this perch will make quick short dashes for food.

Most of the species are found in the warm, tropical waters of the Pacific and Indian Oceans.

This family contains about 34 species of which at least six are known from this area.

The following species is not described or illustrated:

Cirrhitichthys aprinus (Cuvier), 1829, This species has been recorded from Hawaii from material obtained from the hull of a barge which was towed from Guam to the Pearl Harbor drydock. It normally lives in the southwestern Pacific and Indian Oceans.

THE SMALL HAWK FISH
Also known as Pi-li-ko-'a
112—1 *Paracirrhites arcatus* (Cuvier and Valenciennes), 1829

The body of the pili-ko'a is oblong in shape and compressed. The head is quite deep with a fairly large mouth and strong jaws. The eyes are small and are located high upon the head. The background color of the body is a

eddish brown and the entire body is covered by many, small, light spots ocated on the centers of the scales. The posterior half of the body is marked by a longitudinal stripe along the upper side. There is an interesting small patch above and behind the eye which is enclosed by U-shaped border of three colors. Adults will reach a length of about ix inches.

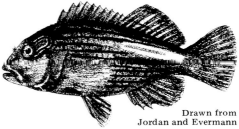

Drawn from
Jordan and Evermann

The distribution of this species extends from Hawaii southward to entral Polynesia, westward through Micronesia and Melanesia, through the last Indies, and across the Indian Ocean to the coast of Africa and the Red ea.

FORSTER'S HAWK FISH
Also known as Pi-li-ko-ʻa and Hi-lu pi-li-ko-ʻa
112—2 *Paracirrhites forsteri* (Bloch and Schneider), 1801

The pili-koʻa has an oblong, compressed body with a large head, mouth, nd jaws; the eyes are placed high upon the head. The color of the body is rownish above and yellowish white below. The front of the body is marked vith dark brown or black spots and the posterior half is marked by orizontal bands. This is one of the larger species and will reach a length of ine or ten inches.

The distribution of this species extends from Hawaii southward to central Polynesia, westward through Micronesia and Melanesia, through the East ndies, and across the Indian Ocean to the coast of Africa and the Red Sea.

THE HARD-HEADED HAWK FISH
Also known as Po-ʻo pa-ʻa, ʻO-ʻo-pu po-ʻo pa-ʻa, and ʻO-ʻo-pu ka-i
112—3 *Cirrhitus pinnulatus* (Bloch and Schneider), 1801

The poʻo-paʻa has an oblong, somewhat compressed body which is stout nd heavy anteriorly. The head is heavy, the mouth is large, and the eyes are

317

small and are placed high upon the head. The background color of the bod
is whitish. The upper parts of the body and fins are marked with rec
brown, and bluish spots and hues.

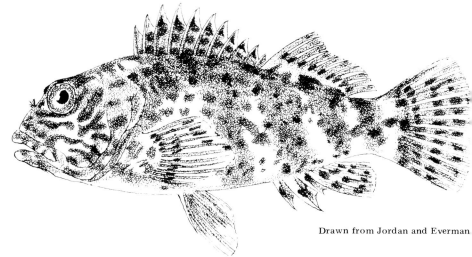

This is an edible, inshore species which will reach a length of about nin
or ten inches.

The distribution of this species extends from Hawaii southward to cen
tral Polynesia, westward through Micronesia and Melanesia, through the Eas
Indies, and across the Indian Ocean to the coast of Africa and the Red Sea

In some books it will be listed under the name of *Cirrhitus alternatu*
Gill, 1862.

THE BANDED HAWK FISH
Also known as Pi-li-ko-'a, Po-'o pa-'a, and 'O-'o-pu ka-i
112—4 *Cirrhitops fasciatus* (Bennett), 1828
This po'o-pa'a is a small species with an oblong, compressed body. It i

eddish brown in color and is marked by broad, vertical, white bars and by a
lack area on the operculum. Adult specimens measure from four to five
inches in length.

The distribution of this species includes Hawaii, southern Japan, and
islands in the western Indian Ocean; it doubtless occurs in some of the intervening areas.

In some books this species will be listed under the name of *Paracirrhites
inctus* (Gunther), 1860.

THE TWO-SPOT HAWK FISH
112—5 *Amblycirrhitus bimacula* (Jenkins), 1903

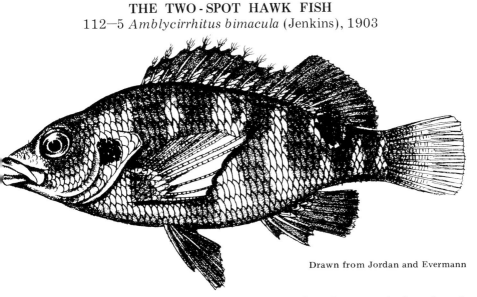

Drawn from Jordan and Evermann

This hawkfish is a small species with uniformly curved dorsal and
ventral outlines which lead to a tapering head and a pointed snout. Some
unusual fringes festoon the membranes of the dorsal fin. The side of the
body is marked by two, large, nearly-round, black spots; one is located on
the gill cover and the other just below the end of the dorsal fin. Adults
measure about three inches in length.

The distribution of this species extends from Hawaii southward to central Polynesia, westward through Micronesia and Melanesia, through the East
Indies, and across the Indian Ocean to Africa.

Some books will list this species under the name of *Cirrhitoidea
bimacula* (Jenkins), 1903.

THE LONG-SNOUTED HAWK FISH
112—6 *Oxycirrhites typus* Bleeker, 1857
This little fish has an elongated body which is compressed and which
leads to a slender, pointed head and snout. The body color is white or
whitish and overlaid with a network of maroon bars of which four are
longitudinal and nine are vertical. Adult specimens measure between three

and four inches in length. The habitat of this fish is in the black coral areas possibly between about 50 and 300 feet in depth.

The distribution of this species appears to extend from western Mexico across the tropical Pacific and Indian Oceans to the coast of Africa.

The first specimens from the Hawaiian area were obtained by biologists Robert A. Morris and Donald E. Morris off Oahu in July, 1961.

THE LONG-FINNED HAWK FISH OR STEEN FISH FAMILY

113 *Family Chilodactylidae (Cheilodactylidae)*

This family consists of but a few species which are related to the *Cirrhitidae* or true hawk fishes and which are sometimes included within that family. They differ from the *Cirrhitidae* in having a longer dorsal fin of 18 spines, while the cirrhitids have only 10 or 12 spines. Only one species is known from this area.

THE STRIPED HAWK FISH
Also known as Ki-ka-ka-pu
113—1 *Chilodactylus vittata* Garrett, 1864

The body of this fish is elongated, strongly compressed, and deep in the area behind the head. The body is basically white in color and is marked by wide, diagonal, dark brown or black bands. Large specimens will reach about ten inches in length.

The habitat of this species is at depths below 75 or 100 feet. It is adept at hiding in the crevices of the coral and is rarely seen or captured.

The distribution of this species seems at present to be limited to the Hawaiian area.

In some books this species may be listed as *Goniistius vittatus* (Garrett), 1864.

THE MACKEREL AND TUNA FISH FAMILY
Including the Bonitos, Skipjacks, Albacores, and the Wahoo
114* *Family Scombridae*
(Thunnidae, Cybiidae, Katsuwonidae, Scomberomoridae)

The members of the family of tuna fishes have smooth, beautifully contoured, torpedo-shaped bodies. The dorsal and ventral outlines of the body are nearly identical in their curvatures and extend from a pointed, conical snout and head in front to a very small caudal peduncle at the base of the tail. The dorsal fin has nine or more rather weak spines which may be completely depressed into a groove on the back. The soft dorsal and anal fins are more or less fixed in position and fairly stiff; they are followed in turn by a series of five to ten detached finlets. The caudal peduncle bears from one to three lateral keels and continues into a strong, lunate caudal fin. Scales are present in some species, absent in others, and may be restricted to an area on the front of the body known as a corselet. Most members have a large mouth, weak teeth, and very wide gill openings. The bodies of these fishes are usually a metallic blue or blue-green color above and lighter blue, silvery, or white below.

The mackerels and tunas are carnivorous fishes and feed upon squids, crustacea, and other fishes. They are speedy swimmers, often live in large schools, and are known to migrate long distances in the sea.

The distribution of the family is world-wide in warm and temperate seas; some species will occasionally invade colder waters; there are none in fresh water.

The family contains over 60 species of which at least 15 are known from this area.

The following species are not described or illustrated:

Auxis tapeinosoma Bleeker, 1854. This frigate mackerel from the western Pacific

* See Appendix.

Ocean and the area of the East Indies has been recorded from Hawaii. It ha
been discovered in schools of *Auxis thazard* (Lacepede), 1801, which i
resembles very closely.

Auxis thynnoides Bleeker, 1855. This frigate mackerel has been recorded fror
Hawaii mixed within schools of *Auxis thazard* (Lacepede), 1801, which i
very closely resembles.

Sarda chilensis (Cuvier and Valenciennes), 1831. This bonito is an eastern Pacifi
species which inhabits the coast line from California to Chile. It is uncom
mon in this area.

THE WAHOO FISH
Also known as O-no, Pacific King-fish, Queen-fish, and Peto
114—1   *Acanthocybium solandri* (Cuvier and Valenciennes), 1831

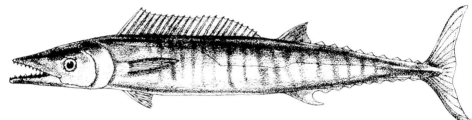

The ono or wahoo is a very elongated, mackerel-like fish with a slender
sharp-pointed head. There are eight or nine finlets on the upper and lowei
side of the body just behind the soft dorsal and anal fins. The cauda
peduncle bears a lateral keel and the tail is large and heavy. The mouth is
large and contains teeth which are triangular in shape and very closely set
The color of the body is dark blue above and silvery beneath; the sides are
marked by between 24 and 30, irregular, dark, vertical bars. Large
specimens may reach six feet and weigh as much as 120 pounds; most are
smaller and weigh nearer 30 pounds.

The ono is a carnivorous fish and feeds upon other fishes and squids.
It is active, savage, and strong, and has been known to take bites from the
sides of other tuna fishes. It is a pelagic species and lives a solitary life at the
surface of the sea.

The distribution of this species is world-wide in warm water.

THE JAPANESE OR TINKER MACKEREL FISH
Also known as the 'O-pe-lu pa-la-hu, 'O-pe-lu pa-ka, Pacific Chub Mackerel,
Pacific Mackerel, Japanese Chub Mackerel, and Saba
114—2 *Scomber japonicus* Houttouyn, 1782

This mackerel has a slender, cylindrical, stream-lined body which is not
compressed. The head is slender and conical and terminates in a conical
snout with a large mouth containing teeth which are small, pointed, and
curved. The eye is quite large and is partly covered by a large, adipose
eyelid. The scales are small and completely cover the body. The dorsal fins
are widely separated and both the soft dorsal fin and the anal fin are
followed by about five finlets. The caudal peduncle is not compressed and

ears two lateral keels. The color of the body is a blue or blue-green above
nd silvery below. The sides of the body are marked by about 30 irregular,
ertical, zig-zag bands. The fins are yellowish. Large specimens are reported
o reach 26 inches in length, but most individuals will measure about 15
nches.

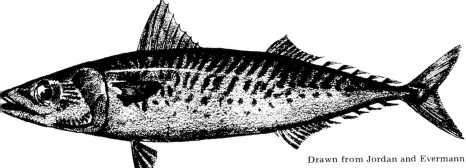

Drawn from Jordan and Evermann

The distribution of this species includes the warmer temperate and
tropical waters of the Pacific, Indian, and Atlantic Oceans.

THE FRIGATE MACKEREL FISH
Also known as the Ke-'o ke-'o and Mexican Skipjack
114—3 *Auxis thazard* (Lacepede), 1802

The frigate mackerel has the general appearance of a small tuna fish.
The body is robust, not noticeably compressed, and possesses a head and
snout which are conical and pointed. The dorsal fins are widely separated
and the soft dorsal fin and anal fin are followed by eight and seven finlets,
respectively. As in other fishes, the caudal peduncle is small and in this
species bears a single, strong keel. The color of the body is bluish green
above and silvery below. The upper half of the body behind the corselet
(of scales) is marked by black spots and short, somewhat wavy bars which
run backward and upward. There are no markings on the belly. Large
specimens may reach as much as 24 inches, but most are 10 to 14 inches in
length.

They are carnivorous, pelagic fishes which sometimes mix with the
kawa-kawa and are occasionally caught with trolling hooks in those schools.

Their flesh is dark and, although edible, is not regarded as superior tasting
The distribution of this species is world-wide in the tropics.

THE SKIPJACK TUNA FISH

Also known as A-ku, A-ku ki-na-'u (young), Skipjack, Oceanic Bonito,
Striped Tuna, and Little Tunny
114—4 *Katsuwonus pelamis* (Linnaeus), 1758

The body of the skipjack tuna is oblong, robust, and spindle-shaped
and bears a large, long, conical head. The skin is smooth and a corselet
(of scales) covers most of the front of the body. The dorsal fins are united
at their base, the pectoral fins are short, and the finlets following the soft
dorsal and anal fins usually number eight above and seven below. The color
of the body is a dark, shining, metallic blue-black above and silvery white
below; the sides of the belly are marked with four or five, dark
longitudinal stripes.

Skipjacks live in schools of various sizes on the high seas where they
continually search for the fishes, squid, and crustacea on which they feed
When feeding on small fishes at the surface, they are usually accompanied
by noddy turns and other sea birds which likewise feed on small species
of fishes; it is these birds which enable the fishermen to locate the schools
of tuna.

The growth rate of this fish has been studied and it has been discovered
that it grows about eighteen inches the first year, ten inches the second year,
and about four inches the third year; in three years this fish will make a
growth of about 32 inches. Although some individuals will reach a length of
40 inches and 50 pounds, most specimens will measure about 32 inches
in length.

The distribution of this species is world-wide in warm water.

THE WAVY - BACK SKIPJACK FISH

Also known as Ka-wa ka-wa, Ka-wa ka-wa ki-na-'u (young), Po-ho po-ho,
Black Skipjack, Bonito, Little Tunny, and False Albacore
114—5 *Euthynnus affinis* (Cantor), 1850

The kawa-kawa is a small tuna with a robust body and a conical,

pointed head and snout. The front of the body is covered by a corselet (of scales) but the remainder of the body is without scales. The pectoral fins are rather short and there are eight finlets above and seven below. The color of the body is a dark blue or blue-green above and silver beneath. About 12, wavy, dark, diagonal lines ornament the upper, posterior area of the body. A few black spots usually occur on the head and are nearly always present on the sides of the body in the area below the pectoral fins. Most individuals measure less than 20 inches in length, but some have been known to measure as much as 30 inches or more.

The kawa-kawa travels in schools and feeds upon surface fishes, crustacea, and squid. It lives in open water but always remains reasonably close to a shore line. Although the adults always remain at sea, the young may enter bays and harbors. This fish is captured for food wherever it occurs; the flesh is edible, but dark in color, and not particularly tasty.

The distribution of this species is world-wide in warm water.

In some books this species will be listed under the name of *Euthynnus alletteratus* (Rafinesque), 1810 or as *Euthynnus yaito* Kishinouye, 1915; some scholars think that there is more than one species represented here.

THE STRIPED BONITO OR ORIENTAL BONITO FISH
114—6 *Sarda orientalis* (Temminck and Schlegel), 1842

This bonito fish has a slender, fusiform body and somewhat resembles a tuna; the body shape, however, is less slender in the young and only becomes more elongated as the fish matures. The mouth is large and contains large, curved teeth. Scales cover the entire body. The finlets number seven or eight above and five or six below. The color of the body is dark bluish above

and silvery on the belly. The upper part of the body is marked by about seven, dark, longitudinal stripes which appear nearly horizontal, but actually run slightly upward and backward to end at the middle on the back. Large specimens have been reported to reach over 30 inches in length, but most are considerably smaller.

The distribution of this species is world-wide in warm water.

It should not be confused with the Atlantic Bonito, *Sarda sarda* (Bloch), 1793, of the Atlantic Ocean and the Mediterranean Sea or with the Pacific Bonito, *Sarda chilensis* (Cuvier and Valenciennes), 1831, which inhabits the eastern Pacific Ocean from California to Chile.

THE PACIFIC LONG-FINNED TUNA FISH
114—7 *Kishinoella zacalles* Jordan and Evermann, 1926

Drawn from Jordan and Evermann

This uncommon and little known species resembles a small yellow-fin tuna. It has a very robust body, a large head, and a very large caudal keel. The dorsal and anal fins are low and are each followed by nine finlets; the first dorsal finlet is very small and is reported as attached to the soft dorsal fin. The pectoral fin is very long and pointed and reaches beyond the origin of the soft dorsal fin or even as far as the middle of the soft dorsal fin. The color of the body is reported as steel blue above and gray beneath; the head is silvery in color. The pectoral fins have black edges and tips, the spinous dorsal fin is yellow, and the soft dorsal fin is silvery at the base and yellow distally. Specimens usually weight less than 20 pounds and do not exceed more than 25 or 30 pounds.

This fish is not well known and appears to be often erroneously identified as a yellow-fin tuna and included with that species.

The distribution of this species includes the Hawaiian area.

THE ALBACORE FISH
Also known as 'A-hi, 'A-hi pa-la-ha, Long-finned Tuna,
European Albacore, Atlantic Albacore, and Alalunga
114—8 *Thunnus alalunga* (Bonnaterre), 1788
The albacore has the robust, spindle-shaped body of the tunas. It may be recognized by its large eyes and by the very long pectoral or shoulder fins,

which in this species extend backward beyond the beginning of the soft dorsal and anal fins. The dorsal finlets are eight or nine in number and the ventral finlets number either seven or eight; the usual numbers are eight and seven, respectively. The color of the body is a blackish blue above and silvery on the sides and belly. The anal finlets have no yellow color. Although specimens have been known to reach a weight of 80 or 90 pounds, most individuals are far smaller; very few ever exceed a weight of 40 pounds.

The albacore is a very important food fish, contains white flesh, and is canned in large quantities.

The distribution of this species is world-wide in warm seas and in the warmer parts of temperate seas.

THE YELLOW-FIN TUNA FISH
Also known as 'A-hi and Allison Tuna
114—9 *Thunnus albacares* (Bonnaterre), 1788

The yellow-fin tuna has a more elongated body and a smaller head than other large tunas. The pectoral fins are long and the second dorsal and the anal fins reach an extraordinary development in this species. When young, the second dorsal and anal fins are not especially noteworthy; but, as the fish grows in size, they become greatly elongated and in some cases may nearly reach the caudal fin; this long-finned adult has long been regarded as a separate species in some areas and called the Allison tuna. There are usually eight or nine dorsal finlets and seven, eight, or nine ventral finlets. The color of the body is blackish blue above, yellow on the sides, and silvery on the belly. The dorsal fin, the anal fin, all finlets, the outer edge of the caudal fin, and the eyes are all yellow in color. The inside of the pectoral fin is blackish and the pelvic fins are yellowish in color but are tipped with blackish hues. The belly may show about twenty, slightly oblique, broken lines which are very pale in color. Although this fish has been reported to exceed eight feet in length and to weigh well over 400 pounds, most specimens are less than 100 pounds.

The yellow-fin tuna is a fish of the open sea where it feeds upon pelagic fishes, squids, and crustacea.

The distribution of this species includes all warm seas.

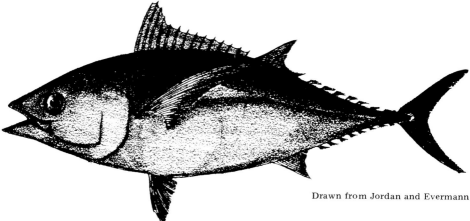

Drawn from Jordan and Evermann

Some scholars prefer the name of *Neothunnus macropterus* (Temminck and Schlegel), 1844, for this species.

THE BIG-EYE TUNA FISH
Also known as 'A-hi, 'A-hi po-'o nu-i (big head), and Shibi
114—10 *Thunnus obesus* Lowe, 1839

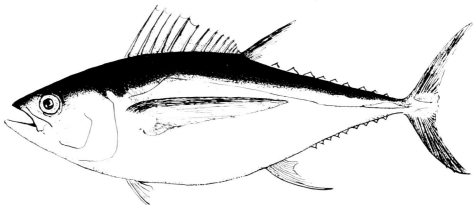

The big-eye tuna may be recognized by its extremely plump and robust body, by its relatively large head, and by its unusually large eyes. The pectoral fins are proportionately longer in young individuals than in mature specimens; this long fin may cause it to be confused for a moment with the albacore which it somewhat resembles. The finlets usually number nine above and nine below. The color of the body is blackish and grayish blue above, the sides shade to silvery, and the belly is likewise silvery. The pectoral fins are black, the ventral fins are grayish, and the anal fin is mostly white with a yellow tip. The finlets show dull, faint, yellowish hues and are each crossed by a broad, sharply-defined, angular, black bar. Although large

328

specimens may reach a length of about six feet and weight well over 300 pounds, most individuals weigh less than 150 pounds.

The big-eye tuna is a fish of the high seas which feeds upon other fishes, squid, and crustacea. It seems to live nearer the surface in temperate seas and in warmer seas to occur at depths below 100 feet.

The distribution of this species is world-wide in warm water.

Some publications may list this species under the name of *Parathunnus sibi* (Temminck and Schlegel), 1842.

THE BLUE-FIN TUNA FISH
Also known as 'A-hi, Black Tuna, Great Tuna, Great Albacore, Short-finned Tuna, European Tuna, and other names.
114—11 *Thunnus thynnus* (Linnaeus), 1758

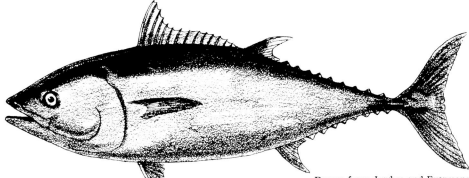

Drawn from Jordan and Evermann

The blue-fin tuna is the largest bony fish in the sea. It has a robust body which tapers rapidly to the tail, a large head, small eyes, and short pectoral fins. The finlets number from eight to ten above and from seven to nine below. The lateral line makes a peculiar, sharp bend over the pectoral fin. The color of the body is a metallic black, bluish, or grayish above and becomes progressively lighter ventrally. The belly is grayish and is marked with vague, faint, transverse rows of lines and dots. Most specimens weight about 250 pounds, but they have been known to reach a length of over ten feet and a weight of over 1,500 pounds.

The distribution of this species includes all of the tropical and warmer temperate seas of the world.

Confusion surrounds the identification and naming of these large fishes. Some scholars include all of these fishes under the name of *Thunnus thynnus;* some prefer to call the Pacific species by the name of *Thunnus orientalis* Temminck and Schlegel, 1842; some regard the fishes in various geographical areas of the world as subspecies of *T. thynnus;* other specialists suggest that perhaps the fish of each geographical area is a distinct species.

THE MARLIN AND SAIL-FISH FAMILY
115 *Family Istiophoridae (Histiophoridae)*

The marlins and the sail-fishes have elongated bodies which are quite robust in some species and more slender in others. They all possess a spear on the head which is an extension of the upper jaw; these spears are nearly round in cross-section, while those of the swordfishes are much wider and quite flat in cross-section. The dorsal fin is very long and varies in height depending upon the species; this long dorsal fin is followed by a small second dorsal fin of six or seven rays which is located just forward of the caudal peduncle. The anal fin is likewise divided into two parts; the first part has two spines and from 11 to 14 rays; the second part is small, has six or seven rays, and is located opposite the second dorsal fin. The pectoral fins are long, narrow, and curved and are located low upon the body. The ventral or pelvic fins are very long and very slender; in the sail-fishes they consist of one spine and two or three rays, while in the marlins they have been reduced to a single spine. The caudal peduncle bears two keels or ridges on each side and a tail with lobes which are high, narrow, and stiff. Teeth are present in the mouth but they are very small in size. The surface of the body is covered with long, pointed scales.

Marlins and sail-fishes are active, voracious, carnivorous fishes of the deep sea. They eat all manner of fishes and squid and, because of their large size, are able to swallow whole tunas and other large species.

They inhabit the tropical and warmer temperate seas of the world.

Of approximately ten known species, at least five species are known from this area.

THE SHORT-BILLED SPEAR-FISH
115—1* *Tetrapterus angustirostris* Tanaka, 1914

Drawn from Tanaka

The short-billed spear-fish is a small, slender species with a long, compressed body. In general appearance, it resembles a sail-fish except for the dorsal fin which is low and long; the anterior ray of this dorsal fin is the longest, a feature helpful in separating it from other species. The spear of this fish is much shorter than those of the other species in this family and extends only a comparatively short distance beyond the lower jaw. The color pattern of the body in life is without stripes or other significant markings. The back and the first dorsal fin are a deep, metallic blue; the

* See Appendix.

sides are silvery grey; and the belly is whitish. After death this color fades and the back becomes a dark, slaty gray and the dorsal fin becomes blackish. Adult specimens average about 40 pounds in weight; they usually weigh less than 60 pounds and rarely exceed 100 pounds in weight and six feet in length.

This spear-fish is an oceanic species and is not found along coast lines. It feeds upon squid and small fishes.

The distribution of this species includes the tropical central and western Pacific Ocean, the coast of Chile, and the Indian Ocean.

THE SAIL - FISH
Also known as A-'u le-pe
115—2* *Istiophorus platypterus* (Shaw and Nodder), 1791

Drawn from Walford

The sail-fishes have a smaller and more slender, compressed body than the marlins. The dorsal fin is high and folds into a groove on the back of the body. The anal fin is divided into two parts; the first part is quite large, while the second part is small, is equal in size to the second dorsal fin, and is located directly below it. The pectoral fins are curved and pointed; the pelvic or ventral fins are reduced to two, long, strap-like appendages consisting of two or three rays which fit into grooves on the lower side of the belly. The caudal peduncle bears two keels or ridges on each side and is followed by the caudal fin which is large, narrow, and widely forked. The entire body is covered with elongated scales. The color of the body is purplish blue above and yellowish gray below. The sides are marked with a series of vertical bars composed of white spots. The dorsal fin is a dark, brilliant blue color and is marked with numerous, small blue spots. Most sail-fishes average between 30 and 50 pounds in weight. There are records of some specimens which have weighed over 200 pounds and measured 11 or 12 feet in length.

Sail-fishes are pelagic species which live in deep water. They are rarely caught by trolling and are occasionally taken on tuna long-line gear. They have a habit of leaping when hooked and are therefore of great interest to sport fishermen.

* See Appendix.

331

The distribution of sail-fishes has long been a puzzling problem. Some ichthyologists believed that there is but one species of sail-fish which is distributed in all warm seas while others believed that there are separate species in the Atlantic, Pacific, and Indian Oceans. Recent studies now show that there is but a single species with a world-wide distribution.

THE SILVER OR BLACK MARLIN FISH
Also known as A-'u, Black Marlin (Central and South America, New Zealand), and White Marlin (Japan) or Shirokajiki
115—3* *Makaira indica* (Cuvier), 1831

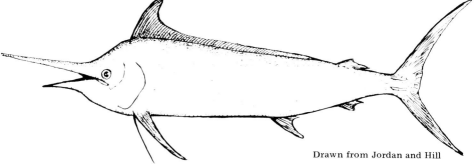

Drawn from Jordan and Hill

This marlin is a large, heavy-bodied species which is most easily identified by its pectoral fins which are permanently extended and which cannot be folded against the sides of the body. The body is more robust than either *M. nigricans* or *T. audax* and proportionally deeper through the pectoral region of the body than either species. The first dorsal fin is very low and the slender pelvic fins are short compared to other species. The color of the body is whitish when alive, but on dying changes to a metallic bluish gray above and to a whitish color below. After several hours, the color of the upper part of the body changes to a dark, leaden gray color. This species is usually reported to be without stripes, but some have observed faint stripes on the body after death. Most individuals weigh from 200 to 350 pounds, but some have been known to exceed 1,500 pounds and 14 feet in length. These large specimens seem to have been females. Some scholars regard this as the largest member of this family.

The distribution of this species includes the tropical and warmer temperate waters of the Pacific and Indian Oceans.

THE BLUE MARLIN FISH
Also known as A-'u, Pacific Blue Marlin, Black Marlin, and Kurokajiki
115—4* *Makaira nigricans* Lacepede, 1802

The blue marlin has a deep and robust body which is not laterally compressed in the area of the anal fin as in *M. audax*. The dorsal fin is relatively low and the first dorsal ray is shorter than the greatest depth of the

* See Appendix.

body. The pectoral fins can be folded back against the sides of the body; this feature is useful in separating this species from *M. indica* which has a stiff and rigid pectoral fin which cannot be folded against the body without breaking the joint where it attaches. The lateral line in this species is very faint, obscure, and inconspicuous and, when visible, divides into a reticulated pattern; this pattern may sometimes be seen when the skin is dry or when a piece of skin has been removed and held before a light.

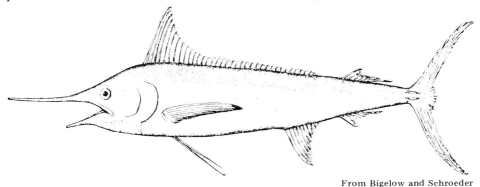

From Bigelow and Schroeder

The color of the body in fresh specimens is a brilliant, deep, metallic blue with vertical stripes. Following death the blue color changes to a leaden gray color with brownish hues wherever the skin has been rubbed. The stripes likewise disappear following death, except possibly in young specimens; this leads to confusion with the striped marlin, *T. audax;* however, it should be remembered that *M. nigricans* has a lower dorsal fin, a more robust body, is not laterally compressed in the area of the anal fin, and has the usual lateral line described above; none of these features occur in *T. audax.* Most specimens weigh between 300 and 400 pounds, however some have been known to exceed 1,400 pounds and 11 feet in length. One specimen caught off Oahu in November, 1954, by George Parker weighed 2,002 pounds.

This marlin is a pelagic species which is often captured by trolling and on long-line tuna gear. It is the most common species of marlin in the Hawaiian area.

The distribution of this species includes the tropical Pacific, Indian, and Atlantic Oceans.

THE STRIPED MARLIN FISH
Also known as A-'u, Mitsukuri's Marlin, Makajiki (True Marlin), and Akakajiki (Red Marlin)
115—5[*] *Tetrapterus audax* (Philippi), 1887

The striped marlin is a smaller marlin than the two preceeding species and presents a less robust body which is laterally compressed, particularly in the area of the anal fin. As usual in these fishes, the dorsal and anal fins are divided into two parts, with the second portions being nearly equal in size and opposite in position; the caudal peduncle bears the usual two keels

[*] See Appendix.

on each side. In this species, the first dorsal ray is as long or longer than the greatest depth of the body; in this feature, it differs from *M. nigricans* where the ray is shorter. The ventral fins consist of a single, long spine. The lateral line is simple in pattern, but it is difficult to see. The color of the body is a deep, metallic, cobalt blue above and whitish on the belly. The sides are marked by a series of vertical stripes. Following death the bright blue color fades to a dark bluish gray or leaden gray and the stripes persist in a faded condition.

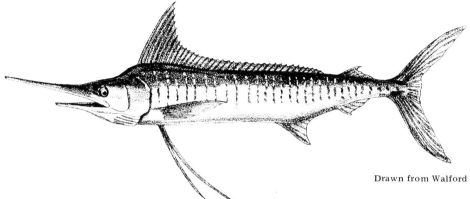

Drawn from Walford

The average size of this species is about 80 pounds. A few individuals may exceed 500 or 600 pounds, but they are believed to never exceed 1,000 pounds. Large specimens of 400 or 500 pounds are easily confused with *M. nigricans;* small specimens are also difficult to identify.

This is a pelagic species which is captured by trolling and by long-line fishing gear. It is the second most abundant species in Hawaii.

The distribution of this species extends across the entire tropical Pacific Ocean and adjoining areas of warm water.

This species appears in many publications under the name of *Tetrapterus mitsukurii* Jordan and Snyder, 1901; this name honors Dr. Kakichi Mitsukuri, formerly a professor of zoology in the Imperial University at Tokyo. It is also known as *Makaira audax* (Philippi), 1887.

THE BROAD-BILL SWORD-FISH FAMILY
116 *Family Xiphiidae*

This family contains but a single living species, the broad-bill sword-fish, although other species are known to have existed in prehistoric times. The body of this fish is elongated, sub-cylindrical, and bears a large, rigid tail at one end and a spear at the other. This spear, for which this fish is so famous, is an extension of the upper jaw and may be as much as one-third of the total body length; it is flat in cross-section and has rather sharp edges. There is no lateral line upon the body and a single, strong ridge or keel is present on the side of the caudal peduncle. The dorsal fin is in two parts, a large and high anterior section placed above the pectoral fins, and a small and low posterior fin located just forward of the caudal peduncle; both of these fins have only soft rays. The anal fin is likewise in two parts, a large and a small fin; the anal fin also bears only soft rays. It is interesting to note that both the dorsal and anal fins are continuous in very young specimens and subsequently develop into two fins as the fish develops. The pelvic or ventral fins are absent. Teeth are present in young sword-fish but are absent in the adult. Young individuals possess scales, but these too have disappeared by the time the fish reaches 30 inches in length.

Although the sword-fish is related to the marlins, it differs from them in the absence of the scales, teeth, and ventral fins; it also has only a single keel upon the caudal peduncle, a high short dorsal fin, and a flat spear.

THE BROAD-BILL SWORD-FISH
Also known as A-ʻu ku
116—1 *Xiphias gladius* Linnaeus, 1758

The body of the sword-fish tapers rather uniformly from front to back. The pectoral fins are long, narrow, and curved, and are mounted low upon the sides of the body. The eye is large and reported to be blue. The very young sword-fish is different in appearance from the adult. The young have a single, continuous dorsal and anal fin; both jaws are elongated and toothed; and the surface of the body is covered with spiny plates and scales. All of these features disappear with growth and are absent by the time the fish reaches a half pound in weight, except the scales which persist until the fish is about 30 inches in length. The color of the body varies greatly; the upper surfaces may be black, dark gray, purple, leaden blue, and possibly brownish; the lower surfaces are whitish or yellowish and show a silvery iridescence; the fins are brown. Large specimens may reach as much as 20 feet in length and weigh over 1,000 pounds; however, most specimens are less than 500 pounds.

Sword-fishes live a solitary life upon the high seas. They are rarely seen near land and they are rarely seen at the surface when the sea is rough. During calm weather they are often observed swimming slowly at the surface and at this time may be approached and harpooned. They are carnivorous and feed upon all manner of fishes and squid. Their mouth is large and capable of swallowing tunas and other fishes whole.

Sword-fishes are eagerly sought after by fishermen and usually bring a good price; their flesh is red, very fine tasting, and is commonly served in restaurants.

Sword-fishes are reported to have the unusual habit of ramming ships and other objects with their swords, often to their own destruction. The

ancient poet Oppian relates this silly habit most beautifully in the following lines:

> "*Nature her bounty to his mouth confined,*
> *Gave him a sword, but left unarmed his mind.*"

The distribution of this species includes all tropical seas and all temperate seas which are warmer than about 50° F.

THE DEEP-SEA SNAKE MACKEREL OR ESCOLAR FISH FAMILY
117 *Family Gempylidae (Acinaceidae)*

The snake mackerels are mackerel-like fishes with bodies which are elongated, band-shaped, and compressed. Scales may cover the body, be reduced in size, or be entirely absent in some species. In the dorsal fin, the spinous portion is longer than the soft or rayed portion which follows it; these fins are united at their base. The soft dorsal and anal fins are usually followed in most species by one or more finlets. In this family, the caudal fin is forked, quite small, and weak; there are no keels on the caudal peduncle. The pectoral fins are very short and the ventral or pelvic fins may be developed or rudimentary. The mouth is large with a projecting lower jaw and contains sharp, compressed teeth of which some are large and fang-like. The species which live at the surface usually exhibit bright, metallic, silvery colors, while those which inhabit deeper water may be violet, black, brown, or other colors.

Most gempylids are medium-sized, carnivorous fishes. Some live at the surface, some at moderate depths, and some inhabit deeper water. All are edible, although some have oily flesh and are not particularly tasty.

The distribution of this family includes the warmer waters of tropical and temperate seas.

This family contains about 22 species of which at least six are known from this area.

THE OIL-FISH
Also known as Wa-lu, Scour Fish, and Plain-tail
117—1 *Ruvettus pretiosus* Cocco, 1829

The oil-fish is a rather large species with a slender, spindle-shaped body which is covered by small, rough, bony plates with short spines. The dorsal fin is divided into an anterior, spinous portion containing between 13 and 15 spines and a posterior, soft dorsal fin containing between 16 and 18 rays. Both the soft dorsal fin and the anal fin below are followed by two, separate finlets. The tail is deeply forked and there are no keels upon the caudal peduncle. The pectoral and pelvic fins are small. There is no lateral line. The head is large and exhibits a projecting lower jaw. The color has been reported as brownish above with darker areas; it is lighter below. Large specimens will reach a length of six feet and weigh over 100 pounds.

The habitat of this fish seems to be at depths between 500 and 2,500

feet. The flesh of the oil-fish is reported to be white, flaky, soft, and oily. It is reported as edible, but appears to cause diarrhea and is therefore not recommended; the common name "scour fish" seems to suggest that it should not be eaten.

The distribution of the oil-fish is world-wide in warm water including the Mediterranean Sea.

The accompanying photo is of a mounted specimen in the Waikiki Aquarium.

THE BERMUDA CAT - FISH OR RABBIT FISH
117—2 *Promethichthys prometheus* (Cuvier and Valenciennes), 1831

This gempylid fish has a slender, elongated, fusiform body and a large, conical head with large eyes. The mouth is likewise large and full of long, sharp teeth including two canine teeth in the front of each jaw. The dorsal fin is long and contains 19 spines; it is followed by the soft dorsal fin and then by two finlets; the anal fin, which is about equal in size and opposite the soft dorsal fin, is likewise followed by two finlets. The pectoral fins are small and the ventral or pelvic fins have been reduced to a pair of spines which are located on the belly just forward of the pectoral fins. The lateral line is present and contains a rather unusual downward curve in the area above the pectoral fins. The color of the body is steel blue above and silvery gray below; the dorsal fins are black and there are various other black markings on the body. Most specimens are 15 or 16 inches in length, although some have been captured which measured 24 inches.

The habitat of this fish is near the bottom at depths between 500 and 2,500 feet.

The distribution of this species is apparently circumtropical.

SMITH'S ESCOLAR FISH
117—3 *Lepidocybium flavobrunneum* (Smith), 1849

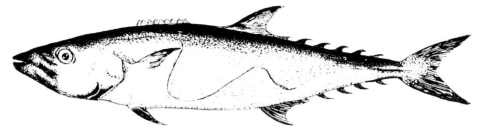

This escolar is a medium-sized fish which superficially resembles a tuna. The dorsal fin is divided into a spinous dorsal containing between nine and twelve spines and a soft dorsal fin of 16 or 17 rays; this is followed by four, five, or six finlets. The anal fin, which is about equal in size and opposite to the soft dorsal fin, is followed by four finlets. The lateral line is useful in identifying this fish for it begins high on the side of the body and pursues an irregular wavy course to end in a lateral keel on the caudal peduncle. The mouth contains a single series of curved, incisor-like teeth. The color of the body is reported to become nearly black in large, old specimens. Large individuals will reach a weight of at least 100 pounds and a length of at least four feet.

This is a rare fish which lives in deeper water and which is occasionally captured on long-line tuna gear. The flesh is reported to be oily. Very little is known about this fish and specimens are very uncommon.

The distribution is believed to be circumtropical.

THE SNAKE MACKEREL FISH
Also known as Ha-u-li, Ha-u-li-u-li, and Ha-u-li-u-li pu-hi
117—4 *Gempylus serpens* Cuvier, 1829

This amazing, snake-like fish has a slender, elongated, ribbon-like body with a large head, large eyes, and a large mouth filled with fang-like teeth. The skin is smooth and is without scales except for a few behind the eye and at the base of the tail. The spinous portion of the dorsal fin is very long and bears from 28 to 32 spines; this is followed by the soft dorsal fin and by five to seven detached finlets. The anal fin is equal in size and opposite the soft dorsal fin and is likewise followed by about six finlets. The lateral line has two branches, both of which begin below the first spine of the dorsal fin; the upper line runs parallel to the dorsal fin and ends at its base; the lower line extends along the side of the body to the base of the tail. The caudal fin is small and forked; the pectoral fins are quite small and pointed; and the

pelvic fins have been reduced to a pair of spines and are located below the base of the pectoral fins. The color of the body is a uniform, dark slate-blue. Most specimens measure about 30 inches, but there are records of specimens reaching five feet in length.

The habitat of the snake mackerel is the open sea from the surface down to several hundred feet. It is sometimes captured on tuna long-line fishing gear.

The distribution of this species is world-wide in tropical and warm temperate seas.

THE DEEP-WATER GEMPYLID FISH
117—5 *Epinnula magistralis* Poey, 1854

Like the other members of this family, the body is elongated and spindle-shaped; the sides are slightly compressed so that the body is oval in cross-section. The surface of the body is covered with minute, delicate scales which are easily brushed off; there are no lateral keels at the base of the tail; and there are two lateral lines on each side of the body of which one is placed high on the body and follows in general the upper profile, and the other is low on the body and follows the ventral profile. The spinous dorsal fin with its 16 spines is joined to the soft dorsal fin which follows it; in this species there are no detached finlets and all vertical fins are without scales. The caudal fin is deeply forked and divided into two lobes of which the lower lobe is slightly smaller than the upper. The ventral fins are located behind the pectoral fins and under their lower angle. The anal fin resembles the soft dorsal fin but is slightly shorter. The length of the body of the Cuban specimen from which this species was described measured about 39 inches. Hawaiian specimens have been smaller.

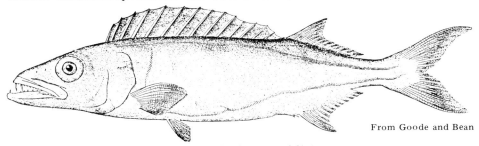

From Goode and Bean

The color of the body is bluish above and lighter on the sides and belly. The fins have a reddish hue and at least the dorsal fin may be iridescent. The iris is reported to be white.

The habitat of this gempylid is in depths of 500 feet or more.

The distribution of this species seems to include the warmer waters of the tropical Atlantic and Pacific Oceans.

THE WORLD-WIDE GEMPYLID FISH
117—6 *Nealotus tripes* Johnson, 1865

The body of this rare fish is very much elongated and compressed and in this feature resembles the other members of this family. The body is covered with large scales which are scattered over the surface, but do not overlap. There is a single lateral line. The dorsal fin is long and contains 20 or 21 spines; the soft dorsal and anal fins are about equal and opposite and each are followed by two finlets. The head has a nearly straight profile above and the eyes are large. The mouth is also large and the lower jaw is longer than the upper jaw. There are three, large, fang-like teeth in the upper jaw and a pair of canine teeth in the front of the lower jaw. The color of the head and body is black, the pectoral and caudal fins are dark brown, and the inside of the mouth and the peritoneum are likewise black. Most specimens have measured ten inches or less in length.

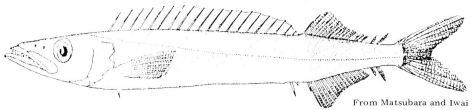

From Matsubara and Iwai

The habitat of this gempylid is in deep water. One Hawaiian specimen was captured at about 2,000 feet. For this reason, very few specimens are known to scientists.

The distribution of this species is apparently world-wide in warm water.

This species resembles *P. prometheus*, but may be separated from it by the number of spines in the spinous dorsal fin. *P. prometheus* has 18 spines; *N. tripes* has 20 or 21 spines.

THE CUTLASS OR HAIR-TAIL FISH FAMILY
Also known as the Blade Fishes
118 *Family Trichiuridae*

The cutlass fishes possess a body which is greatly elongated, narrow, and compressed and which tapers rather uniformly from the head to the tail where it terminates in a very small, V-shaped caudal fin or simply ends in a point. The surface of the body is without scales and a lateral line is present from the head to the tail. The dorsal fin begins just behind the head, is very long, and extends for the full length of the body. Although continuous, it includes a shorter spinous portion and a longer, soft-rayed portion; the spines and rays are difficult to separate. A small anal fin, containing many short spines, is present. The ventral fins are either absent or are represented by a pair of small, flat, scale-like spines. The head of these fishes somewhat resembles that of a barracuda and contains a projecting lower jaw and a large mouth filled with large, strong, unequal teeth. The color of most species is a bright, silvery hue. Some species will reach a length of five feet. They are edible fishes and some are regularly used as food.

The family is widely distributed in all warm seas where its members live from surface waters down to intermediate depths.

Of nearly two dozen species, at least one is known from this area.

THE SLENDER CUTLASS FISH
118—1 *Benthodesmus tenuis* (Gunther), 1877

This fish is a slender species and possesses a long, tapering body which is without scales. Like other members of this family, the dorsal fin extends from the head to the end of the body. The mouth is large, barracuda-like in appearance, and contains large, strong, unequal teeth. The body is uniformly silvery in color. Hawaiian specimens have measured from eight to about 25 inches in length.

Trichiurus lepturus

From Goode and Bean

The habitat of this species seems to be in waters of intermediate depth. Hawaiian specimens have been captured off north Maui and in Kaiwi Channel between Oahu and Molokai at depths between about 1,000 and 2,000 feet.

The distribution of this fish includes Hawaii, the central Pacific area, and Japan.

The accompanying figure is of a related species, *Trichiurus lepturus* L., 1758, which inhabits the Atlantic, Indian, and western Pacific Oceans.

THE SQUARE-TAIL FISH FAMILY
119 *Family Tetragonuridae*

The members of this family of fishes have long, cylindrical bodies and a long, low spinous dorsal fin followed by a higher soft dorsal fin. They also have two lateral keels on each side of the tail, plate-like scales with keels, an esophagus with lateral sacs, and unusual teeth.

They inhabit the high seas of all temperate and tropical oceans between the 45th parallels.

The group contains about three species of which at least one is known from this area.

CUVIER'S SQUARE-TAIL FISH
119—1 *Tetragonurus cuvieri* Risso, 1810

Cuvier's square-tail fish is cylindrical in shape with torpedo-like outlines. The spinous dorsal fin is long and low and contains between 15 and 21 spines; the soft dorsal fin is higher than the spinous dorsal fin and follows immediately behind it. The tail bears two keels on each side. The scales are present as keeled plates with five or six keels each; these scales are connected in rows, are very tough, and are almost impossible to remove. To some, these scales appear to have been "carved from wood". The head contains eyes of moderate size and a mouth which is quite large and V-shaped when viewed from the front. The color of the body is reported to be dark brown or nearly black. Most specimens measure between 10 and 15 inches in length; the maximum length is about 24 inches.

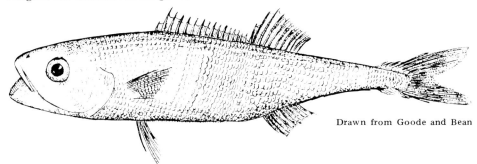

Drawn from Goode and Bean

The habitat of this fish includes the open sea from the surface down to several hundred feet.

The distribution is world-wide in tropical and warmer temperate seas.

THE RUDDER FISH AND SHEPARD FISH FAMILY
120 *Family Nomeidae (Psenidae, Centrolophidae)*

The fishes in this family range in size from small to medium and have oval, elongated, compressed bodies which are covered with scales. The dorsal fin is either deeply cleft or divided into two, the tail is forked, and the ventral fins are large, attached to the belly, and can be depressed into a groove; these ventral fins change in size and shape with growth in some species. The lateral line is arched and the throat bears the unusual, heavy wall at its rear.

The members of the family are all marine and are pelagic on the high seas of tropical and warmer temperate regions.

At least six species of this family are known from this area.

This family should not be confused with the *Kyphosidae* which are also known as rudder fishes.

THE BLUE BOTTLE OR MAN-O-WAR FISH
120—1 *Nomeus gronovii* (Gmelin), 1789

This little fish has an oval, compressed body which is quite elongated and to which is attached a long, trailing, deeply-forked tail. The dorsal fin is separated into two parts and the pelvic fins, which are very large and spectacular, are fan-shaped and may be folded into a groove along the belly. The color of the body is bluish above and silvery on the sides and belly; however, the ground color of this fish is overshadowed by about five, black, saddle-shaped areas which extend down the sides of the body, either as solid bands or as variously scattered and shaped spots and blotches. Most specimens are three inches or less, but some have been reported to approach

six inches in length.

The habitat of this fish is underneath large jelly-fishes; it also lives under the Portuguese Man-O-War, *Physalia.*

The distribution of this species includes all tropical seas.

THE ARAFURA SEA NOMEID FISH
120—2 *Psenes arafurensis* Gunther, 1888

This rare little fish had an oval body which is deep and compressed. The head is large but short and bears large eyes and a large mouth which is inclined downward. The color of this fish is reported as silvery, particularly in front; the body is marked on the posterior parts with faint cross-bars which extend downward and which are sometimes broken into spots and blotches. Specimens measure from two and one-half to four inches in length.

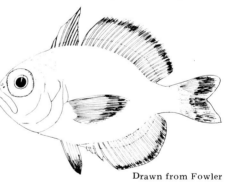

Drawn from Fowler

The habitat of this little fish is beneath jelly-fishes.

The distribution of this species includes the Arafura Sea south of New Guinea, Hawaii, and doubtless wide areas in the adjoining Indo-Pacific region.

THE TROPICAL NOMEID FISH
120—3 *Psenes cyanophrys* Valenciennes, 1833

This little fish has a compressed, oval body, a curved lateral line, and a deeply-forked tail. The color of the body is brownish; in addition, each scale bears a light spot which together form light, longitudinal lines. Because a blue line is present on the head above the eye, it is sometimes called the "blue eyebrow fish". The dorsal, anal, and pelvic fins are dark in color,

while the pectoral and caudal fins are light yellow. The young are reported to have faint cross-bars. The maximum length is reported to be about five inches.

This is a pelagic species which dwells in the open ocean.

The distribution of this species includes the tropical and warmer temperate waters of the Pacific, Atlantic, and Indian Oceans.

GUNTHER'S NOMEID FISH
120—4 *Cubiceps pauciradiatus* Gunther, 1882

This nomeid fish is an uncommon species. The body is elongated, spindle-shaped, and compressed through its entire length including the caudal peduncle. The upper and lower profiles are rather uniformly curved and the mouth is small and short. The dorsal fin is divided into two parts; the anterior, spinous portion has eleven spines; the posterior, soft portion has one spine and 17 rays. The anal fin contains three spines and 14 soft rays. The caudal fin is deeply-forked, long, slender, and pointed. The pectoral fin is longer than the head, about twice the length of the ventral fin, and reaches as far an the anus. The pelvic or ventral fins fit into grooves on the ventral side of the body; in front of these fins the abdomen is compressed to form a ridge along its ventral border. The color of the body has been described as brownish or purplish brown. The fins are lighter in color. The insides of the mouth and the gill cavity are black. Specimens have measured about five inches in length.

This is an uncommon species which is rarely seen or captured, although some specimens have been recovered from the spewings of tuna fishes.

The distribution of this oceanic species extends from Hawaii to central Polynesia, westward into Melanesia and the East Indies, and doubtless elsewhere in adjoining seas.

EVERMANN'S NOMEID FISH
120—5 *Ariomma evermanni* Jordan and Snyder, 1907

This uncommon fish has an elongated, fusiform body with scales arranged in longitudinal rows. The head bears a mouth which is small and

hort and eyes of moderate size which lack the adipose eyelids of *A. lurida*.
The dorsal fin is divided into two parts; the caudal peduncle is small and
bears two, small, oblique keels; and the caudal fin is deeply forked. The
lateral line lies high on the side of the body and follows the curve of the
dorsal outline. The body is a dark, chocolate-gray color above and somewhat silvery on the sides; the belly is pinkish. Although most specimens
have measured about one foot in length, it is known to reach a length of at
least 24 inches.

This is a fish of the open sea.

The distribution of this species includes the Hawaiian area and doubtless adjoining regions.

This species was named for Dr. Barton Warren Evermann, American
ichthyologist and student of Hawaiian fishes, who was associated with the
U.S. Bureau of Fisheries and later with the California Academy of Sciences
as head of the Steinhart Aquarium in San Francisco.

This species appears in some books under the name of *Cubiceps
thompsoni*, Fowler, 1923.

The accompanying photo is of a fish caught off the Kona coast of
Hawaii by Mr. Charles Yamamoto in late October, 1972.

THE LURID NOMEID FISH
120—6 *Ariomma lurida* Jordan and Snyder, 1904

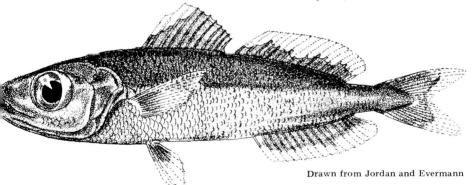

Drawn from Jordan and Evermann

The body of this fish is elongated and somewhat compressed. The
head is large and bears enormous eyes which are partly covered by an

anterior, adipose eyelid and by a larger, posterior, adipose eyelid; the iris is brown. The caudal fin is rather slender and deeply forked. The maximum size for adult specimens seems to be about 12 inches.

The distribution of this species includes the Hawaiian area and undoubtedly a much larger area in the Indo-Pacific region.

A specimen of this rare fish was caught in 1962 by Mr. Haruyoshi Ichimasa. He reports that it was captured by hook and line in 120 feet of water off the Ala Wai Yacht Harbor in Honolulu.

THE SAND PERCH FISH FAMILY
121 *Family Mugiloididae (Parapercidae, Pinguipedidae)*

The sand perches are a small family of small fishes which are not well defined. They possess elongated bodies which are covered with small scales; scales also cover the head. The side of the body is marked by a single lateral line which is usually high on the body anteriorly and then drops to the center of the side posteriorly. The dorsal fin is usually continuous, but is occasionally separated and often deeply notched; the caudal fin is not forked; and the anal fin has either one weak spine or is without spines and contains between 18 and 20 soft rays. The pelvic fins, which have one spine and five rays, are placed far forward on the body and are inserted under the base of the pectoral fin or anterior to it and in front of the origin of the dorsal fin. There is only one spine on the opercle, there are no bony stays across the cheek, and there are two pairs of nostrils of which the anterior pair is tubular.

Members of this family live in sea-weeds or over sandy bottoms along the shore line; a few species inhabit deep water.

The distribution of this family includes the Pacific and Indian Oceans and the southern Atlantic Ocean along the coast of South America.

At least three species are known from this area.

GILBERT'S SAND PERCH
121—1 *Pteropsaron incisum* Gilbert, 1905

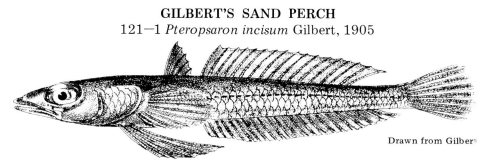

Drawn from Gilbert

The body of this sand perch is long, slender, and rounded and is covered with cycloid scales except for the cheeks. The dorsal fin is completely separated into a spinous dorsal portion with four or five spines and a long soft dorsal fin which is a bit shorter than the anal fin below it. The number of scales in a longitudinal row is about 30. The caudal fin is rounded in this species. The eyes are large and the snout is pointed. The olor of the spinous dorsal fin is black except for a small, white tip on the irst dorsal spine. The side of the body is marked in the middle with four, oblong, bright, yellowish green spots. The length of known specimens seems o be between two and three inches.

This is a deep water species taken in dredges from various locations below 500 feet. It occurs in the Hawaiian area and doubtless in adjoining reas.

SCHAUINSLAND'S SEA PERCH
121—2 *Parapercis schauinslandi* (Steindachner), 1900

This sea perch has an elongated, compressed body which is covered with small scales which number about 60 in a longitudinal row. The lateral ine begins high on the body and then descends to continue along the midline of the side. Although the dorsal fin is notched, the anterior and posterior portions are connected by a low membrane. The caudal fin is lunate or deeply concave and the upper and lower rays are filamentous. The spinous dorsal fin is reddish in color and the soft dorsal fin which follows is marked by a row of black spots. The head is marked by a red line with a yellow border which passes through the eye. The side of the body is marked by rosy blotches; the lower side is white. Specimens may reach as much as seven inches in length, but most measure between four and five inches in length.

The habitat of this fish seems to extend from shallow water down to depths beyond 100 feet.

The distribution of this species includes the Hawaiian area and doubtless the adjoining areas to the south and west.

This species is named for Dr. Schauinsland, Director of the Bremen Museum, who collected fishes from Hawaii and elsewhere during a voyage in the Pacific Ocean in 1896 and 1897.

THE ROSY GREEN SEA PERCH
121—3 *Neopercis roseoviridis* Gilbert, 1905

The body of this little fish is long and slender and bears a wide, depressed head with a short snout and large eyes. The dorsal fin is continuous and lacks the notch between its anterior spinous portion and its posterior soft-rayed portion; the caudal fin is rounded in outline. The color of the body is a light rose above and is crossed by wide, vertical, green bars.

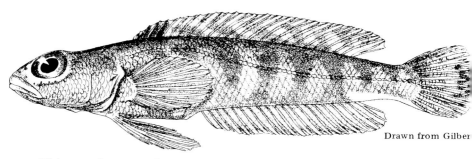

This species was first described from two specimens less than thre
inches long which were dredged from about 600 feet in 1902 by th
Albatross off the northeast coast of the island of Maui.

THE SAND DIVER FISH FAMILY
122 *Family Bembropsidae (Pteropsaridae, Bembropidae)*

This is a small family of fishes with slender, rounded, depressed bodies
The head is likewise flattened and bears a large mouth, eyes which are
located high on the sides of the head, and a skinny flap behind the maxillary
bone. The dorsal fin is divided into two parts and the ventral or pelvic fin
are placed far forward on the body.

These fishes primarily inhabit the tropics of the Atlantic, Pacific, and
Indian Oceans.

At least three species are known from this area.

THE DUCK-BILLED BEMBROPSID FISH
122—1 *Bembrops filifera* Gilbert, 1905

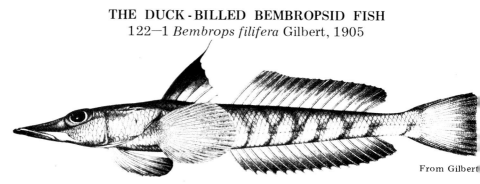

This uncommon fish from deep water has a long, slender body with a
dorsal fin which is divided and a lateral line which curves slightly upward
then downward, and thereafter continues along the middle of the side
toward the tail. The head is slender and bears a long, flattened, duck-shaped
beak with a projecting lower jaw. The eyes are quite large and are placed
high on the sides of the head. The color of the body was olive brown after
preservation in alcohol.

This species was first described from two specimens about nine inches
long which were captured in a dredge at a depth of about 1,000 feet by the
steamer *Albatross* in 1902 off the northeast coast of Maui.

THE GOLDEN-SPOTTED BEMBROPSID FISH
122—2 *Chrionema chryseres* Gilbert, 1905

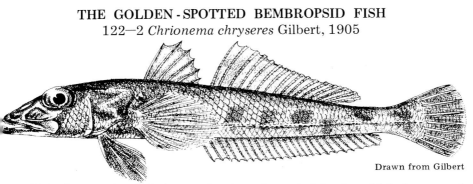

Drawn from Gilbert

This deep water fish has a slender, elongated body which is covered with small scales. The head is slender and bears a wide, elongated, depressed snout and a projecting lower jaw. The dorsal fin is divided and the caudal fin is rounded. The color of the body in life is olive-green mottled with darker brown above and white below. The sides are marked by a series of dark blotches of alternating sizes. Golden yellow spots are variously placed over the head and back.

This species was first described from a single specimen which measured about eight inches in length and which was captured in 1902 by the steamer *Albatross* in a dredge at a little over 1,000 feet off the south coast of Oahu.

THE SCALY-HEADED BEMBROPSID FISH
122—3 *Chrionema squamiceps* Gilbert, 1905

From Gilbert

The body of this little fish is long and slender and is covered with small scales. The head bears a flattened snout, a protruding lower jaw, and large eyes which are situated high on the sides of the head. The dorsal fin is divided and the anal fin, although long, is shorter than in *C. chryseres;* the anal fin of this species has 18 rays while *C. chryseres* has 24 rays. The color of the body is light olive above and whitish below; the sides are mottled with darker blotches. It will reach about four inches in length.

This species was first described from a single specimen which measured about two and one-half inches in length and was captured in 1902 by the steamer *Albatross* in a dredge at a depth of a little more than 600 feet off the north coast of Maui.

THE TRICHONOTID OR
SAND DIVER FISH FAMILY
123 *Family Trichonotidae*

The trichonotid fishes are small, slender species with rounded elongated bodies and pointed heads. The dorsal and anal fins are very long extend nearly to the base of the tail, and contain very weak spines which ar very difficult to distinguish from rays. In some species, the lateral line run along the body near the base of the anal fin and terminates near the end o the anal fin. The mouth is large, the teeth are small and weak, and in som species the lower jaw projects beyond the upper jaw. Some of these fishe have curious eye shades which function as eyelids and probably protect th eyes from intense light. The color of many species is very light or trans parent; they are very sparsely pigmented and therefore difficult to see.

The habitat of the sand divers is over sandy bottoms in shallow, shore line waters of tropical fresh-water and warmer seas. Here they dive, burrow and live in the sand, often with their eyes exposed.

This is a family of diverse genera which have been gathered together fo taxonomic convenience. There is a good presentation of these genera by Dr. Leonard Schultz in *U. S. National Museum Bulletin* 202, Volume 2 1960, pp. 273-277.

This is a small group which is distributed through Pacific, Australian and Indian seas. At least two species are known from this area.

COOKE'S SAND DIVER
123—1 *Crystallodytes cookei* Fowler, 1923

From Fowler

Cooke's sand diver is a small, elongated fish with long dorsal and ana fins containing about 37 rays each. The body is smooth and without scale except for those along the lateral line. The head is pointed in front and bears small eyes. The lower jaw does not project as it does in *Kraemeria bryani (Kraemeriidae)*, another sand-living species with which it might be confused. The color is nearly transparent and glassy; the back is marked by eleven clusters of small spots which are grouped into saddles along the back It is an extremely difficult fish to see. It will reach a length of possibly four inches, although most specimens are smaller.

The distribution of this species is at present limited to the Hawaiian Islands.

This species was named in honor of Mr. Charles Montague Cooke, III, who captured the first specimen on November 5, 1922, at Laie Beach, Oahu.

DONALDSON'S SAND DIVER
123—2 *Limnichthys donaldsoni* Schultz, 1960

Donaldson's sand diver is a very small, slender, elongated fish with long dorsal and anal fins, each with about 24 rays, and a body which is completely covered with scales. The head is depressed, the snout is flattened, and the eyes are large and located high upon the sides of the head. The body is translucent in color and measures about one inch in length; it is one of the very smallest of marine fishes.

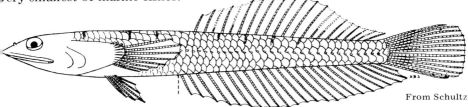

From Schultz

The distribution of this species includes the Hawaiian area, Micronesia, and doubtless other adjoining areas in the central Pacific Ocean.

This species was named in honor of Dr. Lauren R. Donaldson (1903-   ) of the School of Fisheries at the University of Washington in Seattle, a famous ichthyologist who specialized in the development of better strains of trout and salmon. He was a long time friend of the author.

Some scholars groups this species and a few other sand divers into a family known as the *Limnichthyidae*.

THE CHAMPSODONTID FISH FAMILY
124 *Family Champsodontidae (Centropercidae)*

These small fishes have an elongated, cylindrical body which is covered with rough scales. The head is of good size and bears a large mouth with long, slender teeth. The eyes are placed high on the head and have spines located above them. The dorsal fin is divided into two parts; the spinous dorsal consists of four or five spines and the soft dorsal has one spine and between 18 and 21 rays. The anal fin has one spine and 17 or 18 rays. The ventral or pelvic fins have one spine and five rays and are placed anterior to the pectoral fins. This family is a bit unusual in that it has two lateral lines on each side with transverse branches.

The champsodontids are carnivorous in their habits; they live in schools in moderately deep water and often rise to the surface during the night.

This is a small Indo-Pacific group of small species and contains but one genus.

At least one species of this family occurs in this area.

THE FRINGED CHAMPSODONTID FISH
124—1 *Champsodon fimbriatus* Gilbert, 1905

The body of this species is elongated and is completely covered with scales including the head. The dorsal fin is divided into a spinous dorsal with four spines and a soft dorsal with 19 rays. The anal fin has 17 rays and the caudal fin is widely forked. The head is large and bears moderately large eyes which are placed high on the sides; the mouth is large, the lower jaw is large and projects beyond the upper jaw, and the tongue is missing. The body contains the two lateral lines characteristic of this family. The color of this fish is dusky brownish above and silvery below; the sides are marked with wide, faint, dark cross-bars and the upper surface is speckled with black spots; the fins are whitish in color.

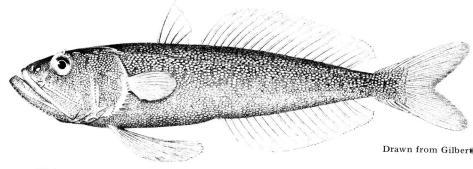

Drawn from Gilbert

This species was first described from specimens measuring about four inches in length which were captured in a dredge by the schooner *Albatross* in 1902 at a depth between 732 and 858 feet in the Pailolo Channel between Molokai and Maui.

THE SWALLOWER FISH FAMILY

125 *Family Chiasmodontidae*

The swallowers are a small group of fishes which have the astonishing ability to swallow other fishes which are larger than themselves. When their stomachs are empty, they present a normal, fish-like appearance, but when they have engulfed another fish, they may present a very bizarre, gorged, inflated appearance. The body is elongated and tapering, quite cylindrical, and is without scales, although it exhibits a few small spines. There are two dorsal fins and the ventral fins are placed far forward on the body. The head bears a large mouth which extends backward well beyond the eyes. The teeth are long and sharp and may be depressed. The operculum bears one blunt spine.

Swallowers inhabit all deep seas.

At least one species is known from this area.

A specimen of a swallower, possibly *Kali indica* Lloyd, 1909, measuring about eight inches in length, was captured at a depth of about 2,500 feet off the Hamakua coast of Hawaii. The figure shown here is of *Kala indica*.

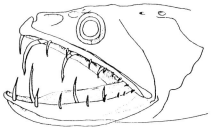

From Johnson

352

THE SCALELESS OR
COMB-TOOTHED BLENNY FISH FAMILY

126 *Family Blenniidae*

(Salariidae, Runulidae, Aptoclinidae, Chaenopsidae, Xiphasiidae)

The blennies are a large group of mostly small, agile fishes which have elongated, compressed, scaleless bodies. Their heads are quite large and bear eyes placed high upon them. The mouth is placed low upon the head and the snout is short, blunt, and rounded. The head is usually covered with a variety of crests, ridges, fringes, head flaps, or tentacles known as cirri. The teeth are small and are closely set in a single series; some species have large, curved, canine teeth farther back in the jaws. The dorsal fin is long and may contain a deep notch dividing it into two parts; it usually contains 12 flexible spines and 12 or more dorsal rays. The anal fin is long and has two spines which are usually buried in the flesh. The caudal fin is free or sometimes may be fused with the dorsal and anal fins. The ventral or pelvic fins contain but one spine and two to four rays and are placed anterior to the pectoral fins; this feature is useful in separating the blennies from the gobies. The color of the blennies varies from bright colors to dull, camouflaged designs. In some species the sexes are of different colors. In most species the characteristic colors fade rapidly after death.

Blennies are bottom dwellers and frequent coral heads, tide pools, crevices in stones, sea shells, and sea weeds. They include both carnivorous and herbivorous forms and represent a very wide variety of habits including some species which come out of the water for short intervals.

The blennies are a very large family of about 300 species which are world-wide in tropical and warmer temperate seas; of this family, at least 13 species are known from this area.

THE SHORT-BODIED BLENNY FISH
Also known as Pa-o-'o ka-u-i-la and 'O-'o-pu pa-o-'o

126—1 *Exallias brevis* (Kner), 1868

From Jordan and Evermann

The body of this blenny is short and compressed, the eyes are placed high on the head with a flap above each, the mouth is low, and the snout i nearly vertical. The dorsal fin has a deep notch dividing the anterior portion with its 12 spines from the posterior portion with its 13 rays. The ana fin has two spines; in the male they are blackish and are imbedded in fleshy pads; in the female the first anal spine is imbedded in the genital pad. The basic color of the body is a variable, pale, creamy, yellowish brown to orange color. The entire body is covered with round, brown or black spots. The maximum length of this species is about six inches, although most specimens will range in length from about two and one-half to four and one-half inches.

The habitat of this fish is on the outer edge of the reef from where the waves are active downward to a depth of 35 feet or more.

The distribution of this species extends from Hawaii southward to central Polynesia, westward through Micronesia and Melanesia, through the East Indies, and into the Indian Ocean as far as Ceylon.

THE SPOTTED-CHEEK BLENNY FISH
126—2 *Cirripectus lineopunctatus* Strasburg, 1956

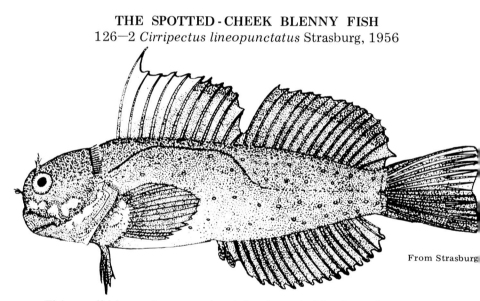

From Strasburg

This small blenny has a moderately elongated body and a comparatively large head; the eyes are placed high upon the head and the mouth is located below a nearly vertical snout. There is an unbranched tentacle above the eye which is useful in its identification. The dorsal fin is continuous and contains 12 spines and 15 rays which are separated by a deep notch. The anal fin has two spines of which the first is embedded in the flesh. The color of the body, head, and fins is a dark brown with lighter areas on the cheeks, upper lip, and at the base of the pectoral fins. There are also rows of small, white or yellow, black-rimmed spots on the sides of the body; often other scattered, small, black dots are present. Known specimens do not exceed three inches in length.

The habitat of this fish is along rocky shores where the surf is strong and in depths from four to ten or more feet.

The distribution of this species at present includes Hawaii and Johnston sland.

It is most easily confused with *C. obscurus* and *C. variolosus*.

THE OBSCURE BLENNY FISH
126—3 *Cirripectus obscurus* (Borodin), 1927

The name of this species is not in keeping with its features for it is a fairly large and colorful species. The body is shorter than most blennies, deeper than most, and compressed. The dorsal fin contains 12 spines and 16 rays and is divided into two parts. The color of the body is a dusky rose in the males and a golden orange in the females; both are covered with small, white dots. The first dorsal fin is plain blackish; some individuals are marked with about eight broken bars on the sides; and there is a dark spot behind the eye. Most specimens measure less than five inches, but some will reach seven inches in length.

The habitat of this species is over rocky bottoms in water between four and 20 feet in depth.

This fish is known from Hawaii.

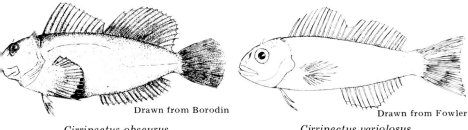

Drawn from Borodin   Drawn from Fowler

Cirripectus obscurus   *Cirripectus variolosus*

THE COMMON BLENNY FISH
126—4 *Cirripectus variolosus* (Cuvier and Valenciennes), 1836

This blenny is a comparatively small, but common, species. The body is rather uniformly colored. The head is brown, sometimes with bright red markings; the body is olive brown to blackish, often with bluish reflections; and the fins are blackish in color with the exception of the upper borders of the dorsal and caudal fins which are reddish, orange, or yellowish. Large specimens will reach a length of about four inches.

The habitat of this fish is over shallow coral bottoms where the water is active at depths from two to 30 or more feet; here it moves about from one hole or hiding place to another.

The distribution of this fish extends from Hawaii, Guam, and southern Japan, southward to Easter Island, central Polynesia, Micronesia and Melanesia, and possibly elsewhere in the Indo-Pacific area.

THE MARBLED BLENNY FISH
126—5 *Entomacrodus marmoratus* (Bennett), 1828

The marbled blenny has the usual, slender, compressed body and large head. The dorsal fin is divided into two parts by a deep notch. The dorsa fin has between 14 and 16 soft rays; the anal fin has two spines and betwee 15 and 17 soft rays. There are two characters which are helpful in distir guishing this species. There is a pair of tentacles on each side of the nec and the tentacle over the eye is branched. This is a multi-colored fish. It i mottled with brownish black, brown, olive brown, and olive green; the bell is white. Large specimens will reach five or six inches in length.

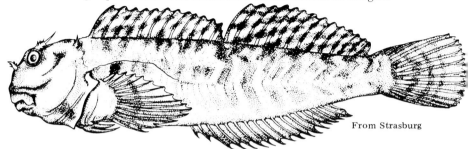

From Strasburg

The habitat of this fish is along rocky coasts in the surf zone; here it lives in nearby crevices and small holes which are protected from heavy wave action. When frightened it is reported to "leap into the surf" and go "skittering across the frothing water just clear of the foam". Its food consists of algae, detritus, and small invertebrate animals.

The distribution of this species includes the Hawaiian area.

STRASBURG'S BLENNY FISH
126—6 *Entomacrodus strasburgi* Springer, 1967

From Springer

This is a very small blenny which is marked in life by a few "reddish brown vertical stripes" on the side of the head in the area of the preopercle. The side of the body is marked by double, vertical, reddish brown bands there are six-pairs of these double band, but the last pair on the caudal peduncle does not extend downward across the entire body. These markings tend to disappear with death and preservation. Large specimens measure less than one and one-half inches in length.

The habitat of this blenny is in "the surge zones on rocky shores at depths not exceeding two meters".

The distribution of this species includes the Hawaiian area.

The name of this species honors Dr. Donald W. Strasburg, ichthyologist and student of Pacific blennies.

THE HUMP-HEADED BLENNY FISH
126—7 *Istiblennius gibbifrons* (Quoy and Gaimard), 1824

This blenny is a long, slender species with a compressed body. The soft dorsal rays are 19 or 20 in number and the anal soft rays number 20 or 21. In this species, the last dorsal ray is not attached to the caudal fin as in *I. zebra*. The head is rounded in outline, has a nearly vertical profile, and lacks the crest which is found in *I. zebra*. The tentacle over the eye is unbranched and there are no tentacles on the neck. The color of the body is a tawny olive; it is darker above than below and is marked on the sides by about eight, double, vertical bars. The males have blue-white spots on the sides of the body; these are not present in the female. Large specimens will reach about five inches in length.

This blenny is a common, shallow water form but is not often observed because of its cunning, secretive nature. It lives in shallow shore line water of two, three, or four feet in depth.

The distribution of this species includes the area from Hawaii, Johnston Island, Marcus Island, and Wake Island southward to central Polynesia and westward through the East Indies and across the Indian Ocean to the coast of Africa.

THE ROCK SKIPPER OR ZEBRA BLENNY FISH
Also known as Pa-o-ʻo and Pa-no-ʻo
126—8 *Istiblennius zebra* (Vaillant and Sauvage), 1875

From Jordan and Evermann

This rock skipper is recognized by a high, fleshy crest on the midline of the head and by the presence of a membrane which attaches the last ray of the soft dorsal fin to the caudal fin. In addition, the dorsal fin is deeply notched, there are no canine teeth, and there are no tentacles or cirri on the side of the neck or top of the head. The color of this fish varies; it has been described as ranging from bluish to black to gray to yellowish brown. The sides are marked with tan or gray vertical bars.

The habitat of this fish is in the tide pools of rocky shores and beaches. It is an active, hardy, alert, little fish and very difficult to capture. It is able to leave the water for short periods and to jump across the land for short distances to other tidal pools. It feeds on the detritus of the bottom.

The distribution of this fish is limited to the Hawaiian area, but does not appear to be found on either Midway Island or Johnston Island.

THE HAWAIIAN BLENNY FISH
126—9 *Ecsenius hawaiiensis* Chapman and Schultz, 1952

This species has been a puzzle to biologists. It is known from 14 specimens collected by Spencer Tinker from among the fouling organisms on the bottom of a large barge in the Pearl Harbor drydock which had been towed there from Guam and the western Pacific.

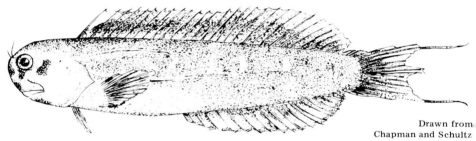

Drawn from
Chapman and Schultz

The body is long with a nearly straight dorsal outline and a rounded head with cirri only near the nasal openings. The dorsal fin is continuous and is attached posteriorly by a membrane to the caudal peduncle. The color in alcohol was plain brown above and lighter below. The sides are marked by five to seven, short, white, vertical bars. The outer edge of the caudal fin is light colored and there is a dark spot behind the eye. The above specimens were all less than three inches in length.

The distribution of this species is at present not known beyond Oahu.

THE LITTLE BROWN BLENNY FISH
126—10 *Enchelyurus brunneolus* (Jenkins), 1903

This blenny is very small and has an elongated, compressed body. The profile of the head is rounded and steep and the eyes are small and placed high upon the head. The dorsal fin has 10 dorsal spines and is continuous, while the anal fin has 19 or 20 soft rays; both of these fins are attached by a membrane to the tail. The color of the body and the tail is a very dark brown or black. Specimens will measure about one inch in length. This species resembles *E. ater* (Gunther), 1877, of the South Pacific. It should not be confused with young specimens of *Cirripectus* since it lacks the tentacles above the eyes and on the neck.

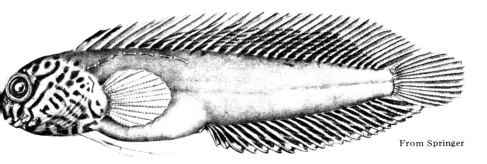

The habitat of this species is in dead coral heads. It is fairly common, but is seldom seen.

The distribution of this species is limited at present to the Hawaiian area.

THE ELONGATED BLENNY FISH
126—11 *Omobranchus elongatus* (Peters), 1855

This species is known from Hawaii from four specimens which appeared in a tank at the Institute of Marine Biology at Moku-o-Loe Island in Kaneohe Bay, Oahu. It is uncertain if they were introduced from central Polynesia, possibly Samoa, or are native to Hawaii. The body of this fish is elongated and compressed and bears a dorsal fin which is continuous. Both the dorsal and anal fins are attached at their posterior end to the caudal peduncle by a membrane. The body is somewhat translucent in appearance and the vertebral column is visible toward the tail. The body color is olive brown with a network of white lines on the upper part, a dull red color on the lower side, and grayish white on the belly. The head is marked by dark, vertical bars. The soft dorsal fin has a bright blue-green spot between the tenth and twelth rays. It reaches a length of at least three inches.

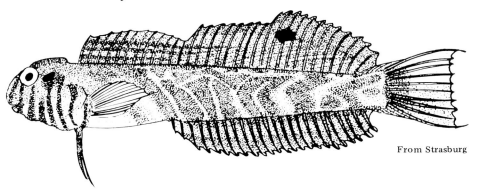

The habitat of this fish is in the shallow waters of the shore line.

The distribution of this species extends from Hawaii southward to central Polynesia, westward through Melanesia and the East Indies, and across the Indian Ocean to the coast of Africa.

THE BLUE-STRIPED BLENNY FISH
126—12 *Plagiotremus rhinorhynchus* (Bleeker), 1852

This unmistakable species has a slender, elongated, compressed, scaleless body. The dorsal fin is continuous and uniform and neither it nor the anal fin are attached to the caudal peduncle or caudal fin. The color of the body is brick red with two, bright, black-edged, blue bands extending along the entire length of the side. The dorsal and anal fins are brick red, the caudal fin is reddish, and the pectoral fins are translucent. It reaches a length of about five inches.

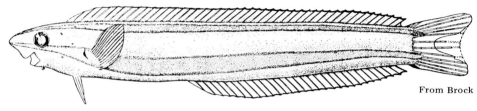

From Brock

The first Hawaiian specimen of this species was procured by Mr. Fernando Leonida, a commercial fisherman, who saw it drop upon the deck of his boat from the open end of a pipe which was part of the frame on the base of his fish trap. The specimen was given to the author who relayed it to Mr. Vernon Brock for further study. Mr. Brock published a description of it and named it *Petroscirtes ewaensis* Brock, 1948, for the Ewa district of Oahu near where it was captured.

Recent studies now seem to indicate that this species was described by Pieter Bleeker in 1852 and that a more correct name for this species is *Plagiotremus rhinorhynchus* (Bleeker), 1852.

The distribution of this fish extends from Hawaii southward to central Polynesia and westward through Micronesia, Melanesia, and the East Indies.

GOSLINE'S BLENNY FISH
126—13 *Plagiotremus goslinei* (Strasburg), 1956

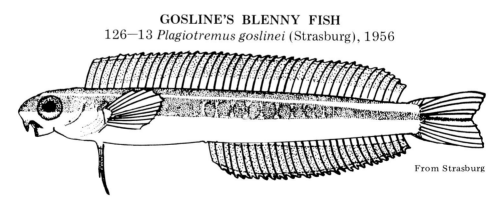

From Strasburg

This small blenny has an elongated, compressed body. The dorsal fin is continuous and contains eight spines and between 34 and 37 soft rays. The anal fin contains two spines and either 29 or 30 soft rays. The color of the body in alcohol is brown above and white below; there is a white, longitudinal line along the upper side of the body and below it a wider, interrupted, longitudinal stripe. The fins are longitudinally banded. Adult specimens measure between two and three inches in length.

This little fish has a pair of gigantic canine teeth in the rear of the lower jaw and combines this feature with the happy habit of biting the exposed bodies of swimmers.

This blenny inhabits shallow, rocky bottoms of the shore where the waves are active. It has also been found in the stomachs of the yellow-fin tuna and dolphin fishes, indicating that it may live in deeper water and there be eaten by these larger fishes.

The distribution of this species is at present limited to the Hawaiian area.

This fish was named by Dr. Donald W. Strasburg in honor of his former teacher, Dr. William A. Gosline, famous ichthyologist and Professor of Zoology at the University of Hawaii from 1948 to 1971.

THE SCALED BLENNY OR CLINID FISH FAMILY

127 *Family Clinidae (Emblemariidae)*

The scaled blennies are a large family of fishes, most of which are of small size. Their bodies are covered with scales, they possess a lateral line, and their caudal fin is never attached to either the dorsal or anal fins.

Some of these fishes have three, separate, dorsal fins; the anterior two fins have spines and the posterior fin has only soft rays. These three-finned fishes are sometimes put in a separate family by some authors and called the *Tripterygiidae.*

In general, this family inhabits the temperate and tropical seas of the southern hemisphere. It is a large family and contains 175 or more species of which at least one species is known from this area.

THE THREE-FINNED BLENNY FISH

127—1 *Tripterygion atriceps* Jenkins, 1903

This little fish has a very small, elongated, compressed body which bears three, separate, dorsal fins. The color of the body is bright red or brownish red and the head is black in the males. The side of the body is

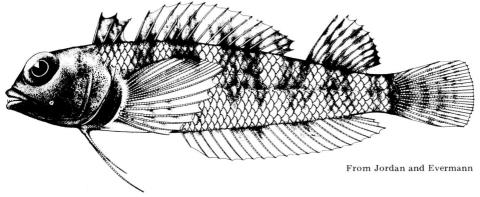

From Jordan and Evermann

marked with from nine to 14 vertical bars which are sometimes combined into as few as six vertical bars. This is a very small fish and will measure one inch in length or perhaps a bit more in adult specimens.

The habitat of this fish is in the coral heads in shallow water. It is reasonably abundant, but it is rarely seen because it remains hidden from view.

The distribution of this species includes the Hawaiian area.

THE CONGROGADID FISH FAMILY
128 *Family Congrogadidae*

These fishes are small, eel-like forms which are without the paired ventral or pelvic fins. Their dorsal and anal fins are long and join with the tail fin to unite these three fins into a single fin. The lateral line is present, but it may be incomplete. This family is found in the Indo-Pacific area.

A member of this family, *Congrogadus marginatus* Vaillant and Sauvage, 1875, was described from a specimen obtained in Hawaii. It was reported as brown in color, as having a deep head, and as marked with a "narrow black border along dorsal fin and upper caudal lobe." It measured about five inches in length.

THE LARVA-LIKE FISH FAMILY
129 *Family Schindleriidae*

These fishes are extremely small and strongly resemble the larval stages of larger fishes; however, they are known to be adult fish because they bear rather large eggs which indicates that they are sexually mature.

The bodies of these fishes are elongated, compressed, transparent, thin, and fragile. The head bears a pair of large, protruding eyes, a short snout, and a mouth which is terminal in position. The body has no scales, no lateral line, and no pigmentation; the skeleton remains primarily cartilaginous with very little evidence of ossification. The dorsal and anal fins are in the posterior half of the body and are composed of simple rays. The dorsal fin is low and continuous and begins somewhat anterior to the anal fin. The caudal fin is small, fan-like, and without lateral keels. The pectoral fins are present, but the pelvic fins are missing. The last few vertebrae are fused into a rod-like structure. The males are somewhat smaller than the females and bear genital papillae. Their bodies are nearly transparent and the internal organs can be seen from the outside. They reach about one inch in length. These fishes appear to be at the larval stage in most of their anatomical features. However, they do reach sexual maturity and produce rather large eggs which can be seen through their transparent bodies.

These fishes are pelagic in their habits and frequent shore lines and protected bays and harbors. They are much more abundant than we realize and usually pass unobserved because of their transparent nature.

Two member of this family are known from this area.

THE LARVA-LIKE FISH
129—1 *Schindleria praematurus* (Schindler), 1930

This species differs from the following species in the number of rays in the fins and also in the vertebral count. This species has 19 rays in the dorsal fin, 11 rays in the anal fin, and 16 rays in the pectoral fin. The vertebral counts range from 38 to 40 including the urostyle. It will reach a length of about one inch.

Drawn from Gosline

The distribution of this species extends from Hawaii southward through central Polynesia to the Tasman Sea and westward through Micronesia and Melanesia; it doubtless includes adjoining regions.

PIETSCHMANN'S LARVA-LIKE FISH
129—2 *Schindleria pietschmanni* (Schindler), 1931

This species is distinguished from *S. praematurus* by its more numerous anal rays and its smaller vertebral count. The anal rays in this species number between 14 and 17; the vertebral count ranges from 34 to 38 including the urostyle. It measures about an inch in length.

The distribution of this species includes the Hawaiian area.

This species is named after Dr. Victor Pietschmann, a native of Germany, who studied Hawaiian fishes during 1927—1928.

THE CUSK EEL FISH FAMILY
130 *Family Ophidiidae*

Cusk eels have elongated, eel-like bodies and superficially resemble eels. Their dorsal fin begins just behind the head and continues backward where it joins the caudal fin. The anal fin is likewise long and extends from about the middle of the body backward to join the caudal fin, thus uniting the three median fins into a single, continuous fin. The pectoral fins are unusually large and possess many rays, but the pelvic fins are greatly reduced in size and possess only one or two rays; these pelvic fins have been moved far forward on the body to a position under the chin, where they now serve as a pair of feelers. Most cusk eels are small in size, usually less than a foot in length; however, there is one species which reaches a length of about five feet.

They are a small group of about three dozen species which live in all temperate and tropical seas.

The following species is not described or illustrated:

Luciobrotula lineata (Gosline), 1954. This species was originally described as *Volcanus lineatus* Gosline, 1954, and included in the Family *Brotulidae*. Some authors like to include it within the *Ophidiidae*. It measures ten inches in length and is brownish in color with bluish black shadings on the head, belly, and fins. It was collected floating in the ocean off the coast of the island of Hawaii at the time of the 1950 eruption of Mauna Loa near where molten lava entered the sea.

BARTSCH'S CUSK EEL FISH
130—1 *Luciobrotula bartschi* Smith and Radcliffe, 1913

This cusk eel has a body which is somewhat elongated posteriorly and laterally compressed and which is covered with small, loose scales. The head is quite long, is depressed above, and exhibits a slightly concave profile. The eyes are small and are dorso-lateral in position; the mouth is large and obliquely placed; there are no barbels beneath the chin; and the operculum bears two spines on its border. The dorsal fin bears between 86 and 91 rays and, like the anal fin, is continuous with the caudal fin. The ventral or pelvic fins each consist of two rays which are divided nearly to their bases; the inner ray is the longest. The fleshy sheaths at the bases of the dorsal and anal fins are also covered with scales. The color of the body is very dark. Specimens measure from ten to sixteen inches in length.

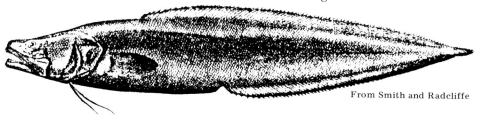

From Smith and Radcliffe

The type specimen, measuring about ten and one-half inches, was captured in the Palawan Passage in the Philippine Islands over a coral and sand bottom at a depth of about 2,250 feet.

The known distribution of this species includes the Gulf of Aden south of the Red Sea, the Philippine Islands, Japan, and Hawaii.

The name of this fish honors the memory of Dr. Paul Bartsch, a conchologist in the U.S. National Museum and a member of the U.S. Bureau of Fisheries Philippine Expedition of 1907—1910 aboard the steamer *Albatross*.

THE DEEP-WATER BLENNY OR BROTULID FISH FAMILY
131 *Family Brotulidae*

The brotulids are an uninspiring, dull-colored array of fishes. They have somewhat elongated, compressed bodies which taper posteriorly to a point at the tail. The dorsal fin is single and continuous and usually merges with the caudal fin which is reduced in size and usually distinct. The anal fin is usually similar to the dorsal fin although shorter. The pectoral fins are quite large and many rayed, while the pelvic fins have been reduced to a very few rays and are located far forward on the body. The body is either scaleless or is covered with very small scales. The lateral line may be present and entire, incomplete, or entirely absent. The head bears eyes in various stages of degeneration; some have well developed eyesight, some have feeble eyesight, and in some the eyes are non-functional and reduced in size. A few species bear barbels or whiskers on the snout or chin.

The habitat of these fishes ranges from fresh to salt water and from the surface to depths of at least four miles. The deep-water species tend to be blind and there are some blind species in the fresh water caves of Cuba and Yucatan. Most of these fishes are timid and are rarely seen by man. Some lay eggs and some bring forth their young alive. A few species will reach three feet in length, some are a foot or more in length, but most of the species are much smaller in size.

Of more than 150 known species, at least nine are known from this area.

Some scholars regard the brotulids *(Brotulidae)* as very closely related to the cusk eels *(Ophidiidae)* and think that these two families should be united into one family under the name of *Ophidiidae.*

The following species are not described or illustrated:

Microbrotula nigra Gosline, 1953. This brotulid is about three inches long. It was first known from a single specimen caught off Waikiki. It was described as small, chunky, and black.

Microbrotula rubra Gosline, 1953. This is a small, bright red species which is known only from the reefs in Kaneohe Bay, Oahu. Specimens less than two inches in length contained large eggs.

Persons wishing to read more concerning the above two species should refer to their original descriptions. See an article by Wm. A. Gosline in *Copeia* 1953(4), pp. 215-225.

The following species were collected on June 3, 4, and 6, 1950, by Dr. William A. Gosline and others off the lava flow from Mauna Loa on the Island of Hawaii. They are all presumed to be deeper water forms brought to the surface by this volcanic activity. For more information see an article by Wm. A. Gosline in *Pacific Science* 8 (1), 1954, pp. 68-83.

Cataetyx hawaiiensis Gosline, 1954. This species was represented by a male which measured about nine and one-half inches in length. It had a bluish black head and an orange body.

Pycnocraspedum armatum Gosline, 1954. This species was represented by a single specimen which measured nearly 12 inches in length and lacked the barbels of other species. Since 1950, this fish has been captured at depths of about 1,000 feet.

Voloanuo lincatuo Gosline, 1954. This species was represented by a female specimen which measured a bit more than ten inches in length. It was described as brown in color over the body and shading into bluish black on the head, belly, and fins. A more recent name for this species is *Luciobrotula lineata* (Gosline), 1954.

THE MANY-WHISKERED BROTULID FISH

Also known as Pu-hi pa-la-ho-a-na, Pu-hi ho-a-na, and Pa-la-ho-a-na

131—1 *Brotula multibarbata* Temminck and Schlegel, 1846

The body of this fish is elongated, quite strongly compressed, and tapers to a point at the tail. The dorsal and anal fins are long and low and

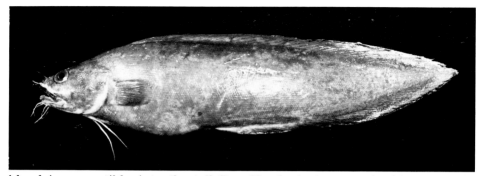

blend imperceptibly into the tail fin. The body is covered with very small scales and the lateral line is present and complete. The head is small and elongated and tapers to a large mouth which is bordered by four long and two shorter barbels on the upper lip and by six barbels on the lower lip. The eye is quite large and is directed upward and forward somewhat. There is a small spine on the upper part of the operculum. The color of the body is reddish brown with silvery reflections. The lips are black and the chin is white. Most adult specimens will measure between 12 and 18 inches, but some are reported to reach as much as 24 inches in length.

The habitat of this fish is in the crevices of the reef. It is sly and secretive and therefore seldom seen. Fishermen do not frequent the areas where it lives and it does not enter fish traps very readily.

The distribution of this species extends from Hawaii southward into central Polynesia, westward through Micronesia and Melanesia, through the East Indies, and across the Indian Ocean to the coast of Africa.

TOWNSEND'S BROTULID FISH
131—2 *Brotula townsendi* Fowler, 1900

This brotulid resembles *B. multibarbata* in its general appearance. The body is compressed posteriorly and the dorsal and anal fins are continuous with the caudal fin. The pelvic fins are reduced to two rays and are placed far forward on the body. The eyes are small and the barbels which surround the mouth consist of three pairs on the snout and three pairs on the chin. The color of the body is greenish to orange brown. The dorsal and anal fins are marked with a broad, orange border and the lips and chin are of a greenish brown. Adult specimens will reach a length of at least eight inches.

The habitat of this fish is in the crevices of the reef. The distribution of this species includes the Hawaiian area, Micronesia, and doubtless some adjoining areas.

This species was named for Mr. J. K. Townsend.

THE PEARL FISH OR CUCUMBER FISH FAMILY
132 *Family Fierasferidae (Carapidae)*

This small family of fishes is famous because of the habit of its members of living inside the body cavities of sea cucumbers, starfishes, sea urchins, clams, oysters, and a few tunicates. Their eggs float in the sea where they pass through larval stages leading to their adult form. While small they hunt up a place to hide; this hiding place is usually within the body of some sea animal, which they enter either head first or tail first through the vent. Some species appear to spend their entire life within their host, usually a sea cucumber, while other species leave the body for short periods of time to seek food.

Pearl fishes are somewhat eel-shaped. They have a rather large head and a long, slender, tapering, transparent body; some are cylindrical in shape while others are compressed. The pectoral fins may be either present or absent, a lateral line is present, but pelvic fins and scales are absent. The anal fin is very long and extends from the vent, which is located under the throat, to the end of the body; the dorsal fin is long and uninterrupted. Most pearl fishes measure less than six inches, although one species will reach as much as 12 inches in length.

Pearl fishes occur in all warm and temperate seas.

There are approximately two dozen species of which at least four species are known from this area.

THE CANINE-TOOTHED PEARL FISH
132—1 *Snyderidia canina* Gilbert, 1905

This rare fish can be recognized most easily by the presence of large, curved, fang-like teeth in the fronts of the upper and lower jaws. The color of the body is a light grayish beneath a covering layer of pigment spots. The peritoneum is black and the interiors of the mouth and gill covers are blackish.

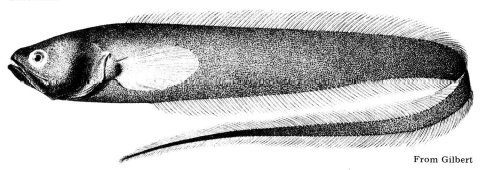

From Gilbert

This species was first described and named from a single specimen measuring 12 inches in length, which was captured in a dredge between 385 and 500 fathoms off the island of Kauai by the steamer *Albatross* in 1902.

In some books this species may be classified within the family *Lycodapodidae.*

THE SLENDER PEARL FISH
132—2 *Encheliophis gracilis* (Bleeker), 1856

The body of this pearl fish is very long, slender, and tapering. The eyes are covered with thick adipose tissue and the mouth is horizontal in position. The anal fin is unusual in that it begins in front of the dorsal fin. The color is variously described as translucent yellowish with some bluish tinges and with some brown or black spots or mottlings; it is darker above than below. It will reach a length of about ten inches.

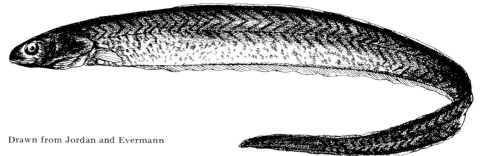

Drawn from Jordan and Evermann

Most specimens have come from the bodies of sea cucumbers, but this fish is known to also inhabit the interiors of starfishes.

The distribution of this species extends from Hawaii southward to central Polynesia, westward through Micronesia and Melanesia, through the East Indies, and across the Indian Ocean to the coast of Africa and the Red Sea.

THE KEELED PEARL FISH
132—3 *Carapus margaritiferae* (Rendahl), 1921

Drawn from Arnold

The body of this fish is long, slender, and strongly compressed and bears a keel on the chest in front of the anal fin. In adult specimens, there are well developed canine teeth in the fronts of both jaws. The lower lip bears a transverse fold. The color of the body is a translucent pink and bears blackish shades at the tip of the tail. When preserved in alcohol, the entire body is white except for the darker marking on the tip of the tail. Large specimens will measure four inches in length.

The habitat of this fish seems to be in rock and pearl oysters and related bivalve mollusks. It also occurs less frequently in sea cucumbers.

The distribution of this species extends from Hawaii southward to Australia, westward through the tropical western Pacific and the East Indies, and across the Indian Ocean to the coast of Africa.

THE INDO-PACIFIC PEARL FISH
132—4 *Carapus homei* (Richardson), 1844

In life, the body of this pearl fish is translucent in color with bluish or reddish shades on the front of the body. The sides are marked with dark cross-bars and some silver areas above the lateral line. There is also a silvery spot between the back of the eye and the upper jaw. Individuals will range in length from four to eight inches.

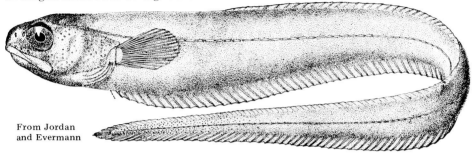

From Jordan
and Evermann

The habitat of this fish includes a variety of animals including sea cucumbers, sea urchins, starfishes, and an ascidian tunicate.

The distribution of this species extends from Hawaii southward to Australia, westward through the tropical Pacific Ocean, through the East Indies, and across the Indian Ocean to the coast of Africa and the Red Sea.

THE SAND-LANCE OR SAND-EEL FISH FAMILY
133 *Family Ammodytidae (Bleekeridae, Hypoptychidae)*

The bodies of these fishes are long, slender, and cylindrical and possess a long, continuous, uninterrupted dorsal fin and usually no pelvic fins. The head is long and pointed and bears a projecting lower jaw which is usually pointed. The mouth is usually large but it contains no teeth. The lateral line is located high on the body where it runs along close to the back; it is incomplete. The body has about 100 scales in a longitudinal series. The tail fin is either forked or concave, but it is not continuous with either the dorsal or the anal fin. In some ways these fishes resemble the snake mackerels *(Gempylidae)*.

The habitat of this small group is in sandy areas where they burrow head first into the sand. They occur in the temperate and tropical areas of the Atlantic, Mediterranean, Pacific, and Indian Oceans.

Of this small family, at least one species is known from this area.

GILL'S SAND LANCE
133—1 *Bleekeria gillii* T.H. Bean, 1894

This species is exceedingly rare and precious little is known about it. Known specimens are from three to six inches in length; some of these were spewed up by tuna fishes which suggests that this fish lives some distance offshore; others have been captured in trawls at depths of nearly 700 feet.

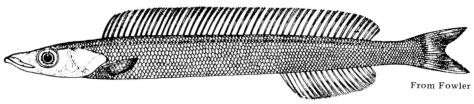

From Fowler

The name of this species honors the memory of Theodore Nicholas Gill (1837-1914), a famous American ichthyologist and zoologist.

THE DRAGONET FISH FAMILY
134 *Family Callionymidae*

The dragonet fishes are nearly all of small size with elongated bodies, flattened heads, and often with long, high, filamentous fins. They possess two dorsal fins of which the first is short and high and contains between two and four spines and the second is longer and lower. The pectoral fins and the caudal fin are large; the ventral or pelvic fins are placed far forward and are attached ahead of the pectoral fins. The mouth is small, terminal, and protruding and contains small, weak teeth only on the jaws. The eyes are placed high upon the sides of the head and are directed upward somewhat. The body is without scales. The gill openings in most species are small, pore-like openings which are placed high upon the side of the body; this is doubtless a result of their life in the sand. Most species measure between four and eight inches in length. The males are often brighter in color than the females and possess longer dorsal and caudal fins.

The dragonet fishes are bottom dwellers and inhabit sandy bottoms from the shallow shore line down to deeper water. They usually lie buried in the sand and may be caught at this time with the aid of screens when the tide is low. Their eggs float to the surface and drift in the plankton while they develop; the young later descend to take up their adult life in the sand.

Dragonet fishes occur in the Atlantic, Pacific, and Indian Oceans.

This family contains more than three dozen species of which at least four are known from this area.

THE BEARDED DRAGONET FISH
134—1 *Pogonemus pogognathus* Gosline, 1959

Drawn from Gosline

This dragonet is a small, flat-headed species which exhibits a fringe of tentances extending forward from the lower jaw. It differs from most others by not having a membrane between the base of the pectoral fin and the inner

370

edge of the ventral or pelvic fin; also the gill openings are wider and are not reduced to a small hole as in most. The color of the body is a yellowish brown with black on the dorsal fin and spots on the body. Adults will reach a length of about one and one-half inches.

The distribution of this species was at first thought to be limited to Hanalei Bay on the island of Kauai.

THE RED-BANDED DRAGONET FISH
134—2 *Synchiropus rubrovinctus* (Gilbert), 1905

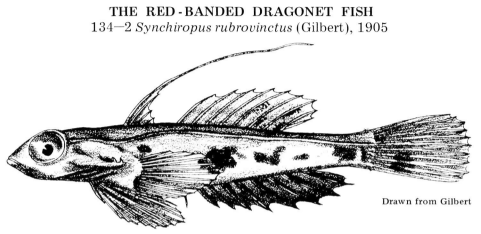

Drawn from Gilbert

This small fish is marked on the back by four, bright, red bars extending nearly to the middle of the side. The lower half of the side is marked by four, irregular, brownish black blotches which are located below the red bars. The dorsal fin is divided with four dorsal spines and eight or nine soft rays; the anal fin has eight rays. Adult fish will reach a length of about one inch.

All known specimens were taken in less than 260 feet.

The distribution of this species was at first limited to the islands of Maui, Molokai, and Lanai.

THE DECORATED DRAGONET FISH
134—3 *Callionymus decoratus* Gilbert, 1905

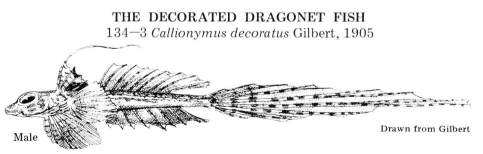

Male

Drawn from Gilbert

This dragonet is a slender species with a complex color pattern. The body is brownish or grayish above and whitish below; the sides are marked by four or five, faint, vertical bars, by many, round, gray spots enclosed by black lines, and by various other irregular markings. The soft dorsal and caudal fins are banded vertically; the anal fin is black. The males have black bars beneath the chin, long caudal fins, and a filament trailing from the first dorsal spine. It will reach 11 inches in length.

The habitat of this fish is over sandy bottoms from the shore line down to over 300 feet.

Female   Drawn from Gilbert

The distribution of this species includes the Hawaiian area.

The following species are thought by some authors to be synonyms of the above species: *Callionymus corallinus* Gilbert, 1905; *Calliurichthys astrinius* Jordan and Jordan, 1922; and *Calliurichthys zanectes* Jordan and Jordan, 1922.

THE BLUE-SPOTTED DRAGONET FISH
134—4 *Callionymus coeruleonotatus* Gilbert, 1905

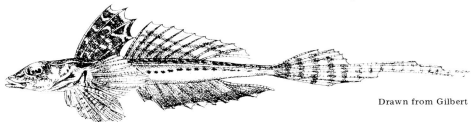

Drawn from Gilbert

This slender, little dragonet fish is dull colored on the upper side of the body and is marked on the sides with golden yellow and bright blue spots and lines. This species is known from a few specimens which were captured in a dredge by the steamer *Albatross* in 1902 off the east side of Maui and in Pailolo Channel between Maui and Molokai at depths between 300 and 1,000 feet.

The distribution of this species includes the Hawaiian area.

THE PRIMITIVE DRAGONET FISH FAMILY

135 *Family Draconettidae*

This small family is related to the *Callionymidae*, but differs from them in having wider gill openings and other features. There are two dorsal fins with three spines in the first fin and 12 to 15 rays in the second. The side of the head bears two large spines which represent the reduced remnants of the operculum and suboperculum.

This small family inhabits deeper water in the North Pacific and North Atlantic Oceans.

At least one member of this group is known from this area.

THE HAWAIIAN DRAGONET FISH
135—1 *Draconetta hawaiiensis* Gilbert, 1905

From Gilbert

This species was first described from a single specimen captured in a dredge by the schooner Albatross in 1902 in Pailolo Channel between Molokai and Maui at a depth between about 700 and 800 feet.

The body of this fish is rather slender, the dorsal fin is divided into two parts, and the sides of the head bear two large diverging spines. The color of this fish when preserved is a light gray with faint traces of five darker cross-bars; the body was also variously marked with darker flecks and spots. It will reach a length of four inches.

The distribution of this species includes the Hawaiian area.

THE SURGEON FISH FAMILY

136 *Family Acanthuridae (Teuthidae, Hepatidae, Acronuridae)*

Surgeon fishes have high, compressed bodies which are covered with very small, shagreen-like scales; this gives their skin a leathery texture somewhat like that of the file fishes and the angler fishes. The lateral line is present and complete and extends from head to tail. The dorsal fin is continuous from front to back and is not notched between the anterior spinous dorsal fin and the soft posterior portion. The eyes are located quite high on the head and the mouth, in contrast, is located rather low on the head and contains a multitude of small teeth. The most significant feature of this family is the presence of spines on the sides of the caudal peduncle. Each side will bear either a single, sharp, hinged spine or one or two sharp, immobile, keel-like plates. A few species bear a single, bizarre looking horn on the front of the head. Members of this family are small or medium in size, but the group includes no large species. Most are of dull or somber hues, but a few species are marked with bright colors.

Nearly all members of this family are vegetarians and live upon the algae which abound in shallow water. Like large, terrestrial, plant-eating animals, these fishes have unusually long digestive tracts to digest this plant food.

Surgeon fishes inhabit all tropical and sub-tropical seas; they are usually found in shallow water near coral reefs.

Of less than 100 species, about two dozen are known from this area.

THE ACHILLES SURGEON FISH
Also known as Pa-ku-'i-ku-'i
136—1 *Acanthurus achilles* Shaw, 1803

This species is most easily recognized by the color markings of the body which contrast with the background color of dark brown to black. The most obvious marking is a large, elliptical, orange-red spot on the side just anterior to the spine and enclosing the spine within its posterior elongation. In addition, there is a red, crescent-shaped area on the tail and a long, narrow, red line at the bases of the dorsal and anal fins. There is also a light blue line under the chin and another on the edge of the operculum below the eye. The body has the

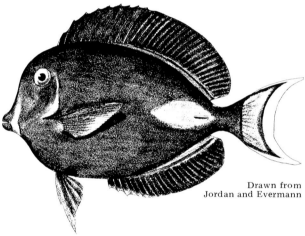

Drawn from
Jordan and Evermann

shape of a tear drop in outline and will reach a length of about ten inches in large specimens.

The habitat of this fish is in the inshore areas near coral reefs where the water is in motion through the surge channels and passage ways of the reef.

The distribution of this species extends from Hawaii southward to central Polynesia and westward through Micronesia and Melanesia. It apparently does not extend to the Philippine Islands, the East Indies, and the Indian Ocean.

LESSON'S SURGEON FISH
136—2 *Acanthurus glaucopareius* Cuvier and Valenciennes, 1829

This species resembles *A. achilles* rather closely. The body is black in color in life and is marked by bright yellow lines at the bases of the dorsal and anal fins. The margins of the dorsal and anal fins are blue and the caudal fin has a large orange area and a white posterior margin. The margin of the operculum is pale yellow, the caudal spine is yellow, and there is a narrow, white stripe around the mouth. The iris is pale yellow in color and there is a white area just below the eye. The pectoral fins are colorless and the pelvic fins are black with a blue outer margin. It should be noted that the color of the body in the accompanying picture has faded from black to gray. Large specimens will reach a length of about eight inches.

The habitat of this fish is in the areas surrounding the coral reefs where the water is actively moving.

The distribution of this species extends from the tropical eastern Pacific westward to Hawaii, central Polynesia, Micronesia, Melanesia, the Philippine Islands, and the islands of the East Indies.

Most scholars regard *Acanthurus aliala* Lesson, 1830, as a synonym of *A. glaucopareius.*

Acanthurus glaucopareius

Acanthurus dussumieri

DUSSUMIER'S SURGEON FISH
Also known as Pa-la-ni
136—3 *Acanthurus dussumieri* Cuvier and Valenciennes, 1835

The palani is somewhat difficult to distinguish from the species of pualu. The body is pale brown with fine, blue, purplish or bluish gray, slightly wavy, horizontal lines. The caudal fin is bright blue in the middle and is marked in this area with many, small, black spots. The dorsal and anal fins are yellow in color and are longitudinally banded with blue until they become an adult. The eyes are connected over the snout by a band of yellow. The caudal spine is white, lies in a white sheath, and is broadly edged with black. Like the na'e-na'e, this species has a gizzard-like stomach and in old age develops a lump upon the front of its snout. Large specimens will reach a length of 16 or 18 inches.

Like other members of this family, the palani is a shore line species which inhabits the deeper waters on the outer edge of the reef.

The distribution of this species extends from Hawaii and southern Japan southward through Melanesia and the Philippines, through the East Indies, and across the Indian Ocean to the coast of Africa.

THE SPOTTED SURGEON FISH
136—4 *Acanthurus guttatus* Bloch and Schneider, 1801

The body of this fish is almost circular in outline and is greatly compressed; it bears a tail which is truncated on the posterior margin. The color of the body and head is brownish above and lighter below. The body is unmistakably marked on the front half by three or four, pale, white, vertical cross-bars and on the posterior half by many, small, round, bluish white spots which extend onto the soft dorsal and anal fins but not onto the tail. Large specimens have exceeded 11 inches, but most are six or eight inches in length.

The habitat of this fish is along the shore line where the waves create currents in surge channels. It is an active species and is not often seen.

The distribution of this species extends from Hawaii southward to central Polynesia, westward through Micronesia and Melanesia, through the East Indies, and across the Indian Ocean to Mauritius.

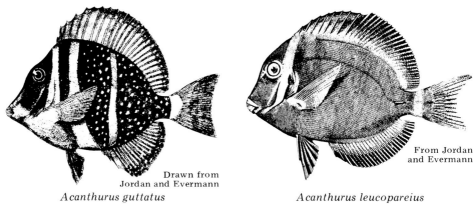

Drawn from
Jordan and Evermann

Acanthurus guttatus

From Jordan
and Evermann

Acanthurus leucopareius

JENKIN'S SURGEON FISH
Also known as Ma-i-ko and Ma-i-ko-i-ko
136—5 *Acanthurus leucopareius* (Jenkins), 1903

This surgeon fish is easily identified by its color markings. The body is brownish in color and is marked by a vertical, white band behind the eye; this band extends from the front of the dorsal fin to the base of the operculum and is bordered by dark brown areas. A white vertical band crosses the base of the tail and a small black spot is present on the top of the caudal peduncle at the rear end of the soft dorsal fin. In life, the body shows faint, bluish, longitudinal lines or rows of spots; these lines are more obvious in young specimens. Most specimens measure between six and eight inches in length, but large specimens will reach as much as ten inches.

The ma-iko-iko is a common species in Hawaii where it lives singly, in small groups, or in schools on the outside of the reef.

The distribution of this species extends from Hawaii southeastward to Easter Island, and westward to Marcus Island in northern Micronesia and possibly some areas in Melanesia. It apparently does not occur in the islands within these three distant points.

Acanthurus leucopareius   *Acanthurus mata*

THE RING-TAILED SURGEON FISH
Also known as Pu-a-lu and Pu-wa-lu
136—6 *Acanthurus mata* Cuvier and Valenciennes, 1835

This is the smaller of the two species known as pualu; both this species and *A. xanthopterus* are hard to distinguish and so bear a common name. The body looks black in life, but it is more likely a very dark greenish gray color. It is longitudinally striped with many fine, closely-set lines of small, light gray spots. The dorsal fin is marked with about eight, lengthwise, dark blue bands, while the anal fin has five or six similar bands. The pectoral fins, in contrast to *A. xanthopterus*, are uniformly brown in color. The caudal fin is dark blue with wavy, vertical lines in the middle and with white at its base. This white area, which encircles the posterior part of the caudal peduncle, is more distinct than in *A. xanthopterus*. The caudal spine is of normal size (larger than in *A. xanthopterus*) and fits into a socket which is bordered by a dark margin. The side of the head is marked by a yellow spot between the eye and the top of the gill slit. This species will exceed 12 inches in length.

The habitat of this pualu is the water on the outside of the reef. It is a fairly abundant fish.

The distribution of this species extends from Hawaii southward to central Polynesia, westward through Micronesia and Melanesia, through the East Indies, and across the Indian Ocean to the Red Sea.

THE BLACKISH BROWN SURGEON FISH
136—7 *Acanthurus nigrofuscus* (Forskal), 1775

This surgeon fish is a small species which closely resembles *A. nigroris*, a larger species. The two species may be identified by their color markings.

The body of this fish is a lavender brown color in life with fine, bluish gray longitudinal lines on the body and small, bright orange spots on the head these color markings disappear in preserved fish. There are small pimples or the side of the head below the eye and there is a black spot at the end o: both the soft dorsal and anal fins where they join the body. The caudal fir is lunate in shape and bears extended upper and lower rays; the curvec posterior margin is marked by a narrow white line. The fins are brownish ir color and there is a narrow, black margin around the groove of the cauda spine. Large specimens will reach a length of about seven inches.

This fish is a very common species in the shallow shore line areas on the outer edge of the reef.

The distribution of this species extends from Hawaii southward tc central Polynesia, westward through Micronesia and Melanesia, through the East Indies, and across the Indian Ocean to the coast of Africa and the Red Sea.

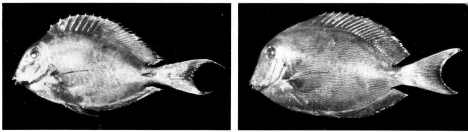

Acanthurus nigrofuscus   *Acanthurus nigroris*

CUVIER'S SURGEON FISH
Also known as Ma-i-ko
136—8 *Acanthurus nigroris* Cuvier and Valenciennes, 1835

In appearance, this species resembles *A. nigrofuscus*, but it is a larger fish and presents slightly different color markings. The body is dark brown in color in life and is marked by narrow, longitudinal, blue lines and by a white band at the base of the tail. The caudal fin is marked with a very narrow white line at its posterior border and the caudal spine lacks the black border found in *A. nigrofuscus*. The median fins are a brownish yellow color and are marked with lengthwise, dull blue bands. Large specimens will reach ten inches in length.

The habitat of the maiko is the shallow waters of the shore line particularly on the outside of the reef. It is a common species.

The distribution of this species extends from Hawaii, including the leeward islands, southward to central Polynesia and westward through Micro-nesia and Melanesia to the East Indies.

THE ORANGE-SPOT SURGEON FISH
Also known as Na-'e-na-'e
136—9 *Acanthurus olivaceus* (Bloch and Schneider), 1801
The identification of this surgeon fish is simplified by the presence of

a large, elongated, horizontal, bright orange band with a purplish black border located just behind the head and above the pectoral fin. The body is

a dark grayish brown color and the caudal fin, which is lunate in shape, bears a vertical white crescent mark and a narrow white border. The snout of large old males grows forward somewhat to produce a convexity or lump in the area in front of the eyes. These fishes also possess an unusual, sub-spherical, gizzard-like stomach. Large individuals will reach a length of 12 inches. Young na'e-na'e are orange-yellow in color and change to brown at about two inches in length.

Na'e-na'e live about the reef on its outer side where the waves are active and the water is deeper.

The distribution of this species extends from Hawaii southward to central Polynesia and westward through Micronesia, Melanesia, the Philippines, and the East Indies.

THE SANDWICH ISLAND SURGEON FISH
Also known as the Ma-ni-ni
136—10 *Acanthurus sandvicensis* Streets, 1877

The manini is a species which is easily recognized by its color pattern. The body is a light gray above, whitish beneath, and is marked by six, black, vertical bars on the sides of the body. The first black bar passes through the eye, the next four mark the side of the body, and the sixth is very short and on the upper side of the caudal peduncle. Large specimens will approach nine inches in length, but most are much smaller.

The manini live in the shallow waters of the reef where it feeds upon fine, filamentous algae.

The distribution of this species is limited to the Hawaiian area.

Some authors regard the Hawaiian manini as a sub-species of *Acanthurus triostegus* (Linnaeus), 1758, a species which is distributed from the Gulf of California westward across the entire tropical Pacific and Indian Oceans to the coast of Africa; it does not occur in Hawaii. *A. sandvicensis* differs from *A. triostegus* in having the second stripe a bit longer and the fin ray counts of the soft dorsal and anal fins somewhat greater. These authors will use the name of *Acanthurus triostegus sandvicensis* Streets, 1877, for this Hawaiian manini.

THOMPSON'S SURGEON FISH
136—11 *Acanthurus thompsoni* (Fowler), 1923

This is a fish of dull, variable colors which is difficult to identify except for the presence of a small dark spot just below the base of the pectoral fin. The color of the body is not uniform and seems to vary from a light bluish gray through dark olive drab to black. The caudal fin is lunate in shape and may be either dark or light depending upon the geographical area from

which it comes. The dorsal and anal fins may appear uniformly dark or may show a narrow blue margin with two, three, or more, longitudinal, yellowish brown bands. Large specimens will reach a length of nearly eight inches.

The habitat of Thompson's fish is on the outside of the reef from possibly 30 or 40 feet to depths of at least 100 feet. It is an uncommon species which lives singly and in small schools.

The distribution of this species extends from Hawaii southward to central Polynesia and westward through Micronesia, Melanesia, the East Indies, the Philippine Islands, and southern Japan.

This fish was named by Dr. Henry Weed Fowler in honor of Mr. John W. Thompson, a staff member of the Bernice P. Bishop Museum. It is a bit unfortunate to be remembered by such a dull fish.

THE YELLOW-FINNED SURGEON FISH
Also known as Pu-a-lu, Pu-wa-lu and Ring-tailed Surgeon Fish
136—12 *Acanthurus xanthopterus* Cuvier and Valenciennes, 1835

The name of pu-a-lu was given to two very similar species of surgeon fishes in old Hawaii; it was the name for both this species and *A. mata.* The body of this species is a uniform purplish gray; however, at some times horizontal, irregular, dark, purplish gray lines will appear upon the body, alternating with the lighter interspaces. This species has the dorsal and anal

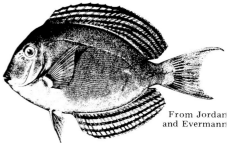

From Jordan and Evermann

fins colored a brownish yellow and marked with three or four alternating blue and yellow-brown bands. (*A. mata* has about eight bands on its dorsal fin.) The outer third of the pectoral fin is yellow in color. (*A. mata* has a uniformly brown pectoral fin.) There is a yellowish area under the eye and an indistinct white band encircles the caudal peduncle at the base of the tail.

he caudal spine is small and the caudal fin has a crescent-shaped margin. This is believed to be the largest member of this genus and will probably reach a length of 24 inches.

The habitat of the paulu is in deeper water off the outer edge of the reef and cliffs and in the deeper bays and inlets.

The distribution of this species extends one-half way around the world; inhabits the tropical waters of the Pacific and Indian Oceans from the coast of western Mexico westward to the coast of east Africa.

THE HAWAIIAN SURGEON FISH
136—13 *Ctenochaetus hawaiiensis* Randall, 1955

The Hawaiian surgeon fish resembles *C. strigosus* but may be separated from it by the following features: it lacks the yellow ring around the eye found in *C. strigosus;* it has an opaque pectoral fin, while the fin of *C. strigosus* is quite transparent; finally, the tail of *C. hawaiiensis* is less emarginate than in *C. strigosus.* The color of the body is a very dark olive-brown color, although it appears black under water. The sides of the body and head are marked by many, fine, lengthwise, yellowish gray lines and the pectoral fins are a dark brown color. The length of large specimens will reach ten inches.

The habitat of this surgeon fish seems to be in the deeper waters along the outer edge of the reef. Specimens have been seen in water only 12 feet deep, but most often occur at depths beyond 50 or 75 feet. It is an uncommon species which has been observed living singly or in small schools.

The distribution of this species extends from Hawaii southeastward to eastern Polynesia, southward to central Polynesia, westward to the Marianas Islands, and doubtless to many adjoining areas.

THE YELLOW - EYED SURGEON FISH
Also known as Ko-le
136—14 *Ctenochaetus strigosus* (Bennett), 1828

The body of the kole is brown in color and is marked with about 35 fine, light blue, longitudinal lines which continue onto the rear of the soft dorsal and anal fins at the back of the body. The eye is encircled by a bright yellow ring, small blue spots cover much of the head, and the chin is purplish in color. The pectoral fins are transparent. Large specimens will reach a length of about seven inches.

The habitat of this little fish is in the shallow waters on the outside of the reef.

The distribution of this species extends from Hawaii southward to central and eastern Polynesia and Australia, then westward through Micronesia, Melanesia and the Philippines, through the East Indies,
and across the Indian Ocean at least as far as Mauritius. This species appar ently does not inhabit this entire area and specimens from various localities within this area show some differences in structure and color.

THE YELLOW SURGEON FISH
Also known as La-'i-pa-la, La-u-'i-pa-la, and La-u-ki-pa-la
136—15 *Zebrasoma flavescens* (Bennett), 1828

The lau-'i-pala is one of the most beautiful of all fishes. Its entire body, except for the white sheath of the caudal spine, is a uniform, chrome yellow color. Immature individuals have the same yellow color pattern as the adults. The body is high, compressed, and covered with small scales. There is a single caudal spine and four, or rarely five, spines in the dorsal fin. Large specimens may reach a length of eight inches.

This is a shore line species which inhabits the waters on both sides of the reef from a few feet in depth to beyond 100 feet. Some observers believe that it is more common on the leeward sides of the islands.

The distribution of this species extends from the Hawaiian area, includ ing Johnston Island, westward through the northern Marshall Islands to Wake, Marcus, Guam, and other Marianas Islands.

A similar species, *Z. scopas* (Cuvier), 1829, has long puzzled scientists because it resembles this species in nearly all details except color. It has been regarded as a darker color phase of *Z. flavescens*, but recent studies seem to indicate that it is a distinct species. It is chocolate brown or blackish in color with fine, wavy, longitudinal, bluish lines on the head and body; it also has a blue, horizontal streak above the pectoral fins. Both species have a golden yellow iris. It is distributed from central Polynesia and Micronesia westward through the East Indies and across the Indian Ocean

Both species occur at Bikini and doubtless at other islands in that area.

THE SAIL-FIN SURGEON FISH
Also known as 'A-pi
136—16 *Zebrasoma veliferum* (Bloch), 1797

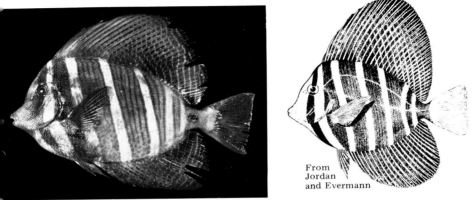

From
Jordan
and Evermann

The sail-fin tang is another unmistakable species. It can likewise be immediately recognized by its large and very high dorsal and anal fins which are purplish brown in color and marked toward the back with narrow, vertical, pale lines. The body is a light yellowish color and is marked with about seven, broad, purplish, vertical bars which are in turn overlaid with a few, narrow, vertical stripes. The caudal fin is brown in color, the pectoral fins are yellowish, and the snout is covered with small white to yellowish spots. Large specimens will reach a length of about 16 inches.

The habitat of this fish is on the outside of the reef, where it seems to show a preference for bays and inlets. It gathers into small schools and may occasionally enter shallower water.

The distribution of this species extends from Hawaii southward to central Polynesia, westward through Micronesia and Melanesia, through the East Indies, and across the Indian Ocean to the coast of Africa.

THE RINGED UNICORN SURGEON FISH
136—17 *Naso annulatus* (Quoy and Gaimard), 1824

The body of this species is typical of the other members of the group in possessing two spines on the caudal peduncle and a horn on the head. The horn of this species is located below the center of the eye and is directed downward slightly so that the longitudinal axis of this horn passes backward through the lower part of the eye. This horn grows slowly with age and in older specimens will extend beyond the mouth. The dorsal fin of this species contains but five spines followed by 28 or 29 soft rays. The color of the body is a dull gray-brown above and is tinged with yellow below. The dorsal and anal fins have a white border with a black line just below it. The pectoral fin is dark brown at its base and lighter at its outer margin. The caudal fin has a yellowish hue and a white margin with a black line just for-

ward of it. The caudal peduncle is marked by an encircling white band from
which this species gets its name; how-
ever, this band apparently is not
visible in all specimens. Large specimens are reported to reach as much as
22 inches in length.

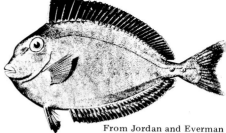

The distribution of this fish
extends from Hawaii southward to
central Polynesia and Queensland,
westward through Micronesia,

From Jordan and Everman

Melanesia, and the Philippine Islands, through the East Indies, and across the
Indian Ocean to the coast of Africa.

The presence of this species in Hawaii is somewhat doubtful. It wa
reported from specimens captured here in 1889 and 1896 but has not beer
reported since that time.

THE UNICORN SURGEON FISH
Also known as Ka-la
136—18 *Naso brevirostris* (Cuvier and Valenciennes), 1835

The name of *brevirostris* for this fish is very misleading. This name
means "short rostrum", but actually this fish has a very long horn in the
older adults. Young specimens do not have a horn, but they slowly begin to
develop one at the site of a lump on their snout. In addition to the horn,
this fish, like other members of the genus *Naso*, bears two spines on the side
of the caudal peduncle. The body of this fish is a greenish gray color and is
marked with a large number of vertical rows of small, dark, short lines or
spots. The dorsal and anal fins are a grayish brown color on their outer
portions, but are darker toward their bases. The posterior third of the
caudal fin is greenish in color. Large specimens will reach 18 inches in
length.

The habitat of this unicorn fish is in the shore line waters on the outer
side of the reef.

The distribution of this species extends from Hawaii southward to
central Polynesia, westward through Micronesia and Melanesia, through the

ast Indies, and across the Indian Ocean to the coast of Africa.

THE SIX-SPINED SURGEON FISH
136—19 *Naso hexacanthus* (Bleeker), 1855

This surgeon fish is a rather plain, drab species with an elongated body and without a horn on its head. The body ranges in color from dark olive-gray to purplish blue. The dorsal and anal fins are a brownish yellow color and are longitudinally marked with light blue stripes. The caudal fin varies n color from a dark blue anteriorly to a greenish color posteriorly. As in other members of the genus *Naso*, there are two spines on each side of the caudal peduncle. It is reported to reach a length of 20 inches; most are much shorter.

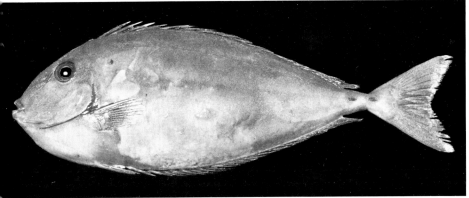

The habitat of this fish is in the deeper water on the outside of the reef. It is a common species and is usually represented in the fish markets.

The distribution of this species extends from Hawaii southward and westward through Micronesia and Melanesia to the East Indies. It is doubt-less more widely distributed.

THE LITURATE SURGEON FISH
Also known as U-ma-u-ma-le-i
136—20 *Naso lituratus* (Bloch and Schneider), 1801

The uma-uma-lei can be identified by the two caudal spines on each side of the tail, each of which is surrounded by a bright orange area. There is no horn on the head of this species. The color of the body is a dark brown or purplish brown. The lips are orange and a yellow line extends from the eye forward and downward in a curve to the corner of the mouth. The dorsal fin has a blue line at the base, then black, and finally a band of white along the outer margin. The anal fin is a brownish orange at its base and white at its margin. The caudal fin has a yellow, crescent-shaped marking, a white posterior border, and, in the case of the males, streamers at the top and bottom of the fin. Large specimens will reach 15 and possibly 18 inches in length.

The habitat of the uma-uma-lei is in the shore line waters on the outside

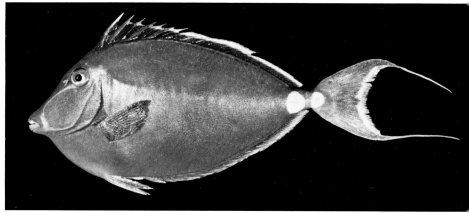

of the reef.

The distribution of this species extends from Hawaii southward to central Polynesia, westward through Micronesia and Melanesia, through the East Indies, and across the Indian Ocean to the coast of Africa and the Red Sea

THE DARK - SPOTTED SURGEON FISH
136—21 *Naso maculatus*, Randall and Struhsaker, 1981

Photo by Dr. John E. Randall

This uncommon surgeon fish has a long, slender body somewhat like that of a mackerel; it is laterally compressed and the dorsal and ventral outlines are uniformly curved from the head to the tail. The body becomes slightly more elongated with age. The dorsal fin usually has six spines, of which the first or second is the longest, and these are followed usually by 26 to 28 rays; the margin of the caudal fin is lunate in shape; and the caudal peduncle bears two bony plates, each of which has a sharp, horizontal keel. The color in both life and in alcohol is brownish or grayish above and paler below. The body and tail are covered with small, round spots and short lines which are more numerous on the upper half of the body Specimens will reach a length of at least 24 inches.

The habitat of this species is in the deeper water on the outside of the reef. Some Hawaiian specimens have been caught in trawl nets at a depth of more than 300 feet.

The distribution of this fish includes the Hawaiian area, Japan, and doubtless many adjoining areas.

The original description of this species may be found in *Copeia* 1981:3, pp. 553-8. This species has long been confused with *N. lopezi* Herre, 1927, a very similar species from the Philippine Islands.

THE LARGE UNICORN FISH
Also known as Ka-la
136—22 *Naso unicornis* (Forskal), 1775

The kala is well known and easily identified as an adult. The dorsal and ventral outlines curve gradually from the deeper anterior part of the body to the caudal peduncle. The body is compressed and is marked posteriorly by two fixed spines on each side of the caudal peduncle. The horn on the head begins to develop when the fish is about five inches in length; it first begins with a bump on the snout at the level of the eyes. The color of the body is a light olive or grayish brown above with faint yellowish hues on the belly. The dorsal and anal fins are longitudinally striped with light blue and brownish yellow. A light blue area surrounds each caudal spine. Large specimens will reach a length of 20 or possibly 24 inches.

The habitat of this fish is determined by its food. It is a plant eater like most surgeon fishes and will enter shallow water to feed on *Sargassum*.

The distribution of this species extends from Hawaii southward to central Polynesia, westward through Micronesia and Melanesia, through the East Indies, and across the Indian Ocean to the coast of Africa and the Red Sea.

THE MOORISH IDOL FISH FAMILY

137 *Family Zanclidae*

The Moorish Idol is the only species in this family. Although i
resembles the butterfly fishes (*Chaetodontidae*) in general appearance, thi
fish is most closely related to the surgeon fishes (*Acanthuridae*), but it lack
the bony plate or spine found on the caudal peduncle of that family. The
body is taller than long, possesses a long protruding snout, and simple
slender, flexible teeth. Only a single species is known.

THE MOORISH IDOL FISH
Also known as the Ki-hi-ki-hi
137—1 *Zanclus cornutus* Linnaeus, 1758

The kihi-kihi is one of the world's most beautiful fishes. It is an un
mistakable species of bizarre shape and beautiful colors and a source o:
delight and inspiration to all who view it. The body is short, high, oval
shaped, and compressed. It is covered with small scales and the lateral line

Drawn from
Jordan and Everman

is present and arched. The dorsal fin
is continuous and includes a long filament which seems to become shorter
with age; the filament arises from the
greatly enlarged third dorsal spine.
The body is vertically striped with
bands of black, white, and yellow; in
addition, there are some narrow, blue
lines on the tail and a red line on the top and sides of the snout. Large
adults will reach a length of about nine inches.

The name of *Z. canescens* Linnaeus, 1758, is a second name which has
long been used for this species and is therefor found in many books. The
young have a strong, sharp, knife-like spine directed backward from above
the corner of the mouth; these spines seem to drop off with age and
another pair of horns develops on the front of the head between the eyes.
Formerly these were regarded as separate species, but they are apparently
the young and the adult phase of the same species.

The habitat of the kihi-kihi is the area near coral reefs.

The distribution of this species includes the warm tropical water from Hawaii to Australia and from the west coast of Central America westward to the coast of Africa and the Red Sea.

THE GUAVINA OR SLEEPER FISH FAMILY
138 *Family Eleotridae*

The sleepers get their name from their habit of resting motionless on the bottom for long periods of time; a few members of this group hover suspended and motionless in the water. These fishes have elongated bodies which are usually covered with scales. They possess two dorsal fins which are most often separated; the second dorsal fin and the anal fin are usually small, equal, and opposite and contain very few rays. The mouth is usually large and there is no lateral line. It is important to note that this family has the ventral or pelvic fins separated and not joined together to form a sucking disc or cup as in the *Gobiidae*. Most members of this family are small in size, but the guavina of Central America and a few other species approach two feet in length.

The habitat of the sleepers includes both fresh water and brackish water; a few species are also marine.

They are distributed throughout most tropical rivers and coast lines.

Of this family, at least three are known from this area.

THE SANDWICH ISLAND SLEEPER
Also known as 'O-'o-pu, 'O-'o-pu 'a-ku-pa, 'O-ku-he, 'A-po-ha,
Ku-he, and 'O-a-u
138—1 *Eleotris sandwicensis* Vaillant and Sauvage, 1875

From Jordan and Evermann

The body of this sleeper is elongated and bears a depressed head with a large mouth and thick, fleshy lips. The body is covered with small scales which number about 75 along the lateral line. It should be remembered that the sleepers have pelvic fins which are separated and should not be confused with the gobies of the genus *Sicydium* which they closely resemble and which have the pelvic fins united to form a sucking cup. The color of the entire body is a dirty, brownish hue above and lighter below. The fins are dark in color and there is a narrow, white edge along the margin of the soft dorsal fin. The side of the head is marked across the cheek with two, blackish, horizontal lines. Large specimens will reach nine inches in length.

The habitat of this 'o'opu is in fresh water streams and in the brackish water of their estuaries; it does not enter the sea.

The distribution of this fish seems to be limited to the Hawaiian area.

THE SMALL SLEEPER
Also known as 'O-'o-pu
138—2 *Eviota epiphanes* Jenkins, 1903

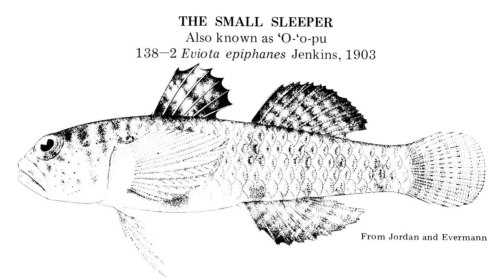

From Jordan and Evermann

This is an elongated, compressed little fish with the two dorsal fins well separated, the caudal fin rounded at its margin, and with the anal fin equal in size to the soft dorsal fin and placed opposite to it. The pectoral fins are large and the pelvic fins below them contain four main rays. The rays on the lower part of each pectoral fin and the four main rays of each pelvic fin give off feather-like branches; these feather-like fin rays make certain the identification of this species. The color of the body varies from bluish green to green to olive brownish; it may have the appearance of a bluish fish covered with green spots. Large specimens will reach a length of one inch. It is one of the smallest species of fishes.

The habitat of this sleeper is along the shore line from very shallow water to depths of about 30 feet where it inhabits coral heads. It is a very common species.

The distribution of this species extends from Hawaii southward to central Polynesia and westward through the East Indies.

RUPPELL'S SLEEPER
Also known as 'O-'o-pu
138—3 *Asterropteryx semipunctatus* Ruppell, 1821

The body of this 'o'opu is elongated, laterally compressed, and covered with scales. The dorsal fin bears six spines of which the first three spines usually bear filaments (not shown); this feature is useful in identifying this species.   The body and fins are uniformly, dark brown in color and are crossed by about six, irregular, obscure, vertical bars and blotches.   The median fins are marked with blue dots and most of the scales likewise bear blue dots. Large specimens will reach a length of about three inches.

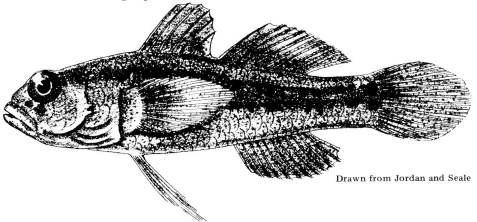

Drawn from Jordan and Seale

The habitat of this little fish is over shallow bottoms in quiet water in areas where dead coral, sand, and silt are present.

The distribution of this species extends from Hawaii southward to central Polynesia, westward through Micronesia and Melanesia, through the East Indies, and across the Indian Ocean to the Red Sea.

THE GOBY FISH FAMILY

139 *Family Gobiidae*

The gobies are a large family of small fishes. Their bodies are usually elongated and robust, without a lateral line, with or without scales, and usually with a large mouth. There are two dorsal fins which are separated in most species, although they may be placed close together. The pelvic or ventral fins are important in identifying the members of this family. These fins are joined in front and behind, either completely or partially, to form a sucking disc or cup on which the fish rests and which is used to attach to rocks, particularly in streams where the fish might otherwise be washed away.   In color most gobies are either a dull greenish or brownish hue, although a few are more brightly colored. Gobies range in length from about two to four inches, although a few do exceed these limits.

One particular goby, *Pandaka pygmaea* Herre, 1927, from the fresh waters of the Philippines is of great biological interest because it measures less than one-half inch when fully grown. It is believed to be the smallest of all vertebrate animals.

Many gobies are commensal in their habits and live associated with other animals; they inhabit the cavities in sponges and the burrows of crabs, shrimps, worms, and other marine animals.   A few gobies with subterranean habits are blind.

The mud skippers, *Periophthalmus*, have developed large eyes and large,

391

strong pectoral fins for jumping. They are found on tide flats and other exposed areas where they await the returning tide or jump from pool to pool.

The eggs of gobies are laid in patches attached to rocks or coral heads by short stalks.

The members of this family are distributed throughout the tropical and warmer temperate seas of the world; a few live in fresh water.

Of more than 400 species in this family, at least 19 are known from this area.

The following species of gobies are not described or illustrated.

Lentipes concolor (Gill), 1860. This goby was described many years ago from specimens taken in streams near Hilo, Hawaii. It has not been seen in recent years. It was a small species, without scales, purplish in color, and with the paired fins exhibiting a pearly iridescence.

Lentipes seminudus Gunther, 1880. This species is based on specimens about two inches long from Honolulu and Maui captured many years ago. It has not been seen since. The body was reported as having no scales on the head and trunk, but with scales on the tail.

THE SMALL, SHINING GOBY
139—1 *Vitraria clarescens* Jordan and Evermann, 1903

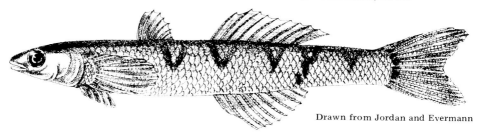

Drawn from Jordan and Evermann

The body of this goby is slender and elongated and bears a head which is flattened on top. The two dorsal fins are well separated and the pelvic fin, which is placed far forward, is completely in front of the first dorsal fin. This appears to be the only goby in this area in which the caudal fin is forked at its posterior margin; this feature is useful in identifying this species. The body color of this fish is nearly transparent, but there are about seven, distinct, pale, brownish, V-shaped marks on the sides of the body; these marks unite over the back. The fins are whitish in color. This is a small fish and will reach a length of about one inch.

The distribution of this fish includes the Hawaiian area and central Polynesia.

THE POINTED-TAIL GOBY
Also known as 'O-'o-pu
139—2 *Oxyurichthys lonchotus* (Jenkins), 1903

The body of this goby is rather long and slender and terminates in a long, pointed tail. The dorsal fin is separated into two parts which are placed close together. The soft dorsal fin and the anal fin are quite long, equal in size, and opposite in location. The body is covered with scales, except for an area on top of the head in front of the first dorsal fin and another area on the lower side in front of the pelvic fins. The body is a pale, transparent color and is marked with about ten, very faint, vertical bars which are scarcely visible. There is a small, dark spot at each anterior nostril, a dark band from the base of the eye to the corner of the mouth, and a dark spot at the base of the pectoral fin. The soft dorsal and caudal fins may show faint, transverse markings. Large specimens may reach a length of about five inches.

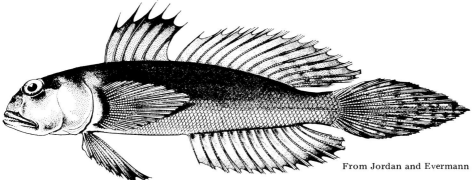

From Jordan and Evermann

The habitat of this species is on the muddy bottoms of brackish water estuaries.

The distribution of this species includes the Hawaiian area.

STIMPSON'S GOBY
Also known as 'O-'o-pu
139—3 *Sicydium stimpsoni* Gill, 1860

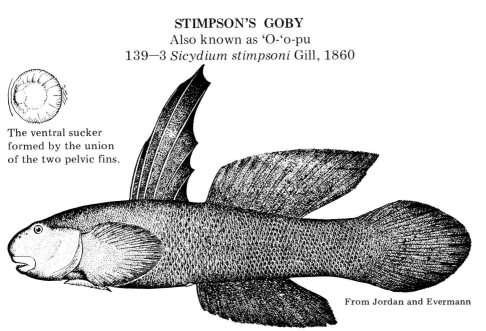

The ventral sucker formed by the union of the two pelvic fins.

From Jordan and Evermann

The body of this goby is long and slender and bears a blunt head, a rounded snout, and a small eye which is placed high on the head. The dorsal fins are high, particularly the first dorsal fin, and the caudal fin is quite large and rounded. The body is completely covered with fine scales. The color of the body is a dark, olive-green hue. There are about 14, indistinct, black bars crossing the back and descending onto the upper part of the sides. The head and cheek are marked with short, darker, irregular lines and there is a dark blotch at the base of the last two dorsal spines. Large specimens will reach a length of about seven inches.

The habitat of this goby is in the fresh water of various island streams.

The distribution of this species includes the larger Hawaiian Islands, the Society Islands, and doubtless other high islands in adjoining areas.

THE SCALELESS GOBY
139—4 *Kelloggella oligolepis* (Jenkins), 1903

From Jordan and Evermann

This little goby has an elongated, compressed body with two dorsal fins, the typical ventral sucker, and no scales upon the body. The body is crossed by about 12, dark, vertical bars which alternate with narrower, white bars. There are a few, short, light bands extending downward and backward from the eye. This is the smallest goby in this area and will reach a length of about one inch.

The home of this little fish is in the tide pools along rocky shore lines.

The distribution of this species includes the Hawaiian area, Easter Island, and doubtless many intervening areas.

THE STRIPED-CHEEK GOBY
Also known as 'O-'o-pu
139—5 *Chonophorus genivittatus* (Cuvier and Valenciennes), 1837

From Jordan and Evermann

The body of this goby is elongated and compressed and bears a rounded head with a large mouth. The upper part of the body is olive-green in color and is marked by about 12 vertical, blackish bands; the belly is whitish and reddish in color. The head is conspicuously marked by a dark band which extends from the eye downward and backward across the cheek to end below the corner of the mouth. Large specimens will reach a length of about six inches.

The habitat of this goby is in the lowland streams and estuaries.

The distribution of this species extends from Hawaii southward to central Polynesia and westward through Micronesia and Melanesia.

THE COMMON GOBY

Also known as 'O-'o-pu na-ke-a, Na-ke-a, No-ke-a, Na-wa-o,
'O-'o-pu le-he (large males), and 'O-'o-pu ku-mu i-ki (female)
139—6 *Chonophorus stamineus* (Eydoux and Souleyet), 1841

The common goby is a short, stout, heavy species with a large, broad head and an equally large and broad mouth. The eyes are small and are set high upon the head. The body is covered with scales except for the head and the breast. The color of the body is a dark olive-brown above and lighter below. The dorsal fins are a pale yellowish color and are crossed by about seven, narrow, horizontal, black bars. There is also a dark area at the base of the caudal fin. Large specimens will reach about 12 inches in length.

The common goby is an abundant species in the fresh water streams and in the estuaries and river mouths of the lowlands.

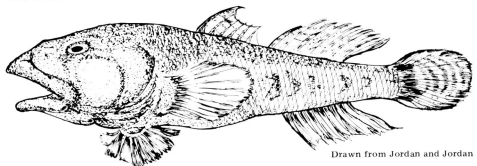

Drawn from Jordan and Jordan

The distribution of this species includes all of the larger islands of Hawaii and doubtless adjacent areas.

In some books this goby will appear under the name of *Chonophorus guamensis* (Valenciennes), 1837.

THE TONGAREVA GOBY

139—7 *Ctenogobius tongarevae* (Fowler), 1927

This little goby has a body which is quite long and compressed. The head, snout, and mouth are broad and the eyes are relatively large. The body is covered with scales except on the head, the breast, and at the bases of the pectoral fins. The color of the body is generally light and the fins are

395

transparent. There are darker areas at the base of the tail, at the bases of the pectoral fins, and below the eyes. Both dorsal fins bear spots on their membranes. This is a very small species and measures less than one inch in length.

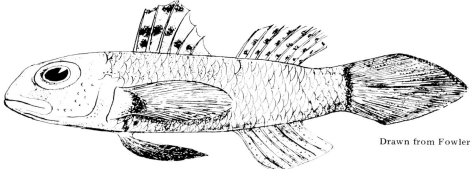

Drawn from Fowler

The specimens taken at Tongareva were captured in tide pools; those from Waikiki, which are believed to be the same species, came from a depth of about 30 feet.

The distribution of this species at present includes Tongareva (Penrhyn Island) and the Hawaiian area.

THE COD-HEAD GOBY
Also known as Pa-o'o 'o-pu-le
139—8 *Bathygobius cotticeps* (Steindachner), 1880

From Jenkins

The head of this goby is heavy, broad, and depressed and its lower surface is quite uniformly flat. Scales cover the body including the cheeks and the operculum. There are two dorsal fins which are of about equal height. The pectoral fins of this goby are unusual in that their upper rays are extended as fine filaments. The body is a dull, brownish hue. Large specimens will reach about five inches in length.

The habitat of this goby includes rocky areas in shallow water.

The distribution of this species is known to include Hawaii and the islands of central Polynesia.

In some books, this fish will appear under the name of *Chlamydes laticeps* Jenkins, 1903.

THE BROWN GOBY
Also known as 'O-'o-pu 'o-hu-ne
139—9 *Bathygobius fuscus* (Ruppell), 1828

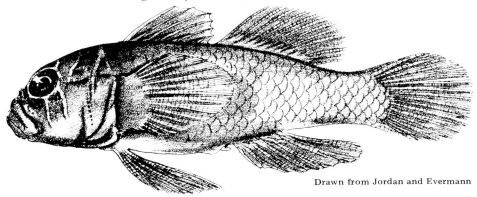

From Jordan and Evermann

The body of this goby is elongated and somewhat cylindrical; it bears a rounded, depressed head and a wide mouth. The upper pectoral rays are definitely silky in color and the caudal fin is rounded. The color of the body is olive above and paler below, but changes widely from a light tan to nearly black to match the bottom over which the goby lives. The head and body are marked with irregular darker spots; both the sides of the head and body are also variously marked with whitish spots. There is usually a dark spot behind the eye. Large specimens will reach a length of about five inches.

The habitat of this goby is in the tide pools where it is usually the most abundant species.

The distribution of this species extends from Hawaii southward to central Polynesia and Queensland, westward through Micronesia and Melanesia, through the East Indies, and across the Indian Ocean to the coast of Africa and the Red Sea.

SMALL RARE GOBY
139—10 *Zonogobius farcimen* (Jordan and Evermann), 1903

Drawn from Jordan and Evermann

This little goby has a rather robust, compressed body and the head, which is quite large, bears a large mouth with thick lips. The fins of this species are quite large and strong and seem to remain erect. In identifying this species, it should be noted that the sucker formed by the ventral fins is

397

incomplete since there is no membrane connecting these fins in front. The color of the body is a yellowish brown with many small dots covering the trunk. The head is marked by three, light lines with darker borders; these pass over the top of the head and down the sides to about the middle of the head. Large specimens reach a length of about one and one-half inches.

The habitat of this goby is in salt water in shallow shore line areas. It is an uncommon species which is rarely captured and very little is known of its habits.

The distribution of this species includes the Hawaiian area.

THE SHORE LINE GOBY
139—11 *Quisquilius eugenius* Jordan and Evermann, 1903

Drawn from Jordan and Evermann

The body of this goby is quite robust and compressed and bears a rather large head with a large mouth and jaws. Scales cover the body except beneath the head and there is no lateral line. In this species and in the following two species of *Quisquilius*, the pelvic fins are not joined together in front by a membrance. The body is brownish black in color and is marked with about 12 alternating light and dark, vertical bands. The pectoral fins are a light, reddish brown. Large specimens will reach a length of about three inches.

The habitat of this goby is in the shallow waters of the shore line; it is often abundant in some areas of dead coral.

The distribution of this species includes the Hawaiian area.

GOSLINE'S SMALL GOBY
139—12 *Quisquilius limbatosquamis* Gosline, 1959

This little goby has an elongated body which is covered with scales except for an area on the back in front of the dorsal fin. Each scale is marked by a light center and a dark ring of pigment spots. The eyes of this fish are directed upward. The body is light in color but is marked with a few, darker but faint, vertical bars. It is known from a few specimens which measured less than one inch in length.

The habitat of this fish is in the shore line waters at depths in excess of

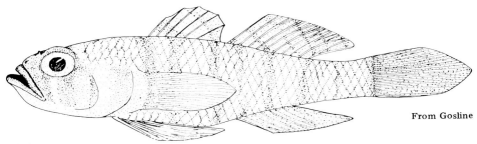

From Gosline

20 feet.

The distribution of this species includes the Hawaiian area.

Persons wishing to read more complete descriptions of this and the two succeeding species should consult *Pacific Science* 13(1), 1959, pp. 67-77.

THE GOLDEN GREEN GOBY
139—13 *Quisquilius aureoviridis* Gosline, 1959

From Gosline

This small, slender goby is completely covered with scales except for the cheek and the operculum. Living specimens are a yellowish green to yellowish brown color and are marked by very faint, darker, vertical bars. Large specimens will reach a length of about three inches.

The habitat of this fish is in the waters of the shore line at depths below 15 feet.

The distribution of this species includes the Hawaiian area.

THE SMALL SHORE LINE GOBY
139—14 *Hazeus unisquamis* Gosline, 1959

This little goby has a slender body which tapers uniformly to the tail. The body is completely covered with scales except for the top of the head anterior to the eyes and the breast in front of the pelvic fins. The cheeks below the eyes contain a single, large, embedded scale from which this species takes its name. The body is light grayish in color and bears narrow, dark borders on the two dorsal fins and a dark, vertical bar across the base of the caudal peduncle. Specimens obtained thus far have measured less than one inch in length. This fish bears a superficial resemblance to *Eviota*

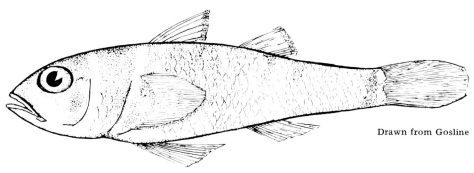

epiphanes (Eleotridae).

The habitat of this goby is in shore line waters at depths of about 20 feet.

The distribution of this species includes the Hawaiian area.

THE CLOUDY GOBY
139—15 *Opua nephodes* E.K. Jordan, 1925

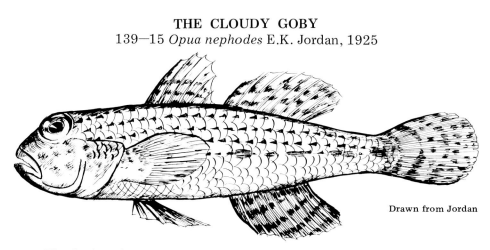

The body of this goby is small and somewhat elongated. The dorsal fins are not large and are separated; the ventral fins are completely united and are free from the belly. The entire body is covered with large scales except for the snout, cheeks, and the lower two-thirds of the operculum. The color of the body is a yellowish white hue and is mottled, streaked, and clouded with olive-brown. The head and the fins are darker in color than the body; this species also lacks a narrow, black border on the dorsal fin. Large specimens will reach a length of two inches.

The habitat of this goby seems to be in the quiet, brackish waters of the shore line.

The distribution of this species includes the Hawaiian area.

THE ANJER GOBY
139—16 *Gnatholepis anjerensis* (Bleeker), 1850

The body of this small goby is elongated and compressed and bears a blunt snout and large eyes. The color of the body is an olive-green hue; it is marked with brown spots and with about seven, incomplete, irregular, vertical cross-bars. The sides of the head often bear small blue dots; in addition, there is a distinctive, narrow, dark bar extending downward from the eye. The spinous dorsal fin is marked by three or four, narrow, horizontal bands. Large specimens will reach a length of about three inches.

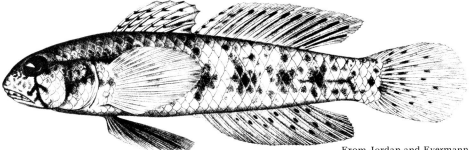

From Jordan and Evermann

The habitat of this species is in shallow water from the shore line down to depths of at least 50 feet.

The distribution of this species extends from Hawaii southward to central Polynesia and westward through Micronesia, Melanesia, and the East Indies.

The name of this species was taken from the town of Anjer near the north-western corner of Java.

GUNTHER'S PACIFIC GOBY
139—17 *Fusigobius neophytus* Gunther, 1877

This small goby has a sharp snout and a projecting lower jaw. The profile of the forehead is nearly straight from the area above the eyes to the tip of the lower jaw. There are no scales on the midline of the nape above the head. The second dorsal fin is as high or higher than the first dorsal fin; the caudal fin is rounded. The color of the body is translucent. There are some scattered spots of a dark orange color and some of black. A larger, black spot is present on the caudal peduncle; there are no dark bars below the eyes. It will reach a length of about four inches.

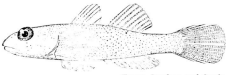

From Jordan and Seale

The distribution of this species includes Micronesia, Hawaii, and central Polynesia.

YONGE'S GOBY
139—18 *Cottogobius yongei* Davis and Cohen, 1968

Yonge's goby is a small, slender species with a compressed body which is covered with ctenoid scales except for the head, the area anterior to the first dorsal fin, and an area on the belly from the rear margin of the disc to the anus. The snout is broad and rounded, the eye is large, and the teeth are likewise quite large. The mouth is large, terminal, and obliquely placed.

This goby may be distinguished from other gobies and identified by the lateral rows of scales which number between 40 and 50, while other gobies range between 25 and 37 rows. The color of the body is transparent to translucent and is marked with alternating, vertical bands of pigmented areas. There are small amounts of red color around the head and body including the margin of the upper jaw, beneath the head, and occasionally on the dorsal fins; the iris is red with a central, golden ring. Most specimens measure less than one inch in length.

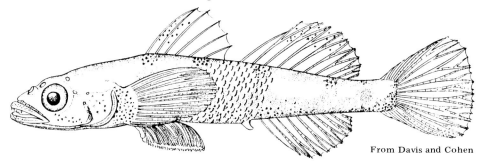

From Davis and Cohen

The habitat of this little goby is on the stalks of an antipatharian sea whip, *Cirrhipathes* species. It has been captured within a few feet of the surface.

The distribution of this goby includes the Hawaiian area, Borneo, and doubtless many intervening areas.

The name of this species honors Sir Maurice Yonge, the Australian zoologist.

MAINLAND'S GOBY
139—19 *Psilogobius mainlandi* Baldwin, 1972

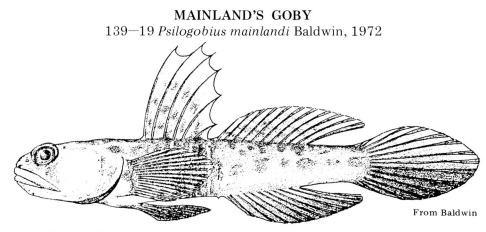

From Baldwin

Mainland's goby is a small species with a slender, compressed body. The head is large and bears a short, blunt snout. The dorsal profile of the head is convex, the jaws are equal in size, and the mouth is moderately large. Scales are absent on the head forward of the first dorsal fin and on the belly forward of the anal fin. The first dorsal fin is high; the third and fourth spines are the largest. In the second dorsal fin, all of the soft rays are branched. The color of the body is a light tan hue. It is marked along the

402

sides by a series of about ten, orange-brown markings. In addition, the body bears small, blue, irridescent spots, some of which may encircle the orange-brown spots. The adults are usually marked on the sides of the body by about six or seven, narrow, blue-white, vertical stripes in the area below the spinous dorsal fin. The anal fin has one flexible spine and about nine, branched rays. The pelvic fins form a disc beneath the body. Most specimens are less than one and one-fourth inches in length.

The habitat of this fish is in the quiet, shallow waters of reef flats, where it is reported to inhabit the burrows of alpheid shrimps.

The distribution of this species includes the Hawaiian area.

The name of this fish honors the memory of Dr. Gordon Beach Mainland, zoologist, who as a young man collected this fish in 1939 in Kaneohe Bay, Oahu, Hawaii.

Persons interested in this species should read the original description in *Pacific Science* 26(1), 1972, pp. 125-128.

THE SAND LANCE FISH FAMILY
140 *Family Kraemeriidae*

The sand lances comprise a small family of small fishes which are related to the gobies (*Gobiidae*) but, unlike the gobies, do not have their ventral fins united to form a sucking disc beneath their bodies. They are without scales, have small eyes which are placed high upon their head, and have a strongly projecting lower jaw. The dorsal and anal fins have 13 or 14 soft rays. In color, they are transparent or glass-like and most difficult to see against any background. Most species range from one to three inches in length.

The members of this family are shore line fishes and inhabit shallow sandy or muddy bottoms of streams, estuaries, lagoons, and quiet shore lines where they are often partially concealed by burrowing.

The distribution of this family seems to extend from Hawaii southward through Polynesia to Australia and westward across the tropical Pacific and Indian Oceans to the coast of Africa.

Of about a dozen species, at least one is known from this area.

BRYAN'S SAND LANCE
140—1 *Kraemeria bryani* Schultz, 1941

This little fish is long and slender and somewhat resembles a small eel. It may, however, be separated from all eels by the presence of caudal and pelvic fins. The head and body are without scales and a lateral line does not seem to be present. The lower jaw is longer than the upper jaw and possesses a fleshy tip. The eyes are small and black and are located close together on the top of the head. The dorsal fin rays number 19 or 20; the anal fin rays number 12 or 13; the pectoral fin rays number three, four, or five; and the pelvic fins have always one spine and five rays. The color of the body is translucent and glassy. Large specimens will reach an inch in length.

This sand lance is a burrowing, sand dwelling, shore line species.

The distribution of this species includes the Hawaiian area and regions to the south and west.

This species has been confused with *K. samoensis* Steindachner, 1906. This species has from three to five pectoral rays, while *K. samoensis* has seven or eight.

Drawn from Pietschmann

The name of this fish honors the work and memory of Edwin Horace Byran, Jr. (1898-   ), long time Curator of Collection at the Bernice Pauahi Bishop Museum in Honolulu.

THE LONG-FINNED CODFISH FAMILY
141 *Family Moridae*

This family is a small group and has often been included partly or entirely within the family of the codfishes (*Gadidae*) to which its members are closely related. They are long bodied fishes with two dorsal fins; the soft dorsal and anal fins are equal in size, opposite in position, and very long in some species. A single barbel is usually present on the chin. Their color is usually black or nearly so; this is in keeping with their deep water habitat.

This family occurs in the deep waters of the Atlantic and Pacific Oceans.

Of this family, at least three species occur in this area.

THE SMALL-SCALED OR LONG-FINNED CODFISH
141—1 *Antimora microlepis* Bean, 1890

This codfish has an elongated, tapering body which is covered with small scales. There are two dorsal fins; the first dorsal fin is very short with an elongated first ray and the second fin is very long and low. The anal fin is about one-half the length of the dorsal fin and bears a low, wide notch. The head is somewhat pointed and bears a large mouth with a small barbel below the tip of the lower jaw; the eyes are round and quite large. The color of the body is reported to vary from a pale, bluish gray or olive-green to black; the pectoral, ventral, and caudal fins are a deep blue color. Specimens from the Atlantic Ocean have reached two feet in length.

There is evidence to indicate that this species is identical to the Atlantic species known as *Antimora rostrata* Gunther, 1878, the species illustrated here.

Pacific specimens have been few in number and have come from deep water. The first two were taken by the steamer *Albatross* off Cape St. James in British Columbia on August 29, 1888, at a depth of 876 fathoms. The third specimen was taken by the *Albatross* on September 3, 1890, off nearby Moresby Island at a depth of 1,588 fathoms. A few specimens are known from Alaska. The *Albatross* captured a single specimen in Hawaii in 1902 off the island of Kauai at a depth between 1,000 and 1,314 fathoms; it measured about 18 inches in length.

From Clemens and Wilby

The distribution of the Pacific specimens seems to extend from northwestern Alaska and the Hawaiian area to southern California. It is doubtless much more widely distributed.

THE ORANGE - FINNED CODFISH
141—2 *Laemonema rhodochir* Gilbert, 1905

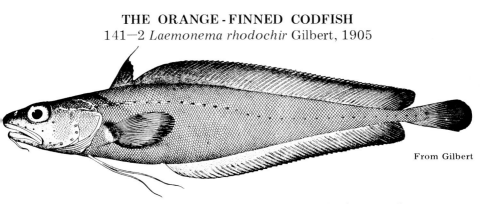

From Gilbert

The body of this codfish is wide and robust in front and tapers to a flat, slender tail. The head is wide, depressed, and rounded in front. The mouth is wide and the chin below it bears two, small barbels at the tip of the lower jaw. The eyes are located high on the head. There are two dorsal fins; the first is short, highest in front, and usually bears a filament extending from the first ray; the second dorsal fin is long and low. The anal fin is long, low, and approximately equal and opposite the soft dorsal fin. The paired pelvic fins are long, slender, and black, and are located well in advance of the pectoral fins. The color of the body is dark, but it shows faint shades of white, blue, orange, pink, and red. The head and body are brownish to black, the belly is bluish gray, and the pectoral fins are orange-red in color. The length of Gilbert's type specimen was about four and one-half inches.

This species was described from a single specimen captured in a dredge by the steamer *Albatross* in 1902 off the south coast of Oahu at a depth between 53 and 211 fathoms. However, on June 5, 1966, Mr. Paul Ebesu of

Honolulu captured a specimen measuring 11 inches with a hook and line between 70 and 90 fathoms off Barbers Point, Oahu, Hawaii.

The distribution of this species is at present limited to the Hawaiian area; it is undoubtedly much more widely distributed.

GRINNELL'S CODFISH
141—3 *Physiculus grinnelli* Jordan and Jordan, 1922

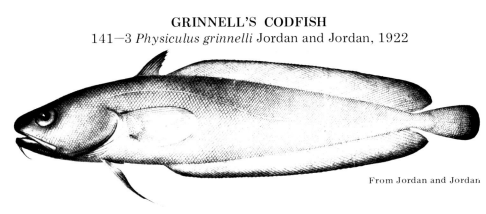

From Jordan and Jordan

This codfish has an elongated body which tapers uniformly to a small tail. There are two dorsal fins, the first of which is short. The soft dorsal and anal fins are very long, nearly equal, and approximately opposite in position. The paired pelvic fins are small and slender and are placed well in advance of the pectoral fins. The chin bears a barbel. The color of the body is dusky above and somewhat lighter below. It will reach a length of at least one foot.

This codfish inhabits deep water. Very little is known about it.

The original description of this species was made from a single specimen, measuring about 12.5 inches in length, which was found in the Honolulu fish market.

The distribution of this species includes the Hawaiian area and doubtless a much larger region adjacent to it.

In some books this species may appear under the name of *Physiculus kaupi* Poey, 1865.

THE BREGMACEROTID FISH FAMILY

142 *Family Bregmacerotidae*

The fishes of this family resemble the codfishes (*Gadidae*) and are combined with that family by many authors.

In this group the first dorsal fin has been reduced to one ray which is located toward the top of the head. The dorsal and the anal fin are not continuous with the caudal fin. The anal fin is deeply notched and the ventral fins are long and reach the beginning of the anal fins.

This family of less than a half-dozen species is known principally for *Bregmaceros macclellandi* Thompson, 1840, a small marine species of less than six inches which is found in the seas from India to China.

The distribution of this small group includes the tropical and warmer temperate seas of the world.

In recent years, a few, small, unidentified specimens of this family have been captured in deep water in this area.

THE GRENADIER OR RAT-TAIL FISH FAMILY

143 *Family Macrouridae*

(Macruridae, Lyconidae, Coryphaenoididae)

The grenadier fishes have a body somewhat like that of the codfishes; but, unlike the cods, the posterior part of the body is long, flat, and tapering and ends in a point rather than in a tail as in the cods. There are two dorsal fins. The first dorsal fin is short and high and possesses rather stiff, branched rays. The second dorsal fin and the anal fin are long, usually about opposite in position, and nearly equal in size and extend backward to meet and join at the end of the body where a tail fin would usually occur; in these fishes the tail or caudal fin is lacking. The pelvic fins, as in the codfishes, are placed far forward on the belly at a point anterior to the pectoral fins. The body is covered with scales which usually bear keels or spines or in some species are smooth. Because these scales do not seem to be firmly attached and the flesh is soft, most specimens captured in deep water have lost many of their scales by the time they arrive at the surface. The snout projects beyond the lower jaw so that the mouth is inferior in position. The tip of the lower jaw usually bears a barbel. There are sensory canals on the head and an air bladder is present. The color of these fishes is usually dull gray or black. Members of this group usually measures less than two feet in length, although a few exceed this length.

The distribution of this family is world-wide in deep water, particularly in northern seas.

Hawaiian specimens are best known through the dredging of the steamer *Albatross* in 1902.

BOWERS' GRENADIER FISH
143—1 *Bathygadus bowersi* Gilbert, 1905

The head of this fish is very large, wide, and deep; thereafter the body tapers uniformly toward the tail. The color of the body is brownish and blackish above and blue-black beneath. It will reach a length of at least 18 inches.

The steamer *Albatross* collected six specimens in 1902 off Bird Island and Kauai at depths between 313 and 876 fathoms.

The distribution of this species includes the Hawaiian area and doubtless surrounding areas.

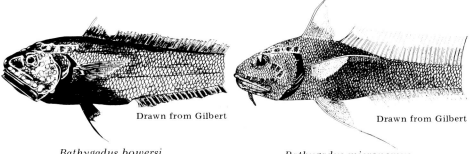

Drawn from Gilbert

Drawn from Gilbert

Bathygadus bowersi

Bathygadus micronemus

THE THREADED GRENADIER FISH
143—2 *Bathygadus micronemus* (Gilbert), 1905

This grenadier has the large head and long, tapering body which are typical of its group. There are long, tapering filaments extending from the beginning of the first dorsal, pectoral, and pelvic fins. The chin bears a small barbel. The color of the body is brownish, grayish, and black.

This species was first described from a single specimen measuring about nine inches in length which was captured in a dredge by the steamer *Albatross* in 1902 in Pailolo channel between Molokai and Maui at a depth between 753 and 787 fathoms.

The distribution of this species includes the Hawaiian area and doubtless other adjoining areas.

THE PLOW-NOSED GRENADIER FISH
143—3 *Coelorhynchus aratrum* Gilbert, 1905

The head of this grenadier bears a long, depressed snout which ends in a slender spine. The head bears three longitudinal ridges on each side; the uppermost is on top of the head near the center, the second passes backward just above the eye and ends near the gill slit, and the third extends from the tip of the snout along the lower side of the head below the eye to the end of the gill slit. The color of the body is described as light brown above with lighter areas below. The fins are mostly darker toward their bases and lighter distally. Specimens have measured as much as 12 inches in length.

This species was first described from a few specimens which were captured by the steamer *Albatross* in 1902 off the south coast of Oahu and in

he Pailolo Channel between Molokai and Maui at depths between 289 and
37 fathoms. In 1891, the steamer *Albatross* captured a single specimen
measuring nearly five inches in length in a beam trawl in the Kaiwi Channel
etween Molokai and Oahu at a depth of about 313 fathoms.

The distribution of this species includes the Hawaiian area and doubt-
ss surrounding areas.

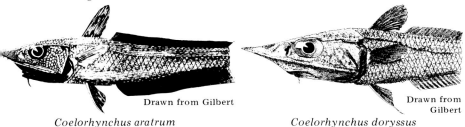

Coelorhynchus aratrum   Drawn from Gilbert   Drawn from Gilbert   *Coelorhynchus doryssus*

THE SPEAR-NOSED GRENADIER FISH
143—4 *Coelorhynchus doryssus* Gilbert, 1905

This species is reported to resemble *C. aratrum*, but has a more slender snout and a larger mouth. The color of the body is a very light gray and
ll of the fins are black. It will reach a length of at least 14 inches.

This species was first described from a few specimens captured by the
teamer *Albatross* in 1902 off the coast of Kauai, off southwestern Oahu,
nd in the Kaiwi Channel between Molokai and Oahu at depths between 192
nd 449 fathoms.

The distribution of this species includes the Hawaiian area and doubt-
ess adjoining areas.

THE SHARP-SNOUTED GRENADIER FISH
143—5 *Coelorhynchus gladius* Gilbert and Cramer, 1897

The most prominent feature of
his fish is a long snout which is
extended to form a strong, horny
pine. The color of the body is black
or blackish over most of its surface.
The fins are both light and dark and
vary with age. There is a dark area
above and behind the base of the
pectoral fins. The specimens mentioned below range in length from
about two and one-half to nine inches.

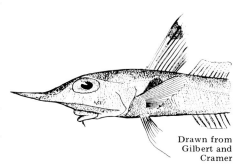

Drawn from
Gilbert and
Cramer

This species was first described from four specimens which were cap-
ured in a beam trawl by the steamer *Albatross* in 1891 in the Kaiwi Channel
etween Oahu and Molokai at a depth of about 295 fathoms. Later six
dditional specimens were captured by the steamer *Albatross* in 1902 off
orthwestern Oahu, southwestern Oahu, and off the eastern coast of Kauai
t depths between 192 and 352 fathoms.

The distribution of this species includes the Hawaiian area and doubt less other adjoining areas.

THE DEEP WATER GRENADIER FISH
143—6 *Coryphaenoides longicirrus* (Gilbert), 1905

In this grenadier the contours of the head are more rounded than in other species. The first dorsal fin is high and short and the pelvic fins bear long, trailing filaments from their anterior borders. The chin bears a small barbel. The color of the body is a dark purplish brown.

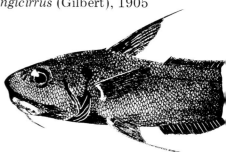

Drawn from Gilber

This species was first described from a single specimen measuring about 23 inches in length which was captured in a dredge by the steamer *Albatross* in 1902 off Kauai at a depth between 1,000 and 1,314 fathoms

The distribution of this species includes the Hawaiian area and doubt less other adjoining areas.

THE BLACK - FINNED GRENADIER FISH
143—7 *Gadomus melanopterus* Gilbert, 1905

The head and the body of this fish are compressed and the body tapers uniformly toward the tail. There are filaments extending from the anterior borders of the first dorsal, pectoral, and pelvic fins and the chin bears a barbel. The color of the body is brownish, dark gray, and black; the fins are jet black in color.

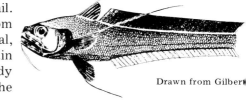

Drawn from Gilber

This species was first described from a single specimen, measuring about 11 inches in length, which was captured in a dredge by the steamer *Albatross* in 1902 off Kauai at a depth between 444 and 478 fathoms.

The distribution of this species includes the Hawaiian area and doubt-less other adjoining areas.

THE COMMON BIG - EYED GRENADIER FISH
143—8 *Hymenocephalus antraeus* Gilbert and Cramer, 1897

This grenadier is characterized by a large, square head with vertical sides, a short rounded snout, very large eyes, and highly developed mucous cavities covering the head. There are two unusual lens-shaped bodies located on the lower surface; one is on the breast, the other on the belly. The color of the body is dark brown and black; the fins are pale. Large specimens reach a length of about eight inches.

This species was first described from 91 specimens which were captured n four hauls with a beam trawl by the steamer *Albatross* in 1891 in the Kaiwi Channel between Molokai and Oahu at depths between 298 and 343 fathoms. When the steamer *Albatross* resumed collecting in 1902, this species proved to be the most abundant grenadier in Hawaii at depths between 250 and 350 fathoms.

This species feeds upon small crustacea. Its eggs are released in late summer.

The distribution of this species includes the Hawaiian area and doubtless adjoining areas.

Drawn from Gilbert and Cramer

THE BLACK GRENADIER FISH
143—9 *Hymenocephalus aterrimus* Gilbert, 1905

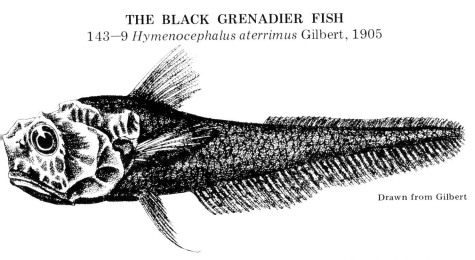

Drawn from Gilbert

The black grenadier has a very large, compressed head which bears a heavy, rounded snout and a large mouth which is obliquely placed at the front of the head. The body tapers uniformly to the tail. Two lens-like structures are located on the ventral surface, one beneath the breast and the other on the belly. The color of the body is quite uniformly black. Large specimens will reach a length of at least seven inches.

This species was first described from specimens captured off Kauai, Niihau, Bird Island, northern and northeastern Molokai, and in the Kaiwi Channel between Molokai and Oahu by the steamer *Albatross* in 1902 at depths between 293 and 800 fathoms.

The distribution of this species includes the Hawaiian area and undoubtedly adjoining areas.

GILBERT'S GRENADIER FISH
143—10 *Hymenocephalus striatulus* Gilbert, 1905

This grenadier resembles *H. antraeus* somewhat, but it differs in having a smaller head, smaller eyes, a more slender body, and more rays in the pelvic fins. The body of this grenadier, including the head, is long, slender and tapering; the eyes are large and slightly elliptical; and the mouth is quite large and obliquely placed. The color of the body is light olive in life; the lower half of the tail is marked by coarse, black, pigment spots; there is also a conspicuous, black, pigment spot at the base of each ray of the anal fin. I will reach a length of five or six inches.

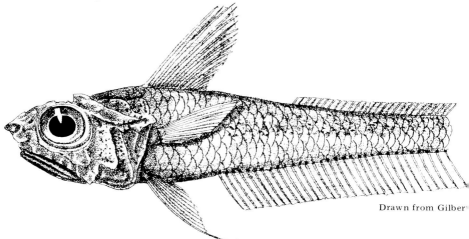

Drawn from Gilber

This species was first described from specimens captured by the steamer *Albatross* in 1902 off southeastern and southwestern Oahu and off Kauai at depths between 192 and 362 fathoms.

The distribution of this species includes the Hawaiian area and doubtless other adjoining areas.

THE SLENDER GRENADIER FISH
143—11 *Hymenocephalus tenuis* Gilbert and Hubbs, 1917

This little grenadier was reported to differ from all other members of its genus in having a cylindrically-shaped head, rather than a compressed head. The body was extremely slender, a barbel was present on the chin, and the color was reported to be yellowish brown above, silvery on the sides and tail, and darker below. It measured three inches in length.

This species was first described in 1917 from a single, possibly immature specimen which was taken by the steamer *Albatross* in 1902 off the south coast of Oahu between 265 and 280 fathoms.

The distribution of this species includes the Hawaiian area and doubtless surrounding areas.

BURRAGE'S GRENADIER FISH
143—12 *Lionurus burragei* (Gilbert), 1905

Burrage's grenadier has a body which is deep and compressed and covered with small scales bearing slender spines. The head is short, high and compressed and bears a snout which ends in a small, median, spiny tubercle and two, smaller, lateral tubercles. The first dorsal fin is short and high and he second dorsal spine, which forms the anterior border of this fin, is marked by about 17 serrations along its anterior border. The lateral line is present and a barbel extends downward from the chin. There is a small, scaleless pit on the lower surface between the pelvic fins. The color of the body is grayish above and shades to blackish below: the cavity of the mouth is whitish. It will reach a length of about ten inches.

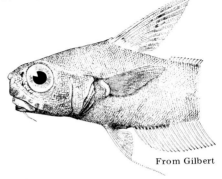

This fish was first described from a single specimen captured in 1902 by the steamer *Albatross* off the south coast of Oahu at a depth between 294 and 330 fathoms.

This species is named for Lieut. G. H. Burrage, U.S.N., who was the Navigating and Executive Officer of the steamer *Albatross* in 1902.

The distribution of this species includes the Hawaiian area and doubtless other surrounding areas.

From Gilbert

Recent studies suggest that *Nezumia burragei* (Gilbert), 1905, is a more correct name for this species.

THE ELONGATED GRENADIER FISH
143—13 *Lionurus ectenes* (Gilbert and Cramer), 1897

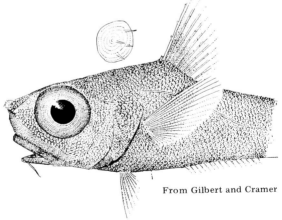

The body of this grenadier is compressed and elongated and terminates in a very slender tail. The head is deep and compressed with vertical sides, the eyes are large, the mouth is small, and a small barbel is attached to the lower jaw. The tip of the snout bears a spiny tubercle at its center and a small, lateral tubercle on each side. The scales which cover the body are small, very thin, and flexible; the second dorsal spine is serrated, and

From Gilbert and Cramer

the outer ray of each pelvic fin is elongated. The color of the body is reported as brownish black in alcohol.

This species was first described from a single specimen about five inches long which was captured by the steamer *Albatross* in 1891 in a beam trawl in Kaiwi Channel between Oahu and Molokai at a depth of 313 fathoms.

The distribution of this species includes the Hawaiian area and doubtless other nearby areas.

Recent studies suggest that *Nezumia ectenes* (Gilbert and Cramer), 1897, is a more correct name for this species.

THE HUMPED GRENADIER FISH
143—14 *Lionurus gibber* (Gilbert and Cramer), 1897

The body of this grenadier is deep and compressed and tapers uniformly to the tip of the tail. The head is likewise deep and compressed and covered with scales on its top and sides; it bears a short snout which is tipped with a small, median, spiny tubercle and a smaller, lateral tubercle on each side. The mouth is obliquely placed and there is a barbel on the chin. The first dorsal fin is high and short with the first, large spine bearing serration

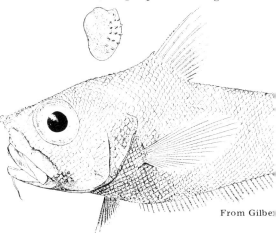

on its anterior border; the second dorsal fin is long, low, and inconspicuous. The pectoral fins are quite long and slender and bear a long filament extending from the outer ray. The body is covered with thin, spiny scales and the lateral line is apparently missing. The color of this fish in alcohol was reported to be brownish to black with dark colored fins. It will reach a length of at least eight inches.

From Gilbert

In 1891 the steamer *Albatross* captured specimens in the Kaiwi Channel between Molokai and Oahu and in 1902 additional specimens were captured off Bird Island, off Kauai, off the western coast of Hawaii, and of the south coast of Molokai. All of the above specimens were taken at depths between 253 and 800 fathoms.

The distribution of this species includes the Hawaiian area and doubtless surrounding areas.

Recent studies suggest that *Sphagemacrurus gibber* (Gilbert and Cramer), 1897, is a more correct name for this species.

THE DULL GRENADIER FISH
143—15 *Lionurus hebetatus* (Gilbert), 1905

The body of this grenadier is short and deep and tapers uniformly to

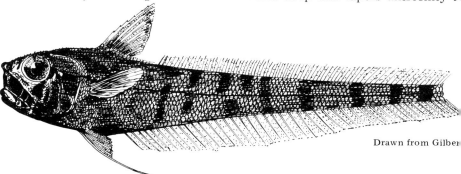

Drawn from Gilbert

he tail. It is covered with scales bearing spines and has a lateral line. The head is quite short and is cuboidal in shape with a vertical anterior profile; he head bears a snout which terminates in a small, smooth tubercle. The irst dorsal fin is short and high and is bordered on its anterior edge with a pine bearing eight serrations; the second dorsal fin is long and very low. The color of the body is grayish above and black on the sides and belly. The nterior of the mouth is whitish. It will reach a length of at least five inches.

This species was first known from a single specimen captured by the teamer *Albatross* in 1902 off the south coast of Oahu at a depth between 299 and 323 fathoms.

The distribution of this species includes the Hawaiian area and doubtless surrounding areas.

Recent studies suggest that *Nezumia hebetatus* (Gilbert), 1905, is a nore correct name for this species.

CRAMER'S GRENADIER FISH
143—16 *Lionurus holocentrus* (Gilbert and Cramer), 1897

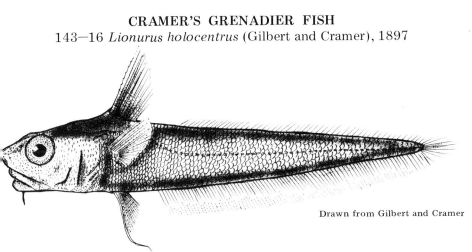

Drawn from Gilbert and Cramer

The body of this grenadier is long, slender, compressed, and covered with scales. The head is likewise slender and compressed and bears a slender, conical snout; this snout ends anteriorly in a median, spiny tubercle which is bordered on each side by a smaller, spiny tubercle. The mouth is small and bears a barbel on its lower jaw. The first dorsal fin is short and high and is margined by the second spine which is serrated along its anterior border and extends as a filament beyond the fin. The pelvic fins each bear eight or nine rays of which the outermost is prolonged into a filament. There is a small, round, naked pit on the belly between the bases of the pelvic fins. The color of the body has been described as light brownish above and darker below. The largest known specimen measured about seven inches in length.

The steamer *Albatross* captured three specimens in Kaiwi Channel between Oahu and Molokai in 1891 and one additional specimen off the south coast of Oahu in 1902. They were taken between 308 and 375 fathoms.

The distribution of this species includes the Hawaiian area and doubtless surrounding areas.

Recent studies suggest that *Nezumia holocentrus* (Gilbert and Cramer) 1897, is a more correct name for this species.

THE KAUAI GRENADIER FISH
143—17 *Lionurus obliquatus* (Gilbert), 1905

The body of this grenadier is long and slender and tapers uniformly toward the tail. The body is covered with scales and bears a lateral line. The head is quite long and bears a snout which ends in a very spiny tubercle which is directed obliquely upward. The first dorsal fin is short and high and is bordered on its anterior margin by a serrated spine; the second dorsal fin is long and very low. The color of this fish is grayish above and black on the sides and lower surfaces.

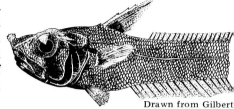
Drawn from Gilbert

This species was first described from a single specimen which measured about six inches in length and which was captured by the steamer *Albatross* in 1902 off the eastern coast of Kauai at a depth between 437 and 632 fathoms.

The distribution of this species includes the Hawaiian area and doubtless surrounding areas.

Recent studies suggest that *Nezumia obliquatus* (Gilbert), 1905, is a more correct name for this species.

THE KAIWI CHANNEL GRENADIER FISH
143—18 *Lionurus propinquus* (Gilbert and Cramer), 1897

The body of this grenadier is long and compressed and is covered with small scales which are loosely attached. The first dorsal fin is high and is bordered by the second spine which is serrated along its anterior margin and which ends in a long filament; the outer ray of the pelvic fins likewise terminates in a filament. The head is of moderate size and compressed and bears a short, broad snout. This snout bears a spiny tubercle at its tip and a single, smaller tubercle on each side. The eyes are quite large and the mouth is comparatively small. A short barbel is present. The color of the body in alcohol is reported to be brownish above and black below. The dorsal fin is lighter below than distally. The length of this grenadier will reach at least ten inches.

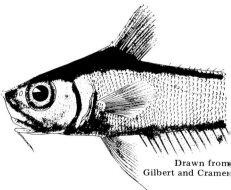
Drawn from
Gilbert and Cramer

Specimens were captured by the steamer *Albatross* in 1891 and again in 1902. They were taken off the east coast of Kauai and in the Kaiwi Channel between Molokai and Oahu at depths between 286 and 411 fathoms.

The distribution of this species includes the Hawaiian area and doubtless adjoining areas.

Recent studies suggest that *Nezumia propinquus* (Gilbert and Cramer), 1897, is a more correct name for this fish.

THE HAWAIIAN GRENADIER FISH
143—19 *Malacocephalus hawaiiensis* Gilbert, 1905

The Hawaiian grenadier has a high, compressed body which is covered with scales and which tapers gradually to the tip of the tail. The head and snout are likewise compressed and covered with scales. The first dorsal fin is short and high with a weak spine on its anterior margin; the second dorsal fin is long and low. There is a small pit on the belly between the bases of the pelvic fins. The color of this fish was described as olive brown above, bluish silvery on the sides, and black below. The fins are mostly black and the interior of the mouth is white. The type specimen measured 14 inches in length.

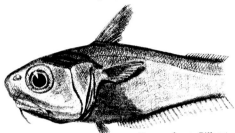
Drawn from Gilbert

This species appears to be quite abundant for it was captured by the steamer *Albatross* both in 1891 and in 1902 at various locations in Hawaii at depths between 165 and 684 fathoms. It feeds upon squids and shrimps.

The distribution of this species includes the Hawaiian area and doubtless adjoining areas.

THE STURGEON-LIKE GRENADIER FISH
143—20 *Mataeocephalus acipenserinus* (Gilbert and Cramer), 1897

This common species has a slender, tapering body and a head which bears a long, flattened snout which projects forward to end in a small, spiny tubercle. The mouth is small and a very small barbel is present below it. The color is described as uniform, pale brown above; however, some specimens exhibit a pattern of light spots in the areas above the lateral line. Individual specimens are known to reach a length of eight inches.

This species was first captured by the steamer *Albatross* in both 1891 and 1902 at many locations. It is reported to be a very abundant species at depths between 200 and 400 fathoms.

The distribution of this species includes the Hawaiian area and doubtless surrounding areas.

THE THORNY-SKINNED GRENADIER FISH
143—21 *Trachonurus sentipellis* Gilbert and Cramer, 1897

The scientific name of this grenadier is obtained from the spiny scales which cover the body and most of the head. The body is moderately deep, compressed, and slender and tapers uniformly to the tip of the tail. The

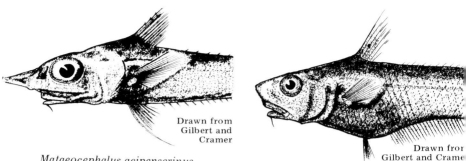

Drawn from
Gilbert and
Cramer

Mataeocephalus acipenserinus

Drawn from
Gilbert and Cramer

Trachonurus sentipellis

head is compressed, square in shape with vertical sides, but with rounded corners and contours and without ridges or angles. A small barbel is present below the chin. The first dorsal fin is short and high and is bordered along its anterior margin by the second dorsal spine; in this case, it should be noted that this spine is smooth and without the serrations along its anterior border which are found in many related species. The color of the body is dark brownish to black; the interior of the mouth is also black. It will reach a length of at least 11 inches.

The steamer *Albatross* captured specimens in 1891 and again in 1902 at various locations off Kauai and in the Kaiwi channel between Oahu and Molokai at depths between 335 and 804 fathoms.

THE ARROW-TOOTHED GRENADIER FISH
143—22 *Ventrifossa atherodon* (Gilbert and Cramer), 1897

The head of this grenadier is compressed and bears pits and depressions upon its upper surface. The snout is short and broad, the eyes are large, and there is a small barbel beneath the chin. The body is compressed and tapers uniformly to the tail. The mouth is large, obliquely placed, and contains arrow-shaped teeth. The outer rays of the pelvic fins are extended as filaments and there is a small, scaleless pit on the belly between the pelvic fins. The color of the body in alcohol is reported as being brown above, silvery on the sides, and bluish black beneath. Large specimens will reach a length of about 15 inches.

This fish is a very abundant species between 250 and 400 fathoms. It feeds upon small crustacea and squids.

The distribution of this species includes the Hawaiian area and doubtless surrounding areas.

THE COMMON GRENADIER FISH
143—23 *Ventrifossa ctenomelas* (Gilbert and Cramer), 1897

This common grenadier has a slender, compressed body which tapers uniformly toward the tail. The head is compressed and has vertical cheeks, large eyes, a broad triangular snout, and a large, obliquely-placed mouth. A barbel is attached to the tip of the lower jaw. There is a small, scaleless pit located on the belly between the bases of the pelvic fins. The color of the

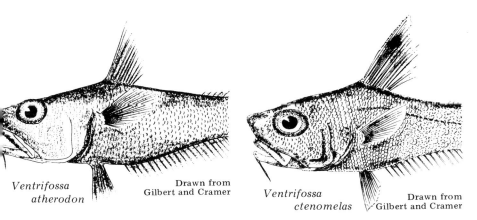

Ventrifossa atherodon
Drawn from Gilbert and Cramer

Ventrifossa ctenomelas
Drawn from Gilbert and Cramer

ody in alcohol is brownish above, silvery and speckled with brown on the ides, and blackish below. The interior of the mouth is white. Large pecimens will reach eight inches in length.

This grenadier is a very common species at depths between 250 and 350 athoms. Its food appears to consist of shrimps and squids.

The distribution of this species includes the Hawaiian area and doubt-ess surrounding areas.

THE SCORPION FISH OR ROCK FISH FAMILY
144 *Family Scorpaenidae*

Scorpion fishes are a family of marine fishes of moderate size with short, moderately compressed bodies and large heads which are also usually compressed. They all possess a strange ridge or bony plate, called "the sub-orbital stay," which extends horizontally across the cheek from below the eye backward to the edge of the preopercle or gill cover. The body surface is usually covered with scales, although in some species they are small, buried in the skin, or even absent. In addition, some species bear dermal flaps or tentacles of skin scattered over the head and nearby areas. The margin of the operculum usually has two spines and the preopercle usually has either four or five points or spines along its margin. The single dorsal fin bears from 12 to 15 spines; the anal fin has from one to four strong spines and from four to eight rays; the tail fin may be either rounded or truncated, but it is never forked; the pelvic fins are placed far forward under the body and contain one spine and from two to five rays; and the pectoral fins are usually fan-like, often with long rays and shorter membranes between them.

These fishes can be dangerous to the uninformed or the unwary for their dorsal, pelvic, and anal spines are strong and sharp and are able to inject poison from the poison-producing tissue along these spines. Since many of these species are camouflaged and concealed by their color, it is important that swimmers and waders wear shoes and gloves and pay great attention to what they touch and where they step.

Scorpion fishes are bottom dwellers, usually near rocks or coral heads. They are poor swimmers and spend most of their time sitting motionless waiting for smaller fishes to pass within reach; at this moment, they open their mouth, draw in water, and leap forward a short distance to capture the passing fish. They are entirely carnivorous in their habits and may therefore be readily caught with hook and line. Most species in this family bear their young alive when the young reach a length of about one-fourth inch.

Scorpion fishes inhabit the tropical and especially the temperate seas of the world from shallow shore line waters down to depths of at least 500 feet. A few enter fresh water.

Of this large family, more than two dozen species are known from this area.

Persons wishing to study Hawaiian scorpion fishes should consult an article by Wm. N. Eschmeyer and John E. Randall in *Proceedings of the California Academy of Sciences*, Fourth Series, 40:11, 1975, pp. 265-334.

BARBER'S SCORPION FISH
144—1 *Dendrochirus barberi* (Steindachner), 1900

The body of this scorpion fish is small and compressed and the mouth and eyes are large. The fins are large and the spines of the dorsal fin are quite long, are usually 13 in number, and project well beyond their connecting membranes. This species may be most easily identified by examining the upper rays of the pectoral fins and noting that they are branched near their free ends. The color of the body is a reddish brown with wide, lighter, vertical markings. Specimens will measure at least four or five inches in length.

The habitat of this scorpion fish is usually around small caves or recesses along rocky ledges as deep as 150 feet where the water is comparatively calm. It is not a rare species.

The distribution of this species is at present limited to the Hawaiian

area.

This species has been previously known under several names including *D. brachypterus* (Cuvier), 1829; *D. chloreus* Jenkins, 1903; and *D. hudsoni* Jordan and Evermann, 1903.

GARMAN'S DEEP WATER SCORPION FISH
144—2 *Ectreposebastes imus* Garman, 1899

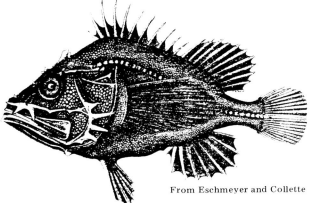

From Eschmeyer and Collette

This deep water scorpion fish has a body which is deep and compressed. The flesh is soft and flabby and the bones and spines are weak; the scales are thin and loosely attached. The dorsal fin has 12 spines and 10 rays; the anal fin has three spines and six rays; and the rays of the pectoral fin are usually 19 in number. The color of the body is black when small, but it changes to maroon and black when it matures. The interior of the mouth is black with orange and red patches. Large specimens are about six inches in length.

The habitat of this fish is in deep water. It has been captured at depths between 1,500 and 2,500 feet.

The distribution of this fish is probably world-wide in deep water. It is known from both sides of the north Atlantic Ocean, from the eastern Pacific Ocean, from Hawaii and the central Pacific, and from Japan.

The word *imus* is a Latin word meaning *lowest* and doubtless refers to the great depth at which this fish lives.

THE SPOT-BEARING SCORPION FISH
144—3 *Iracundus signifer* Jordan and Evermann, 1903

This rare scorpion fish has a rather elongated body which is slightly compressed and which is covered with scales and numerous dermal flaps, particularly on the head. The eyes are prominent and the mouth is large. The dorsal fin is deeply notched and its fourth spine is greatly elongated. It is reddish in life and bears a significant, black

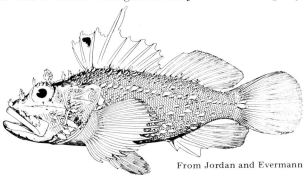

From Jordan and Evermann

spot on the spinous dorsal fin near the edge of the membrane between the second and third spines.

This species was first described from two specimens about four inches long; one of these was captured on the reef at Honolulu and the other seems to have come from the Honolulu fish market. It is an uncommon species.

The distribution of this species includes the Hawaiian area, central Polynesia, and Mauritius in the western Indian Ocean.

THE VERMILLION AND WHITE SCORPION FISH
144—4 *Neomerinthe rufescens* (Gilbert), 1905

This scorpion fish is a small, deep-water species with spines on the head and with dermal flaps, mostly narrow and small, scattered over the head and body, particularly along the lateral line. The color of the body is vermillion and pearly white arranged in irregular blotches. The interior of the mouth is white. The largest known specimen measured about four inches in length.

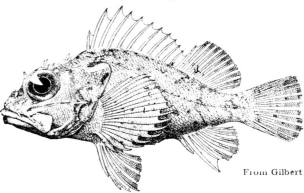

From Gilbert

This species was first described from two specimens captured by the steamer *Albatross* in 1902 off the islands of Kauai and Maui at depths between 41 and 165 fathoms.

The distribution of this species includes the Hawaiian area and doubtless adjoining areas.

In some books this species will be listed as *Helicolenus rufescens* Gilbert, 1905.

THE LARGE-EYED SCORPION FISH
144—5 *Phenacoscorpius megalops* Fowler, 1938

The large-eyed scorpion fish is a small species with oval outlines and a compressed body which is covered by quite large scales. The head is also compressed and bears many, strong, sharp spines. The mouth and the eyes are both large. The lateral line is very short and is found only on a few scales at its origin. The body is reddish in color and bears a prominent spot or dark area on the membranes of the spinous dorsal fin in the area between the 6th and 8th spines. The type specimen measured more than 4 inches (109 mm) and was captured in 1909 off Luzon at a depth of 209 fathoms.

The habitat of this species ranges from about 150 to 2,000 feet in depth. Some specimens have been associated with beds of pink coral.

The distribution of this species includes Hawaii, the Philippine Islands, the East Indies, and doubtless other adjoining areas.

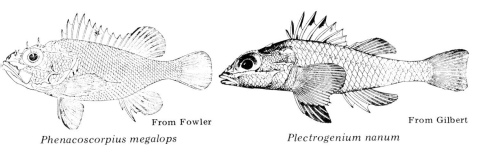

From Fowler

From Gilbert

Phenacoscorpius megalops　　　　*Plectrogenium nanum*

THE SMALL SCORPION FISH
144—6 *Plectrogenium nanum* Gilbert, 1905

The body of this deep-water form is slender, elongated, and only very slightly compressed. The body is covered with rather large scales and a lateral line is present. The head bears large eyes and spines including a horizontal row passing beneath each eye. The dorsal fin is divided in this species. The color of the body is nearly a uniform, rose red. There are some darker shadings on the membranes of the spinous dorsal fin at its outer margin just behind each spine and also at the base of the soft dorsal fin.

This species was first described from 15 specimens captured by the steamer *Albatross* in 1902 at depths between about 150 and 350 fathoms at various locations in the Hawaiian area.

The distribution of this species includes the Hawaiian area, Japan, and doubtless adjoining areas.

THE LARGE-HEADED SCORPION FISH
Also known as 'O-'o-pu ka-i no-hu
144—7 *Pontinus macrocephala* (Sauvage), 1882

This scorpion fish is probably most easily recognized by its long head and bright colors. The head contains a large mouth and is covered with

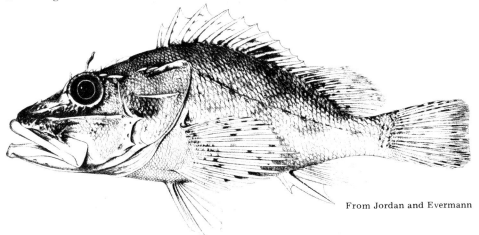

From Jordan and Evermann

scattered spines of which there are two directly behind each eye, two farther back on the operculum, and a horizontal row of about five spines under each eye which ends in a longer spine at the margin of the preopercle. Above each eye is a small, short, fleshy tentacle. The color of the body is a bright orange and reddish hue which is lighter below; it is mottled with darker spots. Large specimens will reach a length of about ten inches.

The habitat of this species is on the outer side of the reef in deeper water. It is caught on hand lines and appears occasionally in the markets.

The distribution of this species at present includes the Hawaiian area and doubtless adjoining areas.

This species will appear in older books under the name of *Merinthe macrocephala* (Sauvage), 1882.

The species, known as *Pontinus spilistius* Gilbert, 1905, is believed to be the young, immature individuals of *P. macrocephala.* In these young forms there is a dark area on the membranes of the spinous dorsal fin; this dark spot becomes less distinct in older individuals.

THE WASP SCORPION FISH
Also known as Lion Fish and Turkey Fish
144—8 *Pterois sphex* Jordan and Evermann, 1903

This is a dangerous fish because of the poison contained in its spines. The name *sphex* is the Greek word for *wasp* and was undoubtedly given to this species because of the severity of its sting.

This scorpion fish has an elongated, compressed body with uniformly curving dorsal and ventral outlines. The spines of the dorsal fin and the rays of the pectoral fins are unusual because they are very long and extend far beyond the membranes connecting them. All of the pectoral rays are unbranched and the upper pectoral rays, in particular, are developed into long, feeler-like filaments. The color of the body is reddish brown; it is marked with light, vertical lines which are more or less in pairs. Most specimens are six or seven inches in length; large specimens might reach ten inches.

The habitat of this fish is in the quiet waters of the shore line. It is a

bold, slow-moving fish and is easily captured. Over zealous collectors can have "the lesson of their life" if they make the mistake of touching this fish.

The distribution of this species includes the Hawaiian area.

THE STRANGE-EYED SCORPION FISH
144—9 *Rhinopias xenops* (Gilbert), 1905

This deep water scorpion fish has a deep, compressed body and prominent eyes; it is covered by an array of dermal flaps. The color of the body is a brilliant vermillion; it is marked with small purplish spots and is mottled with yellowish white below. In addition, there are white spots on the back of the tail and at the bases of the eighth and ninth dorsal spines. It reaches a length of at least six inches.

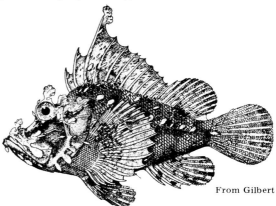

From Gilbert

This species was first known from a single specimen captured in 1902 by the steamer *Albatross* in Auau Channel between Maui and Lanai at a depth between 32 and 43 fathoms.

The distribution of this species includes the Hawaiian area, Japan, and doubtless surrounding areas.

In older books, this species may appear under the name of *Peloropsis xenops* Gilbert, 1905.

BALLIEU'S SCORPION FISH
Also known as Po-'o pa-'a
144—10 *Scorpaena ballieui* Sauvage, 1875

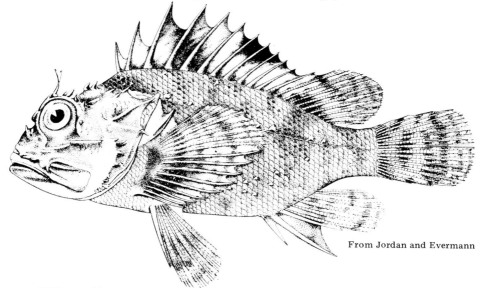

From Jordan and Evermann

This small scorpion fish is a variable species and has been described and named several times by different authors. It is a rather elongated species with the dorsal and ventral outlines approximately opposite and equal. The features which separate it from its relatives have been pointed out by Dr. Wm. Gosline; these include the absence of scales on the cheek and opercle, the pectoral fin with four branched rays and without a sheath of scales at its base, and the attachment of the last dorsal ray by a membrane for most of its length to the caudal peduncle. The color of the body is olive green and whitish and is applied in large irregular areas. The fins contain yellow markings. There are no small, dark spots scattered over the body as in *S. coniorta*. Large specimens, but not small ones, have a black blotch on the posterior part of the spinous dorsal fin. Adult specimens do not appear to exceed four inches in length.

The habitat of this fish includes the shallow shore line areas. It is a common species.

The distribution of this species includes the Hawaiian area, Johnston Island, and doubtless other surrounding areas.

The name of this species honors M. Ballieu, a French consul in Hawaii prior to 1875.

THE RED SCORPION FISH
144—11 *Scorpaena colorata* (Gilbert), 1905
This scorpion fish is a small species with large eyes. The head bears an array of spines and the body has a few, scattered, dermal flaps, particularly along the lateral line. The color of the body is bright reddish; the body is marked with small, dark spots which are scattered over the body, head, and

426

basal parts of the dorsal fin. There is a dark mark on the membrane of the dorsal fin between the eighth and the ninth spines. Specimens will measure about four inches in length.

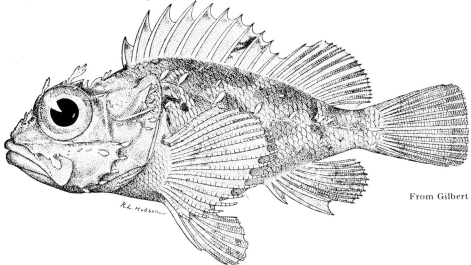

From Gilbert

This is a deep-water species which was first known from specimens captured by the steamer *Albatross* in 1902 off the southern coast of Molokai at depths between 43 and 73 fathoms.

The distribution of this species includes the Hawaiian area and doubtless adjoining areas.

THE SMALL SCORPION FISH
144—12 *Scorpaena coniorta* (Jenkins), 1903

This little fish has a moderately elongated and compressed body with a slightly humped back. The head is quite large and bears large eyes, a large mouth and jaws, a short snout, and an array of many spines. The color of the body is a light olive with large, dark brown areas and mottlings. The head, body, and fins are marked

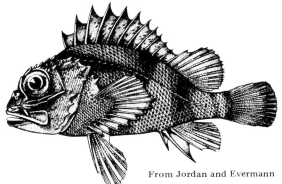

From Jordan and Evermann

with many, small brown spots. The iris is red and there are red or reddish areas on the caudal, anal, and ventral fins. Most specimens measure less than three inches in length.

The habitat includes the shallow, inshore areas downward to depths of possibly 100 feet. It is an abundant species.

The distribution of this species includes the Hawaiian area, Johnston Island, the Line Islands and doubtless other adjoining areas.

JENKIN'S SCORPION FISH
144—13 *Scorpaena galactacma* (Jenkins), 1903

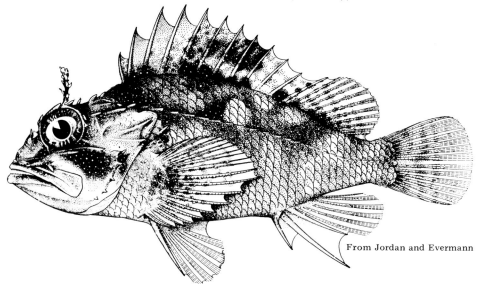

From Jordan and Evermann

    This scorpion fish is small in size and has a body which is laterally compressed. The head is large, compressed, and covered with spines, but it is without scales. The eyes and mouth are both large. The dorsal fin contains twelve spines and nine rays; the fourth spine is the longest. The lateral line extends the full length of the body. The side of the body is marked above by large, irregular, poorly defined, dark, saddle-shaped areas; the body is lighter in color below. There is a large, dark areas on the membrane of the spinous dorsal fin beginning somewhere between the 5th, 6th or 7th spine and extending to the 9th spine. Adult specimens are less than three inches in length.

    The habitat of this species is in the shallow shore line areas where coral and coral rubble occur.

    The distribution of this species includes the Hawaiian area and doubtless adjoining areas.

THE PELE SCORPION FISH
144—14 *Scorpaena pele* Eschmeyer and Randall, 1975

    This fish is one of the smaller species within this family. The body is quite high behind the head and tapers downward toward the tail. The head is large and is covered with spines and both the head and the body are covered with small dermal flaps. The eyes are large and are placed high and quite far forward on the head. The dorsal fin contains 12 spines and the pectoral fin contains 17 rays. The color of the body was described as "mostly red, marbled and spotted with white".

    The habitat of this fish is in the deeper water beyond the shore line. Numerous specimens have been captured in trawls at depths between about 500 and 750 feet.

The distribution of this species includes the Hawaiian area and probably nearby adjoining areas.

The name of this species appears to have been taken from Pele, the ancient Hawaiian goddess of volcanoes.

THE RED CORAL SCORPION FISH
144—15 *Scorpaenodes corallinus* Smith, 1957

This is a very small scorpion fish which was first found and described from the Indian Ocean. It has a rather high compressed body and a small head with a large mouth. The dorsal outline of the body is a sweeping curve, while the ventral outline is nearly straight. The suborbital ridge, which

Photo by John E. Randall

passes horizontally below the eye, has three small spines in a row. The dorsal fin contains 13 spines and only 8 soft rays; the last ray is divided. The anal fin contains three spines and five rays; the last ray is divided. The pectoral fin contains 17 or 18 rays. The body is red in color and is marked by a light area which encompasses the entire caudal peduncle. Hawaiian specimens measure less than two inches in length.

The habitat of this scorpion fish is in coral and rocky areas from shallow water downward to about 60 feet.

The distribution of this species includes the Hawaiian area, central Polynesia, the East Indies, and the western Indian Ocean.

The original description may be found in Rhodes University, *Ichthyological Bulletin*, 1957, 4:64-65, 68, figure 5, plate 3E.

THE HAIRY SCORPION FISH
144—16 *Scorpaenodes hirsutus* (Smith), 1957

This scorpion fish is a small species of usual proportions. The dorsal fin has 13 spines and usually eight soft rays; the last ray is divided. The anal fin has three spines and five soft rays; the last ray is divided. The pectoral fin has 17 or occasionally 18 rays. The color pattern of the body consists of large, dark mottlings. Hawaiian specimens have been less than two inches in length.

The habitat of this fish is in coral reef areas from shore line to depths of about 125 feet.

Photo by John E. Randall

The distribution of this species extends from Hawaii southward to central Polynesia, westward to Taiwan and southern Japan, through the East Indies, and onward across the Indian Ocean to the coast of Africa and the Red Sea.

For the original description see Rhodes University, *Ichthyological Bulletin*, 1957, 4:63, figure 5, plate 1E.

KELLOGG'S SCORPION FISH
144—17 *Scorpaenodes kelloggi* (Jenkins), 1903

Kellogg's scorpion fish is a small species with a moderately elongated, compressed body and bears some resemblance to *S. parvipinnis.* The head bears many spines to some of which a small dermal flap is attached. There is also a prominent horizontal row of spines across the cheek below the eye which ends in a larger spine at the edge of the opercle. The color of the body is bright brownish, gray, and whitish. There are three, wide, ill-defined, dark, vertical bands across the body. There is a dark blotch below the eye.

From Jordan and Evermann

Most specimens measure less than two inches in length.

The distribution of this species extends from Hawaii to Micronesia and doubtless to adjoining areas.

This fish was named in 1903 in honor of Professor Vernon Lyman Kellogg of the Department of Entomology at Stanford University.

THE SHORE LINE SCORPION FISH
144—18 *Scorpaenodes littoralis* (Tanaka), 1917

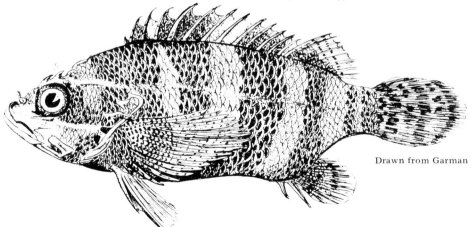

Drawn from Garman

This is a small, uncommon species which exhibits the typical shape of the scorpion fishes. The head is rough and covered with spines. The dorsal fin has 12 spines and nine rays; the last ray is divided. The anal fin has three spines and five rays; the last ray here is likewise divided. Dr. Yachiro Okada describes the color as "dark red with 3 light grayish red cross-bars on the side; there is a black blotch, slightly larger than the pupil, on the lower edge of the opercle and 3 blackish brown stripes radiating downwardly from the lower edge of the eye." The length of the body will reach at least four inches.

The habitat of this species "appears to be rocky or coral areas and coves".

The distribution of this species includes Hawaii, Japan, and doubtless many adjoining areas.

Dr. Wm. N. Eschmeyer and Dr. John E. Randall suggest that the species reported in Hawaii as *S. guamensis* (Quoy and Gaimard), 1824, is probably *S. littoralis,* since *S. guamensis* does not occur in Hawaii.

THE SMALL - FINNED SCORPION FISH
144—19 *Scorpaenodes parvipinnis* (Garret), 1864

The body of this little scorpion fish is elongated and compressed and covered with scales. The dorsal fin is very low and has the basal portion of the whole dorsal fin covered with a sheath of scales. The mouth is large, the eyes are placed high upon the front half of the head, and there are but few dermal flaps. How-

Photo by John E. Randall

ever, the head is covered with scattered spines and a row of spines extends horizontally under the eye to end posteriorly in a larger spine at the opercle. Minute filaments cover the body. The color of the flesh is reddish in life; it is marked with large vertical shadings. It will reach a length of about six inches.

This species inhabits shallow, shore line water where it is relatively common. It is often found hiding under coral heads.

The distribution of this species extends from the Hawaiian area southward into central Polynesia and westward into Micronesia.

THE MOLOKAI SCORPION FISH
144—20 *Scorpaenopsis altirostris* Gilbert, 1905

This scorpion fish is a small, deep water species with a large compressed head and large eyes. The head bears an assortment of spines. Dermal flaps are scattered over the head and body, particularly along the lateral line; the dermal flaps above the eyes are particularly large. The color of the head and snout is purplish; the body is mottled with reddish, greenish, bluish, and white hues; the belly is white in color. The known specimens were less than three inches in length.

This species was described from six specimens captured by the steamer

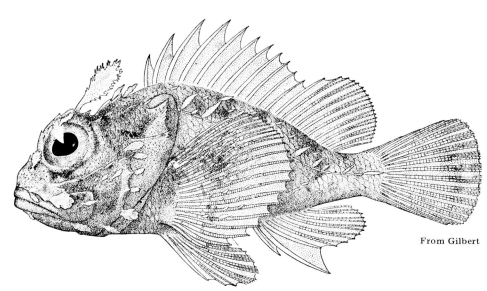

From Gilbert

Albatross in 1902 off the south coast of Molokai at a depth between 43 and 73 fathoms.

The distribution of this species includes the Hawaiian area and doubtless adjoining areas.

THE SHORT-BROWED SCORPION FISH
144—21 *Scorpaenopsis brevifrons* Eschmeyer and Randall, 1975

This is a small scorpion fish with a large head and robust body. The head is covered with spines and dermal flaps occur on both the head and body. The dorsal fin has 12 spines and 9 rays; the last ray is divided. The highest part of the dorsal fin is in the area between the third and sixth spines. The anal fin has three spines and five rays; the last ray is likewise divided.

Photo by John E. Randall

The pectoral fin usually has 19 rays although it may range from 18 to 20 rays; the upper rays are branched at their tips in mature specimens. Eschmeyer and Randall described the color in life as variable; their description follows:

> "Upper part of body and most of head brownish to gray with bluish-green to green areas and some yellow, mottled with white. Lower parts with more red and orange. Pelvic fin red, streaked with white, mostly white distally. Anal fin with prominent white bar across anterior base, greenish in middle, otherwise red streaked with white. Dorsal fin mostly pale, mottled with brown, orange, and green."

The spinous dorsal fin is usually marked with a dark spot near its center. Large specimens will reach a length of nearly five inches.

The habitat of this scorpion fish is in the shallow waters of the shore line to depths of about 100 feet.

The distribution of this species at present includes only the Hawaiian area. It is doubtless more widely distributed.

JENKIN'S SCORPION FISH
Also known as No-hu and No-hu 'o-ma-ka-ha
144—22 *Scorpaenopsis cacopsis* Jenkins, 1901

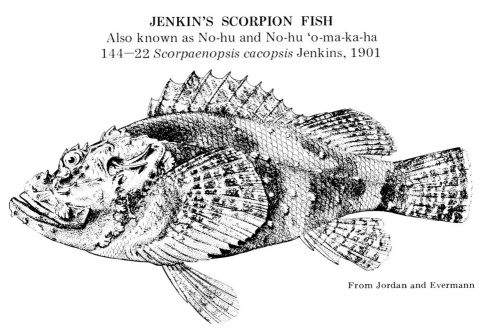

From Jordan and Evermann

The body of this nohu is moderately elongated and resembles its relatives. The head is large and rough and there is an elevated prominence between the eyes and the end of the snout. The eyes are small and the mouth is large and placed at an angle of about 45 degrees. The color of the body is varied and most unevenly distributed. It includes rusty, reddish brown hues, white, and yellow; these colors are scattered, blotched, and spotted in an irregular manner over the body. It is lighter in color below. Large specimens will reach a length of at least 20 inches.

The habitat of this fish is on the outer edge of the reef at depths below 20 feet. It is reasonably common and occasionally appears in markets.

The distribution of this species includes Hawaii and doubtless adjoining areas.

THE HUMPED SCORPION FISH
Also known as No-hu and No-hu 'o-ma-ka-ha
144—23 *Scorpaenopsis diabolus* Cuvier, 1829

The nohu is a stocky, heavy-bodied species with a back which is elevated below about the first five dorsal spines. The head is large and rough-looking with ridges, depressions, spines, and dermal flaps. The mouth is placed at an angle of about 45 degrees and the lower jaw bears a small knob at its tip. The eyes are small and are located high on the head so as to

project above the dorsal outline of the head. The color of the body is gray except under the pectoral fins where it is black, red, orange, and yellow. Large specimens will reach a length of about 12 inches.

The habitat of this species is in the quiet, shallow waters of the shore line. It is occasionally encountered sitting on the bottom in one or two feet of water at low tide. It is almost invisible and is usually noticed only when it moves and thereby exposes the bright colors beneath the pectoral fins.

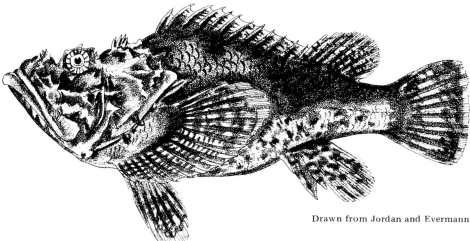

Drawn from Jordan and Evermann

The distribution of this species extends from Hawaii southward to central Polynesia, westward through Micronesia and Melanesia, through the East Indies, and across the Indian Ocean to the coast of Africa and the Red Sea.

In Hawaii, this fish has previously and usually been listed as *S. gibbosus* (Bloch and Schneider), 1801. Recent studies indicate that *S. gibbosus* is an Indian Ocean species and that the Hawaiian species should be known as *S. diabolus.*

FOWLER'S SMALL SCORPION FISH
144—24 *Scorpaenopsis fowleri* (Pietschmann), 1934

Fowler's scorpion fish is possibly the smallest species in this family for mature individuals have measured about 1.5 inches in length. The head is rough and bears many small spines, but there are no dermal flaps on the

body. The dorsal fin has 12 spines and nine rays; the last ray is divided. The anal fin has three spines and five rays; the last ray is likewise divided. The pectoral fin is helpful in identifying this species, because it has but 16 rays, while most others have 17 rays. It is very difficult to distinguish from the young of other species. The color of living specimens is described as "body and fins mottled with red and white."

Drawn from Pietschmann

The habitat of this small fish seems to be from shallow water down to about 100 feet.

The distribution of this species includes Hawaii, central Polynesia, the Marshall Islands, and doubtless many adjoining areas.

The name of this species honors the memory of Dr. Henry Weed Fowler, ichthyologist and student of Indo-Pacific fishes.

GUENTHER'S SCORPION FISH
144—25 *Setarches guentheri* Johnson, 1862

Drawn from Gilbert and Cramer

The body of this scorpion fish is elongated somewhat and strongly compressed; the upper and lower outlines are nearly opposite and equal. The body is covered with very small scales, there are no dermal flaps, and the lateral line consists of a broad, membraneous tube lying outside the scales.

The pectoral fins are very large and the caudal fin is truncated in shape with rounded corners. The color of the body is reddish. Dark specks are scattered over the body and in some places are so dense as to form shaded areas. Larger specimens approach eight inches in length.

The steamer *Albatross* captured specimens in 1891 and 1902 at many locations in the Hawaiian area at depths between about 100 and 350 fathoms.

This fish is widely distributed and extends from Hawaii westward across the entire tropical Pacific and Indian Oceans and on into the western Atlantic Ocean.

This species has been listed in many books as *Setarches remiger* (Gilbert and Cramer), 1897; this last name is a synonym and should be discarded.

THE THREE-SPINED SCORPION FISH
144—26 *Taenianotus triacanthus* Lacepede, 1802

This little scorpion fish has a head and body which are high and extremely compressed. The body is without scales but is covered with short, dermal cirri and a few dermal flaps about the head. The dorsal fin is high, long, and continuous and connects by a membrane to the tail. There seems to be three color phases

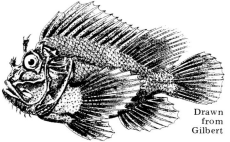

Drawn from Gilbert

of this species: one yellow, one red, and one black. The yellow phase will be found in some books under the name of *T. citrinellus* Gilbert, 1905. Large

436

specimens will reach a length of about four inches.

The habitat of this fish is in coral and algae beds from the shore line down to depths of at least 400 feet, particularly where wave action is strong.

The distribution of this species extends from Hawaii southward to central Polynesia and westward through Micronesia and Melanesia, through the East Indies, and onward across the Indian Ocean to the coast of Africa.

THE DWARF ROCK FISH OR VELVET FISH FAMILY

145 *Family Caracanthidae*

The caracanthids are a very small group of fishes which are related to the scorpion fishes and occasionally included in that family. They are small, nearly circular in outline, and extremely compressed. Their bodies are covered with a blanket of small, velvet-like villae or papillae except upon the fins. The dorsal fin has seven or eight spines and there are either two or three spines on the operculum. The ventral fins are present, but are rudimentary and somewhat difficult to locate.

The habitat of all members of this family is in the coral heads where the water is in motion. They are poor swimmers and remain hidden deep in the coral colony.

The distribution of this family is limited to the tropical Indo-Pacific area. Of this small group, at least two species are known from this area.

THE SPOTTED CARACANTHID FISH

145—1 *Caracanthus maculatus* (Gray), 1831

The body of this fish is small, oval in outline, and extremely compressed. The entire body except for the fins is covered with a coating of small, velvet-like papillae. The color of the body is a slate blue above and olive gray beneath. Most of the body is covered with dark, reddish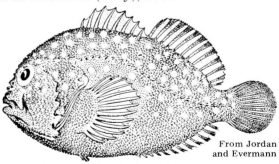

From Jordan and Evermann

spots. Large specimens will not exceed two inches in length.

The habitat of this fish is in the coral heads where there is moving water.

This species is distributed from Hawaii southward to central Polynesia, westward through Micronesia and Melanesia, through the East Indies, and across the Indian Ocean.

GRAY'S CARACANTHID FISH
145—2 *Caracanthus unipinnus* (Gray), 1831

The body of this species resembles that of *C. maculatus* in general outline and structure. It lacks the dark, reddish spots of *C. maculatus* and does
not have the dorsal fin as deeply notched as in that species. The color of the
body is reported as dark buff to brown above and lighter below. Large
specimens will not exceed two inches in length.

The habitat of this fish is in the coral heads of *Acropora* and other
stony corals.

The distribution of this species extends from Hawaii and Wake Island
southward to central Polynesia, westward through Micronesia and Melanesia,
through the East Indies, and across the Indian Ocean.

THE FLAT-HEAD FISH FAMILY
146 *Family Platycephalidae (Bembradidae, Bembridae)*

The flat-head fishes have long, slender, tapering bodies and a head
which is greatly depressed. The head bears a long snout, a large mouth, and
an array of spines. There are two, separate dorsal fins and the pelvic fins are
widely separated in keeping with their sedentary life.

Flat-head fishes are bottom dwellers and live in estuaries and on the
continental shelves. Here they seek out the muddy bottoms where they
settle into the mud with only their eyes showing. Some species are
numerous, particularly in southern Australia, and are captured in trawls for
food.

This family is distributed from Hawaii, Japan, and China southward to
Australia and westward across the Indian Ocean to Africa and the eastern
Atlantic Ocean.

Of several dozen species, at least one occurs in this area.

THE ROSY FLAT-HEAD FISH
146—1 *Bembradium roseum* Gilbert, 1905

Drawn from Gilbert

The body of this flat-head fish is long and spindle-shaped and tapers
uniformly toward the tail. The head is long, narrow, and depressed and
bears a long snout, a large mouth, large eyes, and an array of spines. The

color of the body is an olive hue with reddish colors on the upper part of the body and on the head. The belly is a dull white. Known specimens have not exceeded four inches in length.

This species was first described from two specimens captured in 1902 by the steamer Albatross in the Pailolo Channel between Molokai and Maui at a depth of 138 fathoms.

The distribution of this species includes the Hawaiian area and doubtless adjoining areas.

THE RAT-TAIL OR FLAT-HEAD FISH FAMILY
147 *Family Hoplichthyidae (Oplichthyidae)*

This family includes a small group of unusual, deep-water fishes with large flat heads and long slender bodies. The scales which normally cover the body are absent and their place is taken in part by a longitudinal series of bony scutes or plates which cover a portion of the back and sides. There are two dorsal fins.

The distribution of this family includes the Pacific and Indian Oceans from Hawaii and Japan southward and westward.

Of this small family, at least two species are known from this area.

THE YELLOW RAT-TAIL FISH
147—1 *Hoplichthys citrinus* Gilbert, 1905

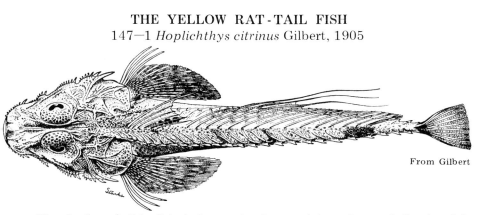

From Gilbert

The body of this fish is long, slender, and tapering and the head is flattened and bears a wide snout. The back and sides of the body are covered in part by a longitudinal series of 27 bony plates. The color of this fish is a bright, lemon yellow or orange-yellow above, including the fins, and a white or silvery color beneath. A black blotch is present at the base of the last dorsal spine. Known specimens are less than eight inches in length.

This species was first described from specimens captured in 1902 by the steamer *Albatross* at a number of locations in Hawaii between 116 and 220 fathoms. The diet of this fish includes crabs and other fishes.

The distribution of this species includes the Hawaiian area and doubtless adjoining area.

THE DEEP WATER RAT-TAIL FISH
147—2 *Hoplichthys platophrys* Gilbert, 1905

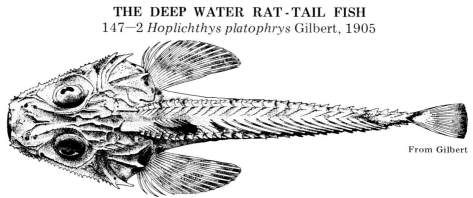

From Gilbert

This small, rare, deep water fish has a long, slender, tapering body and a wide, flat head. The back and sides are covered in part by a longitudinal series of 27 plates. The color of this fish in alcohol was described as light olive. The spinous dorsal fin is marked with a broad, black bar. The single known specimen measured three inches in length.

This species was described from a single specimen, possibly immature, which was captured in 1902 by the steamer *Albatross* off Laysan Island at a depth of 351 fathoms.

Recent studies seem to indicate that this specimen is a young of *H. citrinus;* this species is therefore probably not valid.

THE ARMORED SEA ROBIN FISH FAMILY
Also known as Crocodile Fish and Deep-water Gurnards
148 *Family Peristediidae (Triglidae)*

The fishes of this family are very unusual looking, deep water forms. They possess an elongated, spindle-shaped body which tapers uniformly toward the tail. The head is wide, low, depressed, narrowed toward the front, and completely covered with bony plates. Extending forward from each side of the head is an amazing, horn-like, bony projection which gives this fish a most bizarre appearance. The body is likewise covered with smaller, movable, bony plates, each bearing a curved spine. The mouth is usually small, placed beneath the head, and bears no teeth. The dorsal fin is usually continuous, but it may be either deeply notched or completely divided. Most species are a light reddish color.

The habitat of these fishes is on the bottoms of all temperate and tropical seas. They are sluggish, feeble animals which grope over the ocean bottom for their food.

Of less than 20 species, at least two are known to occur in this area.

105—20 *Caranx ignobilis*

105—10 *Gnathanodon speciosus*

110—6 *Labroides phthirophagus*

109—1 *Dascyllus albisella* (upper)
104—17 *Chaetodon fremblii* (lower)

110 *Pseudojuloides cerasinus*
Blue Male (upper); Reddish Female (lower)

110—40 *Halichoeres ornatissimus*

Plate 17

110—2 *Bodianus bilunulatus* Photo by James H. O'Neill

Photo by James H. O'Neill
110—19 *Hemipteronotus taeniourus* (adult)

Photo by Scott Johnson
110—19 *Hemipteronotus taeniourus* (young)

Photo by James H. O'Neill
110—32 *Coris gaimardi* (adult)

Photo by Scott Johnson
110—32 *Coris gaimardi* (young)

Plate 18

110—26 *Thalassoma lutescens*   Photo by James H. O'Neill

110—29 *Gomphosus varius* (male)   Photo by James H. O'Neill

110—31 *Coris flavovittata*   Photo by James H. O'Neill

110—34 *Coris venusta*   Photo by James H. O'Neill

Plate 19

Photo by James H. O'Neill
110—35 *Stethojulis balteata*

Photo by Scott Johnson
111—9 *Calotomus zonarcha*

111—7 *Scarus sordidus* Photo by Karl Frogner

112—4 *Cirrhitops fasciatus* Photo by James H. O'Neill

Plate 20

112—6 *Oxycirrhites typus*

Photo by James H. O'Neill

Photo by Frank W. Adams

112—2 *Paracirrhites forsteri* (adult)

Photo by Scott Johnson

112—1 *Paracirrhites arcatus*

112—2 *Paracirrhites forsteri* (sub-adult)

Photo by Frank W. Adams

Plate 21

113—1 *Chilodactylus vittata*

136—1 *Acanthurus achilles*

126—12 *Plagiotremus rhinorhynchus*

136—2 *Acanthurus glaucopareius*

136—3 *Acanthurus dussumieri*

136—7 *Acanthurus nigrofuscus*

136—14 *Ctenochaetus strigosus*

Plate 22

136—9 *Acanthurus olivaceus*

136—15 *Zebrasoma flavescens*

136—16 *Zebrasoma veliferum*

136—20 *Naso lituratus*
Nighttime Coloration

136—20 *Naso lituratus*
Daytime Coloration

Plate 23

137—1 *Zanclus cornutus*

Photo by Frank W. Adams

Plate 24

Photo by Frank W. Adams
139—18 *Cottogobius yongei*

Photo by James H. O'Neill
144—1 *Dendrochirus barberi*

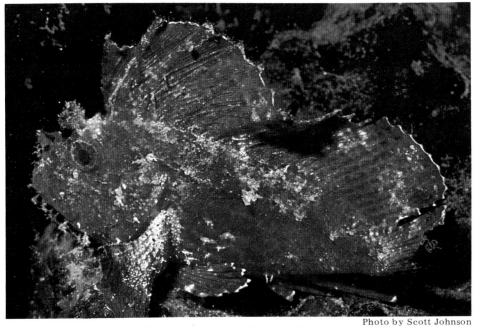

Photo by Scott Johnson
144—26 *Taenianotus triacanthus* (reddish color phase)

Photo by Scott Johnson
144—26 *Taenianotus triacanthus*
(light color phase)

Photo by James H. O'Neill
144—26 *Taenianotus triacanthus*
(dark color phase)

Plate 25

144—8 *Pterois sphex*

Photo by Frank W. Adams

Photo by Karl Frogner
157—9 *Xanthichthys mento*

149—1 *Dactyloptena orientalis*

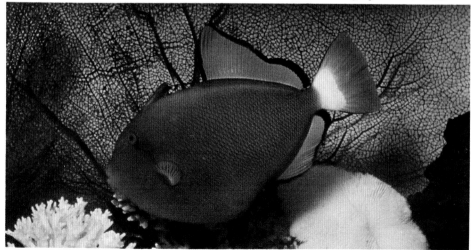

157—4 *Melichthys vidua*

Photo by Douglas Faulkner

Plate 26

157—6 *Rhinecanthus rectangulus*

Photo by James H. O'Neill

Photo by Frank W. Adams

104—17 *Chaetodon fremblii* (upper) and 157—7 *Sufflamen bursa* (lower)

Plate 27

158—1 *Pervagor spilosoma*　　　Photo by Scott Johnson

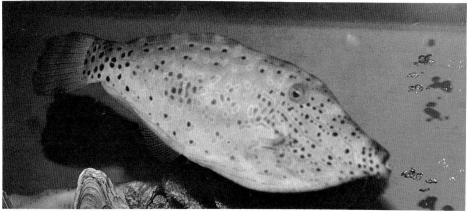

159—2 *Osbeckia scripta*　　　Photo by James H. O'Neill

Photo by Frank W. Adams

160—1 *Ostracion meleagris* (male)

Plate 28

160—1 *Ostracion meleagris* (female)   Photo by Scott Johnson

160—4 *Lactoria fornasini*   Photo by Scott Johnson

162—1 *Arothron hispidus*   Photo by Scott Johnson

Plate 29

163—4 *Canthigaster jactator* Photo by Scott Johnson

163—1 *Canthigaster amboinensis* Photo by James H. O'Neill

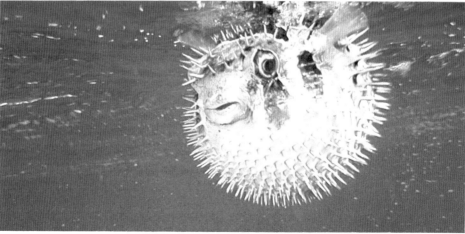

164—1 *Diodon holacanthus* Photo by Scott Johnson

Plate 30

164—1 *Diodon holacanthus*

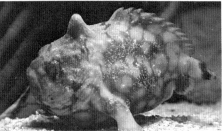

167—4 *Antennatus bigibbus*

167 *Antennarius* species

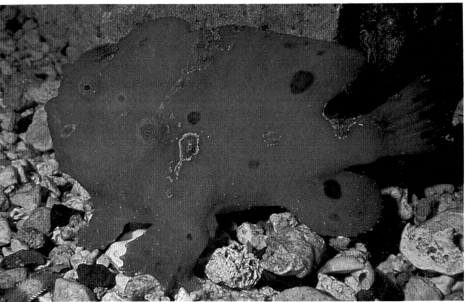

167—5 *Antennarius chironectes*

Plate 31

167—7 *Antennarius moluccensis* Photo by Frank W. Adams

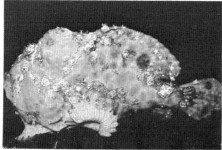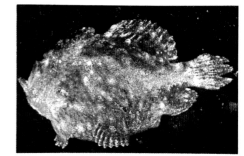

Photo by Douglas Faulkner 167—7 *Antennarius moluccensis*

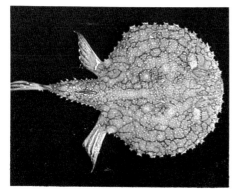

Dorsal 169—3 *Halieutaea retifera* Photos by Spencer Tinker
Ventral

Plate 32

THE SMALL ARMORED SEA ROBIN
148—1 *Peristedion hians* Gilbert and Cramer, 1897

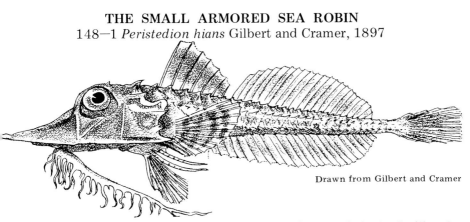

Drawn from Gilbert and Cramer

The skull of this fish is covered with bony plates and the body likewise is encased in several series of movable, spongy, bony plates, each of which bears a sharp, recurved spine. The number of plates covering the body is as follows: dorsal series, 30 plates; upper lateral series, 34 plates; lower lateral series, 25 plates; and the ventral series, 26 plates. A single, bony horn extends forward from each corner of the snout. The chin bears a large barbel with many branches. The color of the body is a dull reddish hue. The spinous dorsal fin is black. Adult specimens apparently reach a length of about eight inches.

This species was described from specimens obtained in 1891 and 1902 by the steamer *Albatross* in various locations about Hawaii. It is apparently fairly common at depths between 225 and 350 fathoms. It is a bottom dweller and feeds upon small crustaceans.

The distribution of this species includes the Hawaiian area.

More recent books may list this species as *Satyrichthys hians* (Gilbert and Cramer), 1897.

THE LARGE ARMORED SEA ROBIN
148—2 *Peristedion engyceros* Gunther, 1871

The body of this sea robin is long and slender and tapers uniformly to the tail. The head is wide and flat and narrows toward the snout which is nearly square in outline. The two forward corners of the snout each bear a slender horn which projects directly forward. These horns are parallel to each other and are separated by a distance equal to their length. The plates which cover the body are arranged in the following longitudinal rows: dorsal series, 29 or 30 plates; upper lateral series, 34 or 35 plates; lower lateral series, 23 or 24 plates; and the ventral series, 26 or 27 plates. The color of the upper side of the body is pink with yellowish tinges; it is white below. The specimen in the accompanying photograph measured 13 inches in length.

The habitat of this fish is on sandy bottoms at depths between 150 and 250 fathoms. The steamer *Albatross* captured 60 specimens at 17 different dredging stations at the time of its visit to Hawaii in 1902.

The distribution of this species includes the Hawaiian area and

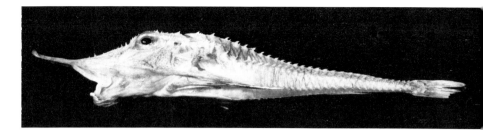

doubtless adjoining area.

    Recent books may list this species as *Satyrichthys engyceros* (Gunther) 1871.

THE FLYING GURNARD FISH FAMILY
149 *Family Dactylopteridae (Cephalacanthidae)*

These gurnards have a rather slender body which tapers quite uniformly to the tail. The head is short and blunt and is covered above with bones which are united to form a shield over the top of the head. The preopercle bears a large, long, strong spine which projects backward. There are two dorsal fins on the back which may be separated by a small, immovable spine between them. In front of the dorsal fin is a single, great, tall, elongated spine. The pectoral fins are enormous in size and quite fan-shaped; the first five or six rays of this fin are detached and are used to explore the sandy bottom beneath the fish. The pelvic fins are placed far forward on the body and used somewhat as legs to support the fish off the ocean floor.

These gurnards are bottom living forms and, in spite of their name, are unable to fly. They occur in all warm and tropical seas except the eastern Pacific Ocean.

This family includes only two or three species of which at least one is known from this area.

THE EASTERN FLYING GURNARD FISH
Also known as Lo-lo-a-'u and Pi-na-o
149—1 *Dactyloptena orientalis* (Cuvier and Valenciennes), 1829

The body of this gurnard is elongated, nearly circular in cross-section, and tapers gradually to the tail. The head is quite large, somewhat box-like in shape, and bears rather large eyes and a small mouth; from the side this head looks somewhat like that of a frog. The body is covered with scales including four, keel-like scales which are found low on the side of the body

near the tail. The dorsal fin is in two parts. The spinous dorsal fin has th
first two spines separated from the rest and placed farther forward on th
body; of these two spines, the first is very long and conspicuous. Th
pectoral fins are enormous, fan-like in
shape, and are the most astonishing
feature of this fish. The paired pelvic
fins are placed far forward under the
body and are used as legs to keep the
fish off the ocean floor; the fish is
able to take steps with them and to
walk slowly along upon them. The
color of the body is a dull, greenish
blue above and whitish below; it is
marked on the body and pectoral fins
with dark spots which have orange
edged. It will reach a length of about 15 inches.

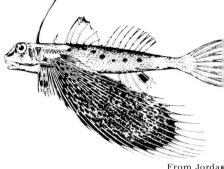

From Jordan
and Everman

The habitat of this fish is in the shallow waters of the shore line and in
deeper water beyond the reef; here it spends the major portion of its time
upon the bottom. It is easily captured with a hook and line. It is very
doubtful if it can fly or even sail through the air for more than three or four
feet.

The distribution of this fish extends from Hawaii and Japan southward
to central Polynesia, westward through Micronesia and Melanesia, through
the East Indies, and across the Indian Ocean to the coast of Africa.

THE SEA-MOTH OR SEA-DRAGON FISH FAMILY
150 *Family Pegasidae*

The sea moths are small fishes of very unusual appearance. Their
bodies are covered by a series of bony rings; these rings are fused on the
front of the body to form a rigid body shell, while the rings on the posterior
portion of the body are not fused together and therefore permit limited
movement of the abdomen and tail. The head bears a long snout or rostrum
which ends in a knob in some species. The eyes are of medium size and the
mouth, which is placed below the head, is small and toothless. The dorsal
fin is short and small and bears only five rays. The anal fin is small and the
pelvic fins are likewise reduced.

The habitat of these fishes is on the bottom in moderately deep water.
They are reported to prefer beds of sea weeds.

These fishes were undoubtedly named by von Linne for *Pegasus*, the
winged horse of ancient Greek mythology.

The distribution of this family includes the warm tropical seas of the
western Pacific and Indian Ocean; they extend from Hawaii to Australia,
from Japan to the East Indies, and westward across the Indian Ocean to the
coast of Africa.

Of about one-half dozen species, at least one is known from this area.

THE HAWAIIAN SEA-MOTH FISH
150—1 *Pegasus papilio* Gilbert, 1905
The bony plates which cover the body are fused to form a box-like shell

Above and Below: Dorsal Views

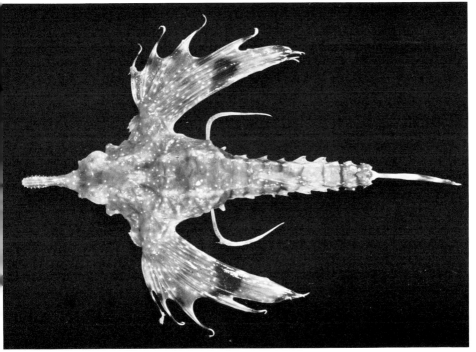

over most of the forward part of the body; the plates on the posterior portion of the body are fused so as to form eight, movable rings which cover the body from the anterior, box-like shell to the tail. A conspicuous feature of the head is a long, slender snout which ends in a knob that is covered with short spines. The dorsal and anal fins are small, the pectoral fins are extremely large and fan-like, and the ventral or pelvic fins have been reduced to a single filament. The color of the body seems to be variable. Most specimens were either olive or yellowish olive above; the upper side is mottled with reddish and speckled with small, white spots. A broad, dark band extends across the middle of the pectoral fins. The lower surface of the body is whitish. Large specimens will reach a length of about three inches.

The habitat of this species is in moderately deep water. The specimens captured in 1902 in the dredging by the steamer *Albatross* were taken between 24 and 83 fathoms. Specimens are obtained by fishermen and others from time to time.

The distribution of this species includes the Hawaiian area and doubtless adjoining areas.

THE TURBOTS OR
LEFT-EYED FLOUNDER FISH FAMILY

Also known as the Sand Dabs, Bastard Halibut, and Brills

151 *Family Bothidae (Paralichthyidae, Scophthalmidae)*

The flounders and their relatives are amazing fishes because of their unusual habit of swimming on their side. They begin life swimming in an upright position as other fishes do, but, as they begin to assume their adult form and while still very small, they turn over on their side and remain on their side for the remainder of their life. The upper side develops color in the particular pattern of that species, but the lower surface remains white. The eye, which was originally on the lower side, slowly moves until it is located upon the upper side of the head; this means that the upper side of the head now has two eyes and the lower side has none. Many other things about these fishes are unequal and asymmetrical; the pectoral and pelvic fins are unequal, the eyes are unevenly placed, and the mouth is twisted and uneven.

The fishes of this family are all flat-bodied, oval in outline, and usually have their eyes upon the left side of their head. These fishes therefore have the right side of their body down and the left side uppermost. Their bodies are covered with small or medium-sized scales and their lateral line is single, without branches, and is greatly curved at its anterior end. The fins possess no spines and are unusual in various details. The dorsal fin is long and usually begins above the eye or anterior to it; the anal fin is long and continuous; and the caudal fin is free and not attached to either the dorsal or anal fins as in the tongue fishes. The pelvic fins have six or fewer segmented rays and are unequal, uneven, and off center. The pelvic fin of the upper side is usually placed exactly on the abdominal ridge, but the fin on the lower or right side is placed above the midline and its first ray is slightly farther back than the first ray of the upper side. The head is also compressed and bears a rather large mouth with a prominent lower jaw which is tipped with a small knob. In this family, the margin of the preopercle is free and is not embedded in the skin as in the soles.

The members of this family are bottom dwellers; here they lie unnoticed or partly buried in the sand with only their eyes showing. From this position, they make short dashes to capture small fishes and crustaceans. Although most members of this family are small or medium in size, a few get quite large; all are edible.

The distribution of this family extends from shallow to deep water in all tropical and temperate seas.

Of this large family, about a dozen species are known from this area.

THE WEAK FLOUNDER
151—1 *Arnoglossus debilis* (Gilbert), 1905

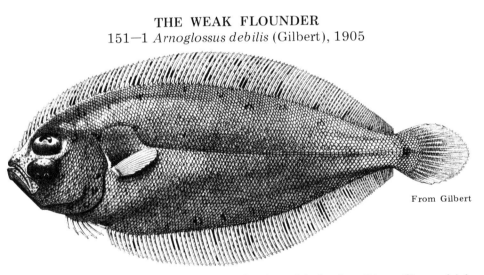

From Gilbert

This small flounder has a rather slender, thin body with outlines which curve uniformly toward the tail. There is a slight indentation in the outline of the snout just in front of the upper eye. The dorsal fin begins far forward on the snout and extends to the caudal peduncle; the anal fin is about equal in size but has a shorter base. In this species the caudal rays are forked. The right pectoral fin is much smaller than the left, but they both have 13 rays. The left pelvic fin has a longer base and is situated on the ridge of the abdomen but is deflected to the left at the rear. The color of the body is olive brown above with fine specklings; it is semi-transparent. Known specimens have reached a length of seven inches.

This species is based upon specimens dredged in 1902 by the steamer *Albatross* at various locations in Hawaii at depths between 122 and 220 fathoms.

The distribution of this species includes the Hawaiian area.

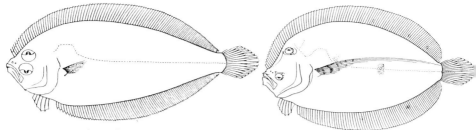

Arnoglossus debilis   *Bothus mancus*

THE COMMON FLOUNDER
Also known as Pa-ki-'i and Mo-e-o-ne
151—2 *Bothus mancus* (Broussonet), 1782
This is a common species, but difficult to identify.   The body is

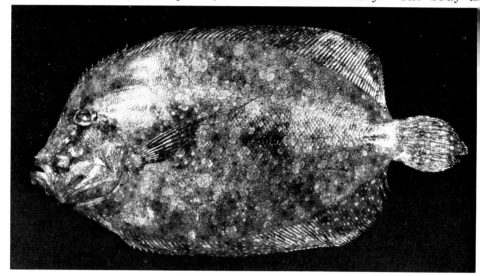

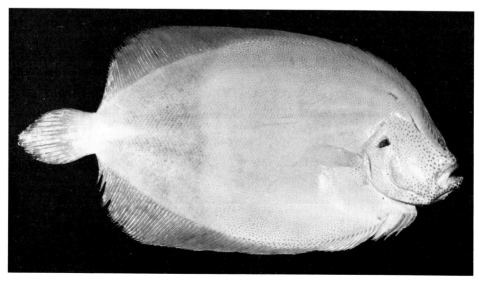

elliptical in shape with uniformly curving upper and lower outlines. The dorsal fin begins far forward on the snout and contains about 100 rays; the anal fin contains between 74 and 80 rays. The caudal fin is bluntly pointed. The upper or left pectoral fin is long and has filamentous rays which extend to the base of the caudal fin. The head bears a small oblique mouth and contains from nine to eleven gill rakers on the lower limb of the first gill arch; the upper limb contains no gill rakers. The eyes are quite small and a bit unusual in that the lower eye is placed completely in advance of the upper eye. The color of the body is brownish with an irregular pattern of mottlings, blotches, and spots. There are two, large, irregular, dark areas on the upper side of the body between the head and the tail. One of these spots is located just behind the base of the pectoral fin and the other is midway between the base of the pectoral fin and the tail. The lower surface of the body is white, but contains faint brown specklings on the head. Large specimens measure between 14 and 16 inches.

The females of this species differ from the males and may even be mistaken for different species. In the females, the eyes are closer together, the left or upper pectoral fin lacks the long filaments, and there is no bony tubercle on the snout.

The habitat of this fish is in the shallow waters of the shore line where the bottom is sandy.

The distribution of this species extends from Hawaii southward to central Polynesia, westward through Micronesia and the East Indies, and across the Indian Ocean to the coast of Africa.

THE SPOTTED FLOUNDER
151—3 *Bothus pantherinus* (Ruppell), 1828
The body of this flounder is slightly more elongated than that of *B. mancus.* The dorsal fin has between 80 and 90 rays and the anal fin

has about 70 rays. Some of the rays of the pectoral fin in the male are produced into long filaments which may extend beyond the end of the tail. The ventral fins are close together; the left fin is slightly larger than the right. The eyes are prominent, but the lower eye is not completely in advance of the upper eye as in *B. mancus.* The color of the body is brownish with spotting and mottling in an irregular pattern. There are two darker areas along the side of the body which are equally spaced between the lower eye and the tail. The body is covered with irregular areas with dark borders. Large specimens will reach a length of about 18 inches.

The males and females of this species are unlike in some particulars and may be mistaken for other species. The females have the eyes placed closer together, the upper pectoral fin does not have the long filaments found in the males, and there is no bony tubercle on the snout of the females.

The habitat of this fish is in shallow water where there is a sandy bottom. It is a common species.

The distribution of this species extends from Hawaii southward to central Polynesia, westward through Micronesia and the East Indies, and across the Indian Ocean to the coast of Africa.

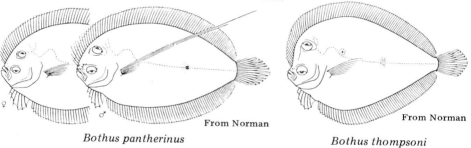

From Norman

Bothus pantherinus

From Norman

Bothus thompsoni

THOMPSON'S FLOUNDER
151—4 *Bothus thompsoni* (Fowler), 1923

This small fish was first described as a new species under the name of *Platophrys thompsoni* Fowler, 1923, from a single Hawaiian specimen which measured less than five inches in length. In the years which followed, this species was regarded as a synonym of *Bothus bleekeri* Steindachner, 1861, and was listed under it. Recent studies by Dr. Paul Struhsaker and others indicate that *B. thompsoni* is a valid species from Hawaii and that *B. bleekeri* probably does not occur in this area.

Thompson's flounder is a small species with an oval outline. The head is deep, the eyes are widely separated, and the mouth is small. The rays in the dorsal fin number between about 84 and 95, while the rays in the anal fin are usually between 64 and 70 in number. The rays of the pectoral fin of the upper side number between 10 and 14 and are not elongated, while in *B. bleekeri* they number only 8 or 9 and are elongated. The caudal rays are usually 16 in number, while in most other species of *Bothus* they are usually 17 in number. The color of the body is white below; older males may show a dusky white color anteriorly. The upper surface is a light olive green color.

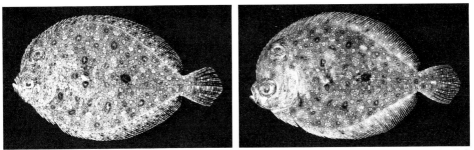

Photos by John E. Randall

Female   Male

There is a significant, single, large, dark spot on the midline of the body about two-thirds of the distance to the tail; in addition, there are two, smaller, dark spots near the pectoral fin. Light blue spots are scattered over the entire head, body, and fins. The eyes of males are father apart than those of females. Known specimens are less than five inches in length.

The habitat of this fish is on the sandy bottoms at depths between about 200 and possibly 400 feet.

The distribution of this species includes the Hawaiian area.

The name of this species honors the memory of Mr. John W. Thompson, an artist and exhibit specialist at the Bernice Pauahi Bishop Museum in the early years of this century.

GILBERT'S RARE FLOUNDER
151—5 *Chascanopsetta prorigera* Gilbert, 1905

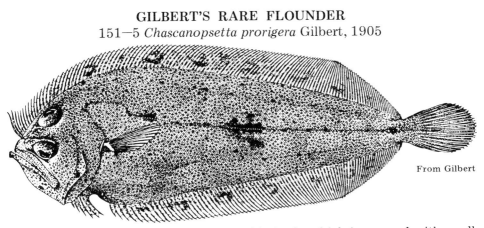

From Gilbert

This small flounder has a slender, thin body which is covered with small scales. The head is quite large and deep and bears a rather large mouth which is placed at an angle of about 45 degrees; the lower jaw projects a short distance beyond the upper jaw. The upper eye is placed slightly behind the lower eye. The color of the body is a light olive brown with speckles of a lighter brown color. Three, small, irregular, darker blotches are located along the lateral line. Large specimens will reach a length of about 12 inches.

This species was described from a single specimen measuring over nine inches in length which was captured in 1902 by the steamer *Albatross* off the north coast of Maui at a depth between 178 and 202 fathoms.

The distribution of this species includes the Hawaiian area.

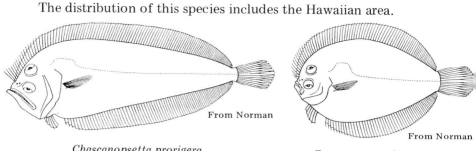

Chascanopsetta prorigera　　From Norman

Engyprosopon hawaiiensis　　From Norman

THE HAWAIIAN FLOUNDER
151—6 *Engyprosopon hawaiiensis* Jordan and Evermann, 1903

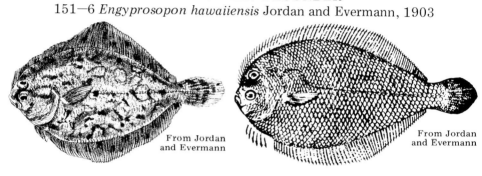

From Jordan
and Evermann

From Jordan
and Evermann

This little flounder is somewhat elongated, has a body which is deepest at about the end of the pectoral fin, and has an unusually deep head. The body is covered with large scales and the lateral line is strongly arched in front and thereafter is straight. The eyes are small and widely separated. The left pectoral fin is short and pointed and the caudal fin is rounded. The color of the body is olive brown with darker areas which may have the shape of incomplete circles. There may also be about four, curved, incomplete, darker cross-bars on the caudal fin. The lower side of the body is a creamy white. Adult specimens measure about four inches in length. The habitat of this fish is in the shallow waters of the shore line.

The distribution of this species includes the Hawaiian area.

GILBERT'S SMALL FLOUNDER
151—7 *Engyprosopon xenandrus* Gilbert, 1905

The body of this small flounder is only moderately elongated. The dorsal and ventral outlines are quite uniformly curved except for a down-ward curve in front of the upper eye and an indentation above the lower eye near the beginning of the dorsal fin. The body is covered with large scales and the lateral line contains a high arch anteriorly and thereafter extends straight to the tail. The eyes are quite large and well separated, both possess a spine on their anterior margin, and the males bear a semi-circular mem-brane around the posterior side of the eye. The color of the body is grayish with blackish shades and mottlings including three, irregular, blackish areas

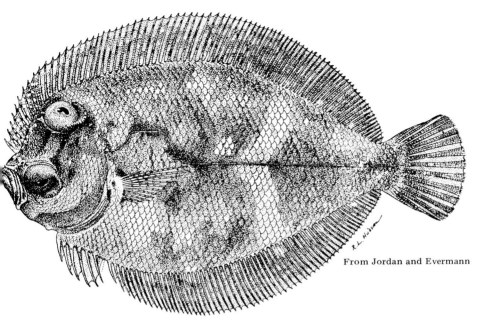

From Jordan and Evermann

on the sides, and two, dark, parallel lines connecting the eyes. The dorsal fin and the snout are marked anteriorly with yellowish spots. Adult specimens will reach a length of about four inches.

The habitat of this fish is on the sandy bottom on the outer side of the reef; it is reported to be common at depths between 40 and 100 fathoms.

The distribution of this species includes the Hawaiian area.

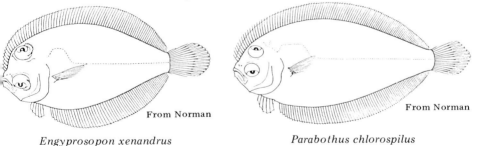

From Norman

From Norman

Engyprosopon xenandrus   *Parabothus chlorospilus*

THE GREEN-SPOTTED FLOUNDER
151—8 *Parabothus chlorospilus* (Gilbert), 1905

This deep-water flounder is somewhat slender in outline, possesses eyes which are quite large and widely separated, and displays a lateral line only upon the left side of the body. The pectoral fin of the upper or left side is about twice the size of the right pectoral fin and has the second and third rays somewhat elongated. The left ventral or pelvic fin is attached to the ridge in front of the anus and has the membrane of the last ray deflected toward the left. The rays of the caudal fin are branched; all other rays are unbranched. The color of the body is an olive gray and is speckled with olive brown. There are several longitudinal series of olive green spots with dark borders on the body and greenish yellow spots on the rostrum.

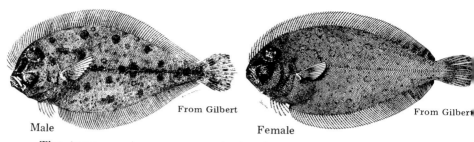

Male   From Gilbert   Female   From Gilbert

The type specimen measured about seven inches in length and was captured in 1902 by the steamer *Albatross* off the north coast of Maui between 78 and 85 fathoms.

Additional specimens described under the name of *Platophrys inermis* Gilbert, 1905, came from depths of over 1,000 feet.

The distribution of this species includes the Hawaiian area.

THE COARCTATE FLOUNDER
151—9 *Parabothus coarctatus* (Gilbert), 1905

This flounder is a slender species which somewhat resembles *P. chlorospilus*. The body has uniformly curving outlines, is covered with small scales, and bears a lateral line only upon the left side. In the dorsal fin, the first ray is inserted on the lower or blind side and the second ray is on the ridge. The color of the body is light olive brown; there are many irregular, green spots of varying sizes each with a darker ring or border; in addition, there is a row of larger spots near the border of the dorsal and anal fins. The dorsal and anal fins are also mottled. Specimens will reach a length of over 11 inches.

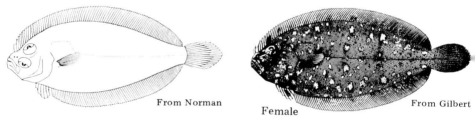

From Norman   Female   From Gilbert

The specimens dredged by the steamer *Albatross* in 1902 came from several Hawaiian islands and were taken at depths between 138 and 220 fathoms.

The distribution of this species includes the Hawaiian area.

THE LONG-JAWED FLOUNDER
151—10 *Pelecanichthys crumenalis* Gilbert and Cramer, 1897

This unusual flounder has a slender body which is very compressed and which tapers uniformly toward the tail. Most of the head and all of the body are covered with small scales. The head is rather obliquely situated and bears an amazingly long and slender lower jaw. The eyes are on the left side of the head and are quite large in size; the upper eye is located farther forward than the lower eye. The color is reported as light brown with darker brown spots. The abdomen, which is unusually short, is marked by vertical, blue-black stripes. It will reach a length of about ten inches.

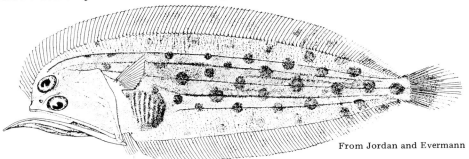

From Jordan and Evermann

Very little is known about this fish. It lives over muddy and sandy bottoms and feeds on small fishes, shrimps, and other small crustacea.

This species was first known from specimens obtained in 1891 and 1902 by the steamer *Albatross* at depths between 238 and 344 fathoms.

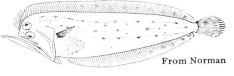

From Norman

The distribution of this species includes the Hawaiian area.

THE ROUND-BODIED FLOUNDER
151—11 *Taeniopsetta radula* Gilbert, 1905

This small, deep water flounder has a flat body which is unusually rounded in outline. The body is covered with small scales and the lateral line is present on the upper surface, but not on the under side. The head is quite short, the eyes are upon the left side, and the mouth is very small. The dorsal fin begins far forward of the eyes, is continuous to the tail, and has the twelfth to the eighteenth rays elongated; the first four rays of the anal fin are likewise extended. The pelvic or ventral fins are

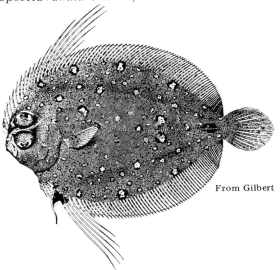

From Gilbert

equal and opposite and contain a spine between them. The color of the body is reported as light olive brown and is marked with darker brown spots and markings. Dark rings are scattered along the bases of the dorsal and anal fins and a dark area is located on the caudal peduncle. This fish will reach a length of about five or six inches.

Little is known of the habits of this flounder. It lives on the bottom in rather deep water and seems to be reasonably common between 50 and 100 fathoms.

The distribution of this species includes the Hawaiian area.

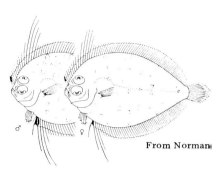

From Norman

THE RIGHT-EYED FLOUNDER AND HALIBUT FISH FAMILY

152 *Family Pleuronectidae (Hippoglossidae, Samaridae, Rhombosoleidae)*

The right-eyed flounders resemble in many ways the members of the Family *Bothidae* or left-eyed flounders. They both begin life in an upright position and later turn onto their side; they both have eyes which migrate from the lower to the upper side of the head; they both lack spines in their fins; they both have oval, compressed bodies with a single, unbranched lateral line; and they both enjoy the same mode of life upon the bottom of the sea.

The differences between these families are also interesting. In this family, the eyes are usually on the right side and the optic nerve to the left eye is always dorsal in position. The pectoral fins are well developed and more equal in size than in the *Bothidae* and, in some species, the left pectoral fin is absent. The pelvic fins are usually symmetrically arranged, possess a short base, and are placed one on each side of the abdominal ridge; however, a few are asymmetrical and have a long base as in the *Bothidae*. The dorsal fin usually begins in the area above the eye and is therefore not as far forward as in the *Bothidae;* the dorsal and anal fins are always free from attachment to the caudal fin. On the head, the preoperculum has a free margin; the jaws on the upper side are straight, while those of the lower side are curved; and the teeth are better developed on the blind side. The eggs of these flounders lack the oil globule which is present in the eggs of the *Bothidae.*

Flounders and halibuts make their home on the continental shelves of arctic, temperate, and tropical seas. Most are marine, but a few species live in estuaries and some are in fresh water. In tropical waters, they are neither abundant nor of large size; several species inhabit deeper water.

Of this large family, at least three species are known from this area.

THE HAWAIIAN RIGHT-EYED FLOUNDER

152—1 *Poecilopsetta hawaiiensis* Gilbert, 1905

This right-eyed flounder has a very thin, elliptical body with dorsal and ventral outlines which are uniformly curved from head to tail. The body is somewhat transparent along its upper and lower margins. The dorsal fin begins at about the middle of the upper eye and, together with the anal fin, extends to the base of the outer caudal ray. The right pectoral fin is longer than the left, has ten rays and a black border, and bears scales upon the rays. The lateral line is arched in front and thereafter extends straight to the tail. The eyes are large and the mouth is small. The color of the body is a brownish hue marked with fine spots; a row of larger, round, dark spots marks the dorsal and anal fins, and there are two black spots at the edge of the caudal fin. It will reach a length of about six inches.

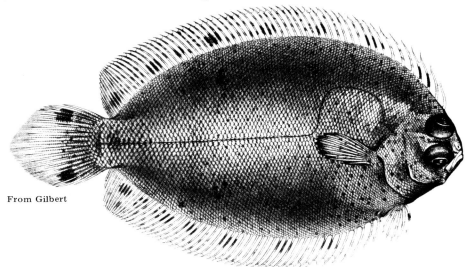

From Gilbert

The steamer *Albatross* captured a few specimens in 1902 off various Hawaiian Islands at depths between 128 and 238 fathoms.

The distribution of this species includes the Hawaiian area.

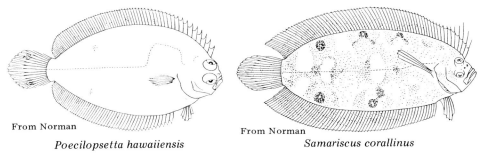

From Norman

From Norman

Poecilopsetta hawaiiensis

Samariscus corallinus

THE CORALLINE - RED FLOUNDER

152—2 *Samariscus corallinus* Gilbert, 1905

The body of this flounder is long and slender with body outlines which are somewhat parallel. The dorsal fin begins above the front of the upper eye where the first few rays have filamentous ends; it thereafter, together with the anal fin, gradually increases in width toward the tail. The right pectoral fin is narrow with four rays, while the lower pectoral fin is absent.

The pelvic fins are symmetrical and contain five rays each; the right pelvic fin is longer than the left. The head is small, the preopercle margin is free, and the mouth, which is set at a very oblique angle, has a prominent lower jaw. The eyes are close together and are separated by a rounded bony ridge; the upper eye is placed slightly behind the lower eye. The color of the body is coralline red above and is irregularly mottled and spotted with pinkish hues, pearl gray, and black. Two, round, black spots with orange centers mark the rear margin of the body. Specimens will measure five inches in length.

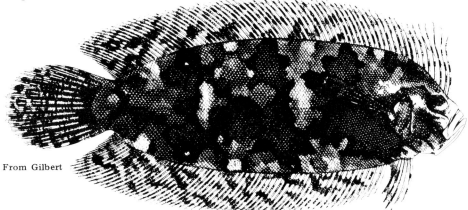

From Gilbert

This species is based upon a few specimens captured in 1902 by the steamer *Albatross* off the south coast of Molokai at depths between 43 and 73 fathoms.

The distribution of this species includes the Hawaiian area.

THE THREE - SPOT FLOUNDER
152—3 *Samariscus triocellatus* Woods, 1966

The body of this flounder is small, somewhat rectangular in outline,

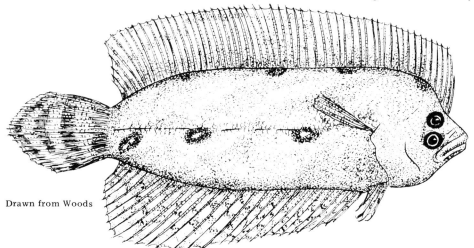

Drawn from Woods

and possesses a lateral line which is nearly straight. The dorsal fin originates on the blind side just ahead of the eye and contains between 64 and 70 fin rays; the anal fin contains between 47 and 56 rays. The pectoral fin is small, slender, and contains five nearly black rays on the upper side; on the blind side this fin contains but one rudimentary ray or is absent. On the head, the margin of the preopercle is free and the eyes, which are placed close together and almost directly above each other, are separated by a bony ridge. The color of the body varies from light to dark brownish hues. Three prominent, round, dark spots with light centers are placed along the side of the body. In addition, the head and body are mottled with small, round spots and larger, oval spots. The dorsal and anal fins are marked with scattered, small, black spots. The caudal fin is mottled on its basal two-thirds, while the distal one-third is marked by small dots which are arranged in curved, vertical rows. It will reach a length of about five inches.

The habitat of this species is in the shallow waters of the shore line; it is common in some areas.

The distribution of this species extends from the Hawaiian area southward and westward to the Marshall Islands.

THE SOLE FISH FAMILY

153 *Family Soleidae (Archiridae, Trinectidae, Synapturidae)*

The soles and the tongue fishes are sometimes difficult to distinguish until it is remembered that in this family the eyes are on the right side of the head, while in the tongue fishes *(Cynoglossidae)* they are on the left side. The bodies of soles are oval and thin and have uniformly curving outlines. The dorsal fin usually begins quite far forward on the snout; both the dorsal and anal fins usually have simple rays; and both fins may be either free or attached to the caudal fin, which in this family is never pointed. The pelvic fins show variety; they may be symmetrical or asymmetrical; some are free from the anal fin, while in some the right pelvic fin is connected to the anal fin. The pectoral fins are rudimentary; the right fin is larger than the left or they may both be absent. All fins are without spines. On the head, the preoperculum is fused with other bones of the gill cover and the margin is hidden by the skin and scales of the head. The lower jaw is never prominent. There are no ribs in this family and the lateral line is single and straight on the body, but it may be arched or branched on the head.

The distribution of this family includes warm temperate and tropical seas; some also live in fresh water.

Of this family, at least one species occurs in this area.

THE KOBE SOLE FISH

153—1 *Aseraggodes kobensis* (Steindachner), 1896

This sole has a moderately slender, compressed body with dorsal and ventral outlines which curve uniformly from head to tail. The eyes are located on the right side of the head, are quite small, and are placed close together. The body is covered with scales and the lateral line is straight. The dorsal fin has about 70 rays and the anal fin has about 51 rays. The color of the upper side is a grayish brown. Large specimens will reach a length of about four inches.

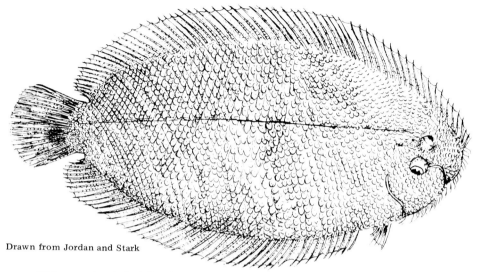

Drawn from Jordan and Stark

This species inhabits the sandy bottoms of shores and bays in southern Japan. It was named for the city of Kobe.

Dr. William A. Gosline has captured specimens in Hawaii at depths of 75 feet and less which he believes are this species. He states that they had the head of a tongue fish *(Cynoglossidae)* but, like the soles *(Soleidae)*, they had their eyes on the right side and had a separate tail.

THE TONGUE FISH OR
TONGUE-SOLE FISH FAMILY

154 *Family Cynoglossidae*

The tongue fishes have tongue-shaped bodies which are rounded in front and which taper rather uniformly to a pointed tail. They are related to the flounders but are more degenerate in their body structures. The dorsal fin begins far forward on the head and, together with the anal fin, proceeds uniformly to the tail to which both are joined. The dorsal and anal fin rays are usually simple and there are no spines on any fins. The pectoral fins are absent in this family and there is but a single pelvic or ventral fin on the left side; this pelvic fin is either free or may be joined to the anal fin. On the head, the preoperculum is fused to other bones and its margin is usually hidden by the skin and scales of the head. The eyes are very small and are situated very close together on the left side. The mouth is small, curved, and very asymmetrical. The lower jaw is never prominent in this family. The lateral line is present on the eyed side and may be either single, double, or triple; it is absent in a few species. Most members of this family are less than 12 inches in length and are therefore of little commercial value.

Tongue fishes inhabit the bottoms of all tropical and temperate seas; many are known only from deep water.

At least two species of this family are known from this area.

THE DEEP-WATER TONGUE FISH
154—1 *Symphurus strictus* Gilbert, 1905

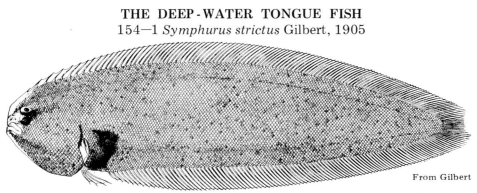

From Gilbert

This little fish is very elongated in form. The head is rounded and the body tapers uniformly toward the posterior end and the tail which in this species is vertically truncated. The dorsal fin contains between 108 and 115 rays; these rays, together with between 95 and 102 anal rays, join 14 caudal rays to form a continuous, confluent fins from just above the eye around the posterior of the body to the anus. The rays of the caudal fin are easily distinguished from those of the dorsal and anal fins. The eyes are small and are placed close together on the left side of the head with the upper eye slightly in advance of the lower eye. The margin of the preoperculum is fused to other bones and is covered by the skin and scales of the head. The mouth is small and is curved. The color of the body is a brownish hue. The peritoneum is jet black in color and is clearly visible through the body wall.

This species is based upon five specimens measuring about four inches

461

in length which were captured in 1902 by the steamer *Albatross* off Kauai and Oahu at depths between 265 and 399 fathoms.

The distribution of this species includes the Hawaiian area.

THE WAVY TONGUE FISH
154—2 *Symphurus undatus* Gilbert, 1905

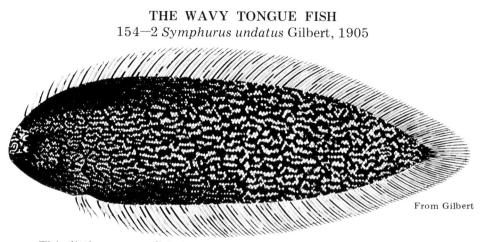

From Gilbert

This little tongue fish has a rounded head and a long, tapering body which ends in a pointed tail. The dorsal fin begins above the middle of the eye and, together with the anal fin, continues without interruption to join the tail. The rays in the dorsal fin number about 103 and about 88 in the anal fin. The left pelvic fin has four rays; the right pelvic fin is missing. On the head, the eyes are set close together on the left side and very nearly in a vertical line. As usual the preopercle is fused to other bones and so its margin is covered by the skin and scales of the head. The mouth is small and curved. The lateral line is not visible. The color of the body is brown; it is everywhere marked by narrow, wavy streaks of light olive which run in all directions and from which this species gets its scientific name. Adult specimens will reach a length of at least six inches.

This species was first described from two specimens measuring about four inches in length which were captured in 1902 by the steamer *Albatross* off the northwest coast of Oahu at a depth between 154 and 216 fathoms.

The distribution of this species includes the Hawaiian area.

THE REMORA FISH FAMILY

155 *Family Echeneidae (Echeneididae)*

Also known as Shark Suckers, Sucker Fishes, and Louse Fishes

The bodies of the remoras are spindle-shaped and taper rather uniformly toward the tail; most are moderately slender, but at least one species is very much elongated.

The most astonishing feature of these fishes is an oval, sucking disc located upon the top of the head. The disc bears within it from 10 to 28 pairs of transverse, movable, louver-like plates which are serrated on their free posterior edge; these plates are surrounded by a fleshy margin which represents the outer lip of the sucking disc. These fishes are without a spinous dorsal fin and it is therefore believed that this sucking disc was developed in ancient times from the anterior half of the dorsal fin. This disc is so arranged that the remora has to move forward to release its suction. As the host fish swims forward and the friction and pressure of the water increase, the sucking disc clings more tightly to the host.

The body of these fishes is smooth to the touch, although it is covered with minute scales; the lateral line is present and follows a straight course along the middle of the body toward the tail. The soft dorsal and anal fins are about equal and opposite; the pectoral fins are placed high on the body; and the pelvic fins, which contain one spine and five rays each, are placed close together and far forward on the body; there are no finlets and no caudal keels. The head is flattened, the gill openings are wide, the mouth is large, and the lower jaw projects beyond the upper jaw.

Remoras are alert, agile, carnivorous fishes, which swim actively about whenever their host is feeding. They feed upon various animals in the plankton, scraps from the mouth of their host, possibly parasites, and occasionally faeces.

The remoras should not be considered as parasites because they do not derive their nourishment from their host and they do no harm except to

Below: *Echeneis naucrates* and host.

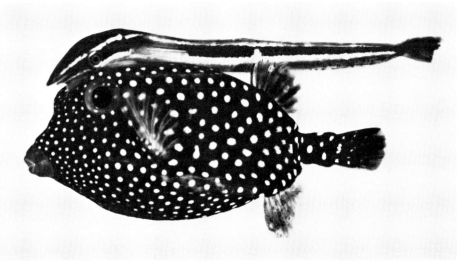

impede the progress of the host.

There are some interesting stories about remoras. It is reported that in some places in the tropics, these fishes are used for fishing. A fishing line is tied to the tail of the remora and it is sent into the sea to look for a host. As soon as the remora has attached itself to a fish, the fisherman slowly pulls the two of them up to the boat.

The ancients, especially the Romans, believed that the remora had unusual power. They believed, among other things, that it could hinder or stop sailing ships. Pliny, the Roman, tells how a remora stopped, out of the entire fleet, the great galley of the Emperor Caligula thereby fortelling his death. They also believed that the sight or presence of a remora could effect the birth of a child and even determine the outcome of lawsuits.

These fishes attach themselves to all manner of hosts. Some remoras show a preference for certain types of hosts, while others will attach themselves to almost anything that swims. Hosts include sharks and rays, all manner of large fishes, turtles, whales, the hulls of ships, and various floating objects.

The distribution of this family is world-wide; they are found in all tropical seas and all warm, temperate waters.

THE LARGE, SLENDER REMORA
Also known as Le-le-i-o-na, O-mo, and Ke-i-ki a ka ma-no
155—1 *Echeneis naucrates* Linnaeus, 1758

Drawn from Bigelow and Schroeder

The body of this remora is very long and slender. The sucking disc on the head usually has between 21 and 28 laminae and is oval in outline, being approximately twice as long as wide. The dorsal and anal fins are very long and are approximately opposite and equal in size. The caudal fin in young individuals is pointed 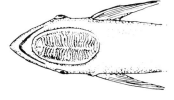 and has the middle ray elongated; in older individuals this fin is either truncate or emarginate. The pectoral fins are pointed and placed high on the body. The color of the body is dark brown. The sides are marked with a black band which extends from the head to the tail and is usually bordered with a white stripe above and below. The caudal fin is edged above and below with white. This is the largest species of remoras and will reach a length of about 36 inches.

The host fish most preferred by this species seems to be the large sharks; it occurs, however, on a very wide variety of other species.

The distribution of this species is world-wide in warm water.

THE LINEATE REMORA
155—2 *Phtheirichthys lineatus* (Menzies), 1791

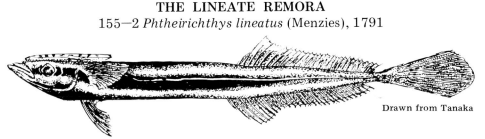

Drawn from Tanaka

The body of this fish is long, slender, and striped somewhat like *Echeneis naucrates*. It is quite easily identified by the sucking disc which contains from 9 to 11 laminae. The pectoral fins are pointed and the caudal fin is rounded with the outer edges sometimes projecting. The color of the body is dark brown above and below. It is marked on the sides with two pale lines; the upper line is just above the lateral line, while the lower stripe is nearer the mid-ventral line. Large specimens will reach a length of 30 inches.

The distribution of this species is world-wide in warm water.

THE WHALE SUCKER OR SOUTHERN REMORA
155—3 *Remora australis* (Bennett), 1840

Drawn from Clemens and Wilby

This remora gets its name from the fact that it is most often found attached to whales. The body of this fish is elongated, depressed anteriorly, and laterally compressed toward the tail. Its most amazing features is the very large sucking disc atop the head. In this species, this sucking disc is about three times as long as it is wide and appears to be nearly half the length of the body; it is wider than the body and usually contains 27 laminae, although it may have as few as 25 of these plates. The head is broad and depressed and bears a pair of small eyes. The lower jaw is narrower than the upper jaw and projects beyond it. The soft dorsal fin has between 20 and 23 rays and the anal fin contains between 20 and 24 rays. The caudal fin is slightly concave and the pectoral fins are rounded in outline. The color of the body varies from dark gray to brown above and is darker on the ventral surface. There is usually a narrow, white border on the dorsal and anal fins. Large specimens may reach 20 inches in length, but most are about one-half that length.

The favorite hosts of this remora are various species of whales including the great blue whale and the smaller dolphins and porpoises.

The distribution of this species is world-wide in warm water. In some books, this species may be listed as *Remilegia australis.*

THE SHORT-FINNED REMORA OR SPEAR-FISH REMORA
155—4 *Remora brachyptera* (Lowe), 1839

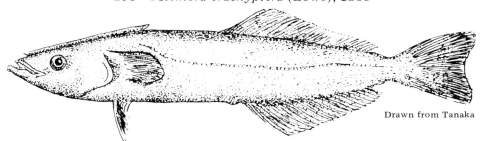

Drawn from Tanaka

The body of this remora appears to be more spindle-shaped and to possess a longer and more robust trunk than most other species. The sucking disc is nearly twice as long as broad and usually contains 15 plates or laminae, although these plates may range in number from 14 to 17 in this species. The dorsal fin contains between 29 and 32 soft rays and is correspondingly longer than the dorsal fin of *R. remora* which has between 22 and 25 rays. The pectoral fins are short and are rounded rather than pointed at their posterior margin. The ventral fins are attached to the abdomen for at least one-half of their length. The color of this remora is a uniform brownish hue over the entire body. Specimens will reach a length of 12 inches, although most are shorter.

The host fishes most preferred by this species seem to be the broad-bill sword-fish and the various species of spear-fishes; it also has been taken less frequently from other large fishes.

The distribution of this species is world-wide in warm water.

THE BONY-FINNED REMORA OR MARLIN SUCKER FISH
155—5 *Remora osteochir* (Cuvier), 1829

The word *osteochir* means "bony hand" and refers to the stiff, ossified, bony rays of the pectoral fins. In specimens over six inches in length, the tips of the pectoral rays extend beyond the membrane; these pectoral rays number between 20 and 24 and are multibranched. This remora resembles *R. remora* but differs in the number of gill rakers and in the sucking disc. Including all rudiments, the gill rakers number between 32 and 35 in *R. remora* and less than 21 in *R. osteochir*. The sucking disc has between 15 and 19 laminae, but never 20. This disc is large in proportion to the body length, may measure from 37 to 40 percent of the standard length, and extends backward well beyond the end of the pectoral fin. In this species, the pelvic fins are attached to the abdomen.

This remora prefers to ride upon the various species of spear-fishes. It doubtless occurs on other species, but apparently this is due to its inability to find its preferred host.

The distribution of this species includes the warm and temperate seas of all oceans.

THE COMMON REMORA
Also known as the Brown Remora
155—6 *Remora remora* (Linnaeus), 1758

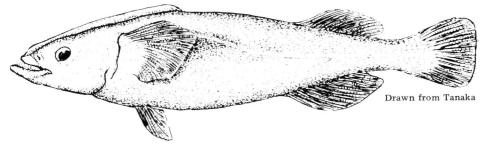

Drawn from Bigelow and Schroeder

This fish is a stout species and possesses a body which is robust anteriorly, quite short, and tapers rapidly toward the tail. While the head is broad and depressed, the posterior portion of the body is laterally compressed and terminates in a caudal fin which is lunate or emarginate in shape. The dorsal fin contains between 22 and 25 rays; this is useful in separating this species from *R. brachyptera* in which the rays are more numerous (29 to 32). The pectoral fins are rounded, short, and broad; the pelvic or ventral fins are attached to the abdomen along their inner margin for about one-half of their length. The sucking disc is about twice as long as wide and contains 17 or 18 plates or laminae; it is longer than the dorsal or anal fin. The color of the body is variously reported as brownish, grayish, black, and violet-black on both the upper and lower sides. Most specimens are less than 18 inches, although a few have been reported as long as 30 inches.

This remora has many hosts including large sharks, mantas, large sunfishes, various bill-fishes, and turtles. It seems to prefer large sharks.

The distribution of this fish is world-wide in warm water.

THE WHITE REMORA OR WHITE SUCKER FISH
155—7 *Remorina albescens* (Temminck and Schlegel), 1850

The body of this species is robust and stout and is not compressed as in other species. The head is short, broad, and depressed and bears a short,

Drawn from Tanaka

blunt snout and eyes which are small and placed high upon the head. The sucking disc contains 12, 13, or 14 laminae, is about one and one-half times as long as wide, and measures about one-third the length of the body. The dorsal fin has between 17 and 22 rays and the anal fin has between 20 and 23 rays; both fins are placed somewhat farther back on the body than in other species. The color of the body has been variously described as brown, grayish brown, or colorless. Large specimens will reach a length of about 12 inches.

The habitat of this remora seems to be on manta rays and a few other large fishes. It is usually found in the mouth and gill cavities.

The distribution of this species is world-wide in warm water.

The photograph below shows a pair of remoras clinging by their suckers to the glass of a window in the old Waikiki Aquarium. Since the sucker is on the top of the head, this is a view of the upper or dorsal side of their body. The outlines of the suckers and the lamellae or plates within the suckers are plainly visible.

The two larger fishes in the background are kala; see item number 136-22 in the text for this species.

THE HORN FISH AND SPIKE FISH FAMILY

156 *Family Triacanthidae (Triacanthodidae)*

The spike fishes, a small group of small fishes, are related to the trigger and file fishes, but are more primitive and less specialized than these two families. Spike fishes possess a small, compressed body which is covered by small, spiny scales which do not overlap. The fins are astonishing in appearance because of their spines. There are two dorsal fins; the first or spinous dorsal fin has between four and six spines of which the first spine is long, slender, and strong; the second dorsal fin and the anal fin below it are without spines and the caudal fin is either rounded or forked. The paired pelvic or ventral fins each possess a single, long, slender, strong spine which is followed by a single, small, weak fin ray.

The habitat of these fishes is in the deeper water beyond the reef.

Some scholars divide the spike fishes into two families. They place those fishes which have a soft dorsal fin with 20 to 26 soft rays, a deeply forked caudal fin, and other characteristics in the Family *Triacanthidae*. In the Family *Triacanthodidae*, they include those species in which the soft dorsal fin has from 12 to 18 soft rays and the margin of the caudal fin is rounded or nearly truncated. These two groups also differ in their scales, teeth, and other details.

This small family occurs in the Atlantic, Pacific, and Indian Oceans, but it is principally an Indo-Pacific group with the most species occuring in the great area from Hawaii and Japan southward to Australia, westward through the tropical western Pacific and the East Indies, and on across the Indian Ocean to the coast of Africa.

At least one species of this family is known from deep water in this area.

GOSLINE'S SPIKE FISH

156—1 *Hollardia goslinei* Tyler, 1968

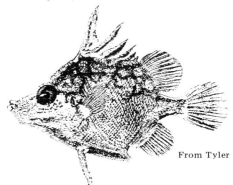

From Tyler

This rare species was first known and described from three Hawaiian specimens from deeper offshore water. One was collected in June, 1950, off the Island of Hawaii near where the lava flow from the eruptions of Mauna Loa entered the sea. The remaining two specimens, which came from beds of red coral, were captured in triangle nets; one of these nets had been set at a depth of 200 fathoms.

The body of this fish is high, compressed, and angular in outline. The head bears large eyes and an elongated snout which ends in a small mouth. The upper profile of the head is straight from the mouth to the eye and from the eye to the dorsal fin, but is depressed to form an angle above the eyes.

The caudal peduncle is long and ends in a fan-shaped tail. The spines of the dorsal fin are long and the pelvic fins possess one long spine and one or possible two rays each. Spiny scales cover the body. The color of the body is pale pinkish or whitish and is marked with a net-like pattern of pinkish lines. Large specimens will reach a length of five and one-half inches.

The habitat of this spike fish seems to be in the beds of red coral at depths approaching 1,000 feet.

The distribution of this species is limited by present knowledge to the Hawaiian area.

The name of this species honors Dr. Wm. A. Gosline, III, an American ichthyologist and University of Hawaii professor from 1948 to 1971.

THE TRIGGER FISH FAMILY
157 *Family Balistidae*

The trigger fishes are rather easily recognized by their flat, deep bodies, their small eyes placed high upon the head, and by their rough, rhomboid-shaped scales, often with small spines, which form a rough, tough covering for the body. There are two dorsal fins. Of these, the first is formed of two or three spines which are placed forward on the body above and behind the eyes. The first of these spines is the largest and may be erected vertically or laid horizontally into a groove on the back. When erected, it is locked in place by the spine behind it and may not be lowered until this second spine has been depressed. The soft dorsal and anal fins are approximately equal and opposite and the caudal fin is either round, truncate, or lunate in shape. The pectoral fins are small and the pelvic fins have been reduced to a small, somewhat movable spine which is placed at the end of a long pelvic bone. The head is angular in outline and bears a long snout which ends in a small mouth containing short, strong jaws. The teeth are reduced to an outer series of eight in each jaw; in addition, the upper jaw contains a second inner series of six plate-like teeth. Most trigger fishes are colorful and are marked with patterns of lines and spots. They range in length from a few inches to two feet.

Trigger fishes are bottom dwellers and usually live in areas of coral reefs. They live a solitary, slow-moving life and spend their days nibbling on a wide variety of bottom animals including crabs, echinoderms, corals, worms, and other fishes. At night, they hide away in crevices where they wedge themselves in place by resting on their pelvic spine and erecting and locking their dorsal spine. Some trigger fishes are capable of making a noise.

Trigger fishes are edible and are eaten in various areas, particularly in the West Indies. However, in many Pacific areas, their flesh is poisonous in varying degrees and eating these fishes is therefore dangerous and is not recommended. In some places their sale in fish markets is prohibited. Eating fishes in which the flesh is poisonous causes a sickness known as fish poisoning or "ciguatera". These poisons seem to be stronger in strictly tropical areas and to get weaker in more northern latitudes.

Trigger fishes are shore line inhabitants of tropical seas including the Mediterranean Sea and the Atlantic, Pacific, and Indian Oceans.

This family includes about 30 species; of this number, at least nine are known from this area.

THE SPOTTED TRIGGER FISH
157—1 *Canthidermis maculatus* (Bloch), 1786

This trigger fish does not closely resemble most other members of its family. The body is slender and elongated and the fins are quite different. The soft dorsal and anal fins are high in front and low at their posterior, thus giving these fish a falcate appearance. The pelvic spine is placed quite far forward on the body and the caudal fin is pointed at the top and bottom and curved outward at the center. The pectoral fins and the mouth are quite small. The body is covered with rough, rectangular scales; there are no spines on the scales. The body is dark in color and is marked by round or oval, light blue spots which are smaller above and in front and larger below and posteriorly. Most specimens are a foot or so in length, but large specimens have measured as much as 22 inches.

The habitat of this trigger fish seems to be in the open sea or at least offshore. It is a much better swimmer than its relatives.

The distribution of this species extends from Hawaii southward to central Polynesia, westward through Micronesia and Melanesia, through the East Indies, and across the Indian Ocean to the coast of Africa. It also occurs in the tropical and sub-tropical Atlantic Ocean. It seems to be world-wide in warm temperate and tropical waters.

THE BROWN TRIGGER FISH
157 2 *Balistes fuscus* (Bloch and Schneider), 1801

This large fish is quite distinctive in appearance. There is a groove in front of the eye, the cheeks are without scales in front, and there are a few enlarged and ossified plates behind the gill openings. The soft dorsal and anal fins are about equal and opposite and both are considerably longer at their anterior ends. There are no spines on the caudal peduncle and the caudal fin possesses extended tips in the adults. The color of this species is reported as variable. The specimens which we have seen were all quite uniformly brown; however, this species is reported to exhibit patterns of lines and spots. It is known to reach a length of at least 20 inches and is therefore one of the very largest members in this family.

The habitat of this fish is in the deeper waters on the outer side of the reef.

The distribution of this species extends from Hawaii southward to central Polynesia, westward through Micronesia and Melanesia, through the East Indies including the Philippines, and westward across the Indian Ocean to the coast of Africa and the Red Sea.

This species is very closely related to *Balistes polylepis* Steindachner, 1876, a large triggerfish from the eastern Pacific, which occurs from California to Equador. If future studies prove that they are identical, they will then both be known as *B. polylepis*.

THE BLACK TRIGGER FISH
Also known as Hu-mu hu-mu 'e-le-'e-le
157—3 *Melichthys niger* (Bloch), 1786

This species is easily identified by its color. In life, the color of the

ɔody is a dark blue-green; this changes on death to a rather uniformly black ːolor. A distinct, horizontal, light blue line extends along the bases of both ːhe soft dorsal and anal fins. There is a groove in front of the eyes, some ɛnlarged ossified plates just behind the gill openings, and seven or eight rows ɔf small spines along the caudal peduncle. Most specimens are eight or nine ɪnches in length; it is known to reach a length of 14 inches and some records ːlaim a length of 20 inches, although this is doubtless an error.

The habitat of this fish is in the areas of the shore line on the outer side ɔf the reef. Here it feeds upon a variety of plant and animal foods.

The distribution of this species is world-wide in most warm temperate ɪnd tropical seas. It occurs from Hawaii and central Polynesia westward ːhrough Micronesia and Melanesia, through the East Indies, and across the ɪndian Ocean to the coast of Africa; it also occurs in the tropical Atlantic Ɔcean.

This species appears in Pacific books under various names including *Melichthys buniva* (Lacepede), 1803, and *M. radula* (Solander), 1848. In ːhe western tropical Atlantic areas, it has been discussed under the name of *M. piceus* (Poey), 1863.

THE RED-TAILED TRIGGER FISH
Also known as Hu-mu hu-mu hi-'u-ko-le and Hu-mu hu-mu u-li
157—4 *Melichthys vidua* (Solander), 1844

Identification of this species may be made from its color pattern. The ːolor of the body varies from dark brown to black. The soft dorsal and anal fins may be pink or white, the caudal fin is pink and white, and the pectoral fins are yellowish. Most specimens are eight or nine inches long; however, it has been reported to reach a length of 15 inches.

The habitat of this fish is in the deeper waters on the outer side of the ːeef.

The distribution of this species extends from Hawaii and the Tuamotu Islands westward through Polynesia, Micronesia, Melanesia, the Philippines and the East Indies, and on across the Indian Ocean to the coast of Africa.

Balistes nycteris (Jordan and Evermann), 1905, is a synonym of *M. vidua*.

THE ACULEATE TRIGGER FISH
Also known as Hu-mu hu-mu nu-ku nu-ku a pu-a-'a
157—5 *Rhinecanthus aculeatus* (Linnaeus), 1758

This is an unmistakable species and the second Hawaiian fish to bear this amazing name. It is very similar to the next species. The body is

homboid in shape with dorsal and ventral outlines which are about equal ¬nd opposite. The head is large and bears a long snout which ends in a small ¬nouth with strong jaws. There are a few osseous plates behind the gill ¬penings and three or four horizontal rows of small spines on the caudal ¬eduncle. The color pattern of the body is astonishing. It is generally ¬rayish with a greenish head and brown patches on the back. Three or four, ¬arrow, blue lines connect the eyes over the top of the head and three blue ¬ines extend downward from each eye. The mouth is edged with a narrow ¬ellow band which continues backward to the base of the pectoral fin. There ¬re four or five, light, diagonal bands extending upward and forward from ¬he anal fin. Large specimens will reach a length of about nine inches.

The habitat of this fish is in the shallow waters on the outer edge of ¬he reef.

The distribution of this species extends from Hawaii and the Marquesas ¬slands westward through central Polynesia, Micronesia, Melanesia, and the ¬hilippines to the coast of China, through the East Indies, and across the ¬ndian Ocean to the coast of Africa and the Red Sea.

THE PIG - NOSED TRIGGER FISH
Also known as Hu-mu hu-mu nu-ku nu-ku a pu-a-ʻa
157—6 *Rhinecanthus rectangulus* (Bloch and Schneider), 1801

Drawn from
Jordan and Evermann

This is one of two trigger fishes which bears the famous, long, Hawaiian name. The body is somewhat rhomboid in shape and has the dorsal and ventral outlines approximately equal and opposite. The head is large and bears a long snout with a small mouth and strong jaws. The eyes are small and are set high upon the head. The color pattern of the body is unusual. The head, back, and upper parts of the body are a brownish yellow; the lower surfaces are white; the eyes are connected over the top of the head by three dark lines; a wide band of black extends from the eyes downward and

475

backward to the anal fin; and the caudal peduncle is encircled with a black band with a pointed, anteriorly-directed extension. It will reach a length of eight or nine inches.

The habitat of this fish is in the shallower water on the outside of the reef. It may be caught with hook and line or with fish traps, but it should not be eaten.

The distribution of this species extends from Hawaii southward to central Polynesia and Australia, westward through Micronesia and Melanesia through the East Indies including the Philippines, and across the Indian Ocean to the coast of Africa and the Red Sea.

THE GREEN AND WHITE TRIGGER FISH
Also known as Hu-mu hu-mu u-ma-u-ma le-i and Hu-mu hu-mu le-i
157—7 *Sufflamen bursa* (Bloch and Schneider), 1801

The body of this trigger fish, like most other members of this group, is oblong and compressed. The head is short, deep, and compressed and bears a long snout which terminates in a small mouth. A pair of small eyes is placed high upon the head. The color of the body is dull green above and white below. These two color areas are separated by a narrow, white line which extends from the corner of the mouth straight to the origin of the anal fin and thence forward to the base of the pelvic spine. The side of the body is marked by two, curved, vertical lines. The first extends through the eye to the base of the pectoral fin; the second extends from the base of the pectoral fin upward and backward onto the body. The interior of the mouth is black. Specimens usually range between six and eight inches in length.

The habitat of this species is in the shore line waters on the outer side of the reef. It is a fairly common species.

The distribution of this species extends from Hawaii and the Marquesas

lands westward through central Polynesia, Micronesia, Melanesia, and the
ast Indies including the Philippines, and on across the Indian Ocean to the
oast of Africa and the Red Sea.

THE BRIDLE-MARKED TRIGGER FISH
Also known as Hu-mu hu-mu mi-mi
157—8 *Sufflamen capistratus* (Shaw), 1804

This drab trigger fish may be most easily identified by the groove in
ront of the eyes, by the enlarged scutes behind the gill openings, and by
even to ten rows of small spines on each side of the caudal peduncle. The
olor of the body is a dull, plain, yellow-brown hue. It is marked by a
ridle-like, yellow band which encircles the mouth and extends backward
rom the corners of the mouth toward the bases of the pectoral fins.
pecimens have been reported to reach the amazing length of 20 inches, but
lost measure between eight and ten inches.

This species is moderately common in the deeper waters on the outer
ide of the reef.

The distribution of this species extends from Hawaii and the Marquesas
Islands westward through central Polynesia, Queensland, Micronesia,
Melanesia, and the East Indies including the Philippines, and on across the
Indian Ocean to the coast of Africa and the Red Sea.

In newer or more recent publications, this species will probably appear
under the name of *Sufflamen fraenatus* (Latreille), 1804.

THE LONG-CHINNED TRIGGER FISH
157—9 *Xanthichthys mento* Jordan and Gilbert, 1882

The body of this fish is oblong and compressed and covered with
rhomboid-shaped scales which are separated by deep, dark lines; these scales,
which cover both the head and body, are especially large on the cheeks. The

head bears a series of five, horizontal lines along the cheek and a single line in front of the eye; there are no enlarged plates behind the gill openings in this species. The eyes are located high on the head and the lower jaw projects beyond the upper one. The fins are brightly colored with pink, orange, and reddish hues; the body is brownish. The females are darker and of more uniform coloration than the males; in the males, the head is darker than the body. Large specimens will reach a length of nearly one foot, but most specimens measure between six and eight inches in length.

The habitat of this fish is in the deeper water on the outer edge of the reef.

The distribution of this species appears to include the warmer waters of the eastern, central, and south Pacific Ocean.

For many years this fish was known in this area as *X. ringens* (Linnaeus), 1758. Recent studies seem to indicate that *X. ringens* is a species of the western Atlantic Ocean and probably does not occur in the Pacific Ocean.

THE FILE FISH FAMILY
158 *Family Monacanthidae*

The file fishes have narrow, compressed bodies which are usually very deep or, in a few species, more elongated and slender. In some species the scales are absent but, when present, are very small and give the skin a rough texture. File fishes have a small mouth which contains six, incisor-type teeth in both the upper and lower jaws; in addition, the upper jaw has a second, inner row of four additional teeth. They have two dorsal fins; the first of these is represented by a large, single spine and by a second, small rudiment behind it. The pelvic fins are absent and the pelvic bones are united to form a single spine which supports a sort of pelvic flap of skin between the chin and the anal fin. The soft dorsal and anal fins are usually about equal in size and opposite in position. In this family, the soft rays in the dorsal fin number between 25 and 38, while the soft rays in the anal fin number between 24 and 36. Some of these fishes have interesting colors, but most are somewhat drab. All are of small or moderate size.

They inhabit the shallow waters of the coast line on both sides of the reef. They are rather slow swimmers, alert to danger, and often hide in plants and crevices. They are primarily vegetarians, but subsist upon a wide variety of food. They are edible but bony, contain little flesh, and are not worth the effort required to prepare them; some are unpalatable.

This family is distributed in the tropical waters of the Atlantic, Pacific, and Indian Oceans. In addition, a few species are found in most temperate seas.

Some scholars include about 75 species in this family; of this number at least six are known from this area.

The following species is not described or illustrated:

Cantherines pardalis (Ruppell), 1835. This species resembles *C. sandwichiensis* and has long been confused with it. However, since they occupy separate areas, their identification is easier. *C. sandwichiensis* seems to be limited to the Hawaiian area, while *C. pardalis* extends from central Polynesia westward to the coast of Africa. These species are discussed by Dr. John Randall in *Copeia*, 1967(2), pp. 331-361.

Cantherhines dumerili (Hollard), 1854

THE FAN-TAIL FILE FISH
Also known as 'O-'i-li le-pa, 'O-'i-le-pa, 'O-'i-li, and 'O-'i-li-'u-wi-'u-wi
158—1 *Pervagor spilosoma* (Lay and Bennett), 1839

This beautiful little fish is most easily recognized by its color. In life the body is yellow in color and is marked with irregular, closely-set, black spots. The tail is orange in color and is marked with small, black spots and a vertical, curved, black, marginal stripe. The cheeks are marked with diagonal, black lines. Young specimens of about two inches in length are silvery in color. Large specimens will reach about five inches in length.

The habitat of this species is in the deeper waters on the outer edge of the reef. Periodically it appears in shallow water in large numbers, usually about January, February, or March, after which time it is sometimes found dead and dry in the wind-rows high on the beach. These dried specimens were used in old Hawaii for fuel.

The distribution of this species includes the Hawaiian area.

THE BLACK-HEADED FILE FISH
158—2 *Pervagor melanocephalus* (Bleeker), 1853

This fish is a widely distributed Indo-Pacific species with several local varieties, of which one variety, *P. melanocephalus johnstonensis* Wood, 1966, is known from Johnston Island and the Hawaiian area. It is dark brownish or blackish in color with black lips, with 8 or 10 dark, wavy lines on its soft dorsal and anal fins, and with some

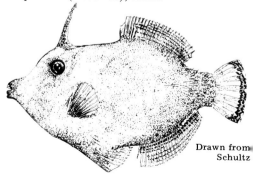

Drawn from
Schultz

480

lark, curved, wavy, longitudinal lines near the posterior margin of the tail. t will reach a length of at least four inches.

The habitat of this fish is on the outer side of the reef. It is very rare in Hawaii.

Persons interested in this species should read Loren P. Woods' account of the *Plectognathida* in *U.S. National Museum Bulletin* 202, Volume 3, 1966, beginning on page 80.

DUMERIL'S FILE FISH
Also known as 'O-'i-li le-pa and 'O-'i-le-pa
158—3 *Cantherhines dumerili* (Hollard), 1854

The body of this file fish is quite deep and extremely compressed. The dorsal and ventral profiles of the head are nearly straight and lead to a small mouth with a projecting lower jaw. The eyes are small and the gill opening is a slit located just above the base of the pectoral fin. The body is covered by a rough, velvety skin, but the scales are small and not visible. The first spine is long and straight and is about equal to the distance between the eye and the corner of the mouth. The soft dorsal and anal fins are both quite high, nearly equal in length, and are placed about opposite each other. The caudal fin is rounded; the pectoral fins are small and usually contain 15 rays. The caudal peduncle is marked on each side by two pairs of spines which curve forward. The color of the body varies from light gray to brownish hues; in older specimens, there are usually about 12, dark, vertical bands marking the posterior half of the body. Young specimens often show white spots scattered over the upper part of the body and occasionally small dark spots. The fins, caudal spines, and the iris of the eye are either yellow or orange in color; a light band encircles the mouth. Large specimens will reach a foot in length.

The distribution of this species extends from the tropical, eastern Pacific islands, Hawaii, and Japan southward and westward through Polynesia, Micronesia, and Melanesia, through the East Indies, and across the Indian Ocean to the coast of Africa.

This has been a difficult species to identify and has previously appeared in books under many names including *C. carolae* (Jordan and McGregor) 1898; *C. howensis* (Ogilby), 1889; and *C. albopunctatus* (Seale), 1901.

THE SANDWICH ISLAND FILE FISH
Also known as 'O-'i-li-le-pa and 'O-'i-le-pa
158—4 *Cantherhines sandwichiensis* (Quoy and Gaimard), 1824

The Sandwich Island file fish is a small species with a compressed body. It is most easily identified by the white spots on the top and bottom of the caudal peduncle; it also lacks the spines on the sides of the caudal peduncle. The soft dorsal fin has between 33 and 36 rays; the anal fin has between 30 and 32 rays; and the pectoral fin has from 12 to 14 rays.

Photo by John E. Randall

The caudal fin is quite straight at its posterior margin and its upper and lower corners are almost square. Dr. John Randall has described the color as "bluish gray . . . with scattered small pale blue spots of variable size on the body, a large white spot anterodorsally on the caudal peduncle and a similar spot ventro-anteriorly on the peduncle; broad region of head around eye with alternating yellow and blue lines . . ." The lips are nearly black and the fins have yellowish hues toward their outer margins. Large specimens will reach about five inches in length.

The distribution of this species includes the Hawaiian area.

THE SHY FILE FISH
158—5 *Cantherhines verecundus* (E. K. Jordan), 1925
This small, rare species has a body which is very deep and greatly compressed. The first dorsal spine is comparatively short, the gill opening is a short slit directly below the eye, and the caudal fin is rounded at the end. The soft dorsal fin has between 34 to 36 rays; the anal fin has 31 or 32 rays; and the pectoral fin usually has 13 rays. The color of this fish varies widely and is very changeable. It was described originally as a "dull olive brown". The color varies in intensity and the body is often marked with blotches of lighter and darker hues, rounded spots, and vertical bars. Also various, poorly-defined, saddle-shaped areas occur around the margins of the body. Large specimens will reach a length of five inches. It is an uncommon species.

The distribution of this species includes the Hawaiian area.

GARRETT'S FILE FISH
158—6 *Pseudomonocanthus garretti* (Fowler), 1928

Garrett's file fish is a small species with a body which is compressed, oblong in shape, and covered with small scales. The eyes are quite large, the mouth is small with six teeth in each jaw, and the dorsal and ventral profile of the head are nearly straight. The gill opening lies directly below the eye and the first dorsal spine is located above the posterior half of the eye. The soft dorsal, anal, caudal, and pectoral fins have transparent membranes and contain 33-34, 31-33, 12, and 13-14 soft rays, respectively. Dr. Randall describes the color of young specimens as "pale yellowish with brown stripes..." This color pattern of stripes changes to a spotted pattern on the area of the head in front of the eyes. The length of known specimens ranges from about three to about six inches.

From Randall

The habitat of this fish is not fully known. Some specimens have been captured at depths between 200 and 250 feet.

The distribution of this species appears to extend the entire length of the Hawaiian Island chain.

Persons wishing to know more about this species should consult an article by Dr. John E. Randall in the *Japanese Jour. of Ichthyology* Vol. 21 (4), 1975, pp. 223-226.

From Fowler

THE LEATHER JACKET FISH FAMILY

159 *Family Aluteridae*

The leather jackets are often combined with the file fishes to form a single family known either as the *Monacanthidae* or the *Aluteridae*. Like the file fishes, the leather jackets have very compressed, narrow bodies, but are more elongated in shape. They have two dorsal fins of which the first is reduced to a slender spine or is even absent in some species; this spine, if present, is always located above the eyes. The pelvic fins are absent and the pelvic bones are joined to form a feeble pelvic spine which may be rudimentary or even absent. The skin has a velvety texture and there are usually no visible scales. The mouth is small and is equipped with six, incisor-type teeth in both jaws; in addition, the upper jaw has a second, inner row of four teeth. The soft dorsal and the anal fins are approximately equal in size and opposite in position. In this family, the soft dorsal rays number between 45 and 50, while the anal rays number between 41 and 53. Some species in this small group are beautifully colored and are reported to reach over three feet in length.

The leather jackets make their home in the quiet waters on the outer side of the reef. They are slow swimmers, quite alert, and often attempt to camouflage themselves by hovering vertically in marine vegetation and swaying with the passing currents. Leather jackets are fundamentally vegetarians but they also eat a wide variety of other foods.

Like the file fishes, the leather jackets are not good food fishes. They are bony, have little flesh, and are not worth the effort to prepare them. Some are reported to be unpalatable.

This family is distributed in all warm seas.

Of this small family, at least two species occur in this area.

THE ONE-SPINED LEATHER JACKET

Also known as Lo-u-lu

159—1 *Alutera monoceros* (Osbeck), 1758

The body of this bizarre fish is greatly compressed and elongated, but somewhat less than in *Osbeckia scripta*. In adults, the profile of the snout is

484

convex above and below with a depression or concavity just below the mouth. The body is covered with a velvety skin which gets its texture from the minute scales buried within it. There is a single, thin, weak spine located on the head above the eyes. The soft dorsal and anal fins are approximately equal and opposite; the soft dorsal has between 45 and 50 rays and the anal fin between 47 and 53 rays. The caudal fin is nearly straight on its posterior margin. The color of the body is a dull olive-brown to blackish, while the fins are yellowish. Large specimens are reported to reach a length of 30 inches.

This fish is reported to be edible, but its flesh is too scanty to warrant its preparation.

The distribution of this species includes all warm seas of the Atlantic, Pacific, and Indian Oceans.

THE BLUE-LINED LEATHER JACKET
Also known as 'O-'i-li le-pa and 'O-'i-le-pa
159—2 *Osbeckia scripta* (Osbeck), 1765

The body of this unusual fish is greatly compressed and elongated and the upper profile of the snout is concave. There is a single, long, slender, frail spine on the back above the eyes. The soft dorsal and anal fins are approximately equal and opposite in position. The soft dorsal fin has between 43 and 48 (usually 45) rays, while the anal fin has between 46 and 52 (usually 48) rays. The pectoral fin has 14 rays. The caudal peduncle is deep and compressed and leads into the caudal fin which has parallel upper and lower borders and a rounded posterior margin. The pelvic fins are absent and the pelvic spine which replaces them is also absent in the adults. The scales which cover the body are very small, short, and closely set giving the skin a velvety texture. The mouth is small, the lower jaw is longer than the upper jaw, and there are eight teeth above and six below. The color of this fish is variable, although the pattern is easily recognized. The body is somewhat olive colored and is marked with small brown spots and blue lines. The fins are yellowish. Large specimens are reported to reach a length of 40 inches.

The habitat of this fish is in the quiet waters on the outside of the reef. It is known to occasionally stand in a vertical position, sometimes in marine

vegetation, and to sway with the passing currents. This species is edible, but the scanty quantity of flesh makes its use infrequent.

The distribution of this species includes all warm seas of the Atlantic, Pacific and Indian Oceans.

THE BOX FISH OR TRUNK FISH FAMILY
Including the Cow Fishes or Cucolds
160 *Family Ostraciidae (Ostraciontidae)*

The box fishes are an unmistakable group of marine fishes. Their bodies are covered by a bony, box-like carapace which is composed of plates that are fused together to form a solid, immovable shell from which only the mouth, eyes, and fins protrude. In cross-section, their bodies are either triangular, square, or pentagonal and are flattened or rounded on the lower surface. (Those box fishes with ridges along their lower surface are grouped into the family *Aracanidae*.) None of the species possess a lateral line. There is only one dorsal fin which is placed toward the rear of the body where it is approximately equal and opposite in position to the anal fin. The pectoral fins are small and the pelvic fins are absent. There are no spines in any of these fins. These fishes have small mouths containing about 10 separate teeth in each jaw. In color, these fishes present a variety of patterns. Many are marked with spots or short lines and a few species exhibit beautiful colors. Identification of some species may be puzzling because the males and females are of different colors. Most box fishes are of small size, although some reach as much as 20 inches in length.

Box fishes are shy and timid and live close to the bottom in shallow water where they can hide when threatened. They are poor swimmers and are easily captured. In Polynesia in olden times, box fishes were eaten after they had been roasted.

When excited or molested, these fishes will exude a poison from their skin which is lethal to other fishes. It is therefore a mistake to place these fishes in containers with other fishes, even for short periods of time. This poison does not seem to be harmful to man.

The distribution of this family includes all warm seas.

This is a small family which contains about 20 species. Of this number, at least four species are known from this area.

The following species are not described or illustrated.

Ostracion solorensis Bleeker, 1853. This is a small, dark colored species with a pattern of lines and reticulations. It is without spines. It was erroneously reported from Johnston Island by Fowler and Ball in 1925. It does not occur in this area.

Ostracion cubicus Linnaeus, 1758. This is a large, quadrangular, spineless species with a variable color pattern. It was reported once from Hawaii in 1923 and has not been seen since. It may not occur here.

486

THE SPECKLED BOX FISH

Also known as Pa-hu, Mo-a, Mo-a mo-a wa-ʻa, and ʻA-u wa-ʻa la lu-a

160—1 *Ostracion meleagris camurum* Jenkins, 1901

This box fish is one of the commonest species. It is enclosed in a quadrangular carapace with four, rounded, longitudinal ridges. The back is convex, without a median ridge, and there are no spines. The sexes of this species are of different colors and this fact has led to much confusion. The males are blue, green, and brown with small, white spots on the back and with a golden band across the top of the head between the eyes. The females and all young fish are dark blue-brown in color with small, white spots on the back and sides. Large specimens will reach six inches in length and some have been reported to reach nine inches.

Because Hawaiian specimens differ slightly in color from those to the south and west of Hawaii, they have been declared a subspecies and given the additional name of *camurum*. If you do not regard the Hawaiian form as a variety, this species would be known as *O. meleagris* Shaw, 1796.

The habitat of this box fish is in the quiet water of the shore line. When annoyed or frightened, it releases a poison into the water which kills nearby fishes.

The distribution of this species extends from Hawaii southward to central Polynesia and westward across the entire tropical Pacific and Indian Oceans to the coast of Africa. It has also been reported from Clipperton Rock off the coast of Mexico.

Above: Male   Below: Female

This species has appeared under other names including *O. sebae* Bleeker, 1851, which was described from a male, and *O. lentiginosus* Bloch and Schneider, 1801, which was described from a female.

WHITLEY'S BOX FISH
160—2 *Ostracion whitleyi* Fowler, 1931

The body of this small box fish is quite angular in shape. It possesses four, longitudinal ridges and is without spines. The color pattern of juvenile and female fish is different from that of the males. In males, the body is brown to dark blue and is marked with small, very light blue spots above and by a light blue, lengthwise band placed high upon the side. The lower surface is light in color and is marked by three, large, round spots of which two are forward and one is located posteriorly. The females are marked above by many, small, white spots upon a darker background. The sides are

Above: Male   Above: Male

Above: Male   Below: Female

variously marked with brown-edged, light, longitudinal stripes. The patterns show some variation. Large specimens will reach at least five inches in length.

It inhabits the quiet waters of the shore line including depths of at least 50 or 60 feet.

The distribution of this species extends from Hawaii to the Marquesas Islands, eastern and central Polynesia, and doubtless adjoining areas.

In some books this species is listed as *Ostracion ornatus* Hollard, 1857.

THE MANY-SPINED COW FISH
160—3 *Lactoria diaphanus* (Bloch and Schneider), 1801

This cow fish has a rather unusual body. The upper part is typical of related species, but the lower part is widened, inflated, and bowl-shaped. The carapace is composed of many hexagonal plates, the outlines of which are apparent on the surface. There is a spine above each eye, a spine in the center of the back, one or more spines along the two dorso-lateral ridges, and one or more spines along the ventro-lateral ridges which terminate in a spine on each side of the anal fin. The body shape and the spines change as the fish grows larger. Large specimens are reported to reach a length of 12 inches.

The habitat of this fish is in the shallow, quiet waters of the shore line.

The distribution of this species extends from Hawaii southward to central Polynesia, westward through Micronesia and Melanesia, through the East Indies, and across the Indian Ocean to the coast of Africa. It is also reported from California.

THE FIVE-HORNED COW FISH
160—4 *Lactoria fornasini* (Bianconi), 1846

This cow fish has a five-sided body composed of hexagonal plates. There are five longitudinal ridges on the body, each of which bears a spine.

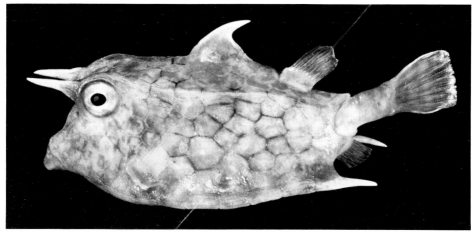

The dorso-lateral ridges pass over the eyes to end in two forward spines; the ventro-lateral ridges pass backward to end in two spines at the end of the body; a fifth spine occupies the center of the mid-dorsal ridge. Large specimens might reach a length of six inches.

The distribution of this species extends from Hawaii southward and eastward through Micronesia and the East Indies to the coast of Africa.

THE KEELED BOX FISH FAMILY
161 *Family Aracanidae*
This family of box fishes resembles the species included within the Family *Ostraciidae* and is often included in that family. They differ from the *Ostraciidae* in having a ridge down the center of the lower side and in having a shorter bony carapace. In the *Ostraciidae*, the bony covering of the body extends posteriorly beyond the dorsal and anal fins, while in the *Aracanidae* the bony carapace ends anterior to the dorsal and anal fins; in addition, there are a few bony plates on the caudal peduncle.

This is a small family which is limited to the warm waters of the Pacific and Indian Oceans. Only one species is known from this area.

THE POINTED OR SPINY BOX FISH
161—1 *Aracana aculeata* (Houttuyn), 1782
The shell of this box fish is marked by six, paired, longitudinal ridges and by a rounded, ventral ridge. The two dorsal ridges each bear a spine near their centers and both lateral ridges bear a series of spines. The caudal peduncle bears some small plates, the eyes are large, and the lateral line is absent. The color of the body is described as a grayish olive above and marked with small, round, brownish green spots; the lower surface is whitish in color. Most specimens measure about four inches in length.

In the Hawaiian area, this species was first known from two specimens dredged in 1902 by the steamer *Albatross* off Laysan Island at a depth between 59 and 163 fathoms.

The distribution of this species includes Hawaii and Japan.

From Tanaka

THE BALLOON FISH FAMILY

Also known as Puffers, Blow Fishes, Globe Fishes, and Toad Fishes

162 *Family Tetraodontidae (Chonerhinidae)*

Balloon fishes have bodies which are heavy, robust, short, and round in cross-section. This body, which incidentally has no ribs, is covered by a tough skin which may be smooth and without scales or may bear small prickles. There is but one dorsal fin which is placed far to the back of the body; below the dorsal fin is an anal fin of approximately equal size. The pectoral fin is rounded on its outer edge and the pelvic fins are absent. In this family, there may be either one or two lateral lines. The mouth contains two teeth or plates in each jaw which are separated by a median suture and which together form a very strong beak. The members of this family have the ability to inflate their bodies with either air or water and are therefore the subject of much curiosity. Most balloon fishes are less than a foot long, but some will reach about 18 inches, and the largest will measure about three feet in length.

Balloon fishes are carnivorous in their habits and live in the quiet waters of shallow shore line areas, or in quiet brackish waters; a few live in fresh water.

Members of this family contain poisons in their bodies which are toxic to humans and which, if eaten in sufficient quantity, will cause death. The Japanese peoples clean these fishes to eliminate most of the poison and thereafter cook and eat them for the "glow" which the poison gives them.

The distribution of this family is world-wide in all warm oceans and in most temperate seas. Of about 90 or more species, at least five are known from this area.

THE SPINY BALLOON FISH
Also known as 'O-'o-pu-hu-e and Ma-ki ma-ki
162—1 *Arothron hispidus* (Linnaeus), 1758

The body of this balloon fish is quite short and the skin which covers it is loose and flabby. The entire body is covered with small spines which become more obvious when the animal is inflated. The color of the body is variable but is basically a gray-brown-green hue. The back is covered with white spots, the belly is marked with longitudinal dark lines, and there is a black circle around the base of the pectoral fin. Most specimens range in length from eight to ten or twelve inches, although some specimens have been reported to reach as much as 20 inches in length.

This balloon fish is a shore line species which inhabits shallow, shore line water and also enters the estuaries and bays where the water is brackish. Like other balloon fishes, this species is able to inflate its body with either air or water. The flesh of this fish is poisonous and should not be eaten.

The distribution of this species extends from Hawaii southward to the northern coast of Australia, westward through Micronesia, Melanesia, and the Philippines, through the East Indies, and across the Indian Ocean to the coast of Africa.

THE SPECKLED BALLOON FISH
162—2 *Arothron meleagris* (Lacepede), 1798

The speckled balloon fish has a body which is rounded in contour and covered by small spines. All of the fins likewise have rounded margins. The color of the body is brown above and brown or light brown below. The body is marked with black mottlings and covered by many, small, white spots. Large

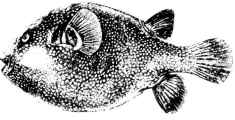

From Jordan
and Evermann

specimens will reach 13 inches in length.

The distribution of this species extends from Hawaii southeastward to the Tuamotu Islands and westward across the entire tropical Pacific Ocean to the Philippine Islands and the East Indies.

This species is also listed as *Arothron meleagris* (Bloch and Schneider), 1801.

BLEEKER'S BALLOON FISH
162—3 *Lagocephalus hypselogeneion* (Bleeker), 1852

The body of this fish is elongated, has somewhat parallel upper and lower outlines, and possesses a rather flat belly. The body is covered with spines on the belly, back, and elsewhere and possesses two lateral lines. The soft dorsal and anal fins are placed near the posterior end of the body and are approximately equal in size and opposite in position. Both are falcate in shape and pointed; they possess eight or nine and seven or eight soft rays, respectively. The margin of the caudal fin is nearly straight. The color of the body is brownish or greenish and is covered with small, brown spots which surround and define larger, gray spots. There is a longitudinal row of larger, golden spots along the posterior half of the side. The belly is white or yellowish. Most specimens are from five to seven inches in length, although some are reported to reach 12 inches.

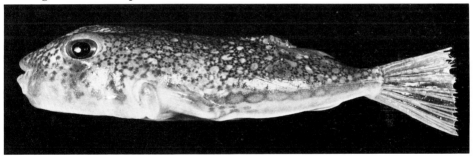

The habitat of this fish is on the bottom of quiet shore line areas to depths of about 400 feet. The flesh of this fish is reported as poisonous and should not be eaten.

The distribution of this species extends from Hawaii southward to central Polynesia and westward across the tropical Pacific and Indian Oceans to the coast of Africa and the Red Sea.

THE PELAGIC BALLOON FISH
162—4 *Lagocephalus lagocephalus* (Linnaeus), 1758

The body of this balloon fish is far more elongated and more slender than that of most other members of this family. The head and snout are long, the eyes are quite large, and the mouth is small. The teeth are pointed at the midline and possess sharp, cutting edges. The soft dorsal and anal fins are placed far back on the body and are approximately equal in size and opposite in position; the dorsal fin has between 12 and 14 rays and the anal

fin has either 11 or 12 rays. The margin of the caudal fin is lunate in shape and the pelvic fins are absent. A fold of skin is present along the lower, posterior part of the body. The belly is covered with scattered spines. The color of the body is blackish blue above, steel blue on the sides, and shades from silvery blue to whitish on the belly. The upper parts of the body are spotted with black. Large specimens will reach a length of about 24 inches.

The habitat of this fish is in the surface waters of the open ocean and occasionally along shore lines.

The distribution of this species includes the warm waters of tropical and sub-tropical areas of the Atlantic, Pacific, and Indian Oceans.

GUNTHER'S BALLOON FISH
162—5 *Sphoeroides cutaneus* (Gunther), 1871

This rare balloon fish is known in this area from a very few specimens. The body is robust and long with a flabby belly. The eyes are quite small, the lips are thick, and the teeth are large. The skin is smooth, but is marked with longitudinal lines or wrinkles. The color of the body is an olive-gray and a pure gray beneath; there is no pattern of markings upon the body. Specimens have ranged in length from nine to 14 inches.

It appears to inhabit deeper water than other members of its family.

The distribution of this species seems to be world-wide in warm water.

THE SHARP-NOSED PUFFER FISH FAMILY

163 *Family Canthigasteridae*

The sharp-nosed puffers resemble the members of the *Tetraodontidae* and are often included within that family by many authors. They differ from the tetraodonts in having no lateral line and in having the outer edge of the pectoral fin either straight or only slightly concave, whereas it is curved in the tetraodonts. The body of these fishes is short, robust, and slightly compressed in cross-section. Their snout is narrower, sharper, and longer than in the tetraodonts and their back is somewhat ridgid. The body is covered by a skin which is somewhat rough to the touch. The teeth are fused to form two plates in the upper jaw and two in the lower jaw; the two plates in each jaw are separated by a median, vertical suture. Like other balloon fishes, the members of this family are able to inflate their bodies. Most of these fishes are attractively colored and all are small in size; none are known to exceed about eight inches in length.

The distribution of this family is world-wide in warm water; most species, however, occur in the tropical Indo-Pacific area.

Of about twenty-three species, at least seven are known from Hawaii. Additional species are listed in the Appendix.

THE AMBOINA PUFFER FISH

Also known as Pu-'u o-la-'i

163—1 *Canthigaster amboinensis* (Bleeker), 1865

The Amboina puffer has a body which is uniformly curved along the dorsal and ventral borders. The soft dorsal fin has 11 or 12 rays and the anal fin has 11 rays. This puffer may be identified by its color when full grown. White spots cover the upper part of the body and the anterior one-half of the tail. Some irregular, dark spots are scattered over the belly and some exceedingly small, dark spots are scattered over the back and head. Bluish lines radiate out from the eyes and a pattern of lines covers the snout, cheeks, and lower jaw. Most specimens are four or five inches long, although

some have been reported to reach a length of ten inches.

The habitat of this fish is in the quiet, shallow waters of the shore line.

The distribution of this species extends from Hawaii and the eastern tropical Pacific southward and westward through Polynesia, Micronesia, Melanesia, the Philippines, the East Indies, and across the Indian Ocean to the coast of Africa.

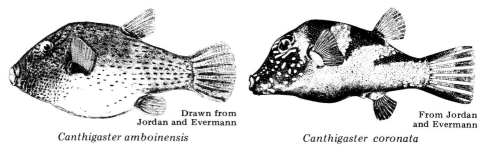

Drawn from
Jordan and Evermann

Canthigaster amboinensis

From Jordan
and Evermann

Canthigaster coronata

THE CROWNED PUFFER FISH
163—2 *Canthigaster coronata* (Vaillant and Sauvage), 1875

This small puffer is covered over the head and body with very small spines. The snout is quite long and is concave above and nearly straight beneath. The color of the body is black and white or yellowish. There are three or four, black, saddle-shaped areas extending from the back down upon the sides. The body is marked by orange spots scattered over the head, back, and sides; the fins are yellowish in color. Large specimens will reach about five inches in length.

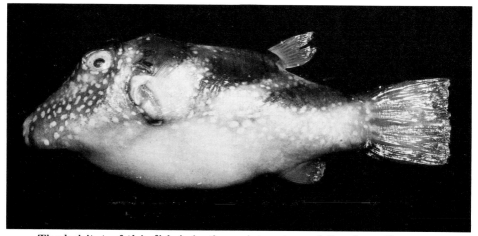

The habitat of this fish is in the quiet waters of the shore line.

The distribution of this species extends from Hawaii southward to northern Australia. westward through Micronesia and Melanesia, through the East Indies, and across the Indian Ocean to the coast of Africa and the Red Sea.

This species has long been known in this area under the name of *C. cinctus* Jordan and Evermann, 1905.

THE RARE KIHEI PUFFER FISH
Also known as Pu-'u o-la-'i
163—3 *Canthigaster epilampra* (Jenkins), 1903

This rare puffer has an oblong, compressed body which is flattened on its sides. The head is quite long and leads into a pointed snout which bears a small mouth with strong, curved teeth which meet at a point in front. Small,

sharp spines occur in single patches on top of the back, below the eyes, and on the belly. The color of the body is dark above and light below. Dark lines occur around the eyes and mouth and at the base of the tail. Most adult specimens measure about four inches in length.

From Jordan and Evermann

This is an uncommon shore line species which occurs from shallow water to depths of at least 300 or 400 feet.

This species was first known from a single specimen which was captured off Kihei, Maui, by Mr. Richard C. McGregor.

The distribution of this species extends from the Hawaiian area southward to central Polynesia, Micronesia, and doubtless to adjoining areas.

Some scholars have listed this species as a synonym of *C. rivulata* (Schlegel), 1850.

The name of *epilampra* is from the Greek *epi* (on, upon) and *lampros* (shining, beautiful) and possibly refers to the color of the body.

THE WHITE - SPOTTED PUFFER FISH
163—4 *Canthigaster jactator* (Jenkins), 1901

This little puffer has a rather long, pointed snout attached to an oval body. The eyes are high on the head, the belly is rounded, and the dorsal and anal fins are placed toward the back of the body. The dorsal and anal fins are about equal in size, but the dorsal fin is placed well forward of the

anal fin. Most of the body is covered with small, rounded, white spots with darker interspaces to form a net-like pattern over the body. There are no spots on the tail fin. Most specimens will measure two and one-half inches or less in length.

The habitat of this fish is in the shallow, quiet waters of the shore line.

The distribution of this species includes the Hawaiian Islands and doubtless adjoining areas.

It should not be confused with *C. solandri* (Richardson), 1845, which has spots on the tail and lines around the eyes; it also resembles *C. janthinopterus* (Bleeker), 1855, in which there are pale streaks crossing the snout; all three of these species have a variously shaped, dark spot or area at the base of the dorsal fin.

SCHLEGEL'S PUFFER FISH
Also known as Pu-'u o-la-'i
163—5 *Canthigaster rivulata* (Schlegel), 1850

This uncommon fish has an oblong, somewhat compressed body and a rather long head and snout. The eye is placed high upon the head and the mouth is small and contains strong teeth. The dorsal fin contains ten rays and is placed well forward of the anal fin. The caudal peduncle is compressed and quite deep. Very small, weak spines occur on the back, cheeks, and belly. The color pattern of the body is composed of irregular lines and spots; the lines predominate on the back and head, while the spots are distributed over the sides. A dark line extends along the midline of the belly. Adult specimens seem to measure between four and five inches in length.

The habitat of this rare fish is in the quiet, shallow waters of the shore line.

The distribution of this species extends from Hawaii westward to Japan, Western Australia, and across the Indian Ocean to the coast of Africa.

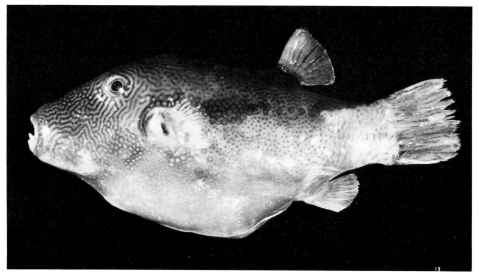

THE PORCUPINE OR BURR FISH FAMILY

164 *Family Diodontidae*

The porcupine fishes have a body which is quite round in cross-section and which is covered with strong spines; these spines are either fixed or movable and, if of the movable type, may be erected to form a thorny covering over the body, especially when the body is inflated. The soft dorsal and anal fins are about equal in size and are placed toward the rear of the body. The caudal fin has a round margin and the pelvic fins are absent. The pectoral fin is broad and has a posterior margin which is concave; this feature is helpful in separating this family from the *Tetraodontidae*. Within the mouth, the teeth are united to form a single, fused, beak-like tooth in each jaw. This wide tooth does not have a vertical, median suture in front as in the *Tetraodontidae*, although it is marked with transverse grooves. There is no lateral line in this family. The body is inflatable with either air or water as in the balloon fishes.

The habitat of these fishes is usually in the quiet waters of the shore line on both sides of the reef. Here they cruise about looking for various invertebrates which they catch and crush with their powerful jaws. Members of this family possess poisonous flesh and should not be eaten. Curio stores occasionally exhibit specimens of these fishes consisting of their dried, inflated skin with erected spines.

The distribution of this family includes all warm tropical seas. The family includes about 15 species of which at least three are known from this area.

THE COMMON PORCUPINE FISH
Also known as 'O-'o-pu hu-e and Ma-ki ma-ki
164—1 *Diodon holacanthus* Linnaeus, 1758

This porcupine fish has an oval, somewhat flabby body which is

covered with two-rooted spines which may be erected when the fish is puffed up with either air or water. The eyes are large and are placed high upon the head. The mouth is of moderate size and bears strong jaws and fused teeth. The color of the body is light brownish above and white beneath. Small, black spots are scattered over the upper parts of the head and body. About seven, large, brown spots are distributed over the upper side of the body; there is one above each eye, one on top of the head, one above each pectoral fin, one in the middle of the back, and one at the base of the soft dorsal fin. Most specimens are less than 12 inches in length, although some are reported to have measured 20 inches in length.

The habitat of this fish is in the quiet shore line waters. It feeds upon crabs, mollusks, and other bottom dwellers.

The distribution of this species is world-wide in warm water.

THE GIANT PORCUPINE FISH
Also known as 'O-'o-pu hu-e, 'O-'o-pu ka-wa, and Ma-ki ma-ki
164—2 *Diodon hystrix* Linnaeus, 1758

This large porcupine fish has a most astonishing appearance. The body is covered with long, two-rooted spines which can be erected. The body tapers uniformly from a very large head toward the tail. The eyes are very large and cow-like in appearance and the mouth has very strong jaws and fused teeth. The soft dorsal and anal fins each have 12 rays. The entire body and fins are covered with small, blue-black spots and a dark band extends across the body below the head. Most specimens measure less than 20 inches in length, but some have been reported as long as 36 inches.

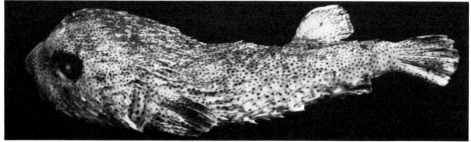

The habitat of this fish is in the quiet waters of the shore line; here it feeds upon a variety of food including crustacea, mollusks, and other forms which it crushes with its great teeth.

The distribution of this species is world-wide in warm water.

GUNTHER'S RARE PORCUPINE FISH
Also known as 'O-'o-pu-hu-e
164—3 *Chilomycterus affinis* Gunther, 1870

The body of this 'o'opuhue is short, robust, and heavy. The head is very large and wide and bears large cow-like eyes which are placed high upon its sides. The mouth is of moderate size and bears its teeth in the form of a large plate; both jaws have a sharp cutting edge. From the head, the body

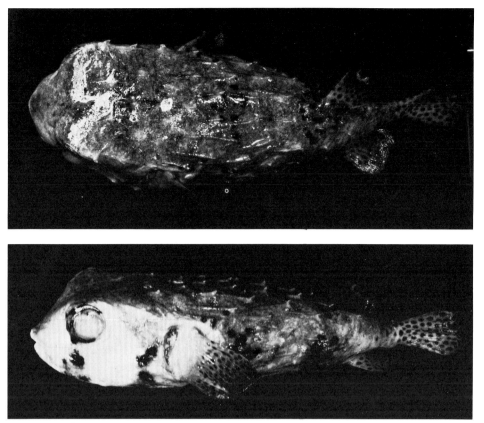

tapers uniformly to the tail. The surface of the body is covered by short, triangular, broad-based spines which are immovable. The body is marked by four, large, irregular, poorly defined, vertical bands; these bands are composed of irregular spots and blotches of varying intensity and are located about as follows: one band passes downward through the front of the eye and its orbit; a second band is placed low in front of the pectoral fin; a third vertical grouping of spots is located just behind the pectoral fin; and the fourth and last vertical group of spots is located just anterior to the dorsal and anal fins. All fins are marked by dark, medium-sized, round or oval spots. This species will reach a length of at least 20 inches.

Very little is known concerning the habits of this porcupine fish because it is an exceedingly uncommon species. It is believed to inhabit the shallow waters of the shore line. Only a few specimens have ever been seen. It is very rare in Hawaii.

The distribution of this species seems to extend across the entire tropical and warmer temperate parts of the Pacific Ocean from Japan to Central America.

THE SUN FISH OR HEAD FISH FAMILY
165 *Family Molidae (Orthagoriscidae)*

The sun fishes are a small family of astonishing species because they appear as if they were cut in half and the posterior half of their body was missing. Their bodies are deep, somewhat oval in shape, and compressed. The caudal peduncle found in most fishes is absent in this group and the normal tail and caudal fin appear to be lacking. The spinous dorsal fin is lacking and the soft dorsal fin and the anal fin are approximately equal in size and opposite in position and are placed at the rear of the body to add to their unusual appearance. The pectoral fins are present, but the pelvic or ventral fins with their accompanying pelvic bones are absent. The skin which covers the body may be rough, possess small plates, or be smooth, depending on the species. The eyes and the mouth are both small. The teeth within the mouth are fused into a single beak-like unit in each jaw, somewhat like those of the porcupine fishes.

The habitat of these fishes is on the high seas. Here they swim lazily about feeding upon any and all small floating creatures. They are not used as food.

The distribution of this family includes all tropical and temperate seas.

This unusual family includes but three species, all of which occur in this area.

THE SMOOTH SUN FISH OR TRUNCATED SUN FISH
Also known as Ma-ku-a, Ku-ne-hi, 'A-pa-hu, and King of the Mackerels
165—1 *Ranzania laevis* (Pennant), 1776

This sun fish is the smallest of the three known species. Its body is more elongated and more compressed than that of the other two species and the end of its tail is more nearly square. The body is covered by a smooth skin in which small, hexagonal plates are buried. The lips, which surround the mouth, form a circular opening to the mouth cavity and cannot be closed.

The body is silvery in color and is marked with vertical patterns of lines, stripes, and dots. Most specimens measure less than 20 inches in length, however, there are records of this fish reaching as much as 30 inches in length.

The habitat of this fish is in the open ocean. It is a surface dweller and feeds upon small animals in the surface waters. It swims by a sculling motion of the dorsal and anal fins. Young specimens live in schools.

The distribution of this species is world-wide in warm water. It occurs in all temperate and tropical seas, but it is nowhere common.

Although there is only one species, this fish may appear in books under any of the following names: *R. truncata* (Retzius), 1785; *R. typus* Nardo, 1840; and *R. makua* Jenkins, 1895.

THE POINT-TAILED SUN FISH
Also known as Ma-ku-a, Ku-ne-hi, and 'A-pa-hu
165—2 *Masturus lanceolatus* (Liénard), 1840

This sun fish resembles the giant sun fish, *Mola mola*, but has a different type of "tail". In this species the "tail" fin has a pointed extension at its center which is absent in *Mola mola*. The body is deep, compressed, and covered with a rough skin. Large specimens are reported to reach a length of seven feet and some have been reported as long as 11 feet.

This is a rare species which inhabits the surface waters of the open ocean. It is rarely captured and very little is known about it.

The distribution of this species seems to be world-wide in warm water, including the Hawaiian area.

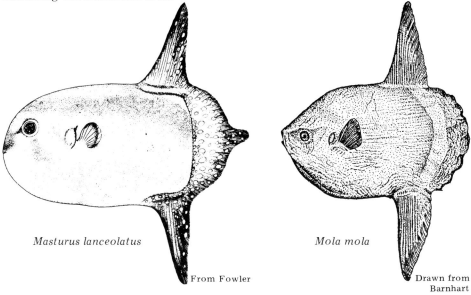

Masturus lanceolatus

From Fowler

Mola mola

Drawn from
Barnhart

THE COMMON OCEAN SUN FISH
Also known as Ma-ku-a, Ku-ne-hi, and 'A-pa-hu
165—3 *Mola mola* (Linnaeus), 1758

The ocean sun fish is an animal curiosity because of its giant size and very bizarre shape. The body is oval in outline, deep, and narrow or compressed. The dorsal and anal fins are high, are of about equal size, and are placed opposite each other. The "tail" is high and short and has a wavy or scalloped margin. The pectoral fins are present, but there is no trace of the

pelvic fins, or of the bones associated with them. The entire body is covered by a thick skin which is leathery in texture and contains patches of tubercles. The eyes and the mouth are both small. The color of the body is a grayish to brownish hue. Specimens have been reported to reach 11 feet in length; these would approach two tons in weight. However, most specimens weigh less than 1,000 pounds.

The habitat of this large fish is in the surface layers of the open ocean. Here it swims lazily about or basks at the surface, often lifting its fins above the water. It feeds upon all of the many kinds of fishes and other animals in the plankton. The flesh of this fish is seldom eaten because it is reported to be tough; it is not poisonous. It is an uncommon species.

The distribution of this species is world-wide in all warm and temperate seas.

The accompanying photo is of a mounted specimen.

THE GOOSE FISH FAMILY
Also known as Monk Fishes, Angler Fishes, and Fishing Frogs
166 *Family Lophiidae*

Goose fishes are bizarre creatures which have adapted their body to life upon the bottom. Their body is broad, depressed, and flabby and their head is extremely wide and flattened. The mouth is likewise very wide, has a projecting lower jaw, and contains an array of rather large canine teeth which may be depressed backward into the mouth. The skin which covers the body is generally smooth and contains many dermal flaps, most of which are located about the head. The spinous dorsal fin is present and contains six spines of which the first three have been modified into slender filaments and placed farther forward than the rest. The first of these slender spines has been developed into a fishing pole, called an *illicium*, which is decorated at its end by a small piece of fuzz and which is waved to attract passing fish. The pectoral fins are large and, as in related families, have elbow-like bends in them. The pelvic fins contain one spine and five rays, are small in size, widely separated, and are placed far forward (jugular) on the body. Most specimens are unattractively colored. Large members have been known to reach a length of about four feet and possibly 50 or more pounds in weight.

The habitat of goose fishes is on the bottom, usually near shore, although a few species prefer deeper water. The eggs of goose fishes are laid scattered through a floating, gelatinous matrix which may measure between one and two feet in width and between 20 and 40 feet in length. Their flesh is edible and they are therefor occasionally found in fish markets.

The distribution of this family is world-wide in both warm and temperate seas.

This small family possesses about a dozen species of which at least one deep water form occurs in this area.

THE DEEP WATER GOOSE FISH
166—1 *Lophiomus miacanthus* Gilbert, 1905

This small goose fish is a dull mottled color over the back and is covered with many white flaps. The lower surface of the body, the inside of the mouth, and the gill cavity are all white in color; the peritonium is black. Known specimens approached six inches in length.

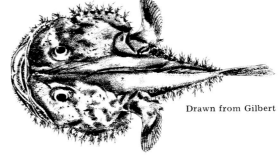

Drawn from Gilbert

This species was first described from specimens captured in 1902 in a dredge by the steamer *Albatross* off various Hawaiian islands at depths between 228 and 312 fathoms.

The distribution of this species includes the Hawaiian area.

THE FROG FISH OR ANGLER FISH FAMILY
Also known as the Fishing Frogs or Toad Fishes
167 *Family Antennariidae*

The angler fishes have rather shapeless, flabby bodies which are covered with a thick, loose skin which is without scales but in which small denticles may be embedded to give some species a feeling of sandpaper. The head is large and bears a pair of small eyes and a very large mouth which opens vertically or nearly so. The teeth within the mouth are small and conical in shape. The gill opening is a small hole located somewhere behind the base of the pectoral fin. The dorsal fin is separated into two parts. The spinous dorsal fin is composed of four, separate spines of which the second and third are often enveloped by skin and the fourth is buried beneath the skin. The first spine, however, is an amazing structure for it has been transformed into a fishing pole and it is from this fishing lure that these fishes get their common names. It consists of a slender, flexible, movable spine at the end of which is usually found a fuzzy, ragged bit of flesh which serves as the lure. This slender spine and the bait together are called the *illicium*. The soft dorsal fin, which is the second half of the dorsal fin, is without spines; the anal fin is likewise spineless. The caudal fin is either rounded or truncated and has nine rays. The pectoral fins resemble feet more than fins and have a bend in them which is similar to an elbow. The pelvic fins are small and have moved far forward on the body so that they lie close together beneath the throat. The members of this family are variously colored, often with protective hues which help to camouflage them in the seaweed or coral where they live. Some are able to slowly change their color. Large specimens may exceed a foot in length.

Angler fishes are sedentary and sluggish in their habits. They sit or "walk" slowly while waiting for small fish to appear. Meanwhile, they wave their bait to attract the fish nearer to their mouth. When the fish is close enough to seize, they jump forward, open the mouth, and the fish is engulfed with the surrounding water. Angler fishes usually inhabit shallow shore line waters where they may be found near coral growths. Some species are pelagic and float about in masses of sea weed. Their eggs are laid in a long, ribbon-like, floating, gelatinous mass.

The distribution of this group extends through the surface and shallow waters of all temperate and tropical seas.

This family includes about 50 species of which at least seven occur in this area.

THE WAIKIKI ANGLER FISH
167—1 *Abantennarius analis* Gosline, 1957

This small species was described from a single specimen which was captured by Dr. William A. Gosline and Dr. John Randall off Waikiki on December 31, 1952. The body is small, globular, compressed, and flabby. The most amazing aspect of this fish is the location of the gill openings. Instead of being located near the head, this species has the gill openings located at the rear of the body just above the base of the anal fin. The water, which enters the mouth and passes through the gills, must therefore pass along the entire side of the body before being released through this remote opening. The first dorsal spine is developed into a lure which is divided at the end; the second dorsal spine is separate and movable; the third dorsal spine lies beneath the skin of the back; and the fourth lies buried in the back. The body is brownish in color and is marked with various darker spots. The caudal, pelvic, and pectoral fins are marked with cross bars. The above specimen measured a little less than two inches in length.

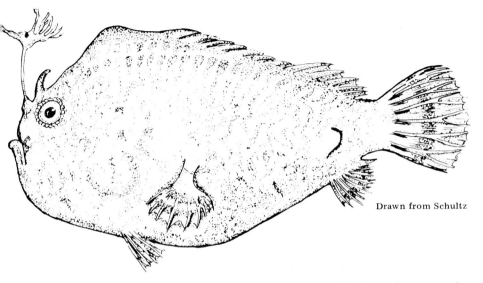

Drawn from Schultz

This species resembles *A. duescus* (Snyder), 1904, but they may be separated by the pectoral fins. In *A. analis* there are ten rays, while in *A. duescus* there are nine rays.

The distribution of this species thus far is limited to the Hawaiian area.

SNYDER'S RARE FROG FISH
167—2 *Abantennarius duescus* (Snyder), 1904

This species is based upon a few small specimens which were captured in a dredge in 1902 by the steamer *Albatross* off Kauai and also between Maui and Lanai at depths between 32 and 75 fathoms.

This species is unusual in having the gill opening on the side of the body midway between the pectoral fin and the anal fin. It has a small, globular body which is almost entirely covered by small prickles. The "bait" and the spine behind it are both very slender and are both tipped with a bit of fleshy fuzz. The color of the body in life was a purplish lilac hue in one specimen; in another, the color was light bronze above and yellowish bronze below. The largest specimens measured less than two inches in length.

The distribution of this species includes the Hawaiian area and undoubtedly surrounding areas.

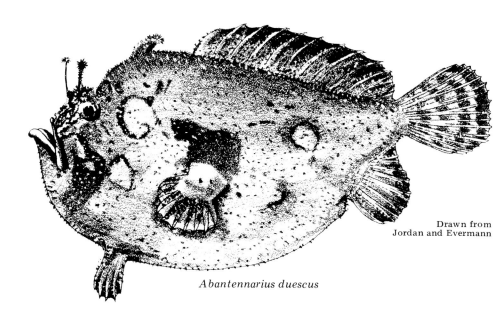

Drawn from
Jordan and Evermann

Abantennarius duescus

CUNNINGHAM'S FROG FISH
167—3 *Phrynelox cunninghami* (Fowler), 1941

This species was originally described from a single Hawaiian specimen about four and one-half inches long. It is a small species with a flabby body and rough skin. The bait and its slender spine are longer than the second spine which follows them. The color of the body is yellowish brown above and lighter below. Six, black lines radiate outward from the eyes and black spots of various shapes and sizes are scattered over the upper and posterior parts of the body and fins.

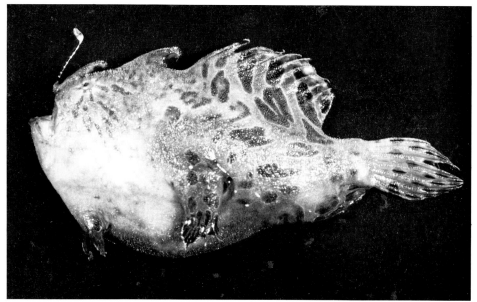

The distribution of this species includes the Hawaiian area.

Dr. Henry W. Fowler named this species for Mr. W. H. Cunningham, who assisted the Academy of Natural Sciences of Philadelphia in the development of their fish collection.

THE RETICULATED FROG FISH
167—4 *Antennatus bigibbus* (Lacepede), 1798

This frog fish is most easily recognized by its color pattern of net-like, brown lines upon a light background. All fins except the dorsal fin have a

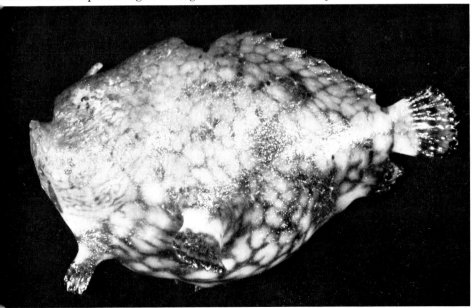

wide, dark brown band across their center and a narrow, dark brown band across their margins. The first dorsal spine is a slender filament with the usual "bait" at its free end; the second spine is free and without significant aspects; and the third spine lies beneath the skin. All fin rays are unbranched in the soft dorsal fin, the pectoral fins, and the pelvic fins; in the anal fin all fin rays are branched. Adult specimens are reported to reach eight inches in length.

The distribution of this species extends from Hawaii and the Tuamotu Islands westward through the tropical Pacific and Indian Oceans to the coast of Africa.

THE VARIABLE FROG FISH
167—5 *Antennarius chironectes* Lacepede, 1798

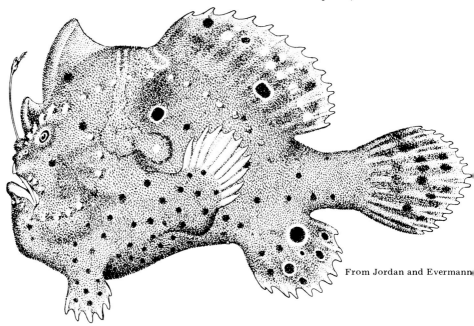

From Jordan and Evermann

This frog fish is a species of great confusion due to the wide variation in its color pattern. It therefore appears in books under a great variety of names. The color of the body is extremely variable and may range from nearly black with only the tips of the rays white through many intermediate stages and shades to light colors with blackish spots on the body, principally on the belly, and with a few scattered ringed spots or ocelli. The first dorsal spine with its "bait" is much longer than the second dorsal spine. The last two or three dorsal rays and the last pelvic ray are divided. All of the rays of the anal fin are divided, while those of the pectoral fins are all simple. It reaches a length of at least eight inches. It bears a resemblance to *A. moluccensis* and should be carefully studied.

The distribution of this species extends from Hawaii southward and westward to the Philippine Islands and the East Indies.

JORDAN'S FROG FISH

167—6 *Antennarius drombus* Jordan and Evermann, 1903

The identity of this species is probably most easily established by examining the dorsal spines. The first dorsal spine is short and slender and bears the "bait"; the second dorsal spine is stiff, excessively curved, and about the same length as the first spine; and the third dorsal spine is covered with skin. As in *A. chironectus*, the last two or three rays of the soft dorsal fin and the last ray of the pelvic fins are divided; all 11 or 12 pectoral rays are divided and no anal rays are divided. The caudal peduncle is very short. The extremely variable color of this species makes quick identification difficult. The basic color is brown to light brown and may be either uniform or marked with spots and blotches. The median fins are finely spotted with brown and the caudal fin is marked by about four, darker cross bars. It will reach a length of at least four inches.

The distribution of this species extends from Cocos Island in the eastern Pacific Ocean to Hawaii and undoubtedly includes adjoining areas.

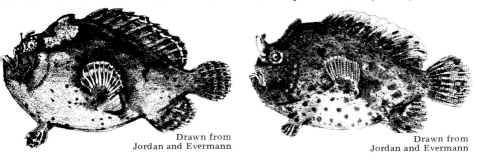

Drawn from
Jordan and Evermann

Drawn from
Jordan and Evermann

THE MOLUCCA ISLANDS ANGLER FISH

167—7 *Antennarius moluccensis* Bleeker, 1855

The Molucca angler fish is a large species and is probably most easily identified by its size; large specimens will reach at least ten and possibly 12 inches in length. The first dorsal spine or fishing pole is small, long, and very slender and bears a small lure at its extremity. When this fishing pole is laid down against the back, it usually extends well beyond the end of the second dorsal spine. There are 13 rays in the soft dorsal fin, the last two of which are divided. The pectoral fin has 11 soft rays of which the last one is divided. In the anal fin all eight rays are divided and the membrane which attaches the anal fin to the caudal peduncle is longer than the membrane which connects the soft dorsal fin above it to the caudal peduncle. The color of this species is both variable and confusing. It ranges from red and brown through various shades to yellow and may or may not be covered with spots, blotches, and areas of various sizes and shapes. It might be described as having a rather mangy appearance which some scholars attribute to the growth of patches of marine algae upon the skin.

The habitat of this fish is about the coral reef where the water is quiet. Here it rests in the crevices of the coral, braced in position with its fins, and

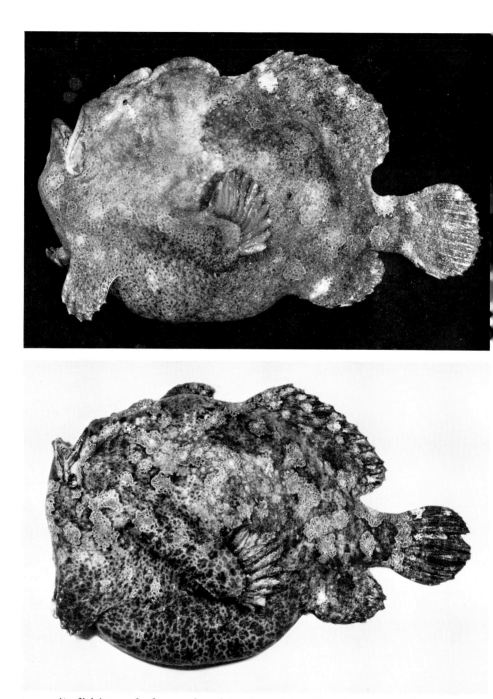

snaps its fishing pole forward and backward to attract passing fishes.

The distribution of this species extends from Hawaii southward to central Polynesia and westward across the tropical, western Pacific Ocean to the East Indies.

This species resembles *A. chironectes;* it appears in some books under the name of *A. commersoni* Cuvier, 1817.

THE ANGLER FISH FAMILY

168 *Family Chaunacidae*

The chaunacid fishes are another group of angler fishes which inhabit deep water. They have flabby bodies which are covered with fine, small spicules which give the skin a texture somewhat like sandpaper. There are two dorsal fins, but the first is represented only by the "fishing pole" or illicium and the other spines normally found in this fin are absent. The mouth is large, opens nearly vertically, and contains many small teeth. The eyes are small. The gill opening is behind the base of the pectoral fin, but both this opening and the pectoral fin are located far back on the body. The belly can be greatly inflated in this family.

The distribution of this group includes the Atlantic, Pacific, and Indian Oceans.

This is a very small family of which only one species is known from this area.

GILBERT'S DEEP WATER ANGLER FISH
168—1 *Chaunax umbrinus* Gilbert, 1905

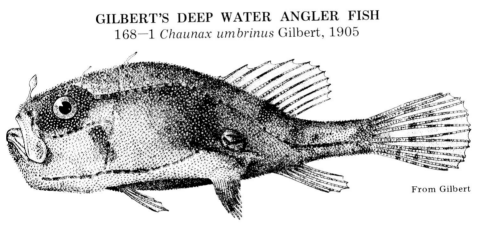

From Gilbert

This little fish was first described from a single specimen captured in a dredge in 1902 by the steamer *Albatross* in Pailolo Channel between Maui and Molokai. It has a flabby body covered with a shagreen-like skin in which fine spicules are embedded. The spinous portion of the dorsal fin is absent except for the "fishing pole" or illicium which represents the first spine. The opening of the gills is behind the base of the pectoral fin, both of which are toward the rear of the body. The color of the body is dark gray above and lighter below and is marked above with darker mottled and blotched areas. The caudal fin is dark in color with lighter cross-bars near its base. The pectoral fins are blackish and are marked with grayish lines at the base. The pelvic fins are yellowish in color. The specimen mentioned above measured 2.1 inches in length. Most specimens approach three inches in length.

The habitat of this species seems to be between about 400 and 1200 feet.

The distribution of this species includes the Hawaiian area.

THE BAT FISH OR SEA BAT FISH FAMILY

169 *Family Oncocephalidae*
(Onchocephalidae, Ogcocephalidae, Malthidae)

The bat fishes are a bizarre, degenerate family with broad, flat, depressed, disc-like heads and bodies and slender, tapering tails. The skin of the body contains no scales, but is usually covered with tubercles and spinules. The pectoral fins are located at the rear of the body and possess an elbow-like bend in them similar to that found in other angler fishes. The pelvic fins are located beneath the center of the disc and are quite widely separated. The spinous portion of the dorsal fin is lacking except for a small "fishing pole" or illicium with a short stalk and "bait". This illicium is located in a tubular cavity from which it may be extended or withdrawn. The mouth is small and the teeth are weak. The gill openings are located far back on the body on the upper side near the axils of the pectoral fins. Some species will reach 12 or 14 inches in length.

Batfishes are bottom dwellers where the terrain is reasonably flat. Here they move slowly about feeding upon small crustacea, fishes, worms, molluscs, and algae. Although a few species occur in shallower water, most inhabit the bottom at moderate or great depths in tropical and warmer temperate seas.

Of approximately 30 species, at least five are known from this area.

JORDAN'S BAT FISH
169—1 *Malthopsis jordani* Gilbert, 1905

The body of this bat fish is typical of the group and consists of a broad, flat, somewhat triangular disc followed by a slender, tubular portion which tapers uniformly toward the tail. The pectoral fins are located at the rear of the disc and bear the elbow-like joint of this group. The surface of the body is covered with ossicles. The body is grayish or light brownish in color

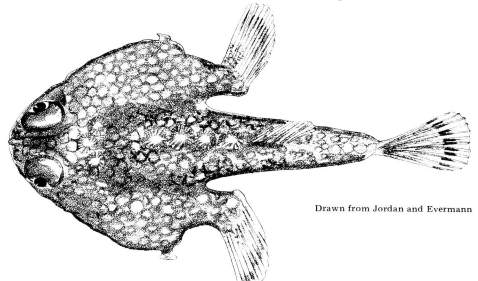

Drawn from Jordan and Evermann

above, lighter below, and is marked above by a net-like pattern of lines and scattered white spots. Most specimens measure about three inches in length.

The habitat of this fish is on the bottom at depths between about 600 and 1,200 feet.

The distribution of this species includes the Hawaiian area, Japan, and doubtless extensive areas in the adjoining regions.

This fish is named for David Starr Jordan, Ph.D., (1851-1931), America's foremost ichthyologist and the first President of Leland Stanford, Jr., University.

CRAMER'S BAT FISH
169-2 *Malthopsis mitrigera* Gilbert and Cramer, 1897

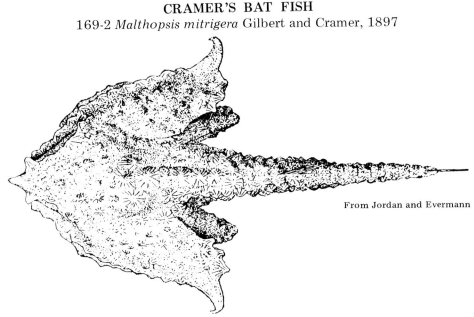

From Jordan and Evermann

This batfish is a small species with a body which consists of a broad, flat, triangular disc and a slender portion tapering toward the tail. The surface of the body is covered with plates or ossicles. The front of the head is vertical, the eyes are quite large, and there is a small illicium (fishing pole) present. Preserved specimens were yellowish in color. Most specimens measure about three inches in length.

This is a bottom dwelling form which lives at depths between about 1,000 and 1,500 feet.

The distribution of this species includes the Hawaiian area, Japan, and undoubtedly extensive areas in the adjoining regions.

THE NET BAT FISH
169—3 *Halieutaea retifera* Gilbert, 1905

The body of this bat fish bears a disc which is nearly circular in outline and a posterior portion which tapers uniformly to the tail. As usual, the pectoral fins are placed at the rear of the disc and the openings from the gills

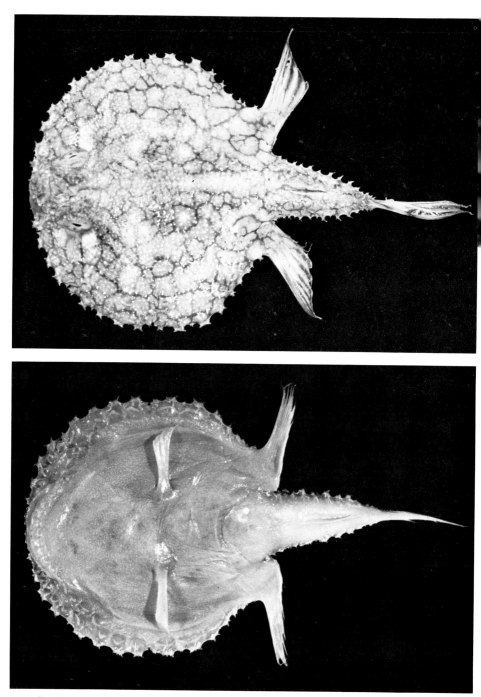

may be located just above them. The color of the body is light olive above and is marked with a net-like pattern of reddish brown lines. The lower surface is light reddish in color with many small white spots. Adult specimens are about four inches in length.

The habitat of this fish is on the bottom at depths from about 300 to

700 or 800 feet. It seems to be a common species at this depth.

The distribution of this species includes the Hawaiian Islands and undoubtedly a much larger area surrounding them.

THE RED BAT FISH
169—4 *Dibranchus erythrinus* Gilbert, 1905

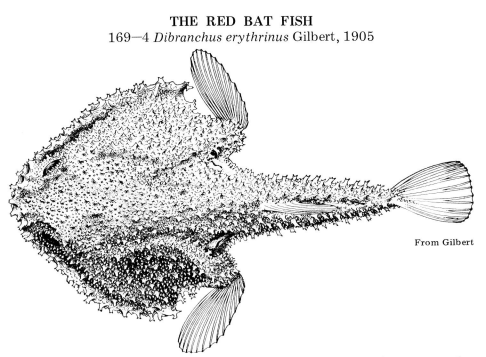

From Gilbert

This species was originally described from a single specimen measuring almost seven inches in length which was captured in 1902 by the steamer *Albatross* in a dredge at a depth between 403 and 477 fathoms off the island of Kauai. The color of the body is a light, carmine red above; the linings of the gill cavities and the abdominal cavity are blackish.

The distribution of this species includes the Hawaiian area.

THE STAR-MARKED BAT FISH
169—5 *Dibranchus stellulatus* Gilbert, 1905

This species was originally described from a single specimen, measuring about two and one-half inches, which was captured in 1902 by the steamer *Albatross* in a dredge off the island of Maui at a depth between 178 and 202 fathoms.

The disc of the body is very flat and is covered over the upper surface with spines from the bases of which lines radiate out to surrounding spines. The color of the body is light olive-brown above and white below. The linings of the mouth, the gill cavities, and the abdomen are white.

The habitat of this species seems to be on bottoms at depths of 1,000 feet or more.

The distribution of this species appears to extend from the Hawaiian area southward and westward to the coast of Africa.

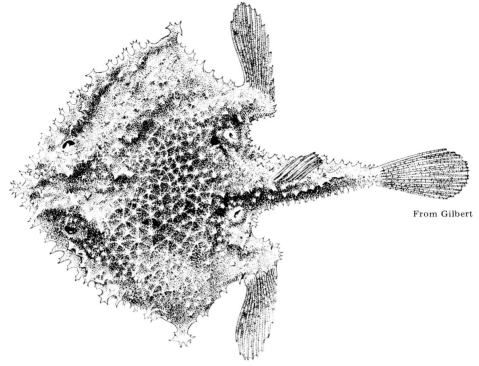

From Gilbert

Dibranchus stellulatus

THE BLACK ANGLER FISH FAMILY
170 *Family Melanocetidae*

The bodies of these fishes are somewhat grotesque in appearance. They have a gigantic head, very small eyes, and an extremely large mouth which opens nearly vertically and which is filled with slender, sharp teeth. The body is deep vertically, bears a hump behind the head, and is covered with a scaleless skin. The spinous dorsal fin is absent except for the illicium or "fishing rod" which represents the first spine. The soft dorsal fin is placed far to the rear of the body. The pectoral fins are small and are placed high upon the sides of the body and forward of the dorsal fin and gill openings. The pelvic fins are absent. Like many fishes from deep water, the bones of the skeleton are light in weight and thin. All species of this family are believed to be black in color.

In some books this family has been combined with the *Ceratiidae*.

Some specimens of this family have been obtained from very deep water about Hawaii. None are described here.

THE DREAMER ANGLER FISH FAMILY

171 *Family Oneirodidae*

These fishes have an interesting, but grotesque appearance. They have a very large head and a short, compressed body which is oval in shape and is usually covered by a scaleless skin, although a few species have a spiny skin. In this family, the dorsal fin has from four to eight soft rays and the anal fin has from four to seven soft rays; both are placed toward the rear end of the body. The first dorsal spine in this family is developed into an unusual and elaborate fishing apparatus called the illicium. This fishing pole has an elbow-like joint which is usually placed nearer to the base of the illicium; the free end of the illicium terminates in an enlarged escal bulb and a light organ.

The males are smaller in size than the females, have eyes which are directed outward, and are free living rather than attached as parasites to the body of the larger females as in some of the other families of angler fishes.

The fishes of this family feed upon a wide variety of deep water animals including smaller fishes, various small crustacea, pteropods, chaetognaths, siphonophores, and other small marine forms.

This family includes about 40 species which are currently divided among 15 genera.

The distribution of this family includes the deep waters of the Atlantic, Pacific, and Indian Oceans.

REGAN'S STRAINER-MOUTH ANGLER FISH

171—1 *Lasiognathus saccostoma* Regan, 1925

From Bertelsen

This angler fish is a small, very bizarre appearing species from deep water. The head is large and the eyes are small. The body is comparatively small, somewhat elongated, and is covered with a smooth, dark skin. The upper jaw is longer than the lower jaw and bears an array of slender, curved teeth of various lengths hanging along its margin. The cleft of the mouth opens horizontally. The dorsal and anal fins have five rays each and are placed toward the back of the body. The fishing pole or illicium is long, jointed, and slender and is tipped with a bulbous esca, denticles, and a light organ.

This species was originally described from a single female specimen about three inches in length from the deep water of the Caribbean Sea.

The distribution of this species includes the Atlantic and Pacific Oceans.

WALTON'S ANGLER FISH
171—2 *Lasiognathus waltoni* Nolan and Rosenblatt, 1975

Walton's angler fish is a small species which closely resembles *L. saccostoma* Regan, 1925. The head is very large and connects to an oval, tapering, compressed body which is covered with a smooth skin. The fishing pole or illicium is long and terminates in a bulbous esca which contains denticles. The jaws are very unequal; the premaxilla bones of the upper jaw extend well forward of the lower jaw. The color of the body was reported as a "deep, chocolate brown".

This species was first known and described from a female specimen measuring a bit less than four inches in length which was captured in 1972 about 750 miles north of Hilo, Hawaii, between the surface and a depth of about 4,500 feet.

The distribution of this species at present includes only the North Pacific Ocean.

The name of this species honors Sir Isaac Walton (1593-1683), an English writer and author of *The Compleat Angler*, a book on fishing which was published in 1653.

Persons wishing to read the original description of this species should consult *Copeia* 1975:1, pp. 60-66. Some scholars place this species within the Family *Thaumatichthyidae*.

THE DEEP-WATER OR HORNED ANGLER FISH FAMILY
172 *Family Ceratiidae*

The deep water angler fishes are a small group of rather degenerate fishes in which the males become attached to the females. When the male fish is young it swims to an appropriate female and attaches itself by its mouth to the side of the female. The mouth then becomes fused into the flesh of the female and the male becomes an attached parasite upon the female and thereafter receives its food from the female through the integrated circulatory system of these two fishes. The female fishes are much larger than the males and have a compressed body which bears a large head. The mouth is large and vertically placed and the eyes are small. There are no scales upon the body and, in this particular family of angler fishes, the pelvic fins are absent. The "fishing pole" or illicium on this family is found only upon the female and consists of a long filament which arises from between the eyes and which bears a bulb at its end. The predominant color in this family is black. Most species in this family are small, but a few attain a larger size.

The habitat of these anglers is on the bottom in both moderate and deeper waters of the Atlantic, Pacific, and Indian Oceans.

Of about 20 species, at least one is known from this area.

KROYER'S DEEP SEA ANGLER FISH
172—1 *Ceratias holboelli* Kroyer, 1844

This species was originally reported in this area from a single specimen, measuring about four inches in length, which was captured in 1902 by the steamer *Albatross* in a dredge off the island of Kauai at a depth between 409 and 550 fathoms.

The body tapers rather uniformly from a very large head toward the tail. The mouth is large, vertically placed, and contains fang-like teeth. The skin of the entire body is set with many, small prickles. In this species, the pelvic fins are absent, the pectoral fins are very small, and the spinous dorsal fin is represented by the single, small illicium; the soft dorsal, anal, and caudal fins are supported by four, four, and nine rays, respectively. It is black in color.

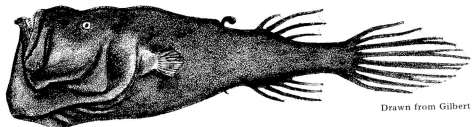

Drawn from Gilbert

The Hawaiian species has long been known as *Myopsaras myops* Gilbert, 1905. However, there is now evidence to indicate that it is the same as the North Atlantic *C. holboelli*, a species which exceeds four feet in length. If this is true, it is doubtless widely distributed.

APPENDIX

THE SHARKS, RAYS, AND CHIMERAS
(Class Chondrichthyes)

THE PACIFIC LARGE-MOUTH SHARK*

A large and most unusual shark was captured on 15 November 1976 about 25 miles northeast of the island of Oahu by a small research vessel operating out of the Hawaii Laboratory of the Naval Ocean Systems Center near Kaneohe, Oahu, Hawaii.

This shark was truly unique and had not previously been seen, studied, or described by any zoologists. It did not fit into any of the existing catagories (namely, Genus, Family, Order, etc.) of sharks and does not appear to be closely related to any known living species of sharks.

The body measured about eleven and one-half feet in total length, weighed about 1,650 pounds, and possessed an enormous mouth. This mouth is bordered by huge jaws and very large, protrusile lips. The teeth within the mouth are all small, somewhat needle-like, and are arrayed in from five to seven rows, but they are absent in the front, central areas of the jaws. The interior of the mouth is lined with a silvery skin which is doubtless luminescent. The tongue is large and thick.

The trunk of this shark is of proportions which are typical of this group and is covered with denticles of varying sizes and patterns. There are two dorsal fins, both of which are only of medium size. The tail fin is large and is heterocercal in design with the characteristic large upper fin lobe. The anal fin is present, but small. The paired pectoral fins are narrow, slender, and whitish in color beneath and at their tips; the pelvic fins are small. The five gill slits are quite large in size and are placed above and just forward of the pectoral fins. The spiracle is present, the eyes are without nictitating membranes, and the nostrils are not connected by a groove to the mouth.

The habits of this shark are not fully known. The large mouth, small teeth, filaments on the gill arches, and large gill slits indicate that this shark feeds in the same manner as the whale shark, the basking shark, and the large baleen whales. It obviously swims forward with its mouth open and passes great quantities of water through its mouth and gills and, from this water, strains out small fishes, crustacea, and other small forms. Its stomach contained remnants of euphausid crustacea.

* At the time this book went to press this shark had not been properly described and named. Much of the above information is from the "Megamouth News Letter" 1(1, 2, 3), 1976.

The habitat of this new shark is unknown. It was captured at a depth of about 500 feet in an area where the sea is over two and one-half miles deep. The shark had entangled its mouth in a nylon parachute which was being used as a sea anchor and was dead upon arrival at the surface.

The distribution of this shark probably extends over large areas in the deep sea.

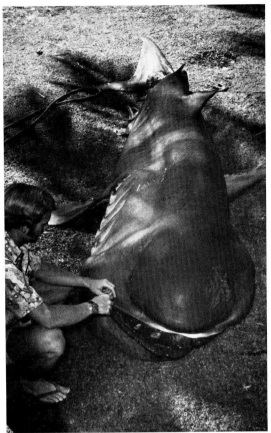

Photo by Terry Luke

Photo by Terry Luke

Photo by the Honolulu Advertiser

THE BONY FISHES
(Class Osteichthyes)

Order Clupeiformes - The Herrings and Related Families

Alepocephalidae (Platyproctidae) - The Slick-head Fishes

The alepocephalid fishes comprise a small family of small to medium sized species. Their body is slender and tapering and may be covered with smooth or keeled scales or by a smooth skin. The dorsal fin is located toward the rear of the back and is placed directly above the anal fin. Phosphorescent spots are usually absent, although a few species have rudimentary spots. The air bladder is absent.

The members of this family are world-wide and inhabit the deep waters of all oceans.

Alepocephalus blanfordii Alcock, 1892, is a deep water species which has been recently discovered in Hawaii. The body of this fish is long, slender, and tapering and is covered with scales of moderate size, except upon the head. The head is covered with black skin beneath which is a "thin layer of gelatinous tissue". The dorsal and anal fins are located far to the rear of the body and are quite small, low, equal, and opposite in position; the caudal fin is forked. The pectoral and pelvic fins are very short and are without scales, although there are scales at the bases of the median fins. The Hawaiian specimens measured about 21 and 23 inches in length.

Two Hawaiian specimens were captured on October 17, 1973, at a depth of about one-fourth mile at a point about six miles west of Kealakekua Bay off the Kona coast of the island of Hawaii.

The distribution of this species includes the Indian Ocean, the Hawaiian area, and doubtless many adjoining areas.

This species is discussed (in English) in the *Japanese Journal of Ichthyology* 22(1), 1975, pp. 1-6 (1 figure).

Bathylaconidae - The Bony-throat Fishes

The bony-throat fishes are a small family of less than a dozen species. They have streamlined, elongated, tapering bodies which are covered with cycloid scales, but there are no scales upon the head in this family. The head bears a small, curved, luminescent organ located just in front of each eye. The pectoral fins are placed very low upon the body and are smaller in size than the pelvic fins. All known species of this family measure less than one foot in length.

The name of "bony-throat" comes from the unusual nature of the branchiostegal rays beneath the throat; in this family they are plate-like and exposed; this feature is not found in any other family of fishes.

The known members of this family occur at depths from about one-fourth mile downward to at least three miles.

This family occurs in the Atlantic and North Pacific Oceans; it is probably much more widely distributed. The best known species within this family is *Bathylaco nigricans* Goode and Bean, 1896, which occurs in the Atlantic, Indian, and eastern Pacific areas.

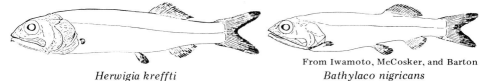

Herwigia kreffti

From Iwamoto, McCosker, and Barton
Bathylaco nigricans

Herwigia kreffti (Nielsen and Larsen), 1970, is a species from deeper water which is now known to occur in Hawaii. The body of this bathylaconid fish is elongated, quite slender, and has the dorsal and ventral profiles approximately equal, opposite, and tapering gradually toward the tail. The dorsal and anal fins are of modest size and are placed toward the rear of the body; the dorsal fin is the larger of the two and begins farther forward on the back. The caudal fin is deeply forked. The pectoral fins are very small and are placed low on the body. The single Hawaiian specimen measured about nine inches in length and was captured in 1973 in a mid-water trawl off the west coast of the island of Hawaii.

The distribution of this species includes the warmer waters of the Atlantic Ocean, the Indian Ocean, the Hawaiian area, and doubtless many adjoining areas.

This species was named for Herr G. Krefft of the Institut fur Seefischerei in Hamburg, Germany.

This species is discussed (in English) in the *Japanese Journal of Ichthyology* 23(1), 1976, pp. 55-59 (1 figure).

50 *Muraenidae* - The Moray Eels

50- *Anarchias seychellensis* Smith, 1962, is known from Marcus Island eastward to Hawaii, Tahiti, and Easter Island. See text and photo by Randall and McCosker in *Nat'l Hist. Museum of Los Angeles County, Contrib. To Science* 264, 1975, pp. 10-13.

50- *Gymnothorax buroensis* (Bleeker), 1857, occurs from the Indian Ocean eastward to Hawaii, the Galapagos Islands, Panama, and Costa Rica.

50-10 *Gymnothorax eurostus* (Abbott), 1861, occurs from Taiwan and the Ryukyu Islands eastward to Hawaii, northeastern Australia, and Easter Island.

50-12 *Gymnothorax goldsboroughi* Jordan and Evermann, 1903, is regarded by some authors as a synonym of *G. nudivomer* (Gunther), 1866, a species known from the Red Sea, off East Africa, and from Hawaii and the Marquesas Islands. See *Pacific Science* 26(3), 1972, pp. 310-317 (Appendix, Note 3).

50- *Gymnothorax javanicus* (Bleeker), 1859, is the largest moray eel in Hawaii; it will exceed seven feet in length and 60 pounds in weight. It occurs in the East Indies, central Polynesia, and Hawaii. For more details see an unpublished thesis by Richard E. Brock in the University of Hawaii Hamilton Library.

50- *Gymnothorax nuttingi* Snyder, 1904, is regarded by some authors as a synonym of *G. pictus* (Ahl), 1789. See *Pacific Science* 26(3), 1972, pp. 310-317 (Appendix, Note 2).

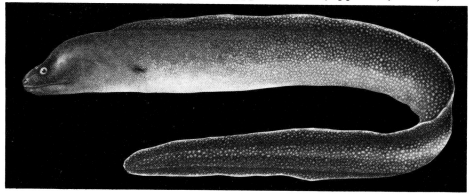

From Jordan and Evermann

From Jordan and Evermann

50-   *Gymnothorax pictus* (Ahl), 1789, occurs from the Indian Ocean eastward to the Galapagos Islands.

50-15   *Gymnothorax rueppelliae* (McClelland), 1845, seems to be the correct name for the species previously known as *G. petelli* (Bleeker), 1856. See an article by McCosker and Rosenblatt in *Proc. of the California Academy of Sciences*, 4th series, 40(13), 1975, pp. 417-427 (2 figures).

50-18   *Gymnothorax xanthostomus* Snyder, 1904, is likewise regarded by some authors as a synonym of *G. nudivomer* (Gunther), 1866. See *Pacific Science* 26(3), 1972, pp. 310-317 (Appendix, Note 3).

50-   *Gymnothorax* species, an unidentified, shallow-water moray eel from the southwestern coast of Oahu.

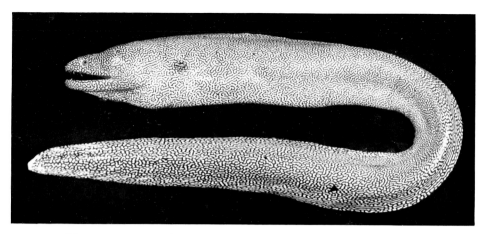

50-   *Gymnothorax* species, an unidentified, shallow-water moray eel from the southwestern coast of Oahu.

51 *Moringuidae* - The Thread Eels

51-   *Moringua ferruginea* Bliss, 1883, occurs from Mauritius eastward to Hawaii and Easter Island.

53 *Congridae* - The Conger Eels

53-   *Congrina aequoria* (Gilbert and Cramer), 1897, is the correct name for *Rhechias armiger* Jordan, 1921, a badly damaged specimen recovered from the sea off the Island of Hawaii following a lava flow into the sea.

53-01   *Conger cinereus* Ruppel, 1828, is the correct name for the species described as *Veternio verrens* Snyder, 1904. See *Copeia* 1970(2), pp. 366-367.

55 *Ophichthyidae* - The Snake Eels

55-   *Ichthyapus vulturus* (Weber and de Beaufort), 1916, is a more correct name for *Caecula platyrhynchus* Gosline, 1951. It is a variable species which occurs from the Seychelles eastward to Hawaii and Easter Island.

55-   *Phaenomonas cooperae* Palmer, 1970, is now known from Hawaii. See *Pacific Science* 29(4), 1975, pp. 361-363.

55-   *Schismorhynchus labialis* Seale, 1917, is known from Hawaii and the central and western Pacific Ocean.

Order Beryciformes - The Squirrel Fishes and Related Families

79   *Holocentridae* - The Squirrel Fishes

Students who are interested in the Genus *Myripristis* should consult a revision of this genus by David W. Greenfield in *Natural History Museum of Los Angeles County, Science Bulletin 19*, 1974. It is an excellent treatise of 54 pages and well illustrated.

79-12   *Myripristis amaenus* (Castelnau), 1873, has long been known in Hawaii as *M. argyromus* Jordan and Evermann, 1903.

79-13   *Myripristis berndti* Jordan and Evermann, 1903, has long been erroneously known in Hawaii as *M. murdjan* (Forsskal), 1775. *M. murdjan* extends from the Red Sea eastward across the Indian Ocean, through the many islands of the East Indies, and into the tropical western Pacific Ocean, but it does not occur in the Hawaiian area or in the Society Islands and the Tuamoto Archipelago to the east.
See Randall, John E. and Paul Gueze. "The Holocentrid Fishes Of The Genus *Myripristis* . . .". Nat'l Hist. Museum of Los Angeles, Contrib. In Science. 1981. No. 334, pp. 1-16 (12 colored figures). This is an excellent treatise.

79-15   *Myripristis kuntee* Cuvier and Valenciennes, 1831, was long known in Hawaii as *M. multiradiata* Gunther, 1874, and is listed in many books under this name.

Order Perciformes - The Perch-like Fishes and Related Families

88 *Serranidae* - The Grouper Fishes

88-   *Caprodon unicolor* Katayama, 1975, has been described as a new species from three specimens which were captured in a trawl off Midway Island in July, 1972, at a depth of about 170 meters (557 feet). This new species resembles *C. schlegeli* in general appearance, but it differs in some details including the size of the head, the number of gill

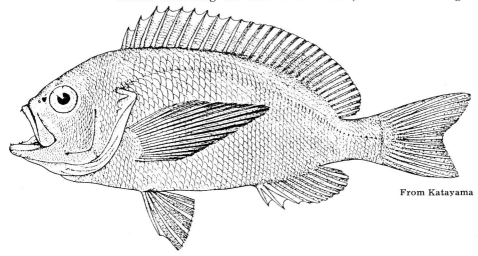

From Katayama

rakers, a straight lower margin of the maxillary bone, and a more deeply forked tail. In addition, the color of the body was orange-red with a white tip at the end of the caudal fin; it lacked the dusky markings which occur on the side of the body of *C. schlegeli.* It measured about 12 inches in length.

The original description of this species is printed (in English) in the *Japanese Journal of Ichthyology* 22(1), 1975, pp. 13-14 (1 figure).

104 *Chaetodontidae* - The Butterfly Fishes

104-12   *Hemitaurichthys zoster* (Bennett), 1831, is an Indian Ocean species and the similar Hawaiian species should henceforth be known as *H. polylepis* (Bleeker), 1857.

109 *Pomacentridae* - The Damsel Fishes

Students who are interested in this family should consult Gerald Allen's book titled *Damselfishes of the South Seas*, 1975, 240 pp.

109-03   *Abudefduf imparipennis* (Vaillant and Savage), 1875, should henceforth be known as *Plectroglyphidodon imparipennis* (Vaillant and Sauvage), 1875.

109-04   *Abudefduf phoenixensis* Schultz, 1943, should henceforth be known as *Plectroglyphidodon phoenixensis* (Schultz), 1943.

109-05   *Abudefduf sindonis* (Jordan and Evermann), 1903, should henceforth be known as *Plectroglyphidodon sindonis* (Jordan and Evermann), 1903.

109-08   *Pomacentrus jenkinsi* Jordan and Evermann, 1903, should henceforth be known as *Eupomacentrus fasciolatus* (Ogilby), 1889. This species is widely distributed in the tropical western Pacific Ocean; it occurs from Hawaii and Easter Island westward.

109-09   *Chromis leucurus* should be spelled *C. leucura.*

110 *Labridae* - The Wrasse Fishes

110-04   *Bodianus russelli* Gomon and Randall, 1975, has been placed in another genus and should henceforth be known as *Polylepion russelli* (Gomon and Randall), 1975.

114 *Scombridae* - The Mackerels and Tuna Fishes

114-   *Euthynnus lineatus* Kishinouye, 1920, the black skipjack, is occasionally observed in Hawaii. See *Fishery Bulletin* 74(1), 1976, p. 207. It occurs normally off the coasts of the Americas and in the area of the Galapagos Islands. Some scholars regard this small species as a synonym or subspecies of *E. affinis* (Cantor), 1850, the kawakawa of Hawaii, a species which is widely distributed in the Pacific and Indian Oceans.

115 *Istiophoridae* - The Marlins and Sail-fishes

115-01   *Tetrapterus angustirostris* Tanaka, 1914, the short-billed spearfish, is known in Japan as furaikajiki.

115-02   *Istiophorus platypterus* (Shaw and Nodder), 1791, the sail-fish, is known in Japan as the bashokajiki.

115-03   *Makaira indica* (Cuvier), 1831, the black marlin, has been known in Hawaii for many years as the silver marlin. In Japan, this species is known as the shirokajiki.

115-04   *Makaira nigricans* Lacepede, 1802, the blue marlin, appears in some books under the name of *M. ampla* (Poey), 1860. It is known in Japan as the kurokajiki.

115-05   *Tetrapterus audax* (Philippi), 1887, the striped marlin, is known in Japan as the makajiki.

Order *Tetraodontiformes* - The Trigger Fishes and Related Families

163 *Canthigasteridae* - The Sharp-nosed Puffer Fishes

163-6   *Canthigaster inframacula* Allen and Randall, 1977, resembles *C. rivulata* and is most easily identified by a single black spot about the size of the eye and located on the lower side of the body a bit below and behind the center of the side. It measures about four inches in length. At present, this species is known only from Hawaii. It was described from four specimens captured in a trawl off the north side of Oahu in 1972 at a depth somewhere between 400 and 500 feet.

The original description of this species is to be found in an article by Gerald R. Allen and John E. Randall titled "Review of the Sharpnose Puffer Fishes . . ." in the *Records of The Australian Museum* (at Sydney) 1977, 30 (17), pp. 475-517. This article contains descriptions of the 22 Indo-Pacific species; in addition, it contains 21 colored illustrations, four black and white photographs, and one drawing. It is an excellent reference.

163-7   *Canthigaster solandri* (Richardson), 1844, is marked on the body and caudal fin (but not on other fins) by many, light-colored spots upon a reddish or brownish background. The eye is surrounded by many, light-colored, radiating lines and a dense black ocellus is present on each side of the body at the base of the dorsal fin. The spots vary widely in size between individuals. The body measures about three inches in length.

It is distributed from Hawaii and the Tuamotu Islands westward through the warm waters of the Pacific and Indian Oceans to the coast of Africa. The article by Allen and Randall mentioned above contains three colored photographs of this species.

INDEX

I

II

III

CORRECTIONS

Page	Number	As Printed	Correct To Read
89	38	*Aulopidae*	
90	38-2	*Hime japonicus* (Gunther), 1880	Remarks: Possibly an undescribed species of *Aulopus*.
115	50	*Muraenidae*	
125	50-15	*Gymnothorax pettelli* (Bleeker), 1856	*Gymnothorax rueppelliae* (McClelland), 1845, See Appendix p. 527.
131	55	*Ophichthidae*	
131	55-	*Caecula platyrhynchus* Gosline, 1951	*Ichthyapus vulturus* (Weber and de Beaufort), 1916. See p. 528.
141	60	*Belonidae*	
143	60-3	*Strongylura appendiculata* (Klunzinger), 1871.	*Tylosurus acus* (Lacepede), 1803.
169	79	*Holocentridae*	
176	79-10	*Ostichthys pillwaxi* Steindachner, 1893	*Ostichthys oligolepis* (Whitley), 1941. Remarks: *O. pillwaxi* is a synonym of *O. archiepiscopus*.
191	88	*Serranidae*	
197	88-10	*Epinephelus tauvina* (Forsskal), 1775	Remarks: The identity of this species is uncertain. This large species may possibly be *E. lanceolatus* (Bloch), 1790.
199	88-14	*Pikea maculata* Doderlein and Steindachner, 1883	*Liopropoma maculatum* (Doderlein and Steindachner), 1883.
230	98	*Mullidae*	
230	98-1	*Upeneus arge* Jordan and Evermann, 1903	*Upeneus taeniopterus* Cuvier, 1829.
236	99	*Kyphosidae*	
236	99-1	*Kyphosus cinerescens* (Forsskal), 1775	Remarks: Photo is believed to be *Kyphosus biggibus* Lacepede, 1802.
240	104	*Chaetodontidae*	
245	104-10	*Heniochus acuminatus* (Linne), 1758	*Heniochus diphreutes* Jordan, Tanaka, and Snyder, 1913.
254	105	*Carangidae*	
262	105-15	*Carangoides ferdau* (Forskal), 1775	Remarks: Photo is of doubtful validity.
273	109	*Pomacentridae*	
275	109-3	*Abudefduf imparipennis* (Vaillant and Sauvage), 1875	*Plectroglyphidodon imparipennis* (Vaillant and Sauvage), 1875.
275	109-4	*Abudefduf phoenixensis* Schultz, 1943	*Plectroglyphidodon phoenixensis* (Schultz), 1943.
276	109-5	*Abudefduf sindonis* (Jordan and Evermann), 1903	*Plectroglyphidodon sindonis* (Jordan and Evermann), 1903.
277	109-8	*Pomacentrus jenkinsi* Jordan and Evermann, 1903	*Stegastes fasciolatus* (Ogilby), 1889.
277	109-9	*Chromis leucurus* Gilbert, 1905	*Chromis leucura* Gilbert, 1905.
279	110	*Labridae*	
282	110-4	*Bodianus russelli* Gomon and Randall, 1975	*Polylepion russelli* (Gomon and Randall), 1975.
308	111	*Scaridae*	
310	111-3	*Scarus formosus* Cuvier and Valenciennes, 1839	Remarks: This is a synonym of *Scarus dubius* Bennett, 1828.
310	111-4	*Scarus forsteri* Cuvier and Valenciennes, 1839	Remarks: This is a synonym of *Scarus psittacus* Forskal, 1775.
311	111-5	*Scarus lauia* Jordan and Evermann, 1903	Remarks: This is a synonym of *Scarus dubius* Bennett, 1828.
353	126	*Blennidae*	
359	126-11	*Omobranchus elongatus* (Peters), 1855	*Omobranchus rotundiceps obliquus* (Garman), 1903.
479	158	*Monacanthidae*	
483	158-6	*Pseudomonacanthus garretti* (Fowler), 1928	*Thamnaconus garretti* (Fowler), 1928.

ADDITIONAL SPECIES

Family Number	Scientific Name	Common Name and Remarks
	Alepocephalidae	
	Alepocephalus blanfordii Alcock, 1892	A deep water species. See Appendix page 524.
	Bathylaconidae	
	Herwegia krefftι (Nielsen and Larsen), 1970	A deep-water species. See Appendιx page 525.
50	*Muraenidae*	
	Anarchias seychellensis Smith, 1962	A moray eel. See Appendix page 526.
	Gymnothorax javanicus (Bleeker), 1859	A very large moray eel, 7+ feet. See Appendix page 526.
51	*Moringuidae*	
	Moringua ferruginea Bliss, 1833	A thread eel. See Appendix page 528.
53	*Congridae*	
	Congrina aequoria (Gilbert and Cramer), 1897 (*Rhechias armiger* Jordan,1921)	A conger eel. See Appendix page 528.
55	*Ophichthidae*	
	Phaenomonas cooperae Palmer, 1970	A snake eel. See Appendix page 528.
56	*Synaphobranchidae*	
	Dysommina brevirostre (Facciola), 1887	A deep-water eel.
	Dysommina muciparus (Alcock), 1891	A deep-water eel.
	Dysommina rugosa Ginsburg, 1951	A deep-water eel.
	Meadia abyssalis (Kamohara), 1952	A deep-water eel.
60	*Belonidae*	
60-3	*Tylosurus acus* (Lacepede), 1803	A needle fish, 30+ inches.
79	*Holocentridae*	
	Ostichthys archiepiscopus (Valenciennes), 1862	A squirrel fish.
88	*Serranidae*	
	Anthias bicolor Randall, 1979	A small, yellowish (above) and pinkish (below) grouper 4+ inches.
	Anthias ventralis Randall, 1979	A small orange-yellow grouper, 2+ inches.
	Caprodon unicolor Katayama, 1975	See Appendix page 529
	Cromileptes altivelis (Cuvier and Valenciennes), 1828	A spotted grouper, 16+ inches, possibly introduced into Hawaii
	Luzonichthys earlei Randall, 1981	A small, salmon-red grouper, 2+ inches.
		An additional species is known from post-larval specimens.
	Plectranthias helenae Randall, 1980	A small serranid species.
	Plectranthias nanus Randall, 1980	A small serranid species.
	Plectranthias winniensis Tyler, 1966	A small serranid species.
94	*Emmelichthyidae*	
	Emmelichthys karnella Heemstra and Randall, 1977	A boga fish.
	Emmelichthys struhsakeri Heemstra and Randall, 1977	A boga fish
95	*Lutjanidae*	
	Pristipomoides auricilla (Jordan, Evermann, and Tanaka), 1927	A snapper, 15+ inches.

Family Number	Scientific Name	Common Name and Remarks
98	*Mullidae*	
	Upeneus vittatus (Forsskal), 1775	A goatfish, 8+ inches, possibly introduced into Hawaii.
99	*Kyphosidae*	
	Kyphosus cinerascens (Forsskal), 1775	A rudder fish or chub.
	Kyphosus vaigiensis (Quoy and Gaimard), 1824	A rudder fish or chub, 15+ inches.
101	*Pentacerotidae*	
	Pentaceros richardsoni A. Smith, 1849	A boar fish or armorhead, 9+ inches.
104	*Chaetodontidae (Pomacanthidae)*	
	Centropyge multicolor Randall and Wass, 1974	A small angel fish 3+ inches.
110	*Labridae*	
	Halichoeres marginatus Ruppell, 1835	A small wrasse fish, 3½+ inches.
	Suezichthys tripunctatus Randall and Kotthaus, 1977	A deep-water wrasse fish.
	Thalassoma quinquevittatum (Lay and Bennett), 1839	A small wrasse fish, 3+ inches.
111	*Scaridae*	
	Scarus psittacus Forsskal, 1775	A parrot fish previously known as *S. forsteri* Cuvier and Valenciennes, 1839.
114	*Scombridae*	
	Euthynnus lineatus Kishinouye, 1920	The black skipjack. See Appendix page 531.
118	*Trichiuridae*	
	Assurger anzac (Alexander), 1916	A very long, slender cutlass fish, 7-8+ feet.
120	*Nomeidae (Centrolopidae)*	
	Hyperoglyphe japonica (Steindachner and Doderlein), 1885	A rudder fish or drift fish, 20+ inches.
136	*Acanthuridae*	
	Acanthurus lineatus (Linnaeus), 1758	A brightly colored surgeon fish, 8+ inches.
139	*Gobiidae*	
	Discordipinna griessingeri Hoese Fourmanoir, 1978	A small goby, 1+ inches.
	Nemateleotris magnificus Fowler, 1938	A small, colorful goby, 1½ inches.
	Ptereleotris heteropterus (Bleeker), 1855	A East Indian species, 49+ mm.
	Trimma taylori Lobel, 1979	A small goby named in honor of Dr. Leighton Taylor.
157	*Balistidae*	
	Xanthichthys auromarginata (Bennett), 1831	A trigger fish
163	*Canthigasteridae*	
163-6	*Canthigaster inframacula* Allen and Randall, 1977	A sharp-nosed puffer, 4+ inches. See Appendix page 531.
163-7	*Canthigaster solandri* (Richardson), 1844	A sharp-nosed puffer, 3+ inches. See Appendix page 532.
167	*Antennariidae*	
	Antennarius nummifer (Cuvier), 1817	A small frog fish, 1½+ inches.

Persons interested in recent new records of fishes from Hawaii should consult the following reference: Randall, John E. "New Records of Fishes from the Hawaiian Islands." PACIFIC SCIENCE 34:3, July, 1980, pp. 211-232. This is a good article and includes 13 figures and a bibliography of 64 references.